ROMAN COINS AND THEIR VALUES

The Emperor Nero
depicted on a gold aureus
minted in Rome, circa AD *64–65*
(No. 1927 in catalogue; *photo by* Andrew Daneman × 5.5:1)

ROMAN COINS

AND THEIR VALUES

The Millennium Edition

DAVID R. SEAR

Volume I

The Republic and The Twelve Caesars
280 BC–AD 96

LONDON 2000

© 2000 Spink and Son Ltd
69 Southampton Row
Bloomsbury
London, WC1B 4ET

ISBN 1 902040 35 X

Reprinted 2001, 2006

Set in 8/9pt Times by Columns Design Ltd, Reading
Printed in Great Britain at The University Press, Cambridge

INTRODUCTION

The original edition of Sear's *Roman Coins & Their Values* was published by Seaby thirty-six years ago and has since been through four revisions (1970, 1974, 1981 and 1988). However, the publication of the 'Millennium Edition' marks a radical departure from previous traditions. An expansion of the listings and an increase in the number of illustrations (all of which are now incorporated in the text) have necessitated a new two-volume format, like the companion work on Greek coins.

This first volume covers a period of approximately 375 years, from the origins of the Roman coinage in the Republican period, in the opening decades of the 3rd century BC, down to the violent end of the second Imperial dynasty, the Flavian, in AD 96. Volume II, which will span about two decades longer than Volume I, will continue the chronological sequence from the accession of Nerva, the 'thirteenth Caesar' and first of the 'Adoptive' emperors, down to the fall of the Western Empire in the eighth decade of the 5th century and the death of the Eastern Emperor Zeno in 491.

Those familiar with the earlier editions of this work will immediately be aware of the transformation which has taken place, particularly in the coverage of the Roman Republican series, the uniformity of which has facilitated the inclusion of a virtually complete listing of types in all metals. Unlike volume I of *Roman Silver Coins*, the arrangement is purely chronological and identification will be simplified by the high density of illustrations appearing in this section of the catalogue. The bronzes are less fully illustrated, the enduring nature of the designs for each denomination in the post-211 BC series making the categorization of these coins a relatively simple matter.

Commencing with the Imperatorial section the listings, by necessity, are of a more selective nature (though complete coverage of this intermediate series will be found in my recently published work *The History and Coinage of the Roman Imperators, 49–27 BC*). The same holds true of the Imperial segment of the catalogue, commencing in 27 BC, though the number of types included shows a significant increase over previous editions (note especially the expansion in the listings of gold) and the proportion of illustrated coins is much greater than before. The brief selection of 'Colonial and Provincial Coinage' previously included at the end of each reign has now been replaced by a more comprehensive listing of the coins of Roman Egypt struck at Alexandria. Other provincial issues are no longer dealt with here as they receive much fuller treatment in my 1982 book *Greek Imperial Coins and Their Values*.

Throughout the catalogue the current market valuations have been expressed in two currencies (pounds sterling and US dollars) and in at least two grades of preservation – usually 'VF' and 'EF' for precious metal coins of all series, and 'F' and 'VF' for base metal coins of the Republic together with the billon and bronze issues of Roman Egypt. For most Imperial *aes* (*sestertii, dupondii, asses*, etc.) a third grade ('EF') has been added as better preserved coins of this series are rather more frequently encountered. These changes have resulted from the preferences expressed over the past few years by collectors and dealers with whom I have corresponded or had personal contact. For the sake of clarity, the grades now appear under each catalogue entry; this has the added advantage of allowing more flexibility in expressing valuations for individual types and series which may only occur in lower grades by virtue of their place of mintage or the circumstances of the issue.

A new feature of the listings in the Imperatorial and Imperial sections of the catalogue is the inclusion of the mint and precise date of each type. Recent scholarship has improved our understanding of the chronology of much of the Roman coinage and I consider it important that collectors and students should benefit from the more accurate information being made available on this important topic. On a similar theme, it will be noticed that a more scientific chronological approach has now been adopted in the presentation of the material (though for ease of reference Cohen's alphabetical arrangement has generally been retained within each denominational listing). This is particularly relevant for the complex coinages of the Julio-Claudian era which have always presented the cataloguer with a serious challege. Thus, the coins issued in the names of the parents of the Emperor Claudius (Nero Claudius Drusus and Antonia) will be found listed under the reign of Claudius, where they properly belong; and the posthumous coinage of Germanicus is divided between those types struck under his son, Caligula, and the later issues of his brother Claudius. Use of the detailed index and the extensive cross references provided in the text should facilitate the easy location of any required type. Still on the subject of chronology, the tables of 'Titles and Powers' previously included at the beginning of certain reigns have now been replaced by a more comprehensive presentation of 'Principal Chronological Criteria of the Imperial Coinage' at the commencement of the Imperial section of the catalogue. With the expansion of the coverage of the coins of Roman Egypt in this edition the Alexandrian regnal dates for each reign have been incorporated into the data provided in this table.

The introductory articles from earlier editions have been retained, though revisions have been made where called for by advances in scholarship. In the revised and expanded Glossary collectors should now be able to find satisfactory answers to the majority of those 'frequently asked' questions on technical term's commonly used in the description of Roman coin types. Equally helpful should be an entirely new section explaining the meanings of many of the most regularly encountered abbreviations found in the inscriptions on Roman coins. I well remember my own early frustrations in trying to come to grips with the bewildering variety of contractions employed by the Roman die-engravers in their renderings of obverse and reverse legends. This new feature should provide valuable assistance in this difficult learning process and render a little more comprehensible what may sometimes appear to the beginner as a hopeless jumble of letters.

I have long considered the historical background information to be of prime importance in the presentation of catalogue listings of Greek and Roman coinage. Accordingly, I have fully revised the biographical sketches at the commencement of each reign and under certain subsidiary headings. Additionally, readers will notice that much information has been added on the significance of individual coin types within the catalogue itself and cross references provided to similar representations in other series. My invariable aim has been to enhance the enjoyment of the hobby of ancient coin collecting by drawing attention to its potential role as a natural gateway to the study of history. In the case of Roman coins this can lead to a fuller understanding and appreciation of a truly remarkable civilization which lies at the very foundations of our modern culture. As we stand on the brink of a new millennium I believe it is vital not only to look forward to the future – exciting as that may be – but also to be keenly aware of the events of the past which have brought us to where we are today. Rome has contributed hugely to that past and still exerts a powerful influence on late 20th century society in Europe and America – on our languages, our basic concepts of law and order, and on our governmental institutions. Indeed, it is hardly overstating the case to quote the words of E.A. Freeman in his Introduction to the English translation of Mommsen's *History of Rome:* 'The history of Rome is the greatest of all historical subjects, for this simple reason, that the history of Rome is in truth the history of the world'.

In conclusion, I should like to express my gratitude to all of those individuals who so willingly gave of their time and expertise in order to assist in the success of this ambitious undertaking. Firstly, I should like to thank those dealers who bravely responded to my request to participate in the updating of current market values by providing their views on price levels of certain basic types within the series. I am keenly aware that this work must frequently have impinged on other more pressing business commitments, and it should serve as an indication of the unselfish attitude of many professionals in the ancient coin trade that they are prepared to make real sacrifices in the cause of disseminating information to collectors. The following is an alphabetical listing of those who cooperated in this project: Harlan Berk of Chicago, IL.; Giulio Bernardi of Trieste, Italy; Dwayne Bridges of The Roman Connection, Dallas, TX; Tom Cederlind of Portland, OR; Kirk Davis of Claremont, CA; Allan and Marnie Davisson of Cold Spring, MN; Kenneth Dorney of Redding, CA; Matt Geary of Praetorian Numismatics, Philadelphia, PA; Rob Golan of Hillsborough, NC; Ira Goldberg of Beverly Hills, CA; Jonathan Kern of Lexington, KY; Herb Kreindler of Dix Hills, NY; Gavin Manton of Lennox Gallery Ltd., London; Chris Martin of C.J. Martin (Coins) Ltd., Southgate, London; Michael Marx of M & R Coins, Worth, IL; David Miller of Hemel Hempstead, England; Wayne Phillips of Phillips Ranch, CA; Paul Rabin of Zürich, Switzerland; Steve Rubinger of Antiqua Inc., Woodland Hills, CA; Dr. Arnold R. Saslow of Rare Coins & Classical Arts Ltd., South Orange, NJ; Fred Shore of Schwenksville, PA; Hans Voegtli of Münzen und Medaillen AG, Basel, Switzerland; and Bill Warden of New Hope, PA. In addition, Rick Ponterio of Ponterio & Associates Inc., San Diego, CA kindly provided many original photographs from his past auctions. My sincere thanks to them all!

Special mention is due to Tory Freeman of Freeman & Sear, Los Angeles, who gave valuable production assistance in the preparation of the illustrations at a time of heavy business commitments; to my good friend Barry Rightman of North Hills, CA, who, over a period of more than a year, has given unstintingly of his time and numismatic knowledge in categorizing the enormous (but unsorted) photo library from which most of the illustrations for this book have been drawn; and to Andrew Daneman, formerly of Numismatic Fine Arts and now resident in Denmark, whose unparalleled skill as a numismatic photographer has contributed in no small part to the visual impact of this catalogue. As always, my gratitude goes out to my wife Margaret for her forbearance and support during the slow and often difficult creation process of this complex revision.

DAVID R. SEAR
Los Angeles
November 1999

GLOSSARY

(For a comprehensive treatment of this subject, see John Melville Jones,
'A Dictionary of Ancient Roman Coins')

Abacus
: a wooden tablet with moveable counters used for making arithmetical calculations. It is often identified as the object appearing as an invariable attribute of Liberalitas.

Acrostolium
: the prow-stem of a warship, i.e. the curved decorative extension of the stem-post.

Adlocutio
: (or allocutio), the act of addressing or haranguing a gathering of military personnel, the word normally accompanies a scene depicting the emperor atop a low platform.

Adventus
: the arrival of an emperor in Rome or in one of the great provincial centres. Usually accompanying a depiction of him on horseback, but on the coinage of the much-travelled Hadrian also showing him as a standing figure, together with a personification of the region or city of his destination (ADVENTVI AVG GALLIAE, ADVENTVI AVG ALEXANDRIAE, etc.). See also Profectio.

Aegis
: a small cloak, decorated with a gorgon's head at the centre, associated in mythology with Zeus (Jupiter) and his daughter Athena (Minerva). It was employed as a decorative feature of the portrait busts of many of the Roman emperors, appearing first on the coinage under Nero.

Aes
: non-precious metal (copper, bronze, brass) used for the production of coinage (hence the abbreviation 'Æ').

Ancile
: a shield of distinctive form (narrow central section of oval shape with broad curving extensions at top and bottom). It was a particular attribute of Juno Sospita and was associated with the Salian priesthood of Mars.

Aplustre
: the curved decorative extension of the stern-post of a warship, usually of spread form composed of several frond-like elements.

Apex
: the hat worn by certain Roman priests, originally referring to the rod or spike surmounting the headdress.

Aquila
: (see Legionary eagle)

Aspergillum
: a whisk or sprinkler associated with religious rituals, appearing on the coinage as a symbol of the Roman priesthood of the Pontifices (this word was not used by the ancient authors and is of relatively modern derivation).

Biga
: a chariot drawn by a team of two animals, usually horses.

Billon
: an impure alloy containing less than 50% of silver, sometimes declining to less than 5%. It is especially associated with the debased imperial tetradrachms of Alexandria and with the Roman antoninianus denomination in the 3rd century, though it is commonly encountered in the 4th century also.

Binio
: a double unit, a term most commonly applied to the gold multiple aurei of the 3rd century which frequently show the emperor with a radiate crown.

Brockage
: a mis-struck piece resulting from the failure of the mint personnel to remove a coin which had stuck in the reverse or upper die after minting. As a result, the next blank to be struck received the impression of the obverse of the previous coin instead of that of the reverse die, thus producing a coin with two obverses (one of them incuse and a mirror version of the other). Brockages are most commonly encountered on denarii of the Roman Republic, but

occur also on coins of all denominations in the Imperial series. Reverse brockages are much rarer and more difficult to explain as they would require a new blank to be placed on top of an existing piece which had remained in the obverse or lower die after striking.

Caduceus the staff of Mercury, messenger of the gods, usually winged and ornamented with snakes.

Carpentum a two-wheeled enclosed carriage permission to use which in central Rome was initially granted only to married women and, from early Imperial times, was restricted to a very select few. Carpenta appear on coins of a number of empresses in the 1st and 2nd centuries AD, drawn by mules and most frequently in connection with posthumous honours.

Christogram the Christian monogram, consisting of the Greek letters *Chi* and *Rho* (CR = [Khr]istos).

Cippus a squared stone pillar, usually bearing a commemorative inscription and set up as a monument or boundary marker.

Cista (or cista mystica), a basket used for housing sacred snakes in connection with the initiation ceremony into the cult of Bacchus (Dionysus).

Cognomen one of the three principal elements of a Roman name (*praenomen, nomen, cognomen*) it indicated the family name of the individual (*e.g.* Gaius Julius CAESAR). Usually acquired by an ancestor as a nickname indicating a personal characteristic the *cognomen* was afterwards inherited, thus becoming a family designation.

Congiarium a ceremony in which the emperor distributed money to the citizenry. On the coinage of the 1st and 2nd centuries AD it is usually commemorated by an elaborate scene depicting the emperor atop a lofty platform, sometimes accompanied by the personification Liberalitas and with the legend CONGIARIVM or an abbreviated form (see also Liberalitas).

Conjoined (see Jugate)

Contorniate late Roman *aes* medallions which appear to have been produced in Rome in the late 4th and 5th centuries and are characterized by an incised border surrounding the obverse and reverse types. The designs are pagan and clearly betray a close connection with the circus and amphitheatre. They may well be associated with the anti-Christian sympathies of many of the late Roman aristocracy. Their purpose is unknown, though it has been speculated that they were used as entrance tokens, as counters in a board game, or as new-year's gifts. Like the earlier non-monetary medallions they have been excluded from this catalogue as they do not form part of the Roman coinage.

Cornucopiae (plural cornuacopiae), the horn of plenty signifying prosperity, it is usually depicted overflowing with fruits and other agricultural produce. Although occasionally shown on its own, it more commonly appears as an attribute of an allegorical personification.

Curule chair a folding stool with curved legs, it was symbolic of the highest or 'curule' magistracies in Rome (consulship, praetorship, and curule aedileship). It was said to derive from the seat placed in the royal chariot from which the Etruscan kings dispensed justice.

Decastyle (see Tetrastyle)

Decennalia the tenth anniversary of an emperor's rule, marked by the redemption of previous vows (*vota soluta*) and the undertaking of new ones (*vota suscepta*). It was often commemorated on the coinage by a depiction of the emperor sacrificing at an altar or by an inscription within a votive wreath. The quinquennalia (five years) and vicennalia (twenty years) were similarly celebrated, the latter of course far less frequently (see also Vota).

Decursio a word used to describe rapid military manoeuvres, especially equestrian. Scenes of Nero galloping on horseback, accompanied by one or more of his soldiers, feature prominently on sestertii of AD 64–7.

Designatus   qualifies an individual who has been elected to future office but has not yet taken up the appointment. Most commonly encountered on the Imperial coinage on issues belonging to the end of the year, just prior to the emperor's assumption of a new consulship on January 1st (e.g. COS II DES III P P).

Diademed   wearing a form of head-dress indicating royalty. An eastern custom adopted by the Greek kings and queens of the Hellenistic age, the diadem is not generally worn by Roman emperors until the late Roman period, commencing with Constantine (though empresses are frequently depicted diademed at a much earlier period). The late Imperial diadem was usually ornamented with pearls and/or rosettes.

Die   the stamp from which a coin blank receives its design through the process of striking. Although very few have survived from ancient times, it seems clear that Greek and Roman dies were made of bronze or of iron and bore designs engraved usually in intaglio to produce a coin type in relief. The lower or anvil die would have received the obverse design and was engraved on the flat face of a cylinder which was then inserted into a circular aperture in an anvil block. The reverse die was engraved on the flat face of a cone or wedge. The top of this would have received the hammer blow after it had been placed above the heated blank which was resting on the anvil die. It has been estimated that this simple process could have produced at least ten thousand coins from a single pair of dies, possibly far more in the case of softer precious metals.

Distyle   (see Tetrastyle)

Equestrian   relating to horse-riding, the word derives from the Latin *equus* ('horse') . In the Roman social order the *Equites* formed a class second only to the senators. They originated from men who were selected for their special military abilities and were provided with a horse for the service of the state in wartime.

Exercitus   'army'. Encountered on Hadrian's series of coins issued to honour the provincial armies throughout his Empire (EXERCITVS SYRIACVS, EXERC BRITANNICVS, etc.). More general types celebrate the military establishment with inscriptions such as GLORIA EXERCITVS and VIRTVS EXERCITI. Also used in appeals for loyalty during unsettled times (CONCORDIA EXERCITVVM, FIDES EXERCITVVM).

Exergue   the small space (generally on the reverse of a coin) below the principal type, from which it is usually separated by the 'exergual' line. On the later Roman coinage it was utilized for the main element of the mint mark.

Fasces   literally 'faggots', it was used to describe bundles of rods bound together which, accompanied by an axe, symbolize the authority of the highest Roman magistrates.

Field   the area surrounding the principal obverse or reverse type, in which may be placed subsidiary symbols or letters (often elements of the mint mark on coins of the later Empire).

Flan   (also planchet), the metal blank of correct size and weight which has been prepared for striking between a pair of dies.

Fourrée   a plated counterfeit coin with base metal core, usually in imitation of a silver denomination, though occasionally of gold. This normally indicates an unofficial product, though some fourrée appear to have been produced from official dies at the mint.

Gens   a group of Roman families sharing a common *nomen*, indicated by the second element of a personal name. Thus, Gaius Julius Caesar and the Republican moneyer Lucius Julius Bursio both belonged to the *Gens Julia*, whilst Gnaeus Pompeius Magnus was a member of the *Gens Pompeia* (see also Nomen).

Graffiti	'scratches', letters and other marks scratched on the surface of a coin in ancient times to identify its owner.
Hexastyle	(see Tetrastyle)
Hybrid	(also mule), a coin on which the obverse and reverse designs are incorrectly combined.
Incuse	a design which is recessed into the surface of the flan rather than protruding in relief. Although frequently encountered on Greek coins this characteristic is very rare in the Roman series, being confined to the legends on certain quadrigati and denarii of the Republican series.
Janiform	two heads joined back to back in the manner of the god Janus.
Jugate	(also conjoined), two or more heads placed side by side. Not commonly encountered on Roman coins, though it does appear in both the Republican and Imperial series.
Labarum	a late Roman military standard ornamented with the Christian monogram (Christogram).
Laureate	wearing a wreath composed of laurel leaves. Originally associated with the god Apollo, and the standard head-dress of the emperors until the late Roman period.
Legend	the principal inscription appearing on the obverse and reverse of a coin, as opposed to a mint mark or mark of value.
Legionary eagle	(also aquila), the principal standard of the Roman legion. Normally affixed to a spear, the eagle was usually made of silver, this being the metal visible at the greatest distance.
Liberalitas	a ceremony in which the emperor distributed money to the citizenry. On the coinage of the 2nd and 3rd centuries AD it is usually commemorated by an elaborate scene depicting the emperor atop a lofty platform, accompanied by the personification Liberalitas and with the legend LIBERALITAS or an abbreviated form. Sometimes the figure of Liberalitas appears alone (see also Congiarium).
Lituus	a short curving staff used in religious ceremonies of divination to mark out an area for the observation of birds. It appears on the coinage as a symbol of the Roman priesthood of the Augures.
Lyre	a string instrument with a rounded sound box at the bottom, traditionally made from the shell of a tortoise, and thin curving arms forming the uprights of the frame. It was believed to have been invented by the Greek god Hermes (Roman Mercury).
Manus Dei	'Hand of God', a Christian image which appears on some coins from the late 4th century onwards in the form of a right hand holding a diadem above the emperor's head. The symbolism indicates that the temporal ruler of the Empire is receiving divine sanction for his authority.
Mappa	originally the white napkin dropped by an emperor or magistrate as a starting signal at the Circus, in late Roman iconography it came to be a used as one of the principal attributes of the consuls.
Mint mark	letters and symbols indicating the place of mintage of a coin and sometimes also the responsible workshop (*officina*) within the establishment. The precise form of the mark can often be a useful indication of chronology.
Modius	a measure of wheat, or any dry or solid commodity, containing the third part of an amphora. In form it resembled an inverted bucket standing on three legs. Serapis is usually shown wearing it on his head to denote his portrayal as god of the corn supply.
Mule	(see Hybrid)
Mural crown	(see Turreted)
Nimbate	wearing a nimbus or halo surrounding the head. Indicating an aura of glory or power, it was associated with the sun god Sol (Greek Helios) who was sometimes shown with a radiate nimbus in place of the usual radiate crown.

Antoninus Pius was the first emperor to appear nimbate (on the reverse of a sestertius) and although seen more frequently in the late Roman period it was never a common iconographic feature.

Nomen (see also Gens), one of the three principal elements of a Roman name (*praenomen, nomen, cognomen*) it indicated the clan to which the individual's family belonged (e.g. Gaius JULIUS Caesar). It was borne also by women (with a feminine ending, e.g. JULIA).

Obverse from the Latin obversus ('turned towards') the obverse is the 'front' of a coin bearing what is considered to be the more important of the two designs struck on a flan. The earliest Greek coins bore only a single type engraved on the lower (anvil) die, whilst the upper (punch) die consisted of a simple raised square. This effectively held the flan in place during striking and produced the well known incuse which typifies the reverses of the archaic Greek coinage. The anvil die thus came to be regarded as providing the chief element of a coin's design.

Octastyle (see Tetrastyle)

Officina one of the separate workshops within a mint establishment. From the mid-3rd century AD the products of an officina are often identified by a letter or numeral in the reverse field or exergue. Later, they are sometimes combined with the mint name, e.g. R P = 2nd officina of Roma; ANT D = 4th officina of Antioch.

Orichalcum brass, a yellowish alloy of copper with zinc. It was used extensively for coinage in the Imperial period, principally for the sestertius and dupondius denominations. As the dupondius was not significantly heavier than its half, the copper as, orichalcum was clearly more highly prized, perhaps being officially overvalued to the benefit of the government.

Palladium a statue of Pallas-Athena (hence the name) reputedly stolen from Troy and subsequently brought to Italy by Aeneas. It was held in great reverence by the Romans who, because of its renowned protective powers, regarded it as the guardian of their city.

Parazonium a short sword or large dagger worn at the waist, it is usually depicted sheathed.

Patera a shallow bowl or dish without handles, it was frequently used in religious ceremonies for pouring libations or scattering grain and salt. It also served as a symbol of the priesthood of the Septemviri Epulones.

Petasus a flat hat, with or without a brim, especially associated with Mercury (Greek Hermes), the messenger of the gods. When depicted on Roman coins the petasus of Mercury is normally winged as an indication of his swiftness.

Pileus a conical felt hat associated with the Dioscuri (Castor and Pollux), twin sons of Jupiter; with Vulcan (Greek Hephaistos), god of iron and fire; and with Ulysses (Greek Odysseus), hero of Homer's *Odyssey*. The pileus was also symbolic of freedom, as it was given to former slaves who had been granted their freedom, hence its use as a symbol of Libertas.

Planchet (see Flan)

Plated (see Fourrée)

Praenomen one of the three principal elements of a Roman name (*praenomen, nomen, cognomen*) it indicated the personal name of the individual within his family (e.g. GAIUS Julius Caesar). It was selected from a relatively small number of recognized *praenomina*, the most common of which were Aulus (abbreviated A.), Decimus (D.), Gaius (C.), Gnaeus (Cn.), Lucius (L.), Marcus (M.), Publius (P.), Quintus (Q.), Servius (Ser.), Sextus (Sex.), Tiberius (Ti.), and Titus (T.).

Profectio the departure of an emperor from Rome at the commencement of a journey or military campaign. He is usually shown mounted, though is sometimes on foot (see also Adventus).

Quadriga	a chariot drawn by a team of four animals, usually horses.
Quinquennalia	(see Decennalia)
Radiate	decorated with rays, like those of the sun, this term is usually applied to the spiky crown sometimes worn by emperors as an alternative to a wreath. Normally indicating a double denomination (dupondius = two asses, antoninianus = two denarii) it derives from the headdress of the sun-god Sol (Greek Helios) and implies an association of the emperor with the divinity. The equivalent attribute for empresses was a crescent moon behind the shoulders, symbolic of the goddess Luna (Greek Selene).
Redux	'bringing back', this epithet was often applied to the goddess Fortuna in the sense that she was being invoked to protect the emperor on his return journey to Rome, both by sea and by land (the former represented by Fortuna's attribute of a rudder, the latter by a wheel placed beneath the seat of her throne or beside her standing figure).
Reverse	from the Latin *reversus* ('turned away') the reverse is the 'back' of a coin bearing what is considered to be the subordinate of the two designs struck on a flan. The earliest Greek coins bore only a single type engraved on the lower (anvil) die, whilst the upper (punch) die consisted of a simple raised square. This effectively held the flan in place during striking and produced the well known incuse which typifies the reverses of the archaic Greek coinage. The punch die thus came to be regarded as providing only the secondary element of a coin's design.
Rostrum	the beak or ram of a warship, often with three prongs (*rostrum tridens*). Those captured by C. Maenius from the fleet of the neighbouring city of Antium in 338 BC were used to adorn the speakers' platform in the Roman Forum. Thus, this structure acquired the name *rostra* ('beaks'), hence the word rostrum in modern English.
Serratus	*serrati* were Roman Republican denarii with notched or serrated edges, produced by chiselling the blank prior to striking. This practice was confined to specific issues and was especially common in the late 2nd century BC through the early decades of the 1st century. The reason for the contemporaneous production of *serrati* and regular denarii remains uncertain.
Signum	(see Standard)
Simpulum	an earthenware ladle with long handle used by the Pontifices for pouring wine at sacrifices. It appears on the coinage as a symbol of this important priesthood.
Sistrum	a ceremonial rattle which appears as an attribute of the Egyptian goddess Isis. It is also held by the personification of the province *Aegyptus* on Hadrian's coinage commemorating his visits to various parts of the Empire.
Standard	a military ensign (*signum*) borne by a *signifer* as an emblem of a cohort within a legion. It took the form of a pole or spear surmounted by a hand and with additional decorations on the shaft, including *phalerae* (metal discs), wreaths, and emblems commemorating the battle honours won by the unit.
Tetrastyle	used to describe a building (usually a temple) showing four columns along its façade. Also distyle (two columns), hexastyle (six columns), octastyle (eight columns), and decastyle (ten columns).
Thyrsus	the staff of Bacchus (Greek Dionysos) usually surmounted by a pine cone and wreathed with tendrils of vine or ivy.
Togate	clad in a toga, the cloak worn by Roman citizens on formal occasions.
Trident	a three-pronged fishing spear, the regular attribute of Neptune.
Triga	a chariot drawn by a team of three animals, usually horses.
Tripod	a three-legged stand, usually serving to support a seat or a large bowl (*cortina* = Greek *lebes*). It was especially associated with Apollo, because the priestess of the god at Delphi transmitted prophecies while seated on a

tripod. At Rome, it also served as a symbol of the priesthood of the Quindecimviri Sacris Faciundis, who had charge of the Sibylline oracles.

Triskeles (Latin *triquetra*), 'three-legs', a device comprising three human legs joined at the hip and radiating from a central point. On Roman coins it symbolizes Sicily. Because of its shape, the island was sometimes called *Trinacria* ('three-cornered').

Trophy the arms of a vanquished enemy, attached to a vertical shaft with cross piece, set up to commemorate a notable victory and often appearing on coins with captives at its foot.

Turreted wearing a crown in the form of a city wall with towers or battlements (normally an attribute of Cybele or a city goddess and often called a mural crown).

Vexillum a military standard consisting of a square-shaped piece of cloth bearing a device suspended from a cross bar attached to a pole. Originally a standard of the legionary cavalry, in Imperial times it was used by auxiliary cavalry units (*alae*) and was borne by the senior standard-bearer, the *vexillarius*. It was also used by detached units (*vexillatio*). Its primary function seems to have been that of a commander's flag used for signalling. Miniature vexilla were awarded as military decorations.

Vicennalia (see Decennalia)

Victimarius an attendant at a ceremonial sacrifice whose task was to slay the sacrificial animal.

Vota (plural of *votum*). A vow made to a god in order to obtain a divine favour stipulated in advance. The granting of the request obliged the vower to fulfil his promise. This usually took the form of a sacrifice to the deity or an offering to his (or her) temple. Public *vota* in Imperial times were normally for the welfare of the emperor over a stated period of time (five or ten years) and were regularly undertaken (*vota suscepta*) and hopefully paid (*vota soluta*). Sometimes they were more specific, relating to the safety of the emperor on a particularly hazardous journey or military campaign, or the current state of his health. The undertaking and fulfillment of these public vows was frequently recorded on the coinage and in the late Empire especially may provide useful evidence for the chronological arrangement of issues (see also Decennalia).

LEGEND ABBREVIATIONS

Roman coin inscriptions contain numerous abbreviations which are rarely separated by punctuation marks. The following are amongst the commonest forms and collectors should try to familiarize themselves with these before attempting to transcribe legends.

AVG
: = *Augustus*, the honorific title bestowed on Octavian by the Senate on 16 January 27 BC and thereafter adopted by all of his successors as an indication of their supreme authority. [On some earlier coins of the Imperatorial period the abbreviation 'AVG' may be used to designate membership of the Augures, one of Rome's four principal priestly colleges].

C or CAES
: = *Caesar*, originally a *cognomen* of the Julia *gens*. In 49 BC Gaius Julius Caesar (later dictator) initiated the period of civil conflict which led to the downfall of the Republic and the establishment of autocratic rule under his heir, Octavian (Augustus). After the extinction of the Julio-Claudian dynasty Caesar was adopted as an imperial title by their successors. It was also borne by the heir to the throne prior to his assumption of supreme authority.

CONOB
: = *Constantinopolis Obryza*, 'Pure Gold of Constantinople'. This form of mint mark, appearing in the exergues of late Roman and Byzantine solidi and fractional gold denominations, had its origins in the second half of the 4th century. 'Obryza', a word of obscure derivation, indicated that the gold from which the coin had been struck had been tested and was guaranteed pure. Initially, other mints employed a similar formula (ANTOB for Antioch, MDOB for Mediolanum, etc.) but eventually CONOB came to be utilized universally, without regard to the actual place of mintage. An important variation appearing at a number of western mints was COMOB. This may have had a slightly different meaning, the COM possibly indicating the office of *Comes Auri* ('Count of Gold'), the official charged with the responsibility of supervising the Imperial gold supplies in the western provinces of the Empire (see also under MINTS AND MINT MARKS OF THE LATER ROMAN EMPIRE).

COS
: = *Consul*, the highest annually elected magistracy of the Roman Republic. From 509 BC until the fall of the Republic two consuls were appointed each year to act as temporary heads of state. Consuls continued to hold office under the Imperial constitution and quite frequently the emperor himself, or his heir, occupied the position (see also under 'DATING ROMAN IMPERIAL COINS').

D N
: = *Dominus Noster*, 'Our Lord'. Introduced under the First Tetrarchy in the early years of the 4th century AD. Common after the middle of the century when it replaced IMP (erator) at the beginning of inscriptions.

DD NN
: = *Dominorum Nostrorum*, the plural of *Dominus Noster*.

III VIR/IIII VIR
: = *Triumvir/Quattuorvir*, 'One of Three/Four Men'. This title was used to describe the annual mint magistrates (usually three in number, but sometimes four) of the Republic and early Empire. This appointment formed an important step in the progression (*cursus honorum*) of a public career, possibly leading to an eventual consulate. The full title was *Tres Viri/Quattuor Viri Aere Argento Auro Flando Feriundo* ('Three/Four Men for the Casting [and] Striking of Bronze, Silver [and] Gold'). This sometimes appears on the coinage, notably the reformed *aes* denominations of Augustus where it is rendered as III VIR A A A F F.

III VIR R P C	= *Triumvir Reipublicae Constituendae*, 'One of Three Men for the Regulation of the Republic'. The title adopted in November of 43 BC by the three Caesarian leaders (Mark Antony, Octavian and Lepidus) when they formed the Second Triumvirate to oppose the tyrannicides Brutus and Cassius.
IMP	= *Imperator*, 'Commander'. Under the Republic it came to designate a victorious general whose success was enthusiastically acclaimed by his troops. For its later development as an Imperial title, see under 'DATING ROMAN IMPERIAL COINS'.
PERP or PP	= *Perpetuus*, 'Continuous'. In the early Empire this indicated the holding of a specific office for life, e.g. CENS(or) PERP(etuus) under Domitian. However, from the late 5th century into Byzantine times it replaced the traditional 'P F', standing on its own as an Imperial title immediately preceding that of Augustus.
P F	= *Pius Felix*, 'Dutiful' (to the gods, the State, and to one's family) and 'Happy' (in good fortune and success). From the mid-3rd to the late 5th centuries AD these titles often immediately preceded that of Augustus, until superseded by 'PP' (*Perpetuus*).
P M	= *Pontifex Maximus*, 'Greatest of the Pontifices'. The sixteen Pontifices formed one of the four senior colleges of priests in Rome and were charged with the supervision of ceremonies connected with the state religion. The head of the Pontifices was the Pontifex Maximus (a title still borne by the Pope today). Augustus received the title in 13 BC on the death of its last Republican holder, the former Triumvir Lepidus. Thereafter, it was normally assumed by each emperor at the time of his accession (see also under 'DATING ROMAN IMPERIAL COINS').
P P	= *Pater Patriae*, 'Father of his Country'. Augustus received this title in 2 BC and it was subsequently adopted by most of his successors at the time of their accession (see also under 'DATING ROMAN IMPERIAL COINS'). An earlier version (*Parens Patriae*) had been bestowed on Cicero after his exposure of the Catiline conspiracy in 63 BC and on Caesar in the final months of his life.
S C	= *Senatus Consulto*, 'by Decree of the Senate'. Sometimes expressed more fully as EX S C. Referring to the authority by which the issue was made. Appears on most Imperial *aes* until the mid-3rd century, but also occasionally on precious metal issues of the Republic and early Empire.
S P Q R	= *Senatus Populusque Romanus*, 'The Roman Senate and People'. The traditional formula expressing the joint authority of the conscript fathers and the common citizenry. Although having little meaning in Imperial times it continues to appear quite regularly on the coinage down to the time of Constantine the Great.
TR P	= *Tribunicia Potestas*, 'Tribunician Power'. Established in the early days of the Republic, the office of Tribune of the Plebs ultimately carried with it wide ranging powers and protections, including inviolability of person. On 1 July 23 BC Augustus obtained a lifetime grant of the tribunician power, an important step in the establishment of an autocracy as it gave him the absolute right of veto as well as the authority to convene the Senate. The tribunician power was generally assumed at the commencement of each new reign, though some emperors had already received it during their predecessor's reign (e.g. Tiberius, Titus, Marcus Aurelius, etc.). It is of special interest when followed by a numeral as this allows a coin to be assigned to its precise year of issue, the tribunician power being renewed annually for the purpose of regnal dating (see also under 'DATING ROMAN IMPERIAL COINS').

THE DENOMINATIONS OF THE ROMAN COINAGE

The earliest coinage of central Italy, known as *Aes Grave*, was of bronze, the various pieces being cast and not struck. Previous to the currency of these, irregular lumps of bronze (*Aes Rude*) and cast bronze bars or ingots bearing designs on both sides (*Aes Signatum*) were in use, although these may have been used as bullion exchangeable by weight rather than as money. *Aes Grave* was first issued by the Roman Republic about 280 BC, but the Romans soon realized that in order to facilitate commerce with other Italian and and non-Italian states it was also necessary to have a more convenient coinage comprising silver denominations and struck bronzes. Accordingly, they introduced silver *didrachms* and bronze *double litrae* and *litrae* closely resembling the coinages of the cities of Magna Graecia. Some years later, between the First and Second Punic Wars, the coinage underwent certain modifications. This resulted in the introduction of a new series of *Aes Grave*, the standardized types of which were subsequently adopted as the norm for most of the later issues of Republican bronze; and a fundamental change in the design of the silver coinage, which saw the large scale production of *quadrigatus-didrachms* bearing a janiform head of the Dioscuri on obverse and Jupiter in a four-horse chariot (quadriga) on reverse. The following table shows the obverse types and relative values of the various bronze denominations, the common reverse type being the prow of a galley:

As	head of Janus	mark of value I	= 12 *unciae*
Semis	head of Saturn	mark of value S	= 6 *unciae*
Triens	head of Minerva	mark of value 4 pellets	= 4 *unciae*
Quadrans	head of Hercules	mark of value 3 pellets	= 3 *unciae*
Sextans	head of Mercury	mark of value 2 pellets	= 2 *unciae*
Uncia	head of Roma	mark of value pellet	

(The mark of value is usually shown on both sides of the coin).

Struck bronze as of 211–206 BC (no. 627)

In the closing years of the 3rd century BC the crisis of the Second Punic War was responsible for a complete restructuring of the Roman currency system. The *Aes Grave* underwent a rapid series of weight reductions and were gradually superseded by lighter struck bronze coins, the transition being complete by *circa* 211 BC. The same date also saw the abandonment of the silver *quadrigatus-didrachm* in favour of the *denarius*, a smaller and lighter piece valued at 10 *asses* (mark of value X). Seven decades later the *denarius* was re-tariffed at 16 *asses* (mark of value XVI), a value

Aes Grave as of 225–217 BC (no. 570)

Silver didrachm of 280–275 BC (no. 22)   Silver quadrigatus-didrachm of 215–213 BC
                                                                        (No. 32)

Silver denarius of 206–194 BC (no. 54)   Silver victoriatus of 211–206 BC (no. 49)

Silver quinarius of 211–206 BC   Gold 60-as of 211–208 BC
          (no. 44)   (no. 3)

Silver sestertius of
211–206 BC (no. 46)

which it retained into the Imperial period. The *denarius* was destined to be the principal denomination of both the Republican and the Imperial monetary systems until its replacement by the *double denarius* (*antoninianus*) in the mid-3rd century AD. At the same time as the inauguration of the *denarius* (*circa* 211 BC) two fractional silver pieces were also introduced. However, the *quinarius* or *half denarius* (mark of value V = 5 *asses*) and the *sestertius* (mark of value IIS = 2 asses and a semis) were struck only for the first few years following the reform of *circa* 211 BC, though both were to be revived at a much later date. The *victoriatus* (so-called because of its reverse type of Victory crowning a trophy) was another new denomination resulting from the reform of *circa* 211 BC. In weight it was the same as the pre-reform *drachm* or *half quadrigatus* and was the equivalent of three-quarters of the *denarius*. Its primary purpose was for circulation amongst Greek communities, principally those of southern Italy, but with the expansion of Rome's horizons following her victory over the Carthaginians in the Second Punic War the denomination gradually lost its importance and was finally discontinued about 170 BC.

Gold aureus of Brutus, 42 BC   Gold quinarius of Tiberius (no. 1761 var.)
(no. 1430)

Gold coins were seldom issued and formed no part of the regular coinage in the Republican period. They were struck usually for military purposes at times of emergency and all types are now rare. In the period of civil strife following the assassination of Julius Caesar on the Ides of March, 44 BC, gold was issued by and for many of the contenders for political power, notably the Triumvirs Mark Antony and Octavian and the Republican leaders Brutus and Cassius. The gold issues of Octavian (later Augustus) eventually evolved into the first Roman Imperial gold coinage.

No regular Republican bronze was issued after about 82 BC, but once Augustus had achieved supreme power and restored peace to the Roman world he resumed the large scale production of *aes* as part of his re-organization of the currency system (*circa* 18 BC). Authority for the minting of gold and silver was retained by Augustus, but the orichalcum (brass) and copper coins were issued under the nominal control of the Senate, as evidenced by the ubiquitous formula 'S C' (*Senatus Consulto*). Initially, the names of the responsible moneyers appeared prominently on the Augustan *aes* (as on the coinage of the Roman Republic), but this practice ceased after about 4 BC.

Gold issues now became a regular part of the coinage and the various denominations of the re-organized system are shown in the following table:

Gold *aureus*	=	25 silver *denarii*
Gold *quinarius*	=	$12\frac{1}{2}$ silver *denarii*
Silver *denarius*	=	16 copper *asses*
Silver *quinarius*	=	8 copper *asses*
Brass *sestertius*	=	4 copper *asses*
Brass *dupondius*	=	2 copper *asses*
Copper *as*	=	4 copper *quadrantes*
Brass *semis*	=	2 copper *quadrantes*
Copper *quadrans*		

Copper as of Tiberius (no. 1770)   Copper quadrans of Augustus (no. 1693)

The *dupondius* and *as*, though of similar size, could be distinguished by the colour of the metal (yellow brass, red copper), the radiate head of the emperor only coming into use as a regular feature of the former coin at a later date. Other than a small early Augustan issue the silver *quinarius* was not struck during the Julio-Claudian period. It was revived by Galba in AD 68 and thereafter its production continued under the Flavian emperors and their successors.

Silver cistophorus of Claudius (no. 1838)   Brass semis of Nero (no. 1979)

At certain Asian mints – notably Ephesus and Pergamum – Augustus and some of his successors continued to strike the large silver pieces known as *cistophori*, equal in value to three *denarii*. Coins of this size and value, bearing as one of their types the Dionysiac snake-basket or *cista mystica*, had been the chief currency of the kingdom of Pergamum in Asia Minor (later the Roman province of Asia) from early in the 2nd century BC. Although in the Imperial period the types of the *cistophorus* were more in accord with the general style of Roman issues the coin was still recognizable to the people of *provincia Asia* and readily passed current.

Nero (AD 54–68), who, with all his faults, was a man of innovation and artistic appreciation, took a keen interest in the Imperial coinage and this led him to institute the experimental issue of an *as* and a *quadrans* struck in orichalcum (brass) in addition to those of copper. Whether his ultimate intention was to discard copper altogether is uncertain, but with the exception of a few isolated issues the experiment did not survive his suicide in AD 68 which ended the Julio-Claudian dynasty.

Brass *sestertii* of the 1st and 2nd centuries AD are amongst the most attractive of all the coins in the Roman series. They frequently bear interesting types which, because of the large size of the flan, are rendered in great detail, thus adding to the visual impact of these handsome pieces. When in the finest condition *sestertii* are much sought-after by collectors and consistently realize high prices. Although their smaller flans do not provide the same scope, the *dupondii* and *asses* also are

Brass sestertius of Hadrian

Brass dupondius of Vespasian   Silver quinarius of Domitian

often beautiful examples of the Roman engraver's art. In the 3rd century, however, the weight and the artistic level of the *sestertius* and its fractions underwent a decline. In fact, by the time the Emperor Trajan Decius (AD 249–51) introduced his experimental *double sestertius*, showing the emperor wearing a radiate crown, the coin weighed little more than many of the *sestertii* of the Julio-Claudian era. Although not continued by Decius' immediate successors, the *double sestertius* was incorporated into his *aes* coinage by the Gallic usurper Postumus (AD 260–268).

Brass double sestertius of Trajan Decius   Gold aureus of Nero (no. 1927)

The weight of the *aureus* and the *denarius*, as well as the fineness of the latter, were reduced by Nero as part of his currency measures undertaken in AD 64. Successive emperors – always pressed for money – carried on the evil process until, by the reign of Caracalla, the *denarius* contained barely 40% silver. This emperor further debased the coinage by introducing a new denomination of similar metal which, although only equivalent in weight to about one and a half *denarii*, was

Silver denarius of Trajan   Silver antoninianus of Pupienus

apparently officially tariffed as the equivalent of two. This new piece, which we know as an *antoninianus* (after Caracalla's official name Antoninus), always shows the emperor wearing a radiate crown instead of the laurel-wreath of the *denarius*. In the case of empresses, the larger silver denomination is distinguished by the addition of a crescent placed beneath the bust.

Silver autoninianus of Otacilia Severa   Billon antoninianus of Aurelian

By the middle of the 3rd century the *antoninianus* had driven the *denarius* out of circulation. With the acute political and economic crisis which was afflicting the Empire at this time the *antoninianus* became increasingly debased until, by the latter part of the sole reign of Gallienus (AD 260–68), it was reduced to a mere base metal coin of diminished size with only a tiny silver content. Aurelian, in his reform of the coinage (*circa* AD 273), restored the *antoninianus* to something like its original size and fixed the silver content at about 5% (perhaps indicated by the 'XXI' mark which it frequently bore in the exergue). He also revived the *denarius* (struck in the same metal as the *antoninianus*) and attempted to reintroduce *aes*, principally *asses*. Prior to this reform *antoniniani* of Gallienus' successor Claudius II Gothicus (AD 268–70) and of the Gallic usurper Tetricus (AD 270–73) had been extensively imitated by unofficial mints in the West, chiefly in Britain and Gaul. Although sometimes reasonably competent copies of the originals, many of these *'barbarous radiates'* are quite grotesque as well as being much smaller than the officially minted coins. With Aurelian's reconquest of the Gallic Empire and his subsequent measures to regularize the currency these imitations were demonetized and quickly disappeared from circulation.

Silver argenteus-siliqua of Diocletian   Billon follis of Diocletian

Thus, by the closing decades of the 3rd century, Rome's Imperial coinage bore little resemblance to the system instituted by Augustus almost three centuries before. The silver coinage had become hopelessly debased; *aes* production had virtually ceased, despite Aurelian's attempt to restore it in AD 273; and gold, though still retaining its fineness, was no longer struck on a consistent weight standard. The time was ripe for radical reform and, beginning about AD 294, the Emperor Diocletian undertook a series of measures with the object of restoring confidence in the Imperial coinage. The most important of the changes was the introduction of two new denominations: the *siliqua* (commonly referred to as the *argenteus*), a silver coin of approximately the same weight and fineness as the reformed Neronian *denarius*; and the *follis*, a large billon coin containing about 5% silver. Production of the *antoninianus* was now discontinued, though a coin of similar appearance remained in issue for about a decade following the reform. This piece no longer bore the mark 'XXI' on the reverse and it contained no trace of silver. It is referred to in this catalogue as a *post-reform radiate*.

Bronze post-reform radiate of Diocletian   Gold solidus of Constantine I

Constantine the Great (AD 307–37) made further changes to the monetary system. In place of the *aureus*, which was currently being struck at 60 to the pound of gold (5.4 grams), he introduced into the western provinces a new and lighter coin called the *solidus*, which was produced at 72 pieces to the pound (4.5 grams). With the defeat of Constantine's eastern rival Licinius (AD 308–24) production of the *solidus* became universal throughout the Empire. The *aureus* was still occasionally struck thereafter, but its issue was generally confined to the celebration of special occasions. Two gold fractional denominations accompanied the *solidus*, though they were never produced in the same quantities as the larger piece. The *semissis* was the equivalent of a *half solidus*, while the *9–siliqua* piece (also called the *one and a half scripulum*) was the equivalent of three-eighths of a *solidus*. Before the end of the 4th century this curious and seemingly inconvenient denomination was replaced by a *one-third solidus* or *tremissis*.

Silver argenteus-siliqua of Constantius II   Silver miliarensis of Constans

In AD 325 Constantine resumed production of the Diocletianic *siliqua* or *argenteus* which had lapsed after about AD 310. At the same time he introduced the larger silver *miliarensis* which was one-third heavier than the *siliqua* (four scruples instead of three) and the same weight as the gold *solidus* (4.5 grams). A few years later, after the death of Constantine, a heavier version of the *miliarensis* was introduced. This *'heavy miliarensis'* was struck at 60 to the pound, the same weight as the old gold *aureus* (5.4 grams). Both versions of the *miliarensis* remained in issue over a considerable period of time, extending even into the Byzantine period. The *siliqua*, however, soon underwent some fundamental changes. About AD 357 Constantius II, the last surviving son of Constantine I, reduced the weight of the *siliqua* from 1/96 of a pound (3.375 grams or three scruples) to 1/144 pound (2.25 grams or two scruples). In consequence, the lighter version of the *miliarensis* now became a *double siliqua*.

Silver reduced siliqua of Julian II   Billon centenionalis of Constantine II

The late Roman bronze coinage presents many problems. The billon *follis* denomination, introduced by Diocletian in the final decade of the 3rd century, soon began to decline in size and weight. Its original weight of about 10 grams was, by *circa* AD 318, down to about one-third of that level and it became clear to Constantine that measures needed to be undertaken to stabilize the situation. Accordingly, a new billon coin, weighing a little over 3 grams, was introduced at this time at the mints under the western emperor's control. This was extended to all the mints of the Empire after the defeat of Licinius in AD 324. The name of this new coin is not certainly known, though it appears likely that it was called a *centenionalis* (most cataloguers refer to it simply as *'Æ 3'*). In AD 330 the weight of the *centenionalis* itself began to decline, just as its predecessor had done, and by AD 336 its weight was down to a mere 1.7 grams. With the political troubles consequent on Constantine's death in 337 remedial measures were delayed for more than a decade and it was not until about AD 348 that Constantius II and Constans reformed the bronze coinage by introducing

Billon maiorina of Constantius II   Billon half maiorina of Constans

several new denominations to replace the *centenionalis* – the billon *maiorina*, struck on two weight standards (5.2 grams and 4.5 grams) and a *half maiorina*, weighing about 2.6 grams. Once again, the nomenclature is not certain and the *maiorina* has frequently been referred to in previous catalogues as a *centenionalis*. Unfortunately, the new arrangement was destined to have the same chequered history as its predecessors, with a rapid decline in size and weight culminating in a tiny billon piece weighing only 1.9 grams by the end of Constantius' reign in AD 361. The picture was further complicated by the issues of a western usurper Magnentius (AD 350–53) who, in obvious financial straits towards the end of his reign, attempted to replace the billon *maiorina* with a larger bronze piece. This initially weighed over 8 grams, but underwent a series of rapid reductions as the rebel regime neared its violent end.

A final brave attempt to revive the ailing late Roman bronze coinage was made by Julian II late in his reign (AD 363). Interestingly, the introduction of a large billon piece weighing about 8.25 grams looks remarkably like an attempt to restore the Diocletianic *follis*, inviting speculation that the pagan emperor had the deliberate intention of reverting to the last coinage reform of pre-Christian times. The experiment was, of course, short-lived and the denomination was soon abandoned by his Christian successors. More lasting was another denomination introduced by Julian – a bronze *'Æ 3'* weighing just under 3 grams and closely resembling the Constantinian billon *centenionalis* of AD 318. This revived *centenionalis* survived into the 5th century and although, like

Billon restored follis of Julian II   Bronze restored centenionalis of Julian II

other 4th century bronze denominations, its weight tended to decline with the passage of years there was actually an attempt to restore it to its original level in AD 395. Another bronze denomination which appeared in the closing decades of the 4th century was an '*Æ 2*' introduced by the western emperor Gratian *circa* AD 379. Although struck in bronze rather than billon, this piece was otherwise reminiscent of the *maiorina* introduced three decades before and may be considered a revival of that denomination. It was to last until AD 395 when it was demonetized under the terms of a rescript preserved in the *Codex* Theodosianus (ix. 232), though there were still a few isolated

Bronze restored maiorina of Theodosius I   Bronze half centenionalis
or nummus of
Magnus Maximus

issues of '*Æ 2s*' during the course of the 5th century. Also appearing about AD 379 was a new '*Æ 4*' denomination, presumably representing the half of the revived *centenionalis*. This diminutive coin was to have a much longer history, eventually becoming the only bronze denomination in regular issue as the disastrous 5th century progressed. Also known as the *nummus*, the latest miserable examples of the '*Æ 4*' frequently weigh less than 1 gram, being almost indistinguishable from imitations produced by the various barbarian tribes who were now invading and occupying former Roman territory. Unofficial 'barbarous' copies of late Roman bronze coinage had been produced from Constantinian times onwards, many of them imitated from the post-348 *maiorinae* of Constantius II with reverse legend **FEL TEMP REPARATIO** and type soldier spearing fallen horseman.

Gold semissis of Zeno   Gold tremissis of Leo I

In AD 498 the Emperor Anastasius carried out a sweeping reform of the bronze coinage. This introduced a whole new range of denominations, each being a multiple of the old *nummus* and bearing its mark value conspicuously on the reverse (*e.g.* M = *40 nummi*, K = *20 nummi*, I = *10 nummi*, etc.). As the introduction of these novel coins marks an almost complete break with the traditions of the Roman coinage, the Anastasian *aes* reform has been considered a convenient point at which to commence the Byzantine series, though no adjustments to the precious metal coinage were made at this time.

THE REVERSE TYPES OF THE IMPERIAL COINAGE

Although most collectors of Roman Imperial coins begin by attempting to acquire a selection of portraits of the emperors and their families, it is in the remarkable array of reverse types that the unique interest and historical value of the series will be found. Moreover, a sound knowledge of these types will often make it possible to attribute a coin even when the legends are obscure (especially important when coins from excavations are being used as archaeological evidence).

I. DEITIES AND PERSONIFICATIONS

In the following notes it is proposed briefly to outline the more important types (the chief deities of the Roman pantheon and a few other divinities which achieved great popularity in the Roman World) and their customary attributes, after which the principal personifications, which constitute the majority of the reverse types, will be dealt with.

As of Caracalla

Aesculapius. The god of medicine and healing, he is shown as a man of mature years, holding a staff about which a snake twines. He is often accompanied by a small figure representing his attendant, Telesphorus.

His image appears on Roman Provincial ('Greek Imperial') coins at a number of mints, including Epidaurus, where the great temple of **Asklepios** was situated, and Pergamum, where there was a celebrated sanctuary of the god (the Asklepieion) which was greatly embellished during the reign of Hadrian.

Antoninianus of Trebonianus Gallus (Apollo)

Apollo. The sun-god, Apollo, was also god of music and the arts, of prophecy, and the protector of flocks and herds: he is usually depicted with a lyre. Amongst his titles are CONSERVATOR, PALATINVS (as protector of the imperial residence on the Palatine), and PROPVGNATOR. He appears at intervals on the Imperial coinage from Augustus to Carausius and then, like most pagan types, falls out of use in the 4th century.

On Roman Provincial coins Apollo is a frequent type, appearing on the Alexandrian series as Apollo Aktios or Pythios, and on coins of Ephesus with the title Hikesios, indicating his role as protector of suppliants. On colonial bronzes of Apamea he is named APOLLO CLARIVS, after his sanctuary at Clarus near Colophon. More commonly encountered are depictions of the god without name or title.

Denarius of Septimius Severus

Bacchus. Under his ancient Italian name of **Liber,** the god of wine occasionally appears as a coin type. He is generally shown holding a wine-cup and thyrsus and is accompanied by his attendant panther. Sometimes his head only is depicted, crowned with vine or ivy leaves. On a coin of Gallienus the panther appears on its own, with the legend LIBERO P CONS AVG. Few emperors, however, adopted Bacchus as a coin type.

In the Roman Provincial series, however, **Dionysos** was a very popular type and occurs on the coins of many cities.

Dupondius of Claudius

Ceres. In the 1st and 2nd centuries AD Ceres appears frequently as a coin type and is generally shown holding ears of corn to symbolize her function as presiding goddess of agriculture. Sometimes she bears a torch to signify her search in the darkness for her lost daughter Proserpina, who had been abducted to Hades by Pluto. The epithet most most commonly applied to her is Frugifera ('bearing fruits').

On Roman Provincial coins she appears as the goddess **Demeter,** sometimes accompanied by her daughter Persephone (the Greek name for Proserpina).

Aureus of Julia Domna (Cybele)

Cybele. Of Asian origin, the Mother of the Gods was not commonly depicted as a Roman coin type, except in the 2nd and early 3rd centuries AD. She is usually shown wearing a turreted crown and holding a tympanum (small drum or tambourine), and is either in a car drawn by lions or enthroned between the animals. The accompanying legend is normally MATER DEVM or MATRI MAGNAE, or a similar variant.

Many Greek cities have **Kybele** on their coins during the Imperial period, her cult being very popular in Asia Minor.

Sestertius of Faustina Junior

Diana. The sister of Apollo, Diana was regarded as the moon-goddess and is sometimes represented with a lunar crescent above her forehead. When given the title of LVCIFERA ('the light-bringer') she is depicted holding a long torch, symbolic of moonlight. She was also protectress of the young and deity of the chase. In the latter role she is equipped with bow and arrows and is sometimes accompanied by a hound or deer. Her other titles include CONSERVATRIX and VICTRIX. As DIANA EPHESIA she appears as a cultus-figure on Asian cistophori of the reigns of Claudius and Hadrian.

The most famous shrine of Diana (or **Artemis** as she was called by the Greeks) was the celebrated Artemision at Ephesus, one of the Seven Wonders of the World. It is mentioned in the *Acts of the Apostles* (19, 27) and some of the local issues of the city show the statue of Artemis Ephesia either alone or within a representation of the famed temple. The cult of Artemis Ephesia was widespread and was honoured on the coinages of many cities, utilizing similar types.

Follis of Maxentius

The Dioscuri. The twins Castor and Pollux, sons of Jupiter and Leda, appear frequently on the Republican coinage and their mounted figures galloping side by side was selected as the exclusive type for the denarius during its initial phase of issue and the principal type for the first seven decades. Invariably, their headdress is the conical pileus, often surmounted by a star to denote divinity. In Imperial times, however, the Dioscuri are rarely featured. Castor alone stands beside his horse on gold of Commodus and silver of Geta, whilst both figures make a final appearance on the early 4th century coinage of Maxentius.

On the Roman Provincial coinage the **Dioskouroi** appear on the issues of a number of cities, notably the Ionian mint of Phocaea, and sometimes they are represented solely by their pilei surmounted by stars.

Aureus of Carausius

Hercules. Son of Jupiter by the mortal Alcmene, Hercules was a popular coin type from the 1st century AD until the time of Constantine the Great. He can always be recognized by his splendid physique and by his constant attributes of club and lion's skin. Commodus, who regarded Hercules as his tutelary deity and even, in his final years, appears to have believed himself a reincarnation of the demi-god, struck many medallions and coins bearing either the figure of Hercules or types relating to him. At a later date, Postumus issued a series bearing types alluding to the various 'labours'. The titles of Hercules are many, and include CONSERVATOR, DEFENSOR, ROMANVS, and VICTOR.

Many Roman Provincial mints depicted **Herakles,** especially those named Heraclea after the demi-god. Under Antoninus Pius the mint of Alexandria issued a remarkable series of bronze hemidrachms illustrating the deity's extraordinary exploits.

Small bronze of the time of Julian II

Isis. Of purely Egyptian origin, Isis, the wife of Osiris, became one of the most popular deities with the Romans and even had several temples dedicated to her in the Imperial capital. She rarely appears, however, on the Imperial coinage, though she is sometimes shown in the company of Serapis. Her normal attribute is the sistrum (rattle), but on a coin of Julia Domna she nurses the infant Horus.

Isis also appears on a number of Roman Provincial issues, especially, of course, on the coinage of Alexandria. Sometimes her head only is shown, and sometimes she is represented as Isis Pharia, holding a sail billowing in the wind, with or without a representation of the celebrated Pharos (lighthouse) of Alexandria.

As of Hadrian (Janus)

Janus. Although the double head of Janus was the regular obverse type of the Republican *as* throughout almost the entire period of its issue, the deity very seldom appears on any of the issues of the emperors. He was the god of beginnings, looking both to past and future, and the first month of the year was named after him. He appears at infrequent intervals as a reverse type – a full-length figure holding a sceptre – and the *Ianus Geminus* ('Twin Janus') features on an extensive issue of *aes* under Nero. When there was peace throughout the Empire the doors of this small shrine were ceremonially closed – an event sufficiently rare to warrant commemoration on the coinage.

Aureus of Julia Soaemias

Juno. The sister and consort of Jupiter is depicted as a tall matron, either seated or standing, holding a patera and a sceptre. She is frequently accompanied by a peacock and on certain posthumous issues of empresses the bird may appear alone, either standing or in flight, bearing the deceased Augusta to heaven (the same role fulfilled by Jupiter's eagle in the case of deified emperors). The temple of Juno Moneta on the Capitoline Hill was of special importance from a numismatic standpoint as the Roman mint was established in its vicinity in Republican times. Eventually, this led to the use of the word *moneta* to mean 'mint' and later 'money', though its original meaning as an epithet of Juno is unknown. Her titles include REGINA, LVCINA (referring to her role as the presiding deity of childbirth), CONSERVATRIX, and VICTRIX.

The representations of **Hera** on Roman Provincial issues are far less frequent than those of her consort Zeus, though she does appear at Chalcis in Euboea and at the Bithynian mint of Nicomedia. On an Alexandrian tetradrachm of Nero the veiled bust of Hera Argeia (Hera of Argos) is shown, identified by the accompanying legend HPA APΓEIA.

Sestertius of Domitian

Jupiter. Jove, or Jupiter, Optimus Maximus ('the Best and Greatest), is usually depicted as a tall bearded man in the prime of life, nude or semi-nude, holding a thunderbolt in his right hand and a sceptre in his left. Sometimes standing, sometimes enthroned, the figure of the Father of the Gods must have been a familiar sight to every Roman from the numerous statues erected in his honour in Rome and in all the principal cities of the Empire. On some coins he is depicted holding a small figure of Victory, or his attendant eagle, instead of a thunderbolt: often the eagle is shown standing at his feet. He may also be represented by an eagle alone, both on regular issues and on posthumous coins of deified emperors. The titles of Jupiter are numerous: they include CONSERVATOR, CVSTOS (Protector of the emperor), LIBERATOR, PROPVGNATOR, STATOR (the Stayer of armies about to flee), TONANS (the Thunderer), TVTATOR, and VICTOR. One unusual representation of the god is as a child seated on the back of the nymph Amalthea's goat, with the legend IOVI CRESCENTI, "to the Growing Jupiter". This appears on a coin of the young Caesar

Valerian, son of Gallienus, and clearly implies a comparison between the young prince and the young god.

On Roman Provincial coins representations of **Zeus** are legion and often are accompanied by one of his many titles, such as Kapetolios (referring to the Roman Capitoline Jupiter), Kasios (referring to his worship on Mount Casium in Syria), and Olympios (at Alexandria).

Antoninianus of Gallienus

Luna. The moon-goddess is usually equated with Diana Lucifera and only appears with her own name on coins of Julia Domna and Gallienus.

Her Greek counterpart, **Selene,** appears rather more frequently on the Roman Provincial coinage and sometimes her head is shown conjoined with that of the sun-god Sol.

The crescent-moon, which is symbolic of Luna, sometimes occurs as a type, usually in association with a number of stars. In the 3rd century the crescent of Luna appears at the empress's shoulders on the obverses of *antoniniani* and *dupondii* to indicate the double value of these denominations (cf. also under Sol).

Antoninianus of Elagabalus

Mars. The god of war – always a popular deity with the Romans – appears frequently as a coin type down to the time of Constantine the Great. He is usually shown with his spear and shield, or with a trophy instead of the latter indicating success in a military campaign. He is sometimes nude, except for a helmet and cloak, and sometimes in full armour. When given the title of PACIFER he bears the olive-branch of Peace, though in this connection one remembers the words which Tacitus puts into the mouth of a British chieftain who, referring to the Romans, says 'They make a desert and call it peace'. Amongst the other titles of Mars are CONSERVATOR, PROPVGNATOR (the Champion of Rome), VLTOR (the Avenger), and VICTOR.

Mars, known to the Greeks as **Ares,** appears on a few Roman Provincial issues, but his name or titles are rarely given.

Sestertius of Herennius Etruscus (Mercury)

Mercury. The messenger of the gods was reverenced as the patron of artists, orators, travellers, merchants and, curiously, thieves. He is one of the least frequent of the major deities to appear as a coin type in Imperial times, though his head had been the standard obverse type for the *sextans* and *semuncia* denominations on the Republican coinage. He is generally depicted wearing the winged cap or petasus and carrying a purse and a caduceus. The latter is occasionally used alone as a coin type, notably on the smaller denominations.

On Roman Provincial coins the Greek **Hermes** was only adopted as a type by some half-dozen cities, appearing without name or title.

As of Claudius

Minerva. The counterpart in Roman mythology of the Greek **Pallas Athene,** Minerva frequently appears on coins, particularly those of Domitian who regarded her as his special tutelary deity. A war-like goddess, she usually bears a spear and a shield and is equipped with helmet and aegis. Sometimes she holds a small figure of Victory or is accompanied by her attendant bird, the owl. Minerva guided men in the dangers of war, where victory is gained by prudence, courage, and perseverance. She was also goddess of wisdom and patroness of the arts. Amongst her titles are PACIFERA, bringer of Peace, and VICTRIX.

On the Roman Provincial issues she is sometimes named as Athena, with perhaps an additional title such as Areia (at Pergamum), Ilias (at Ilium), and Argeia (at Alexandria).

Denarius of Claudius

Nemesis. Originally associated with the concept of rightful apportionment, Nemesis came to be regarded as the avenger of crimes and punisher of wrong-doers. Her complex character led to many local interpretations of her role as a goddess and sometimes she was associated with other deities, such as Aequitas, Pax, and Victory, who appeared to be able to assist her in the fulfillment of her various functions. Nemesis makes comparatively few appearances on the Imperial coinage. When she does, she is depicted winged, holding a caduceus or olive-branch, and sometimes with a snake at her feet. A curious gesture especially associated with this goddess is the drawing out of a fold of drapery from her breast. This has been explained as expressing the idea of aversion by spitting upon her bosom inside the opened garment. It was said that humans could avoid her anger by making this same gesture.

Depictions of Nemesis on the Roman Provincial coinage are rather more frequent. Here, she is not always winged and is typically shown holding a bridle or cubit-rule with a wheel at her feet. Occasionally, two Nemeses may appear standing face to face. This relates to a legend in which the twin Nemeses of Smyrna appeared in a vision to Alexander the Great commanding him to refound the city.

As of Agrippa

Neptune. The god of the sea had appeared only infrequently on the later Republican coinage, the first occasion being on a silver *quinarius* of the moneyer L. Rubrius Dossenus in 87 BC. In Imperial times his depictions were more varied, though they remained sporadic. He is usually represented holding a dolphin and a trident, but sometimes holds an acrostolium (the prow ornament of a galley) instead of the former. The prow itself may be shown beside him, sometimes with his right foot resting on it.

Poseidon, the Greek counterpart of Neptune, is of rare occurrence as a type on the Roman Provincial coinage. However, he does appear at Rhodes, with the name Poseidon Asphaleios ('bringing safety'), and at Alexandria as Poseidon Isthmios (referring to the Isthmus of Corinth).

Sestertius of Nero

Roma. The goddess who personified the city of Rome (and in a wider sense the Empire which she had conquered) is usually represented helmeted and in armour, holding a small figure of Victory, or a wreath, and a parazonium. She is often seated on a pile of arms representing the spoils of war. When the Roman Empire became Christian, the type continued in use as a personification of the city or the state, much as the figure of Britannia is regarded today.

Roma also appears on the coinage of Alexandria, identified by the accompanying legend ΡΩΜΗ.

Alexandrian tetradrachm of Hadrian

Serapis. This deity was a creation of Ptolemy I of Egypt who wished to establish a cult in which his native Egyptian subjects and their new Greek rulers could participate together, thereby fostering a spirit of national unity. Thus, the Egyptians would be able to recognize the characteristics of Osiris and the Greeks would see Zeus, Hades, and Asklepios. The idea appears to have been a resounding success, as Serapis quickly became established as a major deity and later achieved enormous popularity in Rome and throughout the Empire, many splendid temples being erected in his honour.

He appears intermittently on the Roman Imperial coinage from the time of Hadrian onwards and is usually shown raising his right hand and holding a sceptre. On his head he frequently wears a modius and the triple-headed dog Cerberus, guardian of the infernal regions, sometimes sits at his feet. Late in the 2nd century the Emperor Commodus invoke his special protection on a remarkable series inscribed **SERAPIDI CONSERV AVG**, and the early Severan emperors also showed great favour to the cult of Serapis, Septimius himself being of African birth.

Serapis appears on the coins of a number of Roman Provincial mints, principally, of course, on those of Alexandria. Sometimes his bust is shown conjoined with that of the Egyptian goddess Isis, the consort of Osiris.

Antoninianus of Aurelian

Sol. The sun-god frequently appears as a type during the 3rd century and the early decades of the 4th, down to the advent of Christianity under Constantine. He is usually depicted nude, or almost so, wearing a radiate crown and holding a globe or a whip. Sometimes he is shown in his chariot drawn by four lively horses and occasionally his bust only occurs as a type. His titles include **COMES** ('Companion') and **INVICTVS** ('Unconquered'). When he is styled **ORIENS**, a name which properly refers to the eastern or rising sun, it may be taken as alluding to the rising fortunes of the emperor using the type.

Helios, the Greek equivalent of Sol, appears in the Roman Provincial series on the coins of a number of Greek cities. Sometimes his head is shown conjoined with that of the moon-goddess Selene (Roman Luna).

The radiate crown, which the emperor is usually shown wearing on the *dupondius* and *antoninianus* denominations (as well as the rare *double sestertius*), may be taken as an allusion to his position as the earthly personification of the sun-god. Similarly, from the time of Julia Domna to the end of the 3rd century, the empress is normally depicted on the same denominations with a crescent at her shoulders, this being a reference to the moon-goddess Luna. In both instances these distinctions also indicated the double value of the denomination (two *asses*, two *denarii*, and two *sestertii* respectively).

Colonial bronze of Deultum in Thrace

The Three Graces. The Gratiae, or Charites (Euphrosyne, Aglaia, and Thalia), were minor deities who personified the ideals of beauty, gentleness, and friendship. They were attendants of Aphrodite (Roman Venus) and they especially favoured poetry and the arts. Their images, consisting of a standing group of three nude female figures, do not appear on the Imperial coinage. However, the type was used by a number of mints in the Roman Provincial series, including Marcianopolis, Argos, Itanus, Naxos, and Magnesia ad Maeandrum, as well as the colonial mint of Deultum in Thrace. Statues of the Graces were popular throughout the Roman world and the Museum at Cyrene possesses one of the Hadrianic period. The type inspired Italian medallists as late as the 16th century.

Denarius of Julia, daughter of Titus

Venus. The goddess of beauty and love was a favourite Roman coin type from Republican times until early in the 4th century. Amongst her titles are **CAELESTIS, FELIX, GENETRIX,** and **VICTRIX,** and she is usually depicted fully, or almost fully, clothed. Sometimes she holds an apple, sometimes a helmet and a sceptre, and occasionally she is accompanied by Cupid (Greek Eros). In those instances where she is shown semi-nude she is usually posed with her back modestly turned towards the spectator. Julius Caesar, who claimed descent from the goddess, depicted her on many of his coins, generally holding a small figure of Victory.

On Roman Provincial coins the goddess **Aphrodite** was sometimes adopted as a coin type, often because in or near the issuing city there was an important temple dedicated to the deity. In a few cases, such as at Corinth and Cnidus, the representation of the goddess is known to have been copied from a statue for which the issuing city was famous.

As of Caligula (Vesta)

Vesta. One of the most honoured deities of the Romans, Vesta was the special protectress of the family hearth and was worshipped as a goddess of the Roman state as well as by individuals as the guardian of family life. Following a number of appearances on the later Republican coinage (including a depiction of her temple in the Forum) she was represented on the coins of many emperors, from Caligula to Gallienus, as a matron holding a patera and a sceptre, or a torch, a simpulum, or the Palladium. The well-known *as* of Caligula, with a seated figure of the goddess, is perhaps one of the best examples of her image as a coin type. The distinctive circular temple of Vesta also appears from time to time, often in connection with its restoration following some disastrous fire. The titles of Vesta include MATER and SANCTA.

Her Greek counterpart **Hestia** rarely appears on the Roman Provincial coinage, despite the universality of her cult in the Greek world. One of the few possible exceptions is the city of Maeonia in Lydia, where coins were issued depicting both the goddess and her temple (she is not named, however, and the identification has been contested).

Antoninianus of Valerian

Vulcan. The Roman god of iron and fire was of Italic origin and was regarded as the chief deity of smiths and ironworkers. He seldom occurs as a coin type, but when featured he wears a conical hat (pileus) and holds attributes appropriate to the blacksmith's trade, such as a hammer and tongs. His earliest appearance had been on bronze *dodrantes* of 127–126 BC on which his head was shown as the obverse type, wearing a pileus and with tongs over his shoulder. The last appearance was on *antoniniani* of the joint reign of Valerian and Gallienus, on which the god appears at work within a tetrastyle temple, accompanied by the legend DEO VOLKANO. These coins were minted in Gaul where the cult of Vulcan was especially popular.

It was natural that the Roman Vulcan should be equated with the Greek **Hephaistos,** the son of Hera and Zeus and husband of Aphrodite. He appears at a number of Greek mints in the Roman Provincial series and is sometimes depicted seated on a rock, forging the shield of Achilles, as described by Homer.

We can now proceed briefly to summarize the chief allegorical personifications which appear on the Imperial coinage. In the following list, the Latin name of each is given first, followed in brackets by the Greek equivalent (where used on a provincial issue). Then comes the closest English rendering of the name, and finally the attributes normally associated with the personification. Feminine names are listed first, in alphabetical order, followed by the masculine, which are far fewer in number.

FEMALE

Abundantia
(Severus Alexander)

Aequitas (Macrianus)

Aeternitas (Faustina Sr.)

Abundantia (Euthenia). Abundance, Plenty. Holds cornucopiae and corn-ears, or is shown emptying the former.

Aequitas (Dikaiosyne). Equity, Fair Dealing. Holds scales and cornucopiae or sceptre.

Aeternitas. Eternity, Stability. Holds globe, torch, phoenix, or sceptre, or the heads of the Sun and Moon.

Annona
(Antoninus Pius)

Clementia (Hadrian)

Concordia
(Julia Paula)

Annona. The Annual Grain Supply of Rome. Holds corn-ears and cornucopiae, usually with modius and ship's prow beside her.

Clementia. Clemency, Mercy. Holds branch and sceptre, and sometimes leans on a column.

Concordia (Homonoia). Concord, Harmony. Holds patera and cornucopiae or sceptre. As Concordia Militum, holds two standards.

Constantia   Fecunditas   Felicitas (Julia Mamaea)
(Claudius)   (Faustina Jr.)

Constantia. Constancy. Her right hand raised to her face. Sometimes in military attire, also holding spear. [Confined to the coinage of the reign of Claudius].

Fecunditas. Fertility (of an empress). Holds child, or children, and sceptre. Sometimes the children are depicted standing at her feet.

Felicitas (Eutycheia). Happiness, Prosperity. Holds caduceus and cornucopiae or sceptre. Sometimes depicted leaning on a column.

Fides Militum   Fortuna (Domitian)   Hilaritas (Hadrian)
(Maximinus I)

Fides. Good Faith, Loyalty, Trustworthiness. Holds patera and cornucopiae or corn-ears and basket of fruit. As Fides Militum, holds two standards or standard and sceptre.

Fortuna (Tyche). Fortune. Holds rudder, sometimes resting on globe, and cornucopiae; a wheel may be shown beside her. Sometimes her attributes include an olive-branch or a patera.

Hilaritas. Rejoicing. Holds long palm and cornucopiae, sceptre or patera; is sometimes accompanied by one or two children.

Indulgentia
(Antoninus Pius)

Justitia (Nerva)

Laetitia
(Gordian III)

Indulgentia. Indulgence, Mercy. Holds patera and sceptre.

Justitia. Justice. Holds olive-branch, or patera, and sceptre; rarely (on posthumous coins of Constantine) she holds a pair of scales.

Laetitia. Joy, Gladness. Holds wreath and sceptre, or occasionally rudder on globe in place of the latter, or may rest her left hand on an anchor.

Liberalitas (Severus
Alexander)

Libertas (Claudius)

Moneta (Domitian)

Liberalitas. Liberality. Holds tessera (or abacus) and cornucopiae.

Libertas (Eleutheria). Freedom, Liberty. Holds pileus (conical hat) and sceptre.

Moneta. Mint, Money. Holds scales and cornucopiae. Sometimes represented as the Three Monetae (gold, silver and *aes*), each with a pile of metal (or coins) at her feet.

Nobilitas (Geta)

Ops (Antoninus Pius)

Pax (Severus
Alexander)

Nobilitas. Nobility, High Birth. Holds Palladium and sceptre.

Ops. Power, Prosperity, Aid. Holds sceptre or corn-ears. [Confined to the coinages of Antoninus Pius and Pertinax].

Patientia. Endurance, Patience. Holds sceptre.

Pax (Eirene). Peace. Holds olive-branch and sceptre, cornucopiae or caduceus.

Pietas (Julia   Providentia (Caracalla)   Pudicitia (Herennia
Maesa)   Etruscilla)

Pietas (Eusebeia). Piety, Dutifulness. Often veiled, holds patera and sceptre; sometimes shown sacrificing at an altar and holding a box of incense.

> 'Roman piety unites in one whole, reverence for the gods, devotion to the Emperor, affection between the Augusti or between the Augustus and the people, tenderness of parents to sons, respect or affectionate care of the latter for their parents, and in general, love of one's neighbour, or in one word Religion' (Gnecchi).

Providentia (Pronoia). Foreseeing. Holds rod, with which she sometimes points to a globe at her feet, and sceptre. In the 3rd century she is often shown holding the globe. The legend may also accompany types which express the concept of *providentia* in more symbolic ways.

Pudicitia. Modesty, Chastity. Holds sceptre and is usually veiled.

Salus (Maximinus I)   Securitas (Antoninus Pius)

Salus (Hygieia). Health, Safety, Welfare. Holds sceptre and patera from which she feeds a snake coiled round an altar; or holds the snake in her arms and feeds it from the patera.

Securitas. Security, Confidence. Holds patera or sceptre, and may be depicted leaning on a column, legs crossed; sometimes sits back at ease in a chair.

| Spes (Claudius) | Uberitas (Trajan Decius) | Victoria (Antoninus Pius) |

Spes (Elpis). Hope. Holds flower, and is usually shown walking and slightly raising the drapery of her dress behind.

Uberitas *or* **Ubertas.** Fruitfulness, Abundance. Holds cornucopiae and purse or bunch of grapes (possibly even a cow's udder).

Victoria (Nike). Victory. Winged, holding a wreath and a palm; may be shown with a shield, which she sometimes inscribes, or erecting a trophy.

MALE

| Bonus Eventus (Antoninus Pius) | Genius (Hadrian) |

Bonus Eventus. Good Outcome. Holds patera over altar, and cornucopiae.

Genius. Spirit. Holds patera and cornucopiae, sometimes with altar at feet. Most frequently appears as Genius of the Roman People (GENIVS POPVLI ROMANI), but is represented in a variety of other forms, such as Genius of the Senate (bearded and togate), Genius of the Emperors (and Caesars), and Genius of the Army (with military standard). In the early 4th century he sometimes holds the head of Serapis.

Honos (Marcus Aurelius)   Virtus (Hadrian)

Honos. Honour. Holds olive-branch or sceptre and cornucopiae. Sometimes appears in association with another male personification, Virtus.

Virtus. Valour, Bravery. Usually depicted in complete armour, holding Victory or parazonium and spear, or with spear and shield. Sometimes appears in association with another male personification, Honos.

It should be emphasized that the foregoing notes do not pretend to do anything like justice to the subject, about which, indeed, a lengthy book could be written. It is hoped, however, that the information provided, although brief, will be found of interest and may lead collectors of the series to study the subject in more detailed works.

II. REPRESENTATIONS OF THE EMPEROR AND HIS FAMILY

In addition to monopolizing the obverses of Roman Imperial coins, the emperors and their families also make frequent appearances as reverse types.

Agrippa as a   Nero on horseback
reverse type of
Augustus

Augustus set the precedent by authorizing his representation as the victor of Actium and conqueror of Egypt riding in a triumphal quadriga on the reverse of a denarius issued in the autumn of 30 BC. Several other types of Augustus followed during his long reign, including several of 13 BC depicting both the emperor and his trusted friend and colleague, Marcus Agrippa. With the exception of Tiberius, the Julio-Claudian emperors made increasingly frequent appearances on the reverses of their coins. Nero, the last representative of the dynasty, is depicted distributing gifts to the people, haranguing his troops, taking part in military exercises on horseback, and even singing to his own accompaniment on a lyre, in the guise of Apollo.

Titus in triumphal procession

Domitian sacrificing
during Secular Games

In the Flavian period, Vespasian and Titus appear most frequently in connection with two main themes – the quelling of the Jewish Revolt and the recovery of the Roman State following the Civil Wars of AD 68–69. Vespasian is shown raising a kneeling female figure (the State) on one of his *aurei*, and both father and son are depicted riding in their chariots in the triumphal procession which celebrated the victory in Judaea. Domitian appears as conqueror of the German tribes on a *sestertius* which shows him standing in military attire, a personification of the Rhine reclining at his feet. This emperor's most interesting appearances, however, are in connection with the Secular Games of AD 88, when he is depicted as a participant in various ceremonies, often with the temple of Jupiter Capitolinus as a backdrop.

Hadrian arriving in
Mauretania

Antoninus Pius crowning
the king of Armenia

The Golden Age of Trajan, Hadrian, and the Antonine emperors produced a great variety of interesting reverse types depicting the emperor. Trajan, the great warrior, is shown at full gallop thrusting his spear at a Dacian enemy, whilst Hadrian's famous peregrinations spanning his vast Empire are fully documented on the coinage. Antoninus' stature as a statesmen is suitably illustrated by a *sestertius* which shows a togate figure of the emperor in the act of creating a new king of Armenia by placing a diadem on the head of the monarch. With the recurrence of bitter frontier wars under Marcus Aurelius, he, and his co-emperor Lucius Verus, are frequently depicted in military scenes. One type shows Aurelius standing amidst four standards, whilst on a coin of Verus the emperor spears a fallen eastern enemy as he gallops past. The first joint reign in the history of the Empire is commemorated by a type showing togate figures of the two emperors clasping right hands.

The megalomania of Commodus is quite evident on several of his reverse types, as well as on the obverses which show his head clad in the lion's skin of Hercules. A type common to both *sestertius* and *as* feature the emperor dressed as a priest and ploughing with a yoke of two oxen, symbolic of his insane notion to refound the city of Rome and give to it the new name of *Colonia Lucia Antoniniana Commodiana.*

Elagabalus as
priest of the sun-
god

Severus Alexander in
consular procession

The military anarchy which crippled the Empire for a large part of the 3rd century led to a decline in the representation of the emperor in any guise other than as commander-in-chief of the armed forces. Septimius Severus is shown togate, as *Fundator Pacis* ('Founder of the Peace'), on one type, but he and his sons usually appear in scenes of military significance. Elagabalus, who was far from being a soldier, is often depicted in his role as Chief-Priest of the Syrian Sun-God, providing a brief interlude in this martial period. Elagabalus' cousin and successor, Severus Alexander, wears the civilian toga while sacrificing over a tripod-altar, but most of his representations are military in character. Over the next few decades the Roman citizen, observing the reverses of the coins he handled, saw his ruler represented only in a few rather stereotyped poses, usually standing in military attire or mounted on horseback. Few other types break the monotony, although Gallienus, the type content of whose coinage is generally more interesting than that of other emperors of the period, is depicted in a greater variety of poses. In one of these, he raises a kneeling figure representing the Gallic provinces. Soon after this type was struck, however, the region was lost by Gallienus to the usurper Postumus and remained independent of the central government for the following fourteen years.

Magnus Maximus
and Flavius Victor
enthroned

Arcadius
trampling on
captive

Towards the end of the 3rd century successive emperors were often shown receiving a figure of Victory from the hands of Jupiter and this type continued in use into the early years of the 4th century. With the adoption of Christianity by Constantine and the subsequent slow demise of pagan traditions coin types in general became more limited in number and monotonous in content. The emperor usually appears as the champion of the new faith, holding a labarum (Christian standard) and a figure of Victory (which was now becoming equated with the Christian Angel). The Victory-Angel also appears on a series of later 4th century post-Constantinian gold *solidi*, hovering between two emperors enthroned side by side. By this time the Empire had become more or less permanently divided into eastern and western halves, with at least two emperors reigning simultaneously.

The grandsons
of Augustus

The sisters of Caligula

Representations of empresses and princes (and in a few rare instances deceased parents) as reverse types occur throughout most of the period, although there were very few Imperial heirs (as opposed to youthful co-emperors) after the Caesarship of Julian II (AD 355–60). In the early Empire, the emperor's relatives appeared most often on the reverses of his own coins, as their own coinages were very small, where they existed at all. Thus, we see Gaius and Lucius Caesars standing side by side on the reverse of their grandfather Augustus' most prolific issue of *aurei* and *denarii*, and the Empress Livia seated on the reverse of her son Tiberius' principal precious metal type (the 'Tribute Penny' of the Bible). Caligula, on one of his *sestertii*, has a most interesting reverse type depicting his three sisters, Agrippina, Drusilla and Julia. On the reverses of some of his *aurei* and *denarii* Claudius featured the portraits of his fourth wife, Agrippina, and his step-son, Nero; whilst the brief reign of Vitellius in AD 69 produced several interesting family types depicting the emperor's young children and his deceased father, the celebrated Lucius Vitellius.

Hostilian as 'Prince
of the Youth'

Faustina Junior as
'Mother of the Camps'

From the Flavian period, the princes (or 'Caesars') began issuing substantial coinages in their own right, and from the early part of the 2nd century the empresses also were given a much larger share of the total output of the mint. The Caesars, where they appear on the reverses of their own coins, are usually represented as 'Prince of the Youth' (**PRINCEPS IVVENTVTIS**). The Caesar Marcus Aurelius, who served an unprecedented term of over two decades as heir under Antoninus Pius (AD 139–161) was accorded an extensive coinage of his own, and additionally his head appears as the reverse type on a whole range of denominations of Antoninus himself. Empresses appear in a variety of roles as reverse types, often in the guise of some female deity. Faustina Junior, wife of

Marcus Aurelius, features on a number of types as 'Mother of the Camps' (MATER CASTRORVM), a reference to her devotion to the interests of the soldiers during her husband's arduous military campaigns, the hardships of many of which she shared. Another reverse type seen frequently on the coinages of empresses, particularly in the early decades of the 3rd century, shows the Augusta and the Augustus clasping hands, often in commemoration of the actual imperial nuptials.

Septimius Severus and his family

Before closing this brief survey of imperial representations as reverse types, mention should be made of the uniquely extensive series of 'dynastic coins' issued under Septimius Severus (AD 193–211). These depict his wife, Julia Domna, his daughter-in-law, Plautilla, and his two sons, Caracalla and Geta, as well as himself. All these pieces are in the *aureus* and *denarius* denominations and all are rare or very rare. The obverses usually show a single bust, though occasionally two are represented, whilst the reverses have one, two, or even three imperial portraits. Perhaps the most celebrated coin in this series is the *aureus* of Severus issued in AD 201 displaying as its reverse type a remarkable facing portrait of the empress between the confronted busts of her two sons. But despite the seeming promise of continuity, this phase of the Severan dynasty was destined to be extinct within a mere sixteen years of this issue.

III. TYPES OF MILITARY CONQUEST AND VICTORY

During the five centuries of its existence the Roman Empire was involved in numerous wars and campaigns, some expansionist, some defensive, and some domestic. Many of these were commemorated on the coinage, one of the earliest instances being a type of Octavian (Augustus) with crocodile reverse and legend AEGYPTO CAPTA. This refers to the defeat of Antony and Cleopatra in 30 BC and the subsequent annexation of the former Ptolemaic kingdom to the Empire of Rome.

| Claudius triumphing for his British conquest | Captive Judaea (Vespasian) | Captive Germania (Domitian) |

The invasion of Britain in AD 43 was well recorded on the gold and silver coinage of Claudius, with a type depicting the arch erected in Rome to commemorate the conquest. The great Jewish Revolt, which began under Nero in AD 66, was a serious embarrassment to the Romans, coming, as it did, at a time of acute political upheaval in the Empire which saw the rapid succession of four emperors during the years AD 68 and 69. The rebellion in Judaea was actually crushed by the general Vespasian and his son Titus who used their success in this campaign to seize the Imperial throne and establish a new dynasty, the Flavian. Vespasian gave great publicity to his victory in the East on a large output of coins in all metals, known collectively as the 'Judaea Capta' series. One of the commonest types appears on *aurei* and *denarii* and depicts a captive Judaea seated at the foot of a Roman trophy. The German wars of Vespasian's younger son, Domitian, are also commemorated by a large number of types, one of which shows a female German captive in despair seated upon a shield.

Captive Dacia
(Trajan)

Captive
Armenia
(Lucius Verus)

Pile of Sarmatian arms
(Marcus Aurelius)

Trajan's expansionist policy in the early 2nd century led to prolonged campaigns in several widely separated theatres of war. Undoubtedly, his greatest achievement was the conquest of Dacia. This received considerable publicity on the coinage, with no fewer than twelve main types alluding to the event. The eastern wars of AD 163–5 also received extensive notice on the coinages of the joint emperors Marcus Aurelius and Lucius Verus. A notable type in this series shows captive Armenia seated amidst arms. Much of the final decade of Aurelius' rule was taken up with warfare on the harsh northern frontier, and a *sestertius* struck in AD 177 depicts a large pile of arms, symbolic of the successful conclusion of the German and Sarmatian Wars.

Commemoration of victory in northern Britain (Caracalla) and in Germany (Maximinus I)

Septimius Severus' numerous campaigns in both the East and West are well documented on the Imperial coinage, but perhaps the series of greatest interest to British students is the one which commemorates the events of AD 208–11. During this period Severus and his elder son Caracalla campaigned on the northern frontier in Britain and restored Hadrian's Wall, which appears to have suffered damage in the troubled period more than a decade before. Caracalla's Parthian 'war' received some notice on the coinage, and even Macrinus' inglorious encounter with Artaban of Parthia was celebrated as a VICTORIA PARTHICA on coins of all metals. More deserving of commemoration were Maximinus' victories in Germany in AD 235 and *aes* of the following year shows the emperor being crowned by Victory.

The second half of the 3rd century was a disastrous period for Roman arms, with large parts of the Empire succumbing to foreign attack and much of what remained being rent by internal rebellion. Miraculously, however, the situation was restored by a succession of short-lived but very strong military rulers, known collectively as the 'Illyrian' emperors, foremost amongst whom were Claudius Gothicus (AD 268–70), Aurelian (270–75) and Probus (276–82). A coin of this period struck by Aurelian's ephemeral successor, Tacitus, celebrates a victory over the Goths with the inscription VICTORIA GOTTHI.

Victory over the
Goths (Tacitus)

Captive Alamanni
(Crispus)

In the 4th century commemorative reverse types became increasingly rare. One of the last to be issued depicts a personification of the Alamanni (a confederation of Germanic tribes) seated in captivity at the foot of a trophy. This appears on a gold *solidus* of Crispus Caesar, eldest son of Constantine, issued at Trier in AD 319–20. The young prince had led a successful campaign against the Alamanni in 318. A similar contemporary type bears the legend FRANCIA instead of ALAMANNIA and records success against the Franci (Franks), another Germanic people who were later to conquer Gaul and give it the name of France.

IV. LEGIONARY TYPES, ETC

The 'legionary' series forms a compact group within the Roman coinage, most of it having being issued by just five rulers over a period of about 325 years, from the battle of Actium to the late 3rd century AD. Those of Mark Antony (issued 32–31 BC) and Septimius Severus (AD 193) are similar in that both have the same basic reverse type – a legionary eagle between two standards. In contrast, the later 3rd century issues of Gallienus, Victorinus and Carausius interestingly bear the actual badges of the various legions, e.g. a lion for the *IIII Flavia* and a capricorn for the *XXII Primigenia*. The primary reason for the issue of these exceptional types was to inspire the loyalty of the troops whose legions were being honoured. Curiously, in some cases those troops appear not to have been under the command of the emperor issuing the coins. In such instances it must be assumed that what we are seeing is a very artful use of the propaganda value of the coinage, *i.e.* an attempt to win over the loyalty of an opponent's army by means of flattery.

Standards of
Legio XIV
Gemina (Severus)

Badge of Legio
XXII Primigenia
(Gallienus)

Another series of exceptional interest is the 'Army' coinage produced by Hadrian (AD 117–38) in the closing years of his reign. This honoured the army comprising the legionary garrison of each military province (EXERC BRITANNICVS, EXERCITVS SYRIACVS, etc.) and was mostly confined to the large *sestertius* denomination. It was connected with the emperor's keen interest in the military establishment, and in particular the strengthening of the defences of the frontier regions (the policy which led to the construction of Hadrian's Wall in Britain and the German *limes*). These coins, all of which are very rare today, depict the emperor addressing his soldiers from a platform, or saluting them whilst mounted on horseback. Related types of Hadrian and Antoninus Pius refer to military discipline and are inscribed DISCIPLINA AVG.

In addition to calls for allegiance and discipline aimed at specific legions and armies there were also pleas for loyalty addressed to the military in general. This sometimes came at times when that loyalty was in doubt. Thus, on coins of Nerva (AD 96–8), whose brief regime was very unpopular with the soldiers, we see clasped hands holding a legionary eagle set on a prow, accompanied by the legend CONCORDIA EXERCITVVM; whilst much later, the short-lived Gallic usurper Marius (AD 268) used a similar type on his coinage, though on this occasion clasped hands only were shown encircled by the legend CONCORDIA MILITVM. The 'valour of the soldiers' (VIRTVS MILITVM) was proclaimed on a large issue of silver *argentei*, or *siliquae*, issued under the rulers of the First Tetrarchy at the end of the 3rd century; and the 'renown of the army' (GLORIA EXERCITVS) was celebrated on an extensive series of small billon *centenionales* introduced in the closing phase of Constantine's reign and carried on for some years after his death by his sons.

Appeal for loyalty to
the military (Nerva)

Captured German
shields (Domitian)

Many other types of military and naval significance may be found amongst the reverses of the Roman coinage. Noteworthy are a *denarius* of Octavian (Augustus) displaying a naval trophy; a *dupondius* of Domitian depicting two German shields crossed over a vexillum, trumpets and spears; and a coin of Trajan, of the same denomination, with a fine representation of a cuirass (body-armour). Naval power, in the form of a war-galley, was featured in the later 3rd century on coins of the Gallic usurper Postumus and on those of the British usurpers Carausius and Allectus.

V. GEOGRAPHICAL TYPES

The Roman Empire was a unique association of peoples and cultures, such as the Mediterranean World had never seen before and has not witnessed since. What had formerly been a patchwork of Hellenistic monarchies, independent city states and Celtic tribes was miraculously transformed by the genius of Rome and her code of laws into one great political entity, and held together not so much by force of arms as by the *Pax Romana*.

Female personifications of many of the provinces within this vast State were depicted on several coin series during the Imperial period, and even particular cities and rivers receive occasional notice (the latter normally appearing as a bearded male figure in a reclining attitude).

Denarii of Augustus and Galba featuring the city of Emerita and heads of the 'Three Gauls'

An early *denarius* of Augustus' reign shows the city gate and defensive walls of *Emerita* in Spain, a colony which was founded in 25 BC and populated by Roman soldiers whose term of service had expired (*emeritus*). Galba, in AD 68, issued a remarkable type showing three small female heads accompanied by the legend TRES GALLIAE. These represented the three great divisions of the province of Gaul – Narbonensis, Aquitania and Lugdunensis –in recognition of the support which he received from the western provinces during his revolt against Nero's tyrannical rule. Dacia, the province added to the Empire by Trajan, is commemorated on *sestertii* and *dupondii* of that emperor, identified by the legend DACIA AVGVST PROVINCIA. The type shows Dacia seated on a rock, accompanied by two children, symbolic of future generations of Dacians who could now look forward to an era of peace under the protection of omnipotent Rome.

Germany, Cappadocia, Egypt and the Nile, all featured on the coinage of Hadrian

The coinage of Hadrian provides us with a far more complete geographical survey of the Roman World than that of any other emperor. His extensive travels all over his vast Empire were commemorated on several remarkable series of coins, mostly issued towards the end of his reign when he had finally returned to Italy. In addition to honouring most of the provinces, two cities (Alexandria and Nicomedia) receive special attention, as does the River Nile (NILVS). The following is a list of the provinces whose personifications appear on Hadrian's coinage: Britain; Spain; Gaul; Germany; Italy; Sicily; Noricum; Dacia; Macedonia; Moesia; Thrace; Achaea; Asia; Bithynia; Phrygia; Cilicia; Cappadocia; Judaea; Arabia; Egypt; Africa; Mauretania.

Hadrian's successor, Antoninus Pius, also issued a 'provincial' series of coins, in this case to celebrate the remission of half of the *aurum coronarium* ('crown-gold'). This was a demand made by the emperor on the communities of the Empire (and sometimes even on foreign states) at the time of his accession and on certain anniversaries of his rule. Antoninus' remission of half of this burdensome tax at the time he came to the throne was greeted with much enthusiasm and led to the production of an extensive series of *aes* coinage depicting crown-bearing personifications of various provinces (and even of the Parthian kingdom). The advancement of the Roman frontier in Britain to the line of the new Antonine Wall prompted the issue of several attractive Britannia types on *sestertii* of AD 143. This was followed more than a decade later by another type (mostly on *asses*) depicting the personification of the island province in an attitude of dejection and commemorating the quelling of a serious tribal uprising. An elegant personification of Italy, seated on a globe, appeared on a variety of denominations in AD 140, possibly in anticipation of the celebration of Rome's 900th anniversary in 147.

Britannia and Asia on sestertii of Antoninus Pius

Geographical types are less commonly encountered on coins struck in the second half of the 2nd century. Marcus Aurelius has an *as* showing a reclining figure of the River Tiber, whilst Commodus issued two *sestertius* types, one with Italia seated on a large globe, the other a very rare depiction of a standing Britannia. At the very end of the century, Clodius Albinus, in rebellion against Septimius Severus, struck a *denarius* featuring the Genius of the City of Lugdunum in Gaul.

Genius of Lugdunum (Clodius Albinus)

Dacia and the Pannoniae on sestertii of Trajan Decius

During the course of the 3rd century there was a continued decline in the frequency of geographical references on the Imperial coinage. Septimius Severus makes mention of Italy, Africa and Carthage, and half-way through the century Trajan Decius honours the provinces of Dacia and the two Pannoniae with standing figures of their personifications. Dacia appears again on coins of Claudius Gothicus and Aurelian, and the Pannonian provinces are commemorated by Quintillus, Aurelian and Julian. The city of Siscia receives special notice on *antoniniani* of both Gallienus and Probus, and a reclining figure of the Rhine is depicted on coins of the Gallic usurper Postumus. Britannia makes her final appearance on the Roman coinage clasping hands with the late 3rd century rebel Carausius, who had succeeded in temporarily detaching the island-province from the rule of the central government.

The late Roman coinage of the 4th and 5th centuries contain very few geographical references amongst their reverse types. Africa and Carthage occur on *folles* of several of the emperors and usurpers in the early years of the century, and one of the last types of any geographical significance is found on the Constantinopolitan silver and billon coinage of the unfortunate young prince Hanniballianus (AD 335–7). This shows a reclining figure of the river-god Euphrates and its appearance at this time is made all the more remarkable by comparison with the general lack of imagination being shown in the selection of reverse types in the closing years of Constantine's reign.

Africa (Diocletian)

The Euphrates
(Hanniballianus)

VI. ARCHITECTURAL TYPES

The Romans were great builders, a fact attested by the many splendid examples of their architecture which are still to be seen in countries all over the Mediterranean World and in northern Europe. Many of the emperors took a special pride in adorning the capital, and other cities, with edifices which were not only functional (such as the great market of Nero and Trajan's *Basilica Ulpia*), but often possessed considerable architectural merit as well. Doubtless, Rome's autocrats were also well aware of the excellent potential for long-term survival of such structures and saw them as a means of perpetuating their prestige in people's minds. A number of these buildings were displayed on the coins (usually at the time of their construction or renovation) and these reverse types form one of the most sought-after groups within the Roman coinage.

Augustus issued a number of architectural types, a very early example being the temple of Divus Julius depicted on *aurei* and *denarii* of 36 BC, when the building was still under construction. Also appearing on his pre-27 BC coinage is a representation of the *Curia Julia* (the Senate House in the Forum) which was dedicated by Augustus on 28 August 29 BC. On the later Augustan coinage a variety of architectural types are featured, mostly on *denarii*: these include the *Arcus Augusti*, which replaced the earlier Actian arch; the temples of Jupiter Tonans and of Mars Ultor (both on the Capitol); the *Porta Fontinalis* and part of Rome's Servian Wall; and another depiction of a city-gate and defensive walls, this time of the colonial foundation of Emerita in Spain. The celebrated Altar of Lugdunum, dedicated by the emperor in 10 BC, forms the sole reverse type of the Lugdunese *aes* coinage which was produced in considerable quantity in the latter part of the reign.

Temple of Divus   The 'Twin Janus' (Nero)   The Colosseum (Titus)
Julius (Octavian)

As one of his *sestertius* types Tiberius has a depiction of the temple of Concord in the Forum. This building was used to house antique sculpture and is shown adorned with a variety of statues. Caligula features an elaborate representation of the temple of Divus Augustus, also on a *sestertius*; whilst Claudius shows the arch spanning the *Via Flaminia* which was constructed to commemorate his conquest of Britain. Nero, last of the Julio-Claudian emperors, has a number of architectural types which are depicted principally on his handsome *aes* coinage: the *Macellum Magnum*, or Great Market, which was completed in AD 59; the celebrated *Ianus Geminus* ('Twin Janus'), the doors of which were closed with great ceremony to celebrate peace throughout the Empire; an elaborate arch which has since disappeared without trace, probably the one erected to commemorate Corbulo's eastern victories; a remarkable aerial view of the harbour of Ostia, improved under Claudius and Nero; and (on precious metal only) the domed temple of Vesta in the Forum, restored by Nero following its destruction in the great fire of AD 64.

Later emperors eagerly continued the tradition of architectural reverse types. The great Flavian Amphitheatre, known today as the Colosseum, appears on a *sestertius* of Titus under whom the famous edifice was completed and dedicated. A *cistophorus* of Domitian shows the temple of Jupiter Capitolinus, together with the legend **CAPIT RESTIT**, a reference to that emperor's rebuilding of the famous temple following the devastating fire of AD 80. Domitian also has a rare series of *denarii* depicting various temples, identified by Hill as those of Serapis, Cybele, Minerva Chalcidica, and Jupiter Victor, in addition to the Capitoline temple itself. Trajan's coinage has many types of architectural interest, such as the Circus Maximus, restored by Trajan *circa* AD 103; Trajan's celebrated Forum and Basilica; Trajan's Column, erected to commemorate the conquest of Dacia; the 'Danube' bridge (in all probability the *Pons Sublicius* in Rome); a triumphal arch inscribed **I 0 M**; and two octastyle temples, one of which may be that of Divus Nerva.

Trajan's
Column
(Trajan)

The 'Danube' bridge (Trajan)

Temple of Roma
(Antoninus Pius)

The great temple of Venus and Roma, designed by Hadrian himself, appears both on the coinage of its architect's reign and on that of his successor, Antoninus Pius, under whom it was completed. Antoninus also depicts the temple of Divus Augustus, in commemoration of his restoration of the famous edifice (now disappeared without trace). The temple which Antoninus built in honour of his wife Faustina (later dedicated to his memory also) is shown on *denarii* of the deified empress. The ruins of the shell of this structure, enclosing the church of S. Lorenzo in Miranda, are still to be seen in the Roman Forum. A temple of Mercury, of very unusual form, appears on a *sestertius* of Marcus Aurelius, accompanied by the legend **RELIG AVG**; whilst a coin of Commodus of the same denomination features a distyle shrine of Janus.

The famous Arch of Severus, which still stands in all its ancient majesty in the Roman Forum, is depicted on the coinages of both Septimius and Caracalla. A representation of the Circus Maximus, very similar to the one of Trajan, occurs also on *sestertii* of Caracalla struck in AD 213 to commemorate yet another restoration of the structure. Under Severus Alexander several fine architectural types appear, including the Colosseum on an *aureus* and *aes* of AD 223; the Nymphaeum (a monumental fountain at the terminal of the *Aqua Alexandrina*) the ruins of which may still be seen in the Piazza Vittorio Emanuele II; and a very elaborate depiction of the Temple of Jupiter Ultor (or Victor).

Throughout the remainder of the 3rd century architectural reverses occur rather less frequently and are confined in the main to conventional representations of temples, often containing a statue

Temple of
Faustina
(Faustina Senior)

Circus Maximus (Caracalla)

Temple of Juno Martialis
(Volusian)

of Roma. Exceptions to this include a very interesting circular temple dedicated to Juno Martialis, appearing on coins of Trebonianus Gallus and his son Volusian; and a triumphal arch on *aes* of the Gallic usurper Postumus.

With the advent of Christianity as the official state religion in the early part of the 4th century pagan temple types disappear entirely from the coinage. The only subsequent reverses which have any claim to be architectural are the 'camp gate' types, usually on small billon and bronze denominations of the Constantinian era and later; the plan of a military camp on billon *centenionales* of Thessalonica; a bridge over a river on a reduced *centenionalis* of Constantinople; and a distyle shrine with arched roof which occurs on silver *miliarenses* under a number of emperors from Constantine to Valentinian and Valens.

VII. ANIMALS, ETC

For several centuries before the rise of Rome there had been a tradition of featuring animals, birds, fish and insects (as well as various mythological beasts) on the coinages of many of the Greek city-states. Rome inherited this tradition, and although the representation of fauna is less frequent and varied than on coins of the Greek series, they nevertheless form a most appealing group within the Roman coinage.

Crocodile and heifer on the coinage of Augustus

Capricorn
(Vespasian)

Eagle (Domitian)

Crocodile, heifer, bull, wild boar, lion attacking stag, eagle, crab and butterfly, capricorn, Pegasus and Sphinx all appear on the coinage of Augustus, who was the inheritor of the late Republican tradition of great diversity in the selection of coin types. However, during the course of his long reign that tradition was gradually superseded by a more conservative approach to the type content of the new Imperial coinage. Accordingly, the coinages of the later Julio-Claudian emperors feature virtually no representations of animals, other than the elephants drawing the car of

Divus Augustus on a *sestertius* issued by Tiberius, and the eagle appearing on the reverse of a Divus Augustus *as*. The Flavian revival of earlier coin types led to a reintroduction of the tradition of animal depiction on the Imperial coinage. A particularly interesting reverse of this period shows a goat being milked by a goat-herd and another has a sow with its young.

Sow (Antoninus Pius)

In the 2nd century the Pegasus and the griffin appear on several *aes* denominations of Hadrian, whilst his successor Antoninus Pius struck *asses* showing an elephant and a sow suckling its young beneath an oak tree, both types probably having reference to the celebrations connected with the 900th anniversay of the foundation of Rome. An attractive representation of a dove appears on an *aureus* of Antoninus' daughter, the younger Faustina, and elephants occur on an *as* of Commodus and a *denarius* of Septimius Severus.

Elephant, lion and stag on the coinage of Philip I

Hippopotamus
(Otacilia Severa)

The 'king of beasts' is depicted on the coinage of Caracalla, wearing a radiate crown and holding a thunderbolt in its jaws, and several decades later the lion reappears as part of the 'Saeculares' series of Philip I. Similarly, the elephant was popular as a coin type during the first half of the 3rd century, appearing on pieces of Caracalla, Geta, and Philip I. To celebrate Rome's thousandth anniversary in AD 247–8 Philip I staged magnificent games in which many wild beasts were exhibited in the arena of the Colosseum. This resulted in a series of coins featuring the hippopotamus, antelope, stag, and goat, in addition to the lion already mentioned. The city's emblem, the she-wolf suckling the twins Romulus and Remus, also appears as part of this series.

A few years later, during the sole reign of Gallienus (AD 260–68), an extensive series of 'animal' reverses was featured on the debased *antoninianus* denomination. Subsequent to this date such types appear far less frequently and are, in the main, restricted to the 'legionary badge' issues of the usurpers Victorinus in Gaul and Carausius in Britain. The charismatic British usurper also has types showing the milking of a cow, a griffin, and the traditional wolf and twins device.

In the late Empire, the wolf and twins appear on coins of another usurper, Maxentius (AD 306–12), whose policy was to try to revive the past glories of the Imperial capital; and several decades later on small billon pieces (reduced *centenionales*) of the time of Constantine and his successors. In the mid-4th century a phoenix is shown on *half maiorinae* of Constantius II and

Phoenix (Constans)   Bull (Julian II)

Constans; and a very fine representation of a bull, sometimes accompanied by an eagle, occurs on large billon pieces of Julian II towards the end of his short reign (AD 360–63). One of the last animal representations on the Roman coinage is on a tiny bronze *nummus* of the eastern Emperor Leo I (AD 457–74) where a lion appears as a punning allusion to the emperor's name.

VIII. TYPES OF PROPAGANDA

There can be little doubt that the emperors of Rome were fully aware of the value of the Imperial coinage as a tool of propaganda, it being one of the most effective means of mass communication available to them. Everyone, from the provincial governor down to the peasant working the land, was likely to take notice of the ever-changing messages appearing as reverse types on the money which they were daily handling. The government of the day was thus able to present itself and its achievements in surprising detail to almost all of the inhabitants of the vast Empire. However, as it was a means of communication on which the government had a complete monopoly, the propaganda sometimes only told half the truth or was even, on occasions, a complete misrepresentation of reality.

A very large proportion of reverses could be included under the heading of 'Types of Propaganda'. Even the ubiquitous personifications were often intended to proclaim the virtues of the emperor or the good fortune of the age which was lucky enough to witness his enlightened rule. In this brief survey, therefore, mention is made only of those types which have a specific message to convey regarding the wisdom, beneficence and achievements of the emperor.

Augustus early established the propaganda role for the Imperial coinage when he gave extensive coverage to his victory over Cleopatra's Egyptian kingdom which left him sole master of the State and provided the financial resources to carry through his program of reforms. A decade later he produced a whole range of types on his precious metal coinage designed to extract the maximum publicity value from his great diplomatic achievement which led to the restoration in 20 BC of the Roman standards of Crassus and Antony captured years before by the Parthians.

An elegant *sestertius* type of Tiberius proclaims the munificence of the emperor in a reference to the restoration, at his own expense, of several cities in western Asia Minor which had been badly damaged by a severe earthquake in AD 17. Nero publicized his care for the annual corn supply from Egypt on a very attractive *sestertius* type showing an artistic grouping of Annona standing before a seated Ceres, with a ship's stern in the background. The enlightenment and benevolence of Nerva's brief rule is amply attested by his choice of coin types. One *sestertius* shows two mules and a cart, with a legend referring to the measures taken by the emperor to transfer the cost of Imperial posting on the main roads in Italy from the taxpayer to the exchequer. Another represents a distribution scene, or *Congiarium*, depicting the emperor bestowing gifts on the citizenry; whilst others commemorate a special distribution of corn to the urban poor, and the correction of abuses in the collection of the poll tax levied on Jews (*fiscus Iudaicus*).

Restoration of the
Roman standards
(Augustus)

Care for Rome's corn
supply (Nero)

Funding of Imperial posting, corn distribution to the poor, and reform of Jewish poll tax,
all on sestertii of Nerva

A further example of the humanitarianism of this period is to be found on coins of Trajan publicizing the *Alimenta* system. Under this scheme wealthy philanthropists (including emperors from the time of Nerva) made substantial gifts to communities, both in Italy and the provinces, for the purpose of providing sustenance for needy children through agricultural investment. Trajan's successor, Hadrian, in an attempt to gain popularity after having come to the throne under somewhat dubious circumstances, made a grand gesture of cancelling all debts due to the state treasury – a sum equivalent to many millions of pounds. Not surprisingly, this extraordinary act of liberality received full publicity on the coinage, with a remarkable *sestertius* type showing a lictor setting fire to a heap of documents in the presence of three joyful citizens. The notes and bonds were, in fact, publicly destroyed in Trajan's Forum. The orphanage for girls which Antoninus Pius founded in honour of his deceased wife (*Puellae Faustinianae*) is recorded on posthumous *aurei* and *denarii* of Faustina Senior. Antoninus' great stature as a statesman is portrayed on a *sestertius* type where he is shown bestowing a new king on the Quadi, a barbarian tribe who inhabited territory on the left bank of the Danube.

In addition to those already mentioned there are so many other examples of propaganda types on the Roman Imperial coinage that it is simply not possible to do justice to the topic in an article of this scope. It is hoped, however, that many readers will be sufficiently stimulated to pursue on their own their study of this fascinating subject. In the later period the types are generally of a less specific nature, as typified by the *antoniniani* of the joint Emperors Balbinus and Pupienus (AD 238). These all feature clasped right hands accompanied by one of six different forms of legend (e.g. AMOR MVTVVS AVG, CARITAS MVTVA AVGG, etc.) the common aim being to create a public impression of perfect harmony between the ill-matched and, ultimately, ill-fated rulers.

The Alimenta
system (Trajan)

Cancellation of public debts (Hadrian) and
appointment of barbarian king (Antoninus Pius)

Harmony of the joint emperors (Balbinus)

IX. POSTHUMOUS TYPES

Some of the emperors and empresses were publicly deified following their deaths, *i.e.* placed among the official gods of the State, and in most cases commemorative coins were produced in their honour by their immediate successors. The reverse types of these issues form a distinctive group within the Imperial coinage, the same basic types often being repeated through many series of posthumous coins.

Divus Augustus asses struck under Tiberius

The honours paid to Rome's first emperor, Augustus, were of an extraordinary nature and all four of his Julio-Claudian successors struck issues in commemoration of 'Divus Augustus' (Nero only on the Alexandrian coinage). The most extensive of these series was produced under Tiberius and has a wide variety of reverse types, including a thunderbolt, an eagle, the shrine of Vesta on the Palatine, and the altar of Providentia. The eagle and the altar were to become popular types on future posthumous issues.

Aurei and *denarii* struck under Nero in honour of Divus Claudius show an elaborate funerary vehicle drawn by four horses; whilst an intriguing precious metal type produced in AD 80 for Divus Vespasian has two capricorns back to back supporting a shield inscribed S C, a design recalling one of the *sestertius* types of Divus Augustus. A rare *aureus* type of Divus Trajan depicts a radiate phoenix, the fabulous bird which was regarded as a symbol of immortality.

Denarii of Divus Claudius and Divus Vespasian

Despite the alleged strained relationship between Hadrian and his wife Sabina, an interesting coinage was produced in her honour following her death and deification in AD 136. A *sestertius* type shows the new goddess being borne aloft by an eagle. Subsequently, this was to become a popular theme on the posthumous coinages of both emperors and empresses, though in the case of the latter a peacock (symbolic of Juno) usually took the place of Jupiter's eagle. Another posthumous type which achieved popularity during the course of the 2nd century was the so-called 'funeral pyre' (more accurately the crematorium in which the pyre was placed). This pyramidal structure surmounted by a facing quadriga occurs commonly from the time of the coinage of Divus Antoninus Pius onwards. Fragmentary remains of the crematorium of Marcus Aurelius were discovered in the Campus Martius in 1908 and lie below the present Chamber of Deputies.

Denarii of Divus Antoninus Pius and Diva Faustina Senior

Antoninus Pius himself had issued an extensive posthumous coinage in honour of his wife, the elder Faustina, who predeceased him by two decades. In many respects this coinage is unique, both in its large volume and in the diversity of reverse types, many of which would seem to be more in keeping with the coinage of a living empress. Ceres, Juno, Venus, Vesta, and Pietas are amongst a surprising variety of goddesses and personifications making their appearance on this series, the later issues of which probably coincide with various anniversaries of Faustina's deification (fifth, tenth, etc.). The earlier issues are more obviously connected with the apotheosis of the empress, *viz* a funerary car drawn by elephants, an empty throne with peacock beneath, and a flying Victory carrying Faustina to heaven.

The type of an empty throne was revived by Caracalla and Geta on a denarius issued for their deceased and deified father, Septimius Severus, in AD 211. In this case, however, a wreath is shown on the seat to represent the departed Augustus. During the 3rd century the posthumous coinages settled down into a regular and predictable pattern, generally utilizing only a few basic types – an eagle or a large altar for emperors, and a peacock (either standing or bearing the new deity to heaven) for empresses. An intriguing series of *antoniniani* issued by Trajan Decius in AD 250–51 honours the memories of many of the deified emperors dating back to Augustus, each having two reverse types (eagle and altar). In AD 317–18 Constantine the Great issued from several of his mints a series of small bronzes, probably representing two denominations (reduced *folles* and *half folles*),

Diva Paulina borne aloft to heaven

in honour of the deified emperors Claudius II Gothicus (a claimed ancestor), his father Constantius I Chlorus, and father-in-law Maximian. The reverses of these coins exhibit three different types (emperor seated on curule chair, eagle, and lion) and their purpose seems to have been to establish in the public mind Constantine's superior imperial 'pedigree' at a time of intense rivalry with his eastern colleague Licinius.

Antoniniani issued by Trajan Decius in honour of Divus Titus and Divus Nerva

With the advent of Christianity the posthumous coinages inevitably cease, the last emperor to be accorded these honours being Constantine himself (died AD 337). His issues, produced under his three sons, were all of the tiny reduced *centenionalis* denomination ('Æ 4') and were of two main types: one showing a standing figure of the emperor, veiled and togate; the other depicting him in a quadriga being borne aloft to heaven, where the hand of God (*manus Dei*) is extended to greet him.

X. OTHER TYPES

The nine categories of reverse types which have been covered in this brief survey certainly comprise the bulk of the Roman Imperial coinage. There are, however, a number of types which do not classify satisfactorily under any of these groups, and these are described under the following five subheadings.

The Julian comet
(Augustus)

Star (Faustina
Senior)

Crescent moon
and star
(Hadrian)

1. Heavenly Bodies. Objects such as stars and crescent moons make fairly regular appearances on the Imperial coinage. A more unusual representation, on a *denarius* of Augustus, shows the *sidus*

Iulium, the comet with flaming tail which appeared in the heavens shortly after Caesar's assassination and was taken as a sign of the late dictator's divinity. The type depicting a group of stars around a crescent moon was quite popular in the 2nd century and appears on issues of Hadrian, Faustina Senior and Junior, Pescennius Niger, Septimius Severus, and Julia Domna. The type of a single star continued to appear well into the 4th century, the latest example being on silver of Julian II.

2. Inscriptions. It was not unusual, especially in the early Empire, for inscriptions to appear in place of pictorial types on the reverses of coins. The practice was especially common on *aes* denominations and had its origin in the Augustan currency reform of *circa* 18 BC, when *sestertii* and *dupondii* (and later *asses* also) were introduced showing the moneyer's name around a large 'S C' as their reverse type. This was later replaced by an Imperial inscription normally giving the name and titles of the emperor, though sometimes of some other member of the Imperial family. The type was used up until the end of the 1st century AD but does not appear after the reign of Nerva. Another form of epigraphic reverse, showing the inscription in several lines across the field (usually enclosed by a wreath), first appeared under Augustus and became popular from the time of

Drusus, son of Tiberius   Trajan, 'Best of Princes'

Caligula. It continued in use right up until the end of the Roman period in the late 5th century and even extended into early Byzantine times. In the 1st century S P Q R P P OB C S and EX S C OB CIVES SERVATOS are typical examples of the legends shown in this way; and the 2nd century saw the use of inscriptions such as S P Q R OPTIMO PRINCIPI, PRIMI DECENNALES COS III, and VOTA PVBLICA. During the 3rd century the legend VOTIS DECENNALIBVS appeared quite regularly, whilst in the Constantinian era the trend was towards inscriptions giving the emperor's name. Later 4th and 5th

Votive inscription (Trajan Decius)   Votive inscription (Constantius II)

century epigraphic reverses are confined almost exclusively to commemoration of the vows undertaken for various periods of the emperor's rule, e.g. VOT V, VOT V MVLT X, VOTIS XXX MVLTIS XXXX, etc. This type of reverse extended into early Byzantine times, though ultimately the numerals came to be reproduced mechanically from earlier issues without regard to their true meaning. The latest examples appear on Carthaginian silver coins of Justinian I (AD 527–65).

3. Mythological Types. These are rare on the Imperial coinage, except for the representations of the she-wolf suckling the twins Romulus and Remus (this type occurs on the coinages of many of the emperors from Vespasian to Constantine). A *denarius* of Augustus depicts the fate of Tarpeia, the Roman traitress, who admitted the Sabines to the citadel in return for the promise of gold. Instead of giving her their armlets the enemy soldiers, disgusted at her treachery, cast their shields

Aeneas (Antoninus Pius)   Tarpeia (Augustus)   Wolf and twins
(Maxentius)

upon her and crushed her to death. An interesting reverse of Antoninus Pius shows a striding figure of the Trojan prince Aeneas, bearing his aged father Anchises on his shoulders and leading his son Ascanius by the hand. This formed part of a series produced in anticipation of the upcoming 900th anniversary of Rome.

4. Nautical Types. Representations of ships are not uncommon on the Roman coinage and there are even two instances of a 'bird's-eye' view of the harbour installations at Ostia (on *sestertii* of Nero and Trajan). The galley type which appears frequently on the coinage of Hadrian is commemorative of the emperor's numerous voyages during his Empire-wide travels. Similar depictions, though not always so finely rendered, appear on the coins of many of Hadrian's successors (Marcus

Ostia harbour (Nero)   Galley (Hadrian)

Aurelius and Lucius Verus, Commodus, Caracalla, Elagabalus, Postumus, etc.). Especially noteworthy are the galleys shown on the coinages of the British usurpers Carausius and Allectus (AD 287–296) whose regimes depended so heavily on naval power. Even as late as the reign of Theodosius the Great (379–95) there is a type on the *maiorina* ('Æ 2') denomination which shows the emperor standing on a galley with Victory at the helm. One other type which has claim to be included under this heading is the 'dolphin entwined around anchor' reverse which occurs on *aurei* and *denarii* of Titus and Domitian.

5. Symbolic Types. These appear sporadically throughout the entire period of the Roman Imperial coinage and usually have some religious association. Exceptions to this are types such as the *pileus* or felt cap, symbolic of liberty, on *quadrantes* of Caligula; and four young boys at play, representing spring, summer, autumn, and winter, on the coins of several of the emperors from Commodus to Constantine. The thunderbolt, however, which sometimes appears on its own as a reverse type,

Emblems of the
priesthoods
(Augustus)

Thunderbolt
(Antoninus Pius)

does have religious significance, it being symbolic of Jupiter, the chief deity in the Roman pantheon. More obviously of a religious nature are the types which depict various groups of emblems symbolic of the Roman priesthoods, such as the simpulum, lituus, tripod, patera, aspergillum, apex, sacrificial knife, axe, and jug. An early denarius of Nero (under Claudius) shows the first four of these symbols, each one representing one of the priestly colleges (the *Pontifices*, the *Augures*, the *Quindecimviri Sacris Faciundis*, and the *Septemviri Epulones*) to which the young Nero was admitted in AD 51. This type of reverse, which appeared quite frequently up to the end of the 3rd century, was superseded from the time of Constantine by types alluding to Christianity, the new state religion of the Roman Empire. The first representation of the labarum (the Christian standard) occurs on Constantinopolitan *centenionales* of Constantine issued in AD 327, whilst a large Christogram appears in the 350s as the main type on coins of the western usurpers Magnentius and Decentius, and on subsequent issues of Constantius II. The Cross, the supreme symbol of the Christian faith, became popular as a reverse type in the 5th century and occurs most frequenty on the gold *tremissis* denomination.

Christogram
(Magnentius)

Cross
(Romulus
Augustus)

The foregoing notes can make no claim to completeness in describing the various aspects of Roman Imperial reverse types. The topic is so vast that the author can only hope to have stimulated the reader sufficiently to encourage further study in more detailed works. Collectors may also have found here some challenging new themes for the formation of a collection.

Before concluding this section of the introductory material brief mention should be made of the typology of the pre-Imperial Republican series which spans the first two and a half centuries of the Roman coinage. Although Republican coins exhibit an enormous variety of imagery, especially in their later stages, there are few consistent themes which can be traced throughout the series as a whole. The reason for this may be sought in the nature of the issuing authority, for under the Republican constitution responsibility for coin production was in the hands of the annually elected mint magistrates, or moneyers. Initially, during the 3rd century BC, there was little originality shown in the selection of types and the entire process would seem to have been under the control of the Senate as a whole, with the moneyers serving merely in an administrative capacity. Soon after the currency reform of *circa* 211 BC, however, the moneyers' names began to appear on the coins, initially as monograms but soon evolving into longer forms which make identification easier. At this stage the typology of the standard silver coin (*denarius*) is monotonous and clearly under rigid control (head of Roma/Dioscuri galloping) with just occasional variations in the standard design, such as the introduction of the 'Luna in biga' reverse in the first decade of the 2nd century BC and the 'Victory in biga' type in the years before the middle of the century. Around 140 BC, however, there is a clear and dramatic change, with a whole new range of types suddenly appearing. Obviously, some reassessment of the moneyer's role had taken place and his authority had been expanded to include participation in the selection of the design of the coins being struck in his name. This resulted in an explosion of diversity in the types of the *denarius*, many of them making reference to the ancestral history of the individual moneyers. Thus, the types produced by the mint in one year frequently bore no resemblance to those that had preceded them or those that were to follow. Although adding immeasurably to the interest of the series as a whole, this development precludes the possibility of any kind of ordered categorization, there being nothing governing the type selection other than the individual whim of the moneyer. This situation continued to the very end of the series, though with the rise of powerful individuals such as Sulla, Pompey, and Caesar in the final decades of the Republic the selection of types often began to serve the political agendas of the Imperators rather than the vanity of the moneyers. With the triumph of the principle of autocratic rule in the person of Caesar's heir, Octavian, the prerogative of coinage passed under an entirely new authority and one which would certainly not brook interference from any other source. The Imperial coinage was, from first to last, a jealously guarded and vital publicity tool of the emperor.

A series closely related to the Roman Imperial coinage is the Roman Provincial coinage, often referred to as 'Greek Imperial'. Issued from hundreds of mints in Europe, Asia Minor, the Levant, Egypt and North Africa, these coinages served the needs of many local communities, especially in the East, over the first three centuries of the Empire's existence. They exhibit an extraordinary diversity of reverse types many of which make reference to topics of local interest, such as noted architectural features of the city and local festivals and associated games. The names of civic and provincial officials appear quite frequently on these issues, making the series as a whole an invaluable resource for students of Roman provincial administration. With the notable exception of the Alexandrian coinage of Egypt, these issues fall outside the scope of the present work and the reader is referred to the author's companion volume *Greek Imperial Coins and Their Values* as well as to the magisterial new series *Roman Provincial Coinage*.

COUNTERMARKS ON THE AES COINAGE
OF THE EARLY EMPIRE

During the Julio-Claudian period and up to the opening months of Vespasian's reign the practice of countermarking brass and copper coins was quite widespread. These overstrikings served three main purposes: to extend the area in which the coin would be accepted as currency; to prolong the useful life of a coin which had been in circulation over an extended period of time; and to denote that a new authority was converting someone else's issue into its own.

To the first category belong countermarks of the reigns of Augustus and Tiberius which were intended for the use of Roman troops engaged on campaigns, principally in Germany. These include overstrikings such as AVG (with AV in monogram form), AV (in monogram), and IMP (in monogram), all of the time of Augustus; and TIB, TIB IMP (IMP in monogram), and TIB AV (AV in monogram) from the reign of Tiberius. Claudius seems to have followed a similar practice at the time of his invasion of Britain in AD 43, applying countermarks such as TI AV (AV in monogram), T C IMP (MP in monogram), and TI CLAV IM (LAV in monogram).

Countermarks extending the period of circulation of old coins belong mainly to the early years of Nero's reign, when no new *aes* coinage was being produced by the Rome mint. The purpose of this was to withdraw those pieces which had become too worn for continued use and to counter-mark (usually with 'NCAPR') coins which were still in good enough condition to remain in circula-tion for a few years more. A particularly interesting countermark of this period has been noted on a very worn *sestertius*. It contains the legend 'DVP' thus indicating that the piece was being officially authorized to remain in circulation, though only at half of its original value.

In the period of civil strife at the end of Nero's reign and immediately following his death, countermarks such as SPQR, PR, and VITE (VIT in monogram) were employed. The first two were used by Vindex, leader of the anti-Nero uprising in Gaul, and the third was the mark of the Emperor Vitellius. Vindex countermarked *dupondii* and *asses* of Nero, whilst Vitellius used only his *sestertii*. Vespasian, the ruler who eventually emerged victorious from the chaos of the civil wars and went on to found the Flavian dynasty, also countermarked *dupondii* and *asses* of Nero with a monogram of his name. The same emperor was also responsible for a remarkable series of countermarks on silver coins of the Republic and early Empire, possibly applied at the Antioch mint. Being without the facilities to produce a regular coinage to publicize his regime in the early days of his revolt against Vitellius, he adopted the expedient of marking with the legend 'IMP VESP' as many denarii as he could lay his hands on.

Countermarks were rarely applied on Roman coins after this period, but in the Roman Provincial ('Greek Imperial') series they occur quite frequently well into the 3rd century, possibly even as late as the reign of Aurelian (AD 270–75).

ROMAN MINTS FROM AUGUSTUS TO THE REFORM OF DIOCLETIAN

The chaotic monetary system which Octavian inherited on gaining supreme power in 30 BC was the result of decades of civil strife and the eclipse of the Senate as the supreme authority in the Roman World.

In the days of the Republic the issue of coinage was entirely in the hands of the Senate, who annually appointed the monetary magistrates to superintend the operations of the mint. Rome itself was the principal mint, but sometimes, under special circumstances, establishments were utilized in other locations, not always in Italy, though still under the control of the Roman Senate. In the final half century before the overthrow of the Republican constitution a new minting authority appeared in the Roman World – the Imperator. These powerful military commanders in the field assumed the right to produce coinage, and although at first they applied to the Senate for permission to strike money for the payment of their troops this irksome formality was quickly dispensed with. These 'military coinages' gradually started appearing in various parts of the Roman World quite inde-pendently of all Senatorial authority. As a final blow, early in 49 BC the Senate was obliged to flee to Greece at the time of the war between Caesar and Pompey, thus leaving control of the mint of Rome entirely in the hands of Caesar. Following the dictator's assassination on the Ides of March, 44 BC, the Senate looked forward to a restoration of many of the prerogatives it had surrendered during the previous half decade, including its control over the operations of the mint. However, Caesar's youthful heir, Octavian, quickly took charge of the situation in Rome, thereby putting paid to the Senate's hopes of a revival of their authority. Coinage from the Capitoline mint ceased alto-gether in 40 BC and thereafter all the currency needs of the State were provided by military estab-lishments under the control of the Triumvirs Octavian and Mark Antony.

Once Octavian – now called Augustus – had firmly established his constitutional position, in the years following his victory over Antony and Cleopatra, he turned his attention to the much-needed reorganization of the coinage. About 19 BC minting of *aurei* and *denarii* in Rome was resumed after more than two decades, and soon afterwards *aes* coinage was instituted as a regular part of the currency system. However, the new precious metal coinage from Rome was destined to be short-lived and ceased altogether after 12 BC. Augustus had other plans for the creation of a new mint establishment to produce his regular gold and silver issues. A number of provincial mints had been active from the mid-twenties down to about 16 BC, notably in Spain, but the city selected was Lugdunum, the provincial capital of Gaul, where a mint was opened in 15 BC. It soon became the only mint striking in the precious metals and was destined to retain this monopoly down to the time of Nero's currency reform in AD 64. Additionally, the Gallic mint had a substantial output of *aes*, in various denominations, commencing in 10 BC and extending down to the early years of Tiberius' reign. These depicted on the reverse the celebrated 'Altar of Lugdunum' dedicated by Augustus in 10 BC. Another Gallic mint, Nemausus, was also active at this time (and earlier) in the production of dupondii bearing the heads of Augustus and Agrippa on obverse. In the East, the great Asian cities of Ephesus and Pergamum produced large issues of silver *cistophori* (= 3 *denarii*) in the 20s BC, though this coinage ceased after 18 BC and was not revived until the reign of Claudius.

The mint system established by Augustus continued with little change down to the time of the reform enacted by Nero in AD 64. A notable addition was the mint of Caesarea in Cappadocia where silver drachms (and later didrachms and hemidrachms also) were produced from the closing years of Tiberius' reign. Nero's reform saw the return of precious metal minting to Rome for the first time in three-quarters of a century. Lugdunum continued as an important mint, but now striking *aes* denominations to supplement the output of Rome.

The Civil Wars of AD 68–9 occasioned the opening of many new temporary mints, as the various contestants for power required plentiful supplies of coined money to secure the loyalty of their troops. Tarraco, Narbo, Vienne, Nemausus, Lugdunum, Carthage, and an uncertain location in Lower Germany, are all credited with having been Imperial mints at this time. In the East, the revolt of Vespasian against Vitellius' regime led to the opening of other temporary mints, such as Alexandria, Tyre, Antioch, Ephesus, and Aquileia, though none of these was destined to survive for long into the Flavian period. Once Vespasian had emerged as the victor from this complicated series of internal conflicts Rome soon resumed its dominant place as the provider of the Empire's currency. Lugdunum still struck sporadically in *aes* throughout the reign; Ephesus seems to have had a late output of denarii in AD 76; and Samosata in Commagene produced a series of orichacum denominations (*dupondius*, *as*, and *semis*) spanning most of the reign. With the return to more settled conditions, the coinages of the reigns of Vespasian's sons, Titus (AD 79–81) and Domitian (81–96), belong almost entirely to Rome, though silver *cistophori* were produced in Asia, probably at Ephesus.

Throughout most of the 2nd century the mint of Rome exercised a virtual monopoly in the production of the regular Roman coinage. *Cistophori* were still struck at various mints in Asia Minor down to the time of Hadrian, whose output was on an impressive scale, but thereafter production ceases (except for an isolated late issue under Septimius Severus). This period of stability came to an end in the final decade of the century when the Empire was again plunged into civil war through the rivalries of Septimius Severus, Pescennius Niger, and Clodius Albinus. Antioch, the Syrian capital and third city of the Empire, produced coinage for Niger, as did Alexandria and Caesarea; whilst Albinus utilized Lugdunum for his independent coinage between AD 195 and 197. Following the defeat of Niger in 194 or 195 Antioch was disgraced for having served as the seat of opposition to Severus. Accordingly, when coinage was subsequently struck for Severus in Syria this was produced at Emesa, the home of Severus' wife Julia Domna, and later at Laodicea (Alexandria and other eastern mints may also have participated in this coinage). Laodicea was the last of the temporary mints to cease production of Roman denominations under Severus, following the Imperial family's return to Rome after an extended absence in the East (AD 203). Rome, meanwhile, was continuing its steady output of all denominations, and after 203 regained its monopoly of production of the Imperial coinage following a decade of turbulence.

For the next fifteen years Rome remained the sole mint, but with Elagabalus' revolt against Macrinus in AD 218 production of *aurei* and *denarii* recommenced in Syria. Antioch was the probable mint for these issues which extended intermittently into the early years of Severus Alexander. After this, and until the reign of Gordian III (AD 238–44), Rome again struck alone, but this was to be the final period of mint monopoly which the Imperial capital was destined to enjoy. In addition to striking all denominations at Rome, Gordian issued some of his *antoniniani* from at least two other mints. Because of his extensive military operations in the East the Syrian capital of Antioch was, undoubtedly, responsible for part of this provincial coinage. The Balkan mint of Viminacium is the other suggested mint-place for a number of types which clearly are of a style distinct from those attributed to Antioch. The Antiochene issues of *antoniniani* continued under Philip (244–9), Trajan Decius (249–51), and Trebonianus Gallus (251–3); whilst Aemilian (253) issued all of his coins at Rome, with the sole exception of a number of rare *antoniniani* struck at some unidentified mint in the Balkans.

The joint reign of Valerian and Gallienus (AD 253–60) saw some important developments significant of the future move towards total decentralization of the Imperial mint system. A new western mint, probably at Cologne, was opened at this time and another new establishment, located either at Cyzicus in Asia Minor or at Emesa in Syria, commenced operation. Other than the products of Rome, precise mint identification at this time remains problematic because of the lack of explicit mint marks. Antioch certainly seems to have maintained its output of coinage and a Balkan mint, perhaps at Viminacium, seems also to have been active. A notable policy change at this time was the decision to allow provincial mints to strike gold on a regular basis, a precedent which was followed in varying degrees by most of Valerian's successors. This was by no means the first time that mints other than Rome had produced coinage in gold, but from this point on such issues become a normal feature of the Imperial coinage and serve to emphasize the dwindling importance of the capital as the coining centre of the Empire.

During the troubled sole reign of Gallienus (AD 260–68) the beleaguered emperor was forced to revise his father's mint arrangements, due to considerable losses of territory in both the eastern and western halves of the Empire. In the West, the rebellion of Postumus in Gaul (AD 260) meant that the newly-opened mint at Cologne was lost to the central government and to take its place Gallienus opened a new mint at Siscia (Sisak, Croatia). Mediolanum (Milan) also seems to have become active at this time, producing *antoniniani* and gold. In the East, the capture of Valerian by Sapor of Persia in AD 260 inaugurated a period of about twelve years during which Rome exercised very little authority in the eastern provinces, the real power being in the hands of Odenathus and Zenobia, rulers of the desert kingdom of Palmyra. During this period Gallienus certainly produced substantial issues of coinage in the East which are generally assigned to Antioch, though given the prevailing political and military situation in the region it would, perhaps, be preferable to attribute them to Cyzicus. It is possible that other subsidiary mints were also operating at this time in western Asia Minor. Claudius II Gothicus (AD 268–70), the successor of Gallienus, continued to use all of the mints already in operation and available to the central government (Rome, Milan, Siscia, and Cyzicus), whilst *antoniniani* were also struck in his name at Antioch, the Palmyrene rulers having decided to adopt a more conciliatory attitude towards the new regime in Rome.

Aurelian (AD 270–75), the great restorer of Rome's fortunes in the later 3rd century and reformer of the currency, seems to have issued coins from at least eleven mints: Rome; Cologne, Trier, and Lugdunum (the Gallic provinces having been recovered in AD 273); Milan; Ticinum (opened by Aurelian at the time of the currency reform in 273/4 to replace Milan as the northern Italian mint); Siscia; Serdica (another creation of Aurelian); Cyzicus; Antioch (Palmyra having been conquered in 272); and Tripolis in Phoenicia (also opened by Aurelian). Gold was issued at seven of these mints. The Gallic Empire of Postumus had pursued its own policies from AD 260, though Gallienus' recently created mint at Cologne appears to have been retained as the principal source of coinage throughout the thirteen years of the rebel state's existence. Postumus (AD 260–68) seems to have used a secondary Gallic mint for some of his extensive *aes* issues, and a number of *antoniniani* and *aurei* may also be attributed to Milan. The rare coinage of the usurper Laelianus (268) was struck in Lower Germany, either at Moguntiacum (Mainz) or Trier. Postumus' short-lived successor Marius (AD 268) struck most of his coinage at Cologne, though the products of a secondary mint are clearly identifiable and the establishment was probably located at Trier. The final two rulers of the Gallic Empire, Victorinus (268–70) and Tetricus (270–73), would seem to have retained this two-mint system (Cologne and Trier) down to the end of the state's independent existence. Aurelian assumed control of the 'rebel' mints on his defeat of Tetricus in 273, but soon replaced them with a new establishment at Lugdunum.

The final two decades of the period covered by this survey (Tacitus to Diocletian's currency reform, mid-270s to mid-290s) saw few changes in the mint system established by Aurelian. Two new mints appear under Diocletian in the pre-reform period; one of them (Trier) a revival of an establishment utilized by the Gallic usurpers in the late 260s and early 270s; the other (Heraclea in Thrace) an entirely new creation. The independent British Empire of Carausius (AD 287–93) and his successor Allectus (293–6) brought into being several new mints, though only one of these (London) was destined to survive the restoration of the rule of the central government by the Caesar Constantius Chlorus. Camulodunum (Colchester) is usually regarded as the site of the second mint in Britain, though Clausentum (Bitterne) also has its supporters. Products of this mint are usually marked 'C' or 'CL' and the matter cannot be regarded as having been satisfactorily settled. Certain coins of Carausius show a distinctive style and may represent activity on the part of a mint in northwestern Gaul where the usurper's naval superiority allowed him to control some territory, at least in the earlier part of his reign. Rotomagus (Rouen) has been postulated on the basis of local finds, but the attribution can only be regarded as conjectural.

MINTS AND MINT MARKS OF
THE LATER ROMAN EMPIRE

Carthage: follis of Diocletian from
the first officina

Alexandria: follis of Galeria Valeria
from the third officina

  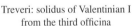

Siscia: maiorina of Constantius II from
the first officina

Treveri: solidus of Valentinian I
from the third officina

Roman Imperial coins began to bear mint marks about the middle of the 3rd century, though the practice had occurred much earlier on *denarii* and *aurei* of Ephesus issued during the reign of Vespasian (AD 69–79). The marks which began to appear – principally on *antoniniani* – from the closing years of Philip I's reign are seldom self-explanatory, normally identifying only the specific workshop or *officina* within the mint. Presumably, these were placed on the coins so that there

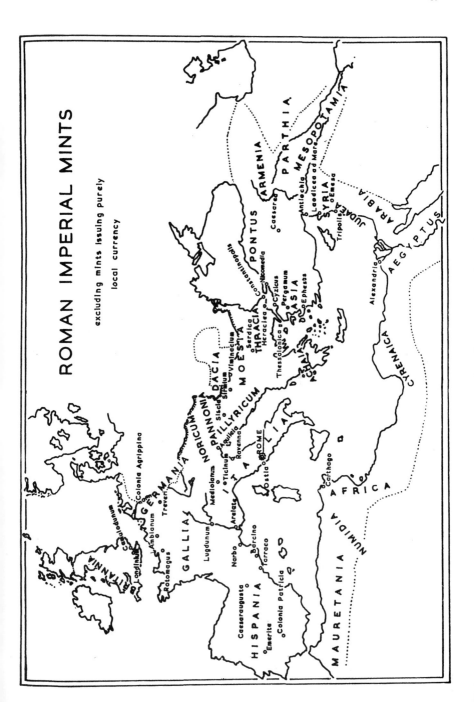

might be some accountability on the part of mint officials and workers. Coins of less than standard weight or fineness could be traced back to those responsible for their production and the culprits suitably dealt with. With the advent of the monetary reform of Diocletian in the final decade of the 3rd century the name of the mint city itself customarily becomes an integral part of the mint mark, though it is sometimes abbreviated to a single initial letter, *e.g.* H = Heraclea, N = Nicomedia. A mint mark is normally placed in the exergual space on the reverse side of the coin and may be composed of up to three elements: firstly, a letter or letters indicating *Pecunia* (P), *Sacra Moneta* (SM), or simply *Moneta* (M); secondly, a letter or letters identifying the mint city, such as LON for Londinium; and finally, a letter or letters showing which of the mint's workshops or *officinae* had produced the coin. At the western mints the *officina* letters are usually Latin – P, S, T and Q standing for *Prima, Secunda, Tertia* and *Quarta*. In the East, however, the system of Greek letter-numerals prevailed, the comparable officina letters being A, B, G and D. Thus, a coin of Alexandria may may bear the mint mark SMALB showing that it was struck in the second officina. Some eastern mints had many *officinae*. Antioch, for example, had fifteen (IE) under Constantius II, and Constantinople eleven (IA). Certain mints sometimes omit the prefix letter or letters, an example being Trier where the commonest forms of mint mark are TRP and TRS. Where PTR and STR occur the prefix letters are *officina* marks placed before instead of after the mint letters. Sometimes the *officina* letter appears in the field rather than the exergue. A small mint, such as London, may have no indication of *officina* (presumably because the mint establishment comprised a single workshop only). Many of the London issues of the Constantinian period are signed simply PLN or PLON.

Under Valentinian I and Valens the letters PS (on silver) and OB (on gold) make their first appearance. These are abbreviations for *pusulatum* ('pure silver') and *obryza* ('pure gold') and they follow the mint letters, *e.g.* TRPS and TROB. Eventually, the form CONOB came to be utilized universally, without regard to the place of mintage, the actual mint letters sometimes appearing as a secondary element in the field. An important variation used at a number of western mints was COMOB. This may have had a slightly different meaning, the COM possibly indicating the office of *Comes Auri* ('Count of Gold'), the official charged with the responsibility of supervising the Imperial gold supplies in the western provinces of the Empire.

In addition to the mint and *officina* letters, symbols, such as a wreath, a crescent, or a palm-branch, are sometimes found in the exergue or in the reverse field. Of rarer occurrence are letters or symbols appearing in the obverse field, usually behind the ruler's head. All of these denote the specific issue to which the coin belongs.

There follows a list of the mints employed at various times from Diocletian's reform down to the end of the Roman period about two centuries later. To list all the complex mint signatures would be a task beyond the scope of this work. However, most of the commoner mint marks are included, though all reference to symbols and officina letters has, of necessity, been omitted. Nevertheless, it is anticipated that the details provided will be sufficient to enable collectors to identify the mints of most of the late Roman coins he or she is likely to encounter.

Alexandria (Egypt): ALE, SMAL. *Operational for Roman currency from ca.* AD *294. Finally closed under Leo I (*AD *457–74).*

Ambianum, more correctly **Civitas Ambianensium,** previously **Samarobriva** (Amiens, France): AMB. *Briefly operational under the usurper Magnentius (a native of the city),* AD *350–53.*

Antioch-on-the-Orontes (Antakyé, Turkey): AN, ANT, ANTOB, SMAN. *Operational down to the time of Zeno, the final issues being of the usurper Leontius (*AD *484–8).*

Aquileia (Udine, Veneto, Italy): AQ, AQVIL, AQOB, AQPS, SMAQ. *Operational from ca.* AD *294. Finally closed in the early years of Valentinian III, soon after* AD *425.*

Arelate/Constantina (Arles, France): A, AR, ARL, CON, CONST, KON, KONSTAN. *Operational from* AD *313 (establishment transferred from Ostia). Finally closed ca.* AD *476.*

(In AD *328 the name of Arelate was changed to Constantina in honour of Constantine II. After his death in 340 the name reverted to Arelate, but in 353 Constantius II changed it back to Constantina. During the 5th century Arelate seems again to have been generally preferred).*

Barcino (Barcelona, Spain): SMBA. *Briefly operational under the usurper Maximus, AD 410–11.*

Camulodunum or **Clausentum** (Colchester or Bitterne near Southampton): C, CL. *Briefly operational under the usurpers Carausius and Allectus, AD 287–96.*

Carthage (near Tunis, Tunisia): K, PK, KART. *Operational AD 296–307 and 308–11.*

Constantinople (Istanbul, Turkey): C, CP, CON, CONS, CONSP, CONOB. *Operational from AD 326 (establishment transferred from Ticinum).*

Cyzicus (Belkis or Balkiz, Turkey): CM, CVZ, CVZIC, CVZIKEN, K, KV, MK, MKV, SMK. *Finally closed under Zeno (AD 474–91).*

Heraclea (Eregli, Turkey): H, HT, HERAC, HERACL, SMH, SMHT. *Operational from ca. AD 291. Finally closed under Leo I (AD 457–74).*

(The old Greek city of Perinthus on the European coast of the Propontis, its name was changed to Heraclea some time during the course of the 3rd century AD).

Londinium (London): L, ML, MLL, MLN, MSL, PLN, PLON, AVG, AVGOB, AVGPS. *Operational AD 287–325, and for a brief period under the usurper Magnus Maximus (AD 383–8).*

Lugdunum (Lyon, France): LG, LP, LVG, LVGD, LVGPS, PL, PLG. *Finally closed under Honorius, ca. AD 418.*

Mediolanum (Milan, Italy): MD, MDOB, MDPS, MED. *Operational intermittently from ca. AD 352 down to the reign of Zeno (AD 474–91).*

Nicomedia (Ismit, Turkey): MN, NIC, NICO, NIK, SMN. *Operational from ca. AD 294 down to the reign of Zeno (AD 474–91).*

Ostia (the port of Rome): MOST, POST. *Operational under the usurper Maxentius and for a brief period under Constantine, AD 308/9–313.*

Ravenna (Italy): RV, RVPS. *Established by Honorius ca. AD 402 and operational down to the time of Zeno (AD 474–91).*

Roma: CORMOB, R, RM, RMPS, ROMA, ROMOB, SMR, VRB·ROM. *Operational down to the time of Zeno (AD 474–91).*

Serdica (Sophia, Bulgaria): SMSD, SER. *Operational briefly ca. AD 303–8 and again in 313–14.*

Sirmium (Sremska Mitrovica, Yugoslavia): SIRM, SIROB, SM (?). *Operational only sporadically, from AD 320–26, 351–64, 379, and possibly also in 393–5.*

Siscia (Sisak, Croatia, Yugoslavia): SIS, SISC, SISCPS, SM (?). *Finally closed in the early 390s, or possibly as late as the reign of Honorius, after the death of Arcadius in AD 408.*

Thessalonica (Thessaloniki, Greece): CHES, COM, COMOB, CONOB, SMTS, TS, TES, TESA, TESOB, THES, THS, THSOB. *Finally closed under Zeno (AD 474–91).*

Ticinum (Pavia, Italy): SMT, T. *Finally closed AD 326 (establishment then transferred to Constantinople).*

Treveri, more correctly **Augusta Treverorum** (Trier, Germany): SMTR, TR, TRE, TRIOB, TRMS, TROB, TROBS, TRPS. *Operational from ca. AD 291. Finally closed under Valentinian III in the late 420s.*

The following mints were reopened in Byzantine times: Alexandria (*ca.* AD 538); Antioch (*ca.* AD 498); Carthage (*ca.* AD 534); Cyzicus (*ca.* AD 518); Nicomedia (*ca.* AD 498); Ravenna (*ca.* AD 555); Rome (*ca.* AD 552); and Thessalonica (*ca.* AD 518).

DATING ROMAN IMPERIAL COINS

The ability to date with a surprising degree of precision many of the coins struck under the Roman Empire provides the student of this remarkably varied series yet another theme for the formation of a collection.

Many people collect Roman Imperial coins in order to assemble a 'portrait gallery' of emperors and empresses; others form their collections on the basis of illustrating the bewildering variety of deities, architectural themes, or commemorations of military campaigns appearing as reverse types; whilst some collectors are attracted by the diversity of mints, scattered throughout the Mediterranean world and northern Europe, at which the Imperial coinage was produced over more than half a millennium. A collection formed on the basis of important dates in Roman history is, however, one theme which most numismatists have probably overlooked and it can be most rewarding.

Thus, one might acquire a coin of AD 70, the year of the capture of Jerusalem by Titus; one of AD 79, which saw the famous eruption of Vesuvius which buried Pompeii and Herculaneum; a coin of Hadrian of the year in which construction began on Hadrian's Wall following the emperor's visit to the province (AD 122); and a coin of Constantine, the first Christian emperor, struck in the year in which he experienced his celebrated 'vision of the Cross' (AD 312). The scope for such a collection is obviously very great, and it has the added advantage of encouraging the collector to undertake his or her own research in order to discover the significance of coins already acquired before pursuing the process further.

One reason for the neglect of this approach is that many collectors are unaware of how to set about dating Roman Imperial coins. It is hoped, therefore, that the following notes, together with the tables of 'Principal Chronological Criteria' appearing in each of the two volumes in this work, will provide much of the necessary information. Users of this new *Millennium Edition* will also notice that in the catalogue entries much fuller information has been provided on the place and time of mintage of each individual type, thus increasing the awareness of chronology.

Tribunicia Potestas (the tribunician power, usually TR P on the coins). The tribunes of the people were first appointed in the early days of the Republic to protect the rights of the lower classes (plebeians) against the powerful aristocrats (patricians). From these humble beginnings the power of the tribunes gradually increased until, under the pretext of defending the rights of the people, they were able to do virtually anything they pleased. This almost unlimited power was drastically curtailed in later Republican times, notably by Sulla, and although many of the rights and privileges of the tribunes were restored after the dictator's death, a few decades later they were again deprived of power by Julius Caesar.

Augustus, in establishing the constitutional basis for his new Imperial rule, quickly realized the advantages to be gained through possession of the power of the tribunes. An added attraction was its popularity with the people, in sharp contrast to the hated titles of *rex* and *dictator*. Accordingly, in 23 BC he had the tribunician power conferred on him for life, thus gathering into his hands many important prerogatives previously enjoyed by the tribunes of the people. He was now empowered to convene and dismiss both the Senate and the Assembly of the People and also to veto any order of the Senate. In addition, the tribunician power rendered his person sacred and inviolable, a valuable asset for an autocrat.

As the emperor wished the tribunician power to be regarded as the basis for his authority it was natural that he should introduce the custom of reckoning the years of his reign by the date of its symbolic annual renewal. The precedent having thus been instituted, this became the normal practice of Augustus' successors and the number of annual renewals of the tribunician power, appearing regularly in the inscriptions on the coinage, provide valuable evidence in establishing the numismatic chronology of each reign. The method employed for selecting the actual date of this annual renewal seems to have varied from reign to reign. Some emperors used the day of its initial conferment (June 27th in the case of Augustus), whilst others preferred the traditional Republican date for the appointment of the tribunes (December 10th). Yet another practice was to renew on January 1st, thus making the tribunician year coincide with the calendar year.

Imperator (usually IMP on the coins). This title, originally meaning 'commander' and used to describe a victorious general, was utilized in several different ways in Imperial times. One use was as a *praenomen* or personal name of the emperor, by virtue of his supreme command over all the legions, auxiliaries, and naval officers comprising the Empire's armed forces. From the reign of Vespasian it was normally placed before all the other names and titles of the emperor and at about the same time it replaced *princeps* as the popular designation of the emperor.

Another use of 'imperator' was to enumerate the victories of the emperor during the course of his reign. Whenever a Roman army achieved some outstanding military success the emperor received an imperatorial acclamation, regardless of whether or not he was personally in command. The numbers of these acclamations are sometimes included in coin inscriptions and when they are frequent, as in the cases of Domitian, Marcus Aurelius, and the early years of Septimius Severus, they can provide valuable chronological evidence.

Consul (usually COS on the coins). The annual office of consul was established immediately after the abolition of the monarchy in Rome in 510 BC and was the highest of the annual magistracies. There were two colleagues in the consulship and during their year of office they wielded an almost regal power over the government of the Republic, only exceeded by that of a dictator appointed on rare occasions in cases of extreme national crisis. Their authority, however, was considerably diminished by the appointment of the tribunes of the people, who were the only magistrates not subject to the consuls. During the final half century of the Republic's existence their influence was frequently compromised by the authority of the powerful military commanders in the field, the imperators. Nevertheless, being the supreme magistrates of the State, the power of the Consuls remained considerable as long as the Republic endured

Under the Empire consuls continued to be appointed. However, although all the grandeur of the office was retained, the holders of the consulship no longer exercised any of the political power of their Republican predecessors. Quite frequently, more than one pair of consuls were appointed for each year and from the reign of Vespasian it was normal for at least five pairs to hold office annually.

The emperor himself would sometimes hold the consulship. If he did so frequently, and advertised the fact regularly on his coins, then it can be a useful indicator of date. In this respect the Flavian emperors were especially helpful: Vespasian held the consulship eight times in ten years; Titus eight times in twelve years; and Domitian seventeen times in twenty-seven years. In marked contrast, Hadrian only held the consulship three times, in the first three years of his 21–year reign. In consequence, the inscription COS III for Hadrian covers the long period AD 119–138.

Pontifex Maximus (usually P M on the coins). The *Pontifex Maximus* was the head of the *Pontifices*, one of the four senior colleges of priests in Rome, who were charged with the supervision of ceremonies connected with the state religion (interestingly, in a remarkable example of long-term continuity this title is still borne by the Pope today). It was a dignity which, once conferred, was held for life and Augustus did not receive it until after the death of Lepidus (Caesar's successor as *Pontifex Maximus*) in 13 BC. Thereafter, it became one of the titles normally assumed by the emperors at the time of their accession.

Prior to the brief rule of Balbinus and Pupienus in AD 238 the title of Pontifex Maximus always went to the senior emperor in the case of a joint reign, the title of *Pontifex* going to the junior partner (this lesser designation usually also applied to the Caesar, or heir to the throne). Balbinus and Pupienus set a precedent for succeeding emperors by sharing the office of *Pontifex Maximus*.

Pater Patriae (usually P P on the coins). This title of honour, meaning "Father of his Country", was conferred on Augustus in 2 BC and was subsequently assumed by most, but not all, of his successors at the time of their accession. Tiberius steadfastly refused the title and some emperors, such as Hadrian and Marcus Aurelius, only accepted it after they had reigned for a number of years. Thus, coins of Hadrian containing P P in their obverse or reverse legends must be dated subsequent to AD 128, at least eleven years after the commencement of his reign.

Armeniacus, Britannicus, Germanicus, Parthicus, *etc.* (usually abbreviated to ARM, BRIT, GERM, PARTH, *etc.* on the coins). These were titles awarded in commemoration of military victories achieved over foreign enemies.

The following will serve as an example in the use of the tables of 'Principal Chronological Criteria' appearing in each of the two volumes in this catalogue. A *sestertius* of Commodus (AD

177–192) bears the legends **M COMMODVS ANT P FELIX AVG BRIT** (on obverse) and **P M TR P XI IMP VII COS V P P S C** (on reverse). Referring to the tables it will be seen that the eleventh year of Commodus' tribunician power spanned the years AD 185–186. As Commodus seems to have renewed his tribunician power on December 10th it is obviously more likely that this piece was struck in 186. However, in order to confirm this some title must be found on the coin to verify the attribution. If we look at the obverse legend we will find that the titles *Pius* (P), *Britannicus* (BRIT) and *Felix* were bestowed on Commodus in AD 183, 184 and 185 respectively and thus provide no assistance in confirming the coin to AD 186. Turning to the reverse legend, we see that Commodus bears the title *Pontifex Maximus* (P M), but according to the table we see that he achieved this status in 180, on the death of his father Marcus Aurelius. His seventh imperatorial acclamation (IMP VII) was in 184 and probably records victories of the Roman governor Ulpius Marcellus in northern Britain; whilst the title of *Pater Patriae* (P P) had been bestowed on him as early as AD 177. This leaves us with **COS V** which, on checking, we will find is the only title which can securely attribute our coin to AD 186 – the year which saw the remarkable mutiny instigated by the army deserter Maternus on the Rhine frontier which was to be spread throughout Gaul and into Spain.

Many issues, of course, do not bear strings of titles enabling them do be dated with great precision, and the coinages of empresses lack all such indications. However, over recent decades much work has been done by scholars on establishing the chronological sequence of issues within specific periods, and in this connection collectors and students are strongly recommended to the works of Dr. Philip V. Hill ('The Undated Coins of Rome, A.D. 98–148' and 'The Coinage of Septimius Severus and his Family of the Mint of Rome, A.D. 193–217', both published by Spink & Son).

ABBREVIATIONS

cuir.	=	cuirassed	laur.	=	laureate
diad.	=	diademed	mm.	=	millimetres
dr.	=	draped	Obv.	=	obverse
ex.	=	exergue	r.	=	right
gm.	=	grammes	rad.	=	radiate
hd.	=	head	Rev.	=	reverse
l.	=	left	stg.	=	standing

CONDITIONS OF COINS IN ORDER OF MERIT

Abbreviation	English	French	German
FDC	mint state	fleur-de-coin	stempelglanz
good EF			
EF	extremely fine	superbe	vorzüglich
nearly EF			
good VF			
VF	very fine	tres beau	sehr schon
nearly VF			
good F			
F	fine	beau	schon
nearly F			
fair	fair	tres bien conservé	sehr gut erhalten
M	mediocre	bien conservé	gut erhalten

ROMAN REPUBLICAN COINAGE, CIRCA 280–41 BC

Principal references:

B = E. Babelon, *Description historique et chronologique des monnaies de la république romaine*. Paris, 1885–6.

BMCRR = H.A. Grueber, *Coins of the Roman Republic in the British Museum*. London, 1910.

CRI = D.R. Sear, *The History and Coinage of the Roman Imperators 49–27 BC*. London, 1998.

CRR = E.A. Sydenham, *The Coinage of the Roman Republic*. London, 1952.

ICC = B.K. Thurlow and I.G. Vecchi, *Italian Cast Coinage*. London and New York, 1979.

RRC = M.H. Crawford, *Roman Republican Coinage*. Cambridge, 1974.

RRM = Michael Harlan, *Roman Republican Moneyers and Their Coins, 63–49 BC*. London, 1995.

RSC = H.A. Seaby, *Roman Silver Coins*, vol. I. 3rd (revised) edition. London, 1978.

The chronology adopted in the following listings generally follows that of Crawford in Roman Republican Coinage.

REPUBLICAN GOLD

Although the origins of the Roman Republican gold coinage extend back to the time of the Second Punic War (late 3rd century BC) the metal was never minted in significant quantities until the chaotic final years of the Republic's existence.

1

2

1   **Stater,** 217–216 BC. Beardless laur. Janiform hd. Rev. ROMA, oath-taking scene, with two warriors and sacrificial pig held by kneeling attendant. RRC 28/1. CRR 69.

VF £10,000 ($16,000) / **EF** £18,000 ($28,800)

2   **Half stater,** 217–216 BC. Similar. RRC 28/2. CRR 70.

VF £5,000 ($8,000) / **EF** 9,000 ($14,400)

3   3 (pentagram)

3   **60-as,** 211–208 BC. Helmeted hd. of bearded Mars r., mark of value ↓X. Rev. ROMA, eagle
    r. on thunderbolt. RRC 44/2. CRR 226.   **VF** £1,000 ($1,600) / **EF** £1,800 ($2,880)
    Rarer varieties exist with symbols anchor, spearhead, pentagram, or staff on the reverse.

4   **40-as,** 211–208 BC. Similar, but with mark of value XXXX. RRC 44/3. CRR 227.
                                               VF £5,000 ($8,000) / **EF** £10,000 ($16,000)

5   5 (ear of corn)

5   **20-as,** 211–208 BC. Similar, but with mark of value XX. RRC 44/4. CRR 228.
                                               VF £1,250 ($2,000) / **EF** £1,800 ($2,880)
    A rarer variety exists with symbol ear of corn on reverse.

6   **Aureus,** 84–83 BC. L SVLLA, diad. hd. of Venus r., Cupid with palm-branch before. Rev.
    IMPER ITERVM, jug and lituus between trophies. RRC 359/1. CRR 760.
                                               VF £12,500 ($20,000) / **EF** £25,000 ($40,000)

7   82 BC. L MANLI PRO Q, helmeted hd. of Roma r. Rev. L SVLLA IM, Sulla in triumphal
    quadriga r., crowned by Victory. RRC 367/4. CRR 756. B *Cornelia* 38.
                                               VF £4,500 ($7,200) / **EF** £9,000 ($14,400)

8   81 BC. Diad. hd. of Venus r. Rev. Q, double cornucopiae. RRC 375/1. CRR 754. B
    Cornelia 32.   (*Unique*)

9   80 BC. A MANLI A F Q, bust of Roma r. in plumed helmet. Rev. L SVLL FELI DIC, equestrian
    statue of Sulla l. RRC 381/1a. CRR 762. B *Cornelia* 46.
                                               VF £15,000 ($24,000) / **EF** £30,000 ($48,000)

10 71 BC. MAGNVS, hd. of Africa r. in elephant's skin, jug behind, lituus before, all in laurel-
    wreath. Rev. PRO COS, Pompey in triumphal quadriga r., horses crowned by Victory. RRC
    402/1b. CRR 1028. B *Pompeia* 6.   **VF** £40,000 ($64,000) / **EF** £75,000 ($120,000)

11 43 BC. Bust of Africa r. in elephant's skin. Rev. L CESTIVS C NORBA PR S C, curule chair sur-
    mounted by Corinthian helmet. RRC 491/1a. CRR 1153. B *Cestia* 1. CRI 195.
                                               VF £2,000 ($3,200) / **EF** £5,000 ($8,000)

12 — C NORBANVS L CESTIVS PR, bust of Sibyl (?) r. Rev. S C, Cybele enthroned in biga of
    lions l. RRC 491/2. CRR 1155. B *Cestia* 3. CRI 196.
                                               VF £2,000 ($3,200) / **EF** £5,000 ($8,000)

11   12

13   **Aureus,** 42 BC. REGVLVS PR, bare hd. of the praetor L. Regulus r. Rev. L LIVINEIVS
      REGVLVS, curule chair dividing six fasces. RRC 494/26. CRR 1108. B *Livineia* 9. CRI 175.
      VF £15,000 ($24,000) / **EF** £30,000 ($48,000)

14   — Rad. hd. of Sol r. Rev. P CLODIVS M F, crescent moon and five stars. RRC 494/20b. CRR
      1114. B *Clodia* 16. CRI 181.   **VF** £2,500 ($3,840) / **EF** £5,500 ($8,800)

15   — Hd. of Ceres r., wreathed with corn. Rev. L MVSSIDIVS LONGVS in corn-wreath. RRC
      494/44a. CRR 1090. B *Mussidia* 1. CRI 185.   **VF** £3,000 ($4,800) / **EF** £7,500 ($12,000)

16

16   — Laur. hd. of Apollo r. Rev. C VIBIVS VARVS, Venus stg. l. beside column, holding mir-
      ror. RRC 494/34. CRR 1137. B *Vibia* 27. CRI 190.
      VF £2,500 ($4,000) / **EF** £5,500 ($8,800)

17   — Helmeted bust of Roma l., holding spear and shield. Rev. C VIBIVS VARVS, Nemesis
      stg. r. RRC 494/35. CRR 1136. B *Vibia* 25. CRI 191.
      VF £3,500 ($5,600) / **EF** £8,500 ($13,600)

18   41 BC. C CLODIVS C F, hd. of Flora r., wreathed with flowers, lily behind. Rev. VESTALIS,
      Vestal virgin seated l., holding bowl. RRC 512/1. CRR 1134. B *Clodia* 12. CRI 316.
      VF £2,750 ($4,400) / **EF** £6,500 ($10,400)

19   — M ARRIVS SECVNDVS F P R, diad. hd. of Fortuna Populi Romani r. Rev. Spear between
      wreath and rectangular phalera. RRC 513/1. CRR 1083. B *Arria* 1. CRI 318.
      VF £10,000 ($16,000) / **EF** £20,000 ($32,000)

20   — L SERVIVS RVFVS, conjoined hds. of the Dioscuri r. in laur. pilei. Rev. Aerial view of the
      citadel and walls of Tusculum, TVSCVL on gateway. RRC 515/1. CRR 1081. B *Sulpicia* 9.
      CRI 323.   **VF** £18,000 ($28,800) / **EF** £35,000 ($56,000)

For other post-49 BC issues of gold, see under Roman Imperatorial Coinage.

REPUBLICAN SILVER

Silver didrachms were first minted by the Roman Republic about 280 BC, probably in connection with King Pyrrhus' invasion of Italy at the behest of the Tarentines. The denominaton continued to be minted down to the middle years of the Second Punic War when, about 211 BC, it was replaced by the silver denarius which remained thereafter the principal coin of the Roman currency system for the following four and a half centuries. In the pre-denarius period a half denomination (drachm) was occasionally struck and after 211 this continued for several decades under the name of victoriatus. The silver fractions of the denarius – its half the quinarius and its quarter the sestertius – were never minted on a regular basis, but were revived from time to time.

THE PRE-DENARIUS COINAGE, CIRCA 280–211 BC

                    22   23

22 **Didrachm,** 280–275 BC. Helmeted hd. of bearded Mars l., oak-spray behind. Rev. ROMANO on tablet below horse's hd r., corn-ear behind. RRC 13/1. CRR 1. RSC 4.
                                              VF £600 ($960) / **EF** £1,250 ($2,000)

23 275–270 BC. ROMANO, laur hd. of Apollo l. Rev. Horse galloping r., star above. RRC 15/1. CRR 4. RSC 6, 6a.   VF £750 ($1,200) / **EF** £1,500 ($2,400)

                    24   25

24 270–265 BC. Diad. hd. of young Hercules r., club and lion's skin over shoulder. Rev. ROMANO, she-wolf stg. r., suckling the twins Romulus and Remus. RRC 20/1. CRR 6. RSC 8.   VF £550 ($880) / **EF** £1,150 ($1,840)

25 265–241 BC. Hd. of Roma r. in Phrygian helmet. Rev. ROMANO, Victory stg. r., attaching wreath to palm-branch. RRC 22/1. CRR 21, 21a. RSC 7, 7a.
                                              VF £700 ($1,120) / **EF** £1,400 ($2,240)

26 241–235 BC. Helmeted hd. of beardless Mars r. Rev. ROMA, horse's hd. r., sickle behind. RRC 25/1. CRR 24. RSC 34.   VF £750 ($1,200) / **EF** £1,500 ($2,400)

26   27

27   **Drachm,** 241–235 BC. Similar. RRC 25/2. CRR 25. RSC 34a.
                                    VF £700 ($1,120) / **EF** £1,400 ($2,240)

28   30

28   **Didrachm,** 235–230 BC. Laur. hd. of Apollo r. Rev. ROMA, horse galloping l. RRC 26/1.
      CRR 27. RSC 37.   **VF** £650 ($1,040) / **EF** £1,350 ($2,160)

29   **Drachm,** 235–230 BC. Similar. RRC 26/2. CRR 28. RSC 38.
                                    VF £800 ($1,280) / **EF** £1,600 ($2,560)

30   **Didrachm,** 230–225 BC. Helmeted hd. of beardless Mars r., club behind. Rev. ROMA,
      horse galloping r., club above. RRC 27/1. CRR 23. RSC 32.
                                    VF £750 ($1,200) / **EF** £1,500 ($2,400)

31   32

31   **Quadrigatus-didrachm,** 225–215 BC. Beardless laur. Janiform hd. Rev. ROMA incuse on
      tablet below Jupiter and Victory in galloping quadriga r. RRC 28/3, etc. CRR 64, etc.
      RSC 23.   **VF** £225 ($360) / **EF** £550 ($880)

32   215–213 BC. Similar, but ROMA in relief on raised tablet. RRC 29/3, etc. CRR 64d, e. RSC
      23/24.   **VF** £250 ($400) / **EF** £600 ($960)

33   — Similar, but ROMA in relief in linear frame. RRC 28/3, etc. CRR 65. RSC 24.
                                    VF £225 ($360) / **EF** £550 ($880)
      A rarer variety exists with symbol ear of corn on reverse.

34   **Quadrigatus-didrachm,** 213–211 BC. Similar, but of debased metal. RRC 28/3. CRR 68.
      RSC 24b.   **VF** £200 ($320) / **EF** £550 ($880)

35   **Quadrigatus-drachm,** 216–214 BC. Beardless laur. Janiform hd. Rev. ROMA (in ex.),
      Jupiter and Victory in galloping quadriga l. RRC 29/4, etc. CRR 67. RSC 25.
                                                         VF £350 ($560) / **EF** £850 ($1,360)

THE EARLY DENARIUS COINAGE, CIRCA 211–155 BC

During the early years of its production the obverse and reverse types of the silver denarius
remained unchanged – helmeted head of Roma right with mark of value X (= 10 asses) behind / the
Dioscuri galloping right, side by side, each holding couched spear, ROMA (initially on tablet, later
in linear frame or in ex.) below. In the following listing these types will be referred to simply as
'Roma hd.' and 'Dioscuri'. In the latter part of the 190s a second reverse type (Luna in biga) made
its initial appearance on the denarius; and a third type (Victory in biga) was introduced in the early
150s.
    The half-denarius (quinarius) and the quarter-denarius (sestertius) bore the same obverse and
reverse types as the denarius (Roma head/Dioscuri), the mark of value being V (= 5 asses) in the
case of the former denomination, IIS (= 2 asses and a semis) on the latter. However, about 208 BC
these two denominations were discontinued and were destined not to be revived for more than a
hundred years.
    The victoriatus, or drachm, received its name from the figure of Victory crowning a trophy
which was its constant reverse type: a head of Jupiter appeared on the obverse. The need for this
denomination disappeared with the rapid expansion of Roman influence in the early decades of the
2nd century and production finally ceased about 170 BC.
    NB Some individual entries in the following listings include multiple variants of symbols and
letters. In such cases the valuations are based on the commonest type and it should be borne in
mind that rarer varieties are worth considerably more (for more detailed information, see Roman
Silver Coins, vol. I).

211–206 BC

36   **Denarius.** Roma hd. Rev. Dioscuri (ROMA incuse). RRC 45/1. CRR 166. BMCRR Italy
      91. RSC 1.   **VF** £450 ($720) / **EF** £1,000 ($1,600)

37   38

37   — Similar, but ROMA only partially incuse. RRC 44/5 CRR 167. BMCRR Italy 90.
      RSC 1a.   **VF** £100 ($160) / **EF** £275 ($440)

38   — Similar, but ROMA in relief. RRC 44/5. CRR 140. BMCRR 1. RSC 2.
                                                         VF £50 ($80) / **EF** £150 ($240)

39 (cornucopiae)   39 (dolphin)

39   **Denarius.** Similar, but with symbol on rev., usually below horses. RRC 50/2, 52/1, 57/2, 58/2; 59/1, 60/1, 61/1, 62/1, 72/3, 73/1, 77/1, 78/1, 79/1, 80/1a, 83/2, 88/2, 89/2, 105/3, 106/3, 108/1, 109/1, 110/1a. CRR 144, 146–7, 149, 151–2, 154, 158, 163, 165, 170, 193, 196, 208, 211, 214, 216, 219, 222, 225, 265, 278, 519. RSC 20a-c, 20f-i, 20k, 20m, 20m*, 20p, 20s, 20w-x, 20z, 20aa-bb, 20jj-kk, 20mm.   *from* **VF** £60 ($96) / **EF** £175 ($280)
      The symbols are extremely varied, some being of considerable rarity. They include: anchor; apex; apex and hammer; beak of prow; caduceus; club; corn-ear; corn-ear and crooked staff; cornucopiae; crescent; dolphin; knife; pentagram; pickaxe; rule; spearhead; staff; Victory; wheel; wreath.

39 (wheel)   40

40   — Similar, but the symbol (branch) is on obv. behind the hd. of Roma. RRC 76/1. CRR 201. RSC 20t.   **VF** £85 ($136) / **EF** £240 ($384)

41 (C AL)   41 (M)

41   — Similar, but with letter or letters (sometimes in monogram form) instead of symbol on rev. RRC 51/1, 74/1, 75/1, 84/1, 104/1, 107/1a-c, 111/1. CRR 155, 171, 187, 198–9, 204–204b, 276. RSC 32–32a, 32d, 32f, *Aelia* 1–2, *Terentia* 2.
                              from **VF** £85 ($136) / **EF** £240 ($334)
      The following letters and monograms have been recorded: AL *(in monogram);* B; C; C AL (AL *ligatured);* C VAR *(VAR in monogram);* M; ROMA *(in monogram).*

42   **Quinarius** (discontinued *circa* 208 BC). Roma hd. Rev. Dioscuri (ROMA in relief). RRC 44/6. CRR 141, etc. RSC 3.   **VF** £55 ($88) / **EF** £160 ($256)

43   — Similar, but with symbol on rev. below horses. RRC 68/2a, 72/4, 73/2, 83/3. CRR 153, 194, 197. RSC 21–21b.   *from* **VF** £65 ($104) / **EF** £185 ($296)
      The following symbols have been recorded: corn-ear; pickaxe; spearhead.

42

44 (H)

44 (MT)   44 (Ω)

44   **Quinarius.** Similar, but with letter and/or monogram on rev., usually below horses. RRC
      63/1, 64/1, 65/1, 74/2, 84/2, 85/1a-b, 86A/1, 97/2, 101/2, 102/2a, 103/2a note; 103/2a-b.
      CRR 156, 159, 161, 172, 174, 174a, 176a, 181, 181a, 183, 185, 188, 200. RSC 33a-33d,
      33f-j, *Aurelia* 9, *Terentia* 3.   *from* **VF** £60 ($96) / **EF** £175 ($280)
      The following letters and monograms have been recorded: AVR *(in monogram);* C· C VAR
      (VAR in monogram); H; KOP AΓ *(both in monogram)* L; M; MA *(in monogram);* MT *(in
      monogram);* Ω; ROMA *(in monogram).*

45   — Similar, but the letter (L) is on obv. below the hd. of Roma. RRC 98A/3. CRR 176a.
      RSC 33e.   **VF** £100 ($160) / **EF** £275 ($440)

46   49

46   **Sestertius** (discontinued *circa* 208 BC). Roma hd. Rev. Dioscuri (ROMA in relief). RRC
      44/7. CRR 142. RSC 4.   **VF** £100 ($160) / **EF** £275 ($440)

47   — Similar, but with ROMA in monogram on rev. below horses. RRC 84/3. CRR189. RSC
      34b.   **VF** £250 ($400) / **EF** £600 ($960)

48   — Similar, but with L on obv. below the hd. of Roma (no monogram on rev.). RRC
      98A/4a. CRR 177. RSC 34a.   **VF** £250 ($400) / **EF** £600 ($960)

49   **Victoriatus.** Laur. hd. of Jupiter r. Rev. Victory stg. r., crowning trophy, ROMA in ex. RRC
      44/1, etc. CRR 83, etc. RSC 9.   **VF** £45 ($72) / **EF** £140 ($224)

50   — Similar, but with symbol in rev. field. RRC 57/1, 58/1, 72/1, 83/1a, 89/1a, 91/1a, 105/1,
      106/1. CRR 209, 212, 217, 220, 223, 233a, 235, 266, 315. RSC 24b-d, 24f, 24l-n, 24r.
                                                   from **VF** £50 ($80) / **EF** £150 ($240)
      *The following symbols have been recorded: club; corn-ear; cornucopiae; crescent; penta-
      gram; spearhead; staff; torque.*

50 (spearhead)   53 (L–T)

51   **Victoriatus.** Similar, but with letter/s or monogram/s in rev. field. RRC 92/1a, 93/1a-b,
      95/1a-b, 97/1c, 98A/1b, 98A/1 note, 101/1, 102/1, 103/1. CRR 111, 113, 115, 117, 118,
      120, 121a, 137. RSC 36b, 36d-e, 36g-i, 36k, 36m.   *from* **VF** £65 ($104) / **EF** £185 ($296)
      The following letters and monograms have been recorded: CROT; KOP AΓ *(both in mono-*
      gram); L; LT *(in monogram);* MP *(in monogram);* MT *(in monogram);* Ο; T; VB *(in mono-*
      gram).

52   — Similar, but with letter on obv. RRC 71/1b, 94/1, 98A/1d. CRR 116, 156 note. RSC 36,
      36j.   *from* **VF** £85 ($136) / **EF** £240 ($384)
      The following letters have been recorded: C *(behind hd. of Jupiter);* L *(below hd.);*
      N *(retrograde, below hd.).*

53   — Similar, but with letters on obv. and rev. RRC 71/1a, 98A/1a, 1c. CRR 112, 132. RSC
      36a, 36f.   *from* **VF** £75 ($120) / **EF** £210 ($336)
      The following letter combinations have been recorded: C–M; L—T.

206–194 BC

54 (knife)

54 (pentragram)   54 (shield and carnyx)

54   **Denarius.** Roma hd. Rev. Dioscuri; symbol below horses. RRC 113/1, 114/1, 115/1,
      116/1a-b, 117A/1, 119/2, 120/2, 121/2, 122/2, 123/1, 124/2, 127/1, 128/1, 129/1. CRR 205,
      244, 246, 249, 252, 255, 258, 261, 263, 268, 268a, 277, 280–81, 290, 290a. RSC 20d–e,
      20j, 20r–s, 20u, 20w–y, 20gg–ii, *Decia* 1, *Horatia* 1. *from* **VF** £60 ($96) / **EF** £175 ($280)
      The following symbols have been recorded: beak of prow; bull butting (left or right); dog;
      female head; knife; meta; pentagram; ram; rudder; shield and carnyx; sow; star; thunder-
      bolt; trident.

55   — Similar, but the symbol (staff) is on obv. before the hd. of Roma. RRC 112/2a. CRR
      240; RSC 20cc.   **VF** £85 ($136) / **EF** £240 ($384)

56 (staff–feather)

56 **Denarius.** Similar, but also with symbol on rev. below horses. RRC 112/2b, 130/1, 131/1. CRR 206, 206 note, 241. RSC 20dd–20ff. *from* **VF** £75 ($120) / **EF** £210 ($336) *The following symbol combinations have been recorded: staff–feather; staff–staff; staff–wing.*

57 (QLC)   57 (VAR)

57 — Similar, but with QLC or VAR (in monogram) on rev. below horses (no symbol on obv.). RRC 125/1, 126/1. CRR 274–5. RSC *Lutatia* 1, *Terentia* 1.
VF £90 ($144) / **EF** £250 ($400)

58 **Victoriatus.** Laur. hd. of Jupiter r. Rev. Victory stg. r., crowning trophy, symbol in field, ROMA in ex. RRC 119/1, 120/1, 121/1, 122/1, 124/1. CRR 247, 250, 253, 256, 259. RSC 24e, 24i–k, 24q. *from* **VF** £65 ($104) / **EF** £185 ($296) *The following symbols have been recorded: dog; knife; meta; sow; thunderbolt.*

59

59 — Similar, but the symbol (staff) is on obv. before the hd. of Jupiter. RRC 112/1. CRR 242. RSC 24p. **VF** £85 ($136) / **EF** £240 ($384)

194–189 BC

60

60   **Denarius.** Roma hd. Rev. Dioscuri; symbol (owl) below horses. RRC 135/1. CRR 282.
      RSC 20v.   **VF** £140 ($224) / **EF** £350 ($560)

61 (L PL H)   61 (P MAE)

61   — Similar, but with moneyer's name in monogram form on rev., usually below horses.
      RRC 132/2, 133/2a–b, 134/1a–b, 138/1. CRR 317, 332, 332a, 334, 334a, 351. RSC *Baebia*
      1, 1a, *Caecilia* 1, *Maenia* 1, *Plautia* 1–2.   *from* **VF** £55 ($88) / **EF** £160 ($256)
      The following monograms have been recorded: L PL H *(sometimes above horses);* ME*; P*
      MAE *(*MAE *only in monogram);* TAMP *(sometimes above horses).*

62 (AV)

62   — Roma hd. Rev. Luna in biga r., moneyer's monogram AV or TAMP above, ROMA in lin-
      ear frame below. RRC 133/3, 136/1. CRR 326, 335; RSC *Aurelia* 1, *Baebia* 3.
                                                      from **VF** £60 ($96) / **EF** £175 ($280)
      The type with TAMP *monogram is of considerable rarity.*

63   **Victoriatus.** Laur. hd. of Jupiter r. Rev. Victory stg. r., crowning trophy, moneyer's mono-
      gram ME or TAMP in field, ROMA in ex. RRC 132/1, 133/1. CRR 318, 336. RSC *Caecilia*
      2, *Baebia* 4.   *from* **VF** £90 ($144) / **EF** £250 ($400)

189–179 BC

64 (AVTR)   64 (L COIL)

64   **Denarius.** Roma hd. Rev. Dioscuri; moneyer's name (sometimes in monogram form)
      below horses. RRC 146/1, 147/1, 152/1a-b, 153/1, 154/1. CRR 287, 341, 341a, 347, 348,
      349. RSC *Autronia* 1, 1a, *Calpurnia* 1, *Coelia* 1, *Domitia* 1, *Quinctilia* 1.
                                              from **VF** £60 ($96) / **EF** £175 ($280)
      The following moneyers' names have been recorded : AVTR *(in monogram);* CN CALP *(ALP
      in monogram);* CN DO; L COIL; SX Q.

65   — Roma hd. Rev. Luna in biga r., holding goad, ROMA in linear frame below. RRC 140/1.
      CRR 339. RSC 5a.   **VF** £50 ($80) / **EF** £150 ($240)

66

66   — Similar, but with moneyer's name TOD below horses, a bird perched on the first letter.
      RRC 141/1. CRR 345. RSC 35.   **VF** £55 ($88) / **EF** £160 ($256)

179–169 BC

67 (ear)   67 (helmet)

67   **Denarius.** Roma hd. Rev. Dioscuri; symbol below horses. RRC 157/1, 165/1a–b, 168/2,
      170/1. CRR 237, 270, 286, 340. RSC 20a, 20h, 20l, 20q.
                                              from **VF** £90 ($144) / **EF** £250 ($400)
      The following symbols have been recorded: anchor; cornucopiae; human ear; helmet.

68 (GR)   68 (MAT)

68 **Denarius.** Similar, but with letter/s or monogram below horses. RRC 155/1, 162/2a-b and note, 169/1, 171/1, 172/1. CRR 285, 289, 291, 320 and note, 330. RSC 32b, 32e, *Furia* 7, *Matiena* 1–2a, *Sempronia* 1. *from* **VF** £65 ($104) / **EF** £185 ($296)
The following letters and monograms have been recorded: D; GR; MA *(in monogram);* MAT *or* MT *(in monogram, sometimes followed by* l*);* PVR *(in monogram).*

69

69 — Roma hd. Rev. Luna in biga r., holding reins (no goad), ROMA in ex. RRC 158/1. CRR 312. RSC 5. **VF** £50 ($80) / **EF** £150 ($240)

70 (fly)   70 (prawn)

70 — Similar, but with symbol below horses. RRC 156/1, 159/2, 163/1. CRR 322, 325, 343. RSC 22–22b. *from* **VF** £85 ($136) / **EF** £240 ($384)
The following symbols have been recorded: feather; fly; prawn.

71

71 — Similar, but with TAL (in monogram) below horses. RRC 161/1. CRR 328. RSC *Juventia* 1. **VF** £175 ($280) / **EF** £425 ($680)

72 **Victoriatus.** Laur. hd. of Jupiter r. Rev. Victory stg. r., crowning trophy, fly or helmet in field, ROMA in ex. RRC 159/1, 168/1. CRR 271, 323. RSC 24g–h.

VF £90 ($144) / **EF** £250 ($400)

73 — Similar, but with MAT or MT (in monogram) in rev. field. RRC 162/1a–b. CRR 321. RSC *Matiena* 3, 3a.

VF £65 ($104) / **EF** £185 ($296)

169–157 BC

74

74 **Denarius.** Roma hd. Rev. Dioscuri; gryphon below horses. RRC 182/1. CRR 283. RSC 20n.

VF £90 ($144) / **EF** £250 ($400)

75 — Roma hd. Rev. Luna in biga r., ROMA in linear frame below, murex-shell above horses, PVR below. RRC 187/1. CRR 424. RSC *Furia* 13.

VF £50 ($80) / **EF** £150 ($240)

157–155 BC

76   77

76 **Denarius.** Roma hd. Rev. Victory in biga r., ROMA in ex. RRC 197/1. CRR 376, etc. RSC 6.

VF £45 ($72) / **EF** £140 ($224)

77 — Similar, but with NAT below horses. RRC 200/1. CRR 382. RSC *Pinaria* 2.

VF £50 ($80) / **EF** £150 ($240)

78

78 — Similar, but with SAR (AR sometimes in monogram) below horses. RRC 199/1a–b. CRR 377. RSC *Atilia* 1–2.

VF £50 ($80) / **EF** £150 ($240)

THE LATER DENARIUS COINAGE, CIRCA 154–41 BC

At the beginning of this period the denarius was the only silver coin being produced by the Roman mint and only three designs had been utilized since the introduction of the denomination more than half a century before (Roma head/Dioscuri; Roma head/Luna in biga; Roma head/Victory in biga). Within a decade or so there began a remarkable proliferation of reverse types and in the final decades of the 2nd century even the obverse design became subject to experimentation. Moneyers' names began to appear in a much fuller form and all of these developments combined to produce a bewildering variety of silver coinage in the final half century of the Republic's existence.

The half-denarius or quinarius, last issued about 208 BC, was reintroduced at the very end of the 2nd century with types reminiscent of the old victoriatus abandoned seven decades before. Thereafter, the quinarius denomination was constantly associated with the winged goddess of victory, a peculiarity which it retained well into Roman Imperial times. This initial revival extended over two decades, until about 81 BC, after which it was again discontinued until its second revival under Caesar's dictatorship in the early 40s BC.

The quarter-denarius or sestertius – never a common denomination under the Republic – had also been abandoned *circa* 208 BC. Its revival did not take place until 91 BC, under the terms of the *lex Papiria*, and was very short-lived. Like the quinarius it reappeared under Caesar about 48 BC, but did not survive his assassination on the Ides of March, 44. When the sestertius was finally reintroduced a quarter of a century later, as part of Augustus' arrangements for his new Imperial coinage, it appeared as a large base metal coin struck in orichalcum (brass).

79   80

79   **Denarius.** C. Scribonius, 154 BC. Helmeted hd. of Roma r., X behind. Rev. Dioscuri galloping r., C SCR below, ROMA in ex. RRC 201/1. CRR 380. RSC *Scribonia* 1.
                                                        VF £50 ($80) / **EF** £150 ($240)

80   — C. Juventius Thalna, 154 BC. Helmeted hd. of Roma r., X behind. Rev. Victory in biga r., C TAL (TAL in monogram) below, ROMA in ex. RRC 202/1a. CRR 379. RSC *Juventia* 7.
                                                        VF £60 ($96) / **EF** £175 ($280)

81   **Denarius serratus.** Similar. RRC 202/1b. CRR 379a. RSC *Juventia* 7a.
                                                        VF £75 ($120) / **EF** £210 ($336)
      A remarkable solitary early example of the curious phenomenon of the notched edge on the denarius which was to become common in later decades.

82   **Denarius.** C. Maianius, 153 BC. Helmeted hd. of Roma r., X behind. Rev. Victory in biga r., C MAIANI (MA and AN in monogram) below, ROMA in ex. RRC 203/1a. CRR 427. RSC *Maiania* 1.   **VF** £50 ($80) / **EF** £150 ($240)

83   84

83   **Denarius.** L. Saufeius, 152 BC. Similar, but with **L SAVF** (**VF** in monogram) below horses. RRC 204/1. CRR 384. RSC *Saufeia* 1.   **VF** £50 ($80) / **EF** £150 ($240)

84   — P. Cornelius Sulla, 151 BC. Similar, but with **P SVLA** (**VL** in monogram) below horses. RRC 205/1. CRR 386. RSC *Cornelia* 1.   **VF** £50 ($80) / **EF** £150 ($240)

85   86

85   — Safra, 150 BC. Similar, but with **SAFRA** below horses. RRC 206/1. CRR 388. RSC *Afrania* 1.   **VF** £50 ($80) / **EF** £150 ($240)
SAFRA *would appear to represent a cognomen only, no stop being inserted after the first letter.*

86   — Decimius Flavus, 150 BC. Helmeted hd. of Roma r., **X** behind. Rev. Luna in biga. r., holding whip, **FLAVS** below, **ROMA** in ex. RRC 207/1. CRR 391. RSC *Decimia* 1.   **VF** £50 ($80) / **EF** £150 ($240)

87   88

87   — C. Junius C.f., 149 BC. Helmeted hd. of Roma r., **X** behind. Rev. Dioscuri galloping r., **C IVNI C F** below, **ROMA** in ex. or in linear frame. RRC 210/1. CRR 392. RSC *Junia* 1.   **VF** £55 ($88) / **EF** £160 ($256)

88   — L. Iteius or Iteilius, 149 BC. Similar, but with **L ITI** below horses. RRC 209/1. CRR 394. RSC *Itia* 1.   **VF** £185 ($296) / **EF** £450 ($720)

89   90

89   **Denarius.** Pinarius Natta, 149 BC. Helmeted hd. of Roma r., X behind. Rev. Victory in biga r.,
     NATTA (TA in monogram) below, ROMA in ex. RRC 208/1. CRR 390. RSC *Pinaria* 1.
                                                            VF £50 ($80) / EF £150 ($240)

90   — Q. Marcius Libo, 148 BC. Helmeted hd. of Roma r., X below chin, LIBO behind. Rev.
     Dioscuri galloping r., Q MARC (MA in monogram) below, ROMA in ex. or in linear frame.
     RRC 215/1. CRR 395. RSC *Marcia* 1.   VF £50 ($80) / EF £150 ($240)
     This marks the first fundamental change in the obverse design of the denarius, the mark of
     value being moved in front of Roma and replaced by the moneyer's cognomen.

                 91   92

91   — L. Sempronius Pitio, 148 BC. Similar, but with PITIO behind hd. of Roma, and L SEMP
     (MP in monogram) below horses. RRC 216/1. CRR 402. RSC *Sempronia* 2.
                                                            VF £50 ($80) / EF £150 ($240)

92   — M. Atilius Saranus, 148 BC. Similar, but with SARAN (AN in monogram) behind hd. of
     Roma, and M ATIL or M ATILI below horses. RRC 214/1. CRR 398–398d. RSC *Atilia* 8–9.
     VF £50 ($80) / EF £150 ($240)

                 93   94

93   — C. Terentius Lucanus, 147 BC. Helmeted hd. of Roma r., crowned by Victory stg. r.
     above X behind. Rev. Dioscuri galloping r., C TER LVC (TE in monogram) below, ROMA in
     ex. RRC 217/1. CRR 425. RSC *Terentia* 10.   VF £50 ($80) / EF £150 ($240)
     The symbolism of Victory crowning Roma, remarkable at this time, would appear to com-
     memorate some notable success in a foreign war.

94   **Denarius.** L. Cupiennius, 147 BC. Helmeted hd. of Roma r., **X** below chin, cornucopiae behind. Rev. Dioscuri galloping r., **L CVP** (**VP** in monogram) below, **ROMA** in ex. RRC 218/1. CRR 404. RSC *Cupiennia* 1.   VF £50 ($80) / **EF** £150 ($240)

95/1   95/2

95   — C. Antestius, 146 BC. Similar, but with **C ANTESTI** (**ANTE** in monogram) behind hd. of Roma, and puppy running r. below horses. RRC 219/1e. CRR 411. RSC *Antestia* 1.

                              VF £50 ($80) / **EF** £150 ($240)
Sometimes the puppy appears on obv. and the moneyer's name on rev.

96   97

96   — M. Junius Silanus, 145 BC. Similar, but with ass's hd. behind hd. of Roma, and **M IVNI** below horses. RRC 220/1. CRR 408, 412. RSC *Junia* 8.   **VF** £45 ($72) / **EF** £140 ($224)

97   — T. Annius Rufus (?), 144 BC. Helmeted hd. of Roma r., **X** behind. Rev. Jupiter in quadriga r., brandishing thunderbolt, **AN RVF** (**AN** and **VF** in monogram) below, **ROMA** in ex. RRC 221/1. CRR 409, 413. RSC *Aurelia* 19.   **VF** £50 ($80) / **EF** £150 ($240)
*This type has traditionally been ascribed to an Aurelius Rufus, but Crawford prefers to identify the moneyer with the consul of 128 BC. Either reading of the **N** monogram is plausible. The reverse represents another departure from the traditional iconography of the Republican coinage, a trend which was soon to gather momentum.*

98   99

98   — Anonymous, 143 BC. Helmeted hd. of Roma r., **X** behind. Rev. Diana in biga of stags r., holding torch, crescent below, **ROMA** in ex. RRC 222/1. CRR 438. RSC 101.

                              VF £55 ($88) / **EF** £160 ($256)
The occurrence of an anonymous issue at this late date is exceptional and surprising.

99   **Denarius.** C. Curiatius Trigeminus, 142 BC. Helmeted hd. of Roma r., X below chin, TRIGE behind. Rev. Juno in quadriga r., crowned from behind by Victory, C CVR (VR in monogram) below, ROMA in ex. RRC 223/1. CRR 436. RSC *Curiatia* 1.

VF £55 ($88) / **EF** £160 ($256)

100   101

100 — L. Julius, 141 BC. Helmeted hd. of Roma r., XVI behind. Rev. Dioscuri galloping r., L IVLI (VL in monogram) below, ROMA in ex. RRC 224/1. CRR 443. RSC *Julia* 1.

VF £50 ($80) / **EF** £150 ($240)

This marks the change in the valuation of the denarius from 10 asses (X) to 16 (XVI).

101 — L. Atilius Nomentanus, 141 BC. Helmeted hd. of Roma r., XVI behind. Rev. Victory in biga r., L ATILI (AT in monogram) below, NOM in ex. RRC 225/1. CRR 444. RSC *Atilia* 16.   VF £600 ($960) / **EF** £1,250 ($2,000)

The extraordinary omission of ROMA on the reverse and its apparent replacement by the moneyer's cognomen remains unexplained.

102   103

102 — C. Titinius, 141 BC. Similar, but with C TITINI below horses and ROMA in ex. RRC 226/1. CRR 445. RSC *Titinia* 7.   VF £85 ($136) / **EF** £240 ($384)

103 — C. Valerius C.f. Flaccus, 140 BC. Similar, but with C VAL C F (VAL in monogram) below horses and FLAC above. RRC 228/1. CRR 441. RSC *Valeria* 8.

VF £60 ($96) / **EF** £175 ($280)

104   105

104 —— Similar, but with X behind Roma instead of XVI. RRC 228/2. CRR 440, 454. RSC *Valeria* 7.   VF £50 ($80) / **EF** £150 ($240)

This issue marks the return to the traditional mark of value 'X' now that the Roman populace was familiar with the retariffing of the denarius at 16 asses.

105 **Denarius.** M. Aufidius Rusticus, 140 BC. Helmeted hd. of Roma r., XVI behind, RVS before. Rev. Jupiter in quadriga r., brandishing thunderbolt, M AVF (AVF or VF in monogram: below, ROMA in ex. RRC 227/1. CRR 446, 458. RSC *Aufidia* 1–1c.

VF £185 ($296) / **EF** £450 ($720)

106   107

106 — M. Aurelius Cotta, 139 BC. Helmeted hd. of Roma r., X behind, COTA before. Rev. Hercules in biga of Centaurs r., holding club, the Centaurs holding branches, M AVRELI (AVR in monogram) below, ROMA in ex. RRC 229/1. CRR 429. RSC *Aurelia* 16.

VF £85 ($136) / **EF** £240 ($384)

107 — A. Spurilius (?), 139 BC. Helmeted hd. of Roma r., X behind. Rev. Luna in biga r., A SPVRI (VR in monogram) below, ROMA in ex. RRC 230/1. CRR 448. RSC *Spurilia* 1.

VF £50 ($80) / **EF** £150 ($240)

Crawford suggests Spurius or Spurinna as possible alternatives for Spurilius.

108   109

108 — C. Renius, 138 BC. Helmeted hd. of Roma r., X behind. Rev. Juno in biga of goats r., C RENI below, ROMA in ex. RRC 231/1. CRR 432. RSC *Renia* 1.

VF £55 ($88) / **EF** £160 ($256)

109 — Cn Gellius, 138 BC. Helmeted hd. of Roma r., X behind, all within laurel-wreath. Rev. Armed figure (Mars?) holding shield, grasping bound female captive in quadriga r., CN GEL or GELI below, ROMA in ex. RRC 232/1. CRR 434. RSC *Gellia* 1.

VF £65 ($104) / **EF** £185 ($296)

This moneyer may be identical with the later 2nd century Roman historian of this name whose 'Annals', although now surviving only in fragments, clearly indicate his wide-ranging antiquarian interests and intimate knowledge of the Hellenistic world.

110   111

110   **Denarius.** P. Aelius Paetus, 138 BC. Helmeted hd. of Roma r., X behind. Rev. Dioscuri gal-
      loping r., P PAETVS below, ROMA in ex. RRC 233/1. CRR 455. RSC *Aelia* 3.
                                                VF £50 ($80) / EF £150 ($240)
      A late revival of the traditional denarius type. The rendering of the moneyer's name in the
      nominative case is an unusual feature.

111   — Ti. Veturius, 137 BC. Helmeted and dr. bust of Mars r., X between back of neck and end
      of crest, TI VET (VET in monogram) behind. Rev. Oath-taking scene, with two stg. warriors
      and sacrificial pig held by kneeling attendant, ROMA above. RRC 234/1. CRR 527. RSC
      Veturia 1.   VF £65 ($104) / EF £185 ($296)
      A remarkable type representing a complete break with the 75-year traditions of the denar-
      ius coinage. The reverse is a revival of the gold coinage of 217–216 BC (see nos. 1 and 2).

112   113

112   — Sex. Pompeius, 137 BC. Helmeted hd. of Roma r., X below chin, jug behind. Rev. She-
      wolf stg. r., suckling the twins Romulus and Remus, fig-tree in background with three
      birds, the shepherd Faustulus stg. r. behind, FOSTLVS on l., SEX POM on r., ROMA in ex.
      RRC 235/1a. CRR 461. RSC *Pompeia* 1.   VF £65 ($104) / EF £185 ($296)

113   — M. Baebius Q.f. Tampilus, 137 BC. Helmeted head of Roma l., X below chin, TAMPIL
      behind. Rev. Apollo in quadriga r., holding laurel-branch, bow and arrow, ROMA below, M
      BAEBI Q F in ex. RRC 236/1a. CRR 489. RSC *Baebia* 12.   VF £45 ($72) / EF £140 ($224)
      An innovative type, with Roma's head turned in the opposite direction and Apollo making
      his first appearance on a Roman denarius. The reversal of the positions of ROMA and the
      moneyer's name was also a novelty.

114   115

114   — Cn. Lucretius Trio, 136 BC. Helmeted hd. of Roma r., X below chin, TRIO behind. Rev.
      Dioscuri galloping r., CN LVCR below, ROMA in ex. RRC 237/1a. CRR 450. RSC *Lucretia* 1.
                                                VF £45 ($72) / EF £140 ($224)
      Another late revival of the traditional denarius type.

115 **Denarius.** L. Antestius Gragulus, 136 BC. Helmeted hd. of Roma r., ✳ (XVI monogram) below chin, GRAG behind. Rev. Jupiter in quadriga r., brandishing thunderbolt, L ANTES (ANTE in monogram) below, ROMA in ex. RRC 238/1. CRR 451, 465. RSC *Antestia 9*.
VF £45 ($72) / EF £140 ($224)
A new mark of value for the denarius is here used for the first time. Resembling a star, it probably represents the numeral XVI *in monogram form.*

116   118

116 — C. Servilius M.f., 136 BC. Helmeted hd. of Roma r., wreath and ✳ (XVI monogram) behind, ROMA below. Rev. Dioscuri galloping apart, C SERVEILI M F in ex. RRC 239/1. CRR 525. RSC *Servilia 1*.
VF £60 ($96) / EF £175 ($280)
ROMA *moves to the obverse for the first time on this novel variation of the Dioscuri type.*

117 — C. Curiatius C.f. Trigeminus, 135 BC. Helmeted hd. of Roma r., X below chin, TRIG (or TRIGE) behind. Rev. Juno in quadriga r., crowned from behind by Victory, C CVR F (VR in monogram) below, ROMA in ex. RRC 240/1. CRR 459, 459a. RSC *Curiatia 2, 2a*.
VF £65 ($104) / EF £185 ($296)
This reproduces the types of the earlier Trigeminus, probably his father (see no. 99).

118 — L. Trebanius, 135 BC. Helmeted hd. of Roma r., X behind. Rev. Jupiter in quadriga r., brandishing thunderbolt, L TREBANI (TR and AN in monogram) below, ROMA in ex. RRC 241/1a. CRR 456. RSC *Trebania 1*.
VF £50 ($80) / EF £150 ($240)

119   122

119 — C. Minucius Augurinus, 135 BC. Helmeted hd. of Roma r., X below chin, ROMA behind. Rev. Column surmounted by statue between two togate figures, C AVG above. RRC 242/1. CRR 463. RSC *Minucia 3*.
VF £55 ($88) / EF £160 ($256)
The reverses of this and the following represent the bronze Columna Minucia outside the Porta Trigemina in the Servian Wall.

120 — Ti. Minucius C.f. Augurinus, 134 BC. Helmeted hd. of Roma r., ✳ (XVI monogram) behind. Rev. Similar to previous, but with TI MINVCI on l., AVGVRINI on r., and ROMA above. RRC 243/1. CRR 494. RSC *Minucia 9*.
VF £55 ($88) / EF £160 ($256)

121 **Denarius.** C. Aburius Geminus, 134 BC. Helmeted hd. of Roma r., ✕ (XVI monogram) below chin, GEM behind. Rev. Mars in quadriga r., holding trophy, spear and shield, C ABVRI (AB and VR in monogram) below, ROMA in ex. RRC 244/1. CRR 490. RSC *Aburia* 1.
VF £50 ($80) / EF £150 ($240)

122 — M. Marcius Mn.f., 134 BC. Helmeted hd. of Roma r., ✕ (XVI monogram) below chin, modius behind. Rev. Victory in biga r., M MARC (MAR in monogram) / ROMA divided by two corn-ears below. RRC 245/1. CRR 500. RSC *Marcia* 8.
VF £50 ($80) / EF £150 ($240)

123 — C. Numitorius, 133 BC. Helmeted hd. of Roma r., ✕ (XVI monogram) below chin, ROMA behind. Rev. Victory in quadriga r., holding wreath, C NVMITORI in ex. RRC 246/1. CRR 466. RSC *Numitoria* 1.
VF £1,750 ($2,800) / EF £3,500 ($5,600)
The extreme rarity of this type is surprising and suggests that the issue was cut short, possibly by the death of the moneyer in office.

124   125

124 — P. Calpurnius, 133 BC. Helmeted hd. of Roma r., ✕ (XVI monogram) behind. Rev. Venus (?) in biga r., crowned by Victory flying l. above, P CALP below, ROMA in ex. RRC 247/1. CRR 468. RSC *Calpurnia* 2.
VF £50 ($80) / EF £150 ($240)

125 — L. Minucius, 133 BC. Obv. Similar. Rev. Jupiter in quadriga r., brandishing thunderbolt, ROMA below, L MINVCI in ex. RRC 248/1. CRR 470. RSC *Minucia* 15.
VF £50 ($80) / EF £150 ($240)

126   127

126 — P. Maenius M.f. Antias (or Antiaticus), 132 BC. Obv. Similar. Rev. Victory in quadriga r., holding wreath and palm, P MAE ANT (MAE and ANT in monogram) below, ROMA in ex. RRC 249/1. CRR 492. RSC *Maenia* 7.
VF £50 ($80) / EF £150 ($240)

127 — M. Aburius M.f. Geminus, 132 BC. Helmeted hd. of Roma r., ✕ (XVI monogram) below chin, GEM behind. Rev. Rad. Sol in quadriga r., holding whip, M ABVRI (AB and VR in monogram) below, ROMA in ex. RRC 250/1. CRR 487. RSC *Aburia* 6.
VF £50 ($80) / EF £150 ($240)

128   129

128   **Denarius.** L. Postumius Albinus, 131 BC. Helmeted hd. of Roma r., ✳ (XVI monogram)
      below chin, apex behind. Rev. Mars in quadriga r., holding trophy, spear and shield, L POST
      ALB (AL in monogram) below, ROMA in ex. RRC 252/1. CRR 472. RSC *Postumia* 1.
                                                        VF £50 ($80) / EF £150 ($240)

129   — L. Opimius, 131 BC. Helmeted hd. of Roma r., ✳ (XVI monogram) below chin, wreath
      behind. Rev. Victory in quadriga r., holding wreath, L OPEIMI below, ROMA in ex. RRC
      253/1. CRR 473. RSC *Opimia* 12.   VF £50 ($80) / EF £150 ($240)
      This moneyer and the next appear to have been brothers and to have held their mint mag-
      istracies simultaneously.

130   — M. Opimius, 131 BC. Helmeted hd. of Roma r., ✳ (XVI monogram) below chin, tripod
      behind. Rev. Apollo in biga r., holding arrow and bow, M OPEIMI below, ROMA in ex. RRC
      254/1. CRR 475. RSC *Opimia* 16.   VF £50 ($80) / EF £150 ($240)

131   132

131   — M. Acilius M.f., 130 BC. Helmeted hd. of Roma r., ✳ (XVI monogram) behind, M
      ACILIVS M F around between double circle of dots. Rev. Hercules in slow quadriga r., hold-
      ing club and trophy, ROMA in ex. RRC 255/1. CRR 511. RSC *Acilia* 4.
                                                        VF £55 ($88) / EF £160 ($256)
      It is tempting to speculate that this novel treatment of the standard obverse type was
      inspired by the mid-2nd century Macedonian tetradrachms with head of Artemis at the
      centre of a shield.

132   — Q. Caecilius Metellus, 130 BC. Helmeted hd. of Roma r., ✳ (XVI monogram) below
      chin, Q METE (ME and TE in monogram) behind. Rev. Jupiter in slow quadriga r., holding
      branch and thunderbolt, ROMA in ex. RRC 256/1. CRR 509. RSC *Caecilia* 21.
                                                        VF £50 ($80) / EF £150 ($240)

133   — M. Vargunteius, 130 BC. Similar, but with M VARG (VAR in monogram) behind hd. of
      Roma. RRC 257/1. CRR 507. RSC *Vargunteia* 1.   VF £50 ($80) / EF £150 ($240)

134   — Sex. Julius Caesar, 129 BC. Helmeted hd. of Roma r., ✳ (XVI monogram) below chin,
      anchor behind. Rev. Venus in biga r., crowned by Cupid behind, SEX IVLI (VL in mono-
      gram) / CAISAR below and in ex., ROMA above. RRC 258/1. CRR 476. RSC *Julia* 2.
                                                        VF £65 ($104) / EF £185 ($296)
      The illustrious name of Caesar here makes its first appearance on the Roman coinage
      three decades before the birth of the dictator.

133   135

135   **Denarius.** Q. Marcius Philippus, 129 BC. Helmeted hd. of Roma r., ✲ (XVI monogram) behind. Rev. Helmeted horseman galloping r., holding spear, Macedonian helmet with goat's horns behind, Q PILIPVS below, ROMA in ex. RRC 259/1. CRR 477. RSC *Marcia* 11.

                                                 VF £60 ($96) / **EF** £175 ($280)
   This reverse seems to allude to the moneyer's cognomen through its depiction of a Macedonian horseman probably representing Philip V.

136   — T. Cloulius (or Cloelius), 128 BC. Helmeted hd. of Roma r., wreath behind, ROMA below. Rev. Victory in biga r., horses rearing, corn-ear below, T CLOVLI in ex. RRC 260/1. CRR 516. RSC *Cloulia* 1.   **VF** £50 ($80) / **EF** £150 ($240)
   The omission of the mark of value at this time is most unusual: it may possibly be concealed in the spokes of the chariot's wheel.

137   139

137   — Cn. Domitius, 128 BC. Helmeted hd. of Roma r., ✲ (XVI monogram) below chin, corn-ear behind. Rev. Victory in biga r., man attacking lion below, CN DOM in ex., ROMA above. RRC 261/1. CRR 514. RSC *Domitia* 14.   **VF** £60 ($96) / **EF** £175 ($280)
   This moneyer may be a Domitius Ahenobarbus, or perhaps a Domitius Calvinus.

138   — Anonymous, 128 BC. Helmeted hd. of Roma r., ✲ (XVI monogram) behind. Rev. Goddess (Pax or Juno Regina) in biga r., holding branch and sceptre, elephant's hd. r., with bell attached, and ROMA below. RRC 262/1. CRR 496. RSC *Caecilia* 38.

                                                 VF £55 ($88) / **EF** £160 ($256)
   Although lacking the moneyer's name it seems certain that this was issued by a Caecilius Metellus, probably either L. Caecilius Metellus Diadematus or L. Caecilius Metellus Delmaticus.

139   — M. Caecilius Q.f. Metellus, 127 BC. Helmeted hd. of Roma r., ✲ (XVI monogram) below chin, ROMA behind. Rev. Macedonian shield with elephant's hd. at centre, M METELLVS Q F around, all within laurel-wreath. RRC 263/1. CRR 480. RSC *Caecilia* 29.

                                                 VF £55 ($88) / **EF** £160 ($256)
   The son of Q. Caecilius Metellus Macedonicus, who defeated the Macedonian pretender Andriscus in 148 BC, this is an early example of a moneyer commemorating his family history on the coinage.

140   141

140 **Denarius.** C. Servilius, 127 BC. Helmeted hd. of Roma r., ✕ (XVI monogram) below chin, lituus behind, ROMA below. Rev. Battle between two mounted horsemen, the one on l. armed with sword, the other with spear, his shield inscribed M, C SERVEIL (VE in monogram) in ex. RRC 264/1. CRR 483. RSC *Servilia* 6.   **VF** £55 ($88) / **EF** £160 ($256)

141 — Q. Fabius Maximus, 127 BC. Helmeted hd. of Roma r., ✕ (XVI monogram) below chin, Q MAX (MA in monogram) before, ROMA behind. Rev. Cornucopiae with thunderbolt placed horizontally in background, all within wreath. RRC 265/1. CRR 478. RSC *Fabia* 5.
                                              VF £60 ($96) / **EF** £175 ($280)

142   143

142 — C. Cassius, 126 BC. Helmeted hd. of Roma r., voting-urn and ✕ (XVI monogram) behind. Rev. Libertas in quadriga r., holding pileus and rod, C CASSI below, ROMA in ex. RRC 266/1. CRR 502. RSC *Cassia* 1.   **VF** £50 ($80) / **EF** £150 ($240)

143 — T. Quinctius Flamininus, 126 BC. Helmeted hd. of Roma r., ✕ (XVI monogram) below chin, apex behind. Rev. Dioscuri galloping r., T – Q divided by Macedonian shield below, ROMA in ex. RRC 267/1. CRR 505. RSC *Quinctia* 2.   **VF** £55 ($88) / **EF** £160 ($256)
It was an ancestor of this moneyer who achieved the celebrated victory over Philip V at Cynoscephalae in 197 BC after which special vows were offered to the Dioscuri. This accounts for the late revival of the traditional reverse type.

144   145

144 — N. Fabius Pictor, 126 BC. Helmeted hd. of Roma r., ✕ (XVI monogram) behind, sometimes with control-letter below chin. Rev. N FABI PICTOR, helmeted and cuir. figure of the Flamen Quirinalis Q. Fabius Pictor seated l., holding apex and spear, shield inscribed QVI/RIN at his side, sometimes with control-letter above, ROMA in ex. RRC 268/1. CRR 517, 517a. RSC *Fabia* 11, 11a.   **VF** £85 ($136) / **EF** £240 ($384)
The first example of the use of control-letters on the denarius coinage. The system was later to be dramatically expanded to include numerals and symbols as well as letters.

145   **Denarius.** C. Caecilius Metellus, 125 BC. Hd. of Roma r., wearing Phrygian helmet, ✶
      (XVI monogram) below chin, ROMA behind. Rev. Jupiter in biga of elephants l., holding
      thunderbolt, crowned by Victory flying r. above, C METELLVS (ME in monogram) in ex.
      RRC 269/1. CRR 485. RSC *Caecilia* 14.   **VF** £90 ($144) / **EF** £250 ($400)

146   — M. Porcius Laeca, 125 BC. Helmeted hd. of Roma r., ✶ (XVI monogram) below chin,
      LAECA behind. Rev. Libertas in quadriga r., holding pileus and rod, crowned by Victory
      flying l. above, M PORC below, ROMA in ex. RRC 270/1. CRR 513. RSC *Porcia* 3.
                                                          VF £50 ($80) / **EF** £150 ($240)

147

147   — Mn. Acilius Balbus, 125 BC. Helmeted hd. of Roma r., ✶ (XVI monogram) below chin,
      BALBVS (AL in monogram) behind, ROMA below, all within wreath. Rev. Jupiter, holding
      thunderbolt and sceptre, in quadriga driven r. by Victory, circular shield below, MN ACILI
      (MN in monogram) in ex. RRC 271/1. CRR 498. RSC *Acilia* 1.
                                                          VF £55 ($88) / **EF** £160 ($256)

148   — Q. Fabius Labeo, 124 BC. Helmeted hd. of Roma r., X below chin, LABEO before, ROMA
      behind. Rev. Jupiter in quadriga r., brandishing thunderbolt, rostrum below, Q FABI in ex.
      RRC 273/1. CRR 532. RSC *Fabia* 1.   **VF** £50 ($80) / **EF** £150 ($240)
      From this point until its final abandonment the mark of value may be represented either by
      the traditional X or by the XVI monogram in star form. This random employment of the two
      varieties is surely without significance and may be taken as evidence that by the final quarter
      of the 2nd century the mark had become nothing more than a decorative design feature.

149   — C. Porcius Cato, 123 BC. Helmeted hd. of Roma r., X behind. Rev. Victory in biga r.,
      C CATO below, ROMA in ex. RRC 274/1. CRR 417. RSC *Porcia* 1.
                                                          VF £45 ($72) / **EF** £140 ($224)

150   — M. Fannius C.f., 123 BC. Helmeted hd. of Roma r., X below chin, ROMA behind. Rev.
      Victory in quadriga r., holding wreath, M FAN C F (AN in monogram) in ex. RRC 275/1.
      CRR 419. RSC *Fannia* 1.   **VF** £45 ($72) / **EF** £140 ($224)

151   — M. Papirius Carbo, 122 BC. Helmeted hd. of Roma r., X below chin, branch behind. Rev.
      Jupiter in quadriga r., brandishing thunderbolt, M CARBO below, ROMA in ex. RRC 276/1.
      CRR 423. RSC *Papiria* 6.   **VF** £45 ($72) / **EF** £140 ($224)

152   — Q. Minucius Rufus, 122 BC. Helmeted hd. of Roma r., X below chin, RVF behind. Rev.
      Dioscuri galloping r., Q MINV below, ROMA in ex. RRC 277/1. CRR 421. RSC *Minucia* 1.
                                                          VF £45 ($72) / **EF** £140 ($224)
      This and the following mark the final appearances of the traditional reverse type for the
      denarius introduced 90 years before.

153   — C. Plutius, 121 BC. Helmeted hd. of Roma r., X behind. Rev. Dioscuri galloping r.,
      C PLVTI below, ROMA in ex. RRC 278/1. CRR 410, 414. RSC *Plutia* 1.
                                                          VF £45 ($72) / **EF** £140 ($224)
      The Plutia gens is unknown to history and Crawford regards this moneyer as a Plautius,
      son of the C. Plautius who was praetor in 146 BC.

154   155

154   **Denarius.** Cn.(?) Papirius Carbo, 121 BC. Helmeted hd. of Roma r., X behind. Rev. Jupiter
        in quadriga r., brandishing thunderbolt, CARB below, ROMA in ex. RRC 279/1. CRR 415.
        RSC *Papiria* 7.   VF £45 ($72) / EF £140 ($224)
        The omission of the moneyer's praenomen is curious, but the issue should be regarded as
        distinct from that of M. Carbo (no. 151). Crawford thinks he is probably the Cn. Carbo
        who held the consulship in 113 BC.

155   — M. Tullius, 120 BC. Helmeted hd. of Roma r., ROMA behind. Rev. Victory in quadriga r.,
        holding palm-branch, wreath above, X below, M TVLLI in ex. RRC 280/1. CRR 531. RSC
        Tullia 1.   VF £45 ($72) / EF £140 ($224)
        The mark of value on the reverse is an unusual feature of this issue, as is the symbol
        (wreath) above the horses.

156   157

156   — M. Furius L.f. Philus, 119 BC. M FOVRI L F, laur. hd. of Janus. Rev. Roma stg. l., crown-
        ing trophy with carnyx and shield on each side, star above Roma, ROMA to r., PHILI (PHI in
        monogram) in ex. RRC 281/1. CRR 529. RSC *Furia* 18.   VF £55 ($88) / EF £160 ($256)
        This radical departure from the conventional iconography of the denarius commemorates
        the victories over the Allobroges and the Arverni in Gaul achieved in 121 BC by Cn.
        Domitius Ahenobarbus and Q. Fabius Maximus (Allobrogicus).

157   **Denarius serratus.** L. Licinius Crassus and Cn. Domitius Ahenobarbus with M. Aurelius
        Scaurus, 118 BC. Helmeted (usually Phrygian) hd. of Roma r., M AVRELI (VR in mono-
        gram) before, ROMA and ✻ (XVI monogram) behind. Rev. Naked Gallic warrior in biga r.,
        with spear, shield and carnyx, SCAVRI (AVR in monogram) below, L LIC CN DOM in ex.
        RRC 282/1. CRR 523, 523a. RSC *Aurelia* 20, 20a.   VF £55 ($88) / EF £160 ($256)

158   — L. Licinius Crassus and Cn. Domitius Ahenobarbus with L. Cosconius, C. Malleolus, L.
        Pomponius, or L. Porcius Licinus, 118 BC. Similar, but Roma wears Attic helmet and is
        encircled by the moneyer's name L COSCO M F, C MALLE C F, L POMPONI CN F (NF in mono-
        gram), or L PORCI LICI; ROMA is omitted; X sometimes appears for ✻; and there is no leg-
        end below horses on rev. RRC 282/2–5. CRR 520–22, 524. RSC *Cosconia* 1, *Poblicia* 1,
        Pomponia 7, *Porcia* 8.   VF £55 ($88) / EF £160 ($256)
        This extraordinary issue, distinguished by flans with serrated edges, was minted at the
        newly-founded city of Narbo, the first Roman colony in Gaul. The two principal magis-
        trates (Licinius Crassus and Domitius Ahenobarbus) producd their coins in association
        with five junior colleagues.

158   160

159   **Denarius.** Q. Marcius (?), C. Fabius (?), and L. Roscius (?), 118/117 BC. Helmeted hd. of
       Roma r., ✕ (XVI monogram) behind. Rev. Victory in quadriga r., holding wreath, ROMA
       below, Ọ MAR C F L R (MAR in monogram) in ex. RRC 283/1a. CRR 541. RSC *Marcia* 16.
                                            VF £55 ($88) / **EF** £160 ($256)
       A rarer variant of this enigmatic issue has the legend C F L R Ọ M *in ex.*

160   — M. Calidius, Q. Caecilius Metellus, and Cn. Fulvius, 117/116 BC. Helmeted hd. of
       Roma r., ✕ (XVI monogram) below chin, ROMA behind. Rev. Victory in biga r., holding
       wreath, M CALID below, Ọ MET CN FL (MET and NF in monogram) in ex. RRC 284/1a. CRR
       539. RSC *Calidia* 1.   **VF** £50 ($80) / **EF** £150 ($240)
       A scarcer variant has CN FOVL *(*NF *and* VL *in monogram) below horses and* M CAL Ọ MET
       *(*AL *and* MET *in monogram) in ex.*

161   — Cn. Domitius, 116/115 BC. Helmeted hd. of Roma r., X behind, ROMA before. Rev.
       Jupiter in slow quadriga r., holding branch and thunderbolt, CN DOMI in ex. RRC 285/1.
       CRR 535. RSC *Domitia* 7.   **VF** £50 ($80) / **EF** £150 ($240)

162   163

162   — Q. Curtius and M. Junius Silanus, 116/115 BC. Helmeted hd. of Roma r., X behind,
       Ọ CVRT before. Rev. Jupiter in quadriga r., brandishing thunderbolt, lituus above, M SILA
       (LA in monogram) below, ROMA in ex. RRC 285/2. CRR 537. RSC *Curtia* 2.
                                            VF £45 ($72) / **EF** £140 ($224)

163   — M. Sergius Silus, 116/115 BC. Helmeted hd. of Roma r., EX S C before, ROMA and ✕
       (XVI monogram) behind. Rev. Helmeted horseman galloping l., holding sword and severed
       Gallic hd. in l. hand, M SERGI below, SILVS in ex., Ọ below horses's forelegs. RRC 286/1.
       CRR 534, 544. RSC *Sergia* 1.   **VF** £45 ($72) / **EF** £140 ($224)
       This issuer strikes as quaestor and by special decree of the Senate (ex senatus consulto).
       Quaestors were the immediate superiors of the moneyers and under unusual circumstances
       occasionally utilized their authority to produce coins.

164   166

164 **Denarius.** Anonymous, 115/114 BC. Hd. of Roma r., in winged and crested Corinthian helmet, X behind, ROMA below. Rev. Helmeted Roma seated r. on pile of shields, holding spear, two birds flying in field to l. and to r., she-wolf suckling twins at Roma's feet. RRC 287/1. CRR 530. RSC 176.   **VF** £55 ($88) / **EF** £160 ($256)
An issue lacking the moneyer's name is surprising and noteworthy at such a late date. The omission must have been his own decision and not the result of a change in government policy. Remarkably, this distinctive reverse type was revived almost 200 years later on an aureus of Titus (see no. 2417).

165 — P. Cornelius Cethegus, 115/114 BC. Hd. of Roma r., wearing Phrygian helmet, ✂ (XVI monogram) below chin, EX S C behind. Rev. Male figure (Dionysus?), wearing Phrygian helmet and holding branch, riding on goat r., CETEGVS below, ROMA in ex., all within ivy-wreath. RRC 288/1. CRR 553. RSC *Cornelia* 18.
                                 VF £4,000 ($6,400) / **EF** £8,000 ($12,800)
Another special issue decreed by the Senate, this is one of the greatest rarities in the entire series.

166 — M. Cipius M.f., 115/114 BC. Helmeted hd. of Roma r., X behind, M CIPI M F before. Rev. Victory in biga r., holding palm-branch, rudder below, ROMA in ex. RRC 289/1. CRR 546. RSC *Cipia* 1.   **VF** £40 ($64) / **EF** £125 ($200)

                167   168

167 — C. Fonteius, 114/113 BC. Beardless laur. Janiform hd. of Dioscuri, ✂ (XVI monogram) below r. chin, control-letter below l. Rev. Galley l., C FONT (NT in monogram) above, ROMA below. RRC 290/1. CRR 555. RSC *Fonteia* 1.   **VF** £55 ($88) / **EF** £160 ($256)

168 — Mn. Aemilius Lepidus, 114/113 BC. Laur. and diad. hd. of Roma r., ✂ (XVI monogram) behind, ROMA (MA in monogram) before. Rev. MN AEMILIO (MN in monogram), equestrian statue r., the horseman holding spear, on base formed by triple-arch containing L–E–P. RRC 291/1. CRR 554. RSC *Aemilia* 7.   **VF** £60 ($96) / **EF** £175 ($280)
The triple-arch has been interpreted as representing either an aqueduct, possibly the Aqua Marcia, or a triumphal arch erected in honour of an ancestor.

169   170

169   **Denarius.** P. Licinius Nerva, 113/112 BC. Helmeted bust of Roma l., holding spear and
      shield, crescent above, ✷ (XVI monogram) before, ROMA behind. Rev. Voting scene show-
      ing two citizens casting their ballots in the Comitium, one being handed his voting tablet
      by an attendant, screen in background surmounted by marker with initial 'P' representing
      the voting tribe, P NERVA (NE in monogram) across upper part of screen. RRC 292/1. CRR
      548. RSC *Licinia* 7.   **VF** £100 ($160) / **EF** £275 ($440)
      One of the most celebrated types of the Republican coinage this depicts the actual voting
      process in the political assembly of the Roman People in the Comitium, where citizens
      voted on business presented to them by magistrates. The area occupied by the Comitium
      was consecrated ground, like a temple, and was located in front of the Senate House in the
      Forum.

170   — L. Marcius Philippus, 113/112 BC. Hd. of King Philip V of Macedon r., wearing diad.
      helmet ornamented with goat's horns, F below chin, ROMA (in monogram) behind. Rev.
      Equestrian statue r. on tablet inscribed L PHILIPPVS, the horseman carrying laurel-branch,
      flower at horse's feet, ✷ (XVI monogram) below tablet. RRC 293/1. CRR 551. RSC
      Marcia 12.   **VF** £80 ($128) / **EF** £225 ($360)

171   173

171   — T. Didius, 113/112 BC. Helmeted hd. of Roma r., ✷ (XVI monogram) below, ROMA (in
      monogram) behind. Rev. Combat between two gladiators, one armed with whip, the other
      with stave, T DEIDI in ex. RRC 294/1. CRR 550. RSC *Didia* 2.
                                                          VF £80 ($128) / **EF** £225 ($360)

172   — L. Manlius Torquatus, 113/112 BC. Helmeted hd. of Roma r., X below chin, ROMA (MA
      in monogram) behind, all within torque border. Rev. Horseman galloping l., holding spear
      and shield, L TORQVA below, Q above, EX S C in ex. RRC 295/1. CRR 545. RSC *Manlia* 2.
                                                          VF £65 ($104) / **EF** £185 ($296)
      The unusual obv. border derives from an ancestor's defeat of a Gaul in single combat lead-
      ing to his acquisition of both his opponent's torque and the cognomen Torquatus. The
      issuer strikes as quaestor by special decree of the Senate (ex senatus consulto).

173 **Denarius.** Cn. Cornelius Blasio Cn.f., 112/111 BC. Hd. of Mars r., wearing crested Corinthian helmet, ✕ (XVI monogram) above, CN BLASIO CN F before, symbol behind. Rev. The Capitoline Triad: Jupiter, holding sceptre and thunderbolt, stg. facing between Juno on l. and Minerva on r., the latter crowning Jupiter, sometimes with palm-branch between Jupiter and Minerva, Greek letter, monogram or symbol in field, ROMA (sometimes divided by eagle) in ex. RRC 296/1. CRR 561–561e. RSC *Cornelia* 19, 20.
VF £80 ($128) / **EF** £225 ($360)
The traditional identification of the obv. head as a portrait of Scipio Africanus is soundly and convincingly rejected by Crawford.

174 — Ti. Quinctius (or Quinctilius), 112/111 BC. Laur. bust of Hercules l., wearing lion's skin, club over r. shoulder. Rev. Desultor galloping l., a second horse at his side, TI – Q divided by rat below, D S S incuse on tablet in ex., control-letter behind. RRC 297/1. CRR 563. RSC *Quinctia* 6.
VF £75 ($120) / **EF** £210 ($336)
The mark of value is here omitted, a characteristic soon to become common and eventually the norm. The formula D S S represents 'de senatus sententia' (see also no. 765).

175 — L. Caesius (or Caesilius), 112/111 BC. Diad. bust of Apollo/Jupiter l., drapery on forward shoulder, brandishing thunderbolt held in r. hand, AP (in monogram) behind. Rev. The two Lares Praestites seated r., each holding sceptre, dog between them, bust of Vulcan l. above, LA (in monogram) in l. field, PRE (in monogram) in r., L CÆSI in ex. RRC 298/1. CRR 564. RSC *Caesia* 1.
VF £65 ($104) / **EF** £185 ($296)

176 — Ap. Claudius Pulcher, T. Mallius or Maloleius (or T. Manlius Mancinus) and Q. Urbinius, 111/110 BC. Helmeted hd. of Roma r., quadrangular device containing circle behind. Rev. Victory in triga r., AP CL T MAL Q VR (MAL and VR in monogram) in ex. RRC 299/1a. CRR 570. RSC *Claudia* 2.
VF £45 ($72) / **EF** £140 ($224)
The identities of the second and third moneyers are quite uncertain and Q VR has often been expanded as quaestores urbani. Crawford believes the MAL monogram is better resolved as MANL. Another variety has T MAL AP CL Q VR (MAL and VR in monogram) in ex. The three-horse chariot (triga) is rarely depicted on the Republican coinage, the only other example being on serrate denarii of C. Naevius Balbus issued some three decades later in the time of Sulla (see no. 309).

177   179

177 — C. Claudius Pulcher, 110/109 BC. Helmeted hd. of Roma r. Rev. Victory in biga r., C PVLCHER in ex. RRC 300/1. CRR 569. RSC *Claudia* 1.   **VF** £45 ($72) / **EF** £140 ($224)

178 — P. Porcius Laeca, 110/109 BC. Helmeted hd. of Roma r., X below chin, ROMA above, P LÆCA behind. Rev. Military figure of a governor stg. l., his r. hand raised, facing togate citizen stg. r., gesturing with r. hand, attendant stg. l. behind governor holding three rods, PROVOCO in ex. RRC 301/1. CRR 571. RSC *Porcia* 4.   **VF** £65 ($104) / **EF** £185 ($296)
An important reverse type illustrating the principle of provocatio, a procedure by which a citizen had the right to appeal to the people against the decision of a magistrate which he considered to represent an abuse of official power.

179 **Denarius.** L. Flaminius Cilo, 109/108 BC. Helmeted hd. of Roma r., X below chin, ROMA behind. Rev. Victory in biga r., holding wreath, L FLAMINI below, CILO in ex. RRC 302/1. CRR 540. RSC *Flaminia* 1. **VF** £40 ($64) / **EF** £125 ($200)

180 — Mn. Aquillius, 109/108 BC. Rad. hd. of Sol r., X below chin. Rev. Luna in biga r., three stars above, a fourth star and MN AQVIL (MN in monogram) below, ROMA in ex. RRC 303/1. CRR 557. RSC *Aquillia* 1. **VF** £65 ($104) / **EF** £185 ($296)

181   183

181 — L. Memmius, 109/108 BC. Young male hd. r., wreathed with oak, ✕ (XVI monogram) below chin. Rev. Dioscuri stg. facing between their horses, each holding spear, L MEMMI in ex. RRC 304/1. CRR 558. RSC *Memmia* 1. **VF** £60 ($96) / **EF** £175 ($280)

182 — Q. Lutatius Cerco, 109/108 BC. Hd. of young Mars r., wearing crested Corinthian helmet, ✕ (XVI monogram) behind, ROMA above, CERCO before. Rev. Galley r., Q LVTATI (VT in monogram) / Q above, all within oak-wreath. RRC 305/1. CRR 559. RSC *Lutatia* 2. **VF** £60 ($96) / **EF** £175 ($280)
Crawford and others have identified the head as that of Roma. However, the features appear to be masculine and it seems preferable to regard it as a youthful depiction of Mars. Cerco strikes in his capacity as quaestor.

183 — L. Valerius Flaccus, 108/107 BC. Winged and dr. bust of Victory r., ✕ (XVI monogram) below chin. Rev. Mars walking l., holding spear and trophy, apex before, corn-ear behind, L VALERI / FLACCI on l. RRC 306/1. CRR 565. RSC *Valeria* 11.
VF £60 ($96) / **EF** £175 ($280)

184   185

184 — Mn. Fonteius, 108/107 BC. Conjoined laur. hds. of the Dioscuri r., ✕ (XVI monogram) below their chins, sometimes with P P before. Rev. Galley r., MN FONTEI (MN and NTE in monogram) above, control-letter below. RRC 307/1. CRR 566–566b. RSC *Fonteia* 7–8.
VF £85 ($136) / **EF** £240 ($384)

185 — M. Herennius, 108/107 BC. Diad hd. of Pietas r., PIETAS (TA in monogram) behind, control-letter below chin. Rev. One of the Catanaean brothers running r., bearing his father on his shoulders, M HERENNI (HE in monogram) on l. RRC 308/1a. CRR 567. RSC *Herennia* 1. **VF** £75 ($120) / **EF** £210 ($336)
Another variety has the control-letter in rev. field to r.

186   187

186   **Denarius.** A. Manlius Q.f. Sergianus, *circa* 118–107 BC. Helmeted hd. of Roma r., **ROMA** before, **SER** behind. Rev. Sol in quadriga to front, rising from the waves, his hd. turned to r., **X** in upper field to l., crescent to r., star on either side of horses, **A MANLI Q F** (**MA** and **NL** in monogram) below. RRC 309/1. CRR 543. RSC *Manlia* 1.

           VF £250 ($400) / **EF** £600 ($960)
This type and the next – both rare issues – cannot be dated with greater precision. They have certain characteristics in common and probably were struck at about the same time.

187   — Cn. Cornelius L.f. Sisenna, *circa* 118–107 BC. Helmeted hd. of Roma r., **X** below chin, **ROMA** before, **SISENA** behind. Rev. Jupiter in quadriga r., brandishing thunderbolt, rad. hd. of Sol l. and crescent above, star on either side, anguipedic giant pierced by thunderbolt below, **CN CORNEL L F** (**NE** in monogram) in ex. RRC 310/1. CRR 542. RSC *Cornelia* 17.

           VF £300 ($480) / **EF** £750 ($1,200)

188   189

188   **Denarius serratus.** L. Cornelius Scipio Asiaticus, 106 BC. Laur. hd. of Jupiter l., control-letter behind or below chin. Rev. Jupiter in quadriga r., brandishing thunderbolt, **L SCIP ASIAG** in ex. RRC 311/1a-b. CRR 576, 576a. RSC *Cornelia* 24b–c.

           VF £45 ($72) / **EF** £140 ($224)
Other varieties have the control-letter on rev., either above or in ex. The reason for the introduction at this time of denarii with notched edges as part of the mainstream coinage of Rome is quite unclear. They had previously been struck a dozen years before in Gaul (see nos. 157–8).

189   — C. Sulpicius C.f., 106 BC. Conjoined laur. hds. of the Dei Penates l., **D P P** before. Rev. The two Dei Penates stg. facing each other, resting on spears and pointing at large sow which lies between them, control-letter above, **C SVLPICI C F** (**LP** in monogram) in ex. RRC 312/1. CRR 572. RSC *Sulpicia* 1.   **VF** £65 ($104) / **EF** £185 ($296)
Crawford's interpretation of this interesting type seems the most convincing: it refers to Aeneas' landing in Lavinium (home of the Sulpicia gens) with the Penates and the subsequent miracle of the great white sow which foretold the founding of Alba Longa.

190   — L. Memmius Galeria, 106 BC. Laur. hd. of Saturn l., control-letter below chin, harpa and **ROMA** behind. Rev. Venus in slow biga r., Cupid flying l. above, **L MEMMI** (**ME** in monogram) / **GAL** in ex. RRC 313/1b. CRR 574. RSC *Memmia* 2.

           VF £55 ($88) / **EF** £160 ($256)
Another variety has the control-letter on rev., below horses.

191   192

191   **Denarius serratus.** L. Aurelius Cotta, 105 BC. Dr. bust of Vulcan r., wearing conical cap
       bound with laurel-wreath, tongs and ✕ (XVI monogram) behind, control-letter below chin,
       all within myrtle-wreath. Rev. Eagle stg. r. on thunderbolt, hd. l., L COT below, all within
       laurel-wreath. RRC 314/1b. CRR 577. RSC *Aurelia* 21.   **VF** £85 ($136) / **EF** £240 ($384)
       Other varieties have the control-letter on rev., below eagle's l. wing, or have control-letters
       on both sides.

192   **Denarius.** L. Thorius Balbus, 105 BC. Hd. of Juno Sospita r., clad in goat's skin, I S M R
       behind. Rev. Bull charging r., control-letter above, L THORIVS below, BALBVS in ex. RRC
       316/1. CRR 598. RSC *Thoria* 1.   **VF** £45 ($72) / **EF** £140 ($224)

193   194

193   — L. Appuleius Saturninus, 104 BC. Helmeted hd. of Roma l.. Rev. Saturn in quadriga r.,
       holding harpa, control-letter above or below, L SATVRN in ex. RRC 317/3a–b. CRR 578,
       578a. RSC *Appuleia* 1.   **VF** £40 ($64) / **EF** £125 ($200)

194   — — Helmeted hd. of Roma l., control-letter behind. Rev. Similar to *obv.*, but with L SAT
       (AT in monogram) behind. RRC 317/1. CRR 579. RSC *Appuleia* 2.
                                                                VF £350 ($560) / **EF** £850 ($1,360)
       The extraordinary duplication on both sides of the obv. and rev. designs on this type and
       the next remains unexplained.

195   196

195   — — Saturn in quadriga r., holding harpa, ROMA in ex. Rev. Similar to *obv.*, but with con-
       trol-letter below and L SATVRN in ex. RRC 317/2. CRR 580. RSC *Appuleia* 3.
                                                                VF £425 ($680) / **EF** £1,000 ($1,600)

196   **Denarius.** C. Coelius Caldus, 104 BC. Helmeted hd. of Roma l. Rev. Victory in biga l.,
       control-letter above, C COIL below, CALD in ex. RRC 318/1a. CRR 582. RSC *Coelia* 2.
                                                    VF £45 ($72) / **EF** £140 ($224)
       Another variety has CALD *below the horses and the control-letter in ex.*

                         197   198

197   — Q. Minucius M.f. Thermus, 103 BC. Hd. of young Mars l., wearing crested helmet. Rev.
       Roman soldier advancing r., fighting with uplifted sword a barbarian soldier before him
       and protecting with shield a fallen comrade at his feet, Q THERM M F (THE and MF in mono-
       gram) in ex. RRC 319/1. CRR 592. RSC *Minucia* 19.   **VF** £55 ($88) / **EF** £160 ($256)

198   — L. Julius L.f. Caesar, 103 BC. Hd. of young Mars l., wearing crested helmet, control-let-
       ter above, CAESAR behind. Rev. Venus in chariot drawn l. by two flying Cupids, lyre
       before, control-letter above, L IVLI L F in ex. RRC 320/1. CRR 593. RSC *Julia* 4.
                                                    VF £55 ($88) / **EF** £160 ($256)

                         199   200

199   — L. Cassius Caeicianus (or Caecianus), 102 BC. Dr. bust of Ceres l., wreathed with corn,
       CÆICIAN (AN in monogram) and control-letter behind. Rev. Yoke of oxen l., control-letter
       above, L CASSI in ex. RRC 321/1. CRR 594. RSC *Cassia* 4.
                                                    VF £65 ($104) / **EF** £185 ($296)

200   — C. Fabius C.f. (Hadrianus?), 102 BC. Veiled and turreted bust of Cybele r., EX A PV
       behind. Rev. Victory in biga r., heron stg. r. before, control-letter below horses, C FABI C F
       in ex. RRC 322/1b. CRR 590. RSC *Fabia* 14.   **VF** £65 ($104) / **EF** £185 ($296)
       EX ARGENTO PVBLICO, *'[struck] from the public silver', here makes its initial appearance
       on a denarius. As all Roman silver coinage was produced from metal withdrawn from the
       state's bullion reserves the reason for its proclamation on this and certain subsequent
       issues is unclear. Crawford connects the phenomenon with the influence of Gaius Marius,
       whose prestige and influence were at their height at this time, interpreting the statement as
       an assertion of the rights of the people. Another variety lacks the* EX A PV *and has a Greek
       control-letter in its place, the control-letter on rev. being omitted.*

201   — L. Julius, 101 BC. Helmeted hd. of Roma r., corn-ear behind. Rev. Victory in biga r.,
       L IVLI below. RRC 323/1. CRR 585. RSC *Julia* 3.   **VF** £60 ($96) / **EF** £175 ($280)

202   203

202 **Denarius.** M. Lucilius Rufus, 101 BC. Helmeted hd. of Roma r., **PV** behind, all within laurel-wreath. Rev. Victory in biga r., **M LVCILI** in ex., **RVF** above. RRC 324/1. CRR 599. RSC *Lucilia* 1.   **VF** £50 ($80) / **EF** £150 ($240)
The proliferation of Victory types at this time would appear to be connected with the military activities of Marius, who defeated the Teutones and Ambrones at Aquae Sextiae in 102 and the Cimbri at Vercellae in 101. **PV** *doubtless represents a more abbreviated form of* **EX A PV** *(see no. 200).*

203   — L. Sentius C.f., 101 BC. Helmeted hd. of Roma r., **ARG PVB** (**AR** in monogram) behind. Rev. Jupiter in quadriga r., holding sceptre and thunderbolt, control-letter above or below, **L SENTI C F** in ex. RRC 325/1. CRR 600, 600a. RSC *Sentia* 1, 1a.
                                             VF £50 ($80) / **EF** £150 ($240)
ARG PVB *provides an expansion of the formula first noted on no. 200.*

204   — C. Fundanius, 101 BC. Helmeted hd. of Roma r., control-letter behind. Rev. Marius as triumphator in slow quadriga r., holding laurel-branch, child seated on near horse, **Q** above, **C FVNDAN** in ex. RRC 326/1. CRR 583. RSC *Fundania* 1.
                                    VF £65 ($104) / **EF** £185 ($296)
A remarkable type commemorating Marius' joint triumph with Q. Lutatius Catulus in 101 BC. Crawford suggests that the young rider on the near horse may be Marius' 8-year-old son. Fundanius strikes as quaestor, though with no reference to special senatorial authority for the issue.

              205   207

205 **Quinarius.** C. Fundanius, 101 BC. Laur. hd. of Jupiter r., control-letter behind. Rev. Victory stg. r., crowning trophy at foot of which is kneeling captive and carnyx, **C FVNDA** (**ND** in monogram) on r., **Q** in ex. RRC 326/2. CRR 584. RSC *Fundania* 2.
                                    VF £50 ($80) / **EF** £150 ($240)
The surprising revival of the quinarius, more than a century after it had gone out of regular production, is clearly associated with Marius' victories againt the Germanic tribes of the Teutones, Ambrones and Cimbri who had lately migrated from Jutland to southern Gaul. Perhaps the coins were struck for distribution to the populace at the time of Marius' triumph, thus setting a precedent for the specialized future role of this unusual denomination. The types were adopted from the old victoriatus which had been discontinued in the 170s.

206 **Denarius.** M. Servilius C.f., 100 BC. Helmeted hd. of Roma r., Greek control-letter behind. Rev. Two dismounted horseman engaged in combat, their horses in background on either side, M SERVEILI C F above control-letter in ex. RRC 327/1. CRR 602. RSC *Servilia* 13.
VF £60 ($96) / **EF** £175 ($280)

207 — P. Servilius M.f. Rullus, 100 BC. Bust of Minerva l., wearing crested Corinthian helmet and aegis, RVLLI behind. Rev. Victory in biga r., holding palm-branch, P below, P SERVILI M F in ex. RRC 328/1. CRR 601. RSC *Servilia* 14. **VF** £55 ($88) / **EF** £160 ($256)
The P *in rev. field appears to be the ultimate abbreviated form of* EX ARGENTO PVBLICO.

208

208 — P. Cornelius Lentulus Marcellinus (son of M. Claudius Marcellus), 100 BC. Bust of young Hercules viewed from behind, his hd. turned to r., shoulders clad in lion's skin and club over l. shoulder, shield behind, control-letter (sometimes Greek) in field to l. or to r., ROMA below. Rev. Helmeted Roma stg. facing, holding spear, crowned by Genius of the Roman People stg. facing on r., holding cornucopiae, control-letter (sometimes Greek) between them or to l., LENT MAR F (NT and MAR in monogram) in ex., all within laurel-wreath. RRC 329/1a–b. CRR 604–604c. RSC *Cornelia* 25–25c.
VF £65 ($104) / **EF** £185 ($296)

209 — — Similar, but with P E S C instead of ROMA below bust of Hercules (the control-letters are always Latin). RRC 329/1c–d. CRR 605, 605a. RSC *Cornelia* 26, 26a.
VF £125 ($200) / **EF** £325 ($520)
The formula P E S C *(= pecunia erogata senatus consulto), 'money paid out by decree of the Senate', seems to refer to some special circumstance surrounding part of the issue of this moneyer.*

210 — L. Calpurnius Piso Caesoninus and Q. Servilius Caepio, 100 BC. PISO CAEPIO Q, laur. hd. of Saturn r., harpa behind, control-symbol above or below. Rev. The two quaestors seated l. side by side on bench between two corn-ears, AD FRV EMV / EX S C in ex. RRC 330/1. CRR 603, 603a. RSC *Calpurnia* 5, 5a. **VF** £60 ($96) / **EF** £175 ($280)
This exceptional type relating to the corn supply is interpreted by Crawford as a joint issue of the Quaestor Urbanus (Caepio) and the Quaestor Ostiensis (Piso). The issue was pro-duced by special decree of the Senate (ex senatus consulto).

211   212

211 **Quinarius.** P. Vettius Sabinus, 99 BC. Laur. hd. of Jupiter r., control-letter behind. Rev. Victory stg. r., crowning trophy, P SABIN between, control-letter on r., Q in ex. RRC 331/1. CRR 587. RSC *Vettia* 1. **VF** £50 ($80) / **EF** £150 ($240)
Sabinus strikes in his capacity as quaestor.

212 **Quinarius.** T. Cloulius (or Cloelius), 98 BC. Laur. hd. of Jupiter r., control-letter behind, before or below. Rev. Victory stg. r., crowning trophy at foot of which is seated captive and carnyx, T CLOVLI (VL in monogram) between, Ω in ex. RRC 332/1. CRR 586–586b. RSC *Cloulia* 2–2b. **VF** £45 ($72) / **EF** £140 ($224)
Cloelius, a known partisan of the Marian faction, strikes as quaestor and celebrates Marius' victories.

213   214

213 — C. Egnatuleius C.f., 97 BC. Laur. hd. of Apollo r., C EGNATVLEI C F (NAT and VL in monogram) behind, Ω below. Rev. Victory stg. l., inscribing shield attached to trophy at foot of which is carnyx, Ω in central field, ROMA in ex. RRC 333/1. CRR 588. RSC *Egnatuleia* 1. **VF** £40 ($64) / **EF** £125 ($200)
This, the last in the current series of quinarii, introduces some new elements in the design. The duplication of 'Ω' suggests that on the reverse it may be intended as a mark of value rather than a designation of the issuer as quaestor.

214 **Denarius.** L. Pomponius Molo, *ca.* 97 BC. L POMPON MOLO, laur. hd. of Apollo r. Rev. Numa Pompilius, holding lituus, stg. r. before altar to r. of which is victimarius l., leading goat, NVMA POMPIL (MA and MP in monogram) in ex. RRC 334/1. CRR 607. RSC *Pomponia* 6. **VF** £100 ($160) / **EF** £275 ($440)

215 — C. Poblicius Malleolus, *ca.* 96 BC. Laur. hd. of Apollo r. Rev. Roma seated l. on shields, holding spear, crowned by Victory stg. behind, C MALL (AL in monogram) on l., ROMA in ex. RRC 335/2. CRR 614. RSC *Poblicia* 4. **VF** £90 ($144) / **EF** £250 ($400)

216 — — Helmeted hd. of Mars r., hammer above, ✖ (XVI monogram) below chin. Rev. Naked warrior stg. l., holding spear, r. foot on cuirass, trophy before, C MAL (AL in monogram) behind, above prow which is sometimes surmounted by caduceus, grasshopper or tablet. RRC 335/3a-e. CRR 615, 615a. RSC *Poblicia* 6–6b. **VF** £65 ($104) / **EF** £185 ($296)
A surprising late revival of the denarius mark of value.

217   218

217 — — Similar, but behind the warrior is voting-tablet (tessera) inscribed C MAL (AL in monogram) and P (sometimes the C MAL is shown below the tablet). RRC 335/3f-g. CRR 615b-c. RSC *Poblicia* 7, 8. **VF** £85 ($136) / **EF** £240 ($384)
Crawford interprets this interesting variant as representing the ballot of a citizen belonging to a tribe with the initial P who is voting for a C. Malleolus.

218 **Denarius.** A. Postumius S(p).f. Albinus, *ca.* 96 BC. Diad. and dr. bust of Diana r., bow and quiver over shoulder, ROMA below. Rev. Three horseman galloping l., fallen warrior and two standards (?) in their path, A ALBINVS S F in ex. (AL sometimes in monogram). RRC 335/9. CRR 613, 613a. RSC *Postumia* 4, 4a.   **VF** £85 ($136) / **EF** £240 ($384)

219 — — Laur. hd. of Apollo r., X below chin, star behind, ROMA (less frequently R) below. Rev. Dioscuri l., holding spears, stg. beside their horses which are drinking at the fountain of Juturna, crescent moon above, A ALBINVS S F (AL sometimes in monogram) in ex. RRC 335/10. CRR 612–612c. RSC *Postumia* 5–6a.   **VF** £75 ($120) / **EF** £210 ($336)

220   221

220 — C. Poblicius Malleolus and A. Postumius S(p).f. Albinus with L. Caecilius Metellus, *ca.* 96 BC. Laur. hd. of Apollo r., A ALB S F before, L METEL behind, sometimes with star or crescent below. Rev. Roma seated l. on shields, holding spear, crowned by Victory stg. behind, C MALL (AL in monogram) on l., ROMA in ex. RRC 335/1a–c. CRR 611, 611a. RSC *Caecilia* 45–46a.   **VF** £55 ($88) / **EF** £160 ($256)

221 — C. Allius Bala, 92 BC. Diad. hd. of female deity r., BALA behind, control-letter (rarely omitted) below chin. Rev. Diana, holding torch and sceptre, in biga of stags r., control-symbol (most commonly grasshopper) below, C ALLI in ex., all within laurel-wreath. RRC 336/1. CRR 595. RSC *Aelia* 4, 4a.   **VF** £55 ($88) / **EF** £160 ($256)

222   223

222 — D. Junius L.f. Silanus, 91 BC. Mask of bearded Silenus r., plough (or ROMA) below, sometimes with Greek control-letter behind, all within torque. Rev. Victory in biga r., holding palm-branch, carnyx below, D SILANVS L F in ex. RRC 337/1a–b. CRR 644, 644a. RSC *Junia* 19–20.   **VF** £85 ($136) / **EF** £240 ($384)

223 — — Diad. hd. of Salus r., sometimes with SALVS (AL sometimes in monogram) below, sometimes with Greek or Latin control-letter below chin, all within torque. Rev. Victory in biga r., holding palm-branch, ROMA below, D SILANVS L F in ex. RRC 337/2a–c. CRR 645, 645a, 645d. RSC *Junia* 18–18c.   **VF** £65 ($104) / **EF** £185 ($296)

224 — — Similar, but the control-letter on obv. (when present) is Latin, and with control-symbol ear, grasshopper or wing instead of ROMA below horses on rev. RRC 337/2d–f. CRR 645b–c. RSC *Junia* 17, 17a.   **VF** £70 ($112) / **EF** £200 ($320)
Crawford considers the symbols in rev. field to be the marks of individual die-engravers.

225

225 **Denarius.** D. Junius L.f. Silanus, 91 BC. Helmeted hd. of Roma r., control-letter behind. Rev. Victory in biga r., control-numeral (I–XXX) above, D SILANVS L F / ROMA in ex. RRC 337/3. CRR 646. RSC *Junia* 15. **VF** £40 ($64) / **EF** £125 ($200)

226 **Sestertius.** D. Junius L.f. Silanus, 91 BC. Helmeted hd. of Roma r., E L P behind. Rev. Victory in biga r., D SILANVS L F in ex. RRC 337/4. CRR 647. RSC *Junia* 21.
F £250 ($400) / **VF** £600 ($960)
The silver sestertius, or quarter-denarius, had not been issued since the time of the Second Punic War almost 120 years before. Its restoration in 91 BC was authorized by the Lex Papiria, hence the formula E(x) L(ege) P(apiria) *on the obv. of this type and on the rev. of sestertii struck the following year by L. Calpurnius Piso Frugi. The denomination then lapsed again for more than four decades until its revival by the Caesarian moneyers in the early 40s BC.*

THE SOCIAL WAR: DENARII OF THE MARSIC CONFEDERATION 90–88 BC

The insensitivity of the Roman government to the legitimate grievances of various Italian peoples ultimately led to a serious military uprising towards the end of 91 BC. The rebel tribes formed a confederation which took its name from the Marsi, a mountain people of central Italy. The federal capital was established at Corfinium, which was renamed Italia. Although the revolt collapsed within two years the Romans heeded the warning and granted citizenship to the Italians, an issue which had been at the heart of the conflict.

The regular coinage of the Marsic Confederation consisted entirely of silver denarii, some with Latin legends, others employing Oscan script. Most issues are anonymous, but a few bear the names of the confederation's leaders. The types are quite diverse, some clearly based on Roman designs, others being original in concept. Considerable stylistic variation suggests that several mints were utilized by the rebel regime, though presumably Corfinium/Italia was the principal location. As this is a non-Roman series only a small representative selection of the known types appears in the following listing.

227   229

227 **Anonymous.** Laur. hd. of Italia l., ITALIA behind. Rev. Oath-taking scene with eight warriors, four on each side, pointing their swords towards sacrificial pig which is held by attendant kneeling at foot of standard, control-letter or numeral in ex. CRR 620–21. BMCRR Social War 3–10. **VF** £550 ($880) / **EF** £1,250 ($2,000)
This reverse is based on the gold stater and half stater of the time of the Second Punic War and the later denarius of Ti. Veturius, 137 BC (see nos. 1 and 2, and 111).

228 **Anonymous.** Similar, but without legend on obv. and with control-numeral in ex. CRR 629. BMCRR Social War 43–7. **VF** £550 ($880) / **EF** £1,250 ($2,000)

229 — Laur. hd. of Italia r., X below chin. Rev. Italia seated l. on shields, holding spear, crowned by Victory stg. behind, ITALIA in ex., control-letter in l. field. CRR 624. BMCRR Social War 14–16. **VF** £650 ($1,040) / **EF** £1,350 ($2,160) *The prototype for this reverse was issued ca. 96 BC by Malleolus, Albinus and Metellus, though Italia has taken the place of Roma (see no. 220).*

230   231

230 — Laur. hd. of Italia l., Oscan legend 'VITELIV' (= ITALIA) behind. Rev. Soldier stg. facing, hd. r., holding spear and sword, his l. foot trampling on Roman standard, recumbent bull on r., Oscan control-letter in ex. CRR 627. BMCRR Social War 19–30. **VF** £500 ($800) / **EF** £1,100 ($1,760)

231 — Bust of Italia r., wearing crested helmet and aegis, crowned by Victory behind. Rev. Two male figures clasping hands, the one on l. holding spear, the other, who has just alighted from ship on r., holding globe (?), control-letter or numeral in ex. CRR 632, 632a. BMCRR Social War 48–9. **VF** £750 ($1,200) / **EF** £1,500 ($2,400) *The interesting rev. type may refer to the embassy sent by the confederates to seek the help of Mithradates of Pontus.*

232 **C. Papius C.f. Mutilus.** Helmeted hd. of Italia r., wreath and ✕ behind, Oscan legend 'MVTIL'\below. Rev. Dioscuri galloping apart, Oscan legend 'C PAAPI C' in ex. CRR 635. BMCRR Social War 31–2. **VF** £1,000 ($1,600) / **EF** £2,000 ($3,200) *This is a very close copy of the denarius issued in 136 BC by C. Servilius M.f. (see no. 116). Mutilus was one of the two consuls appointed by the new confederate government at Corfinium.*

233

233 — Hd. of Italia l., wearing crested helmet, Oscan legend 'MVTIL EMBRATVR' (= MVTIL IMPERATOR) below and before. Rev. Oath-taking scene, with two warriors and sacrificial pig held by bearded attendant kneeling between them, Oscan legend 'C PAAPI C' in ex. CRR 640. BMCRR Social War 39–40. **VF** £850 ($1,360) / **EF** £1,750 ($2,800) *The obv. would appear to be copied from the coinage of Q. Minucius M.f. Thermus issued in 103 BC (see no. 197).*

234 **C. Papius C.f. Mutilus.** Hd. of young Bacchus r., wreathed with ivy, Oscan legend 'MVTIL EMBRATVR' (= MVTIL IMPERATOR) before and below. Rev. Bull r., trampling on she-wolf, Oscan legend 'C PAAPI' in ex. CRR 641. BMCRR Social War 41.

VF £1,250 ($2,000) / **EF** £2,500 ($4,000)

The unequivocal symbolism of the rev. type is the power of Italy and the Samnites over-coming that of Rome.

THE LATER REPUBLICAN DENARIUS COINAGE (CONTINUED)

235/1

235/2

235 **Denarius.** L. Calpurnius Piso L.f. L.n. Frugi, 90 BC. Laur. hd. of Apollo (normally to r., rarely to l.), sometimes with ✕ (XVI monogram) below chin or behind, usually with con-trol-mark in field, sometimes with bead and reel border. Rev. Naked horseman galloping to r. or to l., holding palm-branch, torch, or whip, L PISO FRVGI (or L PISO L F FRVGI, or PISO FRVGI, or similar) below, sometimes with ROMA (sometimes entirely or with MA in mono-gram) below (rarely above), usually with control-mark in field. RRC 340/1. CRR 650–671d. RSC *Calpurnia* 6–12d. VF £45 ($72) / **EF** £140 ($224)

This extraordinarily large and complex issue represents one of the principal war-coinages of the Romans during the conflict with the Marsic Confederation. The control-marks are legion and consist of letters, numerals and symbols in a multitude of combinations on obv. and rev.

236

236 **Quinarius.** L. Calpurnius Piso L.f. L.n. Frugi, 90 BC. Laur. hd. of Apollo r., control-mark/s in field (usually behind). Rev. L PISO FRVGI (or L PISO), Victory stg. r., holding wreath and palm (rarely with sword and spear in l. hand). RRC 340/2. CRR 672–5. RSC *Calpurnia* 13–14. VF £100 ($160) / **EF** £275 ($440)

237 **Sestertius.** L. Calpurnius Piso L.f. L.n. Frugi, 90 BC. Laur. hd. of Apollo r., sometimes with PISO behind. Rev. Horse galloping r., E L P above, FRVGI below. RRC 340/3. CRR 676, 676a. RSC *Calpurnia* 15–16. **F** £150 ($240) / **VF** £350 ($560)

E L P (ex lege Papiria) refers to the restoration of the sestertius denomination in 91 BC under the terms of the Lex Papiria (see also the sestertius of D. Junius Silanus, no 226). Following Piso's issue the denomination lapsed again until its revival by C. Vibius Pansa in 48 BC (see no. 424).

238   239

238 **Denarius.** Q. Titius, 90 BC. Male hd. r. with long pointed beard, wearing winged diad. Rev.
     Pegasus r., Q TITI on tablet below. RRC 341/1. CRR 691. RSC *Titia* 1.
                                                   VF £55 ($88) / **EF** £160 ($256)

239 — — Similar, but with obv. type hd. of young Bacchus or Liber r., wreathed with ivy. RRC
     341/2. CRR 692. RSC *Titia* 2.   **VF** £55 ($88) / **EF** £160 ($256)

                  240   242

240 **Quinarius.** Q. Titius, 90 BC. Winged and dr. bust of Victory r. Rev. Pegasus r., Q TITI
     below. RRC 341/3. CRR 693. RSC *Titia* 3.   **VF** £55 ($88) / **EF** £160 ($256)

241 **Denarius.** C. Vibius C.f. Pansa, 90 BC. Laur. hd. of Apollo r., PANSA behind, control-mark
     below chin. Rev. Ceres walking r., holding torches before her, pig at her feet, C VIBIVS C F
     behind (rarely all within wreath). RRC 342/3. CRR 683–683b. RSC *Vibia* 6–7.
                                                   VF £85 ($136) / **EF** £240 ($384)

242 — — Similar, but with rev. type Minerva in quadriga r., holding trophy and spear, C VIBIVS
     C F in ex. RRC 342/5. CRR 684–684c. RSC *Vibia* 1–2f.   **VF** £50 ($80) / **EF** £150 ($240)
     Rare variants of this type and the next have Victory flying above the quadriga on rev.

243 — — Similar, but Minerva's quadriga is travelling to l. RRC 342/4. CRR 685–6. RSC
     Vibia 3–4.   **VF** £60 ($96) / **EF** £175 ($280)

                  244   245

244 — — Minerva in quadriga l., holding spear and trophy, PANSA in ex. Rev. Minerva in
     quadriga r., holding trophy and spear, C VIBIVS C F in ex. RRC 342/6. CRR 687. RSC
     Vibia 5, 5a.   **VF** £90 ($144) / **EF** £250 ($400)
     A rare variant has Minerva in quadriga to l. on rev.

245   **Denarius.** C. Vibius C.f. Pansa, 90 BC. Mask of bearded Silenus r., wreathed with ivy,
      PANSA behind, control-symbol below. Rev. Mask of bearded Pan r., C VIBIVS C F (IB in
      monogram) below, control-symbol before. RRC 342/1. CRR 689. RSC *Vibia* 8.   **VF** £500
      ($800) / **EF** £1,100 ($1,760)

              246   248

246   —— Similar, but without control-symbols, and the mask of Pan is on obv., with PANSA
      below, and the mask of Silenus is on rev., with C VIBIVS C F (IB in monogram) below. RRC
      342/2. CRR 688. RSC *Vibia* 9.   **VF** £600 ($960) / **EF** £1,250 ($2,000)

247   — M. Porcius Cato, 89 BC. Diad. female bust r., ROMA (MA in monogram) behind,
      M CATO (AT in monogram) below. Rev. Victory seated r., holding patera and palm, some-
      times with ST below seat, VICTRIX (TR in monogram) in ex. RRC 343/1. CRR 596, 596a.
      RSC *Porcia* 5–6.   **VF** £60 ($96) / **EF** £175 ($280)
      The types of this moneyer were utilized more than four decades later by Cato Uticensis for
      his North African coinage in support of the Pompeians opposing Caesar (see nos.
      1381–3).

248   **Quinarius.** M. Porcius Cato, 89 BC. Hd. of young Bacchus or Liber r., wreathed with ivy,
      M CATO (AT in monogram) behind, usually with control-mark below. Rev. Victory seated
      r., holding patera and palm, VICTRIX (TR in monogram) in ex. RRC 343/2. CRR 597–597c.
      RSC *Porcia* 7–7d.   **VF** £45 ($72) / **EF** £140 ($224)

              249   251

249   **Denarius.** L. Titurius L.f. Sabinus, 89 BC. Bare hd. of King Tatius r., bearded, TA (in
      monogram) or palm-branch before, SABIN behind. Rev. Two Roman soldiers running, each
      bearing a Sabine woman in his arms ('rape of the Sabine women'), L TITVRI in ex. RRC
      344/1a-b. CRR 698, 698a. RSC *Tituria* 1–2.   **VF** £60 ($96) / **EF** £175 ($280)

250   —— Similar, but with A PV and palm-branch before hd. of Tatius. RRC 344/1c. CRR
      698b. RSC *Tituria* 3.   **VF** £65 ($104) / **EF** £185 ($296)
      The formula EX ARGENTO PVBLICO, '[struck] from the public silver' (here abbreviated to
      A PV), had previously been used in 102–100 BC at the time of the ascendancy of Gaius
      Marius (see nos 200, 202, 203 and 207). The reason for its employment on this issue is
      quite unclear, though it could be connected with the events of the Social War.

251   —— Obv. Similar to 249. Rev. Tarpeia facing, buried to her waist in shields, trying to
      ward off two soldiers who are about to cast their shields on her, star within crescent moon
      above, L TITVRI in ex. RRC 344/2a–b. CRR 699. RSC *Tituria* 4, 5a.
                                                      VF £60 ($96) / **EF** £175 ($280)

252   253

252   **Denarius.** L. Titurius L.f. Sabinus, 89 BC. Similar, but with obv. as 250. RRC 344/2c. CRR
      699a. RSC *Tituria* 5.   **VF** £65 ($104) / **EF** £185 ($296)

253   — — Bare hd. of King Tatius r., bearded, SABIN behind. Rev. Victory in biga r., holding
      wreath (rarely whip), L TITVRI (VR rarely in monogram) below, control-mark (rarely omit-
      ted) in ex. RRC 344/3. CRR 700–700b. RSC *Tituria* 6–6d.
                                                               VF £60 ($96) / **EF** £175 ($280)

254   255

254   — Cn. Cornelius Lentulus, 88 BC. Helmeted bust of Mars r., viewed from behind, holding
      spear and parazonium, the strap of which is visible over r. shoulder. Rev. Victory in biga r.,
      holding wreath, CN LENTVL in ex. RRC 345/1. CRR 702. RSC *Cornelia* 50.
                                                               VF £40 ($64) / **EF** £125 ($200)

255   **Quinarius.** Cn. Cornelius Lentulus, 88 BC. Laur. hd. of Jupiter r. Rev. Victory stg. r.,
      crowning trophy, CN LENT (NT sometimes in monogram) in ex. RRC 345/2. CRR 703.
      RSC *Cornelia* 51, 51a.   **VF** £40 ($64) / **EF** £125 ($200)

256   257

256   **Denarius.** C. Marcius Censorinus, 88 BC. Conjoined diad. hds. r. of King Numa Pompilius,
      bearded, and King Ancus Marcius, beardless, sometimes with control-mark in field. Rev.
      Desultor galloping r., a second horse at his side, usually with control-mark below, C CENSO
      in ex. RRC 346/1. CRR 713–713g. RSC *Marcia* 18–18f.   **VF** £60 ($96) / **EF** £175 ($280)

257   — — Diad. hd. of Apollo r., sometimes with control-mark in field. Rev. Bridled horse gal-
      loping r., C CENSOR (or C CENSORI) below, usually with control-marks above and in ex.
      RRC 346/2. CRR 714–714f. RSC *Marcia* 19–19h.   **VF** £55 ($88) / **EF** £160 ($256)

258 **Denarius.** L. Rubrius Dossenus, 87 BC. Laur. hd. of Jupiter r., sceptre over shoulder, DOSSEN below. Rev. Empty triumphal quadriga r., thunderbolt on side-panel, surmounted by small wreath-bearing Victory, L RVBRI in ex. RRC 348/1. CRR 705. RSC *Rubria* 1.
VF £50 ($80) / **EF** £150 ($240)
The types of this moneyer appear to express hopes of victory against Marius and his faction.

259 —— Similar, but with obv. type veiled and diad. hd. of Juno r., sceptre over shoulder, DOS behind, and with eagle on thunderbolt on side-panel of quadriga on rev. RRC 348/2. CRR 706. RSC *Rubria* 2.   **VF** £60 ($96) / **EF** £175 ($280)

260   261

260 —— Similar, but with obv. type bust of Minerva r., wearing crested Corinthian helmet and aegis, DOS behind, and the triumphal quadriga on rev. is surmounted by small Victory in biga. RRC 348/3. CRR 707. RSC *Rubria* 3.   **VF** £70 ($112) / **EF** £200 ($320)

261 **Quinarius.** L. Rubrius Dossenus, 87 BC. Laur. hd. of Neptune r., trident over shoulder, DOS–SEN behind. Rev. Victory walking r., holding wreath and palm, snake-entwined altar at her feet, L RVBRI behind. RRC 348/4. CRR 708. RSC *Rubria* 4.
VF £55 ($88) / **EF** £160 ($256)
Crawford interprets the allusion to Aesculapius (the snake-entwined altar) in the light of the devastating plague which broke out in this year.

262 **Denarius.** L. and C. Memmius L.f. Galeria, 87 BC. Laur. hd. of Saturn l., harpa behind, EX S C below, control-letter (usually reversed) below chin. Rev. Venus in slow biga r., Cupid flying l. above, L C MEMIES L F / GAL in ex. RRC 349/1. CRR 712. RSC *Memmia* 8.
VF £55 ($88) / **EF** £160 ($256)
This unusual issue was struck jointly by two brothers, doubtless sons of the moneyer L. Memmius Galeria whose types they imitate (see no. 190). The coins were produced by special decree of the Senate (ex senatus consulto).

263   264

263 — Gargonius (or Gargilius), Ogulnius, and Vergilius (or Verginius), 86 BC. Hd. of Apollo r., wreathed with oak, thunderbolt below. Rev. Jupiter in quadriga r., brandishing thunderbolt, control-letter above, GAR below, OGVL VER or VER OGVL (VL and VE in monogram) in ex. RRC 350A/1a–b. CRR 721, 721a. RSC *Gargilia* 1–2.
VF £185 ($296) / **EF** £450 ($720)
This monetary triumvirate is unusual in that all three members' names appear on each issue. There is also a much larger anonymous issue with identical types (see no. 266).

264 **Denarius.** Gargonius (or Gargilius), Ogulnius, and Vergilius (or Verginius), 86 BC. Similar, but with **OGVL** (VL in monogram) below the horses, and with **GAR VER** (sometimes with **AR** in monogram, always with **VE** in monogram) or **VER GAR** (VE in monogram) in ex. RRC 350A/1c–d. CRR 721b, 721c. RSC *Ogulnia* 1–2.

VF £185 ($296) / **EF** £450 ($720)

265   265   266

265 — — Similar, but with **VER** (VE in monogram) below the horses, and with **GAR OGVL** (VL in monogram) in ex. RRC 350A/1e. CRR 721d. RSC *Vergilia* 1.

VF £185 ($296) / **EF** £450 ($720)

266 — Anonymous, 86 BC. Similar, but without legend or control-letter. RRC 350A/2. CRR 723. RSC 226.   **VF** £40 ($64) / **EF** £125 ($200)
Although obviously connected by type with the signed denarii of Gargonius, Ogulnius and Vergilius the reason for this exceptionally late issue of anonymous coins is unclear.

            267   268

267 — M. Fannius and L. Critonius, 86 BC. Hd. of Ceres r., wreathed with corn, **AED PL** behind. Rev. The two aediles seated r. on subsellium, ear of corn before, **P A** on l., **M FAN L CRIT** (IT in monogram) or **CRI** or **CRT** in ex. RRC 351/1. CRR 717, 717a. RSC *Critonia* 1, 1a.

VF £100 ($160) / **EF** £275 ($440)
This exceptional issue by the plebeian aediles was produced from 'public silver' (P A = publico argento) withdrawn from the state's bullion reserves. Crawford makes the interesting suggestion that these coins (and certain others of the period) were struck from the money bequeathed to the Roman People by Ptolemy X Alexander of Egypt (see also nos. 269 and 273).

268 — L. Julius Bursio, 85 BC. Dr. bust of young male deity r., combining attributes of Apollo (laurel-wreath), Mercury (winged head), and Neptune (trident over shoulder), control-mark behind. Rev. Victory in quadriga r., sometimes with control-mark/s in field, **L IVLI BVRSIO** in ex. RRC 352/1a, c. CRR 728–728f. RSC *Julia* 5–5c.

VF £40 ($64) / **EF** £125 ($200)

269 — Anonymous, 85 BC. Similar, but without moneyer's name or control-symbol on rev., and with **EX A P** in ex. RRC 352/1b. CRR 729. RSC *Julia* 6.

VF £100 ($160) / **EF** £275 ($440)

Although lacking the moneyer's name this issue (together with the following quinarius) clearly forms part of the coinage of L. Julius Bursio. The metal from which it was struck is stated to be ex argento publico ('from the public silver') and Crawford believes it may have been produced from the proceeds of Ptolemy X's legacy to the Roman People (see also nos. 267 and 273).

270   **Quinarius.** Anonymous, 85 BC. Obv. Similar, but without trident over shoulder and no
       control-mark. Rev. Cupid stg. r., breaking thunderbolt over l. knee. RRC 352/2. CRR 730.
       RSC *Julia 7.*   *(Unique)*

271   272

271   **Denarius.** Mn. Fonteius C.f., 85 BC. **MN FONTEI C F** (**MN** and **NT** in monogram), laur. hd.
       of Apollo r., thunderbolt below, sometimes with **AP** monogram below chin or before. Rev.
       Cupid seated on goat stg. r., pilei of the Dioscuri above, thyrsus of Bacchus in ex., all
       within laurel-wreath. RRC 353/1a–c. CRR 724, 724a. RSC *Fonteia* 9–10a.
                                                  VF £55 ($88) / **EF** £160 ($256)

272   —— Similar (without **AP** monogram on obv.), but the pilei are placed on either side of the
       goat on rev. RRC 353/1d. CRR 724b. RSC *Fonteia* 11.   **VF** £75 ($120) / **EF** £210 ($336)

273   — Anonymous, 85 BC. Similar, but with **EX A P** on obv. instead of moneyer's name. RRC
       353/2. CRR 726. RSC *Fonteia* 12.   **VF** £100 ($160) / **EF** £275 ($440)
       *Like the other anonymous denarius type of this year (see no. 269) this unquestionably
       forms part of the moneyer's issue which bears the same types. The formula EX A[RGENTO]
       P[VBLICO] makes its final appearance on these two issues and possibly relates to addi-
       tional bullion made available to the Roman mint as a result of Ptolemy X's will (see also
       no. 267).*

274   276

274   — C. Licinius L.f. Macer, 84 BC. Diad. bust of Apollo l., viewed from behind, brandishing
       thunderbolt, cloak over l. shoulder. Rev. Minerva in quadriga r., holding spear and shield,
       C LICINIVS L F / MACER in ex. RRC 354/1. CRR 732. RSC *Licinia* 16.
                                                  VF £50 ($80) / **EF** £150 ($240)
       *This moneyer was noted as an annalist who wrote a history of Rome in sixteen books, now
       existing only in fragments. He served as praetor in 68 BC but committed suicide several
       years later, having been accused of extortion during his provincial governorship.*

275   **Denarius.** P. Furius Crassipes, 84 BC. Turreted hd. of Cybele r., AED CVR (sometimes with VR in monogram) and deformed foot behind. Rev. Curule chair inscribed P FOVRIVS, CRASSIPES (or CRASSVPES) in ex. RRC 356/1. CRR 735–735b. RSC *Furia* 19–20a.
      VF £55 ($88) / **EF** £160 ($256)
      This issuer strikes as curule aedile, though without reference to senatorial authorization.

276   — L. Cornelius Sulla, 84–83 BC. Diad. hd. of Venus r., Cupid holding palm-branch before, L SVLLA below. Rev. Jug and lituus between two trophies, IMPER above, ITERVM (or ITERV) below. RRC 359/2. CRR 761, 761a. RSC *Cornelia* 29–30.
      VF £85 ($136) / **EF** £240 ($384)
      On this exceptional military issue Sulla strikes in the East as imperator without reference to senatorial authorization, an ominous foreshadowing of the imperatorial age of the 40s and 30s BC. The type was also struck in gold (see no. 6).

277   278

277   — C. Norbanus, 83 BC. Diad. hd. of Venus r., control-numeral behind, C NORBANVS below. Rev. Prow-stem, fasces with axe, caduceus, and ear of corn. RRC 357/1a. CRR 740. RSC *Norbana* 1.   **VF** £100 ($160) / **EF** £275 ($440)

278   — — Similar, but with rev. type ear of corn, fasces with axe, and caduceus. RRC 357/1b. CRR 739. RSC *Norbana* 2.   **VF** £55 ($88) / **EF** £160 ($256)

279   281

279   **Denarius serratus.** Q. Antonius Balbus, 83 BC. Laur. hd. of Jupiter r., S C behind, sometimes with control-letter below or before. Rev. Victory in quadriga r., holding wreath and palm, sometimes with control-letter below, Q ANTO BALB (ANT and AL in monogram) / PR in ex. RRC 364/1. CRR 742–742b. RSC *Antonia* 1–1d.   **VF** £40 ($64) / **EF** £140 ($224)
      This appears to have been the principal coinage of the faction opposed to the return of Sulla to Rome. Balbus strikes as praetor by special decree of the Senate (senatus consulto) and the type anticipates the success of the anti-Sullan cause, a hope which was to be dashed in the battle of the Colline Gate. Denarii with serrated edges had not been struck for more than two decades (see nos. 188–91), but henceforth were to become common down to the mid-60s BC.

280 **Denarius serratus.** Juventius Laterensis, 83 BC. Bare hd. of Jupiter r., **S C** behind, control-letter **B** below, all within laurel-wreath. Rev. Triumphator in slow quadriga l., holding palm-branch and trophy, . . **LATERENS** (**ATE** in monogram) in ex. RRC 358/1. RSC *Juventia* 8.

(Unique)
This remarkable issue, presently known from only a single surviving specimen (unfortunately lacking the moneyer's praenomen), would appear to be another anticipatory type connected with the military confrontation between the Marians and Sulla. Like the coinage of Antonius Balbus this was an emergency issue produced by special decree of the Senate.

281 **Denarius.** L. Marcius Censorinus, 82 BC. Laur. hd. of Apollo r., sometimes with control-symbol behind or before. Rev. The satyr, Marsyas, walking l., his r. arm raised, carrying wine-skin over l. shoulder, column behind, **L CENSOR** before, sometimes with control-letter or numeral on r. RRC 363/1. CRR 737–737f. RSC *Marcia* 24–24d.

VF £55 ($88) / **EF** £160 ($256)

282   283

282 **Denarius serratus.** C. Mamilius C.f. Limetanus, 82 BC. Dr. bust of Mercury r., wearing winged petasus, caduceus over shoulder, control-letter behind. Rev. Ulysses walking r., holding staff, his r. hand extended towards his dog, Argos, **C MAMIL** on l., **LIMETAN** (**TA** in monogram) on r. RRC 362/1. CRR 741. RSC *Mamilia* 6.

VF £85 ($136) / **EF** £240 ($384)

283 **Denarius.** P. Crepusius, 82 BC. Laur. hd. of Apollo r., sceptre over shoulder, usually with control-letter below chin, or with control-symbol below chin and letter behind. Rev. Horseman galloping r., thrusting with spear, control-numeral behind, **P CREPVSI** in ex. RRC 361/1. CRR 738, 738a. RSC *Crepusia* 1–1c.   **VF** £50 ($80) / **EF** £150 ($240)

284

284 — L. Marcius Censorinus, C. Mamilius C.f. Limetanus and P. Crepusius, 82 BC. Veiled, diad. and dr. bust of Venus r., **L CENSORIN** (or **CENSORI** or **CENSOR**) behind. Rev. Venus in biga r., **C LIMETA** (**TA** in monogram) below, **P CREPVSI** in ex., control-numeral above. RRC 360/1b. CRR 736a. RSC *Marcia* 27, 27a.   **VF** £65 ($104) / **EF** £185 ($296)

285 —— Similar, but with **P CREPVS** (or **CREPVSI**) below horses on rev., **C LIMETAN** (or **LIMETA**) in ex., and with **L CENSORIN** (or **CENSOR**) on obv. RRC 360/1a. CRR 736. RSC *Marcia* 25–6.   **VF** £100 ($160) / **EF** £275 ($440)

286   287

286   **Denarius.** L. Cornelius Sulla and L. Manlius Torquatus, 82 BC. L MANLI PRO Q, helmeted
       hd. of Roma r. Rev. Sulla in triumphal quadriga r., holding caduceus, crowned by Victory
       flying l. above, L SVLLA IM (or IMP or IMPE) in ex. RRC 367/1, 5. CRR 757, 757a. RSC
       Manlia 4, 5, 8a.   **VF** £60 ($96) / **EF** £175 ($280)

287   — — Similar, but with obv. legend L MANLI T PRO Q (the T placed sideways), and with L
       SVLLA IM (or IMP) on rev. RRC 367/3. CRR 759. RSC *Manlia* 7–8.
                                                             VF £70 ($112) / **EF** £200 ($320)
       *Another military issue of Sulla, this time probably belonging to the period of civil war in
       Italy in 82 BC. Once again gold aurei were included in the series (see no. 7). The coins also
       bear the name of one of Sulla's lieutenants who is described as proquaestor and was later
       consul (in 65 BC).*

288

288   — C. Valerius Flaccus, 82 BC. Winged and dr. bust of Victory r., control-symbol behind or
       before, or control-letter behind. Rev. C VAL FLA (VAL in monogram), legionary eagle
       between two standards inscribed H (*hastati*) and P (*principes*), EX S C across lower field.
       RRC 365/1. CRR 747–747b. RSC *Valeria* 12–12b.   **VF** £85 ($136) / **EF** £240 ($384)
       *Struck at Massalia by special decree of the Senate (ex senatus consulto) while Flaccus was
       proconsul in Gaul.*

289   291

289   — C. Annius T.f. T.n. Luscus and L. Fabius L.f. Hispaniensis, 82–81 BC. C ANNI T F T N
       PRO COS EX S C, diad. and dr. female bust r., scales before, caduceus behind, usually with
       control-symbol or letter below. Rev. Victory in quadriga r., holding palm, L FABI L F HISP in
       ex., Q above, sometimes with control-letter below. RRC 366/1. CRR 748–748b. RSC
       Annia 2–2b.   **VF** £75 ($120) / **EF** £210 ($336)
       *This issue is connected with Annius' campaign against the renegade Sertorius in Spain and
       was produced by special decree of the Senate. Crawford assigns the coins bearing the name
       of the quaestor Fabius to a mint in northern Italy, those with Tarquitius' name to Spain.*

290   **Denarius.** C. Annius T.f. T.n. Luscus and L. Fabius L.f. Hispaniensis, 82–81 BC. Similar
      (sometimes with control-letter below bust), but without scales and caduceus and with bead
      and reel border on obv. RRC 366/2. CRR 748c–d. RSC *Annia* 3, 3a.
                                                    VF £85 ($136) / **EF** £240 ($384)

291   — — C ANNIVS T F T N PRO COS EX S C, diad. female hd. r., scales before, sometimes with
      control-letter behind. Rev. Victory in slow quadriga r., holding palm, L FABI L F in ex., HISP
      Q above (or L FABI L F HISP in ex., Q above), sometimes with control-letter below horses.
      RRC 366/3. CRR 748e–g. RSC *Annia* 4–5a.   **VF** £85 ($136) / **EF** £240 ($384)

292   — C. Annius T.f. T.n. Luscus and C. Tarquitius P.f., 82–81 BC. Obv. Similar (no control-
      letter). Rev. Victory in biga r., holding palm, C TARQVITI P F in ex., Q below horses, control-
      numeral above. RRC 366/4. CRR 749. RSC *Annia* 1.   **VF** £80 ($128) / **EF** £225 ($360)

293   295

293   — (restored issue of M. Caecilius Q.f. Metellus, moneyer in 127 BC), 82 or 80 BC. Diad.
      hd. of Apollo r., ROMA behind, ✕ (XVI monogram) below chin. Rev. Macedonian shield
      with elephant's hd. at centre, M METELLVS Q F around, all within laurel-wreath. RRC
      369/1. CRR 719. RSC *Caecilia* 30.   **VF** £100 ($160) / **EF** £275 ($440)
      This and the following two types represent a remarkable revival of the issues of the monetary
      triumvirate which had held office approximately forty-five years earlier (see nos. 139–41),
      though with the substitution of Apollo for the Roma head on obv. As well as being compli-
      mentary to several of Sulla's most prominent supporters Crawford suggests that their true
      purpose was to enable Sulla to issue a civil coinage without appointing a new triumvirate of
      moneyers for 82 BC or, alternatively, to celebrate the restoration of the Republic in 80.

294   — (restored issue of C. Servilius, moneyer in 127 BC), 82 or 80 BC. Laur. hd. of Apollo r.,
      ROMA below, ✕ (XVI monogram) below chin, lituus and A or B behind. Rev. Battle
      between two mounted horsemen, the one on l. armed with sword, the other with spear, his
      shield inscribed M, C SERVEIL (VE in monogram) in ex. RRC 370/1. CRR 720. RSC
      Servilia 7.   **VF** £100 ($160) / **EF** £275 ($440)

295   **Denarius.** (Restored issue of Q. Fabius Maximus, moneyer in 127 BC), 82 or 80 BC. Laur. hd.
      of Apollo r., ROMA behind, ✕ (XVI monogram) below chin, Q MAX (MA in monogram) or
      Q MX below, lyre before. Rev. Cornucopiae with thunderbolt placed horizontally in background,
      all within wreath. RRC 371/1. CRR 718. RSC *Fabia* 6.   **VF** £100 ($160) / **EF** £275 ($440)

296   297

296   **Denarius serratus.** A. Postumius A.f. S.n. Albinus, 81 BC. Dr. bust of Diana r., bow and
      quiver over shoulder, bucranium above. Rev. A POST A F S N ALBIN (AL in monogram),
      rock surmounted by togate figure stg. l. before altar, holding sprinkler over sacrificial bull.
      RRC 372/1. CRR 745. RSC *Postumia* 7.   **VF** £60 ($96) / **EF** £175 ($280)

297 **Denarius serratus.** A. Postumius A.f. S.n. Albinus, 81 BC. Veiled hd. of Hispania r., her hair dishevelled, HISPAN behind. Rev. A POST A F S N ALBIN (AL in monogram), togate figure stg. l., extending r. hand towards legionary eagle before him, fasces with axe behind. RRC 372/2. CRR 746. RSC *Postumia* 8.   VF £80 ($128) / **EF** £225 ($360)

298   299

298 — L. Volumnius L.f. Strabo, 81 BC. Laur. hd. of Jupiter r., control-letter behind. Rev. Europa seated on bull galloping l., thunderbolt behind, vine-leaf below, L VOL L F STRAB in ex. (V and L of VOL, TR and AB all in monogram). RRC 377/1. CRR 743. RSC *Volteia* 6.
     VF £325 ($520) / **EF** £800 ($1,280)
The form of this moneyer's name is quite uncertain, Crawford preferring Volumnius to the traditionally accepted Volteius.

299 — C. Marius C.f. Capito, 81 BC. C MARI C F CAPIT, dr. bust of Ceres r., wreathed with corn, control-numeral following legend. Rev. Ploughman conducting yoke of oxen l., control-numeral above, sometimes with S C and control-symbol in ex. RRC 378/1a–b. CRR 744, 744a. RSC *Maria* 7–8.   VF £85 ($136) / **EF** £240 ($384)
It would seem that during his term of office this moneyer was authorized by the Senate to effect a substantial increase in the originally sanctioned volume of his coinage.

300

300 — — Similar, but with obv. legend CAPIT followed by control-numeral, and with C MARI C F / S C in ex. on rev. RRC 378/1c. CRR 744b. RSC *Maria* 9.
     VF £60 ($96) / **EF** £175 ($280)

301   302

301 **Denarius.** Q. Caecilius Metellus Pius, 81 BC. Diad. hd. of Pietas r., stork before. Rev. Elephant walking l., Q C M P I in ex. RRC 374/1. CRR 750. RSC *Caecilia* 43.
     VF £75 ($120) / **EF** £210 ($336)
The issuer strikes as imperator in northern Italy where he was campaigning on behalf of Sulla. The following year he was to be the dictator's colleague in the consulship.

SILVER 129

302 **Denarius.** Q. Caecilius Metellus Pius, 81 BC. Obv. Similar. Rev. Jug and lituus (emblems of the augurate), IMPER in ex., all within laurel-wreath. RRC 374/2. CRR 751. RSC *Caecilia* 44. **VF** £85 ($136) / **EF** £240 ($384)

303 304

303 — Anonymous, 81 BC. Diad. hd. of Venus r. Rev. Double cornucopiae, Q below. RRC 375/2. CRR 755. RSC *Cornelia* 33. **VF** £125 ($200) / **EF** £325 ($520)
This and the following are best explained as emergency Sullan issues in Italy produced in connection with the various military campaigns of the period. There is an aureus of this type (see no. 8).

304 — — Diad. hd. of Venus r., control-letter behind. Rev. Cornucopiae, EX on r., S C on l., all within laurel-wreath. RRC 376/1. CRR 763. RSC *Cornelia* 44.
VF £375 ($600) / **EF** £900 ($1,440)

305

305 **Quinarius.** Anonymous, 81 BC. Laur. hd. of Apollo r. Rev. Victory stg. r., crowning trophy, sometimes with control-mark between, ROMA in ex. RRC 373/1. CRR 609–10. RSC 227–227c and *Claudia* 4. **VF** £55 ($88) / **EF** £160 ($256)
Crawford proposes that this enigmatc type may have been produced by the remnants of the Marian party gathered in Cisalpine Gaul to make their final stand against Sulla. These were the last quinarii to be struck until the Caesarian revival of the denomination more than three decades later.

306 307

306 **Denarius.** L. Procilius L.f., 80 BC. Laur. hd. of Jupiter r., S C behind. Rev. Juno Sospita walking r., brandishing spear and holding shield, snake at her feet, L PROCILI / F behind. RRC 379/1. CRR 771. RSC *Procilia* 1. **VF** £65 ($104) / **EF** £185 ($296)
This moneyer's extensive issue, equally divided between regular denarii and serrati, was authorized by special decree of the Senate – [ex] senatus consulto.

307 **Denarius serratus.** L. Procilius L.f., 80 BC. Hd. of Juno Sospita r., clad in goat's skin, S C behind. Rev. Juno Sospita in biga r., brandishing spear and holding shield, snake below, L PROCILI F in ex. RRC 379/2. CRR 772. RSC *Procilia* 2.   **VF** £60 ($96) / **EF** £175 ($280)

308   309

308 — C. Poblicius Q.f., 80 BC. Helmeted and dr. bust r., ROMA behind, control-letter above. Rev. Hercules stg. l., in combat with the Nemean lion, club at his feet, bow and quiver on l., C POBLICI Q F on right, control-letter above. RRC 380/1. CRR 768. RSC *Poblicia* 9.
VF £65 ($104) / **EF** £185 ($296)

309 — C. Naevius Balbus, 79 BC. Diad. hd. of Venus r., S C behind, sometimes with control-letter below chin. Rev. Victory in triga r., C NÆ BALB (AL in monogram) in ex., sometimes with control-letter or numeral above. RRC 382/1. CRR 769–769b. RSC *Naevia* 6–6b.
VF £45 ($72) / **EF** £140 ($224)
This and the following type represent further large outputs of coinage specially authorized by decree of the Senate, doubtless necessitated by the extensive military operations during the dictatorship of Sulla. The three-horse chariot (triga) is rarely depicted on the Republican coinage, the only other example being on a denarius of Ap. Claudius Pulcher issued in 111/110 BC (see no. 176).

310   311

310 — Ti. Claudius Ti.f. Ap.n. Nero, 79 BC. Diad. and dr. bust of Diana r., bow and quiver over shoulder, S C before. Rev. Victory in biga r., holding palm, TI CLAVD TI F (AVD or VD in monogram) / AP N (AP in monogram) in ex., control-numeral (sometimes preceded by A) below. RRC 383/1. CRR 770, 770a. RSC *Claudia* 5–6.   **VF** £50 ($80) / **EF** £150 ($240)

311 — L. Papius, 79 BC. Hd. of Juno Sospita r., clad in goat's skin, control-symbol (rarely numeral) behind, bead and reel border. Rev. Gryphon leaping r., control-symbol (rarely numeral) below, L PAPI in ex., bead and reel border. RRC 384/1. CRR 773. RSC *Papia* 1.
VF £60 ($96) / **EF** £175 ($280)

312 **Denarius.** M. Volteius M.f., 78 BC. Laur. hd. of Jupiter r. Rev. Tetrastyle temple of Jupiter Capitolinus, M VOLTEI M F below. RRC 385/1. CRR 774. RSC *Volteia* 1.
VF £75 ($120) / **EF** £210 ($336)
This moneyer's coinage exhibits a remarkable variety of types.

312   313

313   **Denarius.** M. Volteius M.f., 78 BC. Hd. of young Hercules r., clad in lion's skin. Rev. The Erymanthian boar running r., **M VOLTEI M F** in ex. RRC 385/2. CRR 775. RSC *Volteia* 2.

         VF £110 ($176) / **EF** £300 ($480)

314   315

314   — — Hd. of young Bacchus or Liber r., wreathed with ivy. Rev. Ceres in biga of snakes r., holding torch in each hand, control-symbol behind, **M VOLTEI M F** in ex. RRC 385/3. CRR 776. RSC *Volteia* 3.   **VF** £75 ($120) / **EF** £210 ($336)

315   — — Dr. bust r., wearing helmet wreathed with laurel, control-symbol behind. Rev. Cybele seated in biga of lions r., Greek letter-numeral control above, **M VOLTEI M F** in ex. RRC 385/4. CRR 777. RSC *Volteia* 4.   **VF** £80 ($128) / **EF** £225 ($360)

316   317

316   — — Laur. hd. of Apollo r. Rev. Snake-entwined tripod, **S C – D T** across field, **M VOLTEI M F** in ex. RRC 385/5. CRR 778. RSC *Volteia* 5.   **VF** £450 ($720) / **EF** £1,000 ($1,600)

317   — L. Cassius Q.f. Longinus, 78 BC. Hd. of young Bacchus or Liber r., wreathed with ivy, thyrsus over shoulder. Rev. Hd. of Libera (Proserpina) l., wreathed with vine, **L CASSI Q F** behind. RRC 386/1. CRR 779. RSC *Cassia* 6.   **VF** £125 ($200) / **EF** £325 ($520)

318   — L. Rutilius Flaccus, 77 BC. Helmeted hd. of Roma r., **FLAC** behind. Rev. Victory in biga r., holding wreath, **L RVTILI** in ex. RRC 387/1. CRR 780, 780a. RSC *Rutilia* 1, 1a.

         VF £45 ($72) / **EF** £140 ($224)

318   319

319   **Denarius.** P. Satrienus, 77 BC. Helmeted hd. of young Mars r., usually with control-
      numeral behind. Rev. She-wolf prowling l., ROMA above, P SATRIE/NVS in ex. RRC 388/1.
      CRR 781, 781a. RSC *Satriena* 1, 1a.   **VF** £80 ($128) / **EF** £225 ($360)

320

320   — L. Rustius, 76 BC. Helmeted hd. of young Mars r., ✱ (XVI monogram) below chin, S C
      behind. Rev. Ram stg. r., L RVSTI in ex. RRC 389/1. CRR 782. RSC *Rustia* 1.
                                                       VF £90 ($144) / **EF** £250 ($400)

321   322

321   — L. Lucretius Trio, 76 BC. Rad. hd. of Sol r. Rev. Crescent moon surrounded by seven
      stars, L LVCRETI below, TRIO above. RRC 390/1. CRR 783. RSC *Lucretia* 2.
                                                       VF £90 ($144) / **EF** £250 ($400)

322   — — Laur. hd. of Neptune r., trident over shoulder, control-numeral behind. Rev. Winged
      boy (deified Palaemon?) riding on back of dolphin r., L LVCRETI / TRIO below. RRC 390/2.
      CRR 784. RSC *Lucretia* 3.   **VF** £80 ($128) / **EF** £225 ($360)

323   — Cn. Cornelius Lentulus Marcellinus, 76–75 BC. Diad. and dr. bust of the Genius of the
      Roman People r., bearded, sceptre over shoulder, G P R above. Rev. Globe between
      wreathed sceptre and rudder, EX – S C in field, CN LEN Q below. RRC 393/1a. CRR 752.
      RSC *Cornelia* 54.   **VF** £60 ($96) / **EF** £175 ($280)
      *Cn. Lentulus strikes in Spain in his capacity as quaestor to the proconsul Pompey, who
      had been sent to the peninsula to assist Q. Caecilius Metellus Pius in the protracted war
      against Sertorius. On the second variety 'quaestor' is replaced by 'curator denariorum
      flandorum' (CVR ✱ FL), meaning 'curator of the casting of denarii', an interesting title the
      origins of which would seem to go back to the very earliest phase of Rome's currency.*

323 324

324 **Denarius.** Cn. Cornelius Lentulus Marcellinus, 76–75 BC. Similar, but with **LENT CVR ✷ FL** or F (NT in monogram) below rev. type. RRC 393/1b. CRR 752a. RSC *Cornelia* 55.
VF £65 ($104) / **EF** £185 ($296)

325 — C. Egnatius Cn.f. Cn.n. Maxsumus (= Maximus), 75 BC. Winged bust of Cupid r., bow and quiver over shoulder, **MAXSVMVS** behind. Rev. Distyle temple of Jupiter Libertas containing stg. figures of the two deities, **C EGNATIVS CN F** below, **CN N** on r., control-numeral on l. RRC 391/2. CRR 788. RSC *Egnatia* 3. **VF** £175 ($280) / **EF** £425 ($680)
The precise location of the temple of Jupiter Libertas is uncertain, though it is known that it was situated on the Aventine and was later restored by Augustus.

326 327

326 — — Diad. and dr. bust of Libertas r., **MAXSVMVS** and pileus behind. Rev. Roma and Venus stg. facing, the former holding spear and sword, her l. foot set on wolf's hd., the latter holding sceptre and with Cupid alighting on her shoulder, rudder set on prow on either side, **C EGNATIVS CN F** (AT in monogram) below, **CN N** on r., control-letter on l. RRC 391/3. CRR 787. RSC *Egnatia* 2. **VF** £140 ($224) / **EF** £350 ($560)

327 **Denarius serratus.** C. Egnatius Cn.f. Cn.n. Maxsumus (= Maximus), 75 BC. Diad. and dr. bust of Venus r., Cupid on shoulder, **MAXSVMVS** behind, sometimes with control-numeral below. Rev. Libertas in slow biga l., crowned by Victory flying r., pileus behind, **C EGNATIVS CN F / CN N** in ex. RRC 391/1. CRR 786, 786a. RSC *Egnatia* 1, 1a.
VF £300 ($480) / **EF** £750 ($1,200)

328 329

328 **Denarius.** L. Farsuleius Mensor, 75 BC. Diad. and dr. bust of Libertas r., **S C** below chin, **MENSOR** before, pileus and control-numeral behind, bead and reel border. Rev. Warrior in biga r., holding spear and reining in horses while he helps togate figure to mount into the chariot, scorpion below, **L FARSVLEI** in ex. RRC 392/1a. CRR 789a. RSC *Farsuleia* 1.
VF £80 ($128) / **EF** £225 ($360)

329 **Denarius.** L. Farsuleius Mensor, 75 BC. Similar, but on obv. the **S C** is behind the hd. of Libertas in place of control-numeral, and on rev. control-numeral appears below horses instead of scorpion. RRC 392/1b. CRR 789. RSC *Farsuleia* 2.

VF £85 ($136) / **EF** £240 ($384)

330   331

330 — C. Postumius Ta . . . . (or At . . . .), 74 BC. Dr. bust of Diana r., bow and quiver over shoulder. Rev. Hound running r., spear below, **C POSTVMI** in ex., usually with **TA** (in monogram) below. RRC 394/1. CRR 785, 785a. RSC *Postumia* 9, 9a.

VF £65 ($104) / **EF** £185 ($296)

331 — L. Cossutius C.f. Sabula, 74 BC. Hd. of Medusa l., winged and entwined with snakes, **SABVLA** behind. Rev. Bellerophon on Pegasus flying r., brandishing spear, **L COSSVTI C F** below, control-numeral behind. RRC 395/1. CRR 790. RSC *Cossutia* 1.

VF £150 ($240) / **EF** £375 ($600)

332 — L. Plaetorius L.f. Cestianus, 74 BC. Diad. and dr. bust of Juno Moneta r., **MONETA** behind, **S C** below chin. Rev. Naked athlete (boxer) running r., holding palm-branch and caestus, **L PLAETORI / L F Q S C** behind and before, sometimes with control-symbol below. RRC 396/1. CRR 792, 792a. RSC *Plaetoria* 2, 2a.   VF £375 ($600) / **EF** £900 ($1,440)
     L. Plaetorius strikes as quaestor in this small issue produced by special decree of the Senate. The duplication of the formula senatus consulto (S C) on both sides of the coin is unusual. The Roman Republican mint was situated next to the temple of Juno Moneta on the Arx, the north summit of the Capitoline Hill.

333   334

333 — P. Cornelius P.f. L.n. Lentulus Spinther, 74 BC. Bare hd. of bearded Hercules r., **Q S C** behind. Rev. The Genius of the Roman People seated facing on curule chair, holding cornucopiae and sceptre, r. foot on globe, crowned by Victory flying l., **P LENT P F** (NT in monogram) on l., **L N** on r. RRC 397/1. CRR 791. RSC *Cornelia* 58.

VF £450 ($720) / **EF** £1,000 ($1,600)
     Another restricted issue produced by special decree of the Senate, doubtless reflecting the unsettled conditions of the period (war with Sertorius in Spain and with Mithradates in the East) and clearly asserting Rome's claim to universal dominion.

334 **Denarius.** Q. Pomponius Rufus, 73 BC. Laur. hd. of Jupiter r., RVFVS before, S C behind. Rev. Eagle stg. l. on sceptre, hd. r., holding wreath in r. claw, control-numeral below, symbol on r., Q POMPONI in ex. RRC 398/1. CRR 793. RSC *Pomponia* 23.
VF £1,500 ($2,400) / **EF** £3,000 ($4,800)
The combination of a pair of control-marks on the same side of the coin is unusual, a characteristic which this issue shares with the following type. The rev. type of the later gold staters of the Thracian (or Scythian) dynast Koson bears a remarkable resemblance to this rare denarius issue (the obv. of Koson's stater is copied from the rev. of one of the denarii of Q. Servilius Caepio Brutus issued in 54 BC).

335 336

335 **Denarius serratus.** Q. Crepereius M.f. Rocus, 72 BC. Bust of Amphitrite r., viewed from behind, dr. with shoulders bare, control-letter before, symbol behind. Rev. Neptune in biga of sea-horses r., brandishing trident, control-letter above, Q CREPEREI (or Q CREPER M F) / ROCVS below. RRC 399/1. CRR 796, 796a. RSC *Crepereia* 1–2.
VF £300 ($480) / **EF** £750 ($1,200)

336 — Mn. Aquillius Mn.f. Mn. n., 71 BC. Helmeted and dr. bust of Virtus r., VIRTVS before, III VIR behind. Rev. Warrior (Mn. Aquillius, consul 101 BC) stg. facing, looking r., holding shield and raising figure of Sicilia who is slumped to l., MN AQVIL (MN in monogram) on r., MN F MN N (both MN in monogram) on l., SICIL in ex. RRC 401/1. CRR 798. RSC *Aquillia* 2.
VF £65 ($104) / **EF** £185 ($296)
The first appearance on the coinage of the triumviral title of a moneyer (III VIR = tresvir).

337 338

337 **Denarius.** L. Axsius (= Axius) L.f. Naso, 71 BC. Hd. of young Mars r., wearing helmet (sometimes crested), NASO below, S C under chin, control-numeral behind. Rev. Diana in biga of stags r., holding spear, two hounds behind, another below stags, control-numeral behind, L AXSIVS L F in ex. RRC 400/1. CRR 794–5. RSC *Axia* 1–2.
VF £275 ($440) / **EF** £675 ($1,080)

338 **Denarius serratus.** Q. Fufius Calenus and P. Mucius Scaevola (Cordus), 70 BC. Conjoined hds. of Honos and Virtus r., the former laur., the latter helmeted, HO behind, VIRT (RT in monogram) before, KALENI below. Rev. Italia stg. r., holding cornucopiae, clasping hands with Roma stg. l., holding spear, r. foot on globe, caduceus above ITAL (TAL in monogram) on l., RO on r., CORDI in ex. RRC 403/1. CRR 797. RSC *Fufia* 1.
VF £100 ($160) / **EF** £275 ($440)

339

339 **Denarius serratus.** T. Vettius Sabinus, 70 BC. Bare hd. of King Tatius r., bearded, **TA** (in monogram) below chin, **SABINVS** behind, **S C** before. Rev. Magistrate in slow biga l., holding staff, ear of corn behind, **IVDEX** above, **T VETTIVS** in ex. RRC 404/1. CRR 905. RSC *Vettia* 2.   **VF** £165 ($264) / **EF** £400 ($640)

340   341

340 **Denarius.** M. Plaetorius M.f. Cestianus, 69 BC. Diad. and dr. female bust (Fortuna?) l., her hair confined in net, usually with control-symbol behind. Rev. Triangular pediment of temple containing representation of anguipede giant, **M PLÆTORIVS** (or similar, the **PL** sometimes in monogram) on entablature, **CEST S C** below. RRC 405/1. CRR 800–800b. RSC *Plaetoria* 9–9f.   **VF** £350 ($560) / **EF** £850 ($1,360)
The temple may be the celebrated sanctuary of Fortuna at Praeneste, home of the moneyer, in which case the female head on obverse would be that of the goddess herself.

341 — — Dr. female bust (Fortuna?) r., her hair in knot, control-symbol behind. Rev. **M PLAETORI CEST S C**, half-length figure of boy facing, holding before him long tablet inscribed **SORS**. RRC 405/2. CRR 801. RSC *Plaetoria* 10.   **VF** £300 ($480) / **EF** £750 ($1,200)
The reverse would appear to symbolize the celebrated oracle at Praeneste known as the Sortes Praenestinae. Each person wishing to determine his or her future cast a lot (sors) in the form of a tablet in order to gain access to the oracle.

342   343

342 — — Dr. bust of Proserpina (Persephone) r., her hair decorated with poppy-heads, usually with control-symbol behind. Rev. Winged caduceus, **M PLAETORI** on r., **CEST EX S C** on l. (sometimes with **M PLAETORI** on l., **CEST S C** on r.). RRC 405/3. CRR 805–6. RSC *Plaetoria* 6, 6a.   **VF** £110 ($176) / **EF** £300 ($480)

343 **Denarius.** M. Plaetorius M.f. Cestianus, 69 BC. Similar, but with rev. type jug and lighted torch. RRC 405/4. CRR 803–4. RSC *Plaetoria* 7–7c.   **VF** £125 ($200) / **EF** £325 ($520)

344 — — Young male hd. (Mercury?) r., with long flowing hair, control-symbol (rarely letter) behind. Rev. Winged caduceus, M PLAETORI on r., CEST EX S C on l. RRC 405/5. CRR 807. RSC *Plaetoria* 5.   **VF** £65 ($104) / **EF** £185 ($296)

345

345 — P. Sulpicius Galba, 69 BC. Veiled hd. of Vesta r., S C behind. Rev. Knife, simpulum and axe (emblems of the pontificate), ÆD or AE on l., CVR on r., P GALB in ex. RRC 406/1. CRR 838–9. RSC *Sulpicia* 6–7.   **VF** £65 ($104) / **EF** £185 ($296)
Galba strikes as curule aedile by special decree of the Senate.

346   347

346 — C. Hosidius C.f. Geta, 68 BC. Diad. and dr. bust of Diana r., bow and quiver over shoulder, GETA before, III VIR behind. Rev. Wild boar r., attacked by hound, usually pierced in shoulder by spear, C HOSIDI C F in ex. RRC 407/2. CRR 903, 903a. RSC *Hosidia* 1, 1a.
VF £60 ($96) / **EF** £175 ($280)

347 **Denarius serratus.** C. Hosidius C.f. Geta, 68 BC. Similar, but the hd. of Diana is not diad., and GETA is behind, III VIR before. RRC 407/1. CRR 904. RSC *Hosidia* 2, 2a.
VF £100 ($160) / **EF** £275 ($440)

348/1   348/2

348 **Denarius.** C. Calpurnius Piso L.f. Frugi, 67 BC. Hd. or bust of Apollo to r. or to l., hair sometimes tied with band, sometimes laur., rarely with bow and quiver or with caduceus over shoulder, control-mark behind. Rev. Naked horseman galloping to r. or to l., occasionally winged, sometimes wearing conical cap, Phrygian cap, causia or petasus, usually

holding palm-branch, torch, or whip, C PISO (or PIS) L F FRV (or FRVGI, or FRVG, or FR) or C PISO FRVGI below, usually with control-mark/s above and/or below. RRC 408/1. CRR 840–878. RSC *Calpurnia* 24–29a. RRM 7.1–4.   **VF** £50 ($80) / **EF** £150 ($240)
C. Piso Frugi was the son-in-law of Cicero to whose interests he was devoted. His coin types are the same as those of his father Lucius who had held the moneyer's office about 90 BC (see no. 235). Gaius' coinage, though much smaller in volume, is equally impressive in its complexity. Crawford's early date has been challenged on the basis of hoard evidence which would seem to indicate a period of issue closer to 60 BC.

349   350

349   **Denarius.** M. Plaetorius M.f. Cestianus, 67 BC. Helmeted and dr. bust of composite deity r., wearing wreath of laurel, corn, poppy and lotus, bow and quiver over shoulder, cornucopiae under chin, CESTIANVS behind, S C before, bead and reel border. Rev. M PLAETORIVS M F AED CVR, eagle stg. on thunderbolt, hd. l., bead and reel border. RRC 409/1. CRR 809. RSC *Plaetoria* 4.   **VF** £65 ($104) / **EF** £185 ($296)
Cestianus strikes as curule aedile by special decree of the Senate. He had earlier struck as moneyer (see nos. 340–44).

350   — — Turreted hd. of Cybele r., forepart of lion behind shoulders, globe under chin, CESTIANVS behind, bead and reel border. Rev. M PLAETORIVS AED CVR EX S C, curule chair, control-symbol on l., bead and reel border. RRC 409/2. CRR 808. RSC *Plaetoria* 3.
                          VF £65 ($104) / **EF** £185 ($296)

351   352

351   — Q. Pomponius Musa, 66 BC. Q POMPONI MVSA, diad. hd. of Apollo r. Rev. Hercules stg. r., playing lyre, club at feet, HERCVLES on r., MVSARVM on l. RRC 410/1. CRR 810. RSC *Pomponia* 8.   **VF** £175 ($280) / **EF** £425 ($680)
This and the following ten varieties comprise the most extensive series of denarii produced by a single Roman Republican moneyer.

352   — — Laur. hd. of Apollo r., lyre-key behind. Rev. Calliope (the Muse of Epic Poetry) stg. r., playing lyre set on column, Q POMPONI on r., MVSA on l. (sometimes reversed, with Q POMPONI on l. and MVSA on r.). RRC 410/2. CRR 811–12. RSC *Pomponia* 9–10.
                          VF £165 ($264) / **EF** £400 ($640)

353   354

353 **Denarius.** Q. Pomponius Musa, 66 BC. Similar, but with scroll tied with cord behind hd. of
     Apollo, and with rev. type Clio (the Muse of History) stg. l., holding open scroll and rest-
     ing elbow on column (Q POMPONI on r., MVSA on l.). RRC 410/3. CRR 813. RSC
     Pomponia 11.   **VF** £165 ($264) / **EF** £400 ($640)

354 — — Similar, but with sceptre behind hd. of Apollo, and with rev. type Melpomene (the
     Muse of Tragedy) stg. facing, looking r., holding club and tragic mask (Q POMPONI on r.,
     MVSA on l.). RRC 410/4. CRR 816. RSC *Pomponia* 14.
                                                       VF £165 ($264) / **EF** £400 ($640)

355   356

355 — — Similar, but with crossed flutes behind hd. of Apollo, and with rev. type Euterpe (the
     Muse of Lyric Poetry) stg. r., holding two flutes (*tibiae*) and resting elbow on column (Q
     POMPONI on l., MVSA on r.). RRC 410/5. CRR 815. RSC *Pomponia* 13.
                                                       VF £165 ($264) / **EF** £400 ($640)

356 — — Similar, but with flower on stalk behind hd. of Apollo, and with rev. type Erato (the
     Muse of Erotic Poetry) stg. r., hd. facing, playing lyre (Q POMPONI on l., MVSA on r.).
     RRC 410/6. CRR 814. RSC *Pomponia* 12.   **VF** £1,500 ($2,400) / **EF** £3,000 ($4,800)
     The reason for the extraordinary rarity of this type remains unexplained.

357   359

357 — — Similar, but with tortoise behind hd. of Apollo, and with rev. type Terpsichore (the
     Muse of Dancing) stg. r., holding plectrum and lyre (Q POMPONI on r., MVSA on l., some-
     times reversed). RRC 410/7a, c. CRR 819a, 820. RSC *Pomponia* 18, 18a.
                                                       VF £165 ($264) / **EF** £400 ($640)

358 **Denarius.** Q. Pomponius Musa, 66 BC. Similar, but with flower on stalk behind hd. of Apollo. RRC 410/7b, d. CRR 819, 820a. RSC *Pomponia* 17, 17a.

VF £165 ($264) / **EF** £400 ($640)

359 — — Similar, but with star behind hd. of Apollo, and with rev. type Urania (the Muse of Astronomy) stg. l., pointing with rod at globe on tripod-stand (Q POMPONI on r., MVSA on l.). RRC 410/8. CRR 823. RSC *Pomponia* 22.

VF £165 ($264) / **EF** £400 ($640)

360 361

360 — — Similar, but with sandal (*calceus*) behind hd. of Apollo, and with rev. type Thalia (the Muse of Comedy) stg. l., holding comic mask and resting l. elbow on column (Q POMPONI on r., MVSA on l., sometimes reversed). RRC 410/9b, c. CRR 821, 821a. RSC *Pomponia* 19–20. **VF** £165 ($264) / **EF** £400 ($640)
A rare variety shows Thalia also holding crook (pedum) in l. hand.

361 — — Similar, but with wreath behind hd. of Apollo, and with rev. type Polymnia (the Muse of Rhetoric) stg. facing in long flowing tunic, her hd. bound with wreath (Q POMPONI on r., MVSA on l., sometimes reversed). RRC 410/10. CRR 817–18. RSC *Pomponia* 15–16.

VF £165 ($264) / **EF** £400 ($640)

362 363

362 — L. Manlius Torquatus, 65 BC. Hd. of Sibyl r., wreathed with ivy, SIBYLLA (or SIBVLLA) below, sometimes all within wreath. Rev. Tripod surmounted by amphora between two stars, L TORQVAT on l., III VIR on r., all within torque. RRC 411/1. CRR 835–837a. RSC *Manlia* 11–12. RRM 8.1–2. **VF** £200 ($320) / **EF** £500 ($800)
Harlan (RRM) dates this rare issue to 59 BC and notes points of similarity to the coinage of C. Calpurnius Piso Frugi which he assigns to the same year.

363 **Denarius serratus.** L. Roscius Fabatus, 64 BC. Hd. of Juno Sospita r., clad in goat's skin, control-symbol behind, L ROSCI below. Rev. Maiden stg. r., feeding snake erect before her, control-symbol behind, FABATI in ex. RRC 412/1. CRR 915. RSC *Roscia* 3. RRM 3.1–2.

VF £60 ($96) / **EF** £175 ($280)
This extensive issue is assigned to 62 BC by Harlan on the basis of hoard evidence.

364   365

364 **Denarius.** L. Cassius Longinus, 63 BC. Veiled and diad. hd. of Vesta l., two-handled cup behind, control-letter before. Rev. Togate citizen stg. l., depositing ballot inscribed V in voting box, LONGIN III V behind. RRC 413/1. CRR 935. RSC *Cassia* 10. RRM 6.1–2.
VF £65 ($104) / **EF** £185 ($296)
An alternative date of 60 BC is proposed for this issue by Harlan, again on the evidence of hoard content. Interestingly, the control-letters on obv. spell out the moneyer's praenomen and nomen, L CASSI *(one* S *reversed).*

365 — L. Furius Cn. f. Brocchus, 63 BC. Dr. bust of Ceres r., wreathed with corn, barley-grain before, corn-ear behind, BROCCHI below, III – VIR across upper field. Rev. Curule chair between two fasces with axes, L FVRI / CN F above. RRC 414/1. CRR 902, 902a. RSC *Furia* 23, 23a.   VF £65 ($104) / **EF** £185 ($296)

366

366 — L. Aemilius Lepidus Paullus, 62 BC. PAVLLVS LEPIDVS CONCORDIA, veiled and diad. hd. of Concordia r. Rev. Togate figure of L. Aemilius Paullus stg. l., touching trophy to l. of which stand King Perseus of Macedon and his two sons as captives, TER above, PAVLLVS in ex. RRC 415/1. CRR 926. RSC *Aemilia* 10. RRM 1.1, 1.3.   VF £55 ($88) / **EF** £160 ($256)
This moneyer was the elder brother of the later triumvir M. Aemilius Lepidus. Harlan dates his extensive issue to 63 BC.

367   368

367 — L. Scribonius Libo, 62 BC. Diad. hd. of Bonus Eventus r., BON EVENT before, LIBO behind. Rev. The Puteal Scribonianum, ornamented with garland between two lyres and hammer (sometimes tongs or anvil) at base, PVTEAL above, SCRIBON below. RRC 416/1. CRR 928. RSC *Scribonia* 8–8b. RRM 2.2–3.   VF £55 ($88) / **EF** £160 ($256)

This small enclosure in the Roman Forum was originally built to protect a sacred spot said to have been struck by lightning. Later, it became the haunt of moneylenders, hence the appearance of various coining implements at the base of the monument (cf. Harlan, pp. 11–13, who dates the issue to 63 BC). The remains of the Puteal Scribonianum were discovered during excavations in 1950.

368   **Denarius.** L. Aemilius Lepidus Paullus and L. Scribonius Libo, 62 BC. Obv. Similar to 366, but CONCORD for CONCORDIA. Rev. Similar to previous, but with PVTEAL SCRIBON above and LIBO below (hammer or tongs at base). RRC 417/1. CRR 927. RSC *Aemilia* 11, 11a. RRM 1.4, 2.1.   **VF** £75 ($120) / **EF** £210 ($336)

369   370

369   — M. Pupius Piso M.f. Frugi, 61 BC. Statue of Mercury as a herm between wreath and two-handled cup. Rev. Sacrificial knife and patera, M PISO M F / FRVGI above, all within laurel-wreath. RRC 418/1. CRR 826. RSC *Calpurnia* 22. RRM 4.2–3.
                                          VF £300 ($480) / **EF** £750 ($1,200)
This moneyer's father, the consul of 61 BC, was originally of the Calpurnia gens but was adopted by a Marcus Pupius whose praenomen and nomen he adopted.

370   — — Similar, but with obv. type bust of Mercury as a herm r., wearing winged diadem, wreath (sometimes with star) behind, two-handled cup before. RRC 418/2. CRR 824–5. RSC *Calpurnia* 23, 23a. RRM 4.1, 4.3.   **VF** £250 ($400) / **EF** £600 ($960)

371   372

371   — M. Aemilius Lepidus, 61 BC. Diad. (or laur. and diad.) hd. of Roma (?) r., sometimes with palm-branch behind, sometimes with simpulum (or two-handled cup) below chin and wreath behind. Rev. M LEPIDVS below equestrian statue of M. Aemilius Lepidus (consul 187 and 175 BC) r., carrying trophy. RRC 419/1. CRR 827–828b. RSC *Aemilia* 20–21b. RRM 5.1, 5.3.   **VF** £90 ($144) / **EF** £250 ($400)
This moneyer later became pontifex maximus in succession to Julius Caesar and in 43 BC formed the Second Triumvirate with Mark Antony and Octavian. For his later coinage, see nos. 1498–1500 and 1521–3.

372   — — Similar, but with additional legend AN XV PR H O C S encircling the equestrian statue on rev. RRC 419/1. CRR 829–830c. RSC *Aemilia* 22–22d. RRM 5.2–3.
                                          VF £100 ($160) / **EF** £275 ($440)

373   374

373   **Denarius.** M. Aemilius Lepidus, 61 BC. Turreted hd. of Alexandria r., **ALEXANDRIA** (or **ALEXSANDREA**) below. Rev. Togate figure of M. Aemilius Lepidus (consul 187 and 175 BC) stg. l., crowning shorter figure of Ptolemy V of Egypt stg. facing, holding sceptre, **M LEPIDVS** in ex., **PONTIF MAX** (**NTIF** in monogram) on r., **TVTOR REG** on l., **S C** above. RRC 419/2. CRR 831–2. RSC *Aemilia* 23–4. RRM 5.6–7.   **VF** £400 ($640) / **EF** £950 ($1,520) *Although nos. 373 and 374 are usually assigned to the period of Lepidus' tenure of the moneyer's office (61 BC) Harlan considers them to be later. This type he dates to 56 BC, associating it with contemporary events in Egypt where the deposed Ptolemy XII Auletes was attempting to regain his throne with Roman help.*

374   — — Laur. and veiled hd. of the vestal virgin Aemilia r., sometimes with simpulum below chin and wreath behind. Rev. View of the Basilica Aemilia et Fulvia, depicted as a two-storied structure with row of shields attached to the columns, **AIMILIA** above, **REF** on l., **S C** on r., **M LEPIDVS** in ex. RRC 419/3. CRR 833–4. RSC *Aemilia* 25–6. RRM 5.4–5.
                                             VF £500 ($800) / **EF** £1,100 ($1,760) *This celebrated structure, the fragmentary remains of which are still visible on the north side of the Forum Romanum, underwent a major renovation beginning in 55 BC and extending over a period of two decades. Harlan believes this coin was issued in 54 BC, just after M. Lepidus' brother Paullus began the refurbishment.*

375   376

375   P. Plautius Hypsaeus, 60 BC. Hd. of Neptune r., trident behind, **P YPSAE S C** before. Rev. Jupiter in quadriga l., brandishing thunderbolt, sometimes with scorpion below horses, **C YPSAE COS / PRIV** in ex., **CEPIT** on r. RRC 420/1. CRR 910, 910a. RSC *Plautia* 11, 11a. RRM 11.1, 11.4.   **VF** £85 ($136) / **EF** £240 ($384) *Hoard evidence now points to this type being later in date than Hypsaeus' joint issue with Scaurus (see nos. 378–9) and Harlan attributes it to 57 BC. The reverse records the capture of Privernum in 329 BC by the consul C. Plautius Decianus who, by a piece of blatant deception on the part of the moneyer, has been transformed into a C. Plautius Hypsaeus.*

376   — — Similar, but with obv. type dr. bust of Leuconoe r., her bejewelled hair bound with triple band, dolphin behind, **P YPSAE S C** before (the **S C** sometimes behind). RRC 420/2. CRR 911–911c. RSC *Plautia* 12–12c. RRM 11.2, 11.4.   **VF** £85 ($136) / **EF** £240 ($384)

377

377 **Denarius.** M. Nonius Sufenas, 59 BC. Hd. of Saturn r., harpa, conical stone and **S C** behind, **SVFENAS** before. Rev. Roma seated l. on pile of arms, holding spear, crowned by Victory stg. l. behind her, **SEX NONI** in ex., **PR L V P F** around. RRC 421/1. CRR 885. RSC *Nonia 1*. RRM 13.1–2.   **VF** £70 ($112) / **EF** £200 ($320)
Harlan dates this issue to 57 BC, again on the evidence of hoard content. The praetor Sextus Nonius Sufenas, nephew of Sulla, is celebrated on the reverse as the initiator of the Victory Games in 81 BC.

378   379

378 — M. Aemilius Scaurus and P. Plautius Hypsaeus, 58 BC. King Aretas of Nabataea, in atti-tude of supplication, kneeling r. beside camel, presenting olive-branch, **M SCAVR** above, **EX – S C** in field, **AED CVR** in ex. Rev. Jupiter in quadriga l., brandishing thunderbolt, **P HVPSAEVS AED CVR** above, **C HVPSAE COS / PREIVER** in ex., **CAPTVM** on r. RRC 422/1a. CRR 912. RSC *Aemilia 9*. RRM 10.2.   **VF** £75 ($120) / **EF** £210 ($336)
There are many minor variations of the legends on the extensive coinage represented by this type and the next.

379 — — Similar, but on obv. **M SCAVR / AED CVR** above camel, **EX – S C** in field, and **REX ARETAS** in ex.; and on rev., scorpion below horses. RRC 422/1b. CRR 913. RSC *Aemilia 8*. RRM 10.1, 11.3.   **VF** £50 ($80) / **EF** £150 ($240)
The precise date of the curule aedileship of Scaurus and Hypsaeus has been recorded, pro-viding a valuable fixed point in the chronology of the later Republican coinage. The remarkable obv. type commemorates the surrender in 62 BC of Aretas III, king of the Nabataean Arabs, to Scaurus himself, the first instance of a moneyer publicizing an event from his own career on the coinage.

380/1   380/2

380   **Denarius.** C. Servilius C.f., 57 BC. Hd. of Flora r., wreathed with flowers, FLORAL PRIMVS
      (AL and MV in monogram) before, lituus behind. Rev. Two soldiers stg. face to face, pre-
      senting swords (rarely with swords crossed), each holding shield, C SERVEIL (RVE in mono-
      gram) in ex., C F on r. RRC 423/1. CRR 890, 890a. RSC *Servilia* 15, 15a. RRM 25.1–3.
      VF £85 ($136) / **EF** £240 ($384)
      Harlan dates this enigmatic issue considerably later (circa 52 BC).

381   382

381   — C. Considius Nonianus, 57 BC. Dr. bust of Venus Erycina r., laur. and diad., C CONSIDI
      NONIANI behind, S C before. Rev. View of the temple of Venus Erycina on rocky promi-
      nence with ERVC at base, circuit of city walls in foreground showing gateway at centre and
      two towers. RRC 424/1. CRR 886–8. RSC *Considia* 1–1b. RRM 14.1–2.
      VF £185 ($296) / **EF** £450 ($720)
      *It would seem that the traditional identification of this temple as the celebrated sanctuary
      of Venus at Eryx in Sicily, a legendary foundation of Aeneas, should be abandoned in
      favour of its counterpart built just outside the Colline Gate, scene of the famous Sullan vic-
      tory in 83 BC. The walls and gateway would then be those of Rome itself, built about 378
      BC though customarily assigned to King Servius Tullius (cf. RRM, pp. 92–3).*

382   — L. Marcius Philippus, 56 BC. Diad. hd. of King Ancus Marcius r., lituus behind, ANCVS
      below. Rev. Aqueduct (the Aqua Marcia) represented as an arcade of five arches sur-
      mounted by equestrian statue r., AQVA MAR (or similar, MAR usually in monogram)
      within the arches, PHILIPPVS on l. RRC 425/1. CRR 919–919c. RSC *Marcia* 28–29c. RRM
      15.1–2.   VF £60 ($96) / **EF** £175 ($280)
      *This moneyer was the step-brother of the young Gaius Octavius (later the Emperor
      Augustus) who was just seven years of age at the time of this issue. The reverse commemo-
      rates the construction in 144 BC of the Aqua Marcia by Q. Marcius Rex, whose statue
      appears above the aqueduct.*

383   384

383   — Faustus Cornelius Sulla, 56 BC. Diad. and dr. bust of Diana r., crescent above, lituus
      behind, FAVSTVS before. Rev. Sulla seated l. between King Bocchus of Mauretania, who
      kneels r. before him, presenting olive-branch, and King Jugurtha of Numidia, who kneels l.
      behind, his hands bound, FELIX on r. RRC 426/1. CRR 879. RSC *Cornelia* 59. RRM
      16.1–2.   VF £250 ($400) / **EF** £600 ($960)
      *Faustus was the son of L. Cornelius Sulla. This remarkable reverse type reproduces the
      device engraved on the dictator's signet ring which commemorated the pivotal event in his*

146   ROMAN REPUBLIC

early career – the betrayal of Jugurtha by his father-in-law Bocchus at Sulla's instigation.
Harlan dates the issues of Faustus as moneyer to 55 BC and those struck ex senatus con-
sulto (see nos. 385–6) to the following year.

384   **Denarius.** Faustus Cornelius Sulla, 56 BC. Diad. bust of beardless Hercules r., his shoulders wrapped in lion's skin, FEELIX behind. Rev. Diana in biga r., holding lituus, stars in
field above and below horses, FAVSTVS below. RRC 426/2. CRR 880–881a. RSC *Cornelia*
60–60b. RRM 16.3–4.   **VF** £150 ($240) / **EF** £375 ($600)

385   386

385   —— Hd. of young Hercules r., clad in lion's skin, S C behind, sometimes accompanied by
FAVSTVS monogram. Rev. Globe surrounded by four wreaths, aplustre and ear of corn in
lower field. RRC 426/4. CRR 882–3. RSC *Cornelia* 61–2. RRM 16.5–6.
                                               VF £100 ($160) / **EF** £275 ($440)
The reverse type commemorates the three triumphs celebrated by Faustus' father-in-law
Pompey the Great, the fourth wreath being his corona aurea awarded in 63 BC.

386   —— Laur., diad. and dr. bust of Venus r., sceptre over shoulder, S C behind. Rev. Three
trophies between jug and lituus, monogram of FAVSTVS in ex. RRC 426/3. CRR 884. RSC
Cornelia 63. RRM 16.7–8.   **VF** £110 ($176) / **EF** £300 ($480)
Three trophies were engraved on the signet ring of Pompey the Great symbolizing his vic-
tories on three continents.

387   388

387   — C. Memmius C.f., 56 BC. Hd. of Ceres r., wreathed with corn, C MEMMI C F before. Rev.
Naked captive kneeling r. at foot of trophy, C MEMMIVS on r., IMPERATOR on l. RRC
427/1. CRR 920. RSC *Memmia* 10. RRM 12.1, 12.5.   **VF** £85 ($136) / **EF** £240 ($384)
Harlan prefers to date this issue to 57 BC. The identity of the imperator Memmius and the
nature of his deeds remain uncertain.

388   —— Laur. hd. of Quirinus r., his long beard in formal ringlets, QVIRINVS behind,
C MEMMI C F before. Rev. MEMMIVS AED CERIALIA PREIMVS FECIT, Ceres seated r., holding
corn-ears and torch, snake at her feet. RRC 427/2. CRR 921. RSC *Memmia* 9. RRM
12.3–4.   **VF** £90 ($144) / **EF** £250 ($400)
The initial staging of the games of Ceres by the aedile Memmius, commemorated on the
reverse, is an event unrecorded in history but presumably predating 210 BC.

389   390

389   **Denarius.** Q. Cassius Longinus, 55 BC. Diad. and veiled hd. of Vesta r., **VEST** (or **VESTA**) before, **Q CASSIVS** behind. Rev. Circular temple of Vesta containing curule chair, voting-urn on l., tablet inscribed **A C** on r. RRC 428/1. CRR 917, 917a. RSC *Cassia* 9, 9a. RRM 23.2–3.   **VF** £90 ($144) / **EF** £250 ($400)
      The celebrated temple of Vesta stood in the Roman Forum and its fragmentary remains are still visible there today. Harlan believes this moneyer's coinage belongs to 53 BC.

390   — — Similar, but with obv. type hd. of Libertas r., **LIBERT** behind, **Q CASSIVS** before. RRC 428/2. CRR 918. RSC *Cassia* 8. RRM 23.2, 23.4.   **VF** £85 ($136) / **EF** £240 ($384)

391

391   — — Young beardless male hd. (Genius of the Roman People?) r., sceptre over shoulder. Rev. Eagle stg. r. on thunderbolt, between lituus and jug, **Q CASSIVS** below. RRC 428/3. CRR 916. RSC *Cassia* 7. RRM 23.5–6.   **VF** £60 ($96) / **EF** £175 ($280)

392   393

392   — P. Fonteius P.f. Capito, 55 BC. **P FONTEIVS P F CAPITO III VIR**, helmeted and dr. bust of Mars r., trophy over shoulder. Rev. **MN FONT TR MIL** (**MN** and **NT** in monogram), horseman galloping r., about to spear warrior below who is attacking a third, disarmed, combatant. RRC 429/1. CRR 900. RSC *Fonteia* 17. RRM 21.1–2.   **VF** £70 ($112) / **EF** £200 ($320)
      Harlan prefers 54 BC for the issues of this moneyer.

393   — — **P FONTEIVS** (**NT** sometimes in monogram) **CAPITO III VIR CONCORDIA**, veiled and diad. hd. of Concordia r. Rev. View of the Villa Publica depicted as a two-storied structure, each level fronted by a row of columns, the lower ones surmounted by arches (sometimes

148   ROMAN REPUBLIC

with iron gratings closing the entrances), the upper storey with sloping roof, T DIDI on l., IMP below, VIL PVB on r. RRC 429/2. CRR 901, 901a. RSC *Didia* 1, 1a. RRM 21.3–5.

VF £200 ($320) / **EF** £500 ($800)
The Villa Publica was situated in the Campus Martius and no trace of the structure is visible today. Originally dating from the 5th century BC the building served a variety of purposes, including the reception of foreign ambassadors. One of its restorations was by T. Didius (consul 98 BC), hence the accompanying legend.

394   395

394 **Denarius.** P. Licinius M.f. Crassus, 55 BC. Laur. and diad. hd. of Venus r., S C behind. Rev. P CRASSVS M F, female figure (Roma?) stg. facing, holding spear and leading horse by bridle, cuirass and shield at her feet. RRC 430/1. CRR 929. RSC *Licinia* 18. RRM 19.1–2.

VF £90 ($144) / **EF** £250 ($400)
This moneyer was the son of the triumvir M. Licinius Crassus whose death, during his invasion of Parthia in 53 BC, hastened the outbreak of civil war between Caesar and Pompey. Publius accompanied his father on the eastern campaign and shared his fate.

395 — A. Plautius, 55 BC. Turreted hd. of Cybele r., A PLAVTIVS before, AED CVR S C behind. Rev. 'Bacchius the Jew' (= Aristobulus of Judaea?), in attitude of supplication, kneeling r. beside camel, presenting olive-branch, BACCHIVS in ex., IVDAEVS on r. RRC 431/1. CRR 932. RSC *Plautia* 13. RRM 18.1–2.   **VF** £80 ($128) / **EF** £225 ($360)
Aulus Plautius strikes as curule aedile. The problematic interpretation of the reverse type appears to have been most successfully resolved by Harlan in RRM (pp. 116–18) who identifies the kneeling figure as Aristobulus, the Jewish high priest, then held captive by Pompey in Rome.

396

396 — Cn. Plancius, 55 BC. Hd. of Macedonia r., wearing causia, CN PLANCIVS before, AED CVR S C behind. Rev. Cretan goat stg. r., bow and quiver behind. RRC 432/1. CRR 933. RSC *Plancia* 1. RRM 17.1–2.   **VF** £70 ($112) / **EF** £200 ($320)
Gnaeus Plancius, a friend of Cicero, strikes as curule aedile. The types recall his military service in Crete, under the proconsul Q. Metellus, and in Macedonia as military tribune under C. Antonius. He later returned to Macedonia as quaestor under the propraetor L. Appuleius Saturninus.

397 398

397 **Denarius.** Q. Servilius Caepio Brutus (= M. Junius Brutus), 54 BC. Hd. of Libertas r., LIBERTAS behind. Rev. L. Junius Brutus (consul 509 BC) walking in procession l. between two lictors, preceded by an accensus, BRVTVS in ex. RRC 433/1. CRR 906. RSC *Junia* 31. RRM 20.1–2. **VF £100 ($165) / EF £275 ($440)**
The most famous of Caesar's assassins in 44 BC M. Junius Brutus lost his father while still a young boy and was adopted by his uncle, Q. Servilius Caepio, thus changing his name to Q. Caepio Brutus. His coin types refer to his illustrious ancestry and his patriotic devotion to the freedom of the Republic. For his later coinage as proconsul and imperator, inluding several portrait types, see nos. 1428–41.

398 —— Bare hd. of L. Junius Brutus (consul 509 BC), bearded, r., BRVTVS behind. Rev. Bare hd. of C. Servilius Ahala (master of horse 439 BC), bearded, r., AHALA behind. RRC 433/2. CRR 907. RSC *Junia* 30. RRM 20.3–4. **VF £165 ($264) / EF £450 ($720)**

399 400

399 —— Q. Pompeius Rufus, 54 BC. Bare hd. of the dictator L. Cornelius Sulla (consul 88 BC) r., SVLLA COS before. Rev. Bare hd. of Q. Pompeius Rufus (consul 88 BC) r., RVFVS COS behind, Q POM RVFI before. RRC 434/1. CRR 908. RSC *Pompeia* 4. RRM 9.1–2.
VF £400 ($640) / EF £1,100 ($1,760)
The moneyer here honours his two grandfathers, coincidentally both consul in the same year (88 BC). This type provides us with the only authentic portrait of the famous dictator to survive from antiquity. Harlan believes the issue should be dated earlier, to circa 58 BC.

400 —— Curule chair between arrow and laurel-branch, Q POMPEI Q F / RVFVS above, COS on tablet below. Rev. Curule chair between lituus and wreath, SVLLA COS above, Q POMPEI RVF on tablet below. RRC 434/2. CRR 909. RSC *Pompeia* 5. RRM 9.3–4.
VF £65 ($104) / EF £185 ($296)

401 —— M. Valerius Messalla, 53 BC. Undraped bust of Roma r., viewed from behind, wearing crested Corinthian helmet, spear over shoulder, MESSAL F (AL in monogram) before. Rev. Curule chair, PATRE COS (TR in monogram) above, S – C in field, sceptre with diadem below. RRC 435/1. CRR 934. RSC *Valeria* 13. RRM 24.1–2.
VF £650 ($1,040) / EF £1,400 ($2,240)
The rev. legend would appear to refer to M. Valerius Messalla Rufus, the moneyer's father and one of the consuls for 53 BC.

401   402

402 **Denarius.** L. Vinicius, 52 BC. Laur. hd. of Concordia r., **CONCORDIAE** (or **CONCORDIAI**) before. Rev. Victory flying r., holding palm-branch to which are attached four wreaths, **L VINICI** before. RRC 436/1. CRR 930, 930a. RSC *Vinicia* 1, 1a. RRM 22.1–2.
VF £225 ($360) / **EF** £550 ($880)
Harlan prefers to date this issue to the preceding year.

403   404

403 — C. Coelius Caldus, 51 BC. Bare hd. of C. Coelius Caldus (consul 94 BC) r., **C COEL CALDVS** before, **COS** below, voting tablet inscribed **L D** behind. Rev. Rad. hd. of Sol r., **CALDVS III VIR** before, circular shield below chin, oval shield (sometimes with **S** above) behind. RRC 437/1a, b. CRR 891–2. RSC *Coelia* 4–5. RRM 26.1, 26.6.
VF £250 ($400) / **EF** £600 ($960)

404 — — Obv. Similar, but with vexillum inscribed **HIS** behind and standard in form of boar below chin (sometimes reversed, with vexillum below chin and boar behind). Rev. Figure of L. Caldus behind table inscribed **L CALDVS / VII VIR EPVL** (VIR and VL in monogram), preparing the feast of Jupiter, flanked by trophy with circular shield on l., and trophy with trumpet and oval shield on r., **C CALDVS** (downward) on l., **I/MP A** (or **AV** in monogram) / **X** on r., **CALDVS III VIR** (**ALD** in monogram) below. RRC 437/2a, 3a. CRR 894, 896. RSC *Coelia* 7, 8. RRM 26.2, 26.5.
VF £225 ($360) / **EF** £550 ($880)

405 — — Similar, but on obv. with trumpet and spear behind hd. and vexillum below chin. RRC 437/4a. CRR 898. RSC *Coelia* 11. RRM 26.3, 26.5.
VF £225 ($360) / **EF** £550 ($880)

406   408

406 — — Similar, but on rev. the trophy with trumpet and oval shield and the inscription **I/M/P / A / X** are on l. of table, and the trophy with circular shield and the inscription **C CALDVS** are on r. RRC 437/4b. CRR 899. RSC *Coelia* 12. RRM 26.3–4.
VF £275 ($440) / **EF** £650 ($1,040)

407 **Denarius.** C. Coelius Caldus, 51 BC. Similar, but with obv. as 404. RRC 437/2b, 3b. CRR 895, 897. RSC *Coelia* 9, 10. RRM 26.2, 26.4. **VF** £275 ($440) / **EF** £650 ($1,040)

408 — Servius Sulpicius, 51 BC. Laur. beardless hd. (Triumphus?) r., SER behind, SVLP (VL in monogram) before. Rev. Naval trophy between naked bound captive stg. on r., point of spear above his hd., and clothed figure wearing petasus on l. RRC 438/1. CRR 931. RSC *Sulpicia* 8. RRM 27.1–2. **VF** £350 ($560) / **EF** £850 ($1,360) *The anepigraphic rev. type would appear to depict the auction of captives following a naval victory.*

409   411

409 — P. Cornelius Lentulus Marcellinus, 50 BC. Bare hd. of M. Claudius Marcellus (consul 222 BC) r., triskeles behind, MARCELLINVS before. Rev. Togate figure of M. Claudius Marcellus advancing r., carrying trophy (*spolia opima*) into tetrastyle temple of Jupiter Feretrius, MARCELLVS on r., COS QVINC on l. RRC 439/1. CRR 1147. RSC *Claudia* 11. RRM 29.1–2. **VF** £275 ($440) / **EF** £650 ($1,040) *Harlan prefers to date this issue to the following year, after the outbreak of the civil war between Caesar and Pompey.*

410 — Q. Sicinius, 49 BC. FORT P R, diad. hd. of Fortuna Populi Romani r. Rev. Palm-branch and caduceus in saltire, wreath above, Q SICINIVS below, III – VIR in field. RRC 440/1. CRR 938. RSC *Sicinia* 5. RRM 30.1–2. CRI 1. **VF** £90 ($144) / **EF** £275 ($440) *See also no. 413.*

411 — Cn. Nerius, 49 BC. Bearded hd. of Saturn r., harpa over shoulder, NERI Q VRB (NE and VR in monogram) before. Rev. Legionary eagle between two standards, L LENT (NT in monogram) on l., C MARC (MA in monogram) on r., COS below. RRC 441/1. CRR 937. RSC *Neria* 1. CRI 2. **VF** £110 ($176) / **EF** £325 ($520) *Nerius strikes as quaestor urbanus and names the two consuls for 49 BC on rev. See also nos. 414–16.*

412   413

412 — Mn. Acilius Glabrio, 49 BC. Laur. hd. of Salus r., SALVTIS behind. Rev. MN ACILIVS III VIR VALETV (MN and TV in monogram), Valetudo stg. l., holding snake and resting on column. RRC 442/1. CRR 922. RSC *Acilia* 8, 8a. RRM 28.1–2. CRI 16, 16a. **VF** £50 ($80) / **EF** £160 ($256)

Harlan prefers to date this issue to the preceding year, prior to Caesar's invasion of Italy, but the huge volume of the coinage would be more appropriate to the circumstances of the civil war.

413   **Denarius.** Q. Sicinius and C. Coponius, 49 BC. Q SICINIVS III VIR, diad. hd. of Apollo r. (rarely l.), star below. Rev. C COPONIVS PR S C, club draped with lion's skin, hd. r. (rarely facing), between arrow and bow. RRC 444/1. CRR 939–40. RSC *Sicinia* 1–2, 4. CRI 3–3b.
                                VF £85 ($136) / **EF** £250 ($400)
Sicinius now strikes as a moneyer in exile in the East, having fled Italy with Pompey following Caesar's invasion. The praetor Coponius commanded the Pompeian fleet.

414   415

414   — L. Cornelius Lentulus and C. Claudius Marcellus, 49 BC. Triskeles, with hd. of Medusa at centre and corn-ears between the legs. Rev. Jupiter stg. r., holding thunderbolt and eagle, LENT MAR (NT and MAR in monogram) on l., COS and harpa r. RRC 445/1. CRR 1029a. RSC *Cornelia* 64. CRI 4.   **VF** £140 ($224) / **EF** £350 ($560)
The exiled consuls for 49 BC here strike in support of Pompey. See also nos. 415–16.

415   — — L LENT C MARC COS (NT and MA in monogram), hd. of Apollo r. Rev Jupiter stg. r., holding thunderbolt and eagle, altar at feet, star and Q on l. RRC 445/2. CRR 1030. RSC *Cornelia* 65. CRI 5.   **VF** £150 ($240) / **EF** £375 ($600)

416

416   — — Hd. of Jupiter r., with long beard. Rev. Cultus-statue of the Ephesian Artemis facing, L LENTVLVS on r., MAR COS (MAR in monogram) or C MARC COS on l. RRC 445/3. CRR 1031, 1031b. RSC *Cornelia* 66, 67a. CRI 6.   **VF** £700 ($1,120) / **EF** £1,500 ($2,400)

417   — L. Hostilius Saserna, 48 BC. Diad. female hd. (Clementia?) r., wreathed with oak. Rev. L HOSTILIVS SASERNA, Victory advancing r., holding caduceus and trophy. RRC 448/1. CRR 951. RSC *Hostilia* 5. CRI 17.   **VF** £85 ($136) / **EF** £250 ($400)

418   — — Hd. of captive Gallic warrior r., chain around neck, shield behind. Rev. Naked Gallic warrior in biga driven r. by charioteer, L HOSTILIVS above, SASERN below. RRC 448/2. CRR 952. RSC *Hostilia* 2. CRI 18.   **VF** £550 ($880) / **EF** £1,250 ($2,000)
The frequent identification of the head as that of the celebrated chieftain Vercingetorix must be regarded as highly conjectural.

418 419

419 **Denarius.** L. Hostilius Saserna, 48 BC. Hd. of female Gallic captive r., with dishevelled hair, carnyx behind. Rev. L HOSTILIVS SASERNA, cultus-statue of Diana (Artemis) facing, with stag and spear. RRC 448/3. CRR 953. RSC *Hostilia* 4. CRI 19.
VF £110 ($176) / **EF** £325 ($520)

420 422

420 — C. Vibius C.f. C.n. Pansa, 48 BC. Mask of bearded Pan r., PANSA below (sometimes with pedum or syrinx behind). Rev. C VIBIVS C F C N IOVIS AXVR, Jupiter Anxurus seated l., holding patera and sceptre. RRC 449/1. CRR 947–948a. RSC *Vibia* 18–19a. CRI 20–20b. **VF** £75 ($120) / **EF** £225 ($360)

421 — — Hd. of young Bacchus or Liber r., wreathed with ivy, PANSA behind. Rev. C VIBIVS C F C N, Ceres advancing r., holding torch in each hand, plough before. RRC 449/2. CRR 946. RSC *Vibia* 16. CRI 21. **VF** £90 ($144) / **EF** £275 ($440)

422 — — Similar, but with rev. type Ceres in chariot drawn r. by two snakes, holding torch. RRC 449/3. CRR 945. RSC*Vibia* 17, 17a. CRI 22, 22a. **VF** £125 ($200) / **EF** £350 ($560)

423 426

423 — — Laur. hd. of Libertas r., LIBERTATIS behind. Rev. C PANSA C F C N, Roma seated r. on pile of arms, resting on sceptre, crowned by Victory flying l. RRC 449/4. CRR 949. RSC *Vibia* 20. CRI 23. **VF** £175 ($280) / **EF** £450 ($720)

424 **Sestertius.** C. Vibius C.f. C.n. Pansa, 48 BC. Laur. and dr. bust of Mercury r., with winged diadem. Rev. Tortoise, C PANSA on l., caduceus on r. RRC 449/5. CRR 950. RSC *Vibia* 21. CRI 24. **F** £450 ($720) / **VF** £1,000 ($1,600)
The first issue of this denomination in over 40 years, the silver sestertius was to enjoy a brief revival under the Caesarian moneyers at Rome down to 44 BC.

425   **Denarius.** C. Vibius C.f. C.n. Pansa and D. Junius Brutus Albinus, 48 BC. Mask of bearded Pan r., C PANSA below. Rev. ALBINVS BRVTI F, clasped hands holding winged caduceus. RRC 451/1. CRR 944. RSC *Vibia* 22. CRI 28.   **VF** £125 ($200) / **EF** £350 ($560)

426   — D. Junius Brutus Albinus, 48 BC. Helmeted hd. of young Mars r. Rev. ALBINVS BRVTI F, two carnyces in saltire, oval shield above, round shield below. RRC 450/1. CRR 941. RSC *Postumia* 11. CRI 25.   **VF** £100 ($160) / **EF** £300 ($480) *Born Decimus Junius Brutus, this moneyer was later adopted into the Postumia gens and changed his name to Decimus Postumius Albinus, though he still styled himself Bruti filius, 'son of Brutus'. He was to be one of the assassins of Caesar on the Ides of March, 44 BC.*

427   427   428

427   — — Hd. of Pietas r., PIETAS behind. Rev. ALBINVS BRVTI F, clasped hands holding winged caduceus. RRC 450/2. CRR 942. RSC *Postumia* 10. CRI 26.   **VF** £90 ($144) / **EF** £275 ($440)

428   — — A POSTVMIVS COS, bare hd. of the consul A. Postumius Albinus r. Rev. ALBINV (or ALBINVS or ALBIN) / BRVTI F in two lines within wreath of corn-ears. RRC 450/3. CRR 943–943b. RSC *Postumia* 13–14a. CRI 27.   **VF** £110 ($176) / **EF** £325 ($520) *The precise identity of the portrait head is uncertain, the consuls of 151 BC and 99 BC being the principal candidates.*

            429   430

429   — L. Plautius Plancus, 47 BC. Hd. of Medusa facing, sometimes flanked by coiled snakes, L PLAVTIVS (or PLAVTIV) below. Rev. Victory facing, her wings spread, conducting four rearing horses, PLANCVS (or PLANCV) below. RRC 453/1. CRR 959–959b. RSC *Plautia* 14–15c. CRI 29, 29a.   **VF** £85 ($136) / **EF** £250 ($400)

430   — A. Licinius Nerva, 47 BC. Laur. hd. of Fides r., FIDES before, NERVA behind. Rev. One-armed horseman galloping r., dragging naked warrior by the hair, A LICINI (or similar) below, III – VIR in field. RRC 454/1–2. CRR 954–5. RSC *Licinia* 23–24c. CRI 30, 30a.   **VF** £110 ($176) / **EF** £325 ($520) *A scarcer variety has A LICINIVS behind the hd. of Fides and NERVA below the horseman.*

431 **Quinarius.** A. Licinius Nerva, 47 BC. Hd. of Minerva r., in crested Corinthian helmet, NERVA behind. Rev. Victory advancing r., A LICINI (or LICINIV) before. RRC 454/3. CRR 956, 956a. RSC *Licinia* 25, 25a. CRI 31. **F** £175 ($280) / **VF** £400 ($640)
The half-denarius here reappears in the moneyers' coinage for the first time in almost 35 years. Unlike the silver sestertius it survived Caesar's downfall in 44 BC, but was only struck sporadically and never formed part of the regular monetary system.

432 **Sestertius.** A. Licinius Nerva, 47 BC. Laur. hd. of Apollo r., NERVA behind. Rev. Victory advancing r., A LICINI (or LICIN) before. RRC 454/4. CRR 957. RSC *Licinia* 26. CRI 32.
F £350 ($560) / **VF** £800 ($1,280)

433 — — Similar, but with rev. type horseman galloping r., holding whip, A LICINI below. RRC 454/5. CRR 958. RSC *Licinia* 27. CRI 33. **F** £400 ($640) / **VF** £900 ($1,440)

434

434 **Denarius.** C. Antius C.f. Restio, 47 BC. Bare hd. of C. Antius Restio (tribune of the plebs 68 BC) r., RESTIO behind. Rev. C ANTIVS C F, naked Hercules advancing r., brandishing club and holding trophy. RRC 455/1. CRR 970. RSC *Antia* 1. CRI 34.
VF £200 ($320) / **EF** £550 ($880)
The obv. portrait is a depiction of the moneyer's father.

435 — — Similar, but with obv. type conjoined diad. hds. of the Dei Penates r., DEI PENATES around. RRC 455/2. CRR 971. RSC *Antia* 2. CRI 35. **VF** £175 ($280) / **EF** £450 ($720)

436 **Quinarius.** C. Antius C.f. Restio, 47 BC. Diad. hd. of Diana r., bow and quiver over shoulder, C ANTIVS behind. Rev. Stag stg. r., RESTIO before. RRC 455/3. CRR 972. RSC *Antia* 3. CRI 36. **F** £150 ($240) / **VF** £350 ($560)

437 **Sestertius.** C. Antius C.f. Restio, 47 BC. Ox's hd. facing, C ANTIVS below. Rev. Lighted altar, RES—TIO in field. RRC 455/4. CRR 973. RSC *Antia* 4. CRI 37.
F £300 ($480) / **VF** £700 ($1,120)

438 — — Similar, but with obv. type bust of Mercury r., in winged petasus, caduceus over shoulder, C ANTIVS behind. RRC 455/5. CRR 974. RSC *Antia* 5. CRI 38.
F £400 ($640) / **VF** £900 ($1,440)

439 — — C ANTIVS, crested Corinthian helmet r. Rev. RESTIO, owl stg. on shield. RRC 455/6. CRR 975. RSC *Antia* 6. CRI 39. **F** £350 ($560) / **VF** £800 ($1,280)

440 **Denarius.** Mn. Cordius Rufus, 46 BC. RVFVS III VIR, conjoined hds. of the Dioscuri r., wearing pilei surmounted by stars. Rev. MN CORDIVS (or similar, MN in monogram), Venus stg. l., holding scales and sceptre, Cupid at shoulder. RRC 463/1. CRR 976–976c. RSC *Cordia* 1–2c. CRI 63, 63a. **VF** £60 ($96) / **EF** £175 ($280)

440   441

441   **Denarius.** Mn. Cordius Rufus, 46 BC. Owl perched on crested Corinthian helmet r., RVFVS
      behind. Rev. MN CORDIVS (MN in monogram), aegis with hd. of Medusa at centre. RRC
      463/2. CRR 978. RSC *Cordia* 4. CRI 64.   VF £125 ($200) / EF £350 ($560)

442

442   —— RVFVS S C, diad. hd. of Venus r. Rev. Cupid riding on back of dolphin r., MN
      CORDIVS (MN in monogram) below. RRC 463/3. CRR 977. RSC *Cordia* 3. CRI 65.
                                                           VF £100 ($160) / EF £300 ($480)

443   **Quinarius.** Mn. Cordius Rufus, 46 BC. MN CORDIVS (or CORDI, MN in monogram), rad.
      hd. of Sol r. Rev. Eagle stg. l. (sometimes to r.), looking back, RVFVS in ex. RRC 463/4.
      CRR 979–979b. RSC *Cordia* 5–5c. CRI 66, 66a.   F £175 ($280) / VF £400 ($640)

444   **Sestertius.** Mn. Cordius Rufus, 46 BC. MN CORDIVS (or CORDI, MN in monogram), diad.
      hd. of Venus r. Rev. RVFVS (sometimes abbreviated), Cupid running r., holding wreath and
      palm. RRC 463/5. CRR 980–980b. RSC *Cordia* 6–7a. CRI 67.
                                                           F £165 ($264) / VF £375 ($600)

445   —— Similar, but with obv. MN CORDIVS (MN in monogram), crested Corinthian helmet r.
      RRC 463/6. CRR 981, 981a. RSC *Cordia* 8–9. CRI 68, 68a.
                                                           F £175 ($280) / VF £400 ($640)

446   447

446   **Denarius.** T. Carisius, 46 BC. Hd. of the Sibyl Herophile r., her hair enclosed in sling. Rev.
      T CARISIVS (or CARISIV) III VIR, Sphinx seated r. RRC 464/1. CRR 983–983b. RSC
      Carisia 10–11a. CRI 69.   VF £150 ($240) / EF £400 ($640)

447 **Denarius.** T. Carisius, 46 BC. Dr. bust of Juno Moneta r., MONETA behind. Rev. Coining implements: anvil die with garlanded punch die above, between tongs and hammer, T CARISIVS (or CARISIV) above, all within laurel-wreath. RRC 464/2. CRR 982–982b. RSC *Carisia* 1–1c. CRI 70. **VF** £90 ($144) / **EF** £275 ($440)
This remarkable type celebrates the Roman mint itself which was situated adjacent to the temple of Juno Moneta on the Arx summit of the Capitoline Hill.

448   450

448 — — Helmeted hd. of Roma r., ROMA behind. Rev. Cornucopiae on globe between sceptre and rudder, T CARISI (or similar) below, all within laurel-wreath. RRC 464/3. CRR 984–984b. RSC *Carisia* 4–5b. CRI 71–71b. **VF** £75 ($120) / **EF** £225 ($360)

449 — — Winged bust of Victory r. Rev. Victory in biga r., T CARISI in ex. RRC 464/4. CRR 986. RSC *Carisia* 2. CRI 72. **VF** £90 ($144) / **EF** £275 ($440)

450 — — Similar, but with S C behind bust of Victory on obv., and on rev. the goddess drives a quadriga. RRC 464/5. CRR 985. RSC *Carisia* 3. CRI 73.
VF £75 ($120) / **EF** £225 ($360)

451 **Quinarius.** T. Carisius, 46 BC. Winged bust of Victory r., palm-branch over shoulder. Rev. Roma seated l. on pile of arms, holding sword and sceptre, T CARISI on r. RRC 464/6. CRR 987. RSC *Carisia* 6. CRI 74. **F** £225 ($360) / **VF** £500 ($800)

452 **Sestertius.** T. Carisius, 46 BC. T CARISIVS, bearded hd. of Silenus r. Rev. Panther walking r., holding thyrsus, III VIR in ex. RRC 464/7. CRR 988, 988a. RSC *Carisia* 12–13. CRI 75.
F £325 ($520) / **VF** £750 ($1,200)

453 — — Diad. hd. of Diana r., bow and quiver over shoulder. Rev. Hound running r., T CARISI (often abbreviated) above or in ex. RRC 464/8. CRR 989, 989a. RSC *Carisia* 7–9. CRI 76, 76a. **F** £165 ($264) / **VF** £375 ($600)

454

454 **Denarius.** C. Considius Paetus, 46 BC. Laur. hd. of Apollo r., sometimes within laurel-wreath, sometimes with border of dots. Rev. Curule chair, C CONSIDIVS above, PAETVS in ex. RRC 465/1. CRR 990, 990a. RSC *Considia* 3–4. CRI 77, 77a.
VF £90 ($144) / **EF** £275 ($440)

455   **Denarius.** C. Considius Paetus, 46 BC. Similar, but with **A** behind hd. of Apollo and with border of dots (sometimes omitted), and on rev. with **C CONSIDI** above curule chair, **PAETI** in ex. RRC 465/2. CRR 991, 991a. RSC *Considia* 2, 2a. CRI 77b-c.
VF £85 ($136) / **EF** £250 ($400)

456   —— Laur. and diad. hd. of Venus r. (sometimes to l.), **PAETI** behind. Rev. Victory in quadriga l., **C CONSIDI** in ex. RRC 465/3–4. CRR 992–3. RSC *Considia* 6–7. CRI 78, 78a.
VF £85 ($136) / **EF** £250 ($400)

457   —— Bust of Minerva r., wearing crested Corinthian helmet and aegis. Rev. Victory in quadriga r, **C CONSIDI** in ex. RRC 465/5. CRR 994. RSC *Considia* 5. CRI 79.
VF £85 ($136) / **EF** £250 ($400)

458   **Quinarius.** C. Considius Paetus, 46 BC. Laur. and diad. hd. of Venus r., **PAETI** behind. Rev. Victory walking r., carrying trophy, **C CONSIDI** before. RRC 465/6b–d, 7b. CRR 995a, 996a-b. RSC *Considia* 8, 9–9b. CRI 80, 80b.   **F** £150 ($240) / **VF** £350 ($560)
Another variety has Victory walking l., with **C CONSIDI** *(or* CONSIDIV *or* CONSIDIVS*).*

459   —— Similar, but Venus is diad. only, and with **PAETVS** on obv. and **C CONSIDIVS** on rev. RRC 465/6a, 7a. CRR 995, 996. RSC *Considia* 8a, 9c. CRI 80a, 80c.
F £165 ($264) / **VF** £375 ($600)
Another variety has Victory walking l.

460   **Sestertius.** C. Considius Paetus, 46 BC. Winged bust of Cupid r., **C CONSIDIVS** (or similar) below. Rev. Double cornucopiae on globe. RRC 465/8. CRR 997–997c. RSC *Considia* 10–11. CRI 81, 81a.   **F** £165 ($264) / **VF** £375 ($600)

461   **Denarius.** L. Papius Celsus, 45 BC. Hd. of Juno Sospita r., clad in goat's skin. Rev. She-wolf stg. r., placing stick on burning brazier to r. of which is eagle fanning the flames with its wings, **L PAPIVS** in ex., **CELSVS III VIR** above. RRC 472/1. CRR 964. RSC *Papia* 2. CRI 82.   **VF** £110 ($176) / **EF** £325 ($520)

462

462   —— Similar, but with obv. type laur. hd. of Triumphus r., trophy over shoulder, **TRIVMPVS** below. RRC 472/2. CRR 965. RSC *Papia* 3. CRI 83.   **VF** £140 ($224) / **EF** £375 ($600)

463   **Quinarius.** L. Papius Celsus, 45 BC. Winged bust of Victory r. Rev. Girl stg. r., feeding snake, **L PAPIVS** behind, **CELSVS** (sometimes omitted) before. RRC 472/3. CRR 966, 966a. RSC *Papia* 4, 4a. CRI 84, 84a.   **F** £185 ($296) / **VF** £425 ($680)

464   **Sestertius.** L. Papius Celsus, 45 BC. Hd. of Mercury r., wearing winged petasus, caduceus over shoulder, **CELSVS** before. Rev. Lyre, sometimes with **L PAPI** or **CELSVS** on r. RRC 472/4. CRR 967–9. RSC *Papia* 5–7. CRI 85–85b.   **F** £325 ($520) / **VF** £750 ($1,200)

465   **Denarius.** Lollius Palicanus, 45 BC. Diad. hd. of Libertas r., **LIBERTATIS** behind. Rev. View of the Rostra in the Roman Forum, ornamented with ships' beaks and surmounted by tribune's bench, **PALIKANVS** (or similar) above. RRC 473/1. CRR 960. RSC *Lollia* 2. CRI 86.   **VF** £150 ($240) / **EF** £400 ($640)

465   466

466   **Denarius.** Lollius Palicanus, 45 BC. Laur. hd. of Honos r., HONORIS behind. Rev. Curule
      chair between two ears of corn, PALIKANVS above. RRC 473/2. CRR 961. RSC *Lollia* 1.
      CRI 87.   **VF** £140 ($224) / **EF** £375 ($600)

467   **Quinarius.** Lollius Palicanus, 45 BC. Diad. hd. of Felicitas r., FELICITATIS behind. Rev.
      Victory in biga r., PALIKANI in ex. RRC 473/3. CRR 962. RSC *Lollia* 3a. CRI 88.
                                                       F £225 ($360) / **VF** £500 ($800)

468   **Sestertius.** Lollius Palicanus, 45 BC. Urn without handles. Rev. Tessera nummaria
      (bronze tag) with ring attached, PALIK–ANVS on r. and l. RRC 473/4. CRR 963. RSC
      Lollia 4. CRI 89.   **F** £350 ($560) / **VF** £800 ($1,280)
      The obv. depicts a money container, whilst the tag on rev. is that used by the money-changers
      (nummularii) to mark their bags of coins as being of guaranteed number and good metal
      and weight.

469/1   469/2

469   **Denarius.** L. Valerius Acisculus, 45 BC. ACISCVLVS, hd. of Apollo r., surmounted by star,
      pickaxe behind, sometimes with laurel-wreath border. Rev. Europa seated on bull r., hold-
      ing billowing veil, L VALERIVS in ex. RRC 474/1. CRR 998, 998a. RSC *Valeria* 16–17.
      CRI 90, 90a.   **VF** £125 ($200) / **EF** £350 ($560)
      The pickaxe (acisculus) represents a punning allusion to the moneyer's cognomen.

470

470   — — Obv. Similar (with laurel-wreath border). Rev. Human-headed owl, wearing crested
      Corinthian helmet, walking r., with two spears (sometimes only one) and shield,
      L VALERIVS in ex. or behind, laurel-wreath border. RRC 474/2. CRR 999–999b. RSC
      Valeria 18–19. CRI 91–91b.   **VF** £175 ($280) / **EF** £450 ($720)

471 **Denarius.** L. Valerius Acisculus, 45 BC. Obv. Similar (with laurel-wreath border). Rev. Hd.
     of the Sibyl Herophile r., her hair enclosed in sling, L VALERIVS before (rarely omitted),
     laurel-wreath border. RRC 474/3. CRR 1000–1001. RSC *Valeria* 14, 15a. CRI 92, 92a.
                                                   VF £500 ($800) / **EF** £1,100 ($1,760)

                     472   473

472 —— ACISCVLVS, laur. hd. of Jupiter r., pickaxe behind, laurel-wreath border. Rev. Snake-
     legged ('anguipedic') giant, his r. hand grasping thunderbolt which has pierced his side, l.
     hand raised, L VALERIVS in ex. RRC 474/4. CRR 1003. RSC *Valeria* 21. CRI 93.
                                                 VF £1,750 ($2,800) / **EF** £3,500 ($5,600)

473 —— ACISCVLVS, rad. hd. of Sol r., pickaxe behind. Rev. Luna in biga r., L VALERIVS in ex.
     RRC 474/5. CRR 1002. RSC *Valeria* 20, 20a. CRI 94.   **VF** £125 ($200) / **EF** £350 ($560)

474 **Quinarius.** L. Valerius Acisculus, 45 BC. Winged bust of Victory r. Rev. ACISCVLVS, pick-
     axe, laurel-wreath border. RRC 474/6. CRR 1004. RSC *Valeria* 22. CRI 95.
                                                      F £200 ($320) / **VF** £450 ($720)

475 **Sestertius.** L. Valerius Acisculus, 45 BC. Double cornucopiae. Rev. ACISCVLVS, pickaxe.
     RRC 474/7. CRR 1005. RSC *Valeria* 23. CRI 96.   **F** £325 ($520) / **VF** £750 ($1,200)

                              476

476 **Denarius.** L. Aemilius Buca, 44 BC. Diad. hd. of Venus r., L BVCA behind. Rev. Sulla
     reclining r. against rock, Luna descending l. from mountain on r., holding torch, Victory
     with spread wings facing in background. RRC 480/1. CRR 1064. RSC *Aemilia* 12. CRI
     164.   **VF** £1,250 ($2,000) / **EF** £2,500 ($4,000)
     Buca was a distant relative of the dictator Sulla and this remarkable type has been inter-
     preted as representing the famous dream which Sulla experienced in 88 BC while advanc-
     ing on Rome to attack Marius. Most of the issues of the four moneyers who held office in
     the fateful year 44 BC were in the name of Julius Caesar (see under Roman Imperatorial
     Coinage). Buca alone struck a denarius with personal types lacking any specific reference
     to the dictatorial regime. Two of the others (M. Mettius and P. Sepullius Macer) issued
     non-Caesarian quinarii and sestertii, but the fourth moneyer, C. Cossutius Maridianus,
     struck only denarii with the dictator's name and portrait.

477   **Quinarius.** L. Aemilius Buca, 44 BC. Diad. hd. of Pax r., **PAXS** behind Rev. **L AEMILIVS BVCA IIII VIR**, clasped hands. RRC 480/24. CRR 1065. RSC *Aemilia* 18. CRI 165.
                                                      F £185 ($296) / **VF** £425 ($680)

478   **Sestertius.** L. Aemilius Buca, 44 BC. Diad. hd. of Luna r., crescent above. Rev. **L AEMILIVS BVCA**, star of six rays. RRC 480/26. CRR 1066. RSC *Aemilia* 19. CRI 166.
                                                      F £300 ($480) / **VF** £700 ($1,120)

479   **Quinarius.** M. Mettius, 44 BC. Hd. of Juno Sospita r., clad in goat's skin, snake behind. Rev. Victory in biga r., **M METTI** in ex. RRC 480/23. CRR 1058. RSC *Mettia* 1. CRI 167.
                                                      F £165 ($264) / **VF** £375 ($600)

480   **Sestertius.** M. Mettius, 44 BC. Diad. hd. of Venus r. Rev. Girl stg. r., feeding snake, **M METTI** behind. RRC 480/28. CRR 1059. RSC *Mettia* 2. CRI 168.
                                                      F £400 ($640) / **VF** £900 ($1,440)

481   **Quinarius.** P. Sepullius Macer, 44 BC. Winged bust of Victory r., diad. and dr. Rev. **P SEPVLLIVS MACER**, Fortuna stg. l., holding rudder and cornucopiae. RRC 480/25. CRR 1078. RSC *Sepullia* 9. CRI 169.   **F** £450 ($720) / **VF** £1,000 ($1,600)

482   **Sestertius.** P. Sepullius Macer, 44 BC. Dr. bust of Mercury r., wearing winged petasus, caduceus over shoulder. Rev. **P SEPVLLIVS**, winged caduceus. RRC 480/27. CRR 1080. RSC *Sepullia* 11–12. CRI 170.   **F** £225 ($360) / **VF** £500 ($800)

        483   484

483   **Denarius.** L. Flaminius Cilo, 43 BC. **IIII VIR PRI FL**, diad. hd. of Venus r. Rev. Victory in biga r., **L FLAMIN** (or **FLAMINI**) below, **CHILO** in ex. RRC 485/2. CRR 1088. RSC *Flaminia* 2, 2a. CRI 171.   **VF** £125 ($200) / **EF** £350 ($560)
      Only three of the four moneyers for this turbulent year can be identified. Of these, Cilo alone struck coins with an imperatorial portrait, that of the late dictator Caesar (see under Roman Imperatorial Coinage). The fractional silver denominations (quinarius and sestertius) were discontinued in the moneyers' coinage after Caesar's assassination.

484   **—** P. Accoleius Lariscolus, 43 BC. **P ACCOLEIVS LARISCOLVS**, dr. bust of Diana Nemorensis r. Rev. Triple cultus-statue of Diana Nemorensis facing, supporting on their shoulders a beam, above which are five cypress trees. RRC 486/1. CRR 1148, 1148a. RSC *Accoleia* 1, 1a. CRI 172, 172a.   **VF** £150 ($240) / **EF** £400 ($640)

485 486

485 **Denarius.** Petillius Capitolinus, 43 BC. Hd. of Jupiter r., **CAPITOLINVS** behind. Rev. The Capitoline temple of Jupiter Optimus Maximus, represented as a richly decorated hexastyle edifice, **PETILLIVS** below. RRC 487/1. CRR 1149. RSC *Petillia* 1. CRI 173.
VF £150 ($240) / **EF** £400 ($640)

486 — — Similar, but with obv. type eagle stg. r. on thunderbolt, wings spread, **PETILLIVS** above, **CAPITOLINVS** below (no legend on rev., though sometimes with **S–F** or **F–S** in field). RRC 487/2. CRR 1150–52. RSC *Petillia* 2–4. CRI 174–174b.
VF £110 ($176) / **EF** £325 ($520)

487/1 487/2

487 — L. Livineius Regulus, 42 BC. **REGVLVS PR** (sometimes omitted), bare hd. of the praetor L. Livineius Regulus r. Rev. Curule chair with three fasces on either side, **L LIVINEIVS** above, **REGVLVS** in ex. RRC 494/27–8. CRR 1109–10. RSC *Livineia* 10–11. CRI 176–7.
VF £125 ($200) / **EF** £350 ($560)
The remarkable coinage of the monetary quattuorvirate for 42 BC comprised extensive issues in gold and silver in the names of the Triumvirs Antony, Octavian and Lepidus, together with Caesar (see under Roman Imperatorial Coinage) as well as personal types of the moneyers themselves.

488 489

488 — — Similar (no legend on obv.), but with rev. type modius between two corn-ears, **L LIVINEIVS** above, **REGVLVS** in ex. RRC 494/29. CRR 1111. RSC *Livineia* 13. CRI 178.
VF £140 ($224) / **EF** £375 ($600)

489 — — Similar, but with rev. type scene of combat between gladiators and wild beasts, **L REGVLVS** in ex. RRC 494/30. CRR 1112. RSC *Livineia* 12. CRI 179.
VF £300 ($480) / **EF** £750 ($1,200)

490 492

490 **Denarius.** L. Livineius Regulus, 42 BC. Similar, but with legend L REGVLVS PR on obv., and with rev. type curule chair between two fasces, REGVLVS F above, PRAEF VR in ex. RRC 494/31. CRR 1113. RSC *Livineia* 8. CRI 180.   **VF** £150 ($240) / **EF** £400 ($640)

491 — P. Clodius M.f., 42 BC. Rad. hd. of Sol r., quiver behind. Rev. Crescent moon and five stars, P CLODIVS / M F below. RRC 494/21. CRR 1115. RSC *Claudia* 17. CRI 182.
   VF £110 ($176) / **EF** £325 ($520)

492 — — Laur. hd. of Apollo r., lyre behind. Rev. Diana Lucifera stg. r., holding long lighted torch in each hand, P CLODIVS on r., M F on l. RRC 494/23. CRR 1117. RSC *Claudia* 15. CRI 184.   **VF** £70 ($112) / **EF** £200 ($320)

493 495

493 — L. Mussidius Longus, 42 BC. Veiled and diad. hd. of Concordia r., CONCORDIA behind. Rev. L MVSSIDIVS LONGVS, clasped hands holding caduceus. RRC 494/41. CRR 1092. RSC *Mussidia* 5. CRI 187.   **VF** £110 ($176) / **EF** £325 ($520)

494 — — Obv. Similar, but sometimes with star or crescent below Concordia'a chin. Rev. L MVSSIDIVS LONGVS, shrine of Venus Cloacina consisting of circular platform, inscribed CLOACIN, surmounted by two statues of the goddess. RRC 494/42. CRR 1093–1093b. RSC *Mussidia* 6–6b. CRI 188–188b.   **VF** £100 ($160) / **EF** £300 ($480)

495 — — Similar, but with obv. type rad. and dr. bust of Sol three-quarter face to r., and sometimes the platform on rev. is inscribed CLOAC. RRC 494/43. CRR 1094, 1094a. RSC *Mussidia* 7, 7a. CRI 189, 189a.   **VF** £150 ($240) / **EF** £400 ($640)

496 — C. Vibius Varus, 42 BC. Hd. of young Bacchus or Liber r., wreathed with ivy. Rev. Panther springing l. towards garlanded altar surmounted by Bacchic mask, thyrsus in background, C VIBIVS in ex., VARVS on r. RRC 494/36. CRR 1138. RSC *Vibia* 24. CRI 192.
   VF £90 ($144) / **EF** £250 ($400)

497   498

497 **Denarius.** C. Vibius Varus, 42 BC. Laur. hd. of bearded Hercules r. Rev. Minerva stg. r., resting on spear and holding Victory, shield at feet, **C VIBIVS** on r., **VARVS** on l. RRC 494/37. CRR 1139. RSC *Vibia* 23. CRI 193.   **VF** £175 ($280) / **EF** £450 ($720)

498 —— Bust of Minerva r., wearing crested Corinthian helmet and aegis. Rev. Naked Hercules stg. l., resting on club and holding lion's skin, **C VIBIVS** on r., **VARVS** on l. RRC 494/38. CRR 1140. RSC *Vibia* 26. CRI 194.
                                        VF £150 ($240) / **EF** £400 ($640)

499 — C. Clodius C.f. Vestalis, 41 BC. **C CLODIVS C F**, hd. of Flora r., wreathed with flowers, lily behind. Rev. Vestal virgin seated l., holding two-handled bowl, **VESTALIS** behind. RRC 512/2. CRR 1135. RSC *Claudia* 13. CRI 317.   **VF** £80 ($128) / **EF** £225 ($360)
The scarce coinage of the college of moneyers for 41 BC was the last to be struck with personal (non-Caesarian) types prior to the closure of the Capitoline mint during the following year. The entire output of the two moneyers who struck in 40 BC (Ti. Sempronius Graccus and Q. Voconius Vitulus) was devoted to issues honouring Octavian and the late dictator, the now-deified Julius Caesar (see under Roman Imperatorial Coinage).

500

500 — M. Arrius Secundus, 41 BC. **M ARRIVS SECVNDVS**, young male hd. (Quintus Arrius or Octavian?) r. Rev. Spear (*hasta pura*) between wreath and rectangular phalera. RRC 513/2. CRR 1084. RSC *Arria* 2. CRI 319.   **VF** £1,350 ($2,160) / **EF** £2,750 ($4,400)

501 —— Similar, but **SECVNDVS** is in ex. on rev. instead of before hd. on obv., and with rev. type two soldiers advancing r., the foremost holding spear and reaching back to grasp one of the two standards held by his companion. RRC 513/3. CRR 1085. RSC *Arria* 3. CRI 320.   **VF** £5,000 ($8,000) / **EF** £10,000 ($16,000)

502   503

502   **Denarius.** C. Numonius Vaala, 41 BC. **C NVMONIVS VAALA**, mature male hd. (an ancestor
      or Julius Caesar?) r. Rev. Soldier advancing l., attacking a palisaded earthwork (*vallum*)
      behind which are two defenders, **VAALA** in ex. RRC 514/2. CRR 1087. RSC *Numonia* 2.
      CRI 322.   **VF** £1,500 ($2,400) / **EF** £3,000 ($4,800)

503   — L. Servius Rufus, 41 BC. **L SERVIVS RVFVS**, bearded male hd. (an ancestor or M. Junius
      Brutus?) r. Rev. The Dioscuri, naked, stg. facing side by side, each holding spear. RRC
      515/2. CRR 1082. RSC *Sulpicia* 10. CRI 324.   **VF** £1,250 ($2,000) / **EF** £2,500 ($4,000)

REPUBLICAN BRONZE

From early times bronze was the traditional medium of exchange amongst the peoples of central
Italy. Economically and culturally this area was backward when compared with the sophisticated
societies of the Greek settlements in the south. For their currency requirements the Romans,
together with their immediate neighbours, made do with irregular lumps of bronze known as *Aes
Rude* and all transactions would have required the use of scales. Towards the close of the 4th century BC a more advanced form of currency came into being in central Italy with the manufacture of
cast bronze bars, or ingots, called *Aes Signatum* bearing a design on each side. Production of these
seems to have extended down to the end of the First Punic War (241 BC). Contemporary with the
Aes Signatum are the earliest issues of bronze coinage proper on circular flans, the *Aes Grave*.
These were produced in a range of denominatons, each clearly marked with its value. Small struck
bronzes (litrae, etc.) were issued collaterally, but these were associated with the silver didrachms
and were intended to facilitate trade with the Greek colonies of the south.
    The crisis of the initial stages of the Second Punic War led to the temporary collapse of the
Roman monetary system. The weights of the *Aes Grave* fell drastically during this period and
increasingly the lower denominations were replaced by struck coins. Eventually, in about 211 BC,
the as itself appeared as a struck coin on the sextantal weight standard, thus bringing the *Aes Grave*
series to a close. Thereafter, struck bronze coins were issued on a regular basis, generally in six
denominations ranging fom the as to its twelfth, the uncia. In line with the contemporary early
denarius coinage the struck bronzes initially were issued anonymously, though symbols and monograms soon began to appear and, eventually, full moneyers' names. Unlike the denarii the types of
the struck bronzes were remarkably conservative, retaining the traditional designs for each denomination introduced in the later stages of the *Aes Grave*. The weight standard fell again in the latter
part of the 2nd century to the uncial level, and under the *Lex Papiria* of 91 BC the final reduction
was made to the semuncial, the standard that was eventually adopted by Augustus for the Roman
Imperial as.
    The final decades of the Republican period, after *circa* 82 BC, saw an almost total cessation of
bronze coinage. There was sporadic local production during the Imperatorial era of the 40s and 30s
BC, but the denominations and weight standards for the most part are uncertain during this revolutionary period (see under Roman Imperatorial Coinage).

CAST CURRENCY: AES RUDE, 5TH–4TH CENTURY BC

505

505　Irregular cast lumps of bronze, with no official stamp or indication of value, ranging in weight from about 8 grams to over 300 grams. BMCRR vol. I, pp. 1–2, 1–11. ICC p. 15 and pl. 2.　　　　　　　　　　　　　　　　　　　　£50 ($80) – £200 ($320)

CAST CURRENCY: AES SIGNATUM, CIRCA 289–241 BC

The weights are variable but the norm seems to be a little over 1,600 grams, making the full ingot the probable equivalent of 5 asses or 5 Roman pounds. Many surviving specimens are fragmentary, cleanly broken in antiquity to represent lesser values.

506　Eagle on thunderbolt, wings spread, hd. r. Rev. Pegasus flying l., sometimes with legend **ROMANOM**. RRC 4/1. ICC AS13–14.　　　**F** £5,000 ($8,000) / **VF** £12,000 ($19,200)

507　Bull stg. r. Rev. Bull stg. l. RRC 5/1. ICC AS18.
　　　　　　　　　　　　　　　　　　　F £4,500 ($7,200) / **VF** £11,000 ($17,600)

508　Ear of corn. Rev. Tripod. RRC 6/1. ICC AS17.　**F** £4,000 ($6,400) / **VF** £10,000 ($16,000)

509　Outside of oval shield. Rev. Inside of oval shield. RRC 7/1. ICC AS15.
　　　　　　　　　　　　　　　　　　　F £4,500 ($7,200) / **VF** £11,000 ($17,600)

510　Sword. Rev. Scabbard. RRC 8/1. ICC AS16.　**F** £5,000 ($8,000) / **VF** £12,000 ($19,200)

511　Amphora. Rev. Spearhead. ICC AS19–20.　**F** £4,500 ($7,200) / **VF** £11,000 ($17,600)

512　Elephant walking r. Rev. Sow stg. l. RRC 9/1. ICC AS21.
　　　　　　　　　　　　　　　　　　　F £6,000 ($9,600) / **VF** £15,000 ($24,000)

513　Anchor. Rev. Tripod. RRC 10/1. ICC AS22.　**F** £4,000 ($6,400) / **VF** £10,000 ($16,000)

514　Filleted trident. Rev. Filleted caduceus. RRC 11/1. ICC AS23.
　　　　　　　　　　　　　　　　　　　F £4,000 ($6,400) / **VF** £10,000 ($16,000)

515　Two feeding chickens face to face, two stars between. Rev. Two trident-heads pointing inwards, two dolphins between. RRC 12/1. ICC AS24.
　　　　　　　　　　　　　　　　　　　F £4,500 ($7,200) / **VF** £11,000 ($17,600)

507

515 Obv.

515 Rev.

518

CAST COINAGE: AES GRAVE, CIRCA 280–211 BC

Initially produced with a variety of obverse and reverse designs and prominent marks of value, the series was standardized about 225 BC with the introduction of the prow of a galley as the constant reverse type combined with the head of a deity on obverse (a different one for each denomination). The pattern established for the bronze coinage at this time was to remain essentially unchanged for the remainder of the Republican period. During the initial decade of the *Aes Grave* series the weight of the as underwent a gradual reduction from the full libral standard of 324 grams to the reduced libral standard of 265 grams, the new level being firmly established by *circa* 269 BC. This standard was maintained for the following half-century until the financial hardships occasioned by the military disasters of the early stages of the Second Punic War resulted in drastic emergency reductions in the weights of the bronze denominations, commencing about 217 BC. This was the death-knell for the *Aes Grave* coinage and over the ensuing half decade the cast as ultimately fell to the sextantal standard of only 44 grams, whilst the fractional denominations were progressively discontinued, their place being taken by equivalent struck pieces. Finally, the as itself was issued as a struck coin (on the sextantal standard) as part of the sweeping currency reform of 211 BC, thus bringing to an end seven decades of *Aes Grave* coinage.

EARLY PHASE: ISSUES WITH VARIED TYPES, CIRCA 280–225 BC

517 **Tressis** (= 3 asses). 269–225 BC. Hd. of Roma r., in Phrygian helmet, III behind. Rev. Six-spoked wheel, III between two of the spokes. RRC 24/1. CRR 57. ICC 29.

(Only two known)

518 **Dupondius** (= 2 asses). 269–225 BC. Similar, but with mark of value II on obv. and rev. RRC 24/2. CRR 58. ICC 30.   F £1,750 ($2,800) / **VF** £4,000 ($6,400)

519 **As.** 280–269 BC. Beardless Janiform hd., I above. Rev. Hd. of Mercury l., in winged petasus, I above. RRC 14/1. CRR 8. ICC 1, 1a.   F £400 ($640) / **VF** £900 ($1,440)

520 — Hd. of Apollo r., I above. Rev. Hd. of Apollo l., I above. RRC 18/1. CRR 15, 51. ICC 8.
F £500 ($800) / **VF** £1,100 ($1,760)

521 **As.** 280–269 BC. Hd. of one of the Dioscuri l., in conical cap. Rev. Hd. of Apollo l. RRC 19/1. ICC 14.   *(Unique)*

522 269–225 BC. Similar to 519, but without marks of value, and with sickle behind hd. of Mercury on rev. RRC 25/4. CRR 44. ICC 36.   F £500 ($800) / **VF** £1,100 ($1,760)
This issue may be associated with the silver didrachm coinage and struck bronze litrae with sickle symbol on rev. (see nos. 26–7 and 602) dated by Crawford to 241–235 BC.

523 — Similar to 520, but without marks of value, and with vine-leaf behind hd. on obv., and bunch of grapes behind hd. on rev. RRC 26/5. ICC 46.
F £1,000 ($1,600) / **VF** £2,250 ($3,600)

524 — Hd. of Minerva three-quarter face to r., wearing triple-crested helmet. Rev. Bull stg. r., L (or I or caduceus) above, ROMA in ex. RRC 37/1. CRR 138–9. ICC 43, 43a.
F £850 ($1,360) / **VF** £2,000 ($3,200)

525 **As.** Hd. of Roma r., in Phrygian helmet, I behind. Rev. Six-spoked wheel, I between two of the spokes. RRC 24/3. CRR 59. ICC 31. **F** £750 ($1,200) / **VF** £1,750 ($2,800)

526 — Lion's hd. facing, holding sword in mouth. Rev. Horse's hd. l., sometimes with symbol or letter (caduceus, barley-grain, club, flower, or G) in field. ICC 45, 45a. **F** £800 ($1,280) / **VF** £1,850 ($2,960)

527 — Hd. of Roma r., in Phrygian helmet, I behind. Rev. Hd. of Roma l., in Phrygian helmet, I behind. RRC 21/1. CRR 31. ICC 16. **F** £750 ($1,200) / **VF** £1,750 ($2,800)

528 — Similar, but with club instead of mark of value behind hd. on both sides. RRC 27/5. CRR 38. ICC 23. **F** £750 ($1,200) / **VF** £1,750 ($2,800)
This issue may be associated with the silver didrachm coinage and struck bronze litrae with club symbols on obv. and rev. (see nos. 30 and 604) dated by Crawford to 230–226 BC.

529

529 **Semis** (= half as). 280–269 BC. Hd. of Minerva l., in crested Corinthian helmet, S below. Rev. Hd. of Venus l., S below. RRC 14/2. CRR 9. ICC 2, 2a. **F** £200 ($320) / **VF** £450 ($720)

530

530 **Semis.** 280–269 BC. Pegasus flying r., S below. Rev. Pegasus flying l., S below. RRC 18/2. CRR 16, 52. ICC 9. **F** £225 ($360) / **VF** £500 ($800)

531 — Hd. of Roma l., in Phrygian helmet, S before. Rev. Horned hd. of young Pan l., S before. RRC 19/2. ICC 15. **F** £750 ($1,200) / **VF** £1,750 ($2,800)

532 269–225 BC. Similar to 529, but with sickle behind hd. of Venus on rev. RRC 25/5. CRR 45. ICC 37. **F** £225 ($360) / **VF** £500 ($800)
This issue may be associated with the silver didrachm coinage and struck bronze litrae with sickle symbol on rev. (see nos. 26–7 and 602) dated by Crawford to 241–235 BC.

533 — Similar to 530, but with vine-leaf above Pegasus on obv., and bunch of grapes above Pegasus on rev. Cf. RRC 26/6. ICC 47. **F** £600 ($960) / **VF** £1,300 ($2,080)

534 — Bull's hd. r. Rev. Prow of galley r., S before. ICC 44.
 F £400 ($640) / **VF** £900 ($1,440)

535 — Bull rearing l., usually with S below. Rev. Six-spoked wheel, S between two of the spokes. RRC 24/4. CRR 60. ICC 32. **F** £300 ($480) / **VF** £650 ($1,040)

536 — Hd. of Minerva r., in crested Corinthian helmet, S below. Rev. Hd. of Minerva l., in crested Corinthian helmet, S below. RRC 21/2. CRR 32. ICC 17.
 F £300 ($480) / **VF** £650 ($1,040)

537 — Similar, but with club behind hd. on both sides. Cf. RRC 27/6. CRR 39. ICC 24.
 F £275 ($440) / **VF** £600 ($960)
This issue may be associated with the silver didrachm coinage and struck bronze litrae with club symbols on obv. and rev. (see nos. 30 and 604) dated by Crawford to 230–226 BC.

538 **Triens.** 280–269 BC. Thunderbolt dividing four pellets. Rev. Dolphin r. (sometimes l.), four pellets below. RRC 14/3. CRR 10. ICC 3, 3a. **F** £150 ($240) / **VF** £350 ($560)

539 — Horse's hd. r., four pellets below. Rev. Horse's hd. l., four pellets below. RRC 18/3. CRR 17, 53. ICC 10. **F** £200 ($320) / **VF** £450 ($720)

535

538

540 **Triens.** 269–225 BC. Similar to 538, but with sickle above dolphin r. on rev. RRC 25/6.
CRR 46. ICC 38.   **F** £175 ($280) / **VF** £400 ($640)
*This issue may be associated with the silver didrachm coinage and struck bronze litrae
with sickle symbol on rev. (see nos. 26–7 and 602) dated by Crawford to 241–235 BC.*

541 — Horse cantering l., two pellets above, two below. Rev. Six-spoked wheel, four pellets
between the spokes. RRC 24/5. CRR 61. ICC 33.   **F** £175 ($280) / **VF** £400 ($640)

542 — Thunderbolt dividing four pellets. Rev. Same as obv. RRC 21/3. CRR 33. ICC 18.
                                                   F £200 ($320) / **VF** £450 ($720)

543 — Similar, but with club in field on both sides. RRC 27/7. CRR 40. ICC 25.
                                                   F £200 ($320) / **VF** £450 ($720)
This issue may be associated with the silver didrachm coinage and struck bronze litrae

539

541

with club symbols on obv. and rev. (see nos. 30 and 604) dated by Crawford to
230–226 BC.

544 **Quadrans.** 280–269 BC. Two barley-grains, three pellets between. Rev. Open r. hand, three
pellets on l. RRC 14/4. CRR 11. ICC 4, 4a. **F** £125 ($200) / **VF** £275 ($440)

545 — Boar running l., three pellets below. Rev. Boar running r., three pellets below. RRC
18/4. CRR 18, 54. ICC 11. **F** £175 ($280) / **VF** £400 ($640)

546 269–225 BC. Similar to 544, but with sickle in r. field on rev. RRC 25/7. CRR 47. ICC 39.
F £150 ($240) / **VF** £350 ($560)
*This issue may be associated with the silver didrachm coinage and struck bronze litrae
with sickle symbol on rev. (see nos. 26–7 and 602) dated by Crawford to 241–235 BC.*

547 — Similar to 545, but with vine-leaf above boar on obv., and bunch of grapes above boar
on rev. RRC 26/7. ICC 48. **F** £450 ($720) / **VF** £1,000 ($1,600)

548 **Quadrans.** 269–225 BC. Dog running l. (rarely to r.), three pellets in ex. Rev. Six-spoked wheel, three pellets between the spokes. RRC 24/6. CRR 62. ICC 34, 34a.

F £150 ($240) / **VF** £350 ($560)

549 — Open r. hand, three pellets on l. Rev. Open l. hand, three pellets on r. RRC 21/4. CRR 34. ICC 19. **F** £175 ($280) / **VF** £400 ($640)

550 — Similar, but with club in field on both sides. RRC 27/8. CRR 41. ICC 26.

F £175 ($280) / **VF** £400 ($640)

This issue may be associated with the silver didrachm coinage and struck bronze litrae with club symbols on obv. and rev. (see nos. 30 and 604) dated by Crawford to 230–226 BC.

551 **Sextans.** 280–269 BC. Scallop-shell, two pellets across lower field. Rev. Caduceus between two pellets. RRC 14/5. CRR 12. ICC 5, 5a. **F** £100 ($160) / **VF** £225 ($360)

552

552 — Hd. of one of the Dioscuri r., in conical cap, two pellets behind. Rev. Hd. of the other Dioscurus l., in conical cap, two pellets behind. RRC 18/5. CRR 19, 55. ICC 12, 12a.

F £150 ($240) / **VF** £350 ($560)

553 269–225 BC. Similar to 551, but with sickle in r. field on rev. RRC 25/8. CRR 48. ICC 40.

F £125 ($200) / **VF** £275 ($440)

This issue may be associated with the silver didrachm coinage and struck bronze litrae with sickle symbol on rev. (see nos. 26–7 and 602) dated by Crawford to 241–235 BC.

554 — Similar to 552, but with vine-leaf behind hd. on obv., and bunch of grapes behind hd. on rev. Cf. RRC 26/8. ICC 49. *(Unique)*

555 — Tortoise. Rev. Six-spoked wheel, two pellets (sometimes omitted) between the spokes. RRC 24/7. CRR 63, 63a. ICC 35, 35a. **F** £125 ($200) / **VF** £275 ($440)

556 — Scallop-shell viewed from outside, two pellets across lower field. Rev. Scallop-shell viewed from inside, rarely with two pellets across lower field. RRC 21/5. CRR 35. ICC 20.

F £110 ($176) / **VF** £250 ($400)

557 — Similar, but with club below shell on both sides. RRC 27/9. CRR 42. ICC 27.

F £110 ($176) / **VF** £250 ($400)

This issue may be associated with the silver didrachm coinage and struck bronze litrae with club symbols on obv. and rev. (see nos. 30 and 604) dated by Crawford to 230–226 BC.

556

559 561

558 **Uncia.** 280–269 BC. Knucklebone and pellet. Rev. Pellet. RRC 14/6. CRR 13. ICC 6, 6a.
F £75 ($120) / **VF** £175 ($280)

559 — Barley-grain and pellet. Rev. Same as obv. RRC 18/6. CRR 20, 56. ICC 13, 13a.
F £85 ($136) / **VF** £200 ($320)

560 269–225 BC. Knucklebone. Rev. Pellet and sickle. RRC 25/9. CRR 49. ICC 41.
F £110 ($176) / **VF** £250 ($400)
*This issue may be associated with the silver didrachm coinage and struck bronze litrae
with sickle symbol on rev. (see nos. 26–7 and 602) dated by Crawford to 241–235 BC.*

561 — Knucklebone viewed from outside, usually with pellet beside. Rev. Knucklebone
viewed from inside. RRC 21/6. CRR 36, 36a. ICC 21. F £85 ($136) / **VF** £200 ($320)
*Thurlow and Vecchi (ICC 21a) record a variety of this type on which the obv. design is
duplicated on the rev. (i.e. knucklebone viewed from outside on both sides).*

562 — Knucklebone viewed from outside, club beside. Rev. Knucklebone viewed from inside,
club beside. RRC 27/10. CRR 43. ICC 28. F £85 ($136) / **VF** £200 ($320)
*This issue may be associated with the silver didrachm coinage and struck bronze litrae
with club symbols on obv. and rev. (see nos. 30 and 604) dated by Crawford to
230–226 BC.*

563 **Semuncia.** 280–269 BC. Acorn. Rev. Σ. RRC 14/7. CRR 14. ICC 7, 7a.
F £65 ($104) / **VF** £150 ($240)

564 269–241 BC. Acorn and Σ. Rev. Same as obv., but Σ retrograde. RRC 21/7. CRR 37. ICC 22.
F £65 ($104) / **VF** £150 ($240)

563

Production of the smallest denomination of the Aes Grave coinage probably ceased during the First Punic War. When reintroduced about 217 BC the semuncia was issued as a struck coin on the semilibral standard (see nos. 619–20).

LATE PHASE: ISSUES WITH STANDARDIZED TYPES (PROW ON REVERSE), CIRCA 225–211 BC

565 **Decussis** (= 10 asses). 215–211 BC. Hd. of Roma r., in Phrygian helmet, X behind. Rev. Prow of galley l., X above. RRC 41/1. CRR 98. ICC 67.
F £7,500 ($12,000) / **VF** £20,000 ($32,000)
The largest denomination of the Aes Grave coinage appeared only in the final phase of the cast coinage. In the currency reform of 211 BC it was replaced by its equivalent in silver, the denarius.

566 **Quincussis** (= 5 asses). 225–217 BC. Bearded hd. of Janus. Rev. Prow of galley r., V above. ICC 50. (*Unique*)
This denomination was the forerunner of the silver quinarius introduced in 211 BC.

567 215–211 BC. Similar to 565, but with mark of value V on both sides. RRC 41/2. ICC 67a.
(*Unique*)

569

570

568   **Tressis** (= 3 asses). 215–211 BC. Similar to 565, but with mark of value III on both sides.
       RRC 41/3a. CRR 99. ICC 68.   **F** £1,500 ($2,400) / **VF** £3,750 ($6,000)
       A unique variant (ICC 68a) has the prow to right.

569   **Dupondius** (= 2 asses). 215–211 BC. Hd of Minerva r., in crested Corinthian helmet, II
       behind. Rev. Prow of galley l., II above. RRC 41/4. CRR 100. Cf. ICC 69.
                                                       F £800 ($1,280) / **VF** £2,000 ($3,200)

570   **As.** 225–217 BC. Bearded hd. of Janus, usually with – (= I) below. Rev. Prow of galley r., I
       above. RRC 35/1. CRR 71–2. ICC 51, 51a.   **F** £400 ($640) / **VF** £1,000 ($1,600)
       Asses of this period were issued on the reduced libral weight standard of ca. 265 grams.

571

571   **As.** 225–217 BC. Similar (without mark of value on obv.), but with prow to l. on rev. RRC 36/1. CRR 78. ICC 57.   **F** £500 ($800) / **VF** £1,250 ($2,000)

572   217–215 BC. Similar, but of the semilibral weight standard (*ca*. 132 grams). RRC 38/1. CRR 89. ICC 63.   **F** £300 ($480) / **VF** £750 ($1,200)

573   215–211 BC. Similar (prow usually to l., rarely to r.), but issued on one of the post-semilibral weight standards. RRC 41/5. CRR 101, 101a. ICC 70, 70a.   **F** £200 ($320) / **VF** £500 ($800)

573

574

The weight of the as during this period declined rapidly from the triental standard of ca.
88 grams to the sextantal of ca. 44 grams.

574   **Semis.** 225–217 BC. Laur. hd. of Saturn l., S below. Rev. Prow of galley r., S above. RRC
       35/2. CRR 73. ICC 52.   **F** £200 ($320) / **VF** £500 ($800)
       Semisses of this period were issued on the reduced libral weight standard of ca. 132
       grams.

575   — Similar, but without mark of value on obv., and with prow to l. on rev. RRC 36/2. CRR
       79. ICC 58.   **F** £250 ($400) / **VF** £600 ($960)

576   217–215 BC. Laur. hd. of Saturn l., S behind. Rev. Prow of galley l., S above. RRC 38/2.
       CRR 90. ICC 64.   **F** £175 ($280) / **VF** £450 ($720)
       Semisses of this period were issued on the semilibral weight standard of ca. 66 grams.

577

577 **Semis.** 215–211 BC. Similar, but sometimes the mark of value is omitted, and the issue is on one of the post-semilibral weight standards (rarely, the hd. of Saturn and/or the prow are turned to r.). RRC 41/6. CRR 102. ICC 71–71c. **F** £125 ($200) / **VF** £300 ($480)
The weight of the semis during this period declined rapidly from the triental standard of ca. 44 grams to the sextantal of ca. 22 grams.

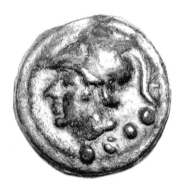

578

578 **Triens.** 225–217 BC. Hd. of Minerva l. (rarely to r.), in crested Corinthian helmet, four pellets below. Rev. Prow of galley r., four pellets below. RRC 35/3. CRR 74. ICC 53, 53a.
F £150 ($240) / **VF** £375 ($600)
Trientes of this period were issued on the reduced libral weight standard of ca. 88 grams.

579 — Similar, but the mark of value is usually omitted on obv., and with prow to l. on rev. RRC 36/3. CRR 80, 80a. ICC 59–60. **F** £200 ($320) / **VF** £475 ($760)

580 217–215 BC. Hd. of Minerva l., in crested Corinthian helmet, four pellets below. Rev. Prow of galley l., four pellets below. RRC 38/3. CRR 91. ICC 65.
F £200 ($320) / **VF** £475 ($760)
Trientes of this period were issued on the semilibral weight standard of ca. 44 grams.

581 215–211 BC. Similar, but issued on one of the post-semilibral weight standards. RRC 41/7a. CRR 103. ICC 72. **F** £150 ($240) / **VF** £375 ($600)
The weight of the triens during this period declined rapidly from the triental standard of ca. 29 grams to the quadrantal of ca. 22 grams.

582

582 **Quadrans.** 225–217 BC. Hd. of young Hercules l., clad in lion's skin, three pellets behind. Rev. Prow of galley r., three pellets below. RRC 35/4. CRR 75. ICC 54.
F £125 ($200) / **VF** £300 ($480)
Quadrantes of this period were issued on the reduced libral weight standard of ca. 66 grams.

583 — Hd. of young Hercules l., clad in lion's skin, club (sometimes three pellets) below. Rev. Prow of galley l., three pellets below. RRC 36/4. CRR 81. ICC 61.
F £160 ($256) / **VF** £400 ($640)

584 217–215 BC. Similar, but with three pellets behind or below hd. of Hercules. RRC 38/4. CRR 92. ICC 66.
F £140 ($224) / **VF** £350 ($560)
Quadrantes of this period were issued on the semilibral weight standard of ca. 33 grams.

585 — Similar, but with ear of corn above prow. RRC 40/1. ICC 66b.
F £275 ($440) / **VF** £600 ($960)
Remarkably, this issue would appear to have been produced in Sicily where most of the known examples have been found.

586 215–211 BC. Hd of young Hercules l., clad in lion's skin, three pellets below. Rev. Prow of galley l., three pellets below. RRC 41/8a. CRR 104. ICC 73.
F £125 ($200) / **VF** £300 ($480)
The final issues of the cast quadrans appear to have been produced on the triental weight standard of ca. 22 grams.

587 **Sextans.** 225–217 BC. Hd. of Mercury l., in winged petasus, two pellets below. Rev. Prow of galley r., two pellets below. RRC 35/5. CRR 76. ICC 55.
F £100 ($160) / **VF** £250 ($400)
Sextantes of this period were issued on the reduced libral standard of ca. 44 grams. From the time of the semilibral weight reduction in 217 BC the sextans was produced only as a struck coin.

588 — Similar, but the mark of value is usually omitted on obv., and with prow to l. on rev. RRC 36/5. CRR 82. ICC 62.
F £125 ($200) / **VF** £300 ($480)

589 **Uncia.** 225–217 BC. Hd. of Roma l., in crested Attic helmet, pellet behind. Rev. Prow of galley r., pellet below or behind. RRC 35/6. CRR 77. ICC 56.
F £75 ($120) / **VF** £175 ($280)
Unciae of this period were issued on the reduced libral standard of ca. 22 grams. From the time of the semilibral weight reduction in 217 BC the uncia was produced only as a struck coin.

STRUCK COINAGE: TOKEN LITRAE, ETC., CIRCA 273–225 BC

Contemporary with the cumbrous cast *Aes Grave* coinage, though apparently commencing a little later (*circa* 273 BC), small struck bronze coins of three denominations were issued by the Roman Republic for almost half a century, probably down to the time of the introduction of the silver quadrigatus about 225 BC. Clearly related to the contemporary silver didrachm coinage (and like them inscribed ROMANO in the earlier phase of production and ROMA after the First Punic War), their purpose was to facilitate commerce with the Greek cities of the south where the large cast *Aes Grave* of central Italy would not have been acceptable.

590   **Double litra.** 273–270 BC. Diad. hd. of Apollo r. (sometimes l.). Rev. Lion walking r., hd. facing, holding in its mouth a broken spear on which it rests l. forepaw, ROMANO in ex. RRC 16/1. CRR 5, 5a. BMCRR Romano-Campanian 23, 27.

F £40 ($64) / **VF** £110 ($176)

591   592

591   230–225 BC. Hd. of young Hercules r., clad in lion's skin, club below. Rev. Pegasus flying r., club above, ROMA below. RRC 27/3. CRR 7. BMCRR Romano-Campanian 51.

F £45 ($72) / **VF** £120 ($192)

592   **Litra.** 273–270 BC. Hd. of Minerva l. (sometimes r.), in crested Corinthian helmet. Rev. ROMANO, horse's hd. r. (sometimes l.). RRC 17/1a–d and i. CRR 3, 3a. BMCRR Romano-Campanian 6, 12, 17.

F £35 ($56) / **VF** £90 ($144)

593   — Similar, but ROMANO appears also on obv., and sometimes with star behind hd. of Minerva (which is always to r.). RRC 17/1e–h. CRR 3b–d. BMCRR Romano-Campanian 13, 14.

F £35 ($56) / **VF** £90 ($144)

The legends on this initial issue of litrae are often blundered and many surviving specimens are probably better classified as contemporary imitations rather than products of the Rome mint.

594   241–235 BC. Hd. of beardless Mars r., in crested Corinthian helmet. Rev. Horse's hd. r., sickle behind, ROMA below. RRC 25/3. CRR 26. BMCRR Romano-Campanian 64.

F £35 ($56) / **VF** £90 ($144)

595   235–230 BC. Laur. hd. of Apollo r. Rev. Horse galloping l., ROMA below. RRC 26/3. CRR 29. BMCRR Romano-Campanian 70.

F £35 ($56) / **VF** £90 ($144)

596   230–225 BC. Hd. of beardless Mars r., in crested Corinthian helmet, club behind. Rev. Horse galloping r., club above, ROMA below. RRC 27/2. CRR 23a. BMCRR Romano-Campanian 53.

F £40 ($64) / **VF** £110 ($176)

597   — Hd. of young Hercules r., clad in lion's skin, club below, L under chin. Rev. Pegasus flying r., bow above, ROMA below. RRC 27/4. CRR 131.

F £50 ($80) / **VF** £140 ($224)

595   598

598   **Half litra.** 235–230 BC. Hd. of Roma r., in Phrygian helmet. Rev. Dog r., l. foreleg raised,
       ROMA in ex. RRC 26/4. CRR 22. BMCRR Romano-Campanian 44.
                                                        F £30 ($48) / **VF** £80 ($128)

599   **Uncertain denomination** (28 mm., 15–19 grams). *Circa* 264 BC. Hd. of Minerva l., in
       crested Corinthian helmet, ROMANO before, control-symbol (plough, helmet, stork, or
       sword) behind. Rev. ROMANO, eagle stg. l. on thunderbolt, looking r., wings spread, sword
       in field to l. RRC 23/1. CRR 30. BMCRR Romano-Campanian 5.
                                                        F £200 ($320) / **VF** £500 ($800)
       Probably struck at the Sicilian city of Messana where the Mamertini (Oscan mercenaries)
       triggered the First Punic War by appealing for military help to both Carthage and Rome.
       The Carthaginians installed a detachment of troops in the city, whilst Rome countered by
       despatching an invasion force which ousted the Punic garrison in 264 BC, the likely occa-
       sion for the issue of these coins.

STRUCK COINAGE: PRE-REFORM FRACTIONS OF
THE AES GRAVE AS, CIRCA 217–211 BC

The economic crisis in the Roman Republic precipitated by the outbreak of the Second Punic War
and Hannibal's invasion of Italy led to a halving in 217 BC of the weight of the *Aes Grave* as, which
was now produced on the semilibral standard of about 132 grams. Worse was to follow, and as the
higher denominations of the bronze coinage became lighter through a rapid series of weight reductions it was no longer practicable to produce the lower value coins by the traditional method of
casting. Accordingly, pieces struck between engraved dies gradually took their place. The transition
was completed by the currency reform of 211 BC by which the *Aes Grave* ceased altogether, the as
itself being issued for the first time as a struck coin on the sextantal weight standard of about
44 grams.

600   **Semis.** 215–211 BC. Laur. hd. of Saturn r., S behind. Rev. Prow of galley r., S above, ROMA
       below. RRC 41/6e.   (*Unique*)
       The rare struck semisses of this period generally weigh about 35 grams (for lighter post-
       reform issues of similar type, see no. 766).

601   — Similar, but with L (Luceria) before prow. RRC 43/2b. CRR 124.
                                                        F £175 ($280) / **VF** £450 ($720)

602   — Similar, but with corn-ear and ROMA above prow, S below. RRC 72/5.   (*Unique*)

603

603 **Triens.** 217–215 BC. Diad. hd. of Juno r., four pellets behind. Rev. Hercules stg. r., attacking with club a centaur r. before him and grasping its hair with his l. hand, four pellets on r., ROMA in ex. RRC 39/1. CRR 93. BMCRR Romano-Campanian 113.
F £500 ($800) / **VF** £1,250 ($2,000)
Struck trientes of this period weigh about 50 grams.

604 215–211 BC. Hd. of Minerva r., in crested Corinthian helmet, four pellets above. Rev. Prow of galley r., ROMA above, four pellets below. RRC 41/7b. CRR 105. BMCRR 44.
F £90 ($144) / **VF** £225 ($360)
Struck trientes of this period vary considerably in weight, ranging from about 28 grams down to 20 grams (for lighter post-reform issues of similar type, see nos. 911, 989 and 1033).

605 — Similar, but with L (Luceria) on obv. (behind or before Minerva), or with L on both sides, behind Minerva and before prow. RRC 43/3. CRR 23a. BMCRR Italy, p. 147, 5.
F £100 ($160) / **VF** £250 ($400)

606

606 **Quadrans.** 217–215 BC. Hd. of young Hercules r., clad in boar's skin, three pellets behind. Rev. Bull charging r., snake below, three pellets above, ROMA in ex. RRC 39/2. CRR 94. BMCRR Romano-Campanian 116.
F £275 ($440) / **VF** £700 ($1,120)
Struck quadrantes of this period weigh about 38 grams.

607 **Quadrans.** 215–211 BC. Similar, but also with corn-ear above bull. RRC 42/2. BMCRR
Romano-Campanian 139.　　　　　　　　　　**F** £150 ($240) / **VF** £350 ($560)
*Struck quadrantes of this period vary considerably in weight, ranging from about 22
grams down to 12 grams. Coins of this type usually weigh about 16 grams (for lighter
post-reform issues, see no. 1043).*

608 — Hd. of young Hercules r., clad in lion's skin, three pellets behind. Rev. Prow of galley r.,
ROMA above, three pellets below. RRC 41/8b. CRR 106. BMCRR 53.
　　　　　　　　　　　　　　　　　　　　F £90 ($144) / **VF** £225 ($360)
For lighter post-reform quadrantes of similar type, see nos. 1037 and 1195.

609 (obverse and reverse transposed)

609 **Sextans.** 217–215 BC. She-wolf stg. r., suckling the twins Romulus and Remus, two pellets
in ex. Rev. Eagle stg. r., holding flower in its beak, two pellets behind, ROMA before. RRC
39/3. CRR 95. BMCRR Romano-Campanian 120.　　　　**F** £125 ($200) / **VF** £300 ($480)
Sextantes of this period weigh about 25 grams.

610

610 — Hd. of Mercury r., in winged pegasus, two pellets above. Rev. Prow of galley r., ROMA
above, two pellets below. RRC 38/5. CRR 85. BMCRR 59.　**F** £60 ($96) / **VF** £150 ($240)

611 215–211 BC. Similar. RRC 41/9. CRR 107. BMCRR 72.　　**F** £50 ($80) / **VF** £125 ($200)
*Sextantes of this period vary considerably in weight, ranging from about 15 grams down
to 9 grams (for lighter post-reform issues of similar type, see no. 1204).*

612

612 **Sextans.** 215–211 BC. Similar, but also with corn-ear above prow. RRC 42/3.
                    F £60 ($96) / **VF** £150 ($240)
     For lighter post-reform sextantes of similar type, see no. 1209.

613 — Similar, but with L (Luceria) between the two pellets below prow, and without the corn-
     ear above. RRC 43/4. CRR 128. BMCRR Italy, p. 148, 7.   **F** £75 ($120) / **VF** £175 ($280)
     For lighter post-reform sextantes of similar type, see no. 1223.

614   615

614 **Uncia.** 217–215 BC. Rad. and dr. bust of Sol facing, pellet on l. Rev. Crescent and two
     stars, pellet above, ROMA below. RRC 39/4. CRR 96. BMCRR Romano-Campanian 125.
                    F £80 ($128) / **VF** £200 ($320)
     Unciae of this period weigh about 13 grams.

615 — Hd. of Roma l., in crested Attic helmet, pellet behind. Rev. Prow of galley r., ROMA
     above, pellet below. RRC 38/6. CRR 86. BMCRR 88.   **F** £50 ($80) / **VF** £125 ($200)

616 215–211 BC. Similar, but Roma hd. is to r. RRC 41/10. CRR 108. BMCRR 109.
                    F £40 ($64) / **VF** £100 ($160)
     *Unciae of this period vary considerably in weight, ranging from about 10 grams down to 5
     grams (for lighter post-reform issues of similar type, see no. 1307).*

617 — Similar, but also with corn-ear above prow. RRC 42/4. CRR 195e. BMCRR Italy 79.
                    F £45 ($72) / **VF** £110 ($176)
     For lighter post-reform unciae of similar type, see no. 1310.

618 — Similar, but with L (Luceria) preceding the pellet below prow, and without the corn-ear
     above. RRC 43/5. CRR 129. BMCRR Italy, p. 148, 9.   **F** £50 ($80) / **VF** £125 ($200)
     For lighter post-reform unciae of similar type, see no. 1320.

619 **Semuncia.** 217–215 BC. Turreted and dr. female bust r. Rev. Horseman galloping r., hold-
     ing whip, ROMA below. RRC 39/5. CRR 97. BMCRR Romano-Campanian 136.
                    F £40 ($64) / **VF** £100 ($160)
     Semunciae of this period weigh about 6–7 grams.

619 620

620 **Semuncia.** 217–215 BC. Hd. of Mercury r., in winged petasus. Rev. Prow of galley r., ROMA above. RRC 38/7. CRR 87. BMCRR 129. **F** £35 ($56) / **VF** £90 ($144)

621 215–211 BC. Similar. RRC 41/11. CRR 109. BMCRR 162. **F** £30 ($48) / **VF** £75 ($120)
Semunciae of this period weigh about 4–5 grams (for lighter post-reform semunciae of the type of 620–21, see no. 1360).

622 — Similar, but also with corn-ear above prow. RRC 42/5. BMCRR Italy 87.
F £35 ($56) / **VF** £90 ($144)
For lighter post-reform semunciae of similar type, see no. 1361.

623 — Similar, but with L (Luceria) below prow, and without corn-ear above. RRC 43/6. CRR 130. BMCRR Italy, p. 148, 11. **F** £35 ($56) / **VF** £90 ($144)

624

624 **Quartuncia.** 217–215 BC. Hd. of Roma r., in crested Attic helmet. Rev. Prow of galley r., ROMA above. RRC 38/8. CRR 110. BMCRR 169. **F** £30 ($48) / **VF** £75 ($120)
Weighing about 3–4 grams the quarter-uncia, the smallest denomination of the Roman bronze coinage, was produced only briefly during the period of the semilibral weight standard. With the further decline in the weight of the bronze coinage after 215 BC issue of the experimental quartuncia ceased, never again to be resumed.

STRUCK COINAGE: POST-REFORM ISSUES, CIRCA 211–82 BC

Under the terms of the sweeping currency reform of 211 BC the principal unit of the bronze coinage, the as, was issued for the first time as a struck coin, thus completing the process which had begun about half a decade before with the introduction of struck fractional denominations. Thereafter, bronzes in a range of values (chiefly as, semis, triens, quadrans, sextans and uncia) were produced regularly on the sextantal weight standard, based on an as of about 44 grams. The pattern of development was similar to the contemporary silver denarius, the initial anonymous issues soon being augmented by others bearing symbols, letters and monograms, and eventually superseded by those with fully expanded moneyers' names. There was a marked decline in the volume of the bronze coinage in the second half of the 2nd century BC. After *circa* 146 production of the as was suspended for more than three decades, though some of the fractional denominations remained in issue. This cessation of bronze coinage coincided with the period of large scale type diversification for the silver denarius, with the result that the bronze types remained more or less immobilized in their traditional forms. Some originality was shown in the designs following the resumption of as production about 113 BC, but bronze issues ceased altogether in the time of Sulla about three decades later. There was a partial revival during the Imperatorial period, but the full-scale restoration of the *aes* coinage was delayed until about 18 BC when it was reintroduced by Augustus in an entirely new form.

Because of the lack of diversity in the designs of the post-reform bronze denominations the descriptions in the following listings are, in most instances, given in an abbreviated form. Fuller details are included only where there is any major deviation from the norm. The following are the standard types for each of the principal denominations:

As. Obv. Laur. hd. of bearded Janus, I above. Rev. Prow of galley r., I above or before, ROMA below (usually with symbol, letter/s or monogram above or before).

Semis. Obv. Laur. hd. of bearded Saturn r., S behind. Rev. Prow of galley r., S above or before, ROMA below (usually with symbol, letter/s or monogram above or before).

Triens. Obv. Hd. of Minerva r., in crested Corinthian helmet, four pellets above. Rev. Prow of galley r., four pellets below or before, ROMA above or below (usually with symbol, letter/s or monogram above or before).

Quadrans. Obv. Hd. of young Hercules r., clad in lion's skin, three pellets behind. Rev. Prow of galley r., three pellets below, before or above, ROMA above or below (usually with symbol, letter/s or monogram above or before).

Sextans. Obv. Hd. of Mercury r., in winged petasus, two pellets above. Rev. Prow of galley r., two pellets below or before, ROMA above or below (usually with symbol, letter/s or monogram above or before).

Uncia. Obv. Hd. of Roma r., in crested Attic helmet, pellet behind. Rev. Prow of galley r., pellet below or before, ROMA above or below (usually with symbol, letter/s or monogram above or before).

Dupondius (= 2 asses)

625

625 **211–208 BC.** Hd. of Minerva r., in crested Corinthian helmet. Rev. Prow of galley r., II above, ROMA below. RRC 56/1. CRR 303. BMCRR p. 47.

F £450 ($720) / **VF** £1,000 ($1,600)

Surviving specimens of this very rare denomination are of the same weight as the as, on which they all appear to be overstruck. The dupondius must, therefore, have been regarded as fiduciary or token currency.

626   — Similar, but also with corn-ear above prow and KA (in monogram) before. RRC 69/1.
       CRR 310. BMCRR Appendix 23.   (*Unique*)
       This extremely rare variant appears to be of Sicilian mintage, probably Catana.

As

*Standard type: laur. hd. of bearded Janus, I above. Rev. Prow of galley r., I above or before, ROMA
below (usually with symbol, letter/s or monogram above or before).*

627

627   **211–206 BC.** Anonymous issue, I above prow. RRC 56/2. CRR 143. BMCRR 217.
                                                 F £55 ($88) / **VF** £140 ($224)
       Weight about 44 grams (for lighter asses of similar type, see no. 712).

628

628   — Anchor before prow, I above. RRC 50/3. CRR 145. BMCRR 347.
                                                 F £60 ($96) / **VF** £150 ($240)
       Weight about 36 grams (for lighter asses of similar type, see no. 688).

629   — Similar, but also with Q above prow. RRC 86B/1. CRR 301.
                                                 F £100 ($160) / **VF** £250 ($400)

630   — Branch above prow, I before. RRC 76/2. CRR 202. BMCRR Italy 113.
                                                 F £75 ($120) / **VF** £180 ($288)

631   **211–206 BC.** Caduceus (usually horizontal, rarely vertical) above prow, I before. RRC
       60/2. CRR 164. BMCRR Italy 49.   **F** £75 ($120) / **VF** £180 ($288)

632

632   — Club above prow, I before. RRC 89/3. CRR 213. BMCRR 312.
                                                              F £65 ($104) / **VF** £160 ($256)

633   — Corn-ear above prow, I before. RRC 72/11. CRR 195.   **F** £80 ($128) / **VF** £200 ($320)

634   — Corn-ear and I above prow, **KA** (in monogram) or **IC** before, and with corn-ear below
       hd. of Janus on obv. RRC 69/2. CRR 310a. BMCRR Italy, p. 208.
                                                              F £90 ($144) / **VF** £225 ($360)
       This appears to be of Sicilian mintage, probaby Catana.

635   — Cornucopiae above prow, I before. RRC 58/3. CRR 218. BMCRR 334.
                                                              F £75 ($120) / **VF** £180 ($288)

636   — I and crescent above prow. RRC 57/3. CRR 221. BMCRR 336.
                                                              F £70 ($112) / **VF** £170 ($272)

637   — Dolphin before prow, I above. RRC 80/2. CRR 215. BMCRR 331.
                                                              F £75 ($120) / **VF** £180 ($288)

638   — Hammer and apex above prow, I before. RRC 59/2. CRR 150. BMCRR Italy 44.
                                                              F £65 ($104) / **VF** £160 ($256)

639   — Spearhead above prow, I before (sometimes the positions reversed). RRC 88/3. CRR
       224.   **F** £100 ($160) / **VF** £250 ($400)

640   — I and horizontal staff above prow. RRC 106/4. CRR 210. BMCRR Italy 64.
                                                              F £75 ($120) / **VF** £180 ($288)

641   — Victory and I above prow. RRC 61/2. CRR 148. BMCRR Italy 25.
                                                              F £65 ($104) / **VF** £160 ($256)

642   — Wreath and I above prow. RRC 110/2. CRR 279. BMCRR 326.
                                                              F £75 ($120) / **VF** £180 ($288)

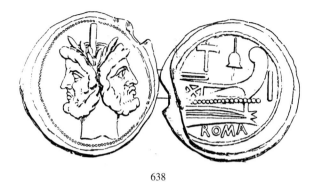

638

643 **211–206 BC.** AVR (in monogram) before prow, I above. RRC 65/2. CRR 162. B *Aurelia* 10.
F £150 ($240) / **VF** £350 ($560)

644 — C before prow, I above. RRC 63/2. CRR 157. BMCRR Italy, p. 189.
F £100 ($160) / **VF** £250 ($400)

645 — CA or C/A (Canusium) before prow, I (sometimes horizontal) above, and usually with CA below hd. of Janus on obv., the mark of value horizontal. RRC 100/1. CRR 309a. BMCRR Italy 265.
F £100 ($160) / **VF** £250 ($400)

646 — I and CN CO above prow, pickaxe (*dolabella*) before. RRC 81/1.
F £200 ($320) / **VF** £450 ($720)
The symbol identifies the cognomen of the moneyer Cn. Cornelius Dolabella.

647 — H before prow, I above. RRC 85/2. CRR 175. BMCRR Italy 203.
F £70 ($112) / **VF** £170 ($272)

648 — L (Luceria) before prow, I above, and with L below hd. of Janus on obv., the mark of value horizontal. RRC 97/22a, 97/28. CRR 304. BMCRR Italy 168.
F £90 ($144) / **VF** £225 ($360)
Some specimens of this type are struck on small flans weighing only about 6 grams.

649 — Similar, but with P instead of L below hd. of Janus. RRC 97/22b.
F £100 ($160) / **VF** £250 ($400)

650 — MA (in monogram) before prow, I above. RRC 64/2. CRR 160. (*Unique*)

651 — Π before prow, I (sometimes horizontal) above, and with Π below hd. of Janus on obv., the mark of value horizontal. RRC 99/1, 99/10. CRR 306. BMCRR Italy 257.
F £100 ($160) / **VF** £250 ($400)
A unique specimen of this type is struck on a small flan weighing only about 6 grams.

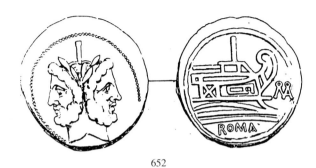

652

652   **211–206 BC. ROMA** (in monogram) before prow, I above. RRC 84/4. CRR 190.
                                                          F £90 ($144) / **VF** £225 ($360)

653   — V before prow, I above. RRC 87/1. CRR 186. BMCRR Italy, p. 199.
                                                          F £90 ($144) / **VF** £225 ($360)

654   **206–194 BC.** Bird and rudder above prow, I before. RRC 117B/1. CRR 292. BMCRR 344.
                                                          F £70 ($112) / **VF** £170 ($272)

655   — Bull (?) charging l. above prow, I before. RRC 116/2.   **F** £100 ($160) / **VF** £250 ($400)

656   — Dog r. (sometimes with foreleg raised) above prow, I before. RRC 122/3. CRR 251.
       BMCRR 489, 490.   **F** £75 ($120) / **VF** £180 ($288)

657   — Helmet above prow, I before. RRC 118/1. CRR 272. BMCRR Italy 374.
                                                          F £75 ($120) / **VF** £180 ($288)

658   — Knife above prow, I before. RRC 120/3. CRR 257. BMCRR 476.
                                                          F £75 ($120) / **VF** £180 ($288)

659   — Meta above prow, I before. RRC 124/3. CRR 260.   **F** £75 ($120) / **VF** £180 ($288)

660   — Beak of prow and I above prow. RRC 114/2. CRR 245. BMCRR 451.
                                                          F £65 ($104) / **VF** £160 ($256)

661   — Ram r. above prow, I before. RRC 123/2.   **F** £100 ($160) / **VF** £250 ($400)

662   — Sow r. above prow, I before. RRC 121/3. CRR 254. **F** £80 ($128) / **VF** £200 ($320)

663   — Staff (horizontal) above prow, I before. RRC 112/3. CRR 210.
                                                          F £80 ($128) / **VF** £200 ($320)

664   — Star above prow, I before. RRC 113/2.   **F** £90 ($144) / **VF** £225 ($360)
       Weight about 34 grams (for lighter asses of similar type, see no. 693).

665   — Thunderbolt before prow, I above. RRC 119/3. CRR 248.
                                                          F £80 ($128) / **VF** £200 ($320)

666   **194–189 BC.** I and crescent above prow. RRC 137/2. CRR 267. BMCRR 579.
                                                          F £90 ($144) / **VF** £225 ($360)

667 **194–189 BC.** Moneyer's monogram **AV** above prow, I before. RRC 136/2. CRR 327.
BMCRR 568.   F £90 ($144) / **VF** £225 ($360)

668 — Moneyer's monogram **L PL H** above prow, I before. RRC 134/2. CRR 333. BMCRR 555.
                                                     F £75 ($120) / **VF** £180 ($288)

669

669 — Moneyer's monogram **ME** above prow, I before. RRC 132/3. CRR 319. BMCRR 536.
                                                     F £65 ($104) / **VF** £160 ($256)

670 — Moneyer's monogram **TAMP** above prow, I before. RRC 133/4. CRR 337. BMCRR
561.   F £75 ($120) / **VF** £180 ($288)

671 **189–179 BC.** Bird with wreath in beak perched on T (rarely **TOD**) above prow, I before.
RRC 141/2. CRR 346. BMCRR 592.   F £80 ($128) / **VF** £200 ($320)
Very rarely, the bird on T is before the prow and the I above.

672

672 — Bull r. and **MD** (in monogram) above prow, I before. RRC 142/1. CRR 299. BMCRR
549.   F £65 ($104) / **VF** £160 ($256)

673 — Shield and **MAE** (in monogram) above prow, I before. RRC 143/1. CRR 375. BMCRR
p. 77.   F £90 ($144) / **VF** £225 ($360)

674 — Ulysses walking r., holding staff, and I above prow, **ROMA** before, **L MAMILI** below.
RRC 149/1a. CRR 369. BMCRR p. 97.   F £90 ($144) / **VF** £225 ($360)

196   ROMAN REPUBLIC

675   **189–179 BC.** Similar, but without moneyer's name, and I is before prow, ROMA below.
      RRC 149/1b.   **F** £100 ($160) / **VF** £250 ($400)

676   — Victory flying r. and spearhead above prow, I before. RRC 145/1. CRR 293. BMCRR
      497.   **F** £70 ($112) / **VF** £170 ($272)

677   — Victory flying r. and L F P (in monogram) above prow, I before. RRC 144/1. CRR 300.
      BMCRR 540.   **F** £70 ($112) / **VF** £170 ($272)

678   — CN DOM above prow, I before. RRC 147/2. CRR 350.   **F** £150 ($240) / **VF** £350 ($560)

679

679   — M TITINI above prow, I before. RRC 150/1. CRR 365. BMCRR 654.
                                                     F £70 ($112) / **VF** £170 ($272)

680   — Q MARI above prow, I before. RRC 148/1. CRR 367. BMCRR 822.
                                                     F £75 ($120) / **VF** £180 ($288)

681   **179–169 BC.** Dolphin r. above prow, I before. RRC 160/1. BMCRR 427.
                                                     F £75 ($120) / **VF** £180 ($288)

682   — Fly r. above prow, I before. RRC 159/3. CRR 324. BMCRR Italy 382.
                                                     F £90 ($144) / **VF** £225 ($360)

683   — Prawn above prow, I before. RRC 156/3. CRR 344.   **F** £100 ($160) / **VF** £250 ($400)

684   — MA (in monogram) above prow, I before. RRC 172/2.   (*Unique*)

685   — MAT (in monogram) above prow, I before. RRC 162/3. CRR 321a. BMCRR 625.
                                                     F £60 ($96) / **VF** £150 ($240)

686   — PVR (in monogram) above prow, I before. RRC 155/2. CRR 331. BMCRR Italy, p. 230.
                                                     F £150 ($240) / **VF** £350 ($560)

687   — TAL (in monogram) above prow, I before. RRC 161/2. CRR 329. BMCRR Italy, p. 232.
                                                     F £150 ($240) / **VF** £350 ($560)

688   **169–157 BC.** Anchor before prow, I above. RRC 194/1. CRR 238. BMCRR 519.
                                                     F £65 ($104) / **VF** £160 ($256)
      Weight about 27 grams (for heavier asses of similar type, see no. 628).

685

689 **169–157 BC.** Ass r. above prow, I before. RRC 195/1. CRR 298. BMCRR 520.
F £65 ($104) / **VF** £160 ($256)

690 — Butterfly (sometimes on vine-branch with grapes) above prow, I before. RRC 184/1. CRR 295–6. BMCRR 504, 518. F £60 ($96) / **VF** £150 ($240)

691 — Caps of the Dioscuri above prow, I before. RRC 181/1. CRR 294. BMCRR 502.
F £70 ($112) / **VF** £170 ($272)

692 — Gryphon and hare's hd. above prow, I before. RRC 182/2. CRR 284. BMCRR Italy 332. F £65 ($104) / **VF** £160 ($256)

693 — Star above prow, I before. RRC 196/1. CRR 264. BMCRR 461.
F £60 ($96) / **VF** £150 ($240)
Weight about 23 grams (for heavier asses of similar type, see no. 664).

694 — Wolf suckling twins above prow, I before. RRC 183/1. CRR 297. BMCRR 514.
F £70 ($112) / **VF** £170 ($272)

695 — A CÆ above prow, I before. RRC 174/1. CRR 355. BMCRR 811.
F £60 ($96) / **VF** £150 ($240)

696

696 — BAL (AL in monogram) above prow, I before. RRC 179/1. CRR 354. BMCRR 608.
F £65 ($104) / **VF** £160 ($256)

697 — C SÆ above prow, I before. RRC 175/1. CRR 357. BMCRR 810. *(Unique)*

698 **169–157 BC.** C SAX (AX in monogram) above prow, I before. RRC 173/1. CRR 360. BMCRR 642.   **F** £60 ($96) / **VF** £150 ($240)

699 — CINA above prow, I before. RRC 178/1. CRR 368. BMCRR 804.   **F** £60 ($96) / **VF** £150 ($240)

700 — MVRENA (MVR in monogram) above prow, I before. RRC 186/1. CRR 373. BMCRR 808.   **F** £60 ($96) / **VF** £150 ($240)

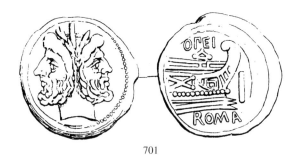

701

701 — OPEI (rarely OPEL) above prow, I before. RRC 190/1. CRR 363. BMCRR 598.   **F** £60 ($96) / **VF** £150 ($240)

702 — OPEIMI (PEIMI in monogram) above prow, I before. RRC 188/1. CRR 362. BMCRR 596.   **F** £75 ($120) / **VF** £180 ($288)

703 — P BLAS above prow, I before. RRC 189/1. CRR 370. BMCRR 788.   **F** £60 ($96) / **VF** £150 ($240)

704 — PAE (in monogram) above prow, I before. RRC 176/1. CRR 358. BMCRR 635.   **F** £65 ($104) / **VF** £160 ($256)

705 — PVR (VR in monogram) above prow, I before. RRC 187/2. CRR 359. BMCRR Italy 424.   **F** £65 ($104) / **VF** £160 ($256)

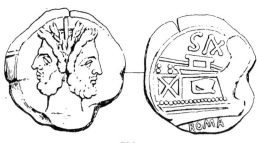

706

706 — SAX (AX in monogram) above prow, I before. RRC 180/1. CRR 361.   **F** £65 ($104) / **VF** £160 ($256)

707   **169–157 BC.** TA (in monogram) above prow, I before. RRC 192/1. CRR 372. BMCRR 793.
                                          F £65 ($104) / **VF** £160 ($256)

708   — TP (in monogram) above prow, I before. RRC 177/1. CRR 353. BMCRR 632.
                                          F £65 ($104) / **VF** £160 ($256)

709   — TVRD (VR in monogram) above prow, I before. RRC 193/1. CRR 366. BMCRR 796.
                                          F £60 ($96) / **VF** £150 ($240)

710   — VAL (in monogram) above prow, I before. RRC 191/1. CRR 356. BMCRR 545.
                                          F £60 ($96) / **VF** £150 ($240)

711

711   — VARO (VAR in monogram) above prow, I before. RRC 185/1. CRR 364. BMCRR 542.
                                          F £65 ($104) / **VF** £160 ($256)

712   **157–155 BC.** Anonymous issue, I above or before prow. RRC 197–198B/1.
                                          F £75 ($120) / **VF** £180 ($288)
       Weight about 21 grams (for the much larger issues of anonymous asses on the heavier sextantal standard, see no. 627).

713   — NAT above prow, I before. RRC 200/2. CRR 383. BMCRR 763.
                                          F £65 ($104) / **VF** £160 ($256)

714   — SAR above prow, I before. RRC 199/2. CRR 378. BMCRR 748.
                                          F £60 ($96) / **VF** £150 ($240)

715   **155–149 BC.** Crescent above prow, I before. RRC 212/1. BMCRR 580.
                                          F £80 ($128) / **VF** £200 ($320)

716   — Mast and sail above prow, I before. RRC 213/1. BMCRR 529.
                                          F £70 ($112) / **VF** £170 ($272)

717   **Q. Caecilius Metellus Macedonicus,** 155 BC. Q ME (ME in monogram) above prow, I
       before. RRC 211/1. CRR 374. BMCRR 603.   **F** £90 ($144) / **VF** £225 ($360)

718   **C. Scribonius,** 154 BC. C SCR above prow, I before. RRC 201/2. CRR 381. BMCRR 733.
                                          F £70 ($112) / **VF** £170 ($272)

719   **C. Maianius,** 153 BC. C MAIANI (MA and AN in monogram) above prow, I before. RRC
       203/2. CRR 428. BMCRR Italy 439.   **F** £65 ($104) / **VF** £160 ($256)

720

720   **L. Saufeius,** 152 BC. Crescent and L SAVF (VF in monogram) above prow, I before. RRC
       204/2. CRR 385. BMCRR 836.   **F** £60 ($96) / **VF** £150 ($240)

721   **P. Cornelius Sulla,** 151 BC. P SVLA above prow, I before, prow-stem decorated with hd. of
       Venus (?) r. RRC 205/2. CRR 387. BMCRR 830.   **F** £65 ($104) / **VF** £160 ($256)

722   **Safra,** 150 BC. SAFRA above prow, dolphin before (no mark of value). RRC 206/2. CRR
       389. BMCRR 675.   **F** £60 ($96) / **VF** £150 ($240)
       SAFRA *would appear to represent a cognomen only, no stop being inserted after the first*
       letter.

723   **C. Junius C.f.,** 149 BC. C IVNI above prow, I before. RRC 210/2. CRR 393. BMCRR 664.
                                                           F £65 ($104) / **VF** £160 ($256)

724   **Q. Marcius Libo,** 148 BC. Q MARC (MA in monogram) above prow, LIBO before (no mark
       of value). RRC 215/2a. CRR 396. BMCRR 702.   **F** £60 ($96) / **VF** £150 ($240)

725   — Similar, but with Q MARC (or Q MAR, MA in monogram) above prow, I before (LIBO
       omitted). RRC 215/2b–c. CRR 367. BMCRR 705, 824.   **F** £65 ($104) / **VF** £160 ($256)

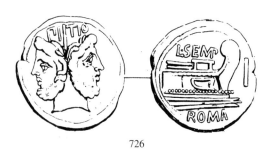

726

726   **L. Sempronius Pitio,** 148 BC. L SEMP (or SEMPR, MP in monogram) above prow, I before,
       and usually with PITIO above hd. of Janus on obv. RRC 216/2. CRR 403. BMCRR 718.
                                                           F £60 ($96) / **VF** £150 ($240)

727   **M. Atilius Saranus,** 148 BC. M ATILI (or ATIL) above prow, I before. RRC 214/2. CRR
       399. BMCRR 692.   **F** £60 ($96) / **VF** £150 ($240)

728

728   **C. Terentius Lucanus,** 147 BC. Wreath-bearing Victory flying r. and C TER LVC (TE in monogram) above prow, I before. RRC 217/2. CRR 426. BMCRR 782.

F £60 ($96) / **VF** £150 ($240)

729   **C. Antestius,** 146 BC. Puppy running r. and C ANTESTI (ANTE in monogram) above prow, I before. RRC 219/2. CRR 407. BMCRR 862. F £65 ($104) / **VF** £160 ($256)

[INTERRUPTION IN PRODUCTION OF THE AS, CIRCA 146–114/113 BC]

730   **C. Fonteius,** 114/113 BC. ROM–A divided by I above prow, anchor before, C FONT (NT in monogram) below. RRC 290/2. CRR 556. BMCRR Italy 617.

F £100 ($160) / **VF** £225 ($360)

731

731   **Cn. Cornelius Blasio Cn.f.,** 112/111 BC. Obv. Laur. hd. of Janus, I above, ROMA around. Rev. CN BLASIO CN F, Victory stg. r., erecting trophy. RRC 296/2. CRR 562. BMCRR Italy 632. F £200 ($320) / **VF** £450 ($720)

732   **C. Sulpicius C.f.,** 106 BC. C SVLPI (LP in monogram) above prow, palm-branch before (mark of value omitted). RRC 312/2. CRR 573. BMCRR 1327.

F £100 ($160) / **VF** £225 ($360)

733   **L. Memmius Galeria,** 106 BC. L MEMMI (ME in monogram) above prow, the stem decorated with hd. of Venus r. and crowned by Cupid before (mark of value omitted). RRC 313/2. CRR 575. BMCRR 1357. F £100 ($160) / **VF** £225 ($360)

734   **C. Fabius C.f. (Hadrianus?),** 102 BC. C FABI C F above prow, heron stg. r. on beak (mark of value omitted). RRC 322/2. CRR 591. BMCRR 1611. F £100 ($160) / **VF** £225 ($360)

735   **P. Cornelius Lentulus Marcellinus,** 100 BC. LENT MAR F (NT and MAR in monogram) above prow, triskeles before (mark of value omitted). RRC 329/2. CRR 606.
                                                                F £100 ($160) / **VF** £225 ($360)

736

736   **L. Pomponius Molo,** *ca.* 97 BC. L POMP (LP and MP in monogram) above prow, I before. RRC 334/2. CRR 608. BMCRR Italy 739.   **F** £90 ($144) / **VF** £200 ($320)

737   **Anonymous (C. Poblicius Malleolus),** *ca.* 96 BC. Hammer above prow, I before. RRC 335/4. CRR 616. BMCRR Italy 708.   **F** £90 ($144) / **VF** £200 ($320)

738   **D. Junius L.f. Silanus,** 91 BC. D SILANVS L F (or similar) above prow (mark of value and ROMA omitted). RRC 337/5. CRR 649. BMCRR 1853.   **F** £75 ($120) / **VF** £175 ($280)

739   **Anonymous (L.P.D.A.P.),** 91 BC. L P D A P above prow (mark of value and ROMA omitted). RRC 338/1. CRR 678. BMCRR 2188.   **F** £110 ($176) / **VF** £250 ($400)
      This legend may be expanded to 'Lege Papiria de assis pondere' and refers to the Lex Papiria of 91 BC by which the weight standard of the bronze coinage was reduced to the semuncial level.

740   **Anonymous,** 91 BC. ROMA above prow (mark of value usually omitted, but sometimes above or before). RRC 339/1. CRR 679. BMCRR 2194.   **F** £90 ($144) / **VF** £200 ($320)

741

741   **L. Calpurnius Piso L.f. L.n. Frugi,** 90 BC. Victory stg. r. on deck of prow, L PISO above, FRVGI below (mark of value and ROMA omitted). RRC 340/4. CRR 677. BMCRR 2179.
                                                                F £90 ($144) / **VF** £200 ($320)

742   **Q. Titius,** 90 BC. Q TITI above prow, I sometimes before (ROMA omitted, mark of value sometimes omitted on obv.). RRC 341/4a–c. CRR 694, 694a. BMCRR 2231, 2234.
                                                                F £75 ($120) / **VF** £175 ($280)

743

743   **Q. Titius,** 90 BC. Similar, but also with control-symbol (ass's hd., caduceus, caps of the Dioscuri, cornucopiae, crescent, dolphin, horse's hd., palm-branch or star) above, behind, before or below prow. RRC 341/4d. CRR 694b. BMCRR 2236.

F £75 ($120) / **VF** £175 ($280)

744

744   **C. Vibius C.f. Pansa,** 90 BC. Laur. hd. of Janus, mark of value sometimes omitted. Rev. Three prows r., usually with palm-branch above, caps of the Dioscuri or I before, moneyer's name above and below, or below only with ROMA above. RRC 342/7. CRR 690–690e. BMCRR 2312–20.   F £90 ($144) / **VF** £200 ($320)
This moneyer's name is represented in a complex variety of forms: C VIBIVS C F PANSA; C VIBIVS; C VIBI; C PANSA; C PASA; C VI PA; C VIB PAN *(PAN in monogram);* C VIBI PA *(PA in monogram);* C VIBI PAN *(AN or PAN in monogram);* C VIBI PANS *(sometimes* AN, PAN, *or* PANS *in monogram);* C VIBI PAS; C VIBI PASA.

745   **L. Titurius L.f. Sabinus,** 89 BC. Moneyer's name above and below prow, usually with Victory or I before, sometimes with palm-branch across (ROMA omitted, mark of value sometimes omitted on obv.). RRC 344/4. CRR 701–701c. BMCRR 2355–63.
F £75 ($120) / **VF** £175 ($280)
This moneyer's name is represented in a complex variety of forms: L TITVRI L F SABINVS *(sometimes* VR *or* TVR *in monogram, sometimes* AB *in monogram, sometimes* IN *in monogram);* L TITVRI·L F SABINS *(AB and* IN *in monogram);* L TITVRI L SABINVS *(AB and sometimes* IN *in monogram);* L TITVRI SABINVS; L TITVR SABINVS; L TITVR SABIN *(AB in monogram).*

746   **Cn. Cornelius Lentulus,** 88 BC. CN LENTVL (rarely with NT in monogram, or LENTV or LENT or LEN) above prow (mark of value and ROMA omitted, mark of value also omitted on obv.). RRC 345/3. CRR 704. BMCRR 2445–7.   F £75 ($120) / **VF** £175 ($280)

747 **C. Marcius Censorinus,** 88 BC. Conjoined hds. r. of Numa Pompilius, bearded, and Ancus Marcius, beardless, **NVMA POMPILI ANCVS** (or **ANCV) MARCI** (**MAR** usually in monogram), *or* **NVMAE** (or **NVMÆ) POMPILI ANCI MARCI** behind and before. Rev. Two arches, beneath which Victory on column and prow r., **C CENSO** above, **ROMA** below. RRC 346/3. CRR 716. BMCRR 2419. **F** £140 ($224) / **VF** £325 ($520)

748

748 — Similar, but with rev. type prow r., stern of another vessel moving in opposite direction behind, Victory on column in background, **C CENSO ROMA** (**MA** sometimes in monogram) above, *or* **C MARCI CENSO** (**MAR** in monogram) above, **ROMA** below. RRC 346/4. CRR 715, 715a. BMCRR 2415. **F** £150 ($240) / **VF** £350 ($560)

749 **L. Rubrius Dossenus,** 87 BC. Laur. hd of Janus, snake-entwined altar between the hds. (no mark of value). Rev. **L RVBRI DOSSEN** (or **DOSSENI, DOSSE,** or **DOSSI**) above prow, **I** before. RRC 348/5. CRR 709. BMCRR 2461. **F** £110 ($176) / **VF** £250 ($400)

750 — Janiform hds. of Hercules l. and Mercury r., club and caduceus below their respective chins. Rev. Prow protruding r. from behind distyle shrine containing snake-entwined altar, **L RVBRI** below, **DOSSE** (or **DOSSEN**) on l. RRC 348/6. CRR 710. BMCRR p. 313. **F** £150 ($240) / **VF** £350 ($560)

751 **Gargonius (or Gargilius), Ogulnius, and Vergilius (or Verginius),** 86 BC. **GAR OGVL VER** or **GAR VER OGVL** (**AR, VL** and **VE** in monogram) above prow, which is turned to l., control-letter above, before or below (mark of value and **ROMA** omitted). RRC 350A/3a-b. CRR 722, 722a. BMCRR 2625–6. **F** £90 ($144) / **VF** £200 ($320)

752

752 — Similar, but with **OGVL GAR VER** or **OGVL VER GAR** (**VL, AR** and **VE** in monogram) above prow. RRC 350A/3c–d. CRR 722b–c. BMCRR 2627–32. **F** £90 ($144) / **VF** £200 ($320)

753   **Gargonius (or Gargilius), Ogulnius, and Vergilius (or Verginius),** 86 BC. Similar, but with VER GAR OGVL or VER OGVL GAR (VE, AR and VL in monogram) above prow. RRC 350A/3e–f. CRR 722d–e. BMCRR 2633.   **F** £90 ($144) / **VF** £200 ($320)

754

754   **Mn. Fonteius C.f.,** 85 BC. MN FONT (MN and NT in monogram) and caps of the Dioscuri above prow, which is turned to l. (mark of value and ROMA omitted). RRC 353/3. CRR 725. BMCRR 2484.   **F** £110 ($176) / **VF** £250 ($400)

755   **C. Licinius L.f. Macer,** 84 BC. Laur. hd. of Janus, I above, C LICINI L F on l. Rev. Prow r., stg. male figure holding sceptre and EX S C MACER above. RRC 354/2. CRR 733. BMCRR 2470.   **F** £110 ($176) / **VF** £250 ($400)

756   — Similar, but moneyer's name omitted on obv. and rev., and the prow usually inscribed with control-letter. RRC 354/3. CRR 734. BMCRR 2471–2.
      F £100 ($160) / **VF** £225 ($360)

757

757   **C. Cassius (Longinus?) and L. (Julius?) Salinator,** 84 BC. Laur. hd. of Janus, crescent above. Rev. Prow r., inscribed D S S, C CASSIVS L SALINAT (AT in monogram) above. RRC 355/1a–d. CRR 731–731b. BMCRR 2473.   **F** £90 ($144) / **VF** £200 ($320)
      The names of both moneyers are sometimes given in an abbreviated or blundered form: C CASSIV, CASSI, CASI, *or* ASSI; L SALINA, SALIN, *or* SALI. *The formula* D S S *represents 'de senatus sententia' (see also no. 174).*

758   — Similar, but with legend L SALINA C CASSIVS above prow. RRC 355/1e–h. CRR 731c–d. BMCRR 2475.   **F** £90 ($144) / **VF** £200 ($320)
      The names of both moneyers are sometimes given in an abbreviated or blundered form: L SALIN, SALI, *or* ALIN; C CASSI.

759   **L. Cornelius Sulla,** 82 BC. L SVL or SVLA (VL in monogram) above prow, IMPE below (mark of value and ROMA omitted). RRC 368/1. CRR 767. BMCRR 2895.

F £250 ($400) / **VF** £550 ($880)

This, the final issue of the as prior to Imperatorial times, was made by Sulla during the period of civil war in Italy in 82 BC.

Dextans

This rare denomination, valued at 10 unciae, was issued briefly by the Luceria mint in the period immediately following the currency reform of 211 BC. It bears the mark of value 'S' followed by four pellets (= a semis and four unciae). Its production was never revived.

760

760   **211–208 BC.** Hd. of Ceres r., wreathed with corn. Rev. Victory in quadriga r., L above, ROMA below, S and four pellets in ex. RRC 97/9, 16 and 23. CRR 305. BMCRR Italy 169.

F £350 ($560) / **VF** £750 ($1,200)

761   — Similar, but with Π behind hd. of Ceres and without L on rev. RRC 99/2a. CRR 308. BMCRR Italy 260.

F £300 ($480) / **VF** £650 ($1,040)

762   — Similar, but with Π on rev., either below horses or in ex. RRC 99/2b-c. CRR 307. BMCRR Italy 259.

F £300 ($480) / **VF** £650 ($1,040)

Dodrans

Another rare denomination, the dodrans was valued at 9 unciae ('S' and three pellets). Its production was limited to two relatively late issues, ca. 127–126 BC.

763   **M. Caecilius Q.f. Metellus,** 127 BC. Dr. bust of Vulcan r., wearing laur. pileus, tongs over shoulder, S and three pellets behind. Rev. Prow r., inscribed M METELLVS, Macedonian shield above, S and three pellets before, ROMA below. RRC 263/2. CRR 481. BMCRR p. 177.

F £300 ($480) / **VF** £650 ($1,040)

764   **C. Cassius,** 126 BC. Similar, but the moneyer's name C CASSI is above the prow (no shield). RRC 266/2. CRR 503. BMCRR 1035.

F £250 ($400) / **VF** £550 ($880)

764

Bes

The bes is known only from a single issue dating from around 126 BC. It was the equivalent of 8 unciae ('S' and two pellets).

765

765   **C. Cassius,** 126 BC. Hd. of Liber r., wreathed with ivy, S and two pellets behind. Rev. Prow r., C CASSI above, S and two pellets before, ROMA below. RRC 266/3. CRR 504. BMCRR p. 154.   **F** £300 ($480) / **VF** £650 ($1,040)

Semis

The semis was valued at half the as (6 unciae). **Standard type:** *laur. hd. of bearded Saturn r., S behind. Rev. Prow of galley r., S above or before, ROMA below (usually with symbol, letter/s or monogram above or before).*

766

766   **211–206 BC.** Anonymous issue, S above prow. RRC 56/3. CRR 143a. BMCRR 229.
                                          F £50 ($80) / **VF** £130 ($208)
        Weight about 22 grams (for a unique heavier pre-reform semis of similar type, see no. 600; and for much lighter late semisses, see no. 901).

767 **211–206 BC.** Anchor before prow, S above. RRC 50/4. CRR 145a. BMCRR 351.
F £60 ($96) / **VF** £150 ($240)
Weight about 20 grams (for lighter semisses of similar type, see no. 824).

768 — Similar, but also with Q above prow. RRC 86B/2. CRR 301a. BMCRR 538.
F £60 ($96) / **VF** £150 ($240)

769 — Branch above prow, S before. RRC 76/3. CRR 203. **F** £70 ($112) / **VF** £170 ($272)

770 — Caduceus above prow, S before. RRC 60/3. CRR 164a. **F** £65 ($104) / **VF** £160 ($256)

771 — Club above prow, S before. RRC 89/4. CRR 213a. **F** £70 ($112) / **VF** £170 ($272)

772 — Corn-ear above prow, S before. RRC 72/12. CRR 195a.
F £65 ($104) / **VF** £160 ($256)

773 — Corn-ear and S above prow, KA (in monogram) or C before. RRC 69/3. CRR 310b.
BMCRR Italy, p. 208. **F** £80 ($128) / **VF** £200 ($320)
This appears to be of Sicilian mintage, probably Catana.

774 — Cornucopiae above prow, S before. RRC 58/4. CRR 218a.
F £65 ($104) / **VF** £160 ($256)

775 — S and crescent above prow. RRC 57/4. CRR 221a. BMCRR 339.
F £65 ($104) / **VF** £160 ($256)

776 — Hammer and apex above prow, S before. RRC 59/3. CRR 150a. BMCRR Italy 46.
F £60 ($96) / **VF** £150 ($240)
This appears to have been struck using two weight standards, one of about 25 grams, the other of only 11 grams.

777 — Spearhead before prow, S above. RRC 88/4. CRR 224a.
F £65 ($104) / **VF** £160 ($256)

778 — S and horizontal staff above prow. RRC 106/5. CRR 210a. BMCRR Italy 67.
F £55 ($88) / **VF** £140 ($224)

779 — Victory and S above prow. RRC 61/3. CRR 148a. BMCRR Italy 29.
F £60 ($96) / **VF** £150 ($240)
This and the following appear to have been struck using two weight standards, one of about 25 grams, the other of only 11 grams.

780 — Wreath and S above prow. RRC 110/3. CRR 279a. BMCRR 329.
F £65 ($104) / **VF** £160 ($256)

781 — AVR (in monogram) before prow, S above. RRC 65/3. CRR 162a. B *Aurelia* 11.
F £90 ($144) / **VF** £225 ($360)

782 — C before prow, S above. RRC 63/3. CRR 157a. BMCRR Italy, p. 189.
F £80 ($128) / **VF** £200 ($320)

783 — CA (Canusium) before prow, S above, and with CA below hd of Saturn on obv. RRC 100/2. CRR 309b. BMCRR Italy 266. F £80 ($128) / **VF** £200 ($320)

784 **211–206 BC.** H before prow, S above. RRC 85/3. CRR 175a. BMCRR Italy 206.
F £65 ($104) / **VF** £160 ($256)

785 — L (Luceria) before prow, S above, and with S (horizontal) below hd. of Saturn on obv.
RRC 97/10. CRR 178a. F £80 ($128) / **VF** £200 ($320)

786 — Similar, but with L below hd. of Saturn (S behind), the L on rev. sometimes omitted.
RRC 97/17, 24. CRR 304a. BMCRR Italy 170. F £75 ($120) / **VF** £180 ($288)

787 — MA (in monogram) before prow, S above. RRC 64/3. CRR 160.
F £100 ($160) / **VF** £250 ($400)

788 — Π and S above prow, and with Π below hd. of Saturn on obv. RRC 99/3. CRR 306a.
BMCRR Italy 261. F £80 ($128) / **VF** £200 ($320)

789 — ROMA (in monogram) before prow, S above. RRC 84/5. CRR 190a. BMCRR Italy 193.
F £55 ($88) / **VF** £140 ($224)

790 — V before prow, S above. RRC 87/2. CRR 186a. BMCRR Italy 238.
F £75 ($120) / **VF** £180 ($288)

791 — Hd. of Ceres r., wreathed with corn, S behind. Rev. Hercules r., grappling with stag, club
behind, ROMA below. RRC 82/1. (*Unique*)
Crawford suggests a Sicilian origin for this extraordinary issue.

792 **206–194 BC.** Bird and rudder above prow, S before. RRC 117B/2.
F £90 ($144) / **VF** £225 ($360)

793 — Dog r. above prow, S before. RRC 122/4. CRR 251a. F £65 ($104) / **VF** £160 ($256)

794 — Helmet above prow, S before. RRC 118/2. CRR 272a. BMCRR Italy, p. 225.
F £65 ($104) / **VF** £160 ($256)

795 — Knife above prow, S before. RRC 120/4. CRR 257a. BMCRR 477.
F £65 ($104) / **VF** £160 ($256)

796 — Meta above prow, S before. RRC 124/4. CRR 260a. BMCRR 496.
F £65 ($104) / **VF** £160 ($256)

797 — Beak of prow above prow, S before. RRC 114/3. CRR 245a. BMCRR 454.
F £65 ($104) / **VF** £160 ($256)

798 — Ram r. above prow, S before. RRC 123/3. (*Unique*)

799 — Sow r. above prow, S before. RRC 121/4. CRR 254a. BMCRR 484.
F £65 ($104) / **VF** £160 ($256)

800 — Staff (horizontal) above prow, S before. RRC 112/4. CRR 210a.
F £65 ($104) / **VF** £160 ($256)

801 — Star above prow, S before. RRC 113/3. CRR 264a. BMCRR 465.
F £65 ($104) / **VF** £160 ($256)
Weight about 17 grams (for lighter semisses of similar type, see no. 829).

802 **206–194 BC.** Thunderbolt before prow, S above. RRC 119/4. CRR 248a.
F £65 ($104) / **VF** £160 ($256)

803 **194–189 BC.** Crescent above prow, S before. RRC 137/3. CRR 267a. BMCRR 581.
F £65 ($104) / **VF** £160 ($256)

804 — Moneyer's monogram AV above prow, S before. RRC 136/3. CRR 327a. B *Aurelia* 3.
F £65 ($104) / **VF** £160 ($256)

805 — Moneyer's monogram L PL H above prow, S before. RRC 134/3. CRR 333a. B *Plautia* 4.
F £80 ($128) / **VF** £200 ($320)

806 — Moneyer's monogram ME above prow, S before. RRC 132/4. CRR 319a. B *Caecilia* 4.
F £65 ($104) / **VF** £160 ($256)

807

807 — Moneyer's monogram TAMP above prow, S before. RRC 133/5. CRR 337a. B *Baebia* 7.
F £65 ($104) / **VF** £160 ($256)

808 **189–179 BC.** Bird (sometimes with wreath in beak) perched on T above prow, S before.
RRC 141/3. CRR 346a. BMCRR 593.   F £60 ($96) / **VF** £150 ($240)

809 — Bull r. and MD (in monogram) above prow, S before. RRC 142/2. CRR 299a.
BMCRR 551.   F £60 ($96) / **VF** £150 ($240)

810 — Shield and MAE (or MA, both in monogram) above prow, S before. RRC 143/2. CRR
375a. B *Maenia* 3.   F £65 ($104) / **VF** £160 ($256)

811 — Ulysses walking r., holding staff, above prow, S before. RRC 149/2c.
F £80 ($128) / **VF** £200 ($320)

812 — Similar, but also with L MAMILI below prow, ROMA vertically before, and S above. RRC
149/2b. CRR 369a. B *Mamilia* 2.   F £75 ($120) / **VF** £180 ($288)

813 — Similar, but RO–MA is above the prow, divided by figure of Ulysses, and S is before.
RRC 149/2a.   F £75 ($120) / **VF** £180 ($288)

814 — Victory flying r. and spearhead above prow, S before. RRC 145/2. CRR 293a.
F £65 ($104) / **VF** £160 ($256)

815 — Victory flying r. and L F P (in monogram) above prow, S before. RRC 144/2. CRR 300a.
BMCRR 541.   F £70 ($112) / **VF** £170 ($272)

816

816 **189–179 BC. M TITINI** above prow, S before. RRC 150/2. CRR 365a. BMCRR 657.
F £60 ($96) / **VF** £150 ($240)

817 — Q MARI above prow, S before. RRC 148/2. CRR 367a. B *Maria* 2.
F £70 ($112) / **VF** £170 ($272)

818 **179–169 BC.** Dolphin r. above prow, S before. RRC 160/2.
F £75 ($120) / **VF** £180 ($288)

819 — Fly r. above prow, S before. RRC 159/4. CRR 324a.   **F** £70 ($112) / **VF** £170 ($272)

820 — MA (in monogram) above prow, S before. RRC 172/3.   **F** £80 ($128) / **VF** £200 ($320)

821 — MAT (in monogram) above prow, S before. RRC 162/4. CRR 321b. BMCRR 627.
F £65 ($104) / **VF** £160 ($256)

822 — PVR (in monogram) above prow, S before. RRC 155/3. CRR 331a. B *Furia* 9.
F £100 ($160) / **VF** £250 ($400)

823 — TAL (in monogram) above prow, S before. RRC 161/3. CRR 329a. BMCRR Italy,
p. 233.   **F** £90 ($144) / **VF** £225 ($360)

824 **169–157 BC.** Anchor before prow, S above. RRC 194/2. CRR 238a. BMCRR Italy 300.
F £65 ($104) / **VF** £160 ($256)
Weight about 12 grams (for heavier semisses of similar type, see no. 767).

825 — Ass r. above prow, S before. RRC 195/2. CRR 298a.   **F** £65 ($104) / **VF** £160 ($256)

826 — Butterfly on vine-branch with grapes above prow, S before. RRC 184/2. CRR 296a.
BMCRR 510.   **F** £65 ($104) / **VF** £160 ($256)

827 — Caps of the Dioscuri above prow, S before. RRC 181/2. CRR 294a.
F £65 ($104) / **VF** £160 ($256)

828 — Gryphon and hare's hd. above prow, S before. RRC 182/3. CRR 284a. BMCRR
Italy 335.   **F** £65 ($104) / **VF** £160 ($256)

829 — Star above prow, S before. RRC 196/2. CRR 264a.   **F** £65 ($104) / **VF** £160 ($256)
Weight about 11 grams (for heavier semisses of similar type, see no. 801).

830 — Wolf suckling twins above prow, S before. RRC 183/2. CRR 297a.
F £70 ($112) / **VF** £170 ($272)

831 **169–157 BC.** A C/E above prow, S before. RRC 174/2. CRR 355a. BMCRR 817.
F £65 ($104) / **VF** £160 ($256)

832 — BAL (AL in monogram) above prow, S before. RRC 179/2. CRR 354a. BMCRR 613.
F £70 ($112) / **VF** £170 ($272)

833 — C SAX (AX in monogram) above prow, S before. RRC 173/2. CRR 360a. BMCRR 648.
F £60 ($96) / **VF** £150 ($240)

834   838

834 — CINA above prow, S before. RRC 178/2. CRR 368a. B *Cornelia* 12.
F £60 ($96) / **VF** £150 ($240)

835 — MVRENA (MVR in monogram) above prow, S before. RRC 186/2. CRR 373a. B *Licinia* 2.
F £65 ($104) / **VF** £160 ($256)

836 — OPEI above prow, S before. RRC 190/2. CRR 363a. BMCRR 601.
F £65 ($104) / **VF** £160 ($256)

837 — OPEIMI (PEIMI in monogram) above prow, S before. RRC 188/2. CRR 362a. B *Opimia* 2.
F £70 ($112) / **VF** £170 ($272)

838 — P BLAS above prow, S before. RRC 189/2. CRR 370a. B *Cornelia* 7.
F £60 ($96) / **VF** £150 ($240)

839 — PAE (in monogram) above prow, S before. RRC 176/2. CRR 358a. B *Aemilia* 3.
F £65 ($104) / **VF** £160 ($256)

840 — PVR (VR in monogram) above prow, S before. RRC 187/3. CRR 359a.
F £70 ($112) / **VF** £170 ($272)

841 — SAX (AX in monogram) above prow, S before. RRC 180/2. CRR 361a. B *Clovia* 2.
F £70 ($112) / **VF** £170 ($272)

842 — TA (in monogram) above prow, S before. RRC 192/2. CRR 372a.
F £65 ($104) / **VF** £160 ($256)

843 — TP (in monogram) above prow, S before. RRC 177/2. CRR 353a.
F £60 ($96) / **VF** £150 ($240)

844 — TVRD (VR in monogram) above prow, S before. RRC 193/2. CRR 366a. BMCRR 799.
F £60 ($96) / **VF** £150 ($240)

845 — VAL (in monogram) above prow, S before. RRC 191/2. CRR 356a. B *Valeria* 2.
F £65 ($104) / **VF** £160 ($256)

846 **169–157 BC.** VARO (VAR in monogram) above prow, S before. RRC 185/2. CRR 364a. B
     Terentia 5.   **F** £65 ($104) / **VF** £160 ($256)

847 **157–155 BC.** Anonymous issue, S before prow. RRC 197–198B/2.
                                                               F £65 ($104) / **VF** £160 ($256)
     Weight about 11 grams (for lighter semisses of similar type, see no. 887).

848

848 — NAT above prow, S before. RRC 200/3. CRR 383a. BMCRR 766.
                                                               F £60 ($96) / **VF** £150 ($240)

849 — SAR above prow, S before. RRC 199/3. CRR 378a. BMCRR 751.
                                                               F £65 ($104) / **VF** £160 ($256)

850 **155–149 BC.** Mast and sail above prow, S before. RRC 213/2.
                                                               F £75 ($120) / **VF** £180 ($288)

851 **C. Scribonius,** 154 BC. C SCR above prow, S before. RRC 201/3. CRR 381a. BMCRR 736.
                                                               F £60 ($96) / **VF** £150 ($240)

852 **C. Maianius,** 153 BC. C MAIANI (MA and AN in monogram) above prow, S before. RRC
     203/3. CRR 428a. BMCRR Italy 444.   **F** £65 ($104) / **VF** £160 ($256)

853

853 **L. Saufeius,** 152 BC. Crescent and L SAVF (VF in monogram) above prow, S before. RRC
     204/3. CRR 385a. BMCRR 839.   **F** £55 ($88) / **VF** £140 ($224)

854 **P. Cornelius Sulla,** 151 BC. P SVLA above prow, S before, prow-stem decorated with hd. of
     Venus (?) r. RRC 205/3. CRR 387a. BMCRR 839.   **F** £60 ($96) / **VF** £150 ($240)

855 **Safra,** 150 BC. SAFRA above prow, dolphin before (no mark of value). RRC 206/3. CRR 389a. B *Afrania* 3.   **F** £60 ($96) / **VF** £150 ($240)
SAFRA *would appear to represent a cognomen only, no stop being inserted after the first letter.*

856 **C. Junius C.f.,** 149 BC. C IVNI above prow, S before. RRC 210/3. CRR 393a. BMCRR 667.   **F** £60 ($96) / **VF** £150 ($240)

857 **Q. Marcius Libo,** 148 BC. Q MARC (MA in monogram) above prow, LIBO before (no mark of value). RRC 215/3. CRR 396c. BMCRR 706.   **F** £60 ($96) / **VF** £150 ($240)

858 **L. Sempronius Pitio,** 148 BC. L SEMP (MP in monogram) above prow, S before. RRC 216/3. CRR 403a. BMCRR 720.   **F** £65 ($104) / **VF** £160 ($256)

859 **M. Atilius Saranus,** 148 BC. M ATILI (or ATIL) above prow, S before. RRC 214/3. CRR 399a. BMCRR 697–8.   **F** £65 ($104) / **VF** £160 ($256)

860   861

860 **C. Terentius Lucanus,** 147 BC. Wreath-bearing Victory flying r. and C TER LVC (TE in monogram) above prow, S before. RRC 217/3. CRR 426a. BMCRR 785.   **F** £60 ($96) / **VF** £150 ($240)

861 **C. Antestius,** 146 BC. Puppy running r. and C ANTESTI (ANTE in monogram) above prow, S before. RRC 219/3. CRR 407a. BMCRR 864.   **F** £65 ($104) / **VF** £160 ($256)

862 **C. Titinius,** 141 BC. C TITINI above prow, S before. RRC 226/2. B *Titinia* 8.   **F** £75 ($120) / **VF** £180 ($288)

863 **C. Valerius C.f. Flaccus,** 140 BC. C VAL C F (VAL in monogram) above prow, S before. RRC 228/3. B *Valeria* 9.   *(Unique)*

864 **C. Renius,** 138 BC. Goat r. above prow, C RENI before (no mark of value). RRC 231/2. CRR 433. B *Renia* 2.   **F** £80 ($128) / **VF** £200 ($320)

865 **Cn. Gellius,** 138 BC. CN GEL (or GELI) above prow, S before. RRC 232/2. CRR 435. BMCRR 920.   **F** £60 ($96) / **VF** £150 ($240)

866 **Sex. Pompeius,** 137 BC. Jug and SEX POM above prow, S before, and with jug instead of mark of value behind hd. of Saturn on obv. RRC 235/2. CRR 462. B *Pompeia* 2.   **F** £65 ($104) / **VF** £160 ($256)

867 **C. Curiatius C.f. Trigeminus,** 135 BC. C CVR F (VR in monogram) above prow, on which Victory stands r. (sometimes omitted), S before. RRC 240/2. CRR 460. BMCRR 944, 946.   **F** £50 ($80) / **VF** £130 ($208)

868

868   **L. Trebanius,** 135 BC. L TREBANI (TR and AN in monogram) above prow, S before. RRC
      241/2. CRR 457. BMCRR 961.   **F** £60 ($96) / **VF** £150 ($240)

869   **C. Minucius Augurinus,** 135 BC. C AVG above prow, S before. RRC 242/2. CRR 464.
      BMCRR 955.   **F** £55 ($88) / **VF** £140 ($224)

870   **Ti. Minucius C.f. Augurinus,** 134 BC. TI AVGVRINI and lituus above prow, S before. RRC
      243/2. CRR 495. B *Minucia* 12.   **F** £65 ($104) / **VF** £160 ($256)

871   **C. Numitorius,** 133 BC. C NVMITORI (or NVMITOR) above prow, S before. RRC 246/2.
      CRR 467. BMCRR 972.   **F** £55 ($88) / **VF** £140 ($224)

872   **P. Calpurnius,** 133 BC. Rev. Ship r., inscribed ROMA, on which stands Victory r. with
      steersman behind, P CALP above, S before, dolphin r. below. RRC 247/2. CRR 469.
      BMCRR 970.   **F** £75 ($120) / **VF** £180 ($288)
      This rev. type represents the first significant variation on the standard design of the post-
      reform bronze coinage. See also no. 1161.

873   **L. Minucius,** 133 BC. L MINVCI above prow, S before. RRC 248/2. CRR 471. BMCRR
      965.   **F** £65 ($104) / **VF** £160 ($256)

874   **M. Fabrinius,** 132 BC. M FABRINI above prow, S before. RRC 251/1. CRR 453. B *Fabrinia* 1.
                                                                    F £60 ($96) / **VF** £150 ($240)

875

875   **L. Opimius,** 131 BC. L OPEIMI and wreath above prow, S before. RRC 253/2. CRR 474. B
      Opimia 13.   **F** £80 ($128) / **VF** £200 ($320)

876   **M. Acilius M.f.,** 130 BC. M ACILI above prow, S before. RRC 255/2. CRR 512. BMCRR
      1120.   **F** £60 ($96) / **VF** £150 ($240)

877　**Q. Caecilius Metellus,** 130 BC. Q MET or METE or METEL, or similar (ME and TE usually in monogram) above prow, S before. RRC 256/2. CRR 510. BMCRR 1056,1059.

　　　　　　　　　　　　　　　　　　　　　　　　F £50 ($80) / **VF** £130 ($208)

On some rev. dies the moneyer's praenomen mistakenly appears as 'C' instead of 'Q'.

878　　　　　　　　　　　880

878　**M. Vargunteius,** 130 BC. M VARG (VAR in monogram) above prow, S before. RRC 257/2. CRR 508. BMCRR 1070.　　　　**F** £55 ($88) / **VF** £140 ($224)

879　**Cn. Domitius,** 128 BC. CN DOM or DOMI or DOME (ME in monogram) above prow, S before. RRC 261/2. CRR 515. BMCRR 1027–8.　　　　**F** £55 ($88) / **VF** £140 ($224)

880　**Anonymous,** 128 BC. Elephant's hd. r. with bell attached above prow, S before. RRC 262/2. CRR 497. BMCRR 1048.　　　　**F** £55 ($88) / **VF** £140 ($224)
Although lacking the moneyer's name it seems certain that this was issued by a Caecilius Metellus, probably either L. Caecilius Metellus Diadematus or L. Caecilius Metellus Delmaticus.

881　**M. Caecilius Q.f. Metellus,** 127 BC. M METELLVS or METELLV (ME always in monogram, TE sometimes so) inscribed on prow, Macedonian shield above, S before. RRC 263/3. CRR 482. BMCRR 1151.　　　　**F** £55 ($88) / **VF** £140 ($224)
The moneyer's name is sometimes omitted.

882　**C. Servilius,** 127 BC. C SERVEILI (VE in monogram) inscribed on prow, lion r. above, S before. RRC 264/2. CRR 484. B *Servilia* 8.　　　　**F** £70 ($112) / **VF** £170 ($272)

883　**Q. Fabius Maximus,** 127 BC. Q MAX (MA in monogram) above prow, S before. RRC 265/2. CRR 479. BMCRR 1160.　　　　**F** £65 ($104) / **VF** £160 ($256)

884

884　**T. Quinctius Flamininus,** 126 BC. T Q above prow, S before. RRC 267/2. CRR 506. BMCRR 1042.　　　　**F** £65 ($104) / **VF** £160 ($256)

885 **C. Caecilius Metellus,** 125 BC. C METEL (or METELLVS with ME and TE in monogram) inscribed on prow, elephant's hd. r. above, S before (ROMA before hd. of Saturn on obv. instead of rev.). RRC 269/2. CRR 486. B *Caecilia* 17.   **F** £65 ($104) / **VF** £160 ($256)

886 **Mn. Acilius Balbus,** 125 BC. MN ACI (MN in monogram) above prow, S before. RRC 271/2. CRR 499. B *Acilia* 2.   **F** £70 ($112) / **VF** £170 ($272)

887 **Anonymous,** 135–125 BC. S before prow. RRC 272/1. BMCRR 244.
   F £65 ($104) / **VF** £160 ($256)
   Weight about 8 grams (for heavier semisses of similar type, see no. 847).

888 **C. Porcius Cato,** 123 BC. C CATO above prow, S before. RRC 274/2.   (*Unique*)

889 **M. Fannius C.f.,** 123 BC. M FAN C F (AN in monogram) above prow, S before. RRC 275/2. CRR 420. BMCRR Italy 471.   **F** £65 ($104) / **VF** £160 ($256)

890 **Cn. Domitius, M. Junius Silanus and Q. Curtius,** 116/115 BC. Obv. CN DOMI before hd. of Saturn. Rev. Harpa, M SILA above, Q CVRTI below. RRC 285/3. CRR 538. BMCRR Italy, p. 259.   **F** £70 ($112) / **VF** £170 ($272)

891 **M. Cipius M.f.,** 115/114 BC. Moneyer's name M CIPI M F before hd. of Saturn, S before prow on rev. RRC 289/2. CRR 547. BMCRR Italy, p. 272.
   F £65 ($104) / **VF** £160 ($256)

892 **C. Fonteius,** 114/113 BC. C FONT (NT in monogram) above prow, S before. RRC 290/3. CRR 556a. B *Fonteia* 3.   **F** £65 ($104) / **VF** £160 ($256)

893 **P. Licinius Nerva,** 113/112 BC. Female dancer r. above prow, S before, and with P NERVA (NE in monogram) before hd. of Saturn on obv. RRC 292/2. CRR 549. B *Licinia* 8.
   F £70 ($112) / **VF** £170 ($272)

894 **Cn. Cornelius Blasio Cn. f.,** 112/111 BC. CN BLASIO (BLA in monogram) above prow, S before (the mark of value on obv. before hd. of Saturn). RRC 296/3. CRR 562a. BMCRR Italy 635.   **F** £70 ($112) / **VF** £170 ($272)

895 **M. Herennius,** 108/107 BC. M HERENNI (HE in monogram) above prow, S before. RRC 308/2. CRR 568. BMCRR 1286.   **F** £70 ($112) / **VF** £170 ($272)

896 **C. Sulpicius C.f.,** 106 BC. C SVLPI (LP in monogram) above prow, palm-branch before (mark of value omitted). RRC 312/3. CRR 573a. B *Sulpicia* 3.
   F £65 ($104) / **VF** £160 ($256)

897   900

897 **L. Memmius Galeria,** 106 BC. L MEMMI (ME in monogram) and mark of value S above prow, the stem decorated with hd. of Venus r. and crowned by Cupid before. RRC 313/3. CRR 575a. BMCRR 1358.   **F** £60 ($96) / **VF** £150 ($240)

898   **L. Pomponius Molo,** ca. 97 BC. L POMP (LP and MP in monogram) above prow, S before (the mark of value on obv. sometimes before hd. of Saturn). RRC 334/3. CRR 608a. BMCRR Italy 740, 742.   **F** £55 ($88) / **VF** £140 ($224)

899   **Anonymous (C. Poblicius Malleolus),** ca. 96 BC. Hammer above prow, S before (the mark of value on obv. sometimes before hd. of Saturn). RRC 335/5. CRR 616a. BMCRR 503 and Italy 710.   **F** £60 ($96) / **VF** £150 ($240)

900   **Anonymous (L.P.D.A.P.),** 91 BC. L P D A P above prow (mark of value and ROMA omitted). RRC 338/2. CRR 678a. BMCRR 2189.   **F** £80 ($128) / **VF** £200 ($320)
This legend may be expanded to 'Lege Papiria de assis pondere' and refers to the Lex Papiria of 91 BC by which the weight standard of the bronze coinage was reduced to the semuncial level.

901   **Anonymous,** 91 BC. S above prow (no symbol or moneyer's name). RRC 339/2. CRR 679a. BMCRR 2196.   **F** £65 ($104) / **VF** £160 ($256)
Weight about 6.5 grams (for the much heavier early semisses of similar type, see nos. 600 and 766).

902   **L. Calpurnius Piso L.f. L.n. Frugi,** 90 BC. L PISO above prow, FRVGI (sometimes omitted) below (mark of value and ROMA omitted). RRC 340/5. CRR 677a, b. BMCRR 2186.
                    F £60 ($96) / **VF** £150 ($240)

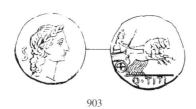

903

903   **Q. Titius,** 90 BC. Obv. Laur. hd. of Apollo r., S behind. Rev. Minerva in quadriga r., Q TITI in ex. RRC 341/5. CRR 695. B *Titia* 5.   **F** £100 ($160) / **VF** £250 ($400)
Remarkably, the types of the three fractional bronze denominations of this moneyer are copied from the silver coinage of his collegue, C. Vibius Pansa (see no. 242).

904   **C. Vibius C.f. Pansa,** 90 BC. C VIBI PA or PAN (PA and PAN both in monogram) above prow, S before (sometimes omitted). RRC 342/8. CRR 690f. B *Vibia* 13.
                    F £65 ($104) / **VF** £160 ($256)

905   **L. Titurius L.f. Sabinus,** 89 BC. L TITVRI (TITVRI in monogram) above prow, SAB below (legends usually retrograde, mark of value and ROMA omitted). RRC 344/5. CRR 701d. BMCRR 2364–5.   **F** £70 ($112) / **VF** £170 ($272)
Rarely, the moneyer's name appears in a fuller form above prow – L TITVRI L F.

906   **Cn. Cornelius Lentulus,** 88 BC. CN LEN above prow, sometimes with trident below (mark of value and ROMA omitted). RRC 345/4. CRR 704a. B *Cornelia* 53.
                    F £70 ($112) / **VF** £170 ($272)

907   **C. Marcius Censorinus,** 88 BC. C CENSORI (or CENSORIN) above prow (mark of value and ROMA omitted). RRC 346/5. CRR 716a. Cf. B *Marcia* 23.
                    F £70 ($112) / **VF** £170 ($272)

906

908   **Anonymous, 86 BC.** S before prow, which is turned to l., ROMA above. RRC 350B/1. CRR
       679a. BMCRR 2205.   **F** £65 ($104) / **VF** £160 ($256)

Quincunx

*The rare 5–uncia denomination was, like its double the dextans, issued briefly by the Luceria mint
immediately following the currency reform of 211 BC. It bears the mark of value five pellets and has
a reverse type similar to the silver denarius. There were no revivals of the quincunx in later periods.*

909

909   **211–208 BC.** Laur. hd. of Apollo r., L behind. Rev. The Dioscuri galloping r., ROMA below,
       five pellets in ex. RRC 97/3, 11. CRR 179. BMCRR Italy 162.
                                                  F £300 ($480) / **VF** £650 ($1,040)
       During the period of issue the weight declines from about 26 grams to 17.5 grams.

910   — Similar, but with Π behind hd. of Apollo. RRC 99/4. CRR 309. BMCRR Italy 262.
                                                  F £250 ($400) / **VF** £550 ($880)
       Weight about 8 grams.

Triens

*The triens was valued at 4 unciae, or one-third of the as. **Standard type:** hd. of Minerva r., in
crested Corinthian helmet, four pellets above. Rev. Prow of galley r., four pellets below or before,
ROMA above or below (usually with symbol, letter/s or monogram above or before).*

911   **211–206 BC.** Anonymous issue, four pellets below prow, ROMA above. RRC 56/4. CRR
       143b. BMCRR 245.   **F** £40 ($64) / **VF** £110 ($176)
       *Weight about 14 grams (for heavier pre-reform trientes of similar type, see no. 604; and
       for lighter issues of later date, see nos. 989 and 1033).*

912 **211–206 BC.** Anchor before prow, four pellets below, ROMA above. RRC 50/5.
F £65 ($104) / **VF** £160 ($256)

913 — Branch above prow, four pellets before, ROMA below. RRC 76/4.
F £70 ($112) / **VF** £170 ($272)

914 — Similar, but with caduceus above prow. RRC 60/4. CRR 164b. BMCRR Italy 51, 347.
F £50 ($80) / **VF** £130 ($208)
This appears to have been struck using two weight standards, one of about 14 grams, the other of only 6 grams.

915 — Similar, but with club above prow. RRC 89/5.
F £80 ($128) / **VF** £200 ($320)

916 — Similar, but the club is behind hd. of Minerva on obv., and with mark of value below prow, ROMA above. RRC 106/6c.
F £75 ($120) / **VF** £180 ($288)
See also no. 926.

917 — Corn-ear and ROMA above prow, four pellets below, and with mark of value behind hd. on obv. RRC 72/6. CRR 195b. BMCRR Italy 77.
F £65 ($104) / **VF** £160 ($256)

918 — Similar, but the mark of value is before prow, ROMA below, and the mark of value on obv. is above hd. RRC 72/13.
F £65 ($104) / **VF** £160 ($256)

919 — Corn-ear above prow, KA (in monogram) or IC before, ROMA below (mark of value omitted on rev.). RRC 69/4. CRR 310c. BMCRR Italy 273.
F £60 ($96) / **VF** £150 ($240)
This appears to be of Sicilian mintage, probably Catana.

920 — Cornucopiae above prow, four pellets before, ROMA below. RRC 58/5a. CRR 218b.
F £60 ($96) / **VF** £150 ($240)

921 — Similar, but the cornucopiae is before prow, mark of value below, and ROMA above. RRC 58/5b.
F £60 ($96) / **VF** £150 ($240)

922 — Crescent and ROMA above prow, four pellets below. RRC 57/5. CRR 221b. BMCRR 342.
F £55 ($88) / **VF** £140 ($224)

923 — Dolphin before prow, four pellets below, ROMA above. RRC 80/3. CRR 215a.
F £80 ($128) / **VF** £200 ($320)

924

924 — Hammer and apex above prow, four pellets before, ROMA below. RRC 59/4. CRR 150b. BMCRR Italy 47, 346.
F £50 ($80) / **VF** £130 ($208)
This appears to have been struck using two weight standards, one of about 17 grams, the other of only 7.5 grams.

925   **211–206 BC.** Spearhead before prow, four pellets below, ROMA above. RRC 88/5. CRR
      224b.   **F** £65 ($104) / **VF** £160 ($256)

926   — Horizontal staff and ROMA above prow, four pellets below, and sometimes with club
      behind hd. on obv. RRC 106/6. BMCRR Italy 71, 73.   **F** £45 ($72) / **VF** £120 ($192)
      Weight about 14 grams (for lighter trientes of similar type, see no. 944).

927   — Victory and ROMA above prow, four pellets below. RRC 61/4. CRR 148b. BMCRR
      Italy 33, 340.   **F** £45 ($72) / **VF** £120 ($192)
      *This appears to have been struck using two weight standards, one of about 17 grams, the
      other of only 7.5 grams.*

928   — AVR (in monogram) before prow, four pellets below, ROMA above. RRC 65/4. CRR
      162b. B *Aurelia* 12.   **F** £80 ($128) / **VF** £200 ($320)

929   — Similar, but with C before prow. RRC 63/4. CRR 157b. BMCRR Italy, p. 189.
                                                    F £75 ($120) / **VF** £180 ($288)

930   — Similar, but with CA (Canusium) before prow, and also below or behind hd. on obv.
      RRC 100/3. CRR 309c. BMCRR Italy 268.   **F** £60 ($96) / **VF** £150 ($240)

931   — Similar, but with H before prow (no letters on obv.). RRC 85/4. CRR 175b. BMCRR
      Italy 210.   **F** £55 ($88) / **VF** £140 ($224)

932   — L (Luceria) before prow, four pellets below, ROMA above, and with L behind or below
      hd. on obv. RRC 97/4, 12, 18, 25. CRR 178b. BMC Italy 163.
                                                    F £60 ($96) / **VF** £150 ($240))
      The mint letter on rev. is sometimes omitted.

933   — MA (in monogram) before prow, four pellets below, ROMA above. RRC 64/4. CRR
      160a.   **F** £70 ($112) / **VF** £170 ($272)

934   — Π before prow, four pellets below, ROMA above, and with Π below hd. on obv. RRC
      99/5. CRR 306b. BMCRR Italy 263.   **F** £65 ($104) / **VF** £160 ($256)

935   — Ω before prow, four pellets below, ROMA above. RRC 86A/2. CRR 182a.
                                                    F £75 ($120) / **VF** £180 ($288)

936   — V before prow, four pellets below, ROMA above. RRC 87/3. CRR 186b. BMCRR Italy
      240.   **F** £65 ($104) / **VF** £160 ($256)

937   **206–194 BC.** Bird and rudder above prow, four pellets before, ROMA below. RRC 117B/3.
      CRR 292a.   **F** £70 ($112) / **VF** £170 ($272)

938   — Dog r. above prow, four pellets before, ROMA below. RRC 122/5. CRR 251b. BMCRR
      491.   **F** £55 ($88) / **VF** £140 ($224)

939   — Helmet before prow, four pellets below, ROMA above. RRC 118/3. CRR 272b. BMCRR
      Italy, p. 226.   **F** £65 ($104) / **VF** £160 ($256)

940   — Knife and ROMA above prow, four pellets below. RRC 120/5. CRR 257b. BMCRR 478.
                                                    F £55 ($88) / **VF** £140 ($224)

941   — Meta above prow, four pellets before, ROMA below. RRC 124/5. CRR 260b.
                                                    F £70 ($112) / **VF** £170 ($272)

942 **206–194 BC.** Beak of prow and ROMA above prow, four pellets below. RRC 114/4. CRR 245b. BMCRR 456. **F** £50 ($80) / **VF** £130 ($208)

943 — Sow r. and ROMA above prow, four pellets below. RRC 121/5. CRR 254b. BMCRR 485. **F** £50 ($80) / **VF** £130 ($208)

944 — Horizontal staff and ROMA above prow, four pellets below, and sometimes with staff before hd. on obv. RRC 112/5. **F** £60 ($96) / **VF** £150 ($240)
Weight about 10 grams (for heavier trientes of similar type, see no. 926).

945 — Star above prow, four pellets before, ROMA below. RRC 113/4. CRR 264b.
F £65 ($104) / **VF** £160 ($256)

946 — Thunderbolt before prow, four pellets below, ROMA above. RRC 119/5. CRR 248b.
F £55 ($88) / **VF** £140 ($224)

947 **194–189 BC.** Crescent above prow, four pellets before, ROMA below. RRC 137/4. CRR 267b. **F** £65 ($104) / **VF** £160 ($256)

948 — Moneyer's monogram AV above prow, four pellets before, ROMA below. RRC 136/4. CRR 327b. **F** £75 ($120) / **VF** £180 ($288)

949 — Moneyer's monogram L PL H above prow, four pellets before, ROMA below. RRC 134/4. CRR 333b. BMC 556. **F** £50 ($80) / **VF** £130 ($208)

950 — Moneyer's monogram ME above prow, four pellets before, ROMA below. RRC 132/5. CRR 319b. B *Caecilia* 5. **F** £65 ($104) / **VF** £160 ($256)

951 — Moneyer's monogram TAMP above prow, four pellets before, ROMA below. RRC 133/6. CRR 337b. B *Baebia* 8. **F** £60 ($96) / **VF** £150 ($240)

952 **189–179 BC.** Bird (sometimes with wreath in beak) perched on T above prow, four pellets before, ROMA below. RRC 141/4. CRR 346b. **F** £55 ($88) / **VF** £140 ($224)

953 — Bull r. and MD (in monogram) above prow, four pellets before, ROMA below. RRC 142/3. CRR 299b. **F** £55 ($88) / **VF** £140 ($224)

954 — Shield and MAE (in monogram) above prow, four pellets before, ROMA below. RRC 143/3. CRR 375b. B *Maenia* 4. **F** £60 ($96) / **VF** £150 ($240)

955 — Ulysses walking r., holding staff, above prow, four pellets before, ROMA below. RRC 149/3b. **F** £75 ($120) / **VF** £180 ($288)

956 — Similar, but with L MAMILI below prow, and RO–MA divided by the figure of Ulysses above. RRC 149/3a. CRR 369b. B *Mamilia* 3. **F** £65 ($104) / **VF** £160 ($256)

957 — Victory flying r. and spearhead above prow, four pellets before, ROMA below. RRC 145/3. CRR 293b. **F** £60 ($96) / **VF** £150 ($240)

958 — Victory flying r. and L F P (in monogram) above prow, four pellets before, ROMA below. RRC 144/3. CRR 300b. B *Furia* 3. **F** £60 ($96) / **VF** £150 ($240)

959 — M TITINI above prow, four pellets before, ROMA below. RRC 150/3. CRR 365b. BMCRR 658. **F** £50 ($80) / **VF** £130 ($208)

958   964

960 **189–179 BC.** Q MARI above prow, four pellets before, ROMA below. RRC 148/3. CRR 367b. B *Maria* 3. **F** £65 ($104) / **VF** £160 ($256)

961 — S FV (FV in monogram) above prow, four pellets before, ROMA below. RRC 151/1. CRR 371a. B *Furia* 17. **F** £80 ($128) / **VF** £200 ($320)

962 **179–169 BC.** Dolphin r. above prow, four pellets before, ROMA below. RRC 160/3. BMCRR 429. **F** £60 ($96) / **VF** £150 ($240)

963 — Fly before prow, four pellets below, ROMA above. RRC 159/5. CRR 324b. **F** £65 ($104) / **VF** £160 ($256)

964 — MAT (in monogram) above prow, four pellets before, ROMA below. RRC 162/5a. CRR 321c. BMCRR 628. **F** £50 ($80) / **VF** £130 ($208)

965 — Similar, but with MAT (in monogram) before prow, four pellets below, and ROMA above. RRC 162/5b. CRR 321f. **F** £55 ($88) / **VF** £140 ($224)

966 — TAL (in monogram) before prow, four pellets below, ROMA above. RRC 161/4. CRR 329b. B *Juventia* 4. **F** £60 ($96) / **VF** £150 ($240)

967 **169–157 BC.** Anchor before prow, four pellets above, ROMA below. RRC 194/3. CRR 238b. **F** £65 ($104) / **VF** £160 ($256)

968 — Ass r. above prow, four pellets before, ROMA below. RRC 195/3. CRR 298b. BMCRR 525. **F** £50 ($80) / **VF** £130 ($208)

969 — Butterfly on vine-branch with grapes above prow, four pellets before, ROMA below. RRC 184/3. CRR 296b. BMCRR 511. **F** £55 ($88) / **VF** £140 ($224)

970 — Gryphon and hare's hd. above prow, four pellets before, ROMA below. RRC 182/4. CRR 284b. **F** £65 ($104) / **VF** £160 ($256)

971 — Star before prow, four pellets below, ROMA above. RRC 196/3. CRR 264c. **F** £55 ($88) / **VF** £140 ($224)

972 — Wolf suckling twins above prow, four pellets before, ROMA below. RRC 183/3. CRR 297b. BMCRR 517. **F** £55 ($88) / **VF** £140 ($224)

973 — A CÆ above prow, four pellets before, ROMA below. RRC 174/3. CRR 355b. BMCRR 820. **F** £50 ($80) / **VF** £130 ($208)

974 **169–157 BC. BAL (AL** in monogram) above prow, four pellets before, **ROMA** below. **RRC** 179/3. CRR 354b. BMCRR 614.   **F** £50 ($80) / **VF** £130 ($208)

975   975   979

975 — **C SAX (AX** in monogram) above prow, four pellets before, **ROMA** below. **RRC** 173/3. CRR 360b. BMCRR 649.   **F** £45 ($72) / **VF** £120 ($192)

976 — **CINA** above prow, four pellets before, **ROMA** below. **RRC** 178/3. CRR 368b. B *Cornelia* 13.   **F** £55 ($88) / **VF** £140 ($224)

977 — **MVRENA (MVR** in monogram) above prow, four pellets before, **ROMA** below. **RRC** 186/3. CRR 373b. B *Licinia* 3.   **F** £55 ($88) / **VF** £140 ($224)

978 — **OPEI** above prow, four pellets before, **ROMA** below. **RRC** 190/3. CRR 363b. BMCRR 602.   **F** £55 ($88) / **VF** £140 ($224)

979 — **OPEIMI (PEIMI** in monogram) above prow, four pellets before, **ROMA** below. **RRC** 188/3. CRR 362b. BMCRR 597*.   **F** £65 ($104) / **VF** £160 ($256)

980 — **P BLAS** above prow, four pellets before, **ROMA** below. **RRC** 189/3. CRR 370b. BMCRR 791.   **F** £50 ($80) / **VF** £130 ($208)

981 — **PAE** (in monogram) above prow, four pellets before, **ROMA** below. **RRC** 176/3. CRR 358b. B *Aemilia* 4.   **F** £65 ($104) / **VF** £160 ($256)

982 — **PVR (VR** in monogram) above prow, four pellets before, **ROMA** below. **RRC** 187/4. CRR 359b. BMCRR Italy 426.   **F** £75 ($120) / **VF** £180 ($288)

983 — **SAX (AX** in monogram) above prow, four pellets before, **ROMA** below. **RRC** 180/3. CRR 361b. BMCRR 604.   **F** £50 ($80) / **VF** £130 ($208)

984 — **TA** (in monogram) above prow, four pellets before, **ROMA** below. **RRC** 192/3. CRR 372b.   **F** £70 ($112) / **VF** £170 ($272)

985 — **TP** (in monogram) above prow, four pellets before, **ROMA** below. **RRC** 177/3. CRR 353b. BMCRR 634.   **F** £55 ($88) / **VF** £140 ($224)

986 — **TVRD (VR** in monogram) above prow, four pellets before, **ROMA** below. **RRC** 193/3. CRR 366b. BMCRR 800.   **F** £50 ($80) / **VF** £130 ($208)

987 — **VAL** (in monogram) above prow, four pellets before, **ROMA** below. **RRC** 191/3. CRR 356b. B *Valeria* 3.   **F** £50 ($80) / **VF** £130 ($208)

988

988 **169–157 BC.** VARO (VAR in monogram) above prow, four pellets before, ROMA below.
RRC 185/3. CRR 364b. B *Terentia* 6.   **F** £60 ($96) / **VF** £150 ($240)

989 **157–155 BC.** Anonymous issue, four pellets before prow, ROMA above. RRC 197–198B/3.
F £65 ($104) / **VF** £160 ($256)
*Weight about 7 grams (for heavier trientes of similar type, see nos. 604 and 911; and for
lighter examples, see no. 1033).*

990 — NAT above prow, four pellets before, ROMA below, and sometimes with mark of value
behind hd. instead of above on obv. RRC 200/4. CRR 383b. BMCRR 767.
F £50 ($80) / **VF** £130 ($208)

991 — SAR above prow, four pellets before, ROMA below. RRC 199/4. CRR 378b. B *Atilia* 5.
F £65 ($104) / **VF** £160 ($256)

992 **155–149 BC.** Mast and sail above prow, four pellets before, ROMA below. RRC 213/3.
F £70 ($112) / **VF** £170 ($272)

993 **C. Scribonius,** 154 BC. C SCR above prow, four pellets before, ROMA below, and sometimes with mark of value behind hd. instead of above on obv. RRC 201/4. CRR 381b.
BMCRR 738.   **F** £45 ($72) / **VF** £120 ($192)

994 **C. Maianius,** 153 BC. C MAIANI (MA and AN in monogram) above prow, four pellets
before, ROMA below. RRC 203/4. CRR 428b. B *Maiania* 4. **F** £50 ($80) / **VF** £130 ($208)

995   996

995 **L. Saufeius,** 152 BC. Crescent and L SAVF (VF in monogram) above prow, four pellets
before, ROMA below. RRC 204/4. CRR 385b. BMCRR 842.
F £50 ($80) / **VF** £130 ($208)

996 **P. Cornelius Sulla,** 151 BC. P SVLA above prow, four pellets before, ROMA below, prow-
stem decorated with hd. of Venus (?) r. RRC 205/4. CRR 387b. B *Cornelia* 4.
F £55 ($88) / **VF** £140 ($224)

997   **Safra,** 150 BC. SAFRA above prow, dolphin before, ROMA below (no mark of value). RRC
         206/4. CRR 389b. B *Afrania* 4.   **F** £55 ($88) / **VF** £140 ($224)
         SAFRA *would appear to represent a cognomen only, no stop being inserted after the first
         letter.*

998   **C. Junius C.f.,** 149 BC. C IVNI above prow, four pellets before, ROMA below. RRC 210/4.
         CRR 393b. BMCRR 668.   **F** £60 ($96) / **VF** £150 ($240)

999   **Q. Marcius Libo,** 148 BC. Q MARC (MA in monogram) above prow, LIBO before, ROMA
         below (no mark of value). RRC 215/4. CRR 396d. BMCRR 708.
                                                         F £50 ($80) / **VF** £130 ($208)

1000   1002

1000   **L. Sempronius Pitio,** 148 BC. L SEMP or SEMPR (MP in monogram) above prow, four pellets
        before, ROMA below. RRC 216/4. CRR 403b. BMCRR 721.
                                                         F £50 ($80) / **VF** £130 ($208)

1001   **M. Atilius Saranus,** 148 BC. M ATILI (or ATIL) above prow, four pellets before, ROMA
        below. RRC 214/4. CRR 399b. BMCRR 699.   **F** £50 ($80) / **VF** £130 ($208)

1002   **C. Terentius Lucanus,** 147 BC. Wreath-bearing Victory flying r. and C TER LVC (TE in
        monogram) above prow, four pellets before, ROMA below. RRC 217/4. CRR 426b. B
        Terentia 13.   **F** £55 ($88) / **VF** £140 ($224)

1003   **C. Antestius,** 146 BC. Puppy running r. and C ANTESTI (ANTE in monogram) above prow,
        four pellets before, ROMA below. RRC 219/4. CRR 407b. B *Antestia* 6.
                                                         F £50 ($80) / **VF** £130 ($208)

1004   **Cn. Gellius,** 138 BC. CN GEL (or GELI) above prow, four pellets before, ROMA below. RRC
        232/3. CRR 435a. BMCRR 921.   **F** £55 ($88) / **VF** £140 ($224)

1005   **L. Antestius Gragulus,** 136 BC. Jackdaw r. and L ANTES (ANTE in monogram) above prow,
        ROMA below (no mark of value), and with GRAG above hd. on obv., four pellets behind.
        RRC 238/2. CRR 452. BMCRR 980.   **F** £60 ($96) / **VF** £150 ($240)

1006   **C. Servilius M.f.,** 136 BC. Mast with pennant and wreath above prow, C SERVEILI M F
        below (no mark of value), and with ROMA below hd. on obv., four pellets behind. RRC
        239/2. CRR 526. B *Servilia* 2.   **F** £65 ($104) / **VF** £160 ($256)

1007   **C. Curiatius C.f. Trigeminus,** 135 BC. C CVR F (VR in monogram) above prow, on which
        Victory stands r. (sometimes omitted), four pellets before, ROMA below, and with mark of
        value behind hd. on obv. RRC 240/3. CRR 460a. B *Curiatia* 4, 8.
                                                         F £55 ($88) / **VF** £140 ($224)

1007   1008

1008 **L. Trebanius,** 135 BC. L TREBANI (TR and AN in monogram) above prow, four pellets before, ROMA below, and sometimes with mark of value behind hd. instead of above on obv. RRC 241/3. CRR 457a. B *Trebania* 3.   **F** £60 ($96) / **VF** £150 ($240)

1009 **C. Minucius Augurinus,** 135 BC. C AVG above prow, four pellets before, ROMA below. RRC 242/3. CRR 464a. B *Minucia* 5.   **F** £55 ($88) / **VF** £140 ($224)

1010 **Ti. Minucius C.f. Augurinus,** 134 BC. TI AVGVRINI and lituus above prow, four pellets before, ROMA below, and with mark of value behind hd. on obv. RRC 243/3. CRR 495a. BMCRR 1007.   **F** £55 ($88) / **VF** £140 ($224)

1011

1011 **C. Aburius Geminus,** 134 BC. C ABVRI GEM (AB and VR in monogram) above prow, four pellets before, ROMA below, and with mark of value behind hd. on obv. RRC 244/2. CRR 491. BMCRR 1001.   **F** £50 ($80) / **VF** £130 ($208)

1012 **M. Marcius Mn.f.,** 134 BC. M MARCI MN F (MAR and MN, sometimes MNF, in monogram) above prow, four pellets before, ROMA below. RRC 245/2. CRR 501. BMCRR 1014.   **F** £50 ($80) / **VF** £130 ($208)

1013 **C. Numitorius,** 133 BC. C NVMITORI (or NVMITOR) above prow, four pellets before, ROMA below. RRC 246/3. CRR 467a. BMCRR 974.   **F** £50 ($80) / **VF** £130 ($208)

1014 **L. Minucius,** 133 BC. L MINVCI above prow, four pellets before, ROMA below, and with mark of value behind hd. on obv. RRC 248/3. CRR 471a. B *Minucia* 17.   **F** £70 ($112) / **VF** £170 ($272)

1015 **P. Maenius M.f. Antias (or Antiaticus),** 132 BC. P MAE ANT M F (MAE, ANT, and MF in monogram) above prow, four pellets before, ROMA below, and with mark of value behind hd. on obv. RRC 249/2. CRR 493. B *Maenia* 8.   (*Unique*)

1016 **M. Fabrinius,** 132 BC. M FABRINI above prow, four pellets before, ROMA below, and with mark of value behind hd. on obv. RRC 251/2. CRR 453a. BMCRR 982.   **F** £50 ($80) / **VF** £130 ($208)

1016   1019

1017   **M. Acilius M.f.,** 130 BC. M ACILI above prow, four pellets before, ROMA below, and with
        mark of value behind hd. on obv. RRC 255/3. CRR 512a. B *Acilia* 6.
                                                        F £70 ($112) / **VF** £170 ($272)

1018   **Q. Caecilius Metellus,** 130 BC. Q METE (ME sometimes in monogram, TE always so) above
        prow, four pellets before, ROMA below, and with mark of value behind hd. on obv. RRC
        256/3. CRR 510a. BMCRR 1060.   **F** £60 ($96) / **VF** £150 ($240)

1019   **M. Vargunteius,** 130 BC. M VARG (VAR in monogram) above prow, four pellets before,
        ROMA below, and with mark of value behind hd. on obv. RRC 257/3. CRR 508a. BMCRR
        1071.   **F** £55 ($88) / **VF** £140 ($224)

1020   **Cn. Domitius,** 128 BC. CN DOMI (or DOM) above prow, four pellets before, ROMA below,
        and with mark of value behind hd. on obv. RRC 261/3. CRR 515a. BMCRR 1029.
                                                     F £55 ($88) / **VF** £140 ($224)

1021   **Anonymous,** 128 BC. Elephant's hd. r. with bell attached above prow, four pellets before,
        ROMA below, and with mark of value behind hd. on obv. RRC 262/3. CRR 497a. B
        Caecilia 40.   **F** £55 ($88) / **VF** £140 ($224)
        *Although lacking the moneyer's name it seems certain that this was issued by a Caecilius
        Metellus, probably either L. Caecilius Metellus Diadematus or L. Caecilius Metellus
        Delmaticus.*

1022

1022   **M. Caecilius Q.f. Metellus,** 127 BC. M METELLVS (ME in monogram) inscribed on prow,
        Macedonian shield above, four pellets before, ROMA below, and with mark of value
        behind hd. on obv. RRC 263/4. CRR 482a. BMCRR 1153. **F** £65 ($104) / **VF** £160 ($256)

1023   **C. Servilius,** 127 BC. C SERVEILI (VE in monogram) inscribed on prow, four pellets below,
        ROMA above. RRC 264/3. CRR 484a. B *Servilia* 9.   (*Unique*)

1024   **T. Quinctius Flamininus,** 126 BC. T Q above prow, four pellets before, ROMA below, and with mark of value behind hd. on obv. RRC 267/3. CRR 506a. B *Quinctia* 4.
F £60 ($96) / **VF** £150 ($240)

1025   **C. Caecilius Metellus,** 125 BC. C METEL inscribed on prow, elephant's hd. r. above, four pellets before, ROMA below, and with mark of value behind hd. on obv. RRC 269/3.
(*Unique*)

1026   **Cn. Domitius, M. Junius Silanus and Q. Curtius,** 116/115 BC. Obv. CN DOMI before hd. of Minerva. Rev. Aegis, M SILA Q CVRTI around. RRC 285/4. CRR 538a. BMCRR Italy, p. 260.   **F** £125 ($200) / **VF** £300 ($480)

1027   **M. Cipius M.f.,** 115/114 BC. Moneyer's name M CIPI M F before hd. of Minerva, four pellets before prow, ROMA below. RRC 289/3. CRR 547a. BMCRR Italy, p. 273.   (*Unique*)

1028   1029

1028   **C. Fonteius,** 114/113 BC. C FONT (NT in monogram) above prow, four pellets before, ROMA below. RRC 290/4. CRR 556b. B *Fonteia* 4.   **F** £60 ($96) / **VF** £150 ($240)

1029   **P. Licinius Nerva,** 113/112 BC. Moneyer's name P NERVA (NE in monogram) before hd. of Minerva, four pellets before prow, ROMA below. RRC 292/3. CRR 549a. BMCRR Italy, p. 276.   (*Unique*)

1030   **L. Pomponius Molo,** ca. 97 BC. L POMP (LP and MP in monogram) above prow, four pellets before, ROMA below. RRC 334/4. CRR 608b. BMCRR Italy 743.
F £50 ($80) / **VF** £130 ($208)

1031   **Anonymous (C. Poblicius Malleolus),** ca. 96 BC. Hammer and ROMA above prow, four pellets below. RRC 335/6. CRR 616b.   **F** £50 ($80) / **VF** £130 ($208)

1032   **Anonymous (L.P.D.A.P.),** 91 BC. L P D A P above prow, four pellets below (ROMA omitted), and with mark of value behind hd. on obv. RRC 338/3. CRR 678b. BMCRR 2192.
F £70 ($112) / **VF** £170 ($272)
This legend may be expanded to 'Lege Papiria de assis pondere' and refers to the Lex Papiria of 91 BC by which the weight standard of the bronze coinage was reduced to the semuncial level.

1033   **Anonymous,** 91 BC. Four pellets below prow, ROMA above (no symbol or moneyer's name). RRC 339/3. CRR 679b.   **F** £70 ($112) / **VF** £170 ($272)
Weight about 4 grams (for heavier trientes of similar type, see nos. 604, 911 and 989).

1034

1034   **Q. Titius,** 90 BC. Obv. Mask of bearded Silenus r., wreathed with ivy, four pellets behind.
Rev. Ceres walking r., holding torches before her, pig at her feet, Q TITI (sometimes retrograde) behind, all within laurel-wreath. RRC 341/6. CRR 696. BMCRR 2237.
                                       F £150 ($240) / **VF** £350 ($560)
*Remarkably, the types of the three fractional bronze denominations of this moneyer are
copied from the silver coinage of his collegue, C. Vibius Pansa (see nos. 241 and 245).*

1035   **L. Titurius L.f. Sabinus,** 89 BC. L TITVR (TITVR in monogram) above prow, SAB below
(mark of value and ROMA omitted). RRC 344/6.   (*Unique*)

1036   **Anonymous,** 86 BC. Four pellets before prow, which is turned to l., ROMA above, and the
mark of value on obv. (when present) may be above or behind hd. RRC 350B/2. CRR
679b. BMCRR 2207.   **F** £55 ($88) / **VF** £140 ($224)

Quadrans

*The quadrans was valued at 3 unciae, or one-quarter of the as. **Standard type:** hd. of young
Hercules r., clad in lion's skin, three pellets behind. Rev. Prow of galley r., three pellets below,
before or above, ROMA above or below (usually with symbol, letter/s or monogram above or before).*

1037

1037   **211–206 BC.** Anonymous issue, three pellets below prow, ROMA above. RRC 56/5. CRR
143c. BMCRR 255.   **F** £40 ($64) / **VF** £110 ($176)
*Weight about 11 grams (for heavier pre-reform quadrantes of similar type, see no. 608;
and for a much lighter issue of later date, see no. 1195).*

1038   — Anchor before prow, three pellets below, ROMA above. RRC 50/6.
                                       F £70 ($112) / **VF** £170 ($272)

1039   — Branch above prow, three pellets before, ROMA below. RRC 76/5. CRR 203a.
                                       F £70 ($112) / **VF** £170 ($272)

1040   — Similar, but with caduceus above prow. RRC 60/5. CRR 164c. BMCRR Italy 52, 348.
                                       F £50 ($80) / **VF** £130 ($208)

This appears to have been struck using two weight standards, one of about 11 grams, the other of only 5 grams.

1041 **211–206 BC.** Similar, but with club above prow. RRC 89/6. CRR 213b.
F £70 ($112) / **VF** £170 ($272)

1042 — Corn-ear above prow, three pellets before, ROMA below. RRC 72/14. CRR 195c.
F £60 ($96) / **VF** £150 ($240)

1043/1   1043/2

1043 — Obv. Hd. of young Hercules r., clad in boar's skin, three pellets behind. Rev. Bull charging r., snake on ground below, corn-ear and three pellets above, ROMA in ex. RRC 69/5, 72/7. BMCRR Romano-Campanian 140, 143. F £90 ($144) / **VF** £225 ($360) *This appears to have been struck using two weight standards, one of about 13 grams, the other of only 6.5 grams (for heavier pre-reform quadrantes of similar type, see no. 607).*

1044 — Cornucopiae before prow, three pellets below, ROMA above. RRC 58/6.
F £70 ($112) / **VF** £170 ($272)

1045 — Crescent and ROMA above prow, three pellets below. RRC 57/6. CRR 221c.
F £70 ($112) / **VF** £170 ($272)

1046 — Dolphin before prow, three pellets below, ROMA above. RRC 80/4. CRR 215b.
F £65 ($104) / **VF** £160 ($256)

1047 — Hammer and apex above prow, three pellets before, ROMA below. RRC 59/5. CRR 150c. F £55 ($88) / **VF** £140 ($224)

1048 — Spearhead before prow, three pellets below, ROMA above. RRC 88/6. CRR 224c.
F £60 ($96) / **VF** £150 ($240)

1049 — Horizontal staff and ROMA above prow, three pellets below, and sometimes with club below hd. on obv. RRC 106/7. BMCRR Italy 74. F £45 ($72) / **VF** £120 ($192) *Weight about 10 grams (for lighter quadrantes of similar type, see no. 1073).*

1050

1050   **211–206 BC.** Victory and **ROMA** above prow, three pellets below. RRC 61/5. CRR 148c. BMCRR Italy 34, 344.   **F** £45 ($72) / **VF** £120 ($192)
This appears to have been struck using two weight standards, one of about 13 grams, the other of only 6.5 grams.

1051   — **AVR** (in monogram) before prow, three pellets below, **ROMA** above. RRC 65/5. CRR 162c. BMCRR Italy 129.   **F** £70 ($112) / **VF** £170 ($272)

1052   — Similar, but with **C** before prow. RRC 63/5. CRR 157c. BMCRR Italy, p. 190.
F £80 ($128) / **VF** £200 ($320)

1053   — Similar, but with **CA** (Canusium) before prow. RRC 100/4a. CRR 309e. BMCRR Italy, p. 206.   **F** £75 ($120) / **VF** £180 ($288)

1054   — Similar, but with **CA** also on obv., below chin of Hercules, and with mark of value above hd. instead of behind. RRC 100/4b. CRR 309d. BMCRR Italy, p. 206, note 2.
F £75 ($120) / **VF** £180 ($288)

1055   — **H** before prow, three pellets below, **ROMA** above, and sometimes with club below hd. of Hercules on obv. RRC 85/5. CRR 175c. BMCRR Italy 212.
F £75 ($120) / **VF** £180 ($288)

1056   — **L** (Luceria) before prow, three pellets below, **ROMA** above (the mark of value on obv. sometimes omitted; rarely, with additional **L** below hd. of Hercules). RRC 97/13c, 19, 26. CRR 178c-d. BMC Italy 212.   **F** £55 ($88) / **VF** £140 ($224)
The weight standard declines from about 16 grams to only 5.5 grams. The heaviest specimens may have been issued before the currency reform of 211 BC.

1057   — Similar, but on obv. the mark of value is below hd. of Hercules, and sometimes with **L** behind. RRC 97/5a, 13a-b. CRR 178d. BMCRR Italy 164.   **F** £60 ($96) / **VF** £150 ($240)

1058   — Similar, but on rev. the mint mark **L** precedes the mark of value below prow, and on obv. the three pellets are disposed one behind hd., two below. RRC 97/5b.
F £75 ($120) / **VF** £180 ($288)

1059   — Obv. Hd. of Mercury r., in winged petasus, three pellets above, **L** below. Rev. Three pellets below prow, **ROMA** above. RRC 97/5c, 13d.   **F** £70 ($112) / **VF** £170 ($272)
The extraordinary abandonment of the standard obv. design of the quadrans in favour of that of the sextans, on this type and the next, remains unexplained.

1060   — Similar, but with **T** before prow. RRC 98A/5.   **F** £80 ($128) / **VF** £200 ($320)

1061   — **MA** (in monogram) before prow, three pellets below, **ROMA** above. RRC 64/5. CRR 160b.   **F** £65 ($104) / **VF** £160 ($256)

1062   — **Π** before prow, three pellets below, **ROMA** above, and with **Π** behind hd. on obv., below the mark of value. RRC 99/6. CRR 306c. BMCRR Italy, p. 204.
F £70 ($112) / **VF** £170 ($272)

1063   — **Ω** before prow, three pellets below, **ROMA** above. RRC 86A/3. CRR 182b. BMCRR Italy 222.   **F** £65 ($104) / **VF** £160 ($256)

1064   **211–206 BC.** ROMA (in monogram) before prow, three pellets below, ROMA above. RRC 84/6. CRR 190b. BMCRR Italy 195.   **F** £55 ($88) / **VF** £140 ($224)

1065   — V before prow, three pellets below, ROMA above. RRC 87/4. CRR 186c. BMCRR Italy 240.   **F** £70 ($112) / **VF** £170 ($272)

1066   **206–194 BC.** Bird and rudder above prow, three pellets before, ROMA below. RRC 117B/4. CRR 292b.   **F** £70 ($112) / **VF** £170 ($272)

1067   — Dog r. above prow, three pellets before, ROMA below. RRC 122/6. CRR 251c. BMCRR 492.   **F** £60 ($96) / **VF** £150 ($240)

1068   — Helmet before prow, three pellets below, ROMA above. RRC 118/4. CRR 272c. BMCRR Italy, p. 226.   **F** £55 ($88) / **VF** £140 ($224)

1069   — Knife and ROMA above prow, three pellets below. RRC 120/6. CRR 257c.   **F** £60 ($96) / **VF** £150 ($240)

1070   — Meta above prow, three pellets before, ROMA below. RRC 124/6. CRR 260c.   **F** £55 ($88) / **VF** £140 ($224)

1071   — Beak of prow and ROMA above prow, three pellets below. RRC 114/5. CRR 245c.   **F** £50 ($80) / **VF** £130 ($208)

1072   — Sow r. and ROMA above prow, three pellets below. RRC 121/6. CRR 254c.   **F** £60 ($96) / **VF** £150 ($240)

1073   — Horizontal staff and ROMA above prow, three pellets below. RRC 112/6b.   **F** £70 ($112) / **VF** £170 ($272)
Weight about 7.5 grams (for heavier quadrantes of similar type, see no. 1049).

1074   — Similar, but the staff is on obv. before hd. of Hercules. RRC 112/6a. CRR 243b. BMCRR 304.   **F** £50 ($80) / **VF** £130 ($208)

1075   — Star above prow, three pellets before, ROMA below. RRC 113/5. CRR 264d.   **F** £65 ($104) / **VF** £160 ($256)

1076   — Thunderbolt before prow, three pellets below, ROMA above. RRC 119/6. CRR 248c.   **F** £65 ($104) / **VF** £160 ($256)

1077   **194–189 BC.** Crescent above prow, three pellets before, ROMA below. RRC 137/5. CRR 267c.   **F** £65 ($104) / **VF** £160 ($256)

1078   — Moneyer's monogram AV above prow, three pellets before, ROMA below. RRC 136/5. CRR 327c.   **F** £70 ($112) / **VF** £170 ($272)

1079   — Moneyer's monogram L PL H above prow, three pellets before, ROMA below. RRC 134/5. CRR 333c.   **F** £70 ($112) / **VF** £170 ($272)

1080   — Moneyer's monogram ME above prow, three pellets before, ROMA below. RRC 132/6. CRR 319c. B *Caecilia* 6.   **F** £60 ($96) / **VF** £150 ($240)

1081

1081   **194–189 BC.** Moneyer's monogram **TAMP** above prow, three pellets before, **ROMA** below.
        RRC 133/7. CRR 337c. B *Baebia* 9.   **F** £65 ($104) / **VF** £160 ($256)

1082   **189–179 BC.** Bird (sometimes with wreath in beak) perched on **T** above prow, three pellets
        before, **ROMA** below. RRC 141/5. CRR 346c.   **F** £55 ($88) / **VF** £140 ($224)

1083   — Bull r. and **MD** (in monogram) above prow, three pellets before, **ROMA** below. RRC
        142/4. CRR 299c.   **F** £65 ($104) / **VF** £160 ($256)

1084   — Shield and **MAE** (in monogram) above prow, three pellets before, **ROMA** below. RRC
        143/4. CRR 375c. B *Maenia* 5.   **F** £65 ($104) / **VF** £160 ($256)

1085   — Ulysses walking r., holding staff, above prow, three pellets before, **ROMA** below. RRC
        149/4b.   **F** £80 ($128) / **VF** £200 ($320)

1086   — Similar, but with **L MAMILI** below prow, and **RO–MA** divided by the figure of Ulysses
        above. RRC 149/4a. CRR 369c. B *Mamilia* 4.   **F** £75 ($120) / **VF** £180 ($288)

1087   — Victory flying r. and spearhead above prow, three pellets before, **ROMA** below. RRC
        145/4. CRR 293c. BMCRR 499.   **F** £55 ($88) / **VF** £140 ($224)

1088   — Victory flying r. and **L F P** (in monogram) above prow, three pellets before, **ROMA**
        below. RRC 144/4. CRR 300c. B *Furia* 4.   **F** £55 ($88) / **VF** £140 ($224)

1089   — **CN DO** above prow, three pellets before, **ROMA** below. RRC 147/3.   (*Unique*)

1090   — **M TITINI** above prow, three pellets before, **ROMA** below. RRC 150/4. CRR 365c.
        BMCRR 659.   **F** £50 ($80) / **VF** £130 ($208)

1091   — **Q MARI** above prow, three pellets before, **ROMA** below. RRC 148/4. CRR 367c.
        BMCRR 825.   **F** £60 ($96) / **VF** £150 ($240)

1092   **179–169 BC.** Dolphin r. above prow, three pellets before, **ROMA** below. RRC 160/4.
        BMCRR 430.   **F** £65 ($104) / **VF** £160 ($256)

1093   — Fly before prow, three pellets below, **ROMA** above. RRC 159/6. CRR 324c.
                                                              F £60 ($96) / **VF** £150 ($240)

1094   — Prawn above prow, three pellets before, **ROMA** below. RRC 156/4. CRR 344a. BMCRR
        587.   **F** £60 ($96) / **VF** £150 ($240)

1095   — **MAT** (in monogram) above prow, three pellets before, **ROMA** below. RRC 162/6a. CRR
        321d. BMCRR 629.   **F** £55 ($88) / **VF** £140 ($224)

1096

1096   **179–169 BC.** Similar, but with **MAT** (in monogram) before prow, three pellets below, and **ROMA** above. RRC 162/6b. CRR 321g. BMCRR Italy 410.   **F** £55 ($88) / **VF** £140 ($224)

1097   — **PVR** (in monogram) above prow, three pellets before, **ROMA** below. RRC 155/4. CRR 331b. BMCRR Italy, p. 231.   **F** £70 ($112) / **VF** £170 ($272)

1098   — **TAL** (in monogram) before prow, three pellets below, **ROMA** above. RRC 161/5. CRR 329c. BMCRR Italy, p. 233.   **F** £65 ($104) / **VF** £160 ($256)

1099   **169–157 BC.** Anchor before prow, three pellets above, **ROMA** below. RRC 194/4. CRR 238c. BMCRR Italy 301.   **F** £55 ($88) / **VF** £140 ($224)

1100   — Ass r. above prow, three pellets before, **ROMA** below. RRC 195/4. CRR 298c. BMCRR 527.   **F** £50 ($80) / **VF** £130 ($208)

1101   — Butterfly on vine-branch with grapes above prow, three pellets before, **ROMA** below. RRC 184/4. CRR 296c. BMCRR 512.   **F** £55 ($88) / **VF** £140 ($224)

1102   — Caps of the Dioscuri above prow, three pellets before, **ROMA** below. RRC 181/3. CRR 294b.   **F** £70 ($112) / **VF** £170 ($272)

1103   — Gryphon and hare's hd. above prow, three pellets before, **ROMA** below. RRC 182/5. CRR 284c. BMCRR Italy 336.   **F** £60 ($96) / **VF** £150 ($240)

1104   — Star before prow, three pellets below, **ROMA** above. RRC 196/4. CRR 264d. BMCRR 466.   **F** £55 ($88) / **VF** £140 ($224)

1105   — Wolf suckling twins above prow, three pellets before, **ROMA** below. RRC 183/4. CRR 297c.   **F** £60 ($96) / **VF** £150 ($240)

1106   — **A CÆ** above prow, three pellets before, **ROMA** below. RRC 174/4. CRR 355c. BMCRR 821.   **F** £45 ($72) / **VF** £120 ($192)

1107   — **BAL** (**AL** in monogram) above prow, three pellets before, **ROMA** below. RRC 179/4. CRR 354c. BMCRR 615.   **F** £50 ($80) / **VF** £130 ($208)

1108

1108   **169–157 BC.** C SAX (AX in monogram) above prow, three pellets before, ROMA below. RRC 173/4. CRR 360c. BMCRR 651.   **F** £45 ($72) / **VF** £120 ($192)

1109   — CINA above prow, three pellets before, ROMA below. RRC 178/4. CRR 368c. BMCRR 807.   **F** £50 ($80) / **VF** £130 ($208)

1110   — MVRENA (MVR in monogram) above prow, three pellets before, ROMA below. RRC 186/4. CRR 373c. B *Licinia* 4.   **F** £60 ($96) / **VF** £150 ($240)

1111   — OPEI above prow, three pellets before, ROMA below. RRC 190/4. CRR 363c. B *Opimia* 10.   **F** £55 ($88) / **VF** £140 ($224)

1112   — OPEIMI (PEIMI in monogram) above prow, three pellets before, ROMA below. RRC 188/4. CRR 362c. B *Opimia* 4.   **F** £55 ($88) / **VF** £140 ($224)

1113   1114

1113   — P BLAS above prow, three pellets before, ROMA below. RRC 189/4. CRR 370c. B *Cornelia* 9.   **F** £55 ($88) / **VF** £140 ($224)

1114   — PAE (in monogram) above prow, three pellets before, ROMA below. RRC 176/4. CRR 358c. B *Aemilia* 5.   **F** £60 ($96) / **VF** £150 ($240)

1115   — PVR (VR in monogram) above prow, three pellets before, ROMA below. RRC 187/5. CRR 359c. BMCRR Italy 427.   **F** £70 ($112) / **VF** £170 ($272)

1116   — SAX (AX in monogram) above prow, three pellets before, ROMA below. RRC 180/4. CRR 361c. BMCRR 606.   **F** £50 ($80) / **VF** £130 ($208)

1117   — TA (in monogram) above prow, three pellets before, ROMA below. RRC 192/4. CRR 372c.   **F** £55 ($88) / **VF** £140 ($224)

1118   — TP (in monogram) above prow, three pellets before, ROMA below. RRC 177/4. CRR 353c.   **F** £50 ($80) / **VF** £130 ($208)

1119   — TVRD (VR in monogram) above prow, three pellets before, ROMA below. RRC 193/4. CRR 366c. BMCRR 803.   **F** £50 ($80) / **VF** £130 ($208)

1120   — VAL (in monogram) above prow, three pellets before, ROMA below. RRC 191/4. CRR 356c. B *Valeria* 4.   **F** £60 ($96) / **VF** £150 ($240)

1121   — VARO (VAR in monogram) above prow, three pellets before, ROMA below. RRC 185/4. CRR 364c.   **F** £50 ($80) / **VF** £130 ($208)

1122   **157–155 BC.** Anonymous issue, three pellets before prow, ROMA below. RRC 197–198B/4.   **F** £70 ($112) / **VF** £170 ($272)
        Weight about 5.5 grams (for lighter quadrantes of similar type, see nos. 1173 and 1194).

1123   1124

1123   **157–155 BC.** NAT above prow, three pellets before, ROMA below. RRC 200/5. CRR 383c. BMCRR 768.   **F** £50 ($80) / **VF** £130 ($208)

1124   — SAR above prow, three pellets before, ROMA below. RRC 199/5. CRR 378c. BMCRR 754.   **F** £50 ($80) / **VF** £130 ($208)

1125   **155–149 BC.** Mast and sail above prow, three pellets before, ROMA below. RRC 213/4.
                           F £65 ($104) / **VF** £160 ($256)

1126   **C. Scribonius,** 154 BC. C SCR above prow, three pellets before, ROMA below. RRC 201/5. CRR 381c. B *Scribonia* 5.   **F** £50 ($80) / **VF** £130 ($208)

1127   **C. Maianius,** 153 BC. C MAIANI (MA and AN in monogram) above prow, three pellets before, ROMA below. RRC 203/5. CRR 428c. BMCRR Italy 445.
                           F £55 ($88) / **VF** £140 ($224)

1128   **L. Saufeius,** 152 BC. Crescent and L SAVF (VF in monogram) above prow, three pellets before, ROMA below. RRC 204/5. CRR 385c. BMCRR 843.
                           F £50 ($80) / **VF** £130 ($208)

1129   **P. Cornelius Sulla,** 151 BC. P SVLA above prow, three pellets before, ROMA below, prow-stem decorated with hd. of Venus (?) r. RRC 205/5. CRR 387c. B *Cornelia* 5.
                           F £65 ($104) / **VF** £160 ($256)

1130   **Safra,** 150 BC. SAFRA above prow, dolphin before, ROMA below (no mark of value). RRC 206/5. CRR 389c. BMCRR 678.   **F** £50 ($80) / **VF** £130 ($208)
       SAFRA would appear to represent a cognomen only, no stop being inserted after the first letter.

1131   **C. Junius C.f.,** 149 BC. C IVNI above prow, three pellets before, ROMA below. RRC 210/5. CRR 393c. BMCRR 669.   **F** £55 ($88) / **VF** £140 ($224)

1132   1133

1132   **Q. Marcius Libo,** 148 BC. Q MARC (MA in monogram) above prow, LIBO before, ROMA below (no mark of value). RRC 215/5. CRR 396e. BMCRR 709.
                           F £55 ($88) / **VF** £140 ($224)

1133   **L. Sempronius Pitio,** 148 BC. L SEMP (MP in monogram) above prow, three pellets before, ROMA below. RRC 216/5. CRR 403c. B *Sempronia* 8.   **F** £50 ($80) / **VF** £130 ($208)

1134   **M. Atilius Saranus,** 148 BC. M ATILI (or ATIL) above prow, three pellets before, ROMA below. RRC 214/5. CRR 399c. B *Atilia* 13.   **F** £50 ($80) / **VF** £130 ($208)

1135   1136

1135   **C. Terentius Lucanus,** 147 BC. Wreath-bearing Victory flying r. and C TER LVC (TE in monogram) above prow, three pellets before, ROMA below. RRC 217/5. CRR 426c. BMCRR 787.   **F** £50 ($80) / **VF** £130 ($208)

1136   **C. Antestius,** 146 BC. Puppy running r. and C ANTESTI (ANTE in monogram) above prow, three pellets before, ROMA below. RRC 219/5. CRR 407c. BMCRR 865.   **F** £50 ($80) / **VF** £130 ($208)

1137   **C. Valerius C.f. Flaccus,** 140 BC. C VAL C F (VAL in monogram) above prow, three pellets before, ROMA below. RRC 228/4. CRR 442. B *Valeria* 10.   **F** £65 ($104) / **VF** £160 ($256)

1138   **C. Renius,** 138 BC. Goat r. above prow, C REN before, ROMA below (no mark of value). RRC 231/3. CRR 433a. B *Renia* 3.   **F** £70 ($112) / **VF** £170 ($272)

1139   **Cn. Gellius,** 138 BC. CN GEL (or GELI) above prow, three pellets before, ROMA below. RRC 232/4. CRR 435b. BMCRR 922–3.   **F** £45 ($72) / **VF** £120 ($192)

1140   **Ti. Veturius,** 137 BC. Rev. Oil-jar attached to thong and strigil, between ROMA on l. and TI VETVR (ET or VETV in monogram) on r. (obv. of standard type). RRC 234/2. CRR 528, 528a. BMCRR Italy, p. 282.   **F** £100 ($160) / **VF** £225 ($360)
Like the denarius of this moneyer (see no. 111) the quadrans is of wholly unconventional design. It has been interpreted as providing evidence that this denomination represented the price of admission to the public baths.

1141   **Sex. Pompeius,** 137 BC. Jug and SEX POM (or PO) above prow, three pellets before, ROMA below, and with mark of value above hd. on obv., jug behind. RRC 235/3. CRR 462a. B *Pompeia* 3.   **F** £75 ($120) / **VF** £180 ($288)

1142   **L. Antestius Gragulus,** 136 BC. Jackdaw r. (sometimes omitted) and L ANTES (ANTE or NTE in monogram) above prow, sometimes with three pellets before, ROMA below. RRC 238/3b–e. CRR 452c–d.   **F** £65 ($104) / **VF** £160 ($256)

1143   — Similar (jackdaw above prow and no mark of value), but with GRAG behind hd. on obv. and three pellets above. RRC 238/3a. CRR 452a–b. Cf. BMCRR 981 (misdescribed).   **F** £65 ($104) / **VF** £160 ($256)

1144   — Similar, but with GRAGV below prow and jackdaw r. above (moneyer's *praenomen* and *nomen* omitted), and with ROMA below hd. on obv. (the mark of value behind). RRC 238/3f. CRR 452e. B *Antestia* 13.   **F** £70 ($112) / **VF** £170 ($272)

1142

1145 **C. Servilius M.f.,** 136 BC. Mast with pennant and wreath above prow, C SERVEILI M F below (no mark of value), and with ROMA below hd. on obv. RRC 239/3. CRR 526a. BMCRR Italy 548.   F £50 ($80) / **VF** £130 ($208)

1146   1147

1146 **C. Curiatius C.f. Trigeminus,** 135 BC. C CVR F (VR in monogram, legend sometimes blundered) above prow, on which Victory stands r. (sometimes omitted), three pellets before, ROMA below. RRC 240/4. CRR 460b. BMCRR 947, 949, 1036.
     F £40 ($64) / **VF** £110 ($176)

1147 **L. Trebanius,** 135 BC. L TREBANI (TR and AN in monogram) above prow, three pellets before, ROMA below. RRC 241/4. CRR 457b. BMCRR 962.
     F £40 ($64) / **VF** £110 ($176)

1148 **C. Minucius Augurinus,** 135 BC. C AVG above prow, three pellets before, ROMA below. RRC 242/4. CRR 464b. BMCRR 956.   F £50 ($80) / **VF** £130 ($208)

1149

1149 **Ti. Minucius C.f. Augurinus,** 134 BC. TI AVGVRINI and lituus above prow, three pellets before, ROMA below. RRC 243/4. CRR 495b. B *Minucia* 14.
     F £50 ($80) / **VF** £130 ($208)

1150 **C. Aburius Geminus,** 134 BC. C ABVRI GEM (AB and VR in monogram, legend sometimes blundered) above prow, three pellets before, ROMA below. RRC 244/3. CRR 491a. BMCRR 1002.   F £40 ($64) / **VF** £110 ($176)

1151 **M. Marcius Mn.f.,** 134 BC. M MARCI MN F (MAR and MN, sometimes MNF, in monogram) above prow, three pellets before, ROMA below. RRC 245/3. CRR 501a. BMCRR 1017.
     F £40 ($64) / **VF** £110 ($176)

1152   1153

1152   **C. Numitorius,** 133 BC. C NVMITORI (or NVMITOR or NVM, sometimes blundered) above prow, three pellets before, ROMA below. RRC 246/4. CRR 467b, e. BMCRR 975.
F £45 ($72) / **VF** £120 ($192)

1153   **P. Calpurnius,** 133 BC. Rev. Ship r., inscribed ROMA, on which stands Victory r. with steersman behind, P CALP above, three pellets before, dolphin r. below. RRC 247/3. CRR 469a. B *Calpurnia* 4.   **F** £60 ($96) / **VF** £150 ($240)
This rev. type represents the first significant variation on the standard design of the post-reform bronze coinage. See also no. 872.

1154   1155

1154   **L. Minucius,** 133 BC. L MINVCI above prow, three pellets before, ROMA below. RRC 248/4. CRR 471b. BMCRR 966.   **F** £50 ($80) / **VF** £130 ($208)

1155   **P. Maenius M.f. Antias (or Antiaticus),** 132 BC. P MAE ANT M F (MAE, ANT, and MF in monogram, legend often blundered) above prow, three pellets before, ROMA below. RRC 249/3. CRR 493a. BMCRR 991.   **F** £40 ($64) / **VF** £110 ($176)

1156   **M. Aburius M.f. Geminus,** 132 BC. M ABVRI M F GEM (or similar, AB, VR, and MF in monogram, legend often blundered) above prow, three pellets before, ROMA below. RRC 250/2. CRR 488. BMCRR 998.   **F** £40 ($64) / **VF** £110 ($176)

1157

1157   **M. Fabrinius,** 132 BC. M FABRINI or FABR (AB sometimes in monogram) above prow, three pellets before, ROMA below. RRC 251/3. CRR 453b. BMCRR 983.
F £40 ($64) / **VF** £110 ($176)

1158   **L. Opimius,** 131 BC. Rev. Club l., L OPEIMI above, ROMA below, all within laurel-wreath (on obv. the hd. of Hercules is bearded). RRC 253/3. CRR 474b. BMCRR 1136.
F £80 ($128) / **VF** £200 ($320)
The unconventional rev. type merely complements the obv. deity.

1159   M. Acilius M.f., 130 BC. M ACILI (or ACIL, sometimes blundered) above prow, three pellets before, ROMA below. RRC 255/4. CRR 512b. BMCRR 1122.
F £50 ($80) / **VF** £130 ($208)

1160   1161

1160   Q. Caecilius Metellus, 130 BC. Q METE (ME and TE usually in monogram, or ET in monogram) or Q MET (MET in monogram, or ME or ET in monogram) above prow, three pellets before, ROMA below. RRC 256/4. CRR 510b. BMCRR 1061.
F £40 ($64) / **VF** £110 ($176)
On some rev. dies the moneyer's praenomen mistakenly appears as 'C' instead of 'Q'.

1161   **M. Vargunteius,** 130 BC. M VARG or VARGV or VAR (VAR usually in monogram) above prow, three pellets before, ROMA below. RRC 257/4. CRR 508b. BMCRR 1073.
F £40 ($64) / **VF** £110 ($176)

1162

1162   **Cn. Domitius,** 128 BC. CN DOMI or DOME (ME in monogram) or DOM or DEOMI or DOMIT above prow, three pellets before, ROMA below. RRC 261/4. CRR 515b, c. BMCRR 1030–31.
F £40 ($64) / **VF** £110 ($176)

1163   **Anonymous,** 128 BC. Elephant's hd. r. with bell attached above prow, three pellets before, ROMA below. RRC 262/4. CRR 497b. BMCRR 1051.   **F** £45 ($72) / **VF** £120 ($192)
Although lacking the moneyer's name it seems certain that this was issued by a Caecilius Metellus, probably either L. Caecilius Metellus Diadematus or L. Caecilius Metellus Delmaticus.

1164   **M. Caecilius Q.f. Metellus,** 127 BC. M METELLVS (ME in monogram) inscribed on prow, Macedonian shield above, three pellets before, ROMA below. RRC 263/5a. CRR 482b. BMCRR 1154.   **F** £45 ($72) / **VF** £120 ($192)

1164

1165   **M. Caecilius Q.f. Metellus,** 127 BC. Similar, but without moneyer's name on prow, and
with club below hd. on obv. Cf. RRC 263/5b (omits club). CRR 482c. BMCRR 1156.
F £50 ($80) / **VF** £130 ($208)

1166   **C. Servilius,** 127 BC. C SERVEILI (VE in monogram) inscribed on prow, three pellets below,
ROMA above. RRC 264/4a.   **F** £60 ($96) / **VF** £150 ($240)

1167   — Similar, but with two corn-ears crossed above prow, three pellets before, ROMA below.
RRC 264/4b. CRR 484b. BMCRR 1171.   **F** £50 ($80) / **VF** £130 ($208)

1168

1168   **Q. Fabius Maximus,** 127 BC. Q MAX (sometimes MA or AX in monogram) above prow,
three pellets before, ROMA below. RRC 265/3. CRR 479a. BMCRR 1161.
F £40 ($64) / **VF** £110 ($176)

1169   **C. Cassius,** 126 BC. C CASSI above prow, three pellets before, ROMA below. RRC 266/4.
(Unique)

1170   **T. Quinctius Flamininus,** 126 BC. T Q above prow, three pellets before, ROMA below.
RRC 267/4. CRR 506b. B *Quinctia* 5.   **F** £55 ($88) / **VF** £140 ($224)

1171   **C. Caecilius Metellus,** 125 BC. C METELL (ME in monogram, TE sometimes so) or METEL or
METE inscribed on prow, elephant's hd. r. above, three pellets before, ROMA below. RRC
269/4. CRR 486a. BMCRR 1184.   **F** £50 ($80) / **VF** £130 ($208)

1172   **Mn. Acilius Balbus,** 125 BC. MN ACIL (MN in monogram) above prow, three pellets
before, ROMA below. RRC 271/3. CRR 499a. BMCRR 1022.
F £65 ($104) / **VF** £160 ($256)

1173   **Anonymous,** 135–125 BC. Three pellets before prow, ROMA below. RRC 272/2. BMCRR
1196.   **F** £55 ($88) / **VF** £140 ($224)
*Weight about 4 grams (for heavier quadrantes of similar type see no. 1122, and for a
lighter issue see no. 1194).*

1174   **Q. Fabius Labeo,** 124 BC. Q FABI above prow, three pellets before, ROMA below. RRC
273/2. CRR 533. BMCRR Italy 500.   **F** £50 ($80) / **VF** £130 ($208)

1175 **C. Porcius Cato,** 123 BC. C CATO above prow, three pellets before, ROMA below. RRC 274/3. CRR 418. BMCRR Italy, p. 250. **F** £65 ($104) / **VF** £160 ($256)

1176 **M. Fannius C.f.,** 123 BC. M FAN C F (AN in monogram) above prow, three pellets before, ROMA below. RRC 275/3. CRR 420a. BMCRR Italy, p. 251. *(Unique)*

1177 **Q. Minucius Rufus,** 122 BC. Q MINV RVF above prow, three pellets before, ROMA below. RRC 277/2. CRR 422. BMCRR Italy 467. **F** £55 ($88) / **VF** £140 ($224)

1178 **C. Plutius,** 121 BC. C PLVTI inscribed on prow, caps of the Dioscuri above, three pellets before, ROMA below. RRC 278/2. **F** £65 ($104) / **VF** £160 ($256)
The Plutia gens is unknown to history and Crawford regards this moneyer as a Plautius, son of the C. Plautius who was praetor in 146 BC.

1179   1180

1179 **Cn.(?) Papirius Carbo,** 121 BC. CARBO inscribed on prow, thunderbolt above, three pellets before, ROMA below. RRC 279/2. CRR 416a. BMCRR Italy, p. 248.
F £75 ($120) / **VF** £180 ($288)
The omission of the moneyer's praenomen is curious, but the issue should be regarded as distinct from that of M. Carbo whose denarii are dated to the preceding year (see no. 151). Crawford thinks he is probably the Cn. Carbo who held the consulship in 113 BC.

1180 **Cn. Domitius, M. Junius Silanus and Q. Curtius,** 116/115 BC. Obv. CN DOMI before hd. of Hercules, the mark of value sometimes above instead of behind. Rev. Club between bow and arrow, M SILA on l., Q CVRTI on r. (positions sometimes reversed). RRC 285/5. CRR 538b. BMCRR Italy 493. **F** £75 ($120) / **VF** £180 ($288)

1181 **M. Cipius M.f.,** 115/114 BC. Moneyer's name M CIPI M F before hd. of Hercules, ROMA below prow (no mark of value on rev.). RRC 289/4. Cf. CRR 547b. BMCRR Italy, p. 273.
(Unique)

1182 **C. Fonteius,** 114/113 BC. C FONT (NT in monogram) above prow, three pellets before, ROMA below. RRC 290/5. CRR 556c. BMCRR Italy 619. **F** £40 ($64) / **VF** £110 ($176)

1183   1185

1183   **P. Licinius Nerva,** 113/112 BC. Moneyer's name P NERVA (NE in monogram) before hd. of Hercules, horse r. above prow, three pellets before, ROMA below. RRC 292/4a. CRR 549b. BMCRR Italy 529.   **F** £40 ($64) / **VF** £110 ($176)

1184   — Similar, but with bird r. instead of horse above prow. RRC 292/4b. CRR 549c.   **F** £55 ($88) / **VF** £140 ($224)

1185   **L. Marcius Philippus,** 113/112 BC. Moneyer's name L PHILIPPVS before hd. of Hercules, cock r. above prow, three pellets before, ROMA below. RRC 293/2. CRR 552. BMCRR Italy 535.   **F** £50 ($80) / **VF** £130 ($208)

1186   **Cn. Cornelius Blasio Cn.f.,** 112/111 BC. CN BLASIO (BLA in monogram) above prow, three pellets before, ROMA below, and with obv. type bust of bearded Hercules l., clad in lion's skin, club over r. shoulder, three pellets behind. RRC 296/4. CRR 562b. BMCRR Italy, p. 297.   **F** £60 ($96) / **VF** £150 ($240)

1187   **M. Herennius,** 108/107 BC. M HERENNI (HE in monogram) and three pellets above prow, ROMA below. RRC 308/3. CRR 568a. BMCRR 1287.   **F** £55 ($88) / **VF** £140 ($224)

                         1188   1189

1188   **C. Sulpicius C.f.,** 106 BC. C SVLPI (LP in monogram) above prow, palm-branch and three pellets before, ROMA below. RRC 312/4. CRR 573b. B *Sulpicia* 4.   **F** £55 ($88) / **VF** £140 ($224)

1189   **L. Memmius Galeria,** 106 BC. L MEMMI (ME usually in monogram) and three pellets above prow, ROMA below, the prow-stem decorated with hd. of Venus r. and crowned by Cupid before. RRC 313/4. CRR 575b. BMCRR 1359.   **F** £45 ($72) / **VF** £120 ($192)

1190   **L. Pomponius Molo,** ca. 97 BC. L POMP (LP and MP in monogram) above prow, three pellets before, ROMA below. RRC 334/5. CRR 608c. BMCRR Italy 744.   **F** £45 ($72) / **VF** £120 ($192)

1191   **Anonymous (C. Poblicius Malleolus),** ca. 96 BC. Hammer and ROMA above prow, three pellets below. RRC 335/7a. CRR 616c. BMCRR Italy 712.   **F** £50 ($80) / **VF** £130 ($208)

1192   — Similar, but the hammer is before prow. RRC 335/7b.   **F** £55 ($88) / **VF** £140 ($224)

1193   **Anonymous (L.P.D.A.P.),** 91 BC. L P D A P above prow, three pellets above or below (ROMA omitted). RRC 338/4. CRR 678c. BMCRR p. 283. **F** £65 ($104) / **VF** £160 ($256) *This legend may be expanded to 'Lege Papiria de assis pondere' and refers to the Lex Papiria of 91 BC by which the weight standard of the bronze coinage was reduced to the semuncial level.*

1194 **Anonymous,** 91 BC. Three pellets before prow (sometimes above), ROMA below (no symbol or moneyer's name). RRC 339/4c–d. CRR 679c.　　**F** £50 ($80) / **VF** £130 ($208)
Weight about 3.25 grams (for heavier quadrantes of similar type, see nos. 1122 and 1173).

1195 — Similar, but ROMA (MA sometimes in monogram) is above prow, the mark of value before or below. RRC 339/4a–b. CRR 679c. BMCRR 2208. **F** £50 ($80) / **VF** £130 ($208)
Weight about 3.25 grams (for much heavier quadrantes of similar type, see nos. 608 and 1037).

1196 **L. Calpurnius Piso L.f. L.n. Frugi,** 90 BC. Obv. Laur. hd. of Apollo r., three pellets behind. Rev. L PISO above prow, FRVGI below (mark of value and ROMA omitted). RRC 340/6a. CRR 677c. BMCRR p. 281.　　**F** £80 ($128) / **VF** £200 ($320)
The unorthodox obv. type is copied from the silver coinage of this moneyer (see nos. 235–7).

1197 — Similar, but with ROMA above prow and three pellets below (moneyer's name omitted). RRC 340/6b.　　**F** £80 ($128) / **VF** £200 ($320)

1198 — Obv. Similar. Rev. Rudder and anchor in saltire, L PISO on l. or on r. RRC 340/6c. CRR 677d. BMCRR 2187.　　**F** £100 ($160) / **VF** £225 ($360)

1199

1199 **Q. Titius,** 90 BC. Obv. Mask of bearded Silenus r., wreathed with ivy, three pellets behind. Rev. Mask of bearded Pan r., Q TITI below. RRC 341/7. CRR 697. BMCRR p. 289.
　　F £150 ($240) / **VF** £350 ($560)
Remarkably, the types of the three fractional bronze denominations of this moneyer are copied from the silver coinage of his collegue, C. Vibius Pansa (see nos. 245–6).

1200 **C. Vibius C.f. Pansa,** 90 BC. Obv. Winged and dr. bust of Victory r. Rev. C VIBI or C VIBI PA (PA in monogram) above prow, three pellets below or before (ROMA omitted). RRC 342/9. CRR 690g. BMCRR 2321.　　**F** £80 ($128) / **VF** £200 ($320)
The obv. type would appear to be copied from the silver quinarii of Pansa's monetary colleague, Q. Titius (see no. 240).

1201 **L. Titurius L.f. Sabinus,** 89 BC. Obv. Laur. hd. of Apollo r., three pellets behind. Rev. L TITVRI (TITVRI in monogram) above prow, SAB below (legends retrograde, mark of value and ROMA omitted). RRC 344/7. CRR 701e. BMCRR 2366.
　　F £80 ($128) / **VF** £200 ($320)

1202 **L. Rubrius Dossenus,** 87 BC. L RVBR above prow (mark of value and ROMA omitted). RRC 348/7. Cf. CRR 711a. Cf. B *Rubria* 8.　　(*Unique*)

1203 **Anonymous,** 86 BC. Three pellets before prow, which is turned to l., ROMA (MA sometimes in monogram) above. RRC 350B/3. CRR 679c. BMCRR 2213.
　　F £50 ($80) / **VF** £130 ($208)

Sextans

The sextans, the sixth part of the as, was valued at 2 unciae. **Standard type:** *hd. of Mercury r., in winged petasus, two pellets above. Rev. Prow of galley r., two pellets below or before,* ROMA *above or below (usually with symbol, letter/s or monogram above or before).*

1204   **211–206 BC.** Anonymous issue, two pellets below prow, ROMA above. RRC 56/6. CRR 143d. BMCRR 263.   **F** £35 ($56) / **VF** £95 ($152)
       Weight about 7 grams (for heavier pre-reform sextantes of similar type, see nos. 610 and 611).

1205   — Anchor before prow, two pellets below, ROMA above. RRC 50/7.
                                                        F £60 ($96) / **VF** £150 ($240)

1206   — Branch above prow, two pellets before, ROMA below. RRC 76/6. CRR 203b.
                                                        F £65 ($104) / **VF** £160 ($256)

1207   — Similar, but with caduceus above prow. RRC 60/6. CRR 164d.
                                                        F £45 ($72) / **VF** £120 ($192)
       This appears to have been struck using two weight standards, one of about 7 grams, the other of only 3 grams.

1208   — Similar, but with club above prow. RRC 89/7. CRR 213c. BMCRR 317.
                                                        F £55 ($88) / **VF** £140 ($224)

1209   — Corn-ear and ROMA above prow, two pellets below. RRC 72/8. CRR 195d. BMCRR Italy 78.   **F** £40 ($64) / **VF** £110 ($176)
       For heavier pre-reform sextantes of similar type, see no. 612).

1210   — Corn-ear above prow, two pellets before, ROMA below. RRC 72/15. CRR 195d.
                                                        F £50 ($80) / **VF** £130 ($208)

1211   — Corn-ear above prow, KA (in monogram) or IC or C before, ROMA below (mark of value omitted on rev.). RRC 69/6. CRR 310d. BMCRR Italy 274, 280.
                                                        F £40 ($64) / **VF** £110 ($176)
       This appears to be of Sicilian mintage, probably Catana.

1212   — Cornucopiae above prow, two pellets before, ROMA below. RRC 58/7a. CRR 218d.
                                                        F £65 ($104) / **VF** £160 ($256)

1213   — Similar, but the cornucopiae is before prow, two pellets below, and ROMA above. RRC 58/7b.   **F** £65 ($104) / **VF** £160 ($256)

1214   — Crescent and ROMA above prow, two pellets below. RRC 57/7. CRR 221d. BMCRR 582.   **F** £65 ($104) / **VF** £160 ($256)

1215   — Hammer and apex above prow, two pellets before, ROMA below. RRC 59/6. CRR 150d.
                                                        F £60 ($96) / **VF** £150 ($240)

1216   — Spearhead before prow, two pellets below, ROMA above. RRC 88/7. Cf. CRR 224d. BMCRR 323.   **F** £50 ($80) / **VF** £130 ($208)

1217   — Horizontal staff and ROMA above prow, two pellets below, and sometimes with club behind hd. on obv. RRC 106/8. BMCRR Italy 75.   **F** £45 ($72) / **VF** £120 ($192)
       Weight about 7 grams (for lighter sextantes of similar type, see no. 1237).

1218   **211–206 BC.** Victory and ROMA above prow, two pellets below. RRC 61/6. CRR 148d.
BMCRR Italy 38, 345.   **F** £40 ($64) / **VF** £110 ($176)
*This appears to have been struck using two weight standards, one of about 8.5 grams, the
other of only 4 grams.*

1219

1219   — AVR (in monogram) before prow, two pellets below, ROMA above. RRC 65/6. CRR
162d. BMCRR Italy 130.   **F** £40 ($64) / **VF** £110 ($176)

1220   — Similar, but with C before prow. RRC 63/6. CRR 157d. BMCRR Italy 187.
                                                  F £40 ($64) / **VF** £110 ($176)

1221   — Similar, but with CA (Canusium) before prow, and also behind or below hd. on obv.
RRC 100/5. CRR 309f. BMCRR Italy, p. 207.   **F** £65 ($104) / **VF** £160 ($256)

1222   — H before prow, two pellets below, ROMA above. RRC 85/6. CRR 175d. BMCRR Italy,
p. 194, note 1.   **F** £65 ($104) / **VF** £160 ($256)

1223   — L (Luceria) dividing two pellets below prow, ROMA above. RRC 97/6b, 14, 20b. CRR
304d. BMCRR Italy 171.   **F** £45 ($72) / **VF** £120 ($192)
*The weight standard declines from about 7 grams to only 3.75 grams (for heavier pre-
reform sextantes of similar type, see no. 613).*

1224   — Similar, but the mint mark L is on obv., below hd. of Mercury. RRC 97/6a, 20a, 27.
BMCRR Italy, p. 185, note 1.   **F** £45 ($72) / **VF** £120 ($192)

1225   — Obv. Hd. of Minerva r. in crested Corinthian helmet, L below chin, two pellets below.
Rev. The Dioscuri galloping r., T below, ROMA in ex. RRC 98A/6. CRR 134. BMCRR
Italy 181.   **F** £80 ($128) / **VF** £200 ($320)
*There is no obvious explanation for this extraordinary temporary abandonment of the
standard design of the sextans utilizing the obverse commonly associated with the triens,
though the head of Mercury had already been employed on contemporary quadrantes from
this mint (see nos. 1059–60).*

1226   1230

1226   — MA (in monogram) or M before prow, two pellets below, ROMA above (the mark of
value sometimes omitted on obv.). RRC 64/6. CRR 160c. BMCRR Italy 119.
                                                  F £40 ($64) / **VF** £110 ($176)
Coins of this issue are sometimes overstruck.

1227 **211–206 BC.** Π dividing two pellets below prow, ROMA above, and also with Π below hd. on obv. RRC 99/7. CRR 306d. BMCRR Italy 264. F £50 ($80) / **VF** £130 ($208)

1228 — Ϙ before prow, two pellets below, ROMA above. RRC 86A/4. CRR 182c. BMCRR Italy 223. **F** £55 ($88) / **VF** £140 ($224)

1229 — ROMA (in monogram) before prow, two pellets below, ROMA above. RRC 84/7. Cf. BMCRR Italy, p. 192, note 1. **F** £65 ($104) / **VF** £160 ($256)

1230 — V before prow, two pellets below, ROMA above. RRC 87/5. CRR 186d. BMCRR Italy 241. **F** £50 ($80) / **VF** £130 ($208)

1231 **206–194 BC.** Bird and rudder above prow, two pellets before, ROMA below. RRC 117B/5. CRR 292c. **F** £65 ($104) / **VF** £160 ($256)

1232 — Dog r. above prow, two pellets before, ROMA below. RRC 122/7. CRR 251d. **F** £55 ($88) / **VF** £140 ($224)

1233 — Helmet before prow, two pellets below, ROMA above. RRC 118/5. CRR 272d. BMCRR Italy, p. 226. **F** £65 ($104) / **VF** £160 ($256)

1234 — Knife and ROMA above prow, two pellets below. RRC 120/7. **F** £65 ($104) / **VF** £160 ($256)

1235 — Meta above prow, two pellets before, ROMA below. RRC 124/7. CRR 260d. **F** £60 ($96) / **VF** £150 ($240)

1236 — Sow r. and ROMA above prow, two pellets below. RRC 121/7. CRR 254d. **F** £50 ($80) / **VF** £130 ($208)

1237 — Horizontal staff and ROMA above prow, two pellets below. RRC 112/7c. **F** £60 ($96) / **VF** £150 ($240)
Weight about 5 grams (for heavier sextantes of similar type, see no. 1217).

1238 — Similar, but the staff is on obv. before hd. of Hercules. RRC 112/7b. CRR 243c. BMCRR 305. **F** £55 ($88) / **VF** £140 ($224)

1239 — Similar, but a staff appears on both obv. and rev. RRC 112/7a. **F** £60 ($96) / **VF** £150 ($240)

1240 — Star above prow, two pellets before, ROMA below. RRC 113/6. **F** £75 ($120) / **VF** £175 ($280)

1241 — Thunderbolt before prow, two pellets below, ROMA above. RRC 119/7. CRR 248d. **F** £50 ($80) / **VF** £130 ($208)

1242 **194–189 BC.** Crescent above prow, two pellets before, ROMA below. RRC 137/6. **F** £65 ($104) / **VF** £160 ($256)

1243 — Moneyer's monogram AV above prow, two pellets before, ROMA below. RRC 136/6. CRR 327d. BMCRR 569. **F** £55 ($88) / **VF** £140 ($224)

1244 — Moneyer's monogram L PL H above prow, two pellets before, ROMA below, and with caduceus over Mercury's shoulder on obv. RRC 134/6. CRR 333d. **F** £50 ($80) / **VF** £130 ($208)

1245   **194–189 BC.** Moneyer's monogram ME above prow, two pellets before, ROMA below. RRC
132/7. CRR 319d. B *Caecilia* 7.   **F** £65 ($104) / **VF** £160 ($256)

1246   — Moneyer's monogram TAMP above prow, two pellets before, ROMA below. RRC 133/8.
CRR 337d. BMCRR 563.   **F** £55 ($88) / **VF** £140 ($224)

1247   **189–179 BC.** Bird with wreath in beak perched on T above prow, two pellets before, ROMA
below. RRC 141/6. CRR 346d.   **F** £60 ($96) / **VF** £150 ($240)

1248

1248   — Bull r. and MD (in monogram) above prow, two pellets before, ROMA below, and with
caduceus over Mercury's shoulder on obv. RRC 142/5. CRR 299d.
F £50 ($80) / **VF** £130 ($208)

1249   — Shield and MAE (in monogram) above prow, two pellets before, ROMA below. RRC
143/5. CRR 375d. B *Maenia* 6.   **F** £60 ($96) / **VF** £150 ($240)

1250   — Ulysses walking r., holding staff, above prow, two pellets before, ROMA below. RRC
149/5b. BMCRR 726.   **F** £65 ($104) / **VF** £160 ($256)

1251   — Similar, but with L MAMILI below prow and RO–MA divided by the figure of Ulysses
above, and with caduceus over Mercury's shoulder on obv. RRC 149/5a. CRR 369d. B
Mamilia 5.   **F** £65 ($104) / **VF** £160 ($256)

1252   — Victory flying r. and spearhead above prow, two pellets before, ROMA below, and with
caduceus over Mercury's shoulder on obv. RRC 145/5. CRR 293d. BMCRR 500.
F £55 ($88) / **VF** £140 ($224)

1253   — Victory flying r. and L F P (in monogram) above prow, two pellets before, ROMA below.
RRC 144/5. CRR 300d. B *Furia* 5.   **F** £55 ($88) / **VF** £140 ($224)

1254   — CN DO above prow, two pellets before, ROMA below. RRC 147/4. B *Domitia* 6.
F £65 ($104) / **VF** £160 ($256)

1255   — M TITINI above prow, two pellets before, ROMA below. RRC 150/5. CRR 365d. B
Titinia 5.   **F** £65 ($104) / **VF** £160 ($256)

1256   — Q MARI above prow, two pellets before, ROMA below. RRC 148/5. CRR 367d.
BMCRR 826.   **F** £50 ($80) / **VF** £130 ($208)

1257   **179–169 BC.** Fly before prow, two pellets below, ROMA above. RRC 159/7. CRR 324d.
BMCRR Italy 383.   **F** £60 ($96) / **VF** £150 ($240)

1258   — MAT (in monogram) above prow, two pellets before, ROMA below. RRC 162/7a. CRR
321e. B *Matiena* 8.   **F** £60 ($96) / **VF** £150 ($240)

1259 **179–169 BC.** Similar, but with MAT (in monogram) before prow, two pellets below, and ROMA above. RRC 162/7b. CRR 321h. BMCRR Italy, p. 237, note 1.
F £60 ($96) / **VF** £150 ($240)

1260 — TAL (in monogram) before prow, two pellets below, ROMA above. RRC 161/6. CRR 329d. BMCRR Italy, p. 234.
F £60 ($96) / **VF** £150 ($240)

1261 **169–157 BC.** Anchor before prow, two pellets above, ROMA below. RRC 194/5. CRR 238d.
F £65 ($104) / **VF** £160 ($256)

1262 — Ass r. above prow, two pellets before, ROMA below. RRC 195/5. CRR 298d.
F £65 ($104) / **VF** £160 ($256)

1263 — Butterfly on vine-branch with grapes above prow, two pellets before, ROMA below. RRC 184/5. CRR 296d.
F £60 ($96) / **VF** £150 ($240)

1264 — Caps of the Dioscuri above prow, two pellets before, ROMA below. RRC 181/4. CRR 294c.
F £65 ($104) / **VF** £160 ($256)

1265 — Gryphon and hare's hd. above prow, two pellets before, ROMA below. RRC 182/6. CRR 284d.
F £60 ($96) / **VF** £150 ($240)

1266 — Star before prow, two pellets below, ROMA above. RRC 196/5. CRR 264e. BMCRR 469.
F £65 ($104) / **VF** £160 ($256)

1267 — Wolf suckling twins above prow, two pellets before, ROMA below. RRC 183/5. CRR 297d.
F £50 ($80) / **VF** £130 ($208)

1268 — A CÆ above prow, two pellets before, ROMA below. RRC 174/5. CRR 355d. B *Caecilia* 12.
F £45 ($72) / **VF** £120 ($192)

1269 — BAL (AL in monogram) above prow, two pellets before, ROMA below, and with caduceus over Mercury's shoulder on obv. RRC 179/5. CRR 354d. BMCRR 617.
F £60 ($96) / **VF** £150 ($240)

1270 — C SAX (AX in monogram) above prow, two pellets before, ROMA below. RRC 173/5. CRR 360d. BMCRR 653.
F £50 ($80) / **VF** £130 ($208)

1271 — CINA above prow, two pellets before, ROMA below. RRC 178/5. CRR 368d. B *Cornelia* 16.
F £50 ($80) / **VF** £130 ($208)

1272 — MVRENA (MVR in monogram) above prow, two pellets before, ROMA below. RRC 186/5. CRR 373d. B Licinia 5.
F £70 ($112) / **VF** £170 ($272)

1273 — OPEI above prow, two pellets before, ROMA below. RRC 190/5.
F £70 ($112) / **VF** £170 ($272)

1274 — OPEIMI (PEIMI in monogram) above prow, two pellets before, ROMA below. RRC 188/5. CRR 362d. B *Opimia* 5.
F £55 ($88) / **VF** £140 ($224)

1275 — P BLAS above prow, two pellets before, ROMA below. RRC 189/5. CRR 370d. BMCRR 792.
F £55 ($88) / **VF** £140 ($224)

1276 — PAE (in monogram) above prow, two pellets before, ROMA below. RRC 176/5. CRR 358d. BMCRR 640.
F £55 ($88) / **VF** £140 ($224)

1277   **169–157 BC.** PVR (VR in monogram) above prow, two pellets before, ROMA below. RRC
        187/6.   **F** £70 ($112) / **VF** £170 ($272)

1278   — SAX (AX in monogram) above prow, two pellets before, ROMA below, and with
        caduceus over Mercury's shoulder on obv. RRC 180/5. CRR 361d. BMCRR 607.
                                                        F £55 ($88) / **VF** £140 ($224)

1279   — TP (in monogram) above prow, two pellets before, ROMA below. RRC 177/5. CRR
        353d.   **F** £70 ($112) / **VF** £170 ($272)

1280   — TVRD (VR in monogram) above prow, two pellets before, ROMA below. RRC 193/5.
        CRR 366d. B *Papiria* 5.   **F** £55 ($88) / **VF** £140 ($224)

1281   — VAL (in monogram) above prow, two pellets before, ROMA below. RRC 191/5. CRR
        356d. B *Valeria* 5.   **F** £65 ($104) / **VF** £160 ($256)

1282   — VARO (VAR in monogram) above prow, two pellets before, ROMA below. RRC 185/5.
        CRR 364d. B *Terentia* 8.   **F** £55 ($88) / **VF** £140 ($224)

1283   **157–155 BC.** NAT above prow, two pellets before, ROMA below. RRC 200/6. CRR 383d. B
        Pinaria 7.   **F** £70 ($112) / **VF** £170 ($272)

1284   — SAR above prow, two pellets before, ROMA below, and sometimes with caduceus over
        Mercury's shoulder on obv. RRC 199/6.   **F** £60 ($96) / **VF** £150 ($240)

1285   **C. Scribonius,** 154 BC. C SCR above prow, two pellets before, ROMA below. RRC 201/6.
        CRR 381d. BMCRR 740.   **F** £65 ($104) / **VF** £160 ($256)

1286   **L. Saufeius,** 152 BC. Crescent and L SAVF (VF in monogram) above prow, two pellets
        before, ROMA below. RRC 204/6. CRR 385d.   **F** £70 ($112) / **VF** £170 ($272)

1287   **Safra,** 150 BC. SAFRA above prow, dolphin before, ROMA below (no mark of value). RRC
        206/6. CRR 389d. Cf. B *Afrania* 6.   **F** £65 ($104) / **VF** £160 ($256)
        SAFRA *would appear to represent a cognomen only, no stop being inserted after the first
        letter.*

1288   **C. Junius C.f.,** 149 BC. C IVNI above prow, two pellets before, ROMA below. RRC 210/6.
        CRR 393d. B *Junia* 6.   **F** £60 ($96) / **VF** £150 ($240)

1289

1289   **Q. Marcius Libo,** 148 BC. Q MARC (MA in monogram) above prow, LIBO before, ROMA
        below (no mark of value). RRC 215/6. CRR 396f. B *Marcia* 6.
                                                        F £55 ($88) / **VF** £140 ($224)

1290   **L. Sempronius Pitio,** 148 BC. L SEMP (MP in monogram) above prow, two pellets before,
        ROMA below. RRC 216/6. CRR 403d. BMCRR 722.   **F** £65 ($104) / **VF** £160 ($256)

1291   **M. Atilius Saranus,** 148 BC. M ATILI above prow, two pellets before, ROMA below, and with caduceus over Mercury's shoulder on obv. RRC 214/6. CRR 399d. B *Atilia* 14.
F £60 ($96) / **VF** £150 ($240)

1292   **C. Terentius Lucanus,** 147 BC. Wreath-bearing Victory flying r. and C TER LVC (TE in monogram) above prow, two pellets before, ROMA below. RRC 217/6. CRR 426d.
F £70 ($112) / **VF** £170 ($272)

1293   **C. Antestius,** 146 BC. Puppy running r. and C ANTESTI (ANTE in monogram) above prow, two pellets before, ROMA below. RRC 219/6.   F £70 ($112) / **VF** £170 ($272)

1294   **C. Servilius M.f.,** 136 BC. Mast with pennant and wreath above prow, C SERVEILI M F below (no mark of value), and with caduceus over Mercury's shoulder on obv., two pellets behind, ROMA below. RRC 239/4. CRR 526b. BMCRR Italy 549.
F £55 ($88) / **VF** £140 ($224)

1295   **C. Curiatius C.f. Trigeminus,** 135 BC. C CVR F (VR in monogram) above prow, on which Victory stands r., two pellets before, ROMA below, and with caduceus over Mercury's shoulder on obv. RRC 240/5. CRR 460c. B *Curiatia* 9 bis (Supplément).   *(Unique)*

1296   **L. Trebanius,** 135 BC. L TREBANI (TR and AN in monogram) above prow, two pellets before, ROMA below, and with caduceus over Mercury's shoulder on obv. RRC 241/5. CRR 457c. B *Trebania* 5.   F £65 ($104) / **VF** £160 ($256)

1297   **Ti. Minucius C.f. Augurinus,** 134 BC. TI AVGVRINI and lituus above prow, two pellets before, ROMA below, and with caduceus over Mercury's shoulder on obv., two pellets behind. RRC 243/5.   F £65 ($104) / **VF** £160 ($256)

1298   **C. Aburius Geminus,** 134 BC. C ABVRI GEM (AB and VR in monogram) above prow, two pellets before, ROMA below, and with caduceus over Mercury's shoulder on obv., two pellets behind. RRC 244/4. CRR 491b. B *Aburia* 4.   *(Unique)*

1299   **C. Numitorius,** 133 BC. C NVMITOR above prow, two pellets before, ROMA below, and with mark of value behind hd. on obv. RRC 246/5. CRR 467c. B *Numitoria* 6.
F £65 ($104) / **VF** £160 ($256)

1300   1302

1300   **M. Fabrinius,** 132 BC. M FABRINI above prow, two pellets before, ROMA below, and with caduceus over Mercury's shoulder on obv., two pellets behind. RRC 251/4. CRR 453c. BMCRR 987.   F £55 ($88) / **VF** £140 ($224)

1301   **M. Acilius M.f.,** 130 BC. M ACILI above prow, two pellets before, ROMA below, and with caduceus over Mercury's shoulder on obv., two pellets behind. RRC 255/5.   *(Unique)*

1302   **M. Vargunteius,** 130 BC. M VARG (VAR in monogram) above prow, two pellets before, ROMA below, and with caduceus over Mercury's shoulder on obv., two pellets behind. RRC 257/5. CRR 508c. B *Vargunteia* 5.   F £60 ($96) / **VF** £150 ($240)

1303 **Anonymous,** 128 BC. Elephant's hd. r. with bell attached above prow, two pellets before, ROMA below, and with caduceus over Mercury's shoulder on obv., two pellets behind. RRC 262/5. CRR 497c. B *Caecilia* 42.   **F** £65 ($104) / **VF** £160 ($256)
Although lacking the moneyer's name it seems certain that this was issued by a Caecilius Metellus, probably either L. Caecilius Metellus Diadematus or L. Caecilius Metellus Delmaticus.

1304 **Cn. Domitius, M. Junius Silanus and Q. Curtius,** 116/115 BC. Obv. CN DOMI before hd. of Mercury. Rev. Caduceus, M SILA on l., Q CVRTI on r. RRC 285/6. CRR 538c. BMCRR Italy, p. 260.   **F** £80 ($128) / **VF** £200 ($320)

1305 **L. Pomponius Molo,** ca. 97 BC. L POMP (LP and MP in monogram) above prow, two pellets before, ROMA below, and with caduceus over Mercury's shoulder on obv. RRC 334/6. CRR 608d. BMCRR Italy 746.   **F** £50 ($80) / **VF** £130 ($208)

1306 **Anonymous (C. Poblicius Malleolus),** ca. 96 BC. Hammer and ROMA above prow, two pellets below, and sometimes with caduceus over Mercury's shoulder on obv. RRC 335/8. CRR 616d.   **F** £60 ($96) / **VF** £150 ($240)

Uncia

The uncia, the twelfth part of the as, represented the basic unit by which most of the larger fractional denominations of the as were denoted. **Standard type:** *hd. of Roma r., in crested Attic helmet, single pellet behind. Rev. Prow of galley r., pellet below or before, ROMA above or below (usually with symbol, letter/s or monogram above or before).*

1307 **211–206 BC.** Anonymous issue, pellet below prow, ROMA above. RRC 56/7. CRR 143e. BMCRR 269.   **F** £30 ($48) / **VF** £85 ($136)
Weight about 3.5 to 4.5 grams (for heavier pre-reform unciae of similar type, see no. 616).

1308 — Anchor before prow, pellet below, ROMA above. RRC 50/8.
        F £60 ($96) / **VF** £150 ($240)

1309 — Caduceus above prow, pellet before, ROMA below. RRC 60/7. CRR 164e.
        F £60 ($96) / **VF** £150 ($240)

1310 — Corn-ear and ROMA above prow, pellet below. RRC 72/9.
        F £50 ($80) / **VF** £130 ($208)
Weight about 3.5 to 4 grams (for heavier pre-reform unciae of similar type, see no. 617).

1311 — Cornucopiae above prow, pellet before, ROMA below. RRC 58/8. CRR 218e.
        F £60 ($96) / **VF** £150 ($240)

1312 — Crescent and ROMA above prow, pellet below. RRC 57/8. CRR 221e.
        F £60 ($96) / **VF** £150 ($240)

1313 — Hammer and apex above prow, pellet before, ROMA below. RRC 59/7. CRR 150e.
        F £60 ($96) / **VF** £150 ($240)

1314 — Spearhead before prow, pellet below, ROMA above. RRC 88/8. Cf. CRR 224e.
        F £60 ($96) / **VF** £150 ($240)

1315 — Horizontal staff and ROMA above prow, pellet below. RRC 106/9. BMCRR Italy, p. 162, note 1.   (*Unique*)

254   ROMAN REPUBLIC

1316   **211–206 BC.** Victory and ROMA above prow, pellet below. RRC 61/7. CRR 148e. BMCRR
        Italy 40.   **F** £45 ($72) / **VF** £120 ($192)

1317   — CA (Canusium) before prow, pellet below, ROMA above, and also with CA below hd. on
        obv. RRC 100/6a. CRR 309g. BMCRR Italy, p. 207.   **F** £55 ($88) / **VF** £140 ($224)

1318   — Similar, but the mint mark CA on rev. is below prow, either preceding or following the
        mark of value. RRC 100/6b–c.   **F** £55 ($88) / **VF** £140 ($224)

1319   — H before prow, pellet below, ROMA above. RRC 85/7. CRR 175e. BMCRR Italy,
        p. 194, note 1.   **F** £45 ($72) / **VF** £120 ($192)

1320   — L (Luceria) and pellet below prow, ROMA above. RRC 97/7c, 15, 21. CRR 304e.
        BMCRR Italy 10 ('Aes Grave'), 173.   **F** £45 ($72) / **VF** £120 ($192)
        The weight standard declines from about 4.5 grams to 2.75 grams (for heavier pre-reform
        unciae of similar type, see no. 618).

1321   — Similar, but the mint mark L is on obv., below hd. of Roma (who sometimes wears
        Phrygian instead of Attic helmet). RRC 97/7a–b. BMCRR Italy 165, 167.
                                                    F £40 ($64) / **VF** £110 ($176)

1322   — Obv. Hd. of Roma r. in Phrygian helmet, L below, pellet behind. Rev. One of the
        Dioscuri galloping r., holding couched spear, T below, pellet behind, ROMA in ex. RRC
        98A/7. CRR 135. BMCRR Italy, p. 187.   **F** £75 ($120) / **VF** £175 ($280)

1323   — Π and pellet (or pellet and Π) below prow, ROMA above. RRC 99/8. CRR 306e.
        BMCRR Italy, p. 205.   **F** £45 ($72) / **VF** £120 ($192)

1324   — Ω before prow, pellet below, ROMA above. RRC 86A/5. CRR 182d. BMCRR Italy,
        p. 196, note 1.   *(Unique)*

1325   **206–194 BC.** Thunderbolt above prow, pellet before, ROMA below. RRC 119/8. Cf. CRR
        248e.   **F** £55 ($88) / **VF** £140 ($224)

1326   **194–189 BC.** Moneyer's monogram AV above prow, pellet before, ROMA below. RRC
        136/7. CRR 327e. B *Aurelia* 7.   **F** £60 ($96) / **VF** £150 ($240)

1327   — Moneyer's monogram TAMP above prow, pellet before, ROMA below. RRC 133/9. CRR
        337e. B *Baebia* 11.   **F** £60 ($96) / **VF** £150 ($240)

1328   **189–179 BC.** Bull r. and MD (in monogram) above prow, pellet before, ROMA below. RRC
        142/6. CRR 299e.   **F** £60 ($96) / **VF** £150 ($240)

1329

1329   — Victory flying r. and L F P (in monogram) above prow, pellet before, ROMA below. RRC
        144/6. CRR 300e. B *Furia* 6.   **F** £65 ($104) / **VF** £160 ($256)

1330   **189–179 BC.** M TITINI above prow, pellet before, ROMA below. RRC 150/6. CRR 365e. B
        Titinia 6.   **F** £60 ($96) / **VF** £150 ($240)

1331   — Q MARI above prow, pellet before, ROMA below. RRC 148/6. CRR 367e. B *Maria* 6.
                                                              F £60 ($96) / **VF** £150 ($240)

1332   **169–157 BC.** Anchor before prow, pellet above, ROMA below. RRC 194/6. CRR 238e.
                                                              F £60 ($96) / **VF** £150 ($240)

1333   — Ass r. above prow, pellet before, ROMA below. RRC 195/6. CRR 298e.
                                                              F £60 ($96) / **VF** £150 ($240)

1334   — Butterfly on vine-branch with grapes above prow, pellet before, ROMA below. RRC
        184/6. CRR 296e.   **F** £60 ($96) / **VF** £150 ($240)

1335   — Wolf suckling twins above prow, pellet before, ROMA below. RRC 183/6. CRR 297e.
                                                              F £55 ($88) / **VF** £140 ($224)

1336   — OPEI above prow, pellet before, ROMA below. RRC 190/6. CRR 363d.
                                                              F £60 ($96) / **VF** £150 ($240)

1337   — PVR above prow, pellet before, ROMA below. RRC 187/7.
                                                              F £60 ($96) / **VF** £150 ($240)

1338   — VAL (in monogram) above prow, pellet before, ROMA below. RRC 191/6. CRR 356e. B
        Valeria 6.   **F** £55 ($88) / **VF** £140 ($224)

1339   — VARO (VAR in monogram) above prow, pellet before, ROMA below. RRC 185/6. CRR
        364e. B *Terentia* 9.   **F** £60 ($96) / **VF** £150 ($240)

1340   **C. Scribonius,** 154 BC. C SCR above prow, pellet before, ROMA below. RRC 201/7. CRR
        381e. B *Scribonia* 7.   **F** £60 ($96) / **VF** £150 ($240)

1341   **C. Maianius,** 153 BC. C MAIANI (MA and AN in monogram) above prow, pellet before,
        ROMA below. RRC 203/6. CRR 428d. B *Maiania* 6.   **F** £60 ($96) / **VF** £150 ($240)

1342   **P. Cornelius Sulla,** 151 BC. P SVLA above prow, pellet before, ROMA below. RRC 205/6.
                                                              (Unique)

1343   **Safra,** 150 BC. SAFRA above prow, dolphin before, ROMA below (no mark of value). RRC
        206/7. B *Afrania* 6 bis (Supplément).   **F** £65 ($104) / **VF** £160 ($256)
        SAFRA *would appear to represent a cognomen only, no stop being inserted after the first
        letter.*

1344   **C. Junius C.f.,** 149 BC. C IVNI above prow, pellet before, ROMA below. RRC 210/7. CRR
        393e. B *Junia* 7.   **F** £60 ($96) / **VF** £150 ($240)

1345   **Q. Marcius Libo,** 148 BC. Q MARC (MA in monogram) above prow, LIBO before, ROMA
        below (no mark of value). RRC 215/7. CRR 396g. B *Marcia* 7.
                                                              F £60 ($96) / **VF** £150 ($240)

1346   **M. Atilius Saranus,** 148 BC. M ATILI above prow, pellet before, ROMA below. RRC 214/7.
        CRR 399e. B *Atilia* 15.   **F** £60 ($96) / **VF** £150 ($240)

1347 **C. Curiatius C.f. Trigeminus,** 135 BC. C CVR F (VR in monogram) above prow, on which Victory stands r., pellet before, ROMA below. RRC 240/6. CRR 460d. B *Curiatia* 6.
(*Unique*)

1348 **C. Minucius Augurinus,** 135 BC. C AVG above prow, pellet before, ROMA below. RRC 242/5. CRR 464d. B *Minucia* 8.
(*Unique*)

1349 **C. Aburius Geminus,** 134 BC. C ABVRI GEM (AB and VR in monogram) above prow, pellet before, ROMA below. RRC 244/5. CRR 491c. B *Aburia* 5.
(*Unique*)

1350 **P. Maenius M.f. Antias (or Antiaticus),** 132 BC. P MAE ANT (MAE and ANT in monogram) above prow, pellet before, ROMA below. RRC 249/4. CRR 493b. B *Maenia* 10.
F £60 ($96) / **VF** £150 ($240)

1351 **M. Aburius M.f. Geminus,** 132 BC. M ABVRI M F GEM (AB, VR, and MF in monogram) above prow, pellet before, ROMA below. RRC 250/3. CRR 488a. B *Aburia* 8.
(*Unique*)

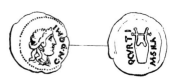

1352

1352 **Cn. Domitius, M. Junius Silanus and Q. Curtius,** 116/115 BC. Obv. Diad. hd. of Apollo r., CN DOMI before, pellet behind. Rev. Lyre, M SILA on l., Q CVRTI on r. (positions sometimes reversed). RRC 285/7. CRR 538d. B *Domitia* 13.
F £75 ($120) / **VF** £175 ($280)

1353 **M. Cipius M.f.,** 115/114 BC. Obv. Hd. of young Hercules r., clad in lion's skin, pellet behind. Rev. Rudder l., M CIPI M F and pellet below, ROMA above. RRC 289/5. CRR 547c. Cf. BMCRR Italy 525.
F £75 ($120) / **VF** £175 ($280)

1354 **C. Fonteius,** 114/113 BC. Rev. Mars in fast quadriga r., C FONT (NT in monogram) below, pellet above, ROMA in ex., and the obv. type is encircled by laurel-wreath. RRC 290/6. CRR 556d. B *Fonteia* 6.
F £75 ($120) / **VF** £175 ($280)

1355 **L. Marcius Philippus,** 113/112 BC. Obv. Laur. hd. of Saturn r., harpa behind, L PHILIPPVS before. Rev. Dog r., pellet above, ROMA in ex. RRC 293/3. CRR 552a. B *Marcia* 14.
F £75 ($120) / **VF** £175 ($280)

1356 **Q. Lutatius Cerco,** 109/108 BC. Obv. Hd. of young Mars r., wearing crested Corinthian helmet, pellet behind. Rev. Q LVTATI (VT in monogram), pellet above, all within oak-wreath. RRC 305/2. CRR 560. B *Lutatia* 5.
F £75 ($120) / **VF** £175 ($280)

1357 **M. Herennius,** 108/107 BC. Rev. Double cornucopiae, M HERENNI (HE in monogram) on l., ROMA on r. RRC 308/4a. CRR 568b. B *Herennia* 4.
F £75 ($120) / **VF** £175 ($280)

1358 — Similar, but without moneyer's name and ROMA is to l. of double cornucopiae. RRC 308/4b. CRR 766.
F £75 ($120) / **VF** £175 ($280)

1359 **L. Hostilius Tubulus,** 105 BC. Rev. L H TVB (TVB in monogram) downwards within oak-wreath, ROMA below. RRC 315/1. BMCRR Appendix 7.
F £65 ($104) / **VF** £160 ($256)

1359

Semuncia

The half uncia, the twenty-fourth part of the as, was the smallest denomination of the post-211 BC Roman Republican coinage. Because of its low value it was most vulnerable to the effects of infla-tion and declining weight standards and, except for a few sporadic 2nd century issues, production virtually ceased after the initial phase of coinage following the currency reform of 211 BC. The types were similar to those used for the sextans, with a head of Mercury in winged petasus on obverse, and the usual prow of a galley on reverse. Most issues lack a mark of value, but when present it takes the form of a 'Σ', or some variant such as 'Є' or '3'.

1360 **211–206 BC.** Obv. Hd. of Mercury r. in winged petasus. Rev. Prow of galley r., ROMA above. RRC 56/8. CRR 143f. BMCRR 277.   **F** £25 ($40) / **VF** £75 ($120)
Weight about 2 grams (for heavier pre-reform semunciae of similar type, see nos. 620–21).

1361 — Similar, but with corn-ear and ROMA above prow. RRC 72/10.
                                                        F £40 ($64) / **VF** £110 ($176)
For heavier pre-reform semunciae of similar type, see no. 622.

1362 — Similar, but with cornucopiae above prow, ROMA below. RRC 58/9.
                                                        F £55 ($88) / **VF** £140 ($224)

1363 — Similar, but with Victory and ROMA above prow. RRC 61/8. CRR 148f. BMCRR Italy, p. 157, note 1.   **F** £55 ($88) / **VF** £140 ($224)

1364 — Similar, but with CA (Canusium) below prow, ROMA above, and also with CA below hd. on obv. RRC 100/7. Cf. CRR 309h. BMCRR Italy, p. 207.
                                                        F £45 ($72) / **VF** £120 ($192)

1365

1365 — Similar, but with L (Luceria) before prow, mark of value Є above, ROMA below, and also with L below hd. on obv. RRC 97/8. CRR 178g. BMCRR Italy, p. 183.
                                                        F £40 ($64) / **VF** £110 ($176)
The mint mark L on rev. is sometimes omitted.

1366 — Similar, but with mark of value Σ and Π below prow, ROMA above (no letter below hd. on obv.). RRC 99/9. CRR 306f. BMCRR Italy, p. 205.   **F** £40 ($64) / **VF** £110 ($176)

1367   **211–206 BC.** Similar, but with mark of value Є (horizontally) below prow, ROMA above
        (no letter or symbol on either side). RRC 106/10.   (*Unique*)

1368   — Obv. Conjoined hds. of the Dioscuri r., wearing laur. pilei, T behind. Rev. The two
        horses of the Dioscuri galloping r., star above each, L in ex. RRC 98A/8. CRR 136.
        BMCRR Italy, p. 187.   **F** £75 ($120) / **VF** £175 ($280)

1369   **179–169 BC.** Obv. Bust of Diana r., bow and quiver over shoulder, mark of value 3 behind.
        Rev. Prow of galley r., dolphin r. above, mark of value e before, ROMA below. RRC 160/5.
                                                         F £55 ($88) / **VF** £140 ($224)

1370   **Anonymous (M. Herennius),** 108/107 BC. Obv. Similar. Rev. Cornucopiae, ROMA on l.
        RRC 308/5.   (*Unique*)
        For the attribution to this moneyer, see nos. 1357–8.

1371   **L. Hostilius Tubulus,** 105 BC. Obv. Similar. Rev. L H TVB (TVB in monogram) downwards
        within oak-wreath, ROMA below. RRC 315/2.   **F** £60 ($96) / **VF** £150 ($240)

1372   **L. Thorius Balbus,** 105 BC. Obv. Laur. female hd. r., mark of value e behind. Rev. L THORI
        (TH in monogram) above mark of value Є (placed horizontally) within oak-wreath, ROMA
        below. RRC 316/2.   (*Unique*)

ROMAN IMPERATORIAL COINAGE, 49–27 BC

Principal references:

B = E. Babelon, *Description historique et chronologique des monnaies de la république romaine.* Paris, 1885–6.

BMCRE = H. Mattingly, *Coins of the Roman Empire in the British Museum*, vol. I. London, 1923.

BMCRR = H.A. Grueber, Coins of the Roman Republic in the British Museum. London, 1910.

C = H. Cohen, *Description Historique des Monnaies Frappées sous l'Empire Romain*, vol. I. 2nd edition. Paris, 1880.

CRI = D.R. Sear, *The History and Coinage of the Roman Imperators 49–27 BC*. London, 1998.

CRR = E.A. Sydenham, *The Coinage of the Roman Republic*. London, 1952.

RIC = C.H.V. Sutherland, *The Roman Imperial Coinage*, vol. I. Revised edition. London, 1984.

RPC = A. Burnett, M. Amandry and P.P. Ripolles, *Roman Provincial Coinage*, vol. I. London and Paris, 1992.

RRC = M.H. Crawford, *Roman Republican Coinage*. Cambridge, 1974.

RSC = H.A. Seaby, *Roman Silver Coins*, vol. I. 3rd (revised) edition. London, 1978.

This brief intermediate series commences with the outbreak of civil war between Caesar and Pompey at the beginning of 49 BC and ends exactly twenty-two years later (January, 27 BC) when Caesar's heir Octavian was given the name Augustus and effectively became the autocratic ruler of the Roman state. The Imperatorial coinage represents the transitional stage between the traditional Republican series and the revolutionary new Imperial coinage of Augustus and his successors.

In its earlier phase (49–45 BC) the Imperatorial series comprised issues bearing the names, though not yet the portraits, of the principal contenders for power. These issues existed side by side with the regular coinage of the Roman moneyers, though in reality these were nothing more than a propaganda tool in the hands of Caesar and his successors who controlled the output of the Capitoline mint almost from the start of the civil war down to the closure of the establishment by Octavian in 40 BC. Additional coinages were produced at various provincial locations by supporters of Pompey and his sons. A major turning point came in January, 44 BC, when Caesar took the unprecedented step of placing his own portrait on the coinage. His assassination followed within three months but, once initiated, this revolutionary innovation was irrevocable and portraiture rapidly became the norm, thus paving the way for the coinage of Imperial Rome.

In the post-Caesarian phase of the Imperatorial coinage (44–27 BC) issues initially were divided between the Triumviral faction, led by Antony, Octavian and Lepidus, and the Republicans, most prominent amongst whom were the tyrannicides Brutus and Cassius. After the pivotal battle of Philippi in the autumn of 42 BC only the two principal Triumvirs, Antony and Octavian, remained to contend for supreme authority in the Roman state. That struggle was finally resolved by the battle of Actium in 31 BC and the subsequent conquest the following year of Antony's last stronghold, the Ptolemaic kingdom of Egypt.

The Imperatorial coinage subdivides conveniently into four major categories: (1) issues of Pompey the Great, his sons and their adherents; (2) issues of Julius Caesar; (3) issues of the Republican tyrannicides and their adherents; and (4) issues of the Triumvirs and their adherents. Between the years 49 and 40 BC it is important to remember that these essentially military coinages must be viewed in association with the contemporary regular silver issues produced by the

Republican moneyers at the Capitoline mint in Rome. These were augmented, between 43 and 41 BC, by an exceptional output of moneyers' gold.

NB From this point in the catalogue the coins described represent only a sample selection of the known types and varieties. For a complete listing of the coins of the Imperatorial period, see 'The History and Coinage of the Roman Imperators, 49–27 BC' by David R. Sear (Spink, 1998).

COINAGE OF POMPEY THE GREAT, HIS SONS AND THEIR ADHERENTS

POMPEY THE GREAT
Proconsul, murdered 48 BC

1374

Gnaeus Pompeius Magnus (Pompey the Great) was born in 106 BC, the son of Gnaeus Pompeius Strabo who was consul in 89 BC and a distinguished commander in the Social War. The young Pompey seems to have had little regard for the normal conventions of Roman aristocratic life, preferring instead to rely on the power and influence vested in him through the command of armies, a trait doubtless inherited from his father. His early military career was certainly an impressive one and by the time he was 25, in 81 BC, he had already assisted the dictator Sulla to achieve supreme power and celebrated a triumph in Rome for his victories in Sicily and Africa. He later went on to achieve further glory in the East through his successes against the Mediterranean pirates and his victory over King Mithradates VI of Pontus. He even took it upon himself to reorganize Rome's territories in the area, creating the new provinces of Syria and Cilicia out of the now defunct Seleucid Kingdom and settling affairs in Judaea. At this point (62 BC) it must have seemed impossible that anyone could mount a serious challenge to the authority of Pompey, but during the 50s that challenge arose in the person of C. Julius Caesar who, through his remarkable conquest of Gaul, was rapidly gaining his own reputation as a military commander of genius. At the close of the decade a struggle for supremacy between the two men appeared inevitable, and early in 49 BC Caesar's lightning invasion of Italy from the north took Pompey completely by surprise and forced him to withdraw hurriedly to Greece. After various preliminary skirmishes the final confrontation took place at Pharsalus in Thessaly on August 9th, 48 BC. The result was an overwhelming victory for Caesar. Pompey, experiencing for the first time in his long military career the anguish of defeat, fled to the coast and took ship for Egypt, cherishing the hope that his great prestige in the East would enable him to re-establish his power and offer a renewed challenge to Caesar. But on hearing of his approach the young Ptolemy XIII and his advisers decided to seek Caesar's favour by murdering his adversary as soon as he stepped ashore. Accordingly, the famous general and imperator met an ignominious end in Egypt on September 28th, 48 BC, leaving Caesar as the most powerful man in the Roman world.

1373

1373   **Silver denarius.** CN PISO PRO Q, hd. of Numa Pompilius r., wearing diad. inscribed
       NVMA. Rev. MAGN PRO COS, prow of galley r. RRC 446/1. CRI 7. BMCRR Spain 62.
       RSC 4. *[Greece, 49–48 BC].*   **VF** £250 ($400) / **EF** £650 ($1,040)

1374   VARRO PRO Q, diad. terminal bust of Jupiter r. Rev. MAGN PRO COS, sceptre between
       dolphin r. and eagle l. RRC 447/1a. CRI 8. BMCRR Spain 64. RSC 3. *[Greece, 49–48 BC].*
                                                         VF £300 ($480) / **EF** £750 ($1,200)

For a gold aureus issued at a much earlier stage of Pompey's career, see no. 10. For posthumous
coins bearing the portrait of Pompey the Great, see under Gnaeus Pompey Junior and under Sextus
Pompey.

SCIPIO
Imperator, committed suicide 46 BC

1376

*Caesar's extended absence in the East (48–47 BC) following his defeat of Pompey at Pharsalus
allowed the remnants of the Pompeian party to regroup in North Africa and to offer renewed opposition to the dictator's supremacy. During the long build up of their forces, spanning the greater
part of the year 47 BC, a considerable coinage, mostly of silver denarii and quinarii, was produced
by the Pompeians to help defray the costs of the growing military establishment under their command. This was augmented by a large output of denarii by King Juba of Numidia bearing the name
and portrait of the colourful, though unpredictable, Pompeian ally. The headquarters of the
Pompeians was at the provincial capital of Utica, about 30 miles north-west of the site of
Carthage, and it seems likely that this was the location of their principal mint. Most of the types
were struck in the name of the Pompeian commander-in-chief, Quintus Caecilius Metellus Pius
Scipio, either solely or with two different legates, P. Licinius Crassus Junianus and M. Eppius. But
despite his illustrious name Scipio was no match for the military genius of his adversary and the
anti-Caesarian movement suffered a devasting setback when the dictator's forces overwhelmed the
Pompeians at Thapsus on 6 February, 46 BC. Cato committed suicide in Utica whilst Scipio, failing
in an attempt to escape by ship, also took his own life.*

1375   **Gold aureus.** METEL PIVS SCIP IMP, hd. of Jupiter r., eagle's hd. l. and sceptre below. Rev.
       CRASS IVN LEG PRO PR, curule chair flanked by corn-ear and dragon's hd., cornucopiae and
       scales above. RRC 460/1. CRI 40. BMCRR Africa, p. 571. B *Caecilia* 48. *[Utica,
       47–46 BC].*   **VF** £60,000 ($96,000) / **EF** £100,000 ($160,000)

1376 **Silver denarius.** Similar. RRC 460/2. CRI 41. BMCRR Africa 4. RSC *Caecilia* 49.
[Utica, 47–46 BC]. **VF** £850 ($1,360) / **EF** £1,750 ($2,800)

1377   1378

1377 CRASS IVN LEG PRO PR, turreted hd. of the city-goddess of Utica r., corn-ear behind,
caduceus before, prow below, uncertain object above. Rev. METEL PIVS SCIP IMP, trophy
flanked by lituus and jug. RRC 460/3. CRI 42. BMCRR Africa 6. RSC *Caecilia* 52.
[Utica, 47–46 BC]. **VF** £750 ($1,200) / **EF** £1,500 ($2,400)

1378 Q METEL PIVS SCIPIO IMP, lion-headed figure of the Genius of Africa stg. facing, holding
ankh, G T – A in upper field. Rev. P CRASSVS IVN LEG PRO PR, Victory stg. l., holding
caduceus and shield. RRC 460/4. CRI 43. BMCRR Africa 8. RSC *Caecilia* 51. *[Utica,
47–46 BC].* **VF** £1,000 ($1,600) / **EF** £2,000 ($3,200)

1379

1379 Q METEL PIVS, laur. hd. of Jupiter r. Rev. SCIPIO IMP, African elephant walking r. RRC
459/1. CRI 45. BMCRR Africa 1. RSC *Caecilia* 47. *[North Africa, 47–46 BC].*
VF £110 ($176) / **EF** £300 ($480)

1380/1   1380/2

1380 Q METELL SCIPIO IMP, hd. of Africa r., laur. and clad in elephant's skin, corn-ear before,
plough below. Rev. EPPIVS LEG F C, naked Hercules stg. facing, r. hand on hip, resting on
club set on rock. RRC 461/1. CRI 44. BMCRR Africa 10, 12. RSC *Caecilia* 50, 50a.
[North Africa, 47–46 BC]. **VF** £165 ($264) / **EF** £400 ($640)
There is considerable variation in the size of the hd. of Africa on coins of this issue.

CATO UTICENSIS
Propraetor, committed suicide 46 BC

1382

M. Porcius Cato, best known to posterity as Cato Uticensis, was born in 95 BC and was the great-grandson of the celebrated Cato the Censor (234–149 BC). A rigid traditionalist in the mould of his illustrious ancestor, Cato's philosophy was that he would prefer to die with the Republic rather than outlive it. The universal respect which he commanded amongst his contemporaries enabled him to arbitrate in the rivalries and disputes which arose between the military leaders of the Pompeian party in North Africa in 47–46 BC. Unfortunately for his cause, Cato insisted on bestowing on Q. Caecilius Metellus Pius Scipio the overall command of the Pompeian forces, merely on the basis of his illustrious name. Because of his relatively low birth the more able and experienced general Titus Labienus was foolishly disbarred from the leadership role. Following Caesar's brilliant victory over the Pompeians at Thapsus Cato initially secured the defences of Utica. However, when the enormity of the defeat became apparent he realized that he had no alternative but to take his own life. With quiet dignity he fell upon his own sword in his private apartments and was given an honourable funeral by the citizens of Utica. Caesar was furious at Cato's grand gesture, realizing that he was far more dangerous as a martyr than as a living oppponent. Generations later the name of Cato Uticensis was still revered as one of the greatest Roman patriots of all time.

1381

1381 **Silver denarius.** M CATO PRO PR, dr. female bust (Roma or Libertas) r., sometimes with ROMA (MA in monogram) behind. Rev. VICTRIX (TR in monogram), Victory seated r., holding patera and palm. RRC 462/1a, c. CRI 46, 46a. BMCRR Africa 15, 17. RSC *Porcia* 9–10. *[Utica, 47–46 BC].* **VF** £125 ($200) / **EF** £325 ($520)
The coin types of Cato Uticensis are copied from those of the moneyer M. Porcius Cato who held office circa 89 BC (see nos. 247–8).

1382 Similar, but Victory holds wreath instead of patera, and always with ROMA (MA in monogram) behind bust on obv. RRC 462/1b. CRI 46b. BMCRR Africa 18. RSC *Porcia* 10a. *[Utica, 47–46 BC].* **VF** £110 ($176) / **EF** £300 ($480)

1383 **Silver quinarius.** M CATO PRO PR, hd. of young Bacchus or Liber r., wreathed with ivy. Rev. VICTRIX (TR in monogram), Victory seated r., holding patera and palm. RRC 462/2. CRI 47. BMCRR Africa 19. RSC *Porcia* 11. *[Utica, 47–46 BC].*
VF £55 ($88) / **EF** £160 ($256)

GNAEUS POMPEY JUNIOR
Elder son of Pompey the Great
Imperator, executed 45 BC

1384

Gnaeus Pompeius was the elder son of Pompey the Great and Mucia and was born in 79 BC. Early in the African War between Caesar and the Pompeians (47–46 BC) he occupied the Balearic Islands and then crossed to Spain to rouse support for the Pompeian cause. There he was joined by the remnants of the Pompeian leadership following Caesar's victory at Thapsus and plans were soon under way for the last desperate stand against the power of the dictator. Concerned about the resurgence of Pompeian activity in the Iberian peninsula Caesar acted quickly and decisively. The issue was brought to battle at Munda on 17 March 45 BC. Caesar's victory brought to an end the first phase of the civil wars which had begun four years earlier with his crossing of the Rubicon. Gnaeus Pompey survived the battle but was later captured and executed. His younger brother Sextus escaped and was later to embark on a whole new career as a naval commander in the period of renewed civil war following Caesar's assassination.

1384   **Silver denarius.** M POBLICI LEG PRO PR, helmeted hd. of Roma r. Rev. CN MAGNVS IMP, Hispania stg. r., presenting palm-branch to Pompeian soldier stg. l. on prow of galley. RRC 469/1a. CRI 48. BMCRR Spain 72. RSC *Pompey the Great 1. [Corduba, 46–45 BC].*
          VF £185 ($296) / **EF** £450 ($720)

1385   CN MAGNVS IMP F, bare hd. of Pompey the Great r. Rev. M MINAT SABIN PR Q, city-goddess Corduba stg. r. amidst heap of arms, holding spear and grasping hand of Pompeian soldier l., disembarking from stern of ship. RRC 470/1a. CRI 49. BMCRR Spain 79. RSC *Pompey the Great 8. [Corduba, 46–45 BC].*
          VF £1,750 ($2,800) / **EF** £3,500 ($5,600)

1386   **Bronze as.** Laur. hd. of Janus, I above. Rev. Prow of galley r., CN MAG (MA in monogram) above, IMP below, I before. RPC 486. RRC 471/1. CRI 53. BMCRR Spain 84. *[Corduba, 45–45 BC].*
          F £185 ($296) / **VF** £450 ($720)

For posthumous coins bearing the portrait of Gnaeus Pompey Junior, see under Sextus Pompey.

SEXTUS POMPEY
Younger son of Pompey the Great
Imperator and Prefect of the Fleet,
executed 35 BC

1387

Sextus Pompey, the younger son of Pompey the Great and Mucia, was born about 67 BC. He was with his father at the time of the latter's murder in Egypt in 48 BC and succeeded in escaping to Africa. Later, following Caesar's victories over the Pompeians at Thapsus (46) and Munda (45), he rallied the survivors and continued to harass the Caesarian generals in Further Spain. After Caesar's assassination in 44 BC the Roman Senate came to an agreement with Sextus and at this time he transferred his base to the important Gallic port of Massilia (modern Marseille) where he anchored his powerful fleet. The following year he was appointed supreme naval commander of the Republic. However, at this time the political situation in post-Caesarian Rome was extremely volatile and a few months later the Senate, under pressure from Octavian, declared Sextus a public enemy. Later still, he was proscribed by the triumviral government in Rome and on receipt of this intelligence, if not before, he set sail from Massilia and seized control of Sicily, using the island as a base for raiding and blockading the Italian mainland. After achieving a string of notable successes in his piratical career, in which he even came close to overthrowing the western triumvir Octavian, Sextus Pompey was eventually defeated by Marcus Agrippa at the naval battle of Naulochus (3 September 36 BC). He managed to escape to Asia Minor, but was soon captured and put to death on Mark Antony's orders.

1387 **Gold aureus.** MAG PIVS IMP ITER, bare hd. of Sextus Pompey r., all within oak-wreath. Rev. PRÆF CLAS ET ORÆ MARIT EX S C (MAR in monogram), confronted bare hds. of Pompey the Great r. and Gnaeus Pompey Junior l., lituus in field to l., tripod to r. RRC 511/1. CRI 332. BMCRR Sicily 13. C *Sextus Pompey, Pompey and Cn. Pompey Jr.* 1. *[Sicily, 42 BC].* **VF** £12,500 ($20,000) / **EF** £30,000 ($48,000)

1388 **Silver denarius.** SEX MAGN IMP SAL, bare hd. of Pompey the Great r. Rev. PIETAS, Pietas stg. l., holding palm-branch and transverse sceptre. RRC 477/1b. CRI 232a. BMCRR Spain 93. RSC *Pompey the Great* 14. *[Spain, 45–44 BC].*
VF £1,200 ($1,920) / **EF** £2,500 ($4,000)

1389 Similar, but with obv. type bare hd. of Gnaeus Pompey Junior l., and legend SEX MAGNVS SAL IMP (AL in monogram). RRC 477/2. CRI 233. BMCRR Spain 94. RSC *Pompey the Great* 15. *[Spain, 45–44 BC].* **VF** £3,500 ($5,600) / **EF** £7,500 ($12,000)

1390   1391

1390 NEPTVNI, bare hd. of Pompey the Great r., trident before, dolphin r. below. Rev. Q NASIDIVS, galley under sail r., star above. RRC 483/2. CRI 235. BMCRR Sicily 21. RSC *Pompey the Great* 20. *[Massilia, 44–43 BC].*
VF £1,100 ($1,760) / **EF** £2,250 ($3,600)

1391 MAG PIVS IMP ITER, diad. hd. of Neptune r., trident over shoulder. Rev. PRÆF CLAS ET ORÆ MARIT EX S C (MAR in monogram), naval trophy set on anchor. RRC 511/2. CRI 333. BMCRR Sicily 15. RSC 1b. *[Sicily, 42 BC].* **VF** £350 ($560) / **EF** £850 ($1,360)

1392 — bare hd. of Pompey the Great r. between jug and lituus. Rev. — Neptune stg. l., holding aplustre and resting r. foot on prow, between the Catanaean brothers Anapias and Amphinomus, each bearing one of his parents on shoulders. RRC 511/3a. CRI 334. BMCRR Sicily 93. RSC *Pompey the Great* 17. *[Sicily, 42–40 BC].*
VF £600 ($960) / **EF** £1,250 ($2,000)

1392   1393

1393   **Silver denarius.** MAG PIVS IMP ITER, the Pharos (lighthouse) of Messana, surmounted by
        statue of Neptune, galley containing legionary eagle moving l. in foreground. Rev. — the
        marine monster Scylla, wielding rudder with both hands. RRC 511/4a. CRI 335. BMCRR
        Sicily 18. RSC 2. *[Sicily, 42–40 BC].*   VF £300 ($480) / **EF** £750 ($1,200)

1394

1394   **Bronze as.** Laur. hd. of Janus, with features of Pompey the Great, MAGN (MA in mono-
        gram) above. Rev. Prow of galley r., PIVS above, IMP below. RPC 671. RRC 479/1. CRI
        336. BMCRR Spain 95. C *Pompey the Great* 16. *[Sicily, 43–36 BC].*
                                                F £110 ($176) / **VF** £300 ($480)

COINAGE OF JULIUS CAESAR

JULIUS CAESAR
Dictator from 49 BC, assassinated 44 BC

1407

*Born in Rome on 13 July 100 BC Gaius Julius Caesar pursued the traditional cursus honorum of
the young aristocrat and did not rise to political prominence until the latter part of the 60s BC. He
was elected to the prestigious lifetime office of pontifex maximus in 63 BC and the next year held a
praetorship followed by a successful military command in Spain. Caesar was now poised to occupy
the highest magistracy of the Republic and in 59 BC he embarked on the first of his five consulships.
Being now in a position to take the initiative in the political game being played out in Rome he proposed a coalition between himself, Pompey, and Crassus which has come to be known as the First*

Triumvirate. Although not an officially constituted body, like the Second Triumvirate sixteen years later, this alliance between the three most powerful and influential men in Rome was a force to be reckoned with and one which could not easily be opposed, even by the Senate. It led to Caesar obtaining a 5-year proconsular command in Gaul which was to provide him with the military prestige and resources which he needed to make his ultimate bid for supreme power a decade later. The delicate balance of power was fatally disrupted in 53 BC when Crassus was defeated and killed in the East during his invasion of Parthian Mesopotamia. Caesar and Pompey were now left to face one another as rivals for supremacy in the Roman world. Matters came to a head in the opening days of the year 49 BC when Caesar invaded Italy from the north, driving Pompey from Rome to seek refuge in Greece. The eventual outcome was Caesar's victory over his rival at Pharsalus (August 9, 48 BC) resulting in Pompey's political downfall and assassination a few weeks later. The struggle between Caesar and the Pompeians, led by the late triumvir's generals and his two sons, continued for several years and was only finally resolved on the battlefield of Munda in Spain (March, 45 BC). Caesar's political preeminence was now undisputed and at the beginning of the year 44 BC the dictator gave orders for his portrait to be placed on the regular silver coinage of Rome. Undoubtedly, this development was instrumental in bringing to a head the grievances of those republicans who feared that Caesar was aiming at the establishment of a monarchy. Accordingly, on the Ides (15th) of March he was struck down by a conspiracy of senators led by M. Brutus and C. Cassius. He had adopted as his heir Gaius Octavius, the grandson of his sister Julia. Remarkably, the young man was willing to take up the heavy mantle of his great-uncle's political ambitions and was destined to become the founder of autocratic government in Rome under the name Augustus.

Lifetime Issues

1395   1396

1395   **Gold aureus. C CAESAR COS TER**, Veiled hd. of Vesta (?) r. Rev. **A HIRTIVS PR**, jug between lituus and axe (emblems of the augurate and pontificate). RRC 466/1. CRI 56. BMCRR 4050. C 2. *[Rome, 46 BC].*   **VF** £850 ($1,360) / **EF** £1,750 ($2,800)

1396   **C CAES DIC TER**, winged and dr. bust of Victory r. Rev. **L PLANC PRAEF VRB** (VR in monogram), sacrificial jug. RRC 475/1a. CRI 60. BMCRR 4118. C 31. *[Rome, 45 BC].*
                                     VF £1,500 ($2,400) / **EF** £3,000 ($4,800)

1397

1397   **CAES DIC QVAR**, diad. bust of Venus r. Rev. **COS QVINC** within laurel-wreath. RRC 481/1. CRI 117. BMCRR 4129. C 20. *[Rome, 44 BC].*   **VF** £2,750 ($4,400) / **EF** £5,500 ($8,800)

1398 **Gold half aureus or quinarius.** Similar to 1396. RRC 475/2. CRI 61. BMCRR 4123. C 32. *[Rome, 45 BC].* VF £3,000 ($4,800) / **EF** £6,000 ($9,600)

1399 1400

1399 **Silver denarius. CAESAR,** elephant walking r., trampling on dragon. Rev. No legend, simpulum, sprinkler, axe and apex (emblems of the pontificate). RRC 443/1. CRI 9. BMCRR Gaul 27. RSC 49. *[Italy, 49 BC].* VF £110 ($176) / **EF** £275 ($440)

1400 Diad. hd. of Clementia (?) r., wreathed with oak, numeral LII (52) behind. Rev. CAESAR, trophy of Gallic arms, axe on r. RRC 452/2. CRI 11. BMCRR 3955. RSC 18. *[Greece, 48 BC].* VF £125 ($200) / **EF** £325 ($520)
The numeral refers to Caesar's age at the time of the issue.

1401 1402

1401 C CAESAR IMP COS ITER, diad. hd. of Venus r. Rev. A ALLIENVS PRO COS, Trinacrus stg. l., r. foot on prow, holding triskeles. RRC 457/1. CRI 54. BMCRR Sicily 5. RSC 1. *[Sicily, 47 BC].* VF £900 ($1,440) / **EF** £2,000 ($3,200)

1402 No legend, diad. hd. of Venus r. Rev. CAESAR, Aeneas moving l., hd. facing, holding Palladium and bearing his father Anchises on l. shoulder. RRC 458/1. CRI 55. BMCRR East 31. RSC 12. *[North Africa, 47–46 BC].* VF £110 ($176) / **EF** £275 ($440)

1403/1 1403/2

1403 DICT ITER COS TERT, hd. of Ceres r., wreathed with corn. Rev. AVGVR PONT MAX, simpulum, sprinkler, jug and lituus (emblems of the augurate and pontificate), D (or M) on r. RRC 467/1. CRI 57, 57a. BMCRR Africa 21, 23. RSC 4, 4a. *[Utica (?), 46 BC].* VF £125 ($200) / **EF** £300 ($480)

1404   1405

1404   **Silver denarius.** No legend, diad. hd. of Venus r., small Cupid at shoulder behind. Rev.
        CAESAR, trophy of Gallic arms between seated male and female captives. RRC 468/1. CRI
        58. BMCRR Spain 89. RSC 13. *[Spain, 46–45 BC].*   **VF** £125 ($200) / **EF** £300 ($480)

1405   — diad. hd. of Venus l., small Cupid at shoulder before, sceptre over shoulder behind,
        lituus on l. Rev. — trophy of Gallic arms between kneeling male and seated female cap-
        tives. RRC 468/2. CRI 59. BMCRR Spain 86. RSC 14. *[Spain, 46–45 BC].*
                                                     VF £175 ($280) / **EF** £400 ($640)

1406   CAESAR DICT QVART, wreathed hd. of Caesar r., lituus behind. Rev. M METTIVS, Juno
        Sospita in galloping biga r. RRC 480/2a. CRI 98. BMCRR 4135. RSC 36. *[Rome, Jan.
        44 BC].*   **VF** £1,600 ($2,560) / **EF** £4,000 ($6,400)
        This is the earliest of Caesar's portrait types.

1407   CAESAR IMP, wreathed hd. of Caesar r., lituus and simpulum behind. Rev. — Venus stg. l.,
        holding Victory and sceptre and resting l. arm on shield set on globe, control-letter (G-L) in
        l. field. RRC 480/3. CRI 100. BMCRR 4143. RSC 34. *[Rome, Jan.–Feb. 44 BC].*
                                                     VF £600 ($960) / **EF** £1,500 ($2,400)
        For a similar type issued posthumously, see no. 1419.

1408   .   1409

1408   CAESAR IM P M, wreathed hd. of Caesar r., crescent behind. Rev. L AEMILIVS BVCA, Venus
        stg. l., holding Victory and sceptre. RRC 480/4. CRI 102. BMCRR 4152. RSC 22. *[Rome,
        Jan.–Feb. 44 BC].*   **VF** £600 ($960) / **EF** £1,500 ($2,400)

1409   CAESAR DICT PERPETVO, wreathed hd. of Caesar r. Rev. L BVCA, fasces and winged
        caduceus in saltire, clasped hands, globe, axe and legend in the four angles. RRC 480/6.
        CRI 103. BMCRR 4157. RSC 25. *[Rome, Feb.–Mar. 44 BC].*
                                                     VF £1,300 ($2,080) / **EF** £3,250 ($5,200)

1410   Obv. Similar. Rev. — Venus seated r., holding Victory and transverse sceptre. RRC 480/7b.
        CRI 104a. BMCRR 4155. RSC 24. *[Rome, Feb.–Mar. 44 BC].*
                                                     VF £900 ($1,440) / **EF** £2,250 ($3,600)

1410　　　　　　　　　　1412

1411　**Silver denarius.** Obv. Similar. Rev. L BVCA, Venus stg. l., holding Victory and sceptre. RRC 480/8. CRI 105. BMCRR 4154. RSC 23. *[Rome, Feb.–Mar. 44 BC].*
　　　　　　　　　　　　　　　　　　　　　VF £600 ($960) / **EF** £1,500 ($2,400)

1412　CAESAR IMP, wreathed hd. of Caesar r., eight-rayed star behind. Rev. P SEPVLLIVS MACER, Venus stg. l., holding Victory and sceptre with star at base. RRC 480/5b. CRI 106a. BMCRR 4165. RSC 41. *[Rome, Jan.–Feb. 44 BC].* **VF** £600 ($960) / **EF** £1,500 ($2,400) *For a similar type issued posthumously, see no. 1420.*

1413　　　　　　　　　　1414

1413　Obv. As 1409. Rev. — Venus stg. l., holding Victory and sceptre, shield at feet to r. RRC 480/10. CRI 107a. BMCRR 4169. RSC 38. *[Rome, Feb.–Mar. 44 BC].*
　　　　　　　　　　　　　　　　　　　　　VF £550 ($880) / **EF** £1,400 ($2,240)

1414　Similar, but hd. of Caesar is also veiled. RRC 480/13. CRI 107d. BMCRR 4173. RSC 39. *[Rome, Feb.–Mar. 44 BC].* **VF** £500 ($800) / **EF** £1,250 ($2,000)

1415

1415　Obv. Similar. Rev. C MARIDIANVS, Venus stg. l., holding Victory and resting l. arm on shield set on globe. RRC 480/16. CRI 111. BMCRR 4185. RSC 9. *[Rome, Feb.–Mar. 44 BC].* **VF** £800 ($1,280) / **EF** £2,000 ($3,200)

1416　**Silver quinarius.** Veiled hd. of Vesta (?) r., simpulum and numeral LII (52) behind. Rev. CAESAR, trophy between wreath and shield. RRC 452/3. CRI 14. BMCRR 3961. RSC 16. *[Greece, 48 BC].* **VF** £400 ($640) / **EF** £1,000 ($1,600) *The numeral refers to Caesar's age at the time of the issue. The half-denarius here reappears for the first time in almost 35 years and was soon also to be resumed on the coinage of the Roman moneyers. Unlike the silver sestertius it survived Caesar's downfall in 44 BC, but was only struck sporadically and never formed part of the regular monetary system.*

1417

1417 **Brass dupondius (?).** CAESAR DIC TER, winged and dr. bust of Victory r., sometimes with star behind. Rev. C CLOVI PRAEF, Minerva advancing l., holding trophy, spears and shield, snake at feet before. RPC 601. RRC 476/1. CRI 62, 62a. BMCRR 4125, 4127. C 7. *[Rome, 45 BC].*   F £150 ($240) / **VF** £350 ($560)

Posthumous Issues

1418 **Gold aureus.** IMP DIVI IVLI F TER III VIR R P C, wreathed hd. of the rejuvenated deified Caesar r., star (*sidus Iulium*) before forehead. Rev. M AGRIPPA COS / DESIG in two lines across field. RRC 534/1. CRI 305. BMCRR Gaul 102. C 33. *[Italy or Gaul, 38 BC].*
VF £14,000 ($22,400) / **EF** £30,000 ($48,000)
The obv. legend refers exclusively to Octavian.

1419   1421

1419 **Silver denarius.** CAESAR IMPER, wreathed hd. of Caesar r. Rev. M METTIVS, Venus stg. l., holding Victory and sceptre and resting l. arm on shield set on globe, control-letter (A-E) in l. field. RRC 480/17. CRI 101. BMCRR 4137. RSC 35. *[Rome, Mar.–Apr. 44 BC].*
VF £600 ($960) / **EF** £1,500 ($2,400)
For a similar type issued during his lifetime, see no. 1407.

1420 Obv. Similar. Rev. P SEPVLLIVS MACER, Venus stg. l., holding Victory and sceptre with star at base. RRC 480/18. CRI 108. BMCRR 4164. RSC 42. *[Rome, Mar.–Apr. 44 BC].*
VF £650 ($1,040) / **EF** £1,600 ($2,560)
For a similar type issued during his lifetime, see no. 1412.

1421 CLEMENTIAE CAESARIS, tetrastyle temple. Rev. — horseman (*desultor*) galloping r., holding whip, a second horse visible in background, wreath and palm-branch behind. RRC 480/21. CRI 110. BMCRR 4176. RSC 44. *[Rome, Apr.–May 44 BC].*
VF £750 ($1,200) / **EF** £1,800 ($2,880)

1422   1423

1422 **Silver denarius.** CAESAR PARENS PATRIAE, wreathed and veiled hd. of Caesar r., lituus
below chin, apex behind. Rev. C COSSVTIVS and MARIDIANVS arranged in form of cross,
A–A–A–F F in the angles. RRC 480/19. CRI 112. BMCRR 4187. RSC 8. *[Rome, Apr.
44 BC].*   **VF** £1,000 ($1,600) / **EF** £2,500 ($4,000)

1423 No legend, wreathed hd. of Caesar r., with idealized features. Rev. L FLAMINIVS IIII VIR,
female deity (Venus or Pax) stg. l., holding caduceus and sceptre. RRC 485/1. CRI 113.
BMCRR 4201. RSC 26. *[Rome, Aug. 43 BC].*   **VF** £2,000 ($3,200) / **EF** £5,000 ($8,000)

1424 CAESAR IMP, wreathed hd. of Caesar r. Rev. P CLODIVS M F, Mars, naked, stg. facing, looking l., holding spear and sword in scabbard. RRC 494/16. CRI 114. BMCRR 4280. RSC
37. *[Rome, 42 BC].*   **VF** £1,400 ($2,240) / **EF** £3,500 ($5,600)

1425   1426

1425 No legend, wreathed hd. of Caesar r., caduceus before, laurel-branch behind. Rev.
L LIVINEIVS REGVLVS, bull charging r. RRC 494/24. CRI 115. BMCRR 4274. RSC 27.
[Rome, 42 BC].   **VF** £900 ($1,440) / **EF** £2,250 ($3,600)

1426 — wreathed hd. of Caesar r. Rev. L MVSSIDIVS LONGVS, cornucopiae on globe between
rudder, on l., and caduceus and apex, on r. RRC 494/39. CRI 116. BMCRR 4237. RSC 29.
[Rome, 42 BC].   **VF** £800 ($1,280) / **EF** £2,000 ($3,200)

1427/1   1427/2

1427 — wreathed hd. of Caesar r., S–C either side of neck. Rev. TI SEMPRONIVS GRACCVS Q
DESIG, legionary eagle between standard, on l., and plough and measuring rod (*decempeda*)
on r. RRC 525/4a. CRI 327a. BMCRR 4319. RSC 47. *[Rome, 40 BC].*
                                     VF £800 ($1,280) / **EF** £2,000 ($3,200)
Another variety has the S–C in rev. field.

1428(1)   1428(2)

1428   **Silver denarius.** No legend, wreathed hd. of Caesar r. Rev. Q VOCONIVS VITVLVS Q
DESIGN, bull-calf walking l., S–C in field. RRC 526/4. CRI 331. BMCRR 4311. RSC 45.
[Rome, 40 BC].   **VF** £800 ($1,280) / **EF** £2,000 ($3,200)
A scarcer variety has the legend DIVI IVLI *on obv. and a lituus behind the hd., whilst* Q
DESIGN *and* S–C *are omitted on rev.*

For other coins depicting Caesar, see under Mark Antony (nos. 1464–5) and Octavian (nos. 1525,
1542 and 1569). For a possible portrait of the dictator on a denarius of the moneyer C. Numonius
Vaala (41 BC), see no. 502.

COINAGE OF THE REPUBLICAN TYRANNICIDES
AND THEIR ADHERENTS

BRUTUS
Proconsul and Imperator,
committed suicide 42 BC

1439

*Marcus Junius Brutus, the tyrannicide, was born about 85 BC and was the son of M. Junius Brutus
and Servilia, daughter of Q. Servilius Caepio. In 77 BC his father was executed at Mutina in
Cisalpine Gaul after surrendering to Pompey on the promise of safe conduct. The young Brutus
was later adopted by his uncle (?) and changed his name to Q. Caepio Brutus. Siding with Pompey
in the civil war of 49–48 BC Brutus was pardoned by Caesar after the battle of Pharsalus. In 46 BC
he was appointed governor of Cisalpine Gaul and two years later praetor urbanus. It was then that
he entered into the conspiracy against Caesar's life, believing that he was filling a noble patriotic
role in ridding Rome of a tyrant and ensuring the survival of constitutional republican government.
Following the dictator's assassination on the Ides (15th) of March, 44 BC, in which he played a
leading part, Brutus quarrelled with Mark Antony and withdrew to Greece where he set about raising an army. In February of the following year the Senate voted him the supreme military command
of all the troops in Illyricum, Macedonia and Achaea. He campaigned successfully against the
Bessi in Thrace and later joined forces with his brother-in-law Cassius Longinus for the inevitable
trial of strength with the triumvirs Antony and Octavian, leaders of the Caesarian party. Two
battles were fought near Philippi in Macedonia in October of 42 BC, both going against the
Republicans thanks to Antony's superior tactical skill. The first resulted in the suicide of Cassius,
Brutus following suit after the disastrous second engagement. Like his father-in-law Cato Uticensis
Brutus came to be regarded as a martyr of the Republican cause. The drama of his suicide was
immortalized by Shakespeare in his play Julius Caesar with the famous words uttered by Antony
"This was the noblest Roman of them all".*

1429   1430

1429   **Gold aureus. M SERVILIVS LEG**, laur. hd. of Libertas r. Rev. Q CAEPIO BRVTVS IMP, trophy.
       RRC 505/4. CRI 206. BMCRR East 85. C 9. *[Sardis (?), summer 42 BC].*
                                          VF £5,500 ($8,800) / **EF** £12,000 ($19,200)

1430   **BRVTVS IMP**, bare hd. of Brutus r., all within laurel-wreath. Rev. **CASCA LONGVS**, com-
       bined military and naval trophy, with prows and shields at base, small L in l. field. RRC
       507/1b. CRI 211. BMCRR East 62. C 14 var. *[Western Asia Minor or Macedonia,
       summer/autumn 42 BC].*   **VF** £35,000 ($56,000) / **EF** £75,000 ($120,000)

1431   1432

1431   **Silver denarius. BRVTVS**, simpulum between axe and knife (emblems of the pontificate).
       Rev. **LENTVLVS SPINT**, jug and lituus (emblems of the augurate). RRC 500/7. CRI 198.
       BMCRR East 80. RSC 6. *[Smyrna (?), early 42 BC].*
                                          VF £400 ($640) / **EF** £1,000 ($1,600)

1432   **LEIBERTAS**, hd of Libertas r. Rev. **CAEPIO BRVTVS PRO COS**, lyre between quiver and laurel-
       branch. RRC 501/1. CRI 199. BMCRR East 38. RSC 5. *[Lycia, spring/summer 42 BC].*
                                          VF £350 ($560) / **EF** £850 ($1,360)

1433   1435

1433   **L SESTI PRO Q**, veiled and dr. bust of Libertas r. Rev. Q CAEPIO BRVTVS PRO COS, tripod
       between axe and simpulum. RRC 502/2. CRI 201. BMCRR East 41. RSC 11.
       [Southwestern Asia Minor, spring/summer 42 BC].   **VF** £450 ($720) / **EF** £1,100 ($1,760)

1434   No legend, hd. of Apollo r., hair in ringlets and bound with taenia and laurel-wreath. Rev.
       Q CAEPIO BRVTVS IMP, trophy between seated male and female captives. RRC 503/1. CRI
       204. BMCRR East 52. RSC 8. *[Lycia, early summer 42 BC].*
                                          VF £1,250 ($2,000) / **EF** £3,000 ($4,800)

1435   **C FLAV HEMIC LEG PRO PR**, dr. bust of Apollo r., lyre before. Rev. Q CAEP BRVT IMP,
       Victory stg. l., crowning trophy and holding palm. RRC 504/1. CRI 205. BMCRR East 55.
       RSC 7. *[Lycia, early summer 42 BC].*   **VF** £800 ($1,280) / **EF** £2,000 ($3,200)

1436   1437

1436   **Silver denarius.** COSTA LEG, laur. hd. of Apollo r. Rev. BRVTVS IMP, trophy. RRC 506/2.
       CRI 209. BMCRR East 59. RSC 4. *[Western Asia Minor or Macedonia, summer/autumn
       42 BC].*   VF £350 ($560) / **EF** £900 ($1,440)

1437   CASCA LONGVS, laur. hd. of Neptune r., trident below. Rev. BRVTVS IMP, Victory walking
       r. over broken sceptre, holding broken diadem and palm. RRC 507/2. CRI 212. BMCRR
       East 63. RSC 3. *[Western Asia Minor or Macedonia, summer/autumn 42 BC].*
                                                           VF £475 ($760) / **EF** £1,200 ($1,920)

1438

1438   L PLAET CEST, laur., veiled and dr. bust of female deity r., hd. surmounted by polos. Rev.
       BRVT IMP, axe and simpulum (emblems of the pontificate). RRC 508/2. CRI 214. BMCRR
       East 66. RSC 2. *[Western Asia Minor or Macedonia, summer/autumn 42 BC].*
                                                           VF £600 ($960) / **EF** £1,500 ($2,400)

1439   BRVT IMP L PLAET CEST, bare hd. of Brutus r. Rev. EID MAR, pileus (cap of Liberty) between
       two daggers. RRC 508/3. CRI 216. BMCRR East 68. RSC 15. *[Western Asia Minor or
       Macedonia, summer/autumn 42 BC].*   VF £22,500 ($36,000) / **EF** £55,000 ($88,000)
       *Probably the most celebrated of all the coin types of ancient Rome, this denarius combines
       the only attested portrait of Brutus on the silver coinage with a reverse which is an
       unabashed celebration of the very act of tyrannicide.*

1440   **Silver quinarius.** Obv. As 1433. Rev. Q CAEPIO BRVTVS PRO COS, Victory advancing r.,
       holding wreath and palm. RRC 502/3. CRI 202. BMCRR East 46. RSC 12. *[Southwestern
       Asia Minor, spring/summer 42 BC].*   VF £600 ($960) / **EF** £1,500 ($2,400)

1441   L SESTI PRO Q, quaestorial chair, against which rests diagonal staff, modius below. Rev. —
       tripod between simpulum and apex. RRC 502/4. CRI 203. BMCRR East 47. RSC 13.
       [Southwestern Asia Minor, spring/summer 42 BC].   VF £300 ($480) / **EF** £750 ($1,200)

1442

1442   LEIBERTAS, diad. hd. of Libertas r. Rev. No legend, stem of prow and anchor in saltire. RRC
       506/3. CRI 210. BMCRR East 39. RSC 5a. *[Western Asia Minor or Macedonia,
       summer/autumn 42 BC].*   VF £150 ($240) / **EF** £375 ($600)
       Although anonymous, there can be little doubt that this type was issued by Brutus.

For coins struck by Brutus as moneyer in 54 BC, see nos. 397–8. For a portrait tentatively identified as that of Brutus on a denarius of the moneyer L. Servius Rufus (41 BC), see no. 503.

CASSIUS
Proconsul and Imperator,
committed suicide 42 BC

1444

Gaius Cassius Longinus had held a high command in the army of Crassus which was so disastrously defeated by the Parthians in 53 BC. Bravely extricating himself from this perilious situation, he rallied the remnants of the Roman forces and successfully organized the defence of Syria, remaining there as proquaestor until 51 BC. In the civil war of 49–48 BC he supported Pompey against Caesar but was pardoned by the latter after Pharsalus. He repaid this kindness by playing a leading role in the conspiracy against the dictator's life which led to Caesar's assassination on the Ides (15th) of March, 44 BC. In the confused period following this event Cassius was forced to leave Rome and eventually made his way to his old province of Syria, over which he soon gained absolute control. Early in 43 BC the Senate gave him and Brutus command over all the eastern provinces, though in the autumn there was a volte-face when both men were declared public enemies under the terms of the lex Pedia which was enacted under coercion from Octavian. After various campaigns of plunder in Asia Minor aimed at strengthening their financial position Brutus and Cassius joined forces and crossed to Europe in September of 42 BC in order to confront the triumvirs. They took up a strong defensive position at Philippi, in eastern Macedonia, prior to the fateful battle with Antony and Octavian which was to decide the future of the Republic. In the first of the two engagements fought in October Cassius' camp was captured and he, believing that the day was altogether lost, committed suicide. Brutus perished several weeks later following his defeat in the second battle.

1443   **Gold aureus.** M AQVINVS LEG LIBERTAS (TA in monogram), diad. hd. of Libertas r. Rev. C CASSI PR COS, tripod surmounted by cauldron and two laurel-branches, fillet hanging on either side. RRC 498/1. CRI 217. BMCRR East 71. C 2. *[Smyrna (?), early 42 BC].*
     VF £6,000 ($9,600) / **EF** £12,500 ($20,000)
   Another variety has IMP *instead of* PR COS *on rev.*

1444   C CASSI IMP LEIBERTAS, diad. hd. of Libertas r. Rev. LENTVLVS SPINT, jug and lituus (emblems of the augurate). RRC 500/2. CRI 220. BMCRR East 76. C 3. *[Smyrna (?), early 42 BC].*   **VF** £4,000 ($6,400) / **EF** £8,000 ($12,800)
   Another variety shows Libertas veiled and draped.

1445   1446

1445   C CASSI IMP, laur. hd. of Libertas r. Rev. M SERVILIVS LEG, aplustre, the branches terminating in flowers. RRC 505/1. CRI 224. BMCRR East 82. C 8. *[Sardis (?), summer 42 BC].*
     VF £5,000 ($8,000) / **EF** £10,000 ($16,000)

1447/1   1447/2

1446   **Silver denarius.** C CASSI IMP, tripod with cauldron, as on rev. of 1443. Rev. As 1444. RRC 500/1. CRI 219. BMCRR East 79. RSC 7. *[Smyrna (?), early 42 BC].*
        VF £1,400 ($2,240) / **EF** £3,500 ($5,600)

1447   As 1444. RRC 500/3. CRI 221. BMCRR East 77–8. RSC 4, 4a. *[Smyrna (?), early 42 BC].*
        VF £250 ($400) / **EF** £600 ($960)

1448   As 1445. RRC 505/2. CRI 225. BMCRR East 83. RSC 9. *[Sardis (?), summer 42 BC].*
        VF £800 ($1,280) / **EF** £2,000 ($3,200)

1449   C CASSEI IMP, laur. hd. of Libertas r. Rev. M SERVILIVS LEG, crab holding alustre in its claws, untied diadem and rose below. RRC 505/3. CRI 226. BMCRR East 84. RSC 10. *[Sardis (?), summer 42 BC].*
        VF £1,000 ($1,600) / **EF** £2,500 ($4,000)

CORNUFICIUS
Imperator, killed in battle 42 BC

1451

Quintus Cornuficius, sometimes called Cornificius, was an orator and poet and a friend of Cicero. He won Caesar's favour in 48 BC through his recovery of Illyricum and its defence against the Pompeian fleet. A grateful dictator rewarded him with the praetorship and he was also appointed to the priestly college of augurs. The governorship of Cilicia followed in 46 BC and two years later, after Caesar's assassination, he took up the governorship of Africa Vetus. However, his loyalty to Caesar, if it ever existed, did not extend to his successors and he refused to hand over his command to Calvisius Sabinus, Antony's nominee for the post. Instead, he held his province for the Senate and at the end of 43 BC he was proscribed by the triumviral government. His territory was reassigned to T. Sextius, governor of Africa Nova, and the issue was decided by a battle near Utica in the early summer of 42 BC in which Cornuficius and his army were massacred by the superior forces of their opponent.

1450   **Gold aureus.** No legend, hd. of Jupiter Ammon l. Rev. Q CORNVFICI AVGVR IMP, Cornuficius, in priestly attire, stg. facing, crowned by Juno Sospita who stands l., holding shield and spear, crow perched on her l. shoulder. RRC 509/1. CRI 227. BMCRR Africa, p. 577. B *Cornuficia* 1. *[Utica (?), spring/summer 42 BC].*
        VF £75,000 ($120,000) / **EF** £125,000 ($200,000)

1451 **Silver denarius.** Similar. RRC 509/2. CRI 228. BMCRR Africa 26. RSC *Cornuficia* 2. *[Utica (?), spring/summer 42 BC].* **VF** £9,000 ($14,400) / **EF** £17,500 ($28,000)

1452 Similar, but with obv. type dr. bust of Africa r., clad in elephant's skin head-dress, two spears behind. RRC 509/4. CRI 230. BMCRR Africa 28. RSC *Cornuficia* 4. *[Utica (?), spring/summer 42 BC].* **VF** £9,000 ($14,400) / **EF** £17,500 ($28,000)

1453 Similar, but with obv. type hd. of Ceres l., wreathed with corn. RRC 509/5. CRI 231. BMCRR Africa 27. RSC *Cornuficia* 3. *[Utica (?), spring/summer 42 BC].* **VF** £8,000 ($12,800) / **EF** £16,000 ($25,600)

MURCUS
Imperator, executed 40/39 BC

1454

L. Staius Murcus was a legate of Caesar in Gaul and Africa (48–46 BC) and probably praetor in 45. Governor of Syria from 44 he was acclaimed imperator the following year, after having secured the surrender of the former Pompeian partisan Caecilius Bassus who was under siege in Apamea. He then gave his support to Cassius and was appointed commander of one of the Republican fleets, a role in which he was very active in 42 BC down to the time of the disaster at Philippi. In 41 BC he joined Sextus Pompey in Sicily, but soon fell from favour and was put to death in 40/39.

1454 **Silver denarius.** No legend, Hd. of Neptune r., trident over shoulder. Rev. **MVRCVS IMP**, Murcus stg. l., raising kneeling figure of Roma (?) r., trophy in background between them. RRC 510/1. CRI 337. BMCRR East 86. RSC *Statia* 1. *[Region of the Ionian Sea, 41 BC].* **VF** £3,250 ($5,200) / **EF** £7,500 ($12,000)

AHENOBARBUS
Imperator, died 31 BC

1456

Gnaeus Domitius Ahenobarbus was, like his father Lucius, a supporter of Pompey in the civil war of 49–48 BC. Pardoned by Caesar, it is uncertain whether he was involved in the dictator's murder in 44 BC, though he did accompany Brutus to Macedonia later in the year and was condemned as an assassin under the lex Pedia in the summer of 43. He commanded one of the Republican fleets and actually achieved a decisive victory on the day of the first battle of Philippi, for which he was saluted imperator. Unfortunately, his success was in a lost cause and following the deaths of Brutus and Cassius he turned to piracy. With seventy ships and two legions under his command he terrorized the ports of the Adriatic until the summer of 40 BC, when he was persuaded by Asinius Pollio to join forces with Antony. Pardoned by the triumvirs under the Pact of Brundisium Ahenobarbus was appointed governor of Bithynia, a post which he held until 35 BC or later. In 32 he was consul with C. Sosius, but was forced to flee to Antony at Ephesus after his colleague had delivered a speech before the Senate bitterly critical of Octavian. Ahenobarbus now became increasingly alarmed over the extent of Cleopatra's proposed participation in the coming war, eventually leading to his desertion to Octavian just prior to the fateful battle of Actium. Already seriously ill with a fever, he died soon afterwards.

1455   **Gold aureus.** AHENOBAR, bare male hd. r., with heavy features. Rev. CN DOMITIVS L F IMP, angled view of tetrastyle temple of Neptune, showing façade and l. side wall, NE–PT in upper field. RRC 519/1. CRI 338. BMCRR East 93. C 1. *[Region of the Adriatic or Ionian Sea, 41–40 BC].*   **VF** £27,500 ($44,000) / **EF** £65,000 ($104,000)
        The identities of the portraits appearing on this type and the next are uncertain, though presumably they are ancestral.

1456   **Silver denarius.** AHENOBAR, bare male hd. r., with slender features. Rev. CN DOMITIVS IMP, prow r., surmounted by trophy. RRC 519/2. CRI 339. BMCRR East 94. RSC *Domitia* 21. *[Region of the Adriatic or Ionian Sea, 41–40 BC].*
                                                VF £500 ($800) / **EF** £1,250 ($2,000)

For a later issue of Ahenobarbus, see under Mark Antony (nos. 1461 and 1472).

LABIENUS
Imperator, executed 39 BC

1457

Son of the Pompeian general Titus Labienus, Quintus Labienus had been sent into Parthia by Cassius in the winter of 43/42 BC to solicit the aid of King Orodes II on behalf of the Republican cause. Although the hoped-for assistance never materialized Labienus did return to Syria more than a year after the battle of Philippi at the head of a Parthian army in company with Orodes' son Pacorus. They proceeded to devastate Syria and Cilicia and then divided their forces, Labienus moving west into Asia Minor and Pacorus south through Syria and down the Phoenician coast to Palestine. Antony was so preoccupied with a dispute with his triumviral colleague Octavian that the invaders had plenty of time to devastate the region at will. But following the Pact of Brundisium in 40 BC the general P. Ventidius was despatched to the East to deal with the deteriorating situation. This he accomplished with remarkable efficiency in a series of brilliant campaigns in 39 and 38 BC, defeating and destroying both the renegade Labienus and the Parthian prince Pacorus.

1457   **Gold aureus.** Q LABIENVS PARTHICVS IMP, bare hd. of Labienus r. Rev. No legend, horse stg. r., with bridle and saddle to which bow-case and quiver are attached. RRC 524/1. CRI 340. BMCRR East 131. C 1. *[Syria or south-eastern Asia Minor, 40 BC].*
                                            VF £30,000 ($48,000) / **EF** £75,000 ($120,000)

1458   **Silver denarius.** Similar. RRC 524/2. CRI 341. BMCRR East 132. RSC 2. *[Syria or south-eastern Asia Minor, 40 BC].*   **VF** £7,500 ($12,000) / **EF** £17,500 ($28,000)

COINAGE OF THE TRIUMVIRS AND THEIR ADHERENTS

MARK ANTONY
Triumvir and Imperator,
committed suicide 30 BC

1477

Marcus Antonius, eldest son of M. Antonius Creticus, was born about 83 BC. Following a somewhat dissolute youth he distinguished himself as a cavalry commander in the East (57–54 BC) after which he joined Caesar's staff in Gaul. He soon became one of Caesar's most trusted lieutenants and as tribune in 49 BC he defended his former commander's interests before a hostile Senate, just prior to the outbreak of the civil war between Caesar and Pompey. Following Caesar's successful invasion of Italy Antony was given supreme command in the country during the dictator's brief absence in Spain, where he defeated the Pompeian generals. The following year (48 BC) he was involved in the military operations in Greece leading up to the final confrontation with Pompey and he commanded Caesar's left wing at the battle of Pharsalus. Problems with Antony's administration in Italy during Caesar's extended absence in the East, following Pharsalus, led to a temporary rift with the dictator and little is heard of him until he held the consulship in 44 BC as Caesar's colleague. On the assassination of the dictator on the Ides (15th) of March Antony became the leader of the Caesarian party, the initial aim of which was to exact retribution on the Republican conspirators. The chief of these, Brutus and Cassius, had withdrawn to the East soon after Caesar's murder and succeeded in assembling an impressive army with which to confront the Caesarians. The issue was decided at the battle of Philippi in October, 42 BC, where Antony's superior tactical skill overwhelmed his opponents. Antony and Octavian, together with M. Aemilius Lepidus, had formed the Second Triumvirate late in 43 BC and these three men now exercised supreme power in the Roman world with Antony clearly in a leadership role. Over the following decade a struggle for supremacy gradually developed between Antony, whose power base was in the East, and the more politically astute Octavian, who held Rome and the West (Lepidus had been eliminated as a political factor by 36 BC). Antony ultimately undermined much of his support among the Roman aristocracy by his close association with Queen Cleopatra of Egypt. He even repudiated his wife, the virtuous Octavia, sister of his triumviral colleague, to facilitate his relationship with Cleopatra by whom he had three children. When the inevitable trial of strength came at the naval battle of Actium (September, 31 BC) Octavian and his lieutenant Agrippa gained a decisive victory over his former colleague, support for whom was rapidly evaporating. Antony and Cleopatra fled back to Egypt and following Octavian's invasion of the Ptolemaic kingdom the following year they both committed suicide at Alexandria. Caesar's heir Octavian, soon to be named Augustus, was left as the supreme authority in the Roman world by virtue of his unquestioned control of the military establishment, the size of which had become enormously inflated over two decades of civil war.

1459   1460

1459   **Gold aureus.** M ANTONIVS III VIR R P C, bare hd. of M. Antony r. Rev. L REGVLVS IIII VIR
        A P F, Hercules seated facing on rock, holding spear and parazonium, shield at side. RRC
        494/2. CRI 143, 143a. BMCRR 4255–6. C 25. *[Rome, 42 BC].*
                                    VF £8,500 ($13,600) / **EF** £17,500 ($28,000)

1460   ANT AVG IMP III V R P C (ANT and AV in monogram), bare hd. of M. Antony r. Rev.
        PIETAS COS, Fortuna stg. l., holding rudder and cornucopiae, stork at feet to l. RRC 516/1.
        CRI 240. BMCRR Gaul 69. C 76. *[Asia Minor, early 41 BC].*
                                    VF £6,000 ($9,600) / **EF** £12,500 ($20,000)
        *The reverse refers to Mark Antony's brother, Lucius, who held the consulship in 41 BC and
        whose cognomen was 'Pietas' in recognition of his fraternal loyalty. See also nos. 1469
        and 1508–10.*

1461   ANT IMP III VIR R P C, bare hd. of M. Antony r., lituus behind. Rev. CN DOMIT
        AHENOBARBVS IMP, prow of galley r., star above. RRC 521/1. CRI 257. BMCRR East 111.
        C 9. *[Corcyra (?), summer 40 BC].*   **VF** £12,000 ($19,200) / **EF** £25,000 ($40,000)

1462   ANT AVG III VIR R P C, galley r., mast with banners at prow. Rev. CHORTIVM PRAETORIARVM,
        legionary eagle between two standards. RRC 544/1. CRI 384. BMCRR East 183. C 8.
        [Patrae (?), 32–31 BC].   **VF** £11,000 ($17,600) / **EF** £22,500 ($36,000)

1463   1465

1463   **Silver denarius.** No legend, veiled hd. of M. Antony r., lituus below chin, jug behind. Rev.
        P SEPVLLIVS MACER, horseman (*desultor*) galloping r., holding whip, a second horse visible
        in background, wreath and palm-branch behind. RRC 480/22. CRI 142. BMCRR 4178.
        RSC 74. *[Rome, Apr.–May 44 BC].*   **VF** £500 ($800) / **EF** £1,250 ($2,000)
        *The first issue bearing Antony's portrait, struck within a month or two of Caesar's assassi-
        nation.*

1464   M ANTON IMP (NT in monogram), bare hd. of M. Antony r., lituus behind. Rev. CAESAR
        DIC, wreathed hd. of Caesar r., jug behind. RRC 488/1. CRI 118. BMCRR Gaul 53. RSC *J.
        Caesar and M. Antony 2. [Cisalpine Gaul, April 43 BC].*
                                    VF £650 ($1,040) / **EF** £1,600 ($2,560)

1465   **Silver denarius.** Similar, but with obv. legend M ANTON IMP R P C (NT in monogram).
       RRC 488/2. CRI 123. BMCRR Gaul 55. RSC J. *Caesar and M. Antony* 3. *[Cisalpine*
       Gaul, Nov. 43 BC].   VF £550 ($880) / **EF** £1,400 ($2,240)
       Struck immediately following the formation of the Second Triumvirate at Bononia.

1466   No legend, bare hd. of M. Antony r. Rev. C VIBIVS VARVS, Fortuna stg. l., holding Victory
       and cornucopiae. RRC 494/32. CRI 149. BMCRR 4293. RSC 4. *[Rome, 42 BC].*
                                               VF £450 ($720) / **EF** £1,100 ($1,760)

                1467   1470

1467   M ANTONI IMP, bare hd. of M. Antony r. Rev. III VIR R P C, distyle temple containing fac-
       ing bust of Sol on disk. RRC 496/1. CRI 128. BMCRR Gaul 60. RSC 12. *[Epirus (?),*
       autumn 42 BC].   VF £275 ($440) / **EF** £650 ($1,040)

1468   IMP, bare hd. of M. Antony r., lituus behind. Rev. M ANTONIVS III VIR R P C, rad. hd. of Sol
       r. RRC 496/3. CRI 129. BMCRR East 89, 91. RSC 70. *[Northern Greece and/or Asia*
       Minor, late 42–early 41 BC].   VF £500 ($800) / **EF** £1,250 ($2,000)

1469   M ANTONIVS IMP III VIR R P C, bare hd. of M. Antony r., lituus behind. Rev. PIETAS COS,
       Pietas stg. l., holding turibulum and cornucopiae surmounted by two storks. RRC 516/5.
       CRI 238. BMCRR Gaul 67, 68. RSC 79. *[Asia Minor, early 41 BC].*
                                               VF £450 ($720) / **EF** £1,100 ($1,760)
       The reverse refers to Mark Antony's brother, Lucius, who held the consulship in 41 BC and
       whose cognomen was 'Pietas' in recognition of his fraternal loyalty. See also nos. 1460
       and 1508–10.

1470   M ANTON IMP AVG III VIR R P C, lituus and jug (emblems of the augurate). Rev. L
       PLANCVS IMP ITER, tall jug between thunderbolt and caduceus. RRC 522/4. CRI 255.
       BMCRR East 118. RSC 22. *[Central Greece, early summer 40 BC].*
                                               VF £600 ($960) / **EF** £1,500 ($2,400)

                1471   1472

1471   No legend, bare hd. of M. Antony r., lituus behind. Rev. M ANT IMP III VIR R P C (NT and
       MP in monogram), caduceus between two cornuacopiae, all resting on globe. RRC 520/1.
       CRI 256. BMCRR East 115. RSC 66. *[Corcyra (?), summer 40 BC].*
                                               VF £600 ($960) / **EF** £1,500 ($2,400)

1472   **Silver denarius.** As 1461 (rev. CN DOMIT AHENOBARBVS IMP, prow r. RRC 521/2. CRI
        258. BMCRR East 112. RSC 10a. *[Corcyra (?), summer 40 BC].*
        VF £600 ($960) / **EF** £1,500 ($2,400)

                        1473   1474

1473   **M ANT IMP III V R P C** (ANT and MP in monogram), bare hd. of M. Antony r., lituus behind.
        Rev. **P VENTIDI PONT IMP** (NT in monogram), naked Jupiter (?) stg. facing, hd. r., holding
        sceptre and branch. RRC 531/1a. CRI 265. BMCRR Gaul 73. RSC 75. *[Cilicia/northern
        Syria, autumn–early winter 39 BC].*   VF £5,000 ($8,000) / **EF** £10,000 ($16,000)

1474   **M ANTONIVS M F M N AVGVR IMP TERT** (MP and RT in monogram), M. Antony, as priest,
        stg. r., holding lituus. Rev. **III VIR R P C COS DESIG ITER ET TERT**, rad. hd. of Sol r. RRC
        533/2. CRI 267. BMCRR East 141. RSC 13a. *[Athens, summer 38 BC].*
        VF £185 ($296) / **EF** £450 ($720)

1475   **ANT AVGVR III VIR R P C**, bare hd. of M. Antony r. Rev. **IMP TER**, trophy, with shields and
        spears at base. RRC 536/4. CRI 270. BMCRR East 147. RSC 17a. *[Northern Syria, late
        summer–autumn 38 BC].*   VF £475 ($760) / **EF** £1,200 ($1,920)

1476   **ANTONIVS AVGVR COS DES ITER ET TERT**, bare hd. of M. Antony r. Rev. **IMP TERTIO III VIR
        R P C**, Armenian tiara, bow and arrow in saltire in background. RRC 539/1. CRI 297.
        BMCRR East 172. RSC 19. *[Antioch (?), autumn 37 BC].*
        VF £750 ($1,200) / **EF** £1,800 ($2,880)

1477   **ANTON AVG IMP III COS DES III III V R P C**, bare hd. of M. Antony r. (artist's signature 'P'
        concealed in hair behind the ear). Rev. **M SILANVS AVG / Q PRO COS** in two lines across
        field. RRC 542/1. CRI 346. BMCRR East 175. RSC 71. *[Athens, summer 32 BC].*
        VF £400 ($640) / **EF** £1,000 ($1,600)
        *This and the following are the only recognized instances of an engraver's signature
        appearing on coins of the Roman Republic.*

1478   Similar, but with rev. type **ANTONIVS / AVG IMP III** in two lines across field. RRC 542/2.
        CRI 347. BMCRR East 177. RSC 2. *[Athens, summer 32 BC].*
        VF £400 ($640) / **EF** £1,000 ($1,600)

                        1479   1482

1479   **ANT AVG III VIR R P C**, galley r., mast with banners at prow. Rev. **LEG V**, legionary eagle
        between two standards. RRC 544/18. CRI 354. BMCRR East 196. RSC 32. *[Patrae (?),
        32–31 BC].*   VF £100 ($160) / **EF** £275 ($440)

284 MARK ANTONY

The celebrated 'legionary' coinage of Mark Antony, produced in all likelihood at his winter headquarters at Patrae just prior to the Actian campaign, honoured twenty-three legions (LEG PRI to LEG XXIII as well as the praetorian cohorts and the cohort of speculatores. A number of the legions have additional types giving their names as well as their numbers. Most varieties are quite commonly encountered, though a few are rare and those honouring the cohorts and the named legions are scarce. LEG PRI is of great rarity. For a 2nd cent. AD restoration of Antony's 'legionary' coinage, see under Marcus Aurelius.

1480   **Silver denarius.** Similar, but with rev. legend LEG XII ANTIQVAE. RRC 544/9. CRI 363. BMCRR East 222. RSC 40. *[Patrae (?), 32–31 BC].*   **VF** £200 ($320) / **EF** £500 ($800)

1481   Similar, but with rev. legend LEG XVII CLASSICAE. RRC 544/10. CRI 373. BMCRR East 223. RSC 50. *[Patrae (?), 32–31 BC].*   **VF** £225 ($360) / **EF** £550 ($880)

1482   Similar, but with rev. legend LEG XVIII LYBICAE. RRC 544/11. CRI 375. BMCRR East 225. RSC 53. *[Patrae (?), 32–31 BC].*   **VF** £250 ($400) / **EF** £600 ($960)

1483   1484

1483   Similar, but with rev. legend CHORTIVM PRAETORIARVM. RRC 544/8. CRI 385. BMCRR East 184. RSC 7. *[Patrae (?), 32–31 BC].*   **VF** £275 ($440) / **EF** £650 ($1,040)

1484   Similar, but with rev. legend CHORTIS SPECVLATORVM and type three standards, each decorated with two wreaths and model of prow. RRC 544/12. CRI 386. BMCRR East 185. RSC 6. *[Patrae (?), 32–31 BC].*   **VF** £275 ($440) / **EF** £650 ($1,040)

1485   M ANTONIVS AVG IMP IIII COS TERT III VIR R P C, bare hd. of M. Antony r. Rev. Victory stg. l., holding wreath and palm, sometimes with D TVR (TVR in monogram) in lower r. field, all within laurel-wreath. RRC 545/1–2. CRI 387–8. BMCRR East 227–8. RSC 11, 81. *[Actium (?), summer 31 BC].*   **VF** £650 ($1,040) / **EF** £1,600 ($2,560)

1486   1487

1486   M ANTO COS III IMP IIII, hd. of Jupiter Ammon r. Rev. ANTONIO AVG SCARPVS IMP, Victory walking r., holding wreath and palm. RRC 546/2. CRI 390. BMCRR Cyrenaica 2. RSC 1. *[Cyrene, summer 31 BC].*   **VF** £350 ($560) / **EF** £850 ($1,360)
A scarcer variety has the obv. legend M ANTONIO COS III IMP IIII.

1487   **Silver quinarius.** M ANT IMP (ANT in monogram), lituus, jug and raven (emblems of the augurate). Rev. No legend, Victory stg. r., crowning trophy. RRC 489/4. CRI 121. BMCRR Gaul 36. RSC 82. *[Transalpine Gaul, summer 43 BC].*   **VF** £90 ($144) / **EF** £250 ($400)

1488   **Bronze as.** L ATRATINVS AVGVR, beardless laur. janiform hd., with features resembling
        M. Antony. Rev. ANTONIVS IMP, prow of galley r. RPC 2226. RRC 530/1. CRI 264.
        BMCRR East, p. 501. C 3. *[Asia Minor (?), 40–39 BC].*

                                           F £300 ($480) / **VF** £750 ($1,200)

The Fleet Coinage (heavy series)

1489

1489   **Bronze sestertius.** M ANT IMP TER COS DES ITER ET TER III VIR R P C (ANT and MP in
        monogram), bare hd. of M. Antony r., facing dr. bust of Octavia l. Rev. L ATRATINVS
        AVGVR COS DESIG , Antony and Octavia (?) stg. in quadriga of hippocamps r., HS in l. field,
        Δ and astragalus (?) below, lituus above. RPC 1453. CRI 279. CRR 1261. C *Octavia and
        M. Antony 5. [Lechaeum (?), summer–autumn 38 BC].*

                                           F £1,250 ($2,000) / **VF** £3,000 ($4,800)
        *Weight about 21 grams. Equivalent issues were produced by the Antonian admirals L.
        Calpurnius Bibulus and M. Oppius Capito.*

1490

1490   **Bronze tressis.** M ANT IMP TERT COS DESIG ITER ET TER III VIR R P C (NT, MP, TE, and RT
        all in monogram), conjoined bare hds. of M. Antony and Octavian r., facing dr. bust of
        Octavia l. Rev. M OPPIVS CAPITO PRO PR PRAEF CLASS F C, three galleys under sail r., Γ and
        triskeles below. RPC 1463. CRI 286. CRR 1266. BMCRR East 154. C *Octavia, M. Antony
        and Octavian 1. [Piraeus (?), summer–autumn 38 BC].*

                                           F £1,250 ($2,000) / **VF** £3,000 ($4,800)
        Equivalent issues were produced by L. Calpurnius Bibulus and L. Sempronius Atratinus.

1491

1491   **Bronze dupondius.** — bare hd. of M. Antony r., facing dr. bust of Octavia l. Rev. — two
       galleys under sail r., caps of the Dioscuri in field, B below. RPC 1464. CRI 287. CRR 1267.
       BMCRR East 155. C *Octavia and M. Antony 12. [Piraeus (?), summer–autumn 38 BC].*
                                                   F £750 ($1,200) / **VF** £1,800 ($2,880)
       *Weight about 15 grams. Equivalent issues were produced by L. Calpurnius Bibulus and L.
       Sempronius Atratinus.*

1492   **Bronze as.** — conjoined hds. of M. Antony and Octavia r. Rev. — galley under sail r., A
       and hd. of Medusa (?) below. RPC 1465. CRI 288. CRR 1268. BMCRR East 164.
       [Piraeus (?), summer–autumn 38 BC].   **F** £450 ($720) / **VF** £1,100 ($1,760)
       *Weight about 8 grams. Equivalent issues were produced by L. Calpurnius Bibulus and L.
       Sempronius Atratinus.*

1493   **Bronze semis.** M ANT IMP TER COS DES ITER ET TER III VIR R P C (ANT and MP in mono-
       gram), bare hd. of M. Antony r. Rev. L BIBVLVS M F PR DESIG, forepart of galley r. RPC
       4092. CRI 277. CRR 1259. BMCRR East 150. Cf. C 97. *[Seleucia (?), summer–autumn
       38 BC].*   **F** £275 ($440) / **VF** £650 ($1,040)
       Equivalent issues were produced by L. Sempronius Atratinus and M. Oppius Capito.

1494

1494   **Bronze quadrans.** M ANT IMP TERT COS DESIG ITER ET TER III VIR R P C (NT, MP, TE, and
       RT all in monogram), janiform hd. (of M. Antony and Octavian?). Rev. M OPPI CAP PRAEF
       CLASS F C, stem of prow, three pellets in field. RPC 1467. CRI 290. Cf. CRR 1270.
       [Piraeus (?), summer–autumn 38 BC].   **F** £250 ($400) / **VF** £600 ($960)
       Equivalent issues were produced by L. Calpurnius Bibulus and L. Sempronius Atratinus.

The Fleet Coinage (light series)

1495

1495   **Bronze sestertius.** Similar to 1489, but weight only about 12 grams. RPC 1459. CRI 291. CRR 1261. BMCRR East 151. *[Tarentum (?), summer 37 BC].*

F £750 ($1,200) / **VF** £1,800 ($2,880)

An equivalent issue was produced by M. Oppius Capito.

1496   **Bronze dupondius.** Similar to 1491, but weight only about 7.5 grams. RPC 1469. CRI 295. CRR 1267. BMCRR East 158. *[Tarentum (?), summer 37 BC].*

F £400 ($640) / **VF** £950 ($1,520)

An equivalent issue was produced by L. Sempronius Atratinus.

1497

1497   **Bronze as.** Similar to 1492, but weight only about 4 grams. RPC 1470. CRI 296. CRR 1268. BMCRR East 165. C *Octavia and M. Antony* 11. *[Tarentum (?), summer 37 BC].*

F £150 ($240) / **VF** £350 ($560)

An equivalent issue was produced by L. Sempronius Atratinus.

MARK ANTONY AND LEPIDUS

1498

Antony entered into an alliance with the pontifex maximus M. Aemilius Lepidus soon after being worsted at Mutina in April, 43 BC by a senatorial army under the joint command of the two consuls and the young Octavian. This embarrassing reverse left Antony particularly vulnerable and he lost no time in seeking the support of Lepidus, who had already assisted him in Rome after Caesar's murder and now, as governor of Gallia Narbonensis and Nearer Spain, had a large army under his command. The two allies later joined forces with Octavian at Bononia to form the Second Triumvirate (November, 43 BC).

1498   **Gold aureus.** M ANTONIVS III VIR R P C, bare hd. of M. Antony r., lituus behind. Rev. M LEPIDVS III VIR R P C, bare hd. of Lepidus r., sprinkler and simpulum behind. RRC 492/2. CRI 125. BMCRR Gaul 46. C *Lepidus and M. Antony* 1. *[Cisalpine Gaul or Italy, Nov.–Dec. 43 BC].*   **VF** £30,000 ($48,000) / **EF** £65,000 ($104,000)

1499

1499   **Silver denarius.** M ANTON IMP (NT in monogram), lituus, capis and raven (emblems of the augurate). Rev. M LEPID IMP, simpulum, sprinkler, axe and apex (emblems of the pontificate). RRC 489/2. CRI 119a. BMCRR Gaul 31. RSC *Lepidus and M. Antony* 2. *[Transalpine Gaul, June 43 BC].*   **VF** £450 ($720) / **EF** £1,100 ($1,760)

1500   **Silver quinarius.** Similar, but with legends M ANT IMP (ANT in monogram) and LEP IMP. RRC 489/3. CRI 120. BMCRR Gaul 33. RSC *Lepidus and M. Antony* 3. *[Transalpine Gaul, June 43 BC].*   **VF** £100 ($160) / **EF** £275 ($440)

For other coins honouring Lepidus, see nos. 1521–3.

MARK ANTONY AND OCTAVIAN

1502

During the early years of their long association the two principal triumvirs honoured each other frequently on their coin issues, beginning with the series commemorating the establishment of the Second Triumvirate in November of 43 BC. These issues ceased abruptly about five years later and Antony and Octavian never even met again after Antony's departure from Italy in the late summer of 37.

1501   **Gold aureus.** M ANTONIVS III VIR R P C, bare hd. of M. Antony r., lituus behind. Rev. C CAESAR III VIR R P C, bare hd. of Octavian r. RRC 492/1. CRI 124. BMCRR Gaul 47. C 4. *[Cisalpine Gaul or Italy, Nov.–Dec. 43 BC].*
VF £6,500 ($10,400) / **EF** £12,500 ($20,000)

1502   M ANT IMP AVG III VIR R P C M BARBAT Q P (MP and AV in monogram), bare hd. of M. Antony r. Rev. CAESAR IMP PONT III VIR R P C, bare hd. of Octavian r. RRC 517/1a. CRI 242. BMCRR East 98. C 7. *[Ephesus, spring–summer 41 BC].*
VF £4,500 ($7,200) / **EF** £8,500 ($13,600)

1503 **Gold aureus.** M ANTON IMP III VIR R P C, bare hd. of M. Antony r. Rev. CAESAR IMP III VIR R P C, bare hd. of Octavian r. RRC 528/1b. CRI 260. BMCRR East 120. *[Italy, late 40–early 39 BC].*   **VF** £5,500 ($8,800) / **EF** £10,000 ($16,000)

1504   1505

1504 **Silver denarius.** As 1502. RRC 517/2. CRI 243. BMCRR East 100. RSC 8. *[Ephesus, spring–summer 41 BC].*   **VF** £400 ($640) / **EF** £850 ($1,360)

1505 M ANT IMP AVG III VIR R P C L GELL Q P (MP and AV in monogram), bare hd. of M. Antony r., jug behind. Rev. CAESAR IMP PONT III VIR R P C, bare hd. of Octavian r., lituus behind. RRC 517/8. CRI 250. BMCRR East 109. RSC 10. *[Asia Minor, autumn 41 BC].*   **VF** £650 ($1,040) / **EF** £1,400 ($2,240)

1506 M ANTON IMP III VIR R P C AVG, bare hd. of M. Antony r. Rev. CAESAR IMP PONT III VIR R P C, bare hd. of Octavian r. RRC 528/3. CRI 251. BMCRR East 123. RSC 2. *[Syria (?), autumn 41 BC].*   **VF** £450 ($720) / **EF** £950 ($1,520)

1507 M ANTON IMP III VIR R P C, bare hd. of M. Antony r., star below. Rev. CAESAR IMP III VIR R P C, bare hd. of Octavian r. RRC 528/2a. CRI 261. BMCRR East 121. RSC 1. *[Italy, late 40–early 39 BC].*   **VF** £450 ($720) / **EF** £950 ($1,520)

For other coins depicting Mark Antony and Octavian, see under Antony's Fleet Coinage and under Octavian and Mark Antony.

MARK ANTONY AND LUCIUS ANTONY

1509

Lucius Antonius was the youngest brother of Mark Antony. He was quaestor in Asia in 50 BC and as tribune six years later he was instrumental in the passing of a law giving Caesar special powers in the appointment of magistrates. During his consulship in 41 he became the focus of opposition to Octavian's regime, a dangerous role in which he was egged on by his assertive sister-in-law Fulvia, wife of Mark Antony. The confrontation between consul and triumvir ultimately led to armed conflict and Lucius took refuge in the strongly defended city of Persusia, confident of the arrival of assistance from his brother's legions stationed in Gaul. But the anticipated help never materialized and Lucius was obliged to capitulate to Octavian, thus ending the so-called Perusine War. Octavian graciously pardoned the former consul's offence and even appointed him to the governorship of Spain, where he died soon afterwards.

1508   **Gold aureus.** M ANT IMP AVG III VIR R P C M NERVA PROQ P (MP, AV, and NE in monogram), bare hd. of M. Antony r. Rev. L ANTONIVS COS, bare hd. of L. Antonius r. RRC 517/4a. CRI 245. BMCRR East 106. C *Lucius Antony and M. Antony* 1. *[Ephesus, summer 41 BC].*   **VF** £10,000 ($16,000) / **EF** £20,000 ($32,000)

1509   **Silver denarius.** Similar. RRC 517/5a. CRI 246. BMCRR East 107. RSC *Lucius Antony and M. Antony* 2. *[Ephesus, summer 41 BC].*   **VF** £650 ($1,040) / **EF** £1,400 ($2,240)

1510

1510   Similar, but with jug behind hd. of M. Antony. RRC 517/5c. CRI 247. BMCRR East 108. RSC Lucius Antony and M. Antony 2b. *[Asia Minor, late summer 41 BC].*   **VF** £850 ($1,360) / **EF** £1,800 ($2,880)

For other reverse types of Mark Antony commemorating his brother's consulship in 41 BC, see nos. 1460 and 1469.

MARK ANTONY AND OCTAVIA

1512

Octavia, the virtuous sister of Octavian, was initially married to C. Claudius Marcellus, consul in 50 BC. His death, a decade later, coincided with the signing of the Pact of Brundisium between Antony and Octavian and the agreement was sealed by the marriage of Antony to his colleague's widowed sister. The couple enjoyed several years of wedded bliss in Athens and in 37 BC Octavia was instrumental in the negotiations leading to the Pact of Tarentum, the last accord to be signed by the two principal triumvirs. Soon after this Octavia was abandoned by Antony and later in the same year he went through a marriage ceremony with Queen Cleopatra of Egypt. Octavia was finally repudiated by her husband in 32 BC, but following his downfall and suicide two years later she took on the responsibility of bringing up all his surviving children, including those by Cleopatra. She died in 11 BC.

1511   **Gold aureus.** M ANTONIVS M F M N AVGVR IMP TER, bare hd. of M. Antony r. Rev. COS DESIGN ITER ET TER III VIR R P C, hd. of Octavia r. RRC 533/3a. CRI 268. BMCRR East 144. C *Octavia and M. Antony* 1. *[Athens, summer 38 BC].*   **VF** £45,000 ($72,000) / **EF** £85,000 ($136,000)

1512 **Silver cistophorus** (= 3 denarii). M ANTONIVS IMP COS DESIG ITER ET TERT, hd. of
M. Antony r., wreathed with ivy, lituus below, all within ivy-wreath. Rev. III VIR R P C, dr.
bust of Octavia r. above cista mystica flanked by two snakes. RPC 2201. CRI 262. CRR
1197. BMCRR East 133. RSC *Octavia and M. Antony* 2. *[Ephesus, summer–autumn
39 BC].*   **VF** £475 ($760) / **EF** £1,200 ($1,920)

1513

1513 — conjoined hds. r. of M. Antony, wreathed with ivy, and Octavia. Rev. — Dionysus,
holding cantharus and thyrsus, stg. l. on cista mystica flanked by two snakes. RPC 2202.
CRI 263. CRR 1198. BMCRR East 135. RSC *Octavia and M. Antony* 3. *[Ephesus, sum-
mer–autumn 39 BC].*   **VF** £425 ($680) / **EF** £1,000 ($1,600)

For other coins depicting Mark Antony and Octavia, see under Antony's Fleet Coinage.

**MARK ANTONY AND MARK
ANTONY JUNIOR**

1514

*Marcus Antonius Junior (called 'Antyllus' by the Greeks) was the elder son of Mark Antony by his
third wife Fulvia. At the conclusion of the Pact of Tarentum in 37 BC he was betrothed to Octavian's
only child, his daughter Julia by his second wife Scribonia. He assumed the toga virilis after his
father's defeat at Actium and was put to death following Octavian's conquest of the Ptolemaic kingdom in 30 BC.*

1514 **Gold aureus.** ANTON AVG IMP III COS DES III III V R P C, bare hd. of M. Antony r. Rev.
M ANTONIVS M F F, bare hd. of M. Antony Junior r. RRC 541/2. CRI 344. BMCRR East
174. C *M. Antony Junior and M. Antony* 1. *[Syria or Armenia, spring–summer 34 BC].*
              VF £60,000 ($96,000) / **EF** £100,000 ($160,000)

CLEOPATRA VII OF EGYPT AND MARK ANTONY

1515

Cleopatra VII, daughter of Ptolemy XII Auletes, was born in 69 BC and became joint ruler of Egypt with her brother Ptolemy XIII on the death of their father in 51 BC. She was temporarily ousted from power by her brother in 48, but was soon reinstated by Julius Caesar who arrived in Egypt immediately following the murder of Pompey the Great. Ptolemy XIII perished when he foolishly attempted to defy Caesar and was replaced as Cleopatra's consort by a younger brother, Ptolemy XIV. The Egyptian queen came to Rome in 46 BC at Caesar's invitation and remained there until the dictator's assassination on the Ides of March, 44, after which she returned to Alexandria. Soon after this Ptolemy XIV died and was replaced by Cleopatra's son, Ptolemy XV (also known as Ptolemy Caesar or Caesarion). Cleopatra claimed that the 3-year-old child was the son of Caesar but the truth of her politically motivated assertion has always been seriously questioned. Her association with Mark Antony began with their meeting at Tarsus in 41 BC and the Roman triumvir spent the winter with her in Alexandria. The following year Cleopatra gave birth to twins – Alexander Helios and Cleopatra Selene. Despite his marriage to Octavian's sister, Octavia, Antony became increasingly involved with the Egyptian queen and eventually, in 37 BC, the couple entered into a political alliance at Antioch and actually went through a wedding ceremony. These developments outraged and alarmed public opinion in Rome and did much to enhance Octavian's position and to undermine Antony's considerable popularity in the West. A third child, Ptolemy Philadelphus, was born to the couple in 36 BC and Cleopatra's political ambitions were clearly revealed when Antony restored to the Egyptian kingdom large areas of former Ptolemaic territory, such as Phoenicia, Palestine, and Cyrenaica. These 'Donations' took place in the Egyptian capital in 34 BC, the same year which had already witnessed Antony's Alexandrian triumph for his Armenian campaign. These momentous events doubtless provided the occasion for the minting of the famous denarius type combining the portraits of the Roman triumvir and the queen of Egypt. Their images had already appeared together on an impressive series of tetradrachms from Syria which appear to have been struck as early as 36 BC (cf. RPC 4094). Antony was defeated by Octavian and Agrippa at the battle of Actium in September, 31 BC. The following year he and Cleopatra committed suicide in Alexandria following Octavian's invasion of Egypt, thus ending the 300–year-old Greek Ptolemaic kingdom.

1515   **Silver denarius.** CLEOPATRAE REGINAE REGVM FILIORVM REGVM, diad. and dr. bust of Cleopatra r., stem of prow before. Rev. **ANTONI ARMENIA DEVICTA**, bare hd. of M. Antony r., Armenian tiara behind. RRC 543/1. CRI 345. BMCRR East 179. RSC 1. *[Alexandria, autumn 34 BC].*   **VF** £1,250 ($2,000) / **EF** £5,000 ($8,000)
On the evidence of the appearance of many surviving specimens coins of this issue did not depict the Roman triumvir as their obverse type. However, given their likely place of mintage this should scarcely occasion much surprise.

FULVIA
Second wife of Mark Antony

1517

The daughter of M. Fulvius Bambalio and Sempronia, Fulvia married Mark Antony about 46 BC and bore him two sons, M. Antony Junior (Antyllus) and Iullus Antonius. She was also briefly mother-in-law of Octavian when her daughter Claudia became the young man's first wife. During the dispute between Octavian and the consul Lucius Antonius in 41 BC she gave active encouragement to her brother-in-law in his bid to overthrow the triumvir, an error of judgement which was to cost her dearly. Although allowed to go free by Octavian following the fall of Perusia Fulvia was bitterly reproached by her husband when they met in Athens and, her spirit broken, she died soon afterwards (40 BC).

1516   **Gold aureus.** No legend, winged hd. of Fulvia as the goddess Victory r. Rev. C NVMONIVS VAALA, soldier advancing l., attacking palisaded earthwork behind which are two defenders. RRC 514/1. CRI 321. BMCRR 4215. C 2. *[Rome, 41 BC].*
          VF £15,000 ($24,000) / **EF** £30,000 ($48,000)

1517   **Silver denarius.** Obv. Similar, but with dr. bust instead of hd. Rev. L MVSSIDIVS LONGVS, Victory in galloping biga r. RRC 494/40. CRI 186. BMCRR 4229. RSC *Mussidia* 4. *[Rome, 42 BC].*
          VF £225 ($360) / **EF** £550 ($880)

1518   **Silver quinarius.** Obv. As 1516. Rev. LVGVDVNI, lion walking r., A – XL (= year 40) in field. RRC 489/5. CRI 122. BMCRR Gaul 40. RSC 4. *[Lugdunum, autumn 43 BC].*
          VF £125 ($200) / **EF** £300 ($480)
   The dates on the reverses of this type and the next refer to Antony's age at the time of the issue.

1519

1519   Similar, but with legends III VIR R P C on obv. and ANTONI IMP on rev., and with date numeral A – XLI (= year 41) in rev. field. RRC 489/6. CRI 126. BMCRR Gaul 48. RSC 3. *[Lugdunum, 42 BC].*
          VF £125 ($200) / **EF** £300 ($480)

GAIUS ANTONY
Proconsul, executed 42 BC

1520

Gaius Antonius, the second son of M. Antonius Creticus and younger brother of Mark Antony, served as a legate of Caesar in 49 BC and was blockaded by a Pompeian fleet on the island of Curicta in the Adriatic. Although forced to surrender he survived this episode and held the praetorship in 44. Assigned the government of Macedonia for the following year he set out for his province at the beginning of 43, but while en route was besieged by M. Brutus in Apollonia, captured, and held hostage (March). Early the following year he was executed on Brutus' orders, ostensibly for attempting to incite the soldiers to mutiny, but more likely as a reprisal for the death of Cicero who had been proscribed by the triumviral government.

1520   **Silver denarius.** C ANTONIVS M F PRO COS, dr. bust of Macedonia r., wearing causia. Rev. PONTIFEX, two simpula and axe (emblems of the pontificate). RRC 484/1. CRI 141. BMCRR East 37. RSC 1. *[Apollonia, Jan.–Mar. 43 BC].*

VF £3,000 ($4,800) / **EF** £6,500 ($10,400)

LEPIDUS
Triumvir and Imperator,
deposed 36 BC, died 13 BC

1522

Marcus Aemilius Lepidus was the younger son of the M. Lepidus who held the consulship in 78 BC. He was a moneyer around 61 BC and as praetor in 49 gave his support to Caesar in the civil war with Pompey. Rewarded with the governorship of Nearer Spain (48–47 BC) he then returned to Rome and held the consulship in 46 with the dictator as his colleague. From 46–44 he served as magister equitum (master of horse) and was thus one of the most influential men in Rome at the time of Caesar's assassination on the Ides of March, 44 BC. In return for the armed support which he gave to Mark Antony at this critical juncture he was granted the title of pontifex maximus held formerly by the dictator. Despite protestations of loyalty to the Republic given to Cicero, Lepidus continued to support Antony and on 27 November 43 BC the two men, together with Caesar's heir Octavian, formed the Second Triumvirate. This was followed by the notorious proscriptions in which many prominent Romans lost their lives on account of their wealth and their political affiliations. Lepidus took no active part in the Philippi campaign in the autumn of 42 BC, remaining instead in Rome to ensure that no trouble arose in the capital. After Philippi he faded into the background, overshadowed by the more powerful personalities of Antony and Octavian. He retained his triumviral rank until 36 BC when he was deposed by Octavian following an attempted coup in Sicily during the war against Sextus Pompey. The remaining 23 years of his life were spent as a state prisoner in the coastal town of Circeii, some 60 miles south of Rome. Lepidus continued as pontifex maximus until his death in 13 BC, the only man other than an emperor to hold this office during the Roman Imperial period.

1521 **Gold aureus. M LEPIDVS III VIR R P C**, bare hd. of Lepidus l. Rev. **L MVSSIDIVS LONGVS**, cornucopiae. RRC 494/13. CRI 162. BMCRR 4232. C 1. *[Rome, 42 BC]*.
VF £30,000 ($48,000) / **EF** £65,000 ($104,000)

1522 Obv. Similar, but hd. of Lepidus r. Rev. **L REGVLVS IIII VIR A P F**, vestal virgin Aemilia stg. l., holding simpulum and transverse sceptre. RRC 494/1. CRI 159. BMCRR 4259. C 3. *[Rome, 42 BC]*.
VF £30,000 ($48,000) / **EF** £65,000 ($104,000)

LEPIDUS AND OCTAVIAN

1523

Lepidus and Octavian were colleagues in the Second Triumvirate from November 43 BC until Lepidus' deposition in the autumn of 36. The precise occasion for this issue by Lepidus is difficult to determine. Crawford regards it as struck from the proceeds of the proscriptions in preparation for the war against Brutus and Cassius. However, the lack of an equivalent type honouring Antony is difficult to explain, especially as Lepidus was much closer to the elder of his two colleagues.

1523 **Silver denarius. LEPIDVS PONT MAX III V** (or **VIR** in monogram) **R P C** (**NT** and **MA** in monogram), bare hd. of Lepidus r. Rev. **CAESAR** (or **C CAESAR**) **IMP III VIR R P C** (**MP** in monogram), bare hd. of Octavian r. RRC 495/2. CRI 140, 140a. BMCRR Africa 30, 31. RSC 2a–c. *[Italy, spring–summer 42 BC]*. VF £900 ($1,440) / **EF** £2,250 ($3,600)
An aureus of this type may also exist, though the only recorded specimen was lost in the great theft from the Paris Cabinet in 1831.

For coins issued by M. Antony honouring Lepidus, see nos. 1498–1500. For coins struck by Lepidus as moneyer in 61 BC, see nos. 371–4.

DOMITIUS CALVINUS
Proconsul and Imperator
in Spain 39–36 BC

1524

Gnaeus Domitius Calvinus, a loyal partisan of Caesar from the time of the outbreak of the Civil War in 49 BC, had a long military career dating back to 62 BC, when he was legate to L. Valerius Flaccus in Asia. He commanded the Caesarian centre at Pharsalus, but six years later was defeated by Ahenobarbus in a naval engagement in the Adriatic at the time of Philippi. 40 BC saw the second of his two consulships (the first had been in 53) and this was followed by a proconsular command in Spain. His success in putting down a revolt of the Cerretani led to him being saluted imperator by his troops, an occasion commemorated by this extraordinary issue of denarii from Osca. On his return to Rome he celebrated a triumph in 36 BC and was responsible for the restoration in marble of the Regia in the Roman Forum.

1524   **Silver denarius.** OSCA, bare male hd. r., with short curly hair and close beard. Rev. DOM
COS ITER IMP, simpulum, sprinkler, axe and apex (emblems of the pontificate). RRC 532/1.
CRI 342. BMCRR Spain 109. *[Osca, 39 BC].*   **VF** £350 ($560) / **EF** £900 ($1,440)
This remarkable type recalls the earlier Iberian silver coinage of Osca.

OCTAVIAN (later AUGUSTUS)
Triumvir, Imperator and Divi filius,
emperor from 27 BC

1558

*The son of C. Octavius (governor of Macedonia in the early 50s BC) and Atia, niece of Caesar,
Gaius Octavius was born on 23 September 63 BC. He lost his father while still a child and was
brought up by his mother. His remarkable political career, which was to span almost six decades,
began when he was adopted as heir by his great-uncle Julius Caesar, thus changing his name to
C. Julius Caesar Octavianus. Although only eighteen at the time of the dictator's assassination on
the Ides (15th) of March, 44 BC, he was already possessed of sufficient political acumen to hold his
own against his principal rival, Mark Antony, who was twenty years his senior. Towards the end of
the following year Antony, Octavian, and Aemilius Lepidus, the pontifex maximus, formed a political alliance known as the Second Triumvirate. Its first task was to defeat the threat posed by the
Republicans led by the tyrannicides Brutus and Cassius. This was accomplished by the battle of
Philippi in 42 BC, a personal achievement of Antony through which he gained a military reputation
far beyond his true abilities. By astute political manœuvring, and with a fair share of Caesarian
luck, Octavian gradually succeeded in dominating the triumviral partnership. The year 36 BC was
pivotal, as it saw the removal of two of his principal rivals – Sextus Pompey, younger son of
Pompey the Great, and the triumvir Lepidus. The final confrontation with Antony was post-
poned until 31 BC and was much facilitated by the eastern triumvir's intimate relationship with
Cleopatra VII, queen of Egypt, a liaison viewed with the utmost suspicion by the Roman people.
Early in September the famous naval battle of Actium was fought in which, through a combination
of the tactical skill of Octavian's lieutenant Agrippa and probable treachery on the part of the
Antonian naval command, the fleet of the eastern triumvir was easily routed and put to flight.
Antony and Cleopatra fled back to Alexandria and Octavian had at last achieved his goal of undisputed mastery of the Roman world. The invasion and conquest of the Ptolemaic kingdom the following year was little more than a formality, though it did result in the suicide deaths of both his
adversaries. The next two years were spent in consolidating his hold on power and planning the
details of a constitutional reorganization. As a result of the changes enacted early in 27 BC, and
over the following four years, Octavian in effect became emperor of Rome, though his receipt from
the Senate of the title 'Augustus' on 16 January 27 is usually taken to mark the commencement of
his reign* (CONTINUED UNDER AUGUSTUS IN ROMAN IMPERIAL SECTION).

1525

1525   **Gold aureus.** C CAESAR COS PONT AVG (NT and AV in monogram), bare hd. of Octavian
r. Rev. C CAESAR DICT PERP PONT MAX (NT and MA in monogram), wreathed hd. of Caesar
r. RRC 490/2. CRI 132. BMCRR Gaul 74. C *J. Caesar and Octavian* 2. *[Italy,
summer–autumn 43 BC].*   **VF** £7,000 ($11,200) / **EF** £15,000 ($24,000)

1526   **Gold aureus.** CAESAR III VIR R P C, bare hd. of Octavian r. Rev. Equestrian statue of
        Octavian l., holding lituus, S C divided by rostrum in ex. RRC 497/1. CRI 136. BMCRR
        Gaul 95. C 245. *[Italy, spring–summer 42 BC].*
                                                VF £4,500 ($7,200) / **EF** £10,000 ($16,000)

1527   C CAESAR III VIR R P C, bare hd. of Octavian r. Rev. L MVSSIDIVS T F LONGVS IIII VIR A P F
        (MV in monogram), naked Mars stg. r., l. foot on shield, holding spear and sword in scab-
        bard. RRC 494/9a. CRI 152a. BMCRR 4227. C 468 var. *[Rome, 42 BC].*
                                                VF £5,500 ($8,800) / **EF** £12,500 ($20,000)

1528   DIVI IVLI F, bare hd. of Octavian r. Rev. TI SEMPRON GRACCVS IIII VIR Q D, Fortuna stg. l.,
        holding rudder and cornucopiae. RRC 525/1. CRI 325. BMCRR 4313. C 522. *[Rome,
        40 BC].*   VF £7,000 ($11,200) / **EF** £15,000 ($24,000)

1529   IMP CAESAR DIVI F III VIR ITER R P C, bare hd. of Octavian r. Rev. COS ITER ET TER DESIG,
        tetrastyle temple of Divus Julius, statue within, DIVO IVL on architrave, star in pediment,
        altar to l. RRC 540/1. CRI 314. BMCRR Africa 32. C 89. *[Italy, spring–summer 36 BC].*
                                                VF £4,500 ($7,200) / **EF** £10,000 ($16,000)

          1530   1532

1530   No legend, bare hd. of Octavian r. Rev. CAESAR DIVI F, equestrian statue of Octavian gal-
        loping l., his r hand raised. RIC 262. CRI 394. BMCRR 4325 (= BMCRE 594). C 73.
        [Rome (?), 32–31 BC].   VF £2,250 ($3,600) / **EF** £5,000 ($8,000)

1531   Obv. Similar. Rev. — Victory in galloping biga r. RIC 260. CRI 402. BMCRR 4323
        (= BMCRE 592). C 67. *[Rome (?), 31–30 BC].*   VF £2,750 ($4,400) / **EF** £6,000 ($9,600)

1532   Obv. Similar. Rev. IMP CAESAR, Victory stg. facing on globe, hd. l., holding wreath and
        vexillum. RIC 268. CRI 417. BMCRR 4356 (= BMCRE 622). C 113. *[Rome (?),
        30–29 BC].*   VF £3,000 ($4,800) / **EF** £7,000 ($11,200)
        *The rev. type would appear to represent the statue of Victory which crowned the apex of the
        roof of the Curia Julia (Senate House) in the Roman Forum (see also no. 1557).*

1533   **Silver cistophorus** (= 3 denarii). IMP CAESAR DIVI F COS VI LIBERTATIS P R VINDEX, laur.
        hd. of Octavian r. Rev. PAX to l. of Pax stg. l., holding caduceus, cista mystica with snake
        on r., all within laurel-wreath. RPC 2203. RIC 476. CRI 433. BMCRR East 248
        (= BMCRE 691). RSC 218. *[Ephesus, 28 BC].*   VF £500 ($800) / **EF** £1,250 ($2,000)

1534   **Silver denarius.** C CAESAR IMP, bare hd. of Octavian r. Rev. S C, equestrian statue of
        Octavian l., his r. hand raised. RRC 490/1. CRI 131. BMCRR Gaul 81. RSC 246.
        [Cisalpine Gaul, spring–summer 43 BC].   VF £350 ($560) / **EF** £850 ($1,360)

1535   Similar, but with obv. legend C CAESAR III VIR R P C, and on rev. the equestrian statue is to
        r. RRC 490/3. CRI 134. BMCRR Gaul 63. RSC 243. *[Cisalpine Gaul, Nov.–Dec. 43 BC].*
                                                VF £400 ($640) / **EF** £1,000 ($1,600)

1536 1539

1536 **Silver denarius.** CAESAR III VIR R P C, bare hd. of Octavian r. Rev. Curule chair of Caesar surmounted by wreath and inscribed CÆSAR DIC PER (AR also in monogram). RRC 497/2a. CRI 137. BMCRR Gaul 76. RSC 55. *[Italy, spring–summer 42 BC].*
VF £275 ($440) / **EF** £650 ($1,040)

1537 CAESAR III VIR R P C, helmeted and dr. bust of youthful Mars r., spear over shoulder. Rev. S–C either side of legionary eagle between two standards, trophy in background. RRC 497/3. CRI 138. BMCRR Gaul 96. RSC 248. *[Macedonia, autumn 42 BC].*
VF £250 ($400) / **EF** £600 ($960)

1538 C CAESAR III VIR R P C, bare hd. of Octavian r. Rev. L LIVINEIVS REGVLVS, Victory stg. r., holding wreath and palm. RRC 494/25. CRI 157. BMCRR 4260. RSC 443. *[Rome, 42 BC].*
VF £350 ($560) / **EF** £850 ($1,360)

1539 Obv. Similar. Rev. BALBVS PRO PR, club. RRC 518/1. CRI 298. BMCRR Gaul 83. RSC 417. *[Italy, late 41 BC].* VF £375 ($600) / **EF** £900 ($1,440)

1540 Obv. Similar. Rev. POPVL IVSSV, equestrian statue of Octavian galloping l., his r. hand raised. RRC 518/2. CRI 299. BMCRR Gaul 79. RSC 227. *[Italy, late 41 BC].*
VF £300 ($480) / **EF** £750 ($1,200)

1541 1543

1541 Obv. Similar. Rev. Q SALVIVS IMP COS DESIG, thunderbolt. RRC 523/1. CRI 300. BMCRR Gaul 88. RSC 514. *[Italy, early 40 BC].* VF £225 ($360) / **EF** £550 ($880)

1542 DIVOS IVLIVS – DIVI F, wreathed hd. of Caesar r., facing bare hd. of Octavian l. Rev. M AGRIPPA COS / DESIG in two lines across field. RRC 534/2. CRI 306. BMCRR Gaul 100. RSC J. *Caesar and Octavian 5. [Italy or Gaul, 38 BC].*
VF £1,500 ($2,400) / **EF** £4,000 ($6,400)

1543 Similar, but with obv. IMP CAESAR DIVI IVLI F, bare hd. of Octavian r. RRC 534/3. CRI 307. BMCRR Gaul 103. RSC 545. *[Italy or Gaul, 38 BC].*
VF £375 ($600) / **EF** £900 ($1,440)

1544   **Silver denarius.** IMP CAESAR DIVI F III VIR ITER R P C, bare hd. of Octavian r. Rev. COS
       ITER ET TER DESIG, simpulum, sprinkler, jug and lituus (emblems of the augurate and pon-
       tificate). RRC 538/1. CRI 312. BMCRR Gaul 116. RSC 91. *[Italy, summer 37 BC].*
                                                        VF £225 ($360) / **EF** £550 ($880)

1545   As 1529 (rev. COS ITER ET TER DESIG, temple of Divus Julius). RRC 540/2. CRI 315.
       BMCRR Africa 33. RSC 90. *[Italy, spring–summer 36 BC].*
                                                        VF £250 ($400) / **EF** £600 ($960)

1546   No legend, bare hd. of Octavian r. Rev. IMP CAESAR DIVI F, round shield with studs. RIC
       543a. CRI 392. BMCRR Gaul 119 (= BMCRE 309). RSC 126. *[Italy or Illyricum,*
       35–34 BC].   **VF** £300 ($480) / **EF** £750 ($1,200)

        1546   1548

1547   Obv. Similar. Rev. CAESAR DIVI F, Venus stg. r., holding helmet and transverse sceptre and
       resting on column, at base of which is shield. RIC 250a. CRI 395. BMCRR 4333
       (= BMCRE 599). RSC 62. *[Rome (?), 32–31 BC].*   **VF** £275 ($440) / **EF** £650 ($1,040)

1548   No legend, diad. hd. of Venus r. Rev. — Octavian, in military attire, advancing l., his r.
       hand extended and holding transverse spear in l. RIC 251. CRI 397. BMCRR 4327 (=
       BMCRE 609). RSC 70. *[Rome (?), 32–31 BC].*   **VF** £250 ($400) / **EF** £600 ($960)

        1549   1550

1549   — diad. hd. of Pax r., olive-branch before, cornucopiae behind. Rev. — Octavian, in mili-
       tary attire, walking r., his r. hand raised and holding spear over shoulder in l. RIC 253. CRI
       400. BMCRR 4329 (= BMCRE 611). RSC 72. *[Rome (?), 32–31 BC].*
                                                        VF £250 ($400) / **EF** £600 ($960)

1550   — bare hd. of Octavian r. Rev. — naked Mercury seated r. on rock, holding lyre. RIC 257.
       CRI 401. BMCRR 4335 (= BMCRE 596). RSC 61. *[Rome (?), 32–31 BC].*
                                                        VF £275 ($440) / **EF** £650 ($1,040)

1551   Obv. Similar. Rev. — Pax stg. l., holding olive-branch and cornucopiae. RIC 252. CRI
       399. BMCRR East 236 (= BMCRE 605). RSC 69. *[Rome (?), 32–31 BC].*
                                                        VF £275 ($440) / **EF** £650 ($1,040)

1552 1553

1552 **Silver denarius.** No legend, bare hd. of Octavian l. Rev. **CAESAR DIVI F**, Victory stg. l. on globe, holding wreath and palm. RIC 254b. CRI 407. BMCRR 4339 (= BMCRE 603). RSC 64. *[Rome (?), 31–30 BC].*   **VF** £275 ($440) / **EF** £650 ($1,040)

1553 — winged bust of Victory r. Rev. — Octavian, as Neptune, stg. l., r. foot on globe, holding aplustre and sceptre. RIC 256. CRI 409. BMCRR 4341 (= BMCRE 615). RSC 60. *[Rome (?), 31–30 BC].*   **VF** £275 ($440) / **EF** £650 ($1,040)

1554 **IMP CAESARI SCARPVS IMP,** open r. hand. Rev. **DIVI F AVG PONT** *(sic)*, Victory stg. r. on globe, holding wreath and palm. RRC 546/6. RIC 534. CRI 413. BMCRR Cyrenaica 5 (= BMCRE 689). RSC 500. *[Cyrene, autumn 31 BC].*   **VF** £850 ($1,360) / **EF** £2,000 ($3,200)

1555 1556

1555 No legend, Victory stg. r. on prow of galley, holding wreath and palm. Rev. **IMP CAESAR,** Octavian in triumphal quadriga r., holding branch. RIC 264. CRI 416. BMCRR 4343 (= BMCRE 617). RSC 115. *[Rome (?), autumn 30 BC].*   **VF** £225 ($360) / **EF** £550 ($880)

1556 — bare hd. of Octavian r. Rev. — trophy set on prow, crossed rudder and anchor at base. RIC 265a. CRI 419. BMCRR 4352 (= BMCRE 625). RSC 119. *[Rome (?), 30–29 BC].*   **VF** £250 ($400) / **EF** £600 ($960)

1557 Obv. Similar. Rev. **IMP CAESAR** on architrave of the Curia Julia (Roman Senate House), with porch supported by four short columns. RIC 266. CRI 421. BMCRR 4358 (= BMCRE 631). RSC 122. *[Rome (?), 30–29 BC].*   **VF** £300 ($480) / **EF** £750 ($1,200) *The official dedication of the Curia Julia (which still stands in the Roman Forum) took place on 28 August 29 BC. For the statue of Victory surmounting the apex of this building, see no. 1532.*

1558 Obv. Similar. Rev. **IMP CAESAR** on architrave of the Actian arch, depicted as a single span surmounted by large statue of Octavian in facing triumphal quadriga. RIC 267. CRI 422. BMCRR 4348 (= BMCRE 624). RSC 123. *[Rome (?), 30–29 BC].*   **VF** £300 ($480) / **EF** £750 ($1,200) *For a later depiction of this arch, see no. 1590.*

1559   1560

1559   **Silver denarius.** No legend, laur. hd. of Octavian, as Apollo, r. Rev. IMP CAESAR, statue of Octavian stg. facing, holding spear and parazonium, on rostral column decorated with anchors and beaks of galleys. RIC 271. CRI 423. BMCRR 4349 (= BMCRE 633). RSC 124. *[Rome (?), 30–29 BC].*   VF £275 ($440) / EF £650 ($1,040)

1560   — laur. hd. of the Actian Apollo r. Rev. — Octavian, as city founder of Nicopolis, ploughing r. with yoke of oxen. RIC 272. CRI 424. BMCRR 4363 (= BMCRE 638). RSC 117. *[Rome (?), 30–29 BC].*   VF £275 ($440) / EF £650 ($1,040)

1561   1562

1561   — bare hd. of Octavian r. Rev. — ithyphallic boundary-stone of Jupiter Terminus, surmounted by laur. facing hd. of Octavian, thunderbolt below. RIC 269a. CRI 425. BMCRR 4360 (= BMCRE 628). RSC 114. *[Rome (?), 30–29 BC].*
          VF £300 ($480) / EF £750 ($1,200)

1562   — laur. hd. of Octavian, as Jupiter Terminus, r., thunderbolt behind. Rev. — Octavian seated l. on curule chair, holding Victory. RIC 270. CRI 427. BMCRR 4362 (= BMCRE 637). RSC 116. *[Rome (?), 30–29 BC].*   VF £325 ($520) / EF £800 ($1,280)

1563   IMP below helmeted hd. of youthful Mars r. Rev. CAESAR around rim of circular shield on top of sword and spear in saltire. RIC 274. CRI 428. BMCRR 4368 (= BMCRE 644). RSC 44. *[Rome (?), 30–29 BC].*   VF £275 ($440) / EF £650 ($1,040)

1564   1568

1564   CAESAR COS VI, bare hd. of Octavian l., lituus behind. Rev. AEGVPTO CAPTA, crocodile r. RIC 275b. CRI 431. BMCRR East 245 (= BMCRE 652). RSC 3. *[Rome (?), 28 BC].*
          VF £1,000 ($1,600) / EF £2,500 ($4,000)

*This type and the next celebrate the conquest of the Ptolemaic kingdom of Egypt in August,
30 BC, the event which removed the last obstacle to Octavian's achievement of supreme
power in the Roman world.*

1565   **Silver denarius.** Similar, but with obv. CAESAR DIVI F COS VI, bare hd. of Octavian r.,
       small capricorn below. RIC 545. CRI 432. BMCRR East 246 (= BMCRE 653). RSC 4.
       [Asia (?), 28 BC].   **VF** £1,200 ($1,920) / **EF** £3,000 ($4,800)

1566   **Silver quinarius.** IMP CAESAR, galley r., with rowers and sail. Rev. DIVI F, Victory stg. l.,
       holding wreath, palm, and rudder. CRI 315A. BMCRR Africa 38. RSC 94. *[Italy,
       spring–summer 36 BC].*   **VF** £500 ($800) / **EF** £1,250 ($2,000)

1567   SCARPVS IMP, open r. hand. Rev. CAESARI DIVI F, Victory stg. r., holding wreath and palm.
       RRC 546/8. CRI 415. BMCRR Cyrenaica 7 (= BMCRE 687). RSC 499. *[Cyrene, autumn
       31 BC].*   **VF** £600 ($960) / **EF** £1,500 ($2,400)

1568   CAESAR IMP VII, bare hd. of Octavian r. Rev. ASIA RECEPTA, Victory stg. l. on cista mystica
       flanked by two snakes. RIC 276. CRI 429. BMCRR East 240 (= BMCRE 647). RSC 14.
       [Rome (?), 29–28 BC].   **VF** £90 ($144) / **EF** £250 ($400)

1569

1569   **Bronze sestertius (or dupondius?).** CAESAR DIVI F, bare hd. of Octavian r. Rev. DIVOS
       IVLIVS, wreathed hd. of Caesar r. RPC 620. RRC 535/1. CRI 308. BMCRR Gaul 106.
       C *J. Caesar and Octavian 3. [Italy, 38 BC].*   **F** £250 ($400) / **VF** £750 ($1,200)

1570

1570   DIVI F, bare hd. of Octavian r., star (*sidus Iulium*) before. Rev. DIVOS / IVLIVS in two lines
       within laurel-wreath. RPC 621. RRC 535/2. CRI 309. BMCRR Gaul 108. C 95. *[Italy,
       38 BC].*   **F** £225 ($360) / **VF** £650 ($1,040)

For a possible portrait of Octavian on denarii of the moneyer M. Arrius Secundus (41 BC), see nos. 500 and 501. For Octavian's post-27 BC issues as Augustus, see below under Roman Imperial Coinage.

OCTAVIAN AND MARK ANTONY

1571

During the early years of their long association the two principal triumvirs honoured each other frequently on their coin issues, beginning with the series commemorating the establishment of the Second Triumvirate in November of 43 BC. These issues ceased abruptly about five years later and Antony and Octavian never even met again after Antony's departure from Italy in the late summer of 37.

1571   **Gold aureus.** C CAESAR IMP III VIR R P C PONT AV (NT and AV in monogram), bare hd. of
       Octavian r. Rev. M ANTONIVS IMP III VIR R P C AVG (AV in monogram), bare hd. of
       M. Antony r. RRC 493/1b. CRI 133. BMCRR Gaul 59. C *M. Antony and Octavian* 3.
       [Cisalpine Gaul, Nov.–Dec. 43 BC].   **VF** £5,500 ($8,800) / **EF** £10,000 ($16,000)

1572   Similar, but with legends CAESAR IMP on obv. and ANTONIVS IMP on rev. RRC 529/1. CRI
       301. BMCRR Gaul 90. C *M. Antony and Octavian* 5. *[Italy, late 40–early 39 BC].*
                                                    VF £4,500 ($7,200) / **EF** £8,000 ($12,800)

1573   **Silver denarius.** CAESAR IMP, bare hd. of Octavian r. Rev. ANTONIVS IMP, caduceus. RRC
       529/2c. CRI 302a. BMCRR Gaul 92. RSC *Augustus* 6a. *[Italy, late 40–early 39 BC].*
                                                    VF £250 ($400) / **EF** £600 ($960)

1574   1575

1574   ANTONIVS IMP, bare hd. of M. Antony r. Rev. CAESAR IMP, caduceus. RRC 529/3. CRI
       303. BMCRR Gaul 94. RSC *M. Antony* 5. *[Italy, late 40–early 39 BC].*
                                                    VF £450 ($720) / **EF** £1,100 ($1,760)
       *Octavian, by omitting his own portrait and relegating his name to the reverse, here
       accords his triumviral colleague a remarkable precedence. Antony's name also appears
       before that of Octavian on the following quinarius.*

1575   **Silver quinarius.** III VIR R P C, veiled and diad. hd. of Concordia r. Rev. M ANTON C
       CAESAR, clasped hands holding caduceus. RRC 529/4b. CRI 304. BMCRR East 128. RSC
       M. Antony 67. *[Gaul, late 39 BC].*   **VF** £80 ($128) / **EF** £225 ($360)

For other coins depicting Octavian and Mark Antony, see under Antony's Fleet Coinage and under
Mark Antony and Octavian.

ROMAN IMPERIAL COINAGE, 27 BC–AD 491

PRINCIPAL CHRONOLOGICAL CRITERIA OF THE IMPERIAL COINAGE FROM 31 BC TO AD 96

Octavian/Augustus

	TR P	IMP	COS	Other Titles	Alexandrian Regnal
31 BC		VI	III		
30 BC			IV		1 (L A)
29 BC		VII	V		1–2 (L A–B)
28 BC			VI		2–3 (L B–Γ)
27 BC			VII	AVGVSTVS	3–4 (L Γ-Δ)
26 BC			VIII		4–5 (L Δ–E)
25 BC		VIII	IX		5–6 (L E–S)
24 BC			X		6–7 (L S–Z)
23 BC	I		XI		7–8 (L Z–H)
22 BC	I–II				8–9 (L H–Θ)
21 BC	II–III				9–10 (L Θ–I)
20 BC	III–IV	IX			10–11 (L I–IA)
19 BC	IV–V				11–12 (L IA–IB)
18 BC	V–VI				12–13 (L IB–IΓ)
17 BC	VI–VII				13–14 (L IΓ–IΔ)
16 BC	VII–VIII				14–15 (L IΔ–IE)
15 BC	VIII–IX	X			15–16 (L IE–IS)
14 BC	IX–X				16–17 (L IS–IZ)
13 BC	X–XI		(Tiberius I)		17–18 (L IZ–IH)
12 BC	XI–XII	XI		P M	18–19 (L IH–IΘ)
11 BC	XII–XIII	XII			19–20 (L IΘ–K)
10 BC	XIII–XIV				20–21 (L K–KA)
9 BC	XIV–XV	XIII (Tiberius I)			21–22 (L KA–KB)
8 BC	XV–XVI	XIV (Tiberius II)			22–23 (L KB–KΓ)
7 BC	XVI–XVII		(Tiberius II)		23–24 (L KΓ–KΔ)
6 BC	XVII–XVIII (Tiberius I)				24–25 (L KΔ–KE)
5 BC	XVIII–XIX (Tiberius I–II)		XII		25–26 (L KE–KS)

Augustus (*cont.*)

	TR P	IMP	COS	Other Titles	Alexandrian Regnal
4 BC	XIX–XX (**Tiberius** II–III)				26–27 (L KS–KZ)
3 BC	XX–XXI (**Tiberius** III–IV)				27–28 (L KZ–KH)
2 BC	XXI–XXII (**Tiberius** IV–V)	XV	XIII	P P	28–29 (L KH–KΘ)
1 BC	XXII–XXIII				29–30 (L KΘ–Λ)
AD 1	XXIII–XXIV				30–31 (L Λ–ΛA)
AD 2	XXIV–XXV				31–32 (L ΛA–ΛB)
AD 3	XXV–XXVI				32–33 (L ΛB–ΛΓ)
AD 4	XXVI–XXVII (**Tiberius** VI)	XVI			33–34 (L ΛΓ–ΛΔ)
AD 5	XXVII–XXVIII (**Tiberius** VI–VII)				34–35 (L ΛΔ–ΛE)
AD 6	XXVIII–XXIX (**Tiberius** VII–VIII)	XVII (**Tiberius** III)			35–36 (L ΛE–ΛS)
AD 7	XXIX–XXX (**Tiberius** VIII–IX)				36–37 (L ΛS–ΛZ)
AD 8	XXX–XXXI (**Tiberius** IX–X)	XVIII			37–38 (L ΛZ–ΛH)
AD 9	XXXI–XXXII (**Tiberius** X–XI)	XIX (**Tiberius** IV)			38–39 (L ΛH–ΛΘ)
AD 10	XXXII–XXXIII (**Tiberius** XI–XII)	(**Tiberius** V)			39–40 (L ΛΘ–M)
AD 11	XXXIII–XXXIV (**Tiberius** XII–XIII)	XX (**Tiberius** VI)			40–41 (L M–MA)
AD 12	XXXIV–XXXV (**Tiberius** XIII–XIV)				41–42 (L MA–MB)
AD 13	XXXV–XXXVI (**Tiberius** XIV–XV)				42–43 (L MB–MΓ)
AD 14	XXXVI–XXXVII (**Tiberius** XV–XVI)	XXI (**Tiberius** VII)			43 (L MΓ)

Tiberius

	TR P	IMP	COS	Other Titles	Alexandrian Regnal
AD 14	XVI			AVGVSTVS	1 (L A)
AD 15	XVI–XVII			P M	1–2 (L A–B)
AD 16	XVII–XVIII				2–3 (L B–Γ)
AD 17	XVIII–XIX				3–4 (L Γ–Δ)
AD 18	XIX–XX		III		4–5 (L Δ–E)
AD 19	XX–XXI				5–6 (L E–S)
AD 20	XXI–XXII				6–7 (L S–Z)
AD 21	XXII–XXIII	VIII	IV		7–8 (L Z–H)
AD 22	XXIII–XXIV (**Drusus** I)				8–9 (L H–Θ)
AD 23	XXIV–XXV (**Drusus** I–II)				9–10 (L Θ–I)
AD 24	XXV–XXVI				10–11 (L I–IA)
AD 25	XXVI–XXVII				11–12 (L IA–IB)
AD 26	XXVII–XXVIII				12–13 (L IB–IΓ)
AD 27	XXVIII–XXIX				13–14 (L IΓ–IΔ)

Tiberius (*cont.*)

	TR P	IMP	COS	Other Titles	Alexandrian Regnal
AD 28	XXIX–XXX				14–15 (L IΔ–IE)
AD 29	XXX–XXXI				15–16 (L IE–IS)
AD 30	XXXI–XXXII				16–17 (L IS–IZ)
AD 31	XXXII–XXXIII	V			17–18 (L IZ–IH)
AD 32	XXXIII–XXXIV				18–19 (L IH–IΘ)
AD 33	XXXIV–XXXV		(Galba I)		19–20 (L IΘ–K)
AD 34	XXXV–XXXVI				20–21 (L K–KA)
AD 35	XXXVI–XXXVII				21–22 (L KA–KB)
AD 36	XXXVII–XXXVIII				22–23 (L KB–KΓ)
AD 37	XXXVIII				23 (L KΓ)

Caligula

	TR P	IMP	COS	Other Titles	Alexandrian Regnal
AD 37	I		I	AVGVSTVS, P M	1–2 (L A-B)
			(Claudius I)		
AD 38	I–III			P P	2–3 (L B–Γ)
AD 39	II–III		II		3–4 (L Γ–Δ)
AD 40	III–IV		III		4–5 (L Δ–E)
AD 41	IV		IV		5 (L E)

Claudius

	TR P	IMP	COS	Other Titles	Alexandrian Regnal
AD 41	I	I–IV		AVGVSTVS, P M	1–2 (L A–B)
AD 42	I–II		II	P P	2–3 (L B–Γ)
AD 43	II–III		III		3–4 (L Γ–Δ)
AD 44	III–IV	V–VII			4–5 (L Δ–E)
AD 45	IV–V	VIII			5–6 (L E–S)
AD 46	V–VI	IX–XI		BRITANNICVS	6–7 (L S–Z)
AD 47	VI–VII	XII–XIII	IV	CENSOR	7–8 (L Z–H)
AD 48	VII–VIII	XIV–XV		CENSOR	8–9 (L H–Θ)
AD 49	VIII–IX	XVI			9–10 (L Θ–I)
AD 50	IX–X	XVII–XX			10–11 (L I–IA)
AD 51	X–XI	XXI–XXIII	V		11–12 (L IA–IB)
			(Vespasian I)		
AD 52	XI–XII	XXIV–XXVI			12–13 (L IB–IΓ)
AD 53	XII–XIII	XXVII			13–14 (L IΓ–IΔ)
AD 54	XIII–XIV				14–15 (L IΔ–IE)

Nero

	TR P	IMP	COS	Other Titles	Alexandrian Regnal
AD 54	I	I		AVGVSTVS	1 (L A)
AD 55	I–II	II	I	P M, P P	1–2 (L A–B)
AD 56	II–III				2–3 (L B–Γ)
AD 57	III–IV	III	II		3–4 (L Γ–Δ)
AD 58	IV–V	IV–V	III		4–5 (L Δ–E)
AD 59	V–VI	VI			5–6 (L E–S)
AD 60	VI–VII	VII	IV		6–7 (L S–Z)
AD 61	VII–VIII	VIII–IX			7–8 (L Z–H)
AD 62	VIII–IX				8–9 (L H–Θ)

Nero (*cont.*)

	TR P	IMP	COS	Other Titles	Alexandrian Regnal
AD 63	IX–X				9–10 (L Ө–I)
AD 64	X–XI				10–11 (L I–IA)
AD 65	XI–XII				11–12 (L IA–IB)
AD 66	XII–XIII	X–XI			12–13 (L IB–IΓ)
AD 67	XIII–XIV	XII			13–14 (L IΓ–IΔ)
AD 68	XIV		V		14 (L IΔ)

Galba

AD 68	I	I		AVGVSTVS, P M	1–2 (L A–B)
AD 69	I		II		2 (L B)

Otho

AD 69	I	I	I	AVGVSTVS, P M	1 (L A)

Vitellius

AD 69	I	I	I	AVGVSTVS, P M, GERMANICVS	1 (L A)

Vespasian

AD 69	I	I–II		AVGVSTVS (**Titus** CAESAR, **Domitian** CAESAR)	1–2 (L A–B)
AD 70	I–II	III–V	II (**Titus** I)	P M, P P	2–3 (L B–Γ)
AD 71	II–III (**Titus** I)	VI–VIII (**Titus** I–II)	III (**Domitian** I)		3–4 (L Γ–Δ)
AD 72	III–IV (**Titus** I–II)	IX (**Titus** III)	IV (**Titus** II)		4–5 (L Δ–E)
AD 73	IV–V (**Titus** II–III)	X (**Titus** IV)	IV (**Domitian** II)	CENSOR (and **Titus**)	5–6 (L E–S)
AD 74	V–VI (**Titus** III–IV)	XI–XII (**Titus** V–VI)	V (**Titus** III, **Domitian** III)		6–7 (L S–Z)
AD 75	VI–VII (**Titus** IV–V)	XIII–XIV (**Titus** VII–VIII)	VI (**Titus** IV)		7–8 (L Z–H)
AD 76	VII–VIII (**Titus** V–VI)	XV–XVIII (**Titus** IX–XII)	VII (**Titus** V, **Domitian** IV)		8–9 (L H–Ө)
AD 77	VIII–IX (**Titus** VI–VII)		VIII (**Titus** VI, **Domitian** V)		9–10 (L Ө–I)
AD 78	IX–X (**Titus** VII–VIII)	XIX (**Titus** XIII)			10–11 (L I–IA)
AD 79	X (**Titus** VIII)	XX (**Titus** XIV)	IX (**Titus** VII, **Domitian** VI)		11 (L IA)

Titus

	TR P	IMP	COS	Other Titles	Alexandrian Regnal
AD 79	VIII–IX	XV		AVGVSTVS, P M, P P	1–2 (L A–B)
AD 80	IX–X		VIII (**Domitian** VII)		2–3 (L B–Γ)
AD 81	X–XI	XVI–XVII			3–4 (L Γ–Δ)

Domitian

	TR P	IMP	COS	Other Titles	Alexandrian Regnal
AD 81	I	I		AVGVSTVS, P M, P P	1 (L A)
AD 82	I–II	I	VIII		1–2 (L A–B)
AD 83	II–III	III–IV	IX	GERMANICVS	2–3 (L B–Γ)
AD 84	III–IV	V–VII	X		3–4 (L Γ–Δ)
AD 85	IV–V	VIII–XI	XI	CENSOR, later PERPETVVS	4–5 (L Δ–E)
AD 86	V–VI	XII–XIV	XII		5–6 (L E–S)
AD 87	VI–VII		XIII		6–7 (L S–Z)
AD 88	VII–VIII	XV–XVII	XIV		7–8 (L Z–H)
AD 89	VIII–IX	XVIII–XXI			8–9 (L H–Θ)
AD 90	IX–X		XV		9–10 (L Θ–I)
AD 91	X–XI				10–11 (L I–IA)
AD 92	XI–XII	XXII	XVI		11–12 (L IA–IB)
AD 93	XII–XIII				12–13 (L IB–IΓ)
AD 94	XIII–XIV				13–14 (L IΓ–IΔ)
AD 95	XIV–XV		XVII		14–15 (L IΔ–IE)
AD 96	XV–XVI				15–16 (L IE-IS)

Principal references:

BMCG = R.S. Poole, *A Catalogue of the Greek Coins in the British Museum*, Alexandria and the Nomes. London, 1892.

BMCRE = H. Mattingly, R.A.G. Carson, *Coins of the Roman Empire in the British Museum*, vols. I–VI. London, 1923–62.

BMCRR = H.A. Grueber, *Coins of the Roman Republic in the British Museum*. London, 1910.

C = H. Cohen, *Description Historique des Monnaies Frappées sous l'Empire Romain*, vols. I–VIII. 2nd edition. Paris, 1880–92.

CBN = J.-B. Giard, *Catalogue des Monnaies de l'Empire Romain*, vols. I–III. Paris, 1976–98.

Cologne = A. Geissen, W. Weiser, *Katalog Alexandrinischer Kaisermünzen der Sammlung des Instituts für Altertumskunde der Universitat zu Koln*. Opladen, 1974–83.

CSS = P.V. Hill, *The Coinage of Septimius Severus and his Family of the Mint of Rome*, AD *193–217*. London, 1977.

Dattari = G. Dattari, *Numi Augg. Alexandrini*. Cairo, 1901.

Milne = J.G. Milne, *Catalogue of Alexandrian Coins*, University of Oxford, Ashmolean Museum. Oxford, 1971.

RIC = H. Mattingly and E.A. Sydenham, P.H. Webb, J.W.E. Pearce, P.M. Bruun, C.H.V. Sutherland, J.P.C. Kent, *The Roman Imperial Coinage*, vols. I–X. London, 1923–94.

RPC = A. Burnett, M. Amandry and P.P. Ripolles, *Roman Provincial Coinage*, vol. I. London and Paris, 1992.

RSC = H.A. Seaby, C.E. King, *Roman Silver Coins*, vols. I–V. London, 1952–87.

UCR = P.V. Hill, *The Dating and Arrangement of the Undated Coins of Rome*, AD *98–148*. London, 1970.

The 'Twelve Caesars' as depicted on their silver denarii

The coinage of the Roman Empire extends over a period of more than five hundred years, from the establishment of autocratic rule in the city on the Tiber by Caesar's heir, Octavian (now called Augustus), down to the accession in Constantinople ('New Rome') of Anastasius I, whose monetary reforms at the end of the 5th century mark the commencement of what is generally termed 'Byzantine' coinage.

For the first two and three-quarter centuries of its production the Roman Imperial coinage maintained a remarkable uniformity. Rome remained the principal mint throughout this lengthy period, though from the later years of Augustus to the coinage reform of Nero in AD 64 the Gallic mint of Lugdunum seems to have been responsible for most of the precious metal issues. The same mint was also active in the large scale production of *aes* from Nero's later years into early Flavian times. Otherwise, provincial minting centres played a significant role only at times of civil war, such as the years following the downfall of Nero in AD 68 and the assassination of Pertinax in 193. Mint marks were almost unknown before the mid-3rd century, though a few had appeared on eastern issues of aurei and denarii in the initial phase of Vespasian's reign.

With the economic and political collapse of the state in the second half of the 3rd century many of the old traditions of the Augustan monetary system disappeared. Production of the *aes* denominations virtually ceased, the silver coinage became hopelessly debased, and there was a rapid decentralization of production, with important new minting centres now being permanently established in the Balkans and in the East. As the imperial residence Rome remained a prominent mint, though it had forever lost its position of pre-eminence.

The sweeping reforms of Diocletian and Constantine in the late 3rd and early 4th centuries brought drastic changes not only to the imperial coinage but also to the way in which the government and defence of the Empire were organized. Being too far removed from the vital frontier regions Rome finally ceased to be the seat of imperial administration. A whole network of mints was now operating throughout the eastern and western provinces of the Empire, supplying the needs of a population which was frequently ruled by a duality or plurality of emperors based in various strategic centres. But the Empire was never again to enjoy the remarkable stability which had been such a feature of the Augustan currency system. Good quality silver coins were reintroduced by Diocletian in the final decade of the 3rd century, but the experiment was short-lived and it was not until ca. 325 that Constantine succeeded in reintegrating the metal back into the monetary system. The history of the *aes* denominations in the 4th and 5th centuries was even more unsettled, with a bewildering succession of reforms and weight reductions which must have seemed almost as incomprehensible to the citizens of the time as they do to numismatists today.

The only real stability in the late Roman currency system was provided by the gold coinage. About AD 310 Constantine the Great introduced a new lighter-weight standard gold denomination known as the solidus. This coin was to have a long and illustrious history extending deep into the Byzantine period. An even more significant innovation by the first Christian emperor was his establishment two decades later of a new imperial capital at Constantinople, on the site of old Byzantium, at the crossroads of Europe and Asia. This was to mark the beginning of a whole new chapter in imperial history. The Christian Empire was to endure for more than a millennium, until the Turkish conquest of 1453, ironically ensuring the survival of much of the science and literature of the classical world of Greece and Rome through its meticulous preservation of pagan writings.

NB The following listings represent only a sample selection of the known types and varieties. For a catalogue of all the silver coins of the Imperial period, see 'Roman Silver Coins' vols. I–V, by H.A. Seaby and C.E. King.

THE TWELVE CAESARS:
1. THE JULIO-CLAUDIAN DYNASTY, 27 BC–AD 68

The Twelve Caesars is a term derived from the *De vita Caesarum* ('The Lives of the Caesars') written by Hadrian's secretary Suetonius (Gaius Suetonius Tranquillus). This somewhat racy biographical work covers Julius Caesar and the first eleven emperors, from Augustus to Domitian, thus encompassing the Julio-Claudian dynasty, the ephemeral emperors of the civil war period (AD 68–69), and the Flavian dynasty.

AUGUSTUS
16 January 27 BC–19 August AD 14

1587

*Through the gradual elimination of all his political rivals over the period 44–30 BC, and the consti-
tutional reorganizations of the early years of his reign, the emperor Augustus had, with the utmost
subtlety, guided the transition of the Roman government from a republic to a monarchy. The
changes enacted in the summer of 23 BC put the finishing touches to this process. In this year he
resigned the consulship, which he had held continuously since 31 BC, receiving in its place proconsular imperium over all of Rome's territories. At the same time he obtained a lifetime grant of the
tribunician power ('tribunicia potestas') thereby acquiring the absolute right of veto. These developments were of immense importance as the gave Augustus, and all of his successors, complete
control of the state. Despite the outward appearance of constitutionality in the form of his authority
Augustus had effected a revolution in the government of the Roman Empire. What was even more
remarkable was that he had accomplished the transformation almost imperceptibly, so awed were
the Roman people with the personal 'auctoritas' of their leader, now generally referred to as the
'princeps'. Under his enlightened administration the Empire prospered and stability was restored
to all aspects of life, from the revival of agriculture in war-torn Italy to the complete reform of the
state's finances and money. The Augustan currency system was to set the pattern for the Roman
Imperial coinage for the first two and three-quarter centuries of its history.*

*Despite his delicate constitution and frequent bouts of ill-health Augustus lived for seventy-
seven years. In the latter part of his life he became increasingly concerned over the question of the
imperial succession, especially as he had begun to outlive not only his contemporaries but also
some of the younger members of the imperial family. His old friend Agrippa expired suddenly and
unexpectedly in 12 BC and even Agrippa's sons, Gaius and Lucius Caesars, grandsons of Augustus,
died tragically in AD 4 and AD 2 respectively. Augustus was left with little choice but to designate
Tiberius, the empress Livia's son by an earlier marriage, as heir to the throne. His relationship
with Tiberius had never been good and this unfortunate turn of events doubtless embittered the
emperor's final years. He died on 19 August AD 14 in the Campanian town of Nola. His legacy was
a peaceful and secure state free from the strife which had characterized the final decades of the
Senate's rule. It was small wonder than when this man passed away there was universal grieving
and a strong desire to honor his memory and commemorate his enormous achievements, which had
affected the lives of every citizen.*

For the titles and powers of this reign, including Alexandrian regnal dates, see table on pp. 305–6.

*The Augustan coinage exhibits many varieties of obv. legend and type. The following are repre-
sented by upper and lower case letters. All others are described in full:*

    A. AVGVSTVS
    B. AVGVSTVS DIVI F
    C. CAESAR
    D. CAESAR AVGVSTVS
    E. CAESAR AVGVSTVS DIVI F PATER PATRIAE
    F. CAESARI AVGVSTO
    G. IMP CAESAR
    H. No legend

    a. Bare hd. of Augustus r.   d. Laur. hd. of Augustus l.
    b. Bare hd. of Augustus l.   e. Oak-wreathed hd. of Augustus r.
    c. Laur. hd. of Augustus r.   f. Oak-wreathed hd. of Augustus l.

1576   1577

1576   **Gold aureus.** Aa. Rev. **ARMENIA CAPTA,** Victory r., kneeling on back of recumbent bull
       and cutting its throat. RIC 514. BMCRE 671 (= BMCRR East 308). CBN 977. C 8.
       [Pergamum, 19–18 BC].   **VF** £7,000 ($11,200) / **EF** £15,500 ($24,800)

The gold aureus dated back only to the time of Sulla in the late 80s BC. Republican and
Imperatorial issues were almost exclusively associated with military activity and were generally
produced by travelling mints under the authority of commanders in the field. The principal exceptions to this were the aurei struck at Rome by the colleges of moneyers in 42 and 41 BC, though
even these were produced under triumviral domination. Augustus transformed the aureus into an
integral part of his new currency system and thereafter it was produced on a regular basis by virtually all of his successors. Over the centuries there were occasional adjustments to the weight standard of the aureus. In the second half of the 3rd century this process became more frequent, and
sometimes quite erratic, as a result of the political and economic disruption which characterized
this period, but the purity of the metal was always carefully maintained. Eventually, during the
early decades of the 4th century, the aureus was gradually superseded by Constantine the Great's
new and lighter standard gold denomination, the solidus.

1577   Ca. Rev. **AVGVSTVS,** heifer walking l. RIC 538. BMCRE 659 (= BMCRR East 281). CBN
       1008. C 26. *[Uncertain eastern mint, after 27 BC].*
                                          VF £9,000 ($14,400) / **EF** £20,000 ($32,000)
       NB The illustration shows a variant with head of Augustus laureate.

1578   1580

1578   Ec. Rev. **C L CAESARES AVGVSTI F COS DESIG PRINC IVVENT,** Gaius and Lucius Caesars
       stg. facing, shields and spears between them. RIC 206. BMCRE 513. CBN 1648. C 42.
       [Lugdunum, 2 BC–AD 4].   **VF** £1,250 ($2,000) / **EF** £2,750 ($4,400)
       *Gaius and Lucius Caesars were the sons of Agrippa and Augustus' daughter Julia (see
       also nos. 1596–7, 1733–5, and 1748–51).*

1579   Bc. Rev. **IMP XII ACT,** Apollo stg. r., holding lyre. RIC 192a. BMCRE 481 (= BMCRR
       Gaul 197). CBN 1443. C 162. *[Lugdunum, 11–10 BC].*
                                          VF £2,500 ($4,000) / **EF** £5,500 ($8,800)
       *In commemoration of the victory over Antony and Cleopatra at the battle of Actium on
       2 Sept. 31 BC.*

1580   **Gold aureus.** Bc. Rev. IMP XIIII, Augustus seated l. on platform, receiving child from bar-
        barian stg. r. before him. RIC 200. BMCRE 492 (= BMCRR Gaul 215). CBN 1451. C 174.
        [Lugdunum, 8 BC].   **VF** £5,000 ($8,000) / **EF** £11,000 ($17,600)

1581   De. Rev. L AQVILLIVS FLORVS III VIR, open six-petalled flower. RIC 308. BMCRE 45
        (= BMCRR 4552). CBN 110. C 363. *[Rome, 19 BC].*
                                                     VF £12,000 ($19,200) / **EF** £26,000 ($41,600)

1582   Fd. Rev. S P Q R, triumphal quadriga r., containing legionary eagle and surmounted by four
        miniature horses galloping r. RIC 107b. BMCRE 390 (= BMCRR 4428). CBN 1182. C
        273. *[Colonia Patricia, 18 BC].*   **VF** £3,500 ($5,600) / **EF** £7,500 ($12,000)
        *This type is to be associated with the temple of Mars Ultor and the negotiated return by the
        Parthians of the legionary standards captured from Crassus and Antony (see also nos.
        1634–5).*

NB Several 4-aureus multiples have also been recorded, though the only unquestionably authentic
example is one found at Pompeii in 1759. It is of the Lugdunum mint and has rev. IMP XV SICIL,
Diana huntress (C 177, illustrated in CBN pl. LXVI, a).

              1583   1584

1583   **Gold quinarius.** Bc. Rev. TR POT XXX, Victory seated r. on globe, holding wreath. RIC
        217. BMCRE 505. CBN 1680. C 317. *[Lugdunum, AD 7–8].*
                                                     VF £1,000 ($1,600) / **EF** £2,250 ($3,600)

First struck by Caesar for his Spanish triumph in 45 BC the gold quinarius, or half-aureus, was reintroduced by Augustus in 11–10 BC. Like its equivalent in silver it was coined only intermittently
and in limited quantities, though it is known for most reigns up to the mid-3rd century. Its purpose
was almost certainly ceremonial and it seems to have been intended for distributions of largess to
government officials at times of public celebration or to high-ranking officers on military
occasions.

1584   **Silver cistophorus** (= 3 denarii). Ga. Rev. AVGVSTVS, Sphinx seated r. RPC 2204. RIC
        527. BMCRE 702 (= BMCRR East 290). CBN 927. RSC 31. *[Uncertain mint in Asia,
        after 27 BC].*   **VF** £3,500 ($5,600) / **EF** £7,500 ($12,000)

The traditional denomination of the province of Asia, with origins dating back to the time of the
later Pergamene kings, the cistophorus was minted extensively under Augustus. Production was
more restricted under most of his successors and Claudius was the only other emperor amongst the
Julio-Claudians to issue cistophori. There was a resumption of production from later Flavian times
until Hadrian, the volume of whose Asian silver rivalled that of Augustus himself, but thereafter
there was an abrupt cessation of minting. An isolated late revival came early in the 3rd century
under Septimius Severus.

1585   Ga, with lituus before. Rev. — capricorn r., hd. l., cornucopiae on back, all within laurel-
        wreath. RPC 2208. RIC 488. BMCRE 698 (= BMCRR East 287). CBN 950. RSC 16a.
        [Pergamum, 27–26 BC].   **VF** £400 ($640) / **EF** £950 ($1,520)

AUGUSTUS 315

1586

1586 **Silver cistophorus** (= 3 denarii). Ga. Rev. — six ears of corn tied together in bundle. RPC 2214. RIC 481. BMCRE 697 (= BMCRR East 264). CBN 918. RSC 32b. *[Ephesus, 24–20 BC].* VF £300 ($480) / **EF** £750 ($1,200)

1587 Ga. Rev. — garlanded altar of Diana (Artemis) with bas-reliefs of two confronted hinds. RPC 2215. RIC 482. BMCRE 694 (= BMCRR East 262). CBN 922. RSC 33. *[Ephesus, 24–20 BC].* VF £325 ($520) / **EF** £800 ($1,280)

1588 IMP IX TR PO V, a. Rev. COM ASIAE, hexastyle temple of Roma and Augustus, the architrave inscribed ROM ET AVGVST. RPC 2219. RIC 506. BMCRE 705 (= BMCRR East 312). CBN 986. RSC 86. *[Pergamum, 19–18 BC].* VF £375 ($600) / **EF** £900 ($1,440)

1589

1589 — Rev. MART VLTO, domed temple of Mars Ultor containing standard. RPC 2220. RIC 507. BMCRE 704 (= BMCRR East 311). CBN 989. RSC 202. *[Pergamum, 19–18 BC].* VF £425 ($680) / **EF** £1,000 ($1,600)

The small temple of Mars the Avenger was situated on the Capitol and was built specially to house the legionary standards of Crassus and Antony recovered by Augustus from Phraates IV of Parthia (see also nos. 1582, 1623–4 and 1632–5).

1590

1590 IMP IX TR PO V Rev. S P R / SIGNIS / RECEPTIS in three lines in the opening of a single-span triumphal arch surmounted by large statue of Augustus in facing triumphal quadriga, IMP IX TR POT V on architrave. RPC 2218. RIC 510. BMCRE 703 (= BMCRR East 310). CBN 982. RSC 298. *[Pergamum, 19–18 BC].* VF £500 ($800) / **EF** £1,150 ($1,840)

This distinctive single-span arch appears to be identical to the structure which had been depicted a decade earlier on Octavian's 'IMP CAESAR' coinage (see no. 1558). In all likelihood this is the 'arcus Octaviani' erected to commemorate the victory at Actium and later demolished to make way for the larger 'arcus Augusti' which celebrated the recovery of the standards from Parthia (see no. 1606). It seems probable that the coins were struck at the time of the levelling of the Actian arch before the precise form of the new edifice had become known to the Asian die-cutters.

1591   1592

1591   **Silver denarius.** Aa. Rev. ARMENIA CAPTA, tiara on l., quiver and bow in case on r. RIC 516. BMCRE 672 (= BMCRR East 304). CBN 995. RSC 11. *[Pergamum, 19–18 BC].*
VF £650 ($1,040) / **EF** £1,500 ($2,400)

Under the Empire, as previously under the Republic, the silver denarius remained the principal denomination of the Roman coinage. In the early years of Augustus' principate Rome shared the issue of denarii and aurei with a number of provincial minting centres and eventually all production came to be concentrated at the Gallic mint of Lugdunum. This important establishment was responsible for the entire output of precious metal coinage in the later years of Augustus and throughout the reigns of the next three emperors, Tiberius, Caligula and Claudius. However, in the post-reform phase of Nero's coinage (after AD 64) Rome reasserted its primacy in this role, a position which it thereafter maintained for almost two centuries. The denarius went unchallenged until the early decades of the 3rd century, but debasement and the introduction of an inflationary double denomination ('antoninianus') led to the rapid disappearance of the historic coin. The process was complete before the middle of the century, marking the end of 450 years of virtually continuous denarius production.

1592   Ha. Rev. AVGVSTVS, capricorn r., holding globe and rudder, cornucopiae on its back. RIC 126. BMCRE 346 (= BMCRR 4374). CBN 1266. RSC 21. *[Colonia Patricia, 18–16 BC].*
VF £275 ($440) / **EF** £600 ($960)
Restorations of this type were made during the revolt of Vindex in Gaul in AD 68 (see no. 2064) and by Nerva in AD 96 (see no. 3075).

1593   1595

1593   Ca. Rev. — heifer stg. r. RIC 475. BMCRE 662 (= BMCRR East 284). CBN 941. RSC 28.
[Pergamum or Samos, 27 or 21–20 BC].   **VF** £400 ($640) / **EF** £900 ($1,440)

1594   **Silver denarius.** M DVRMIVS III VIR HONORI, hd. of Honos r., with features resembling
        Augustus. Rev. AVGVSTVS CAESAR, Augustus in biga of elephants l. RIC 311. BMCRE 52
        (= BMCRR 4560). CBN 191. RSC 427. *[Rome, 19 BC].*
                                            VF £350 ($560) / EF £800 ($1,280)

1595   Da. Rev. C ANTISTIVS REGINVS III VIR, simpulum and lituus above tripod and patera
        (emblems of the four principal priestly colleges). RIC 410. BMCRE 119 (= BMCRR
        4661). CBN 542. RSC 347. *[Rome, 13 BC].*   VF £250 ($400) / EF £550 ($880)

1596   1598

1596   Bc. Rev. C CAES AVGVS F, Gaius Caesar galloping r., legionary eagle between standards
        behind. RIC 199. BMCRE 500 (= BMCRR Gaul 223). CBN 1461. RSC 40. *[Lugdunum,
        8–7 BC].*   VF £225 ($360) / EF £500 ($800)
        *Gaius Caesar was the eldest of the three sons of Agrippa and Augustus' daughter Julia
        (see also nos. 1578, 1597, 1733–5, and 1748–9).*

1597   As 1578 (rev. C L CAESARES AVGVSTI F COS DESIG PRINC IVVENT, Gaius and Lucius
        Caesars standing facing). RIC 207. BMCRE 519. CBN 1651. RSC 43. *[Lugdunum, 2 BC–
        AD 4].*   VF £125 ($200) / EF £275 ($440)

1598   Aa, with lituus behind. Rev. C MARIVS C F TRO III VIR, quadriga galloping r., the car con-
        taining palm-branch. RIC 399. BMCRE 101 (= BMCRR 4644). CBN 517. RSC 456.
        [Rome, 13 BC].   VF £325 ($520) / EF £750 ($1,200)

1599   1600

1599   Da. Rev. C SVLPICIVS PLATORIN, Augustus and Agrippa seated l. on platform ornamented
        with rostra. RIC 407. BMCRE 115 (= BMCRR 4657). CBN 537. RSC 529. *[Rome, 13 BC].*
                                            VF £500 ($800) / EF £1,100 ($1,760)
        *Augustus' lifelong friend and colleague died the year following this issue which probably
        commemorates the renewal of Agrippa's tribunician power.*

1600   Hf. Rev. CAESAR AVGVSTVS, two laurel-branches. RIC 33b. BMCRE 318 (= BMCRR
        Gaul 144). CBN 1285. RSC 48. *[Caesaraugusta, 19–18 BC].*
                                            VF £250 ($400) / EF £550 ($880)

1601   L AQVILLIVS FLORVS III VIR, rad. hd. of Sol r., with features resembling Augustus. Rev.
        CAESAR AVGVSTVS S C, slow quadriga r., the car in form of basket containing corn-ears.
        RIC 303. BMCRE 38 (= BMCRR 4543). CBN 169. RSC 357. *[Rome, 19 BC].*
                                            VF £325 ($520) / EF £750 ($1,200)

1602   1603

1602   **Silver denarius.** Hc. Rev. CAESAR AVGVSTVS S P Q R, shield inscribed CL V between two
       laurel-branches. RIC — (omitted in error, cf. 52a for the aureus of this type). BMCRE 354
       (= BMCRR 4446). CBN 1333. RSC 51. *[Colonia Patricia or Nemausus, 19–18 BC].*
                                                       VF £250 ($400) / **EF** £550 ($880)

1603   TVRPILIANVS III VIR FERON, diad. and dr. bust of Feronia r. Rev. CAESAR AVGVSTVS SIGN
       RECE, Parthian kneeling r., presenting Roman standard. RIC 288. BMCRE 14 (= BMCRR
       4525). CBN 127. RSC 484. *[Rome, 19 BC].*   **VF** £175 ($280) / **EF** £400 ($640)
       *In commemoration of Augustus' diplomatic triumph in securing the restoration of the
       legionary standards captured from Crassus and Antony in their disastrous Parthian cam-
       paigns of 53 and 36 BC. For other types associated with this event, see nos. 1582, 1589–90,
       1606, 1623, and 1632–5).*

1604   1605

1604   S P Q R PARENT CONS SVO (NT in monogram), consular toga over tunic between legionary
       eagle and wreath. Rev. CAESARI AVGVSTO, triumphal quadriga r., surmounted by four
       miniature horses galloping r. RIC 99. BMCRE 397 (= BMCRR 4435). CBN 1191. RSC
       78. *[Colonia Patricia, 18 BC].*   **VF** £175 ($280) / **EF** £400 ($640)

1605   Q RVSTIVS FORTVNÆ ANTIAT, conjoined busts r. of Fortuna Victrix, helmeted and hold-
       ing patera, and Fortuna Felix, diad., both resting on bar with ram's hd. finials. Rev. CAESARI
       AVGVSTO EX S C, ornate rectangular altar inscribed FOR RE. RIC 322. BMCRE 2 (=
       BMCRR 4580). CBN 221. RSC 513. *[Rome, 19 BC].*   **VF** £200 ($320) / **EF** £450 ($720)

1606   S P Q R IMP CAESARI AVG COS XI TR POT VI, a. Rev. CIVIB ET SIGN MILIT A PART
       RECVPER, triple-span triumphal arch surmounted by large group of statuary, comprising
       Augustus in facing triumphal quadriga flanked by two Parthians presenting standard and
       legionary eagle. RIC 134a. BMCRE 428 (= BMCRR 4454). CBN 1232. RSC 84. *[Colonia
       Patricia, 18–17 BC].*   **VF** £350 ($560) / **EF** £800 ($1,280)
       *This depicts the 'arcus Augusti' which was erected on the site of the former Actian arch
       ('arcus Octaviani') to commemorate the return of the Roman standards held as war
       trophies by the Parthians (see also no. 1590).*

1607   Df. Rev. DIVVS IVLIVS, eight-rayed comet (*sidus Iulium*) with tail above. RIC 37b.
       BMCRE 326 (= BMCRR Gaul 138). CBN 1298. RSC 97. *[Caesaraugusta, 19–18 BC].*
                                                       VF £275 ($440) / **EF** £600 ($960)

1607   1608

The 'Julian star' was the comet which appeared in the heavens shortly after Caesar's assassination in 44 BC. It was taken as a sign of the late dictator's divinity (see also nos. 1570 and 1621–2). A restoration of this type was made during the revolt of Vindex in Gaul in AD 68 (see no. 2065).

1608   **Silver denarius.** Hd. Rev. Large altar inscribed FORT RED / CAES AVG / S P Q R in three lines. RIC 54b. BMCRE 360 (= BMCRR 4444). CBN 1349. RSC 106. *[Colonia Patricia or Nemausus, 19–18 BC].*   VF £300 ($480) / **EF** £650 ($1,040)
       This celebrates the safe return of Augustus from the East in 19 BC.

1609   Ba. Rev. IMP X, Augustus seated l. on platform, receiving olive-branches from two soldiers stg. r. before him. RIC 165a. BMCRE 445 (= BMCRR Gaul 157). CBN 1366. RSC 133. *[Lugdunum, 15–13 BC].*   VF £250 ($400) / **EF** £550 ($880)

1610   1611

1610   Ba. Rev. IMP X, bull butting r. RIC 167a. BMCRE 451 (= BMCRR Gaul 163). CBN 1373. RSC 137. *[Lugdunum, 15–13 BC].*   VF £200 ($320) / **EF** £450 ($720)

1611   Ba. Rev. IMP X ACT, the Actian Apollo stg. l., holding plectrum and lyre. RIC 171a. BMCRE 461 (= BMCRR Gaul 175). CBN 1396. RSC 144. *[Lugdunum, 15–13 BC].*
       VF £200 ($320) / **EF** £450 ($720)
       In commemoration of the victory over Antony and Cleopatra at the battle of Actium on 2 Sept. 31 BC.

1612   Ba. Rev. IMP X SICIL, Diana stg. l., looking r., holding spear and bow, hound at her feet. RIC 173a. BMCRE 463 (= BMCRR Gaul 171). CBN 1392. RSC 146. *[Lugdunum, 15–13 BC].*   VF £275 ($440) / **EF** £600 ($960)
       In commemoration of the victory over Sextus Pompey at the battle of Naulochus on 3 Sept. 36 BC.

1613   Da. Rev. IOV TON, hexastyle temple of Jupiter Tonans containing statue of the god stg. l., holding thunderbolt and sceptre. RIC — (omitted in error, cf. 63a for the aureus of this type). BMCRE 363 (= BMCRR 4415). CBN 1098. RSC 179. *[Colonia Patricia, 19 BC].*
       VF £350 ($560) / **EF** £800 ($1,280)
       The temple of Jupiter Tonans was built by Augustus on the Capitol in gratitude for his narrow escape from lightning during the Cantabrian campaign of 26 BC.

1614   1615

1614   **Silver denarius.** Aa. Rev. **IOV OLV**, hexastyle temple of Zeus at Olympia. RIC 472.
       BMCRE 666 (= BMCRR East 257). CBN 936. RSC 182. *[Northern Peloponnese (?), 21
       BC].*   **VF** £400 ($640) / **EF** £900 ($1,440)
       *RIC associates this issue with Augustus' visit to Greece in 21 BC. CBN prefers to assign it
       to the Pergamene mint six years earlier.*

1615   Aa. Rev. **L CANINIVS GALLVS III VIR**, bearded and cloaked barbarian kneeling r., offering
       vexillum. RIC 416. BMCRE 127 (= BMCRR 4678). CBN 560. RSC 383. *[Rome, 12 BC].*
                                          VF £325 ($520) / **EF** £750 ($1,200)

1616   1618

1616   Hc. Rev. **L MESCINIVS RVFVS**, statue of Mars stg. l., holding spear and parazonium, on
       pedestal inscribed **S P Q R / V PR RE / CAES**. RIC 351. BMCRE 86 (= BMCRR 4479). CBN
       331. RSC 463a. *[Rome, 16 BC].*   **VF** £375 ($600) / **EF** £850 ($1,360)
       *This refers to the vows undertaken for the safe return of Augustus from his political and
       military mission to Gaul in 16 BC (see also no. 1641).*

1617   **S C OB R P CVM SALVT IMP CAESAR AVGVS CONS**, bust of Augustus three-quarter face to
       r. on circular shield surrounded by laurel-wreath. Rev. **L MESCINIVS RVFVS III VIR**, similar
       to previous, but pedestal is inscribed **S P Q R V P / S PR S ET / RED AVG**. RIC 356. BMCRE
       90 (= BMCRR 4482). CBN 341. RSC 465b. *[Rome, 16 BC].*
                                          VF £2,500 ($4,000) / **EF** £5,500 ($8,800)
       This type further expresses concerns over the emperor's state of health at this critical time.

1618   **S P Q R / IMP / CAES** on pedestal of equestrian statue of Augustus r., city-walls and gate (the
       Porta Fontinalis) in background. Rev. **L VINICIVS L F III VIR**, cippus inscribed **S P Q R / IMP
       CAE / QVOD V / M S EX / EA P Q IS / AD A DE**. RIC 362. BMCRE 82 (= BMCRR 4474).
       CBN 357. RSC 543. *[Rome, 16 BC].*   **VF** £500 ($800) / **EF** £1,100 ($1,760)
       *The graphic obv. type represents a statue erected in the emperor's honour, probably that
       outside the Porta Fontinalis by which the Via Flaminia entered the city through the old
       Servian Wall. The cippus, set up in Rome's Regio VII, records Augustus' generosity in mak-
       ing special contributions to the public treasury in order to help finance the restoration of
       the public roads. Work on the Via Flaminia was undertaken entirely at his expense, as it
       was necessary to make the route suitable for the frequent passage of armies (see also no.
       1631).*

1619   1622

1619   **Silver denarius.** Da. Rev. M DVRMIVS III VIR, wild boar r., pierced by spear. RIC 317.
BMCRE 61 (= BMCRR 4567). CBN 207. RSC 430. *[Rome, 19 BC].*
VF £325 ($520) / **EF** £750 ($1,200)
*The rev. appears to revive the type issued half a century before by the moneyer C. Hosidius
Geta (see nos. 346–7).*

1620   Da. Rev. — lion on back of stag kneeling l., attacking the base of its victim's neck. RIC
318. BMCRE 65 (= BMCRR 4571). CBN 213. RSC 431. *[Rome, 19 BC].*
VF £375 ($600) / **EF** £850 ($1,360)
*This revives a type which had appeared frequently on the silver coinage of the Greek city
of Velia in southern Italy in the 4th and 3rd cents. BC.*

1621   Ba. Rev. M SANQVINIVS III VIR, youthful laur. hd. of Genius Saeculari Novi r., with features resembling Augustus, four-rayed comet with tail above. RIC 338. BMCRE 71
(= BMCRR 4585). CBN 278. RSC *Julius Caesar and Augustus* 1. *[Rome, 17 BC].*
VF £650 ($1,040) / **EF** £1,500 ($2,400)
*This type and the next are in commemoration of the Ludi Saeculares, the Secular Games
celebrated by Augustus in 17 BC to mark the commencement of a 'New Age' inaugurated by
the Divine Julius and now brought to fruition by his heir. The youthful head on the reverse
has usually been interpreted as that of a rejuvenated Caesar, on the evidence of the comet
('sidus Iulium') which surmounts the portrait. However, there is clearly no resemblance to
the late dictator and it seems more satisfactory to regard it as a personification of the 'New
Age' itself, endowed, like so many of the divine images of Augustus' reign, with the features
of the emperor (cf. A.A. Boyce in ANS NNM 153, pp. 1–11).*

1622   Similar, but with obv. AVGVST DIVI F LVDOS SAE, herald stg. l., clad in long robes and
wearing helmet with two feathers, holding caduceus and shield with star device. RIC 340.
BMCRE 70 (= BMCRR 4584). CBN 273. RSC *Julius Caesar* 6. *[Rome, 17 BC].*
VF £450 ($720) / **EF** £1,000 ($1,600)

1623   1625

1623   Fc. Rev. MAR VLT, domed hexastyle temple of Mars Ultor containing legionary eagle
between two standards. RIC 105a. BMCRE 373 (= BMCRR 4419). CBN 1202. RSC 190.
[Colonia Patricia, 18 BC].   **VF** £225 ($360) / **EF** £500 ($800)
*The small temple of Mars the Avenger was situated on the Capitol and was built specially
to house the legionary standards of Crassus and Antony recovered by Augustus from
Phraates IV of Parthia (see also nos. 1582, 1589, 1624 , 1632, and 1634–5).*

1624 **Silver denarius.** Db. Rev. — domed tetrastyle temple of Mars Ultor containing statue of the god stg. l., holding legionary eagle and standard. RIC 69b. BMCRE 369 (= BMCRR 4411). CBN 1112. RSC 195. *[Colonia Patricia, 19 BC]*. **VF** £250 ($400) / **EF** £550 ($880) *For another depiction of this statue, see no. 1632.*

1625 Da. Rev. **OB / CIVIS / SERVATOS** in three lines within oak-wreath. RIC 77a. BMCRE 378 (= BMCRR 4391). CBN 1154. RSC 208. *[Colonia Patricia, 19 BC]*.
VF £200 ($320) / **EF** £450 ($720)
A restoration of this type was made during the revolt of Vindex in Gaul in AD 68 (see no. 2066).

1626 Da. Rev. **OB CIVIS / SERVATOS** above and below oak-wreath, within which circular shield inscribed **S P Q R / CL V**. RIC 79a. BMCRE 381 (= BMCRR 4393). CBN 1144. RSC 215. *[Colonia Patricia, 19 BC]*. **VF** £225 ($360) / **EF** £500 ($800)

1627 **IMP CAESAR AVGVST**, a. Rev. **P CARISIVS LEG PRO PR**, view of the city-walls of Emerita, with double-portalled gateway in foreground above which, **EMERITA**. RIC 9a. BMCRE 289 (= BMCRR Spain 126). CBN 1036. RSC 397. *[Emerita, 25–23 BC]*.
VF £400 ($640) / **EF** £900 ($1,440)
The colony of Emerita Augusta (modern Mérida) was founded in 25 BC by P. Carisius, governor of Lusitania, for veterans of legions V Alauda and X Gemina who had recently participated in Augustus' campaigns in north-western Spain (see also nos. 1642, 1658 and 1675).

1628   1629

1628 — b. Rev. — trophy erected on heap of Celtiberian arms. RIC 4b. BMCRE 284 (= BMCRR Spain 117). CBN 1061. RSC 402. *[Emerita, 25–23 BC]*.
VF £350 ($560) / **EF** £800 ($1,280)

1629 Da. Rev. **P PETRON TVRPILIAN III VIR**, Pegasus stepping r. RIC 297. BMCRE 23 (= BMCRR 4536). CBN 147. RSC 491. *[Rome, 19 BC]*.
VF £350 ($560) / **EF** £800 ($1,280)

1630 Ec. Rev. **PONTIF MAXIM**, female figure (Livia?) seated r., holding sceptre and branch. RIC 220. BMCRE 545. CBN 1693. RSC 223. *[Lugdunum, AD 13–14]*.
VF £325 ($520) / **EF** £750 ($1,200)
This was the prototype for the standard denarius of Tiberius' reign, the coin which is popularly known as the 'Tribute Penny' of the Bible (see no. 1763).

1631 **S P Q R CAESARI AVGVSTO**, a. Rev. **QVOD VIAE MVN SVNT**, double triumphal arch, surmounted by statue of Augustus crowned by Victory in triumphal quadriga r., the whole placed atop bridge supported by arches. RIC 144. BMCRE 433 (= BMCRR 4463). CBN 1257. RSC 233. *[Colonia Patricia, 17–16 BC]*. **VF** £450 ($720) / **EF** £1,000 ($1,600)
This refers to the extensive measures taken by Augustus to improve the road system in Italy. The depiction on rev. may be that of the Milvian Bridge which carried the Via Flaminia, Italy's great northern highway, across the Tiber just north of Rome. The historian Dio Cassius records the erection of 'statues on arches on the bridge over the Tiber' in commemoration of the emperor's munificence in personally financing the work carried out on the Via Flaminia (see also no. 1618).

1631   1633

1632   **Silver denarius.** Da. Rev. SIGNIS RECEPTIS, Mars Ultor stg. l., looking r., holding legionary
       eagle and standard. RIC 82a. BMCRE 414 (= BMCRR 4405). CBN 1118. RSC 259.
       [Colonia Patricia, 19 BC].   **VF** £275 ($440) / **EF** £600 ($960)
       *The statue of Mars Ultor (shown within his temple on no. 1624) is here depicted as the sole
       type in commemoration of the restoration by the Parthians of the Roman standards cap-
       tured from Crassus and Antony. For other types associated with this event, see nos. 1582,
       1589–90, 1603, 1606, 1623, and 1633–5).*

1633   Da. Rev. — circular shield inscribed CL V, S–P / Q–R above and below, legionary eagle on
       l., standard on r. RIC 86a. BMCRE 417 (= BMCRR 4397). CBN 1132. RSC 265. *[Colonia
       Patricia, 19 BC].*   **VF** £250 ($400) / **EF** £550 ($880)

1634   Fc. Rev. S P Q R, triumphal quadriga r., containing legionary eagle and surmounted by four
       miniature horses galloping r. RIC 108a. BMCRE 392 (= BMCRR 4429). CBN 1178. RSC
       274. *[Colonia Patricia, 18 BC].*   **VF** £275 ($440) / **EF** £600 ($960)
       *This type is to be associated with the temple of Mars Ultor and the restoration by the
       Parthians of the Roman standards. For other depictions of this triumphal car, see nos.
       1582 and 1635.*

1635   1636

1635   Fc. Rev. — domed tetrastyle temple of Mars Ultor, within which triumphal car r., contain-
       ing legionary eagle and surmounted by four miniature horses. RIC 115. BMCRE 389
       (= BMCRR 4427). CBN 1219. RSC 280. *[Colonia Patricia, 18 BC].*
                                                        VF £250 ($400) / **EF** £550 ($880)
       For other depictions of this temple, see nos. 1589 and 1623–4.

1636   Da. Rev. — Victory flying r., holding wreath in both hands, column in background at base
       of which rests shield inscribed CL V. RIC 94. BMCRE 404 (= BMCRR 4382). CBN 1121.
       RSC 289. *[Colonia Patricia, 19 BC].*   **VF** £375 ($600) / **EF** £850 ($1,360)
       NB The illustration shows a variant with head of Augustus wreathed with oak.

1637   Db. Rev. Circular shield inscribed S P Q R / CL V. RIC 42b. BMCRE 335 (= BMCRR Gaul
       130). CBN 1316. RSC 293. *[Caesaraugusta, 19–18 BC].*
                                                        VF £250 ($400) / **EF** £550 ($880)

1637   1638

1638   **Silver denarius.** Ec. Rev. TI CAESAR AVG F TR POT XV, Tiberius in triumphal quadriga r.,
holding branch and eagle-tipped sceptre. RIC 222. BMCRE 512. CBN 1688. RSC 300.
[Lugdunum, AD 13–14].   **VF** £300 ($480) / **EF** £650 ($1,040)
Like the PONTIF MAXIM *rev. (no. 1630) this late type was subsequently adopted for the
coinage of Tiberius' own reign (see nos. 1758–9 and 1762).*

1639   1640

1639   Da. Rev. TVRPILIANVS III VIR, Tarpeia facing, her arms uplifted, buried to her waist in
shields. RIC 299. BMCRE 29 (= BMCRR 4530). CBN 157. RSC 494. *[Rome, 19 BC].*
                                        VF £450 ($720) / **EF** £1,000 ($1,600)
*The inspiration for this type was provided by the coinage of the moneyer L. Titurius
Sabinus issued seven decades before (see nos. 251–2). A star within a crescent moon
appears above Tarpeia on the prototype, a device which features as the principal design on
the following variety.*

1640   Da. Rev. — star within crescent moon. RIC 300. BMCRE 32 (= BMCRR 4532). CBN
161. RSC 495. *[Rome, 19 BC].*   **VF** £400 ($640) / **EF** £900 ($1,440)

1641   S P Q R CAESARI AVGVSTO, a. Rev. VOT P SVSC PRO SAL ET RED I O M SACR, Mars stg. l.,
holding vexillum and parazonium. RIC 150a. BMCRE 438 (= BMCRR 4459). CBN 1242.
RSC 325. *[Colonia Patricia, 17–16 BC].*   **VF** £300 ($480) / **EF** £650 ($1,040)
*This refers to the vows undertaken to Jupiter Optimus Maximus for the health and safe
return of Augustus prior to his departure for Gaul in 16 BC (see also nos. 1616–17).*

1642

1642   **Silver quinarius.** AVGVST, a. Rev. P CARISI LEG, Victory stg. r., crowning trophy. RIC 1a.
BMCRE 293 (= BMCRR Spain 121). CBN 1065. RSC 386. *[Emerita, 25–23 BC].*
                                        VF £110 ($176) / **EF** £275 ($440)
*The colony of Emerita Augusta (modern Mérida) was founded in 25 BC by P. Carisius, gov-
ernor of Lusitania, for veterans of legions V Alauda and X Gemina who had recently participated in Augustus' campaigns in north-western Spain (see also nos. 1627–8, 1658 and
1675).*

1643   **Silver quinarius.** Aa. Rev. No legend, Victory stg. l. on prow, holding wreath and palm.
RIC 474. BMCRE 670 (= BMCRR East 261). CBN 944. RSC 328. *[Northern
Peloponnese (?), 21 BC].*   **VF** £200 ($320) / **EF** £450 ($720)
*RIC associates this issue with Augustus' visit to Greece in 21 BC. CBN prefers to assign it
to the Pergamene mint six years earlier.*

Never a regular part of the Roman monetary system, following these early Augustan issues the silver quinarius disappeared from the Imperial coinage for the remainder of the Julio-Claudian
period. Thereafter, it was struck only in limited quantities, doubtless usually for the purpose of providing imperial largess at public events and on special military occasions.

1644   **Brass sestertius (moneyers' series).** OB / CIVIS / SERVATOS above, within, and below
oak-wreath flanked by two laurel-branches Rev. C ASINIVS C F GALLVS III VIR A A A F F
around large S C. RIC 370. BMCRE 157 (= BMCRR 4494). CBN 372. C 367. *[Rome,
16 BC].*   **F** £80 ($128) / **VF** £200 ($320) / **EF** £750 ($1,200)

Issued only infrequently and in small quantities as a tiny silver coin in Republican times, the sestertius (quarter-denarius) made a dramatic reappearance at Rome about 18 BC as a large and impressive base metal piece struck in yellow orichalcum (brass). In reality, this drastic change had been
anticipated by two decades when Mark Antony issued bronze sestertii as the highest denomination
of his Fleet Coinage. The Augustan sestertii bear the names of the three annually appointed Roman
moneyers, though surprisingly they lack the imperial name itself. The issue extended over four
years and was discontinued after the college of 15 BC had completed its production. Later coins of
this denomination were produced at the Gallic mint of Lugdunum in commemoration of the
famous Altar of Roma and Augustus dedicated by the emperor in 10 BC. These coins have the
emperor's head as their obverse type, but sestertii from the Rome mint did not bear portraits for
more than half a century, the first issues coming under Caligula (AD 37–41). This imposing denomination was to become one of the corner-stones of the Imperial coinage right down to the collapse
of the Augustan monetary system in the economic crisis of the mid-3rd century AD.

1645   Similar, but with moneyer's legend C CASSIVS C F CELER III VIR A A A F F on rev. RIC
374. BMCRE 165 (= BMCRR 4501). CBN 394. C 407. *[Rome, 16 BC].*
F £80 ($128) / **VF** £200 ($320) / **EF** £750 ($1,200)

1646

1646   Similar, but with moneyer's legend C GALLIVS C F LVPERCVS III VIR A A A F F on rev. RIC
377. BMCRE 171 (= BMCRR 4508). CBN 415. C 434. *[Rome, 16 BC].*
F £80 ($128) / **VF** £200 ($320) / **EF** £750 ($1,200)

1647   Similar, but with moneyer's legend C MARCI L F CENSORIN AVG III VIR A A A F F on rev.
RIC 325. BMCRE 178 (= BMCRR 4598). CBN 264. C 454. *[Rome, 18 BC].*
F £80 ($128) / **VF** £200 ($320) / **EF** £750 ($1,200)

1648 **Brass sestertius (moneyers' series).** Similar, but with moneyer's legend C PLOTIVS RVFVS III VIR A A A F F on rev. RIC 387. BMCRE 147 (= BMCRR 4634). CBN 491. C 501. *[Rome, 15 BC].*   **F** £80 ($128) / **VF** £200 ($320) / **EF** £750 ($1,200)

1649 Similar, but with moneyer's legend CN PISO CN F III VIR A A A F F on rev. RIC 380. BMCRE 134 (= BMCRR 4621). CBN 380. C 377. *[Rome, 15 BC].*
F £80 ($128) / **VF** £200 ($320) / **EF** £750 ($1,200)

1650 Similar, but with moneyer's legend L NAEVIVS SVRDINVS III VIR A A A F F on rev. RIC 383. BMCRE 139 (= BMCRR 4626). CBN 460. C 471. *[Rome, 15 BC].*
F £80 ($128) / **VF** £200 ($320) / **EF** £750 ($1,200)

1651 Similar, but with moneyer's legend M SANQVINIVS Q F III VIR A A A F F on rev. RIC 341. BMCRE 191 (= BMCRR 4588). CBN 281. C 520. *[Rome, 17 BC].*
F £80 ($128) / **VF** £200 ($320) / **EF** £750 ($1,200)

1652 Similar, but with moneyer's legend P LICINIVS STOLO III VIR A A A F F on rev. RIC 345. BMCRE 195 (= BMCRR 4595). CBN 302. C 441. *[Rome, 17 BC].*
F £80 ($128) / **VF** £200 ($320) / **EF** £750 ($1,200)

1653 Similar, but with moneyer's legend Q AELIVS L F LAMIA III VIR A A A F F on rev. RIC 323. BMCRE 175 (= BMCRR 4613). CBN 229. C 341. *[Rome, 18 BC].*
F £80 ($128) / **VF** £200 ($320) / **EF** £750 ($1,200)

1654 Similar, but with moneyer's legend T QVINCTIVS CRISPIN SVLPIC III VIR A A A F F on rev. RIC 329. BMCRE 181 (= BMCRR 4602). CBN 248. C 510. *[Rome, 18 BC].*
F £80 ($128) / **VF** £200 ($320) / **EF** £750 ($1,200)

1655 Similar, but with moneyer's legend TI SEMPRONIVS GRACCVS III VIR A A A F F on rev. RIC 348. BMCRE 198 (= BMCRR 4611). CBN 319. C 524. *[Rome, 17 BC].*
F £80 ($128) / **VF** £200 ($320) / **EF** £750 ($1,200)

1656 **Brass sestertius (Lugdunese series).** CAESAR PONT MAX, c. Rev. ROM ET AVG, altar of the cult of Roma and Augustus at Lugdunum, flanked by two columns, each surmounted by statue of Victory. RIC 229. BMCRE 548 (= BMCRR Gaul 203). CBN 1632. Cf. C 239. *[Lugdunum, after 10 BC].*   **F** £700 ($1,120) / **VF** £1,750 ($2,800)
The celebrated 'Altar of Lugdunum' was dedicated by Augustus on 1 August 10 BC, the very day of the birth in the city of the future emperor Claudius. The initial series of aes bearing a representation of the Altar extended over the following three or four years. A later series, including issues in the name of the imperial heir Tiberius, was instituted about AD 10 and continued to the end of the reign.

1657 Similar, but with obv. Ec. RIC 231a. BMCRE 565. CBN 1695. C 236. *[Lugdunum, AD 10–14].*   **F** £600 ($960) / **VF** £1,500 ($2,400) / **EF** £6,000 ($9,600)

1658 **Brass dupondius (Emeritan series).** AVGVST TRIB POTEST, a. Rev. P CARISIVS LEG AVGVSTI, view of the city-walls of Emerita, with double-portalled gateway in foreground above which, EMERITA. RIC 11a. BMCRE p. 54, * note (= BMCRR Spain, p. 377). CBN 1077. C 395. *[Emerita, 23 BC].*   **F** £125 ($200) / **VF** £350 ($560)
The colony of Emerita Augusta (modern Mérida) was founded in 25 BC by P. Carisius, governor of Lusitania, for veterans of legions V Alauda and X Gemina who had recently participated in Augustus' campaigns in north-western Spain. The emperor received his initial grant of tribunician power on 1 July 23 BC (see also nos. 1627–8, 1642 and 1675).

1657

With the exception of several brief revivals during the Imperatorial period, most notably as part of Antony's Fleet Coinage of 38–37 BC, the double-as had not been seen since the time of the Second Punic War, immediately following the currency reform of 211 BC. It now reappeared as part of the new Augustan currency system and, like its double the sestertius, was struck in yellow orichalcum (brass). The emperor's name, though not his portrait, appears on these Augustan dupondii of Rome. Predating by half a decade the initial issue of the denomination in the capital was a small output of dupondii from the Spanish mint of Emerita, produced in the name of the city's founder P. Carisius. The striking of dupondii by the Roman moneyers was discontinued after 15 BC in line with the other *aes* denominations. A later brief experiment was the copper dupondius of the controversial 'triumphal' coinage struck by the three moneyers who held office in 7 BC. However, there may have been more than one denomination involved in this enigmatic series, the true place of which in the later Augustan coinage is still disputed by scholars. At the very end of Augustus' reign the Gallic mint of Lugdunum issued a limited number of dupondii as part of its 'altar' series. Although never minted in quite the same quantities as the sestertius and the as, the dupondius nevertheless remained a vital element of the Roman Imperial coinage down to the collapse of the monetary system in the mid-3rd century AD.

1659   **Brass dupondius (moneyers' series).** AVGVSTVS / TRIBVNIC / POTEST in three lines within oak-wreath. Rev. C ASINIVS GALLVS III VIR A A A F F around large S C. RIC 372. BMCRE 158 (= BMCRR 4495). CBN 378. C 368. *[Rome, 16 BC].*
       F £45 ($72) / **VF** £100 ($160) / **EF** £300 ($480)

1660   Similar, but with moneyer's legend C CASSIVS CELER III VIR A A A F F on rev. RIC 375. BMCRE 166 (= BMCRR 4503). CBN 402. C 408. *[Rome, 16 BC].*
       F £45 ($72) / **VF** £100 ($160) / **EF** £300 ($480)

1661   Similar, but with moneyer's legend C CENSORINVS L F AVG III VIR A A A F F on rev. RIC 326. BMCRE 179 (= BMCRR 4599). CBN 267. C 452. *[Rome, 18 BC].*
       F £45 ($72) / **VF** £100 ($160) / **EF** £300 ($480)

1662   Similar, but with moneyer's legend C GALLIVS LVPERCVS III VIR A A A F F on rev. RIC 378. BMCRE 173 (= BMCRR 4509). CBN 421. C 435. *[Rome, 16 BC].*
       F £45 ($72) / **VF** £100 ($160) / **EF** £300 ($480)

1663   Similar, but with moneyer's legend C PLOTIVS RVFVS III VIR A A A F F on rev. RIC 388. BMCRE 150 (= BMCRR 4637). CBN 496. C 502. *[Rome, 15 BC].*
       F £45 ($72) / **VF** £100 ($160) / **EF** £300 ($480)

1664   Similar, but with moneyer's legend CN PISO CN F III VIR A A A F F on rev. RIC 381. BMCRE 135 (= BMCRR 4622). CBN 439. C 378. *[Rome, 15 BC].*
       F £45 ($72) / **VF** £100 ($160) / **EF** £300 ($480)

1665   **Brass dupondius (moneyers' series).** Similar, but with moneyer's legend **L SVRDINVS III VIR A A A F F** on rev. RIC 384. BMCRE 141 (= BMCRR 4628). CBN 467. C 472. *[Rome, 15 BC].*   **F** £45 ($72) / **VF** £100 ($160) / **EF** £300 ($480)

1666

1666   Similar, but with moneyer's legend **M SANQVINIVS Q F III VIR A A A F F** on rev. RIC 342. BMCRE 193 (= BMCRR 4590). CBN 287. C 521. *[Rome, 17 BC].*   **F** £45 ($72) / **VF** £100 ($160) / **EF** £300 ($480)

1667

1667   Similar, but with moneyer's legend **P STOLO III VIR A A A F F** on rev. RIC 347. BMCRE 197 (= BMCRR 4597). CBN 311. C 440. *[Rome, 17 BC].*   **F** £45 ($72) / **VF** £100 ($160) / **EF** £300 ($480)

1668   Similar, but with moneyer's legend **Q AELIVS LAMIA III VIR A A A F F** on rev. RIC 324. BMCRE 176 (= BMCRR 4614). CBN 236. C 342. *[Rome, 18 BC].*   **F** £45 ($72) / **VF** £100 ($160) / **EF** £300 ($480)

1669   Similar, but with moneyer's legend **T CRISPINVS SVLPICIANVS III VIR A A A F F** on rev. RIC 334. BMCRE 187 (= BMCRR 4607). CBN 254. C 507. *[Rome, 18 BC].*   **F** £45 ($72) / **VF** £100 ($160) / **EF** £300 ($480)

1670   Similar, but with moneyer's legend **TI SEMPRONIVS GRACCVS III VIR A A A F F** on rev. RIC 349. BMCRE 199 (= BMCRR 4612). CBN 324. C 525. *[Rome, 17 BC].*   **F** £45 ($72) / **VF** £100 ($160) / **EF** £300 ($480)

1671   **Copper dupondius? ('triumphal' series).** CAESAR AVGVST PONT MAX TRIBVNIC POT, d, Victory stg. l. behind, adjusting tie of wreath and holding cornucopiae. Rev. **P LVRIVS AGRIPPA III VIR A A A F F** around large **S C**. RIC 426A. BMCRE p. 41, *. CBN 616. C 447. *[Rome, 7 BC].*   **F** £600 ($960) / **VF** £1,750 ($2,800) / **EF** £4,000 ($6,400)
        CBN prefers to classify this and the following two types as 'medallions'. 7 BC was the year of Tiberius' triumph for his military successes in Germany and it is possible that these exceptional issues were in celebration of the occasion.

1671

1672

1672 **Copper dupondius?** ('triumphal' series). Similar, but with moneyer's legend M SALVIVS OTHO III VIR A A A F F on rev. RIC 429. BMCRE 224 (= BMCRR 4689). CBN 685. C 518. *[Rome, 7 BC].* **F** £600 ($960) / **VF** £1,750 ($2,800) / **EF** £4,000 ($6,400)

1673 Similar, but with moneyer's legend M MAECILIVS TVLLVS III VIR A A A F F on rev. RIC 434. BMCRE 217 (= BMCRR 4682). CBN 650. C 450. *[Rome, 7 BC].* **F** £600 ($960) / **VF** £1,750 ($2,800) / **EF** £4,000 ($6,400)

1674 **Brass dupondius (Lugdunese series).** As 1657 (rev. ROM ET AVG, altar of Lugdunum). RIC 232. BMCRE 566. CBN 1707. C 237. *[Lugdunum, AD 10–14].* **F** £55 ($88) / **VF** £130 ($208) / **EF** £325 ($520) *The celebrated 'Altar of Lugdunum' was dedicated by Augustus on 1 August 10 BC, the very day of the birth in the city of the future emperor Claudius. The Lugdunese dupondii all belong to the later phase of minting spanning the final four years of the reign, sestertii and asses only having been produced in the period immediately following the inauguration of the shrine.*

1675 **Copper as (Emeritan series).** CAESAR AVGVS TRIBVN POTEST, a. Rev. P CARISIVS / LEG / AVGVSTI in three lines across field. RIC 22. BMCRE p. 54, * note. CBN 1082. C 393. *[Emerita, 23 BC].* **F** £60 ($96) / **VF** £140 ($224) *The colony of Emerita Augusta (modern Mérida) was founded in 25 BC by P. Carisius, governor of Lusitania, for veterans of legions V Alauda and X Gemina who had recently participated in Augustus' campaigns in north-western Spain. The emperor received his initial grant of tribunician power on 1 July 23 BC (see also nos. 1627–8, 1642 and 1658).*

The as of the reformed Augustan currency system was struck in copper on the semuncial weight standard, which had been mandated by the *Lex Papiria* as far back as 91 BC. The final issues of the denomination under the Republic had been made in the late 80s, but in more recent times, during the political and economic disruptions of the Imperatorial period, many of the military issues of *aes* had reverted to the heavier uncial standard. Predating by seven years the initial production of the denomination at Rome was an issue of asses from the Spanish mint of Emerita, the name of the city's founder P. Carisius forming the reverse type. Unlike the two larger *aes* denominations struck by the moneyers, the as bore an imperial portrait from the very outset of the Roman series, which, in the case of this denomination, was delayed until 16 BC. Nevertheless, it did conform to the same pattern by ceasing after the issues of the following year, though there were brief revivals in 7–6 BC and in AD 10–12. The Gallic mint of Lugdunum participated in the production of asses from 10 BC as a major element of its celebrated 'altar' series. The as was to become one of the principal denominations of the Roman Imperial coinage down to the collapse of the Augustan monetary system in the financial crisis of the mid-3rd century AD.

1676   **Copper as (moneyers' series).** CAESAR AVGVST PONT MAX TRIBVNIC POT, a. Rev. A LICIN NERVA SILIAN III VIR A A A F F around large S C. RIC 437. BMCRE 235 (= BMCRR 4663). CBN 716. C 437. *[Rome, 6 BC].*
　　　　　　　　　　　　　　　　F £45 ($72) / **VF** £110 ($176) / **EF** £275 ($440)

1677   CAESAR AVGVSTVS TRIBVNIC POTEST, a. Rev. C ASINIVS GALLVS III VIR A A A F F around large S C. RIC 373. BMCRE 161 (= BMCRR 4497). CBN 384. C 369. *[Rome, 16 BC].*　　F £45 ($72) / **VF** £110 ($176) / **EF** £275 ($440)

1678   Similar, but with moneyer's legend C CASSIVS CELER III VIR A A A F F on rev. RIC 376. BMCRE 169 (= BMCRR 4506). CBN 409. C 409. *[Rome, 16 BC].*
　　　　　　　　　　　　　　　　F £45 ($72) / **VF** £110 ($176) / **EF** £275 ($440)

1679   Similar, but with moneyer's legend C GALLIVS LVPERCVS III VIR A A A F F on rev. RIC 379. BMCRE 174 (= BMCRR 4510). CBN 428. C 436. *[Rome, 16 BC].*
　　　　　　　　　　　　　　　　F £45 ($72) / **VF** £110 ($176) / **EF** £275 ($440)

1680

1680   Similar, but with moneyer's legend C PLOTIVS RVFVS III VIR A A A F F on rev. RIC 389. BMCRE 153 (= BMCRR 4639). CBN 503. C 504. *[Rome, 15 BC].*
　　　　　　　　　　　　　　　　F £45 ($72) / **VF** £110 ($176) / **EF** £275 ($440)

1681

1681   Similar, but with moneyer's legend CN PISO CN F III VIR A A A F F on rev. RIC 382. BMCRE 137 (= BMCRR 4624). CBN 448. C — (omitted in error). *[Rome, 15 BC].*
　　　　　　　　　　　　　　　　F £45 ($72) / **VF** £110 ($176) / **EF** £275 ($440)

AUGUSTUS   331

1682   **Copper as (moneyers' series).** Similar, but with rev. type diad. hd. of Numa Pompilius r.,
       with long beard (no **S C**). RIC 395. BMCRE p. 28, †. CBN 433. C 379. *[Rome, 15 BC].*
                          F £1,500 ($2,400) / **VF** £4,500 ($7,200)
       *This very rare type forms part of a series which has been the subject of much controversy.
       The group as a whole displays some curious and disturbing features, not least of which is
       the surprising omission of the formula* **S C** *('by decree of the Senate'). Most, if not all,
       specimens exhibit some degree of tooling and it has to be recognized that the authenticity
       of the 'Numa-head' asses is still not universally acknowledged.*

1683   Similar, but with rev. type **L SVRDINVS III VIR A A A F F** around large **S C**. RIC 386.
       BMCRE 144 (= BMCRR 4631). CBN 483. C 473. *[Rome, 15 BC].*
                          F £50 ($80) / **VF** £120 ($192) / **EF** £300 ($480)

1684   **CAESAR AVGVST PONT MAX TRIBVNIC POT,** a. Rev. **M MAECILIVS TVLLVS III VIR A A A F**
       F around large **S C**. RIC 435. BMCRE 220 (= BMCRR 4686). CBN 654. C 448. *[Rome,*
       7 BC].   **F** £50 ($80) / **VF** £120 ($192) / **EF** £300 ($480)

1685

1685   Similar, but with moneyer's legend **M SALVIVS OTHO III VIR A A A F F** on rev. RIC 431.
       BMCRE 226 (= BMCRR 4693). CBN 687. C 515. *[Rome, 7 BC].*
                          F £50 ($80) / **VF** £120 ($192) / **EF** £300 ($480)

1686   Similar, but with obv. type b and with moneyer's legend **P LVRIVS AGRIPPA III VIR A A A F**
       F on rev. RIC 428. BMCRE 214 (= BMCRR 4699). CBN 640. C 446. *[Rome, 7 BC].*
                          F £55 ($88) / **VF** £130 ($208) / **EF** £325 ($520)

1687   Similar, but with obv. type a and with moneyer's legend **SEX NONIVS QVINCTILIAN III VIR**
       A A A F F on rev. RIC 439. BMCRE 237 (= BMCRR 4667). CBN 725. C 474. *[Rome,*
       6 BC].   **F** £50 ($80) / **VF** £120 ($192) / **EF** £300 ($480)

1688   Similar, but with moneyer's legend **VOLVSVS VALER MESSAL III VIR A A A F F** on rev. RIC
       441. BMCRE 241 (= BMCRR 4665). CBN 738. C 538. *[Rome, 6 BC].*
                          F £50 ($80) / **VF** £120 ($192) / **EF** £300 ($480)

1689   **Copper as (dated series).** **IMP CAESAR DIVI F AVGVSTVS IMP XX,** b. Rev. **PONTIF MAXIM**
       TRIBVN POT XXXIIII around large **S C**. RIC 471. BMCRE 275. CBN 883. C 226. *[Rome,*
       AD 11–12].   **F** £50 ($80) / **VF** £125 ($200) / **EF** £375 ($600)
       *The emperor's titles here replace those of the moneyer and set the pattern for the later
       Julio-Claudian aes coinage.*

1689

1690

1690   **Copper as (Lugdunese series).** As 1656 (rev. ROM ET AVG, altar of Lugdunum). RIC
         230. BMCRE 550 (= BMCRR Gaul 209). CBN 1634. C 240. *[Lugdunum, after 10 BC].*
         F £50 ($80) / **VF** £120 ($192) / **EF** £300 ($480)
         *The celebrated 'Altar of Lugdunum' was dedicated by Augustus on 1 August 10 BC, the
         very day of the birth in the city of the future emperor Claudius. The initial series of aes
         bearing a representation of the Altar extended over the following three or four years. A
         later series, including issues in the name of the imperial heir Tiberius, was instituted about
         AD 10 and continued to the end of the reign.*

1691   As 1657 (rev. ROM ET AVG, altar of Lugdunum). RIC 233. BMCRE 567. CBN 1715. C
         237. *[Lugdunum, AD 10–14].*   **F** £55 ($88) / **VF** £130 ($208) / **EF** £325 ($520)

1692   **Brass semis.** As 1657 (rev. ROM ET AVG, altar of Lugdunum). Cf. RIC 234. BMCRE 568.
         CBN 1728. C 238. *[Lugdunum, AD 10–14].*
         F £45 ($72) / **VF** £110 ($176) / **EF** £275 ($440)

The half-as had been last minted under the Republic about 86 BC and in Imperatorial times it
formed part of Antony's Fleet Coinage of 38 BC. It was not included in the early stages of the
Augustan reform of the *aes* coinage and was issued only in the final years of the reign from the
Gallic mint of Lugdunum, where it was struck in yellow orichalcum (brass) and represented the
smallest denomination of the 'altar' series. Production of the semis was on a limited scale under
Augustus' successors and in the later stages of its history the denomination appears generally to
have served only a ceremonial purpose.

1693   1694

1693 **Copper quadrans (moneyers' series).** LAMIA SILIVS ANNIVS, clasped hands holding
caduceus. Rev. III VIR A A A F F around large S C. RIC 420. BMCRE 200 (= BMCRR
4617). CBN 568. C 338/526. *[Rome, 9 BC].*   **F** £15 ($24) / **VF** £35 ($56) / **EF** £95 ($152)

Like its double, the semis, the quarter-as had last appeared as a Republican denomination about
86 BC. Almost half a century later it represented the smallest value in Antony's Fleet Coinage.
Under the reformed Augustan system its reintroduction at Rome was delayed until 9 BC, when it
appeared as a small copper coin lacking both the imperial name and portrait. Issues were made
jointly in the names of all three moneyers (four in the final two years) and with the exception of
7–6 BC, when asses were temporarily reintroduced, the quadrans remained in annual production
down to 4 BC. At this time minting of the diminutive denomination ceased. The Roman quadrantes
of Augustus were minimally augmented by an exceptional issue of orichalcum (brass) quadrantes,
of two types, from the Gallic mint of Lugdunum. The brief production of these probably preceded
the introduction of the moneyers' coinage. With the exception of the reign of Tiberius substantial
issues of quadrantes were made under all the succeeding emperors of the Julio-Claudian dynasty,
but thereafter minting was sporadic and generally only on a very limited scale. Like the semis, in
its final phase the quadrans seems to have become a denomination produced solely for distribution
on occasions of public celebration.

1694 Similar, but with obv. type simpulum and lituus (emblems of the pontificate and augurate).
RIC 421. BMCRE 201 (= BMCRR 4618). CBN 580. C 339/527. *[Rome, 9 BC].*
F £15 ($24) / **VF** £35 ($56) / **EF** £95 ($152)

1695   1700

1695 LAMIA SILIVS ANNIVS, cornucopiae dividing S – C. Rev. III VIR A A A F F, altar. RIC 422.
BMCRE 202 (= BMCRR 4619). CBN 589. C 340/528. *[Rome, 9 BC].*
F £15 ($24) / **VF** £35 ($56) / **EF** £95 ($152)

1696 PVLCHER TAVRVS REGVLVS, clasped hands holding caduceus. Rev. III VIR A A A F F
around large S C. RIC 423. BMCRE 204 (= BMCRR 4574). CBN 601. C 413. *[Rome, 8
BC].*   **F** £15 ($24) / **VF** £35 ($56) / **EF** £95 ($152)

1697 Similar, but with obv. type simpulum and lituus (emblems of the pontificate and augurate).
RIC 424. BMCRE 205 (= BMCRR 4575). CBN 606. C 414. *[Rome, 8 BC].*
F £15 ($24) / **VF** £35 ($56) / **EF** £95 ($152)

1698 PVLCHER TAVRVS REGVLVS, cornucopiae dividing S – C. Rev. III VIR A A A F F, altar. RIC
425. BMCRE 207 (= BMCRR 4577). CBN 611. C 415. *[Rome, 8 BC].*
F £15 ($24) / **VF** £35 ($56) / **EF** £95 ($152)

1699 APRONIVS MESSALLA III VIR, altar. Rev. GALVS SISENNA A A A F F around large S C. Cf.
RIC 443 (misdescribed). BMCRE 243 (= BMCRR 4713). CBN 757. C 352. *[Rome, 5 BC].*
F £12 ($20) / **VF** £30 ($48) / **EF** £85 ($136)

Four moneyers were appointed to hold office each year in 5 and 4 BC, though curiously they continued to style themselves 'triumvir'. The issues of 5 BC are bewilderingly complex, exhibiting a multitude of combinations of the four names on obv. and rev. Four typical examples are catalogued here, but many other varieties exist. The listing in RIC combines the wrong types with the legends.

1700   **Copper quadrans (moneyers' series).** Similar, but with SISENNA APRONIVS III VIR on obv., and GALVS MESSALLA A A A F F on rev. Cf. RIC 459 (misdescribed). BMCRE 260 (= BMCRR 4730). CBN 821. C 420. *[Rome, 5 BC].*
        F £12 ($20) / **VF** £30 ($48) / **EF** £85 ($136)
        ***NB** The illustration is of a 'pattern' struck on an overly large flan.*

1701   Similar, but with GALVS APRONIVS III VIR on obv., and MESSALLA SISENNA A A A F F on rev. Cf. RIC 447 (misdescribed). BMCRE p. 47, 2a. CBN 773. C 374. *[Rome, 5 BC].*
        F £12 ($20) / **VF** £30 ($48) / **EF** £85 ($136)

1702   Similar, but with MESSALLA GALVS III VIR on obv., and APRONIVS SISENNA A A A F F on rev. Cf. RIC 455 (misdescribed). BMCRE 255 (= BMCRR 4725). CBN 805. C 530. *[Rome, 5 BC].*
        F £12 ($20) / **VF** £30 ($48) / **EF** £85 ($136)

1703   P BETILIENVS BASSVS around large S C. Rev. III VIR A A A F F, altar. RIC 465 (misnumbered '456'). BMCRE 265 (= BMCRR 4707). CBN 854. C 376. *[Rome, 4 BC].*
        F £15 ($24) / **VF** £35 ($56) / **EF** £95 ($152)

1704   Similar, but with C NAEVIVS CAPELLA on obv. RIC 466. BMCRE 267 (= BMCRR 4709). CBN 863. C 469. *[Rome, 4 BC].*
        F £15 ($24) / **VF** £35 ($56) / **EF** £95 ($152)

1705   Similar, but with C RVBELLIVS BLANDVS on obv. RIC 467. BMCRE 269 (= BMCRR 4711). CBN 868. C 511. *[Rome, 4 BC].*
        F £15 ($24) / **VF** £35 ($56) / **EF** £95 ($152)

1706   Similar, but with L VALERIVS CATVLLVS on obv. RIC 468. BMCRE 270 (= BMCRR 4712). CBN 873. C 536. *[Rome, 4 BC].*
        F £15 ($24) / **VF** £35 ($56) / **EF** £95 ($152)

1707   **Brass quadrans (Lugdunese series).** Gc. Rev. AVGVSTVS, eagle stg. facing, hd. l., wings spread. RIC 227. BMCRE 561 (= BMCRR Gaul 213). CBN — (cf. p. 54). C 29. *[Lugdunum, 10 BC].*
        F £45 ($72) / **VF** £100 ($160)

1708   Ga. Rev. AVGVSTVS DIVI F, bull butting l. RIC 228. BMCRE 564 (= BMCRR Gaul 212). CBN — (cf. p. 54). C 36. *[Lugdunum, 10 BC].*
        F £50 ($80) / **VF** £110 ($176)

For coins of Divus Augustus and later restorations, see under Tiberius (nos. 1781–91), Caligula (nos. 1806–11 and 1819), Claudius (no. 1891), Nero (no. 2007), Civil Wars (nos. 2064–6, 2068, and 2073), Titus (nos. 2579–85), Domitian (nos. 2892–3), Nerva (nos. 3075–83), Trajan, Hadrian, and Trajan Decius.

Alexandrian Coinage

Following the conquest of the Ptolemaic kingdom in 30 BC the new Roman province of Egypt was organized under the government of a *praefectus* of equestrian rank. This official was directly answerable to Octavian and the whole country was organized as a private estate, a status very different from that of any other Roman province. In effect, Octavian viewed himself as the direct successor of the Ptolemaic rulers and doubtless he was regarded as such by his Egyptian subjects, though their 'pharaoh' now resided elsewhere. Roman senators were strictly excluded from visiting the former Ptolemaic kingdom unless they had Octavian's personal permission to do so. It is scarcely surprisingly that the exceptional closed status of the Egyptian province gave rise to a highly unusual 'local' currency, distinct in many respects from the provincial coinages of Rome's other eastern territories. This was based on the tetradrachm which, from its inception in the 7th Alexandrian year of Tiberius (AD 20–21), was struck in debased silver. From the reign of Claudius (AD 41–54) the Alexandrian billon tetradrachm seems to have been regarded as the equivalent of the Roman denarius. As the series evolved a whole range of fractional bronze denominations was produced, apparently based on the system introduced by Cleopatra, though using a lighter weight standard. Thus, in the listings in this catalogue the large 35 mm. bronze piece, initially struck under Nero, is regarded as a hemidrachm rather than a drachm, with the other denominations being a diobol (30 mm), an obol (25 mm), a hemiobol (20 mm), a dichalkon or quarter-obol (15 mm), and a chalkos or one-eighth obol (10 mm). The types of the Alexandrian coinage are extraordinarily varied and represent a fascinating blend of Graeco-Roman and local Egyptian types. Almost every coin bears a regnal date, a practice inherited from the Ptolemaic kings. This useful feature was retained down to the end of the series which extended to the final decade of the 3rd century and the reign of Diocletian. This made it by far the longest surviving of the 'Greek Imperial' coinages, further evidence of the unique nature of the Alexandrian series. Under Augustus issues were confined to bronze denominations, many of them undated.

1709 **Bronze obol** (80 bronze drachmas = 1 silver obol, 25 mm. diam). ΘΕΟΥ ΥΙΟΥ, bare hd. of Octavian r. Rev. ΚΑΙΣΑΡΟΣ ΑΥΤΟΚΡΑΤΟΡΟΣ, eagle stg. l., cornucopiae to l., P (= 80) to r. RPC 5001. BMCG 1. Cologne 1. Milne (Supplement), p. 1. *[30–28 BC].*
F £100 ($160) / **VF** £250 ($400)
This retains the types of Cleopatra's reformed bronze coinage and must represent the Roman conqueror's initial issue from the Alexandria mint (see also no. 1715).

1710 ΣΕΒΑΣΤΟΣ, bare hd. of Augustus r. Rev. ΚΑΙΣΑΡ, ritual vase. RPC 5005. BMCG 11. Cologne 3. Milne 2. *[After 19 BC].* F £90 ($144) / **VF** £225 ($360)

1711 ΠΑΤΗΡ ΠΑΤΡΙΔΟΣ, laur. hd. of Augustus r. Rev. ΣΕΒΑΣΤΟΣ, six ears of corn tied together in bundle. RPC 5026. BMCG 27. Cologne 10. Milne 12. *[AD 1–5].*
F £80 ($128) / **VF** £200 ($320)

1712 No legend, laur. hd. of Augustus r. Rev. ΣΕΒΑΣΤΟV, capricorn r., L LH (= regnal year 38) above. RPC 5034. BMCG —. Cologne 18. Milne —. *[AD 8–9].*
F £110 ($176) / **VF** £275 ($440)

1713 Obv. Similar. Rev. L MA (= regnal year 41) in oak-wreath. RPC 5061. BMCG 16. Cologne 27. Milne 30. *[AD 11–12].* F £80 ($128) / **VF** £200 ($320)

1714 Similar, but with rev. type Nike stg. l., holding wreath and palm (regnal date in field). RPC 5062. BMCG 4. Cologne 30. Milne 29. *[AD 11–12].* F £80 ($128) / **VF** £200 ($320)

1715 **Bronze hemiobol** (40 bronze drachmas = 1 silver hemiobol, 20 mm). ΘΕΟΥ ΥΙΟΥ, bare hd. of Octavian r. Rev. ΚΑΙΣΑΡΟΣ ΑΥΤΟΚΡΑΤΟΡΟΣ, eagle stg. l., cornucopiae to l., M (= 40) to r. RPC 5002. BMCG 3. Cologne 2. Milne 1. *[30–28 BC].*
F £50 ($80) / **VF** £125 ($200)
This retains the types of Cleopatra's reformed bronze coinage and must represent the Roman conqueror's initial issue from the Alexandria mint (see also no. 1709).

1716 CEBACTOC, bare hd. of Augustus r. Rev. ΚΑΙCAP, simpulum, jug, lituus and axe (emblems of the pontificate and augurate). RPC 5007. BMCG 10. Cologne 4. Milne 7. *[After 19 BC].*
F £40 ($64) / **VF** £100 ($160)

1717 ΣΕΒΑΣΤΟΥ, altar between two laurel-branches. Rev. ΚΑΙΣΑ/ΡΟΣ in two lines within laurel-wreath. RPC 5013. BMCG 17. Cologne 9. Milne 17. *[3–2 BC].*
F £50 ($80) / **VF** £125 ($200)

1718

1718   **Bronze hemiobol.** ΠΑΤΗΡ ΠΑΤΡΙΔΟΣ, laur. hd. of Augustus r. Rev. ΣΕΒΑΣΤΟΣ, double cornucopiae. RPC 5029. BMCG 26. Cologne 13. Milne 21. *[AD 1–5].*
        F £45 ($72) / **VF** £110 ($176)

1719   No legend, laur. hd. of Augustus r. Rev. L MB (= regnal year 42), Nike stg. l., holding wreath and palm. RPC 5073. BMCG —. Cologne — (cf. 31–2 for the obol of this type). Milne — (cf. 32a for the obol). *[AD 12–13].*   **F** £40 ($64) / **VF** £100 ($160)

1720   **Bronze dichalkon** (15 mm). CEBACTOC, altar inscribed K (= 20 bronze drachmas = 1 silver quarter-obol). Rev. KAICAP, cornucopiae. RPC 5009. BMCG 19. Cologne 15. Milne 8. *[After 19 BC].*   **F** £50 ($80) / **VF** £125 ($200)

1721   KAIΣAP, laur. hd. of Augustus r. Rev. ΣΕΒΑΣΤΟΣ, crescent and star. RPC 5021. BMCG 8. Cologne 8. Milne 9. *[3–2 BC].*   **F** £35 ($56) / **VF** £85 ($136)

1722   No legend, laur. hd. of Augustus r. Rev. L M (= regnal year 40) in oak-wreath. RPC 5059. Cf. BMCG 35 (misattributed). Cologne 26. Milne — (cf. 26 for the obol of this type). *[AD 10–11].*   **F** £30 ($48) / **VF** £75 ($120)

1723   **Bronze chalkos** (10 mm). CEBA/CTOC in two lines. Rev. Star. RPC 5011. BMCG 25. Cologne —. Milne —. *[After 19 BC].*   **F** £20 ($32) / **VF** £55 ($88)

1724   Star. Rev. ΣΕΒΑΣΤΟΥ around large L Λ (= regnal year 30). RPC 5031. BMCG —. Cologne —. Milne 24. *[1 BC–AD 1].*   **F** £25 ($40) / **VF** £65 ($104)

For other local coinages of this reign, see *Roman Provincial Coinage,* vol. I, and *Greek Imperial Coins & Their Values,* pp. 1–17.

AUGUSTUS AND AGRIPPA

1731

Marcus Vipsanius Agrippa was born in 63 BC, the same year as his boyhood companion Gaius Octavius (later the emperor Augustus) whose lifelong friend and supporter he was to be. A man with great qualities of leadership and a gifted military strategist, Agrippa remained constantly loyal to Augustus and was largely responsible for the latter's rise to supremacy in the Roman world, being the architect of the victories over Sextus Pompey at Naulochus in 36 BC and over Mark Antony and Cleopatra at Actium five years later. He remained powerful and influential after Augustus' establishment of the principate and in the early years of the reign was clearly regarded as the most likely heir to the throne. On one occasion, during a serious illness in 23 BC, the emperor even handed his old friend his signet ring. But Augustus recovered and despite all the honors heaped upon him Agrippa was destined never to inherit the imperial power. In 21 BC he married Augustus' daughter, Julia, by whom he had three sons (Gaius and Lucius Caesars and Agrippa Postumus) and two daughters (Julia and Agrippina Senior). Through Agrippina the emperors Caligula and Nero were descended from him. Agrippa was very active in both military and civil affairs in various parts of the Empire and during his administration of the eastern provinces he became a close friend of Herod the Great, king of Judaea. Following a mission to Pannonia in 12 BC the robust general suddenly fell ill and died at the age of fifty-one, thus predeceasing the delicate Augustus by more than a quarter of a century.

1725 **Gold aureus.** CAESAR AVGVSTVS, hd. of Augustus r., wreathed with oak. Rev. M AGRIPPA PLATORINVS III VIR, hd. of Agrippa r., wearing combined mural and rostral crown. RIC 409. BMCRE 110 (= BMCRR 4653). CBN 531. Cf. C *Agrippa and Augustus 2. [Rome, 13 BC].*   **VF** £30,000 ($48,000) / **EF** £65,000 ($104,000)
Augustus' lifelong friend and colleague died the year following this issue which probably commemorates the renewal of Agrippa's tribunician power.

1726 1727

1726 **Silver denarius.** Similar, but both heads are bare. RIC 408. BMCRE 112 (= BMCRR 4654). CBN 533. RSC *Agrippa and Augustus 3. [Rome, 13 BC].*
VF £1,500 ($2,400) / **EF** £3,000 ($4,800)

1727 AVGVSTVS COS XI, hd. of Augustus r., wreathed with oak. Rev. M AGRIPPA COS TER COSSVS LENTVLVS, hd. of Agrippa r., wearing combined mural and rostral crown. RIC 414. BMCRE 121 (= BMCRR 4671). CBN 548. RSC *Agrippa and Augustus 1. [Rome, 12 BC].*
VF £2,250 ($3,600) / **EF** £4,500 ($7,200)
Agrippa died in March of this year and it is possible that this type was issued posthumously.

1728 **Brass dupondius.** IMP DIVI F, hds. back to back of Augustus r., bare, and Agrippa l., wearing rostral crown. Rev. COL NEM, crocodile r., chained to palm, wreath with long ties above, two palms below. RPC 522. RIC 154. C *Agrippa and Augustus 7. [Nemausus, after 29/28 BC].*   **F** £75 ($120) / **VF** £175 ($280)
Weight about 16.75 grams. In 27 BC the emperor conferred on this colony of southern Gaul the title of Colonia Augusta Nemausus and the initial issue of dupondii with the heads of Augustus and Agrippa is dated by RPC to this time. However, the omission of the title Augustus in the obv. legend suggests a slightly earlier date, perhaps 29/28 BC. Subsequent revivals of the original type would appear to span the following four decades, with only minor changes to the original design. Curiously, the obverse legend makes reference to the emperor alone with no mention of the identity of the other portrait. An analogy can be drawn with Antony's Fleet Coinage where multiple depictions of portraits are accompanied solely by the name and titles of the eastern Triumvir. The remarkable reverse type commemorates the conquest of Egypt in 30 BC, the theme doubtless being influenced by the settlement in the colony of Egyptian Greeks, veterans from Antony's army which had surrendered to Octavian at Actium. The captive crocodile device is still to be seen in present-day Nîmes.

1729   **Brass dupondius.** Similar. RPC 523. RIC 155. C *Agrippa and Augustus* 7. *[Nemausus,*
         after 16/15 BC].   **F** £50 ($80) / **VF** £125 ($200) / **EF** £350 ($560)
         Weight about 12.50 grams. This initial revival of the Nemausan series on a lighter weight
         standard is probably to be associated with Augustus' visit to Gaul in 16 BC.

1730

1730   Similar, but the hd. of Augustus is laur. instead of bare. RPC 524. RIC 158. C *Agrippa and*
         Augustus 10. *[Nemausus, after 10 BC].*   **F** £45 ($72) / **VF** £110 ($176) / **EF** £300 ($480)
         Despite the death of Agrippa two years before the Nemausan series was again revived to
         coincide with the initial issue of Lugdunese aes in 10 BC.

1731   Similar, but with obv. legend IMP DIVI F P P. RPC 525. RIC 159–60. Cf. C *Agrippa and*
         Augustus 8. *[Nemausus, after AD 10].*   **F** £55 ($88) / **VF** £140 ($224) / **EF** £400 ($640)
         This final revival of the 'crocodile' dupondius appears to coincide with the resumption of
         the Lugdunese aes in AD 10. It is distinguished principally by the addition of the title P P
         (Pater Patriae) on obverse, an honour bestowed on Augustus in 2 BC. Rare examples of
         this variety have an extension to the flan resembling a pig's leg and are explained in RPC
         (p. 153) as probably representing votive offerings.

For the posthumous asses of Agrippa with rev. Neptune, see under Caligula (no. 1812); and for
later restorations, see under Titus (no. 2589), Domitian (no. 2894), and Trajan. For types recording
Agrippa's first designation as consul, see under Octavian (nos.1542–3).

AUGUSTUS AND JULIA

1732

The only child of Augustus, Julia was born in 39 BC and was the daughter of his second wife
Scribonia. Her parents were divorced on the very day of her birth. Betrothed while still a baby to
Mark Antony's son Antyllus, Julia's first marriage was to her cousin Marcellus (25 BC). On his
death she took the much older Agrippa as her husband (21 BC) by whom she had five children. In 11
BC she married a third time, to the future emperor Tiberius, but estrangement followed due, no
doubt, to her alleged licentious conduct. This led to her banishment to the island of Pandateria,
though she was later allowed to move to Rhegium on the mainland. Her mother shared her exile
and remained with her until her death in AD 14, early in the reign of Tiberius.

1732   **Silver denarius.** AVGVSTVS, bare hd. of Augustus r., lituus behind. Rev. C MARIVS TRO
         III VIR, diad. and dr. bust of Julia, as Diana, r., quiver at shoulder. RIC 403. BMCRE 104
         (= BMCRR 4651). CBN 522. RSC *Julia and Augustus* 1. *[Rome, 13 BC].*
                                            VF £2,500 ($4,000) / **EF** £5,500 ($8,800)

For other depictions of Julia, see the following two types.

AUGUSTUS WITH JULIA AND GAIUS & LUCIUS CAESARS

1734

This attractive dynastic type belongs to the period just prior to the death of Agrippa and depicts on reverse his wife, the daughter of Augustus, together with their two sons who were clearly intended for the eventual imperial succession.

1733 **Silver denarius.** AVGVSTVS, bare hd. of Augustus r., lituus behind. Rev. C MARIVS TRO III VIR, hd. of Julia r., surmounted by wreath, between bare hds. r. of Gaius and Lucius Caesars. RIC 404. BMCRE 106. CBN 526. RSC *Caius, Lucius, Julia and Augustus* 1. *[Rome, 13 BC].* VF £5,000 ($8,000) / **EF** £10,000 ($16,000)

1734 Similar, but with obv. AVGVSTVS DIVI F, bare hd. of Augustus r., all within oak-wreath. RIC 405. BMCRE 108 (= BMCRR 4648). CBN 529. RSC *Caius, Lucius, Julia and Augustus* 2. *[Rome, 13 BC].* VF £5,750 ($9,200) / **EF** £11,500 ($18,400)

For another depiction of Julia, see no. 1732. For other depictions of Gaius and Lucius Caesars, see nos. 1578, 1596–7, 1735, and 1748–51.

AUGUSTUS AND GAIUS CAESAR

The young Caesar here appears with his grandfather in the period following his assumption of the toga virilis in 5 BC.

1735 **Bronze obol** (25 mm. diam.) of Alexandria. ΣΕΒΑΣΤΟΣ, laur. hd. of Augustus r. Rev. ΓΑΙΟΣ ΚΑΙΣΑΡ, bare hd. of Gaius Caesar r. RPC 5019. Cologne 7. Milne (Supplement) 10a. *[5–2 BC].* F £200 ($320) / **VF** £500 ($800)

For other depictions of Gaius Caesar, see nos. 1578, 1596–7, 1733–4, and 1748–9.

AUGUSTUS AND TIBERIUS

1736

On the death of his grandson Gaius Caesar in AD 4 Augustus was reluctantly obliged to acknowledge his stepson, Tiberius, as heir to the imperial throne. A decade later Tiberius became Rome's second emperor.

1736 **Gold aureus.** CAESAR AVGVSTVS DIVI F PATER PATRIAE, laur. hd. of Augustus r. Rev. TI CAESAR AVG F TR POT XV, bare hd. of Tiberius r. RIC 225. BMCRE 506. CBN 1681. C *Tiberius and Augustus* 1. *[Lugdunum, AD 13–14].* VF £2,250 ($3,600) / **EF** £5,000 ($8,000)

1737   **Silver denarius.** Similar. RIC 226. BMCRE 507. CBN 1682. RSC *Tiberius and Augustus*
        2. *[Lugdunum, AD 13–14].*   **VF** £750 ($1,200) / **EF** £1,500 ($2,400)

For another depiction of Tiberius on the coinage of Augustus, see no. 1638.

LIVIA

1741

*Livia Drusilla was the daughter of M. Livius Drusus Claudianus and Alfidia and was born on
30 January 58 BC. At about the age of sixteen she was married to Tiberius Claudius Nero, by whom
she had two sons – the future emperor Tiberius, and Nero Claudius Drusus, father of the emperor
Claudius. After a marriage of only four years she was divorced by her husband in 39 BC to leave
her free to marry the triumvir Octavian, later Augustus. Their union was happy, though childless,
and was destined to endure for fifty-three years, until Augustus' death in AD 14. Under the terms of
her husband's will she was adopted into the Julia gens and renamed Julia Augusta. During the
reign of her son, Tiberius, she was obliged to exert more openly the political influence which she
had previously enjoyed behind the scenes. This brought her into conflict with the emperor and may
well have been one of the contributory factors in his remarkable decision to leave Rome in AD 26
and retire permanently to the island of Capreae. Livia died three years later at the age of eighty-
seven and it is an indication of Tiberius' bitterness towards his mother that he refused to authorize
her deification or even to execute her will. The former omission was, however, repaired some years
later under her grandson, the emperor Claudius.*

1738

1738   **Brass sestertius.** S P Q R IVLIAE AVGVST, carpentum drawn r. by two mules. Rev. TI
        CAESAR DIVI AVG F AVGVST P M TR POT XXIIII around large S C. RIC *Tiberius* 51.
        BMCRE *Tiberius* 76. CBN *Tiberius* 55. C 6. *[Rome, AD 22–3].*
                  F £175 ($280) / **VF** £400 ($640) / **EF** £1,500 ($2,400)

1739

1739   **Brass dupondius.** IVSTITIA, diad. and dr. bust of Livia, as Justitia, r. Rev. TI CAESAR DIVI
        AVG F AVG P M TR POT XXIIII around large S C. RIC *Tiberius* 46. BMCRE *Tiberius* 79.
        CBN *Tiberius* 57. C 4. *[Rome, AD 22–3].*
        F £175 ($280) / VF £450 ($720) / EF £1,750 ($2,800)
        For a restoration of this type, see under Titus (nos. 2586–7).

1740

1740   Similar, but with obv. SALVS AVGVSTA, dr. bust of Livia, as Salus, r. RIC *Tiberius* 47.
        BMCRE *Tiberius* 81. CBN *Tiberius* 63. C 5. *[Rome, AD 22–3].*
        F £175 ($280) / VF £450 ($720) / EF £1,750 ($2,800)

1741   PIETAS, veiled, diad. and dr. bust of Livia, as Pietas, r. Rev. DRVSVS CAESAR TI AVGVSTI F
        TR POT ITER around large S C. RIC *Tiberius* 43. BMCRE *Tiberius* 98. CBN *Tiberius* 74.
        C 1. *[Rome, AD 23].*
        F £175 ($280) / VF £450 ($720) / EF £1,750 ($2,800)
        *For a restoration of this type, see under Titus (no. 2588). For other coins of Drusus, son of
        Tiberius, see nos. 1792–4.*

Alexandrian Coinage

1742   **Bronze obol** (25 mm. diam). ΛΙΟΥΙΑ ϹΕΒΑϹΤΟΥ, hd. of Livia r. Rev. No legend, double
        cornucopiae. RPC 5006. BMCG —. Cologne 35. Milne 6. *[After 19 BC].*
        F £150 ($240) / VF £375 ($600)

1743   No legend, hd. of Livia r. Rev. ΠΑΤΡΟϹ ΠΑΤΡΙΔΟϹ, double cornucopiae. RPC 5027.
        BMCG (Supplement) 2637. Cologne 36 Milne 15. *[AD 1–5].*
        F £120 ($192) / VF £300 ($480)

1744   Obv. Similar. Rev. L MA (= regnal year 41 of Augustus), Athena stg. l., holding Nike and
        shield. RPC 5065. BMCG (Supplement) 2633. Cologne 42 Milne 27. *[AD 11–12].*
        F £90 ($144) / VF £225 ($360)
        NB The illustration shows a variant dated regnal year 40 = AD 10–11.

1744   1747

1745   **Bronze hemiobol** (20 mm). ΛΙΟΥΙΑ CEBACTOY, hd. of Livia r. Rev. No legend, eagle stg.
        l., wings closed. RPC 5008. BMCG (Supplement) 2636. Cologne 34. Milne —. *[After
        19 BC].*   **F** £70 ($112) / **VF** £175 ($280)

1746   No legend, hd. of Livia r. Rev. L M (= regnal year 40 of Augustus) in oak-wreath. RPC
        5058. BMCG 32. Cologne —. Milne —. *[AD 10–11].*   **F** £60 ($96) / **VF** £150 ($240)

1747   **Bronze dichalkon** (15 mm). Obv. Similar. Rev. L Δ (= year 4 of Tiberius), two ears of corn
        and two poppies tied together in bundle. RPC 5079. BMCG 61. Cologne 60. Milne 35.
        [AD 17–18]   **F** £50 ($80) / **VF** £125 ($200)

GAIUS CAESAR

1749

*Gaius Caesar, eldest son of Agrippa and Julia and grandson of Augustus, was born in 20 BC. Both
he and his younger brother Lucius were adopted by Augustus in 17 BC and it was clearly the
emperor's hope that one or the other would eventually succeed him. In 5 BC Gaius assumed the
toga virilis, was admitted to the Senate, and was saluted as princeps iuventutis. Four years later he
married Livilla, daughter of Nero Claudius Drusus and Antonia, and in AD 1 became consul while
on an extended tour of the eastern frontier region. During the course of this visit he became
involved in military operations and was seriously wounded at the siege of Artagira in AD 2.
Eighteen months later, on his way back to Rome, he died in Lycia (21 February AD 4).Tragically,
his younger brother Lucius had also died two years previously, so the death of Gaius left Tiberius,
stepson of Augustus, as the only viable candidate for the imperial succession. The tragic loss of his
grandsons was a blow from which the elderly Augustus never fully recovered.*

1748

1748   **Gold aureus.** CAESAR, young bare hd. of Gaius Caesar r., all within oak-wreath. Rev.
        AVGVST, elaborately ornamented candelabrum, all within floral wreath decorated with
        bucrania and paterae. RIC 539. BMCRE 683. CBN 1012. C 1. *[Uncertain mint, 17 BC].*
                              VF £25,000 ($40,000) / **EF** £55,000 ($88,000)

1749 **Silver denarius.** Similar. RIC 540. BMCRE 684. CBN 1013. C 2. *[Uncertain mint, 17 BC].* **VF** £900 ($1,440) / **EF** £2,000 ($3,200)
This type, assigned by Cohen to the eldest grandson of Augustus, has been reattributed to the emperor himself by more recent cataloguers. There remains, however, no convincing explanation of the extremely youthful portrait, the suggestion of a 'rejuvenated' Augustus having no real foundation. The connection of the types with the Ludi Saeculares of 17 BC appears to be well established and this year saw the birth of Gaius' younger brother, Lucius, and the adoption of both by Augustus. Athough the entire legend refers to the emperor, the presence of the name 'CAESAR' alone below the child's portrait would seem to imply a reference to the young heir, the inheritor of his grandfather's name and appearance, at a time when Rome was celebrating the commencement of a new age and looking forward to the perpetuation of the era of peace and prosperity established by Augustus. The usual attribution of this issue to an 'eastern' mint is not supported either by the style of the engraving or by the evidence of provenance.

For other depictions of Gaius Caesar, see nos. 1578, 1596–7, and 1733–5.

LUCIUS CAESAR

1750

Lucius Caesar, second son of Agrippa and Julia and grandson of Augustus, was born in 17 BC. Immediately following his birth both he and his three-year-old brother Gaius were adopted by Augustus, it being the emperor's clear intention that one or the other would eventually succeed him. In 2 BC Lucius assumed the toga virilis and, like his brother three years before, was admitted to the Senate and saluted as princeps iuventutis. Tragically and inexplicably he died at Massilia in southern Gaul whilst en route to Spain (20 August AD 2).

1750 **Bronze semis** (20 mm. diam.) of Julia Traducta in Baetica (Hispania). L CAES, bare hd. of Lucius Caesar r. Rev. IVL TRAD, ear of corn. RPC 103. C 1. *[2 BC–AD 2].*
F £300 ($480) / **VF** £750 ($1,200)

1751 **Æ 20** of Tralles/Caesarea in Asia (Lydia). ΛΕΥΚΙΟΣ ΚΑΙΣΑΡ, bare hd. of Lucius Caesar r., lituus before. Rev. ΚΑΙΣΑΡΕΩΝ, capricorn r., cornucopiae on back. RPC 2651. *[2 BC–AD 2].*
F £350 ($560) / **VF** £850 ($1,360)

For other depictions of Lucius Caesar, see nos. 1578, 1597, and 1733–4.

AGRIPPA POSTUMUS

1752

M. Vipsanius Agrippa Postumus, youngest son of Agrippa and Julia, was born shortly after his father's death in 12 BC, hence his agnomen. Although adopted by his grandfather along with Tiberius following the death of Gaius Caesar in AD 4 his contumacious character and depraved behaviour branded him as unsuitable for high office and he was ultimately condemned by the Senate to permanent exile on the island of Planasia (AD 7). He was put to death soon after the accession of Tiberius in AD 14, his continued existence obviously posing a threat to the security of the new regime.

1752   **Bronze as?** (21 mm. diam.) of Corinth in Achaea. AGRIPPA CAESAR CORINTHI, bare hd. of Agrippa Postumus r. Rev. C HEIO POL/LIONE ITER / C MVSSIO P/RISCO II VIR in four lines within wreath of parsley. RPC 1141. C 1. *[AD 4–5].*   **F** £400 ($640) / **VF** £1,000 ($1,600)

TIBERIUS
19 Aug. AD 14–16 Mar. 37

1770

Tiberius was born in 42 BC, the elder son of the aristocratic Tiberius Claudius Nero, whose name he bore, and Livia Drusilla. When he was only three years of age his parents divorced and Livia married the triumvir Octavian, who was later to become Rome's first emperor under the name Augustus. As a young man Tiberius soon proved himself to be a most competent general and in a military career which was to span more than three decades (20 BC–AD 12) he campaigned extensively in many parts of the Empire. His relationship with his stepfather, however, was always strained and his marriage in 11 BC to Augustus' daughter Julia was most unhappy. This probably contributed to his decision in 6 BC to go into voluntary exile on the island of Rhodes, where he remained for the following eight years. He returned to Rome in AD 2 and on the death of Augustus' grandson Gaius Caesar two years later the emperor was reluctantly obliged to adopt Tiberius and acknowledge him as heir to the throne. Ten years later, on the death of Augustus, he became Rome's second emperor. Although an able administrator Tiberius was suspicious and reclusive by nature and always bore a resentment for the unfair treatment which he felt he had received from his stepfather. His reign was marred by a series of tragedies within the imperial family and by the machinations of the powerful praetorian prefect Sejanus who, prior to his downfall in AD 31, was probably aiming at usurping the imperial power itself. In AD 26 Tiberius once again retired to an island retreat, this time Capreae, and never again set foot in Rome during the remaining eleven years of his life. He died at Misenum on 16 March AD 37 in his seventy-ninth year and was succeeded by his great-nephew Caligula. His own son, Drusus, had died fourteen years before, probably a victim of Sejanus.

    For the titles and powers of this reign, including Alexandrian regnal dates, see table on pp. 306–7.

Pre-accession issues under Augustus

1753   **Brass sestertius.** TI CAESAR AVGVSTI F IMPERATOR V, bare hd. l. Rev. ROM ET AVG, altar of the cult of Roma and Augustus at Lugdunum, flanked by two columns, each surmounted by statue of Victory. RIC *Augustus* 240. BMCRE *Augustus* 572. CBN *Augustus* 1737. C 28. *[Lugdunum, AD 10–11].*
    F £750 ($1,200) / **VF** £1,850 ($2,960) / **EF** £7,500 ($12,000)

1753

1754 **Brass dupondius.** Similar, but with obv. TI CAESAR AVGVST F IMPERAT V, laur. hd. r. RIC *Augustus* 236a. BMCRE *Augustus* 575. CBN *Augustus* 1757. C 33. *[Lugdunum, AD 10–11].* F £50 ($80) / **VF** £120 ($192) / **EF** £300 ($480)

1755 **Copper as.** Obv. Similar, but hd. of Tiberius is bare. Rev. PONTIFEX TRIBVN POTESTATE XII around large S C. RIC *Augustus* 469. BMCRE *Augustus* 271. CBN *Augustus* 878. C 27. *[Rome, AD 10–11].* F £60 ($96) / **VF** £150 ($240) / **EF** £450 ($720)

1756 Similar to 1754, but with obv. legend TI CAESAR AVGVST F IMPERAT VII. RIC *Augustus* 245. BMCRE *Augustus* 585. CBN *Augustus* 1769. C 37. *[Lugdunum, AD 12–14].* F £45 ($72) / **VF** £110 ($176) / **EF** £275 ($440)

1757 **Brass semis.** Similar. RIC *Augustus* 246. BMCRE *Augustus* 588. CBN *Augustus* 1805. C 38. *[Lugdunum, AD 12–14].* F £50 ($80) / **VF** £120 ($192) / **EF** £300 ($480)

For other coins depicting Tiberius struck during the reign of Augustus, see nos. 1638 and 1736–7.

Post-accession issues

1758 **Gold aureus.** TI CAESAR DIVI AVG F AVGVSTVS, laur. hd. r. Rev. Rev. TR POT XVI IMP VII, Tiberius in triumphal quadriga r., holding branch and eagle-tipped sceptre. RIC 1. BMCRE 1. CBN 3. C 45. *[Lugdunum, AD 14–15].* **VF** £1,800 ($2,880) / **EF** £4,000 ($6,400)

1759 Similar, but with TR POT XVII. RIC 3. BMCRE 2. CBN 4. C 47. *[Lugdunum, AD 15–16].* **VF** £1,800 ($2,880) / **EF** £4,000 ($6,400)

1760   1761

1760 Obv. Similar. Rev. PONTIF MAXIM, female figure (Livia?) seated r., holding sceptre and branch. RIC 25. BMCRE 30. CBN 13. C 15. *[Lugdunum, after AD 16].* **VF** £1,250 ($2,000) / **EF** £2,750 ($4,400)

1761 **Gold quinarius.** TI DIVI F AVGVSTVS, laur. hd. r. Rev. TR POT XX, Victory seated r. on globe, holding wreath. RIC 6. BMCRE 14. CBN —. C 50. *[Lugdunum, AD 18–19].*
VF £1,100 ($1,760) / **EF** £2,500 ($4,000)

1762   1763

1762 **Silver denarius.** As 1759 (rev. Tiberius in quadriga). RIC 4. BMCRE 7. CBN 5. RSC 48. *[Lugdunum, AD 15–16].*
VF £275 ($440) / **EF** £625 ($1,000)

1763 As 1760 (rev. PONTIF MAXIM, female seated). RIC 26. BMCRE 34. CBN 16. RSC 16. *[Lugdunum, after AD 16].*
VF £175 ($280) / **EF** £375 ($600)
This type is commonly referred to as the 'Tribute Penny' of the Bible after the well-known New Testament story in St. Matthew's Gospel (22, 17–21).

1764

1764 **Brass sestertius.** CIVITATIBVS ASIAE RESTITVTIS, Tiberius seated l. on curule chair, holding patera and sceptre. Rev. TI CAESAR DIVI AVG F AVGVST P M TR POT XXIIII around large S C. RIC 48. BMCRE 70. CBN 52. C 3. *[Rome, AD 22–3].*
F £200 ($320) / **VF** £500 ($800) / **EF** £2,000 ($3,200)
This publicizes the measures undertaken by Tiberius for the relief of those cities of the province Asia which had been affected by a devastating earthquake in AD 17 centred near the city of Sardis. The type was restored by Titus (see no. 2590).

1765 No legend, empty triumphal quadriga r. Rev. TI CAESAR DIVI AVG F AVGVST P M TR POT XXXVII around large S C. RIC 60. BMCRE 113. CBN 91. C 66. *[Rome, AD 35–6].*
F £175 ($280) / **VF** £450 ($720) / **EF** £1,750 ($2,800)

1765

1766 **Brass sestertius.** — hexastyle temple of Concordia, containing cult-statue and decorated with additional statuary on the roof and flanking the entrance steps. Rev. TI CAESAR DIVI AVG F AVGVST P M TR POT XXXIIX around large S C. RIC 67. BMCRE 132. CBN 119. C 70. *[Rome, AD 36–7].*   F £250 ($400) / **VF** £625 ($1,000) / **EF** £2,500 ($4,000)
This temple, at the northern end of the Forum, was restored by Tiberius during the reign of Augustus and rededicated in AD 10. The building housed many antique statues, hence its elaborately decorated representation on this coin type.

1767

1767 **Brass dupondius.** TI CAESAR DIVI AVG F AVGVST IMP VIII, laur. hd.l. Rev. CLEMENTIAE S C, small facing bust within laurel-wreath at centre of elaborately decorated circular shield. RIC 38. BMCRE 85. CBN 125. C 4. *[Rome, ca. AD 22].*
F £175 ($280) / **VF** £425 ($680) / **EF** £1,500 ($2,400)

1768

1768 Similar, but with rev. legend MODERATIONI S C and the facing bust is encircled by 'petal' motif instead of wreath. RIC 39. BMCRE 90. CBN 129. C 5. *[Rome, ca. AD 22].*
F £175 ($280) / **VF** £425 ($680) / **EF** £1,500 ($2,400)

1769   **Copper as.** TI CAESAR DIVI AVG F AVGVST IMP VII, bare hd. l. Rev. PONTIF MAXIM
        TRIBVN POTEST XVII S C, Livia seated r., holding patera and sceptre. RIC 34. BMCRE 68.
        CBN 41. C 18. *[Rome, AD 15–16].*   **F** £75 ($120) / **VF** £175 ($280) / **EF** £525 ($840)

1770   TI CAESAR DIVI AVG F AVGVST IMP VIII, bare hd. l. Rev. PONTIF MAXIM TRIBVN POTEST
        XXIIII around large S C. RIC 44. BMCRE 91. CBN 68. C 25. *[Rome, AD 22–3].*
                                         F £75 ($120) / **VF** £175 ($280) / **EF** £525 ($840)
        For restorations of this type, see under Titus (nos. 2591–2) and Domitian (no. 2895).

1771

1771   Obv. Similar, but laur. hd. l. Rev. PONTIF MAXIM TRIBVN POTEST XXXVII S C, winged
        caduceus. RIC 59. BMCRE 120. CBN 103. C 22. *[Rome, AD 35–6].*
                                         F £65 ($104) / **VF** £150 ($240) / **EF** £450 ($720)
        For a restoration of this type, see under Titus (no. 2593).

1772

1772   — Rev. PONTIF MAX TR POT XXXIIX S C, rudder superimposed on large banded globe,
        small globe below. RIC 64. BMCRE 135. CBN 122. Cf. C 14. *[Rome, AD 36–7].*
                                         F £65 ($104) / **VF** £150 ($240) / **EF** £450 ($720)
        *This reverse type was 'restored' by Nerva in AD 96 in combination with a Divus Augustus
        obverse (see no. 3079).*

1773   **Copper quadrans.** TI CAESAR DIVI AVG F AVGVSTVS, laur. hd. r. Rev. ROM ET AVG,
        altar of the cult of Roma and Augustus at Lugdunum, flanked by two columns, each sur-
        mounted by statue of Victory. RIC 32. BMCRE 62. CBN 35. C 39. *[Lugdunum, AD
        14–15].*   **F** £55 ($88) / **VF** £140 ($224)

For a later depiction of Tiberius, see no. 2008. For restorations of the coinage of Tiberius, see under
Titus (nos. 2589–92), Domitian (no. 2895), and Trajan.

Alexandrian Coinage

The debased silver tetradrachms, last struck under Cleopatra in 31–30 BC, were revived in the 7th Alexandrian year of Tiberius (AD 20–21).

1774　**Billon tetradrachm.** TIBEPIOΣ KAIΣAP ΣEBAΣTOΣ, laur. hd. of Tiberius r., L Z (= regnal year 7) before. Rev. ΘEOΣ ΣEBAΣTOΣ, rad. hd. of Augustus r. RPC 5089. BMCG 36. Cologne 48. Milne 38. *[AD 20–21].*　　F £60 ($96) / **VF** £150 ($240) / **EF** £375 ($600)

1774   1777

1775　Similar, but with L IΘ (= regnal year 19) on obv., and the hd. of Augustus is to l. RPC 5094. BMCG 44. Cologne 53. Milne (Addenda) 56*. *[AD 32–3].*
F £65 ($104) / **VF** £160 ($256) / **EF** £400 ($640)

1776　Similar, but the hd. of Tiberius is to l., with L KA (= regnal year 21) before, and the hd. of Augustus is to r., with lituus before. RPC 5101. BMCG 48. Cologne 56. Milne —. *[AD 34–5].*　　F £70 ($112) / **VF** £175 ($280) / **EF** £425 ($680)

1777　**Bronze hemiobol** (20 mm). No legend, bare hd. r. Rev. TIBEPIOY, hippopotamus r., L E (= regnal year 5) in ex. RPC 5082. BMCG 57. Cologne 47. Milne 36. *[AD 18–19].*
F £35 ($56) / **VF** £85 ($136)

1778　**Bronze dichalkon** (15 mm). ΣE, bare hd. r. Rev. TI / L Δ (= regnal year 4) in laurel-wreath. RPC 5076. BMCG 60, 63. Cologne 46. Milne —. *[AD 17–18].*
F £30 ($48) / **VF** £75 ($120)

1779　TIBE, bare hd. r. Rev. L Δ (= regnal year 4), eagle stg. l. RPC 5077. BMCG 54. Cologne —. Milne (Supplement) 35a. *[AD 17–18].*　　F £30 ($48) / **VF** £75 ($120)

1780　No legend, bare hd. r. Rev. TIBE, crocodile r., L Δ (= regnal year 4) in ex. RPC 5078. BMCG 51. Cologne —. Milne 33. *[AD 17–18].*　　F £30 ($48) / **VF** £75 ($120)

For other local coinages of this reign, see *Roman Provincial Coinage,* vol. I, and *Greek Imperial Coins & Their Values,* pp. 22–30.

Issues of Tiberius in honour of Divus Augustus

1781　**Gold aureus.** TI CAESAR DIVI AVG F AVGVSTVS, laur. hd. of Tiberius r. Rev. DIVOS AVGVST DIVI F, laur. hd. of Augustus r., star above. RIC 24. BMCRE 29. CBN 1. C *Tiberius and Augustus 3. [Lugdunum, AD 14–16].*
VF £2,250 ($3,600) / **EF** £5,000 ($8,000)
NB The illustration shows a variant with head of Augustus bare.

1781

1782   **Brass sestertius.** DIVVS AVGVSTVS PATER, Augustus, rad., seated l., holding branch and
sceptre, altar at feet. Rev. TI CAESAR DIVI AVG F AVGVST P M TR POT XXIIII around large
S C. RIC 49. BMCRE 74. CBN 50. C *Augustus* 309. *[Rome, AD 22–3].*
    F £175 ($280) / **VF** £450 ($720) / **EF** £1,750 ($2,800)
*This type may represent the statue of Divus Augustus set up near the Theatre of Marcellus
in Rome. Restorations of the issue were made by Titus in AD 80 (see no. 2579) and by
Nerva in AD 96 (see no. 3078). The design was also adapted for issues of Titus honouring
Divus Vespasian (see no. 2573) and of Domitian honouring Divus Titus (see no. 2886).*

1783

1783   DIVO AVGVSTO S P Q R, shield, inscribed OB / CIVES / SER, encircled by oak-wreath and
supported by two capricorns, back to back, globe beneath. Rev. Similar to previous, but
legend ends TR POT XXXVII. RIC 63. BMCRE 109. CBN 93. C *Augustus* 303. *[Rome, AD
35–6].*   **F** £150 ($240) / **VF** £375 ($600) / **EF** £1,500 ($2,400)

1784

1784   DIVO AVGVSTO S P Q R, team of four elephants drawing ornamented car l., surmounted
by seated statue of Augustus, holding branch and sceptre. Rev. Similar to previous, but legend ends TR POT XXXIIX. RIC 68. BMCRE 125. CBN 111. C *Augustus* 308. *[Rome, AD
36–7].*   **F** £150 ($240) / **VF** £375 ($600) / **EF** £1,500 ($2,400)
*This type provided the inspiration for another of Titus' sestertii issued in commemoration
of the deified Vespasian (see no. 2572).*

1785   **Brass dupondius.** DIVVS AVGVSTVS PATER, rad. hd. of Augustus l. Rev. S C, circular
shrine of Vesta on the Palatine, with six columns and domed roof, flanked by two rectangular bases surmounted by statues of a calf and a ram. RIC 74. BMCRE 142. CBN 146. C
Augustus 251. *[Rome, AD 22–3].*   **F** £150 ($240) / **VF** £400 ($640) / **EF** £1,500 ($2,400)
*This shrine was erected near the house of Augustus shortly after the emperor had suc-
ceeded to the office of pontifex maximus following the death of Lepidus in 12 BC. Many
sacred objects were transferred to it from the temple of Vesta in the Forum, the most
important of which was the Palladium, the Trojan statue of Pallas Athene traditionally
brought to Italy by Aeneas. The Aedicula Vestae appeared again on gold issued under
Vespasian (see nos. 2255, 2423 and 2626).*

1786

1786   — Rev. S C, Victory alighting l., wings spread, holding shield inscribed S P Q R. RIC 77.
BMCRE 141. CBN 145. C *Augustus* 242. *[Rome, AD 22–3].*
F £120 ($192) / **VF** £300 ($480) / **EF** £900 ($1,440)
For a restoration of this type, see under Titus (no. 2580).

1787

1787   — Rev. Large S C within oak-wreath. RIC 79. BMCRE 143. CBN 150. C *Augustus* 252.
[Rome, AD 22–6].   **F** £100 ($160) / **VF** £250 ($400) / **EF** £750 ($1,200)

1788

1788   **Copper as.** Obv. Similar, but with star above hd. of Augustus and thunderbolt before. Rev.
S C, Livia seated r., holding patera and sceptre. RIC 72. BMCRE 151. CBN 44. C *Augustus*
244. *[Rome, AD 15–16].*   **F** £75 ($120) / **VF** £175 ($280) / **EF** £425 ($680)

1789

1789 **Copper as.** Obv. As 1785. Rev. PROVIDENT S C, façade of altar-enclosure of the *Ara Providentiae Augusti*, with double panelled door and horns of the altar visible above. RIC 81. BMCRE 146. CBN 131. C *Augustus* 228. *[Rome,* AD *22–30].*
　　　　　　　　　　　　　　F £65 ($104) / **VF** £150 ($240) / **EF** £375 ($600)
The site of the altar dedicated to the 'providence' of Augustus is not known, but it may have been located in the Campus Martius. The type was later revived by Vitellius (see no. 2222) and by Vespasian (see nos. 2360, 2477, and 2657). The original issue was restored by Titus (see nos. 2581–2), by Domitian (see no. 2892), and by Nerva (see no. 3080).

1790

1790 — Rev. S C, eagle stg. facing on globe, hd. r., wings open. RIC 82. BMCRE 155. CBN 136. C *Augustus* 247. *[Rome,* AD *34–7].* **F** £65 ($104) / **VF** £150 ($240) / **EF** £375 ($600)
For restorations of this type, see under Titus (nos. 2583–4), Domitian (no. 2893), and Nerva (no. 3082).

1791

1791 — Rev. S C, winged thunderbolt. RIC 83. BMCRE 157. CBN 141. C *Augustus* 249. *[Rome,* AD *34–7].* 　　　　　　　　　　**F** £65 ($104) / **VF** £150 ($240) / **EF** £375 ($600)
For a restoration of this type, see under Nerva (no. 3081).

See also nos. 1774–6. For later issues in honour of Divus Augustus, see under Caligula (nos. 1806–11 and 1819), Claudius (no. 1891), Nero (no. 2007), Civil Wars (nos. 2064–6, 2068, and 2073), Titus (nos. 2579–85), Domitian (nos. 2892–3), Nerva (nos. 3075–83), Trajan, Hadrian, and Trajan Decius.

DRUSUS

353

Issues of Tiberius in honour of his deceased son Drusus († AD 23)

1792

1792 **Silver drachm.** TI CAES AVG P M TR P XXXV (TR in monogram), laur. hd. of Tiberius r. Rev. DRVSVS CAES TI AVG F COS II TR P IT (TR in monogram), bare hd. of Drusus l. RPC 3622. RIC 86. BMCRE 171. CBN 159. RSC *Drusus and Tiberius* 2a. *[Caesarea in Cappadocia, AD 33–4].* VF £450 ($720) / **EF** £1,100 ($1,760)

For lifetime issues in the name of Drusus, see nos. 1741 and 1793–4.

DRUSUS

1794

The two principal heirs to the imperial throne during the reign of Tiberius were his nephew Germanicus, the elder son of Nero Claudius Drusus and Antonia, and Drusus the younger (born 13 BC), his own son by his first wife Vipsania. Germanicus was adopted by his uncle in AD 4 and became the imperial heir a decade later on the accession of Tiberius. However, the popular young prince was destined to enjoy his new rank for only half a decade. In AD 19, at the Syrian capital of Antioch, Germanicus Caesar died suddenly under mysterious circumstances at the age of only thirty-four. As a result, Tiberius' son Drusus now became heir to the throne and three years later he was granted the tribunician power. A series of bronze coins, in all three principal denominations, was struck in his honour, but soon afterwards he too died prematurely at the age of only thirty-six. It seems likely that he was the victim of the ruthlessly ambitious praetorian prefect Sejanus who had seduced his wife Livilla, sister of the late Caesar Germanicus, and persuaded her to administer poison to her unfortunate husband. Twin sons, Tiberius Gemellus and Germanicus, had been born to the couple in AD 19. Germanicus died in early childhood, but Gemellus survived to be joint-heir with Caligula, only to be murdered by his elder cousin in AD 37 soon after the death of Tiberius.

1793 **Brass sestertius.** No legend, caduceus between two crossed cornuacopiae, each surmounted by bust of one of the twin sons of Drusus, Tiberius Gemellus and Germanicus. Rev. DRVSVS CAESAR TI AVG F DIVI AVG N PONT TR POT II around large S C. RIC *Tiberius* 42. BMCRE *Tiberius* 95. CBN *Tiberius* 72. C 1. *[Rome, AD 23].*
F £225 ($360) / **VF** £550 ($880) / **EF** £2,250 ($3,600)

1793

1794 **Copper as.** DRVSVS CAESAR TI AVG F DIVI AVG N, bare hd. of Drusus l. Rev. PONTIF
TRIBVN POTEST ITER around large S C. RIC *Tiberius* 45. BMCRE *Tiberius* 99. CBN
Tiberius 78. C 2. *[Rome, AD 23].* **F** £75 ($120) / **VF** £185 ($296) / **EF** £450 ($720)
For restorations of this type, see under Titus (nos. 2594–5) and Domitian (no. 2896).

See also nos. 1741 and 1792.

CALIGULA
16 Mar. AD 37–24 Jan. 41

1801

*Gaius Julius Caesar Germanicus was the great-grandson of both of the principal adversaries in
the battle of Actium (31 BC), Mark Antony and Octavian. Born at Antium (modern Anzio) on
31 August AD 12, he was the youngest of the sons of Germanicus and Agrippina Senior. He early
acquired the nickname 'Caligula' from the tiny military boots or 'caligae' that he wore as a young
child during his father's campaigns in Germany. In the latter part of Tiberius' reign Caligula's
mother and two elder brothers all fell victim to the political ambitions of the praetorian prefect
Sejanus. Caligula's youth saved him and in AD 32 he moved to Capreae where he was the constant
companion of his great-uncle, the elderly and reclusive Tiberius. On the emperor's death, in March
AD 37, Caligula ascended the throne and occupied it until his assassination less than four years
later. The excesses and debaucheries of his short reign are well documented and have exercised the
talents and imaginations of authors and film makers in the modern era. In the early months, when
he was probably under the influence of his grandmother Antonia, he showed promise of becoming a
worthy ruler, but later in the year he fell seriously ill and soon began to exhibit clear signs of
insanity. The situation deteriorated rapidly until virtually everyone in the palace and in government circles began to feel personally threatened. Ultimately, a plot was formed amongst the praetorian guard and the emperor was murdered in his palace on 24 January AD 41. In marked contrast
to Caligula's bizarre behaviour the coinage of his reign is notably conservative in character and
there are many types honouring the emperor's relatives, both living and deceased.*

RIC attributes the earlier precious metal issues of this reign, which depict the emperor bare-headed, to the mint of Lugdunum and all subsequent issues, on which he appears laureate, to Rome. CBN prefers to assign them all to Lugdunum and this attribution has been favoured here.

For the titles and powers of this reign, including Alexandrian regnal dates, see table on p. 307.

1795   **Gold aureus.** C CAESAR AVG PON M TR POT III COS III, laur. hd. r. Rev. S P Q R / P P / OB C S in three lines within oak-wreath. RIC 27. BMCRE 29. CBN 37. C 20. *[Lugdunum, AD 40].*   **VF** £5,500 ($8,800) / **EF** £12,500 ($20,000)

1796   **Gold quinarius.** C CAESAR AVG GERMANICVS, bare hd. r. Rev. P M TR POT COS, Victory seated r. on globe, holding wreath. RIC 5. BMCRE 6. CBN p. 61, *. C 14. *[Lugdunum, AD 37].*   **VF** £2,750 ($4,400) / **EF** £6,000 ($9,600)

1797   1798

1797   **Silver denarius.** As 1795. RIC 28. BMCRE 29, note. CBN 39. RSC 21. *[Lugdunum, AD 40].*   **VF** £1,400 ($2,240) / **EF** £3,000 ($4,800)

1798   **Silver drachm.** Obv. as 1796. Rev. IMPERATOR PONT MAX AVG TR POT, simpulum and lituus (emblems of the pontificate and augurate). RPC 3624. RIC 63. BMCRE 102. CBN 161. RSC 12. *[Caesarea in Cappadocia, AD 37–8].*   **VF** £500 ($800) / **EF** £1,250 ($2,000)

1799

1799   **Brass sestertius.** C CAESAR DIVI AVG PRON AVG P M TR P III P P, laur. hd. l. Rev. ADLOCVT COH, Caligula stg. l. on platform, haranguing five soldiers. RIC 40. BMCRE p. 156, *. CBN 100. C 2. *[Rome, AD 39–40].*
         F £650 ($1,040) / **VF** £1,600 ($2,560) / **EF** £6,500 ($10,400)

1800   C CAESAR AVG GERMANICVS PON M TR POT, laur. hd. l. Rev. AGRIPPINA DRVSILLA IVLIA S C, the three sisters of Caligula stg. side by side, with the attributes of Securitas, Concordia, and Fortuna. RIC 33. BMCRE 36. CBN 47. C 4. *[Rome, AD 37–8].*
         F £800 ($1,280) / **VF** £2,500 ($4,000) / **EF** £8,000 ($12,800)

1800

1801

1801   **Brass sestertius.** Obv. As 1799. Rev. **S P Q R / P P / OB CIVES / SERVATOS** in four lines within oak-wreath. RIC 46. BMCRE 58. CBN 101. C 25. *[Rome, AD 39–40].*

   F £400 ($640) / **VF** £1,000 ($1,600) / **EF** £4,000 ($6,400)

1802   C CAESAR DIVI AVG PRON AVG P M TR P IIII P P, Pietas seated l., holding patera and resting l. elbow on statuette, **PIETAS** in ex. Rev. **DIVO AVG S C**, garlanded hexastyle temple of Divus Augustus, before which Caligula stands to l., sacrificing at altar, accompanied by two attendants. RIC 51. BMCRE 69. CBN 118. C 11. *[Rome, AD 40–41].*

   F £300 ($480) / **VF** £750 ($1,200) / **EF** £3,000 ($4,800)

   There were two temples in Rome honouring the deified Augustus, one on the Palatine, the other of uncertain location, possibly behind the Basilica Julia in the depression between the Palatine and Capitoline Hills. The latter, built under Tiberius, was dedicated by Caligula in August, AD 37, an event commemorated by this elaborate architectural type (cf. Hill, 'The Monuments of Ancient Rome as Coin Types', pp. 19–21).

1803   1804

1803   **Copper as.** Obv. As 1800, but emperor is bare-headed. Rev. **VESTA S C**, Vesta seated l., holding patera and sceptre. RIC 38. BMCRE 46. CBN 54. C 27. *[Rome, AD 37–8].*

   F £100 ($160) / **VF** £250 ($400) / **EF** £750 ($1,200)

1804   **Copper quadrans.** C CAESAR DIVI AVG PRON AVG around S C divided by pileus. Rev.
        PON M TR P IIII P P COS TERT around R C C. RIC 52. BMCRE 64. CBN 109. C 7. *[Rome,
        AD 40].*   **F** £25 ($40) / **VF** £55 ($88) / **EF** £125 ($200)
        The abbreviation R C C *has generally been expanded to remissa ducentesima, a reference
        to Caligula's abolition of the tax on auctions originally introduced by Augustus at 1% and
        later reduced to half that level under Tiberius.*

Alexandrian Coinage

Alexandria was virtually inactive during this reign, only a single diminutive bronze type being certainly attributed to the mint by the authors of RPC.

1805   **Bronze chalkos** (10 mm). Rad. hd. of Sol r., L Γ (= regnal year 3) before. Rev. ΓΑΙΟΥ
        above crescent. RPC 5106. BMCG 34 (attributed to Gaius Caesar). Cologne —. Milne —.
        [AD 38–9].   **F** £65 ($104) / **VF** £125 ($200)

For other local coinages of this reign, see *Roman Provincial Coinage,* vol. I, and *Greek Imperial
Coins & Their Values,* pp. 34–9.

Issues of Caligula in honour of Divus Augustus

        1806   1807

1806   **Gold aureus.** C CAESAR AVG GERM P M TR POT COS, bare hd. of Caligula r. Rev. No leg-
        end, rad. hd. of Augustus r., between two stars. RIC 1. BMCRE 1. CBN 1. C *Caligula and
        Augustus* 10. *[Lugdunum, AD 37].*   **VF** £5,500 ($8,800) / **EF** £12,500 ($20,000)

1807   C CAESAR AVG GERM P M TR POT, laur. hd. of Caligula r. Rev. DIVVS AVG PATER
        PATRIAE, rad. hd. of Augustus r. RIC 15. BMCRE 16. CBN 17. C *Caligula and Augustus*
        1. *[Lugdunum, AD 37–8].*   **VF** £5,500 ($8,800) / **EF** £12,500 ($20,000)

1808   **Silver denarius.** As 1806. RIC 2. BMCRE 4. CBN 3. RSC *Caligula and Augustus* 11.
        [Lugdunum, AD 37].   **VF** £1,300 ($2,080) / **EF** £2,800 ($4,480)

1809   C CAESAR AVG GERM P M TR POT, bare hd. of Caligula r. Rev. As 1807. RIC 10. BMCRE
        10. CBN 9. RSC *Caligula and Augustus* 3. *[Lugdunum, AD 37].*
                                                       VF £1,300 ($2,080) / **EF** £2,800 ($4,480)

1810   Similar, but with obv. C CAESAR AVG PON M TR POT III COS III, laur. hd. of Caligula r.
        RIC 24. BMCRE 25. CBN 32. RSC *Caligula and Augustus* 7. *[Lugdunum, AD 40].*
                                                       VF £1,300 ($2,080) / **EF** £2,800 ($4,480)

1811   **Brass dupondius.** DIVVS AVGVSTVS, rad. hd. of Augustus l., dividing S – C. Rev.
        CONSENSV SENAT ET EQ ORDIN P Q R, Augustus (or Caligula) seated l. on curule chair,
        holding branch. RIC 56. BMCRE 88. CBN 134. C *Augustus* 87. *[Rome, AD 37–41].*
                                    F £90 ($144) / **VF** £225 ($360) / **EF** £675 ($1,080)

See also no. 1819.

1811

Issue of Caligula in honour of his deceased grandfather Agrippa († 12 BC)

1812

1812　**Copper as. M AGRIPPA L F COS III**, hd. of Agrippa l., wearing rostral crown. Rev. **S − C** either side of Neptune stg. l., holding dolphin and trident. RIC 58. BMCRE *Tiberius* 161. CBN 77. C *Agrippa* 3. *[Rome, AD 37–41].*

F £65 ($104) / **VF** £150 ($240) / **EF** £600 ($960)

For restorations of this type, see under Titus (no. 2589) and Domitian (no. 2894). For earlier depictions of Agrippa on the coinage of Augustus, see nos. 1725–31.

Issues of Caligula in honour of his deceased father Germanicus († AD 19)

Germanicus was the elder son of Nero Claudius Drusus and Antonia and was born in 15 BC. He lost his father six years later and in AD 4 was adopted by his uncle Tiberius, heir to the imperial throne of Augustus. His military exploits in Germany early in Tiberius' reign further enhanced his reputation and popularity, his clear intention being to emulate his father's achievements in the area. Recalled to Rome by Tiberius in AD 17 Germanicus celebrated a magnificent triumph on 26 May. He was then dispatched to the East to take up a new command, with extraordinary powers over all of Rome's eastern territories. He reduced Cappadocia and Commagene to provincial status, but then offended Tiberius by taking an unauthorized pleasure trip to Egypt, a country which had been barred to senators by Augustus. On returning to Antioch he quarreled with Piso, the governor of Syria, and soon afterwards was stricken with a mysterious illness, which resulted in his death on 10 October AD 19. Piso was suspected of being implicated in the sudden and unexpected demise of the popular prince and later committed suicide, though he always protested his innocence. Germanicus was married to Agrippina Senior, daughter of Agrippa and Julia, and had nine children, one of whom was the future emperor Caligula. The Roman coinage in the name of Germanicus was all produced subsequent to his death. The earlier, more extensive, issues were struck in a range of denominations in all metals under his son, the emperor Caligula (AD 37–41); whilst his brother, the emperor Claudius (AD 41–54), produced a more limited commemorative coinage consisting principally of copper asses.

1813   **Gold aureus.** C CAESAR AVG GERM P M TR POT, bare hd. of Caligula r. Rev. GERMANICVS CAES P C CAES AVG GERM, bare hd. of Germanicus r. RIC 11. BMCRE 11. CBN 14. C *Germanicus and Caligula* 3. *[Lugdunum, AD 37].*

VF £5,500 ($8,800) / **EF** £12,500 ($20,000)

1814

1814   Similar, but Caligula is laur. RIC 17. BMCRE 18. CBN 27. C *Germanicus and Caligula* 1. *[Lugdunum, AD 37–8].*   VF £5,500 ($8,800) / **EF** £12,500 ($20,000)

1815   **Silver denarius.** As 1813. RIC 12. BMCRE 12. CBN 15. RSC *Germanicus and Caligula* 4. *[Lugdunum, AD 37].*   VF £1,500 ($2,400) / **EF** £3,200 ($5,120)

1816   Similar, but with obv. C CAESAR AVG PON M TR POT III COS III, laur. hd. of Caligula r. RIC 26. BMCRE 28. CBN 34. RSC *Germanicus and Caligula* 5. *[Lugdunum, AD 40].*
VF £1,500 ($2,400) / **EF** £3,200 ($5,120)

1817   **Silver didrachm.** GERMANICVS CAESAR TI AVG F COS II, bare hd. of Germanicus r. Rev. Germanicus stg. l., holding spear and crowning King Artaxias of Armenia who stands facing, GERMANICVS on r., ARTAXIAS on l. RPC 3629. RIC 59. BMCRE 104. CBN 164. RSC *Germanicus* 6a. *[Caesarea in Cappadocia, AD 37–8].*
F £3,750 ($6,000) / **VF** £7,500 ($12,000)
This commemorates Germanicus' installation of Artaxias as a Roman vassal in Armenia in AD 18. RPC (following Walker, 'The Metrology of the Roman Silver Coinage') tentatively attributes this and the following type to the reign of Claudius.

1818   **Silver drachm.** Similar. RPC 3630. RIC —. BMCRE 104, note. CBN 165. RSC *Germanicus* 6. *[Caesarea in Cappadocia, AD 37–8].*
F £3,000 ($4,800) / **VF** £6,000 ($9,600)

1819

1819   GERMANICVS CAES TI AVGV COS II G M, bare hd. of Germanicus r. Rev. DIVVS AVGVSTVS, rad. hd. of Augustus l. RPC 3623. RIC 60. BMCRE 105. CBN 163 var. RSC *Germanicus and Augustus* 2. *[Caesarea in Cappadocia, AD 37–8].*
VF £450 ($720) / **EF** £1,100 ($1,760)
RPC attributes this type to the reign of Tiberius, AD 33–4.

1820

1820   **Brass dupondius.** GERMANICVS CAESAR, Germanicus in triumphal quadriga r., holding
        eagle-tipped sceptre. Rev. SIGNIS RECEPT DEVICTIS GERM S C, Germanicus stg. l., his r.
        hand raised, holding legionary eagle in l. RIC 57. BMCRE 93. CBN 140. C *Germanicus* 7.
        [Rome, AD 37–41].   **F** £150 ($240) / **VF** £350 ($560) / **EF** £900 ($1,440)

1821   **Copper as.** GERMANICVS CAESAR TI AVGVST F DIVI AVG N, bare hd. of Germanicus l.
        Rev. C CAESAR AVG GERMANICVS PON M TR POT around large S C. RIC 35. BMCRE 49.
        CBN 73. C *Germanicus* 1. *[Rome, AD 37–8].*
                                      F £70 ($112) / **VF** £175 ($280) / **EF** £425 ($680)

1822

1822   Similar, but with AVG F for AVGVST F on obv., and with rev. legend C CAESAR DIVI AVG
        PRON AVG P M TR P IIII P P. Cf. RIC 50. BMCRE 74. CBN 123. C *Germanicus* 4. *[Rome,*
        AD 40–41].   **F** £70 ($112) / **VF** £175 ($280) / **EF** £425 ($680)
        For restorations of this type, see under Titus (nos. 2598–9) and Domitian (no. 2897).

For later issues honouring Germanicus, see under Claudius (nos. 1904–5).

Issues of Caligula in honour of his deceased mother Agrippina Senior († AD 33)

Born in 15 BC, the elder Agrippina was the daughter of Marcus Vipsanius Agrippa and Julia,
daughter of Augustus. About AD 5 she married Germanicus, elder son of Nero Claudius Drusus,
just after his adoption by his uncle Tiberius. She accompanied her husband on many of his military
campaigns, sharing the hardships of camp life. She also bore him nine children, including the
future emperor Caligula and the empress Agrippina Junior, mother of the future emperor Nero.
Following her husband's early death at Antioch in AD 19 she lived in Rome and became involved in
the opposition to the growing power of the praetorian prefect Sejanus. Unfortunately, she was on
bad terms with the emperor Tiberius, whom she suspected of being implicated in her husband's
mysterious demise. In AD 29 Sejanus succeeded in engineering her arrest and banishment to the
island of Pandateria, where she died of starvation four years later. Her coinage, like that of her
husband, was all issued posthumously, initially under her son, Caligula, and later under her
brother-in-law, Claudius.

1823   **Gold aureus.** C CAESAR AVG GERM P M TR POT, bare hd. of Caligula r. Rev. AGRIPPINA
       MAT C CAES AVG GERM, dr. bust of Agrippina Senior r. RIC 7. BMCRE 7. CBN 11. C
       Agrippina and Caligula 3. *[Lugdunum, AD 37].*
                              VF £5,500 ($8,800) / **EF** £12,500 ($20,000)

1824   Similar, but Caligula is laur. RIC 13. BMCRE 14. CBN 22. C *Agrippina and Caligula* 1.
       [Lugdunum, AD 37–8].   **VF** £5,500 ($8,800) / **EF** £12,500 ($20,000)

1825

1825   **Silver denarius.** As previous. RIC 14. BMCRE 15. CBN 24. RSC *Agrippina and Caligula*
       2. *[Lugdunum, AD 37–8].*   **VF** £1,500 ($2,400) / **EF** £3,200 ($5,120)

1826   Similar, but with obv. legend C CAESAR AVG PON M TR POT III COS III. RIC 22. BMCRE
       23. CBN 33. RSC *Germanicus and Caligula* 6. *[Lugdunum, AD 40].*
                              VF £1,500 ($2,400) / **EF** £3,200 ($5,120)

1827

1827   **Brass sestertius.** AGRIPPINA M F MAT C CAESARIS AVGVSTI, dr. bust of Agrippina Senior
       r. Rev. S P Q R MEMORIAE AGRIPPINAE, carpentum drawn l. by two mules. RIC 55.
       BMCRE 81. CBN 128. C *Agrippina Senior* 1. *[Rome, AD 37–41].*
                 F £450 ($720) / **VF** £1,250 ($2,000) / **EF** £5,000 ($8,000)

For a later issue honouring Agrippina Senior, see under Claudius (no. 1906); and for a restoration
of the Claudian issue, see under Titus (no. 2600).

Issues of Caligula in honour of his deceased brothers Nero and Drusus
(† AD 31 and 33)

*Nero and Drusus Caesars were the eldest and second eldest of the three surviving sons of
Germanicus and Agrippina Senior. Their father died at Antioch in AD 19, and following the equally
sudden and unexpected death of Tiberius' son, Drusus, four years later the two brothers found*

themselves next in line of succession to the throne. Unfortunately, this sealed their fate, for the powerful praetorian prefect Sejanus had designs on the imperial power himself and had almost certainly been responsible for the death of Drusus. Following the death of the emperor's mother, Livia, in AD 29 Sejanus felt free to pursue his ambitions further. Tiberius, now living in exile on Capreae, was informed by the prefect that Nero and his mother were plotting against him. Both were banished and the young prince was put to death two years later. It was now Drusus' turn to fall victim to the ruthless Sejanus. The hapless young prince was arrested in AD 30 and imprisoned in the palace, where he remained for three years until his death. Gaius Caesar, the younger brother of Nero and Drusus, was saved by his youth and following Sejanus' downfall in AD 31 he became the constant companion of the elderly Tiberius in his island retreat. The orichacum dupondii commemorating the late princes were produced by Gaius (Caligula) after he had ascended the imperial throne following the death of Tiberius in AD 37.

1828

1828   **Brass dupondius.** NERO ET DRVSVS CAESARES, Nero and Drusus Caesars on horseback galloping r. Rev. C CAESAR DIVI AVG PRON AVG P M TR P IIII P P around large S C. RIC 49. BMCRE 70. CBN 120. C *Nero and Drusus 2. [Rome, AD 40–41].*

    F £150 ($240) / **VF** £375 ($600) / **EF** £1,000 ($1,600)

CLAUDIUS
25 Jan. AD 41–13 Oct. 54

1839

Tiberius Claudius Drusus was born on 1 August 10 BC at Lugdunum (Lyon) in Gaul, on the very day that Augustus dedicated the great Altar of Lugdunum. He was the younger son of Nero Claudius Drusus, brother of Tiberius, and Antonia, daughter of Mark Antony. Because of serious ill-health, involving some form of paralysis, he was kept out of the public eye. However, despite an apparent uncouthness in his manner Claudius was by no means mentally retarded. Ignored or ridiculed by the other members of his family he devoted himself to scholarship, authoring histories of Etruria and Carthage as well as a continuation of Livy. Unfortunately, none of these works has survived. On the assassination of his nephew Gaius (Caligula) early in AD 41 Claudius was proclaimed emperor by the soldiers of the praetorian guard. Remarkably, despite his disabilities he proved himself to be a surprisingly competent ruler and even added to the territory of the Empire by the invasion and partial conquest of Britain. In his marital affairs, however, he was less fortunate. His third wife, Valeria Messallina, was notorious for her promiscuity and Claudius ordered her execution in AD 48. He then married his own niece, the younger Agrippina, and adopted her

*son Nero as his heir. Claudius' own son, Britannicus, was thus disinherited, presumably because of
the disgrace of his mother Messallina. Claudius died in AD 54 at the age of sixty-three, possibly the
victim by poisoning of his politically ambitious fourth wife. He was succeeded by Nero, who was to
be the last of the Julio-Claudian emperors.*

*RIC attributes all the regular precious metal issues of this reign to the mint of Rome, while
CBN prefers to assign them to Lugdunum. The latter attribution has been adopted in this catalogue. The Roman aes appears to be confined to the first two years of the reign (cf. Giard, CBN II,
p. 27, contra Sutherland, RIC I, pp. 118–19). It was not resumed for two decades thereafter, until
the latter part of Nero's reign, though there was large scale production of imitative aes of Claudian
types. The technical excellence of many of these 'copies', as well as the surprising extent of their
minting, would seem to indicate that some at least were produced with official sanction, possibly in
newly-conquered territory where currency was in short supply. Their value is generally less than
the Roman prototypes, though they possess considerable numismatic interest.*

For the titles and powers of this reign, including Alexandrian regnal dates, see table on p. 307.

The following forms of obv. legend and portrait occur:

    A. TI CLAVD CAES AVG
    B. TI CLAVD CAESAR AVG GERM P M TR P
    C. TI CLAVD CAESAR AVG GERM P M TRIB POT P P
    D. TI CLAVD CAESAR AVG P M TR P (– TR P IIII)
    E. TI CLAVD CAESAR AVG P M TR P VI IMP X (– TR P VIIII IMP XVIII)
    F. TI CLAVD CAESAR AVG P M TR P X IMP P P
    G. TI CLAVD CAESAR AVG P M TR P X IMP XIIX
    H. TI CLAVD CAESAR AVG P M TR P X P P IMP XVIII
    I. TI CLAVD CAESAR AVG P M TR P XI IMP P P COS V
    J. TI CLAVDIVS CAESAR AVG
    K. TI CLAVDIVS CAESAR AVG P M TR P IMP
    L. TI CLAVDIVS CAESAR AVG P M TR P IMP P P

    a. Laur. hd. of Claudius r.
    b. Laur. hd. of Claudius l.
    c. Bare hd. of Claudius l.

           1829   1831

1829 **Gold aureus.** D (TR P) a. Rev. **CONSTANTIAE AVGVSTI**, Constantia seated l. on curule
      chair, her r. hand raised to face. RIC 2. BMCRE 1. CBN 19. C 4. *[Lugdunum, AD 41–2].*
                                    VF £1,750 ($2,800) / **EF** £4,500 ($7,200)

1830 E (TR P VI IMP XI) a. Rev. **DE BRITANN** on architrave of triumphal arch, surmounted by
      equestrian statue l. between two trophies. RIC 33. BMCRE 32. CBN 54. C 17.
      [Lugdunum, AD 46–7].   **VF** £2,000 ($3,200) / **EF** £5,000 ($8,000)
      *The arch commemorating the Claudian conquest of Britain, commencing in AD 43, was
      converted from one of the spans of the Aqua Virgo which carried the aqueduct across the
      Via Flaminia, Rome's principal road to the north (cf. Hill, 'The Monuments of Ancient
      Rome as Coin Types', pp. 50–51).*

1831   **Gold aureus.** Ba. Rev. EX S C / OB CIVES / SERVATOS in three lines within oak-wreath.
        RIC 15. BMCRE 16. CBN 30. C 34. *[Lugdunum, AD 41–2].*
                                                    VF £1,750 ($2,800) / **EF** £4,500 ($7,200)

1832   1833

1832   D (TR P IIII) a. Rev. IMPER RECEPT across battlemented front wall of the praetorian camp,
        with two arched openings, soldier on sentry duty and distyle pedimented building with
        flanking walls within. RIC 25. BMCRE 23. CBN 43. C 43. *[Lugdunum, AD 44–5].*
                                                    VF £2,250 ($3,600) / **EF** £5,500 ($8,800)
        *The praetorian camp was built under Tiberius in AD 22–3 to the north-east of the city, just
        outside the Servian rampart (cf. Hill, 'The Monuments of Ancient Rome as Coin Types',
        p. 99). The praetorian guards were responsible for Claudius' elevation to the throne fol-
        lowing their assassination of Caligula (see also no. 1834).*

1833   D (TR P) a. Rev. PACI AVGVSTAE, winged Pax-Nemesis advancing r., drawing out fold of
        drapery from neck and holding caduceus, snake at feet. RIC 9. BMCRE 6. CBN 21. C 50.
        [Lugdunum, AD 41–2].   VF £1,750 ($2,800) / **EF** £4,500 ($7,200)

1834   — Rev. PRAETOR RECEPT, togate Claudius stg. r., clasping hands with soldier stg. l., hold-
        ing standard with eagle. RIC 11. BMCRE 8. CBN 24. C 77. *[Lugdunum, AD 41–2].*
                                                    VF £2,500 ($4,000) / **EF** £6,500 ($10,400)
        See note following no. 1832.

1835   Ia. Rev. S P Q R / P P / OB C S in three lines within oak-wreath. RIC 63. BMCRE 70. CBN
        72. C 95. *[Lugdunum, AD 51–2].*   VF £1,750 ($2,800) / **EF** £4,500 ($7,200)

1836   **Gold quinarius.** Ba. Rev. VICTORIA AVGVST, Victory stg. r., r. foot on globe, inscribing
        shield set on knee. Cf. RIC 18. BMCRE p. 167, * note (pl. 33, 23). CBN 34. C —.
        [Lugdunum, AD 41–2].   VF £1,500 ($2,400) / **EF** £3,500 ($5,600)

1837   Similar, but with rev. type Victory seated r. on globe, holding wreath. Cf. RIC 17. BMCRE
        p. 167, * note (pl. 33, 24). CBN 36. C 101. *[Lugdunum, AD 41–2].*
                                                    VF £1,500 ($2,400) / **EF** £3,500 ($5,600)

1838

1838   **Silver cistophorus.** Ac. Rev. COM – ASI either side of distyle temple containing stg. fig-
        ures of Claudius crowned by female deity, ROM ET AVG on entablature. RPC 2221. RIC
        120. BMCRE 228. CBN 304. RSC 3. *[Ephesus, AD 41–2].*
                                                    VF £750 ($1,200) / **EF** £1,750 ($2,800)

1839   **Silver cistophorus.** Ac. Rev. DIAN – EPHE either side of tetrastyle temple of the Ephesian
        Diana containing cultus-statue of the goddess. RPC 2222. RIC 118. BMCRE 229. CBN
        298. RSC 30. *[Ephesus, AD 41–2].*   **VF** £850 ($1,360) / **EF** £2,000 ($3,200)

1840

1840   **Silver didrachm.** Bb. Rev. DE BRITANNIS, Claudius in triumphal quadriga r., holding
        eagle-tipped sceptre. RPC 3625. RIC 122. BMCRE 237. CBN 290. RSC 15. *[Caesarea in
        Cappadocia, AD 46–8].*   **VF** £750 ($1,200) / **EF** £1,750 ($2,800)

1841   Bb. Rev. P P / OB CIVES / SERVATOS in three lines within oak-wreath. RPC 3626. RIC 123.
        BMCRE 240. CBN 291. RSC 76. *[Caesarea in Cappadocia, AD 46–8].*
                                        VF £600 ($960) / **EF** £1,250 ($2,000)

1842   **Silver denarius.** E (TR P VI IMP XI) a. Rev. CONSTANTIAE AVGVSTI, as 1829. RIC 32.
        BMCRE 31. CBN 48. RSC 8. *[Lugdunum, AD 46–7].*
                                        VF £700 ($1,120) / **EF** £1,850 ($2,960)

1843   E (TR P VIIII IMP XVI) a. Rev. DE BRITANN on triumphal arch, as 1830. RIC 45. BMCRE
        50. CBN 62. RSC 19. *[Lugdunum, AD 49–50].*   **VF** £750 ($1,200) / **EF** £2,000 ($3,200)

1844   As 1831 (rev. EX S C etc. in wreath). RIC 16. BMCRE 18. CBN 33. RSC 35. *[Lugdunum,
        AD 41–2].*   **VF** £650 ($1,040) / **EF** £1,750 ($2,800)

1845   As 1832 (rev. IMPER RECEPT on praetorian camp). RIC 26. BMCRE 24. CBN 45. RSC 44.
        [Lugdunum, AD 44–5].   **VF** £800 ($1,280) / **EF** £2,100 ($3,360)

1846   Fa. Rev. PACI AVGVSTAE, Pax-Nemesis advancing, as 1833. RIC 52. BMCRE 62 CBN
        66. RSC 65. *[Lugdunum, AD 50–51].*   **VF** £650 ($1,040) / **EF** £1,750 ($2,800)

1847   1848

1847   As 1834 (rev. PRAETOR RECEPT, Claudius and soldier). RIC 12. BMCRE 9. CBN 26. RSC
        78. *[Lugdunum, AD 41–2].*   **VF** £850 ($1,360) / **EF** £2,250 ($3,600)

1848   E (TR P VI IMP XI) a. Rev. S P Q R etc. in wreath, as 1835. RIC 41. BMCRE 45. CBN 59.
        RSC 87. *[Lugdunum, AD 46–7].*   **VF** £650 ($1,040) / **EF** £1,750 ($2,800)

1849

1849   **Brass sestertius.** Ka. Rev. EX S C / OB / CIVES / SERVATOS in four lines within oak-wreath.
        RIC 96. BMCRE 115. CBN 152. C 39. *[Rome, AD 41–2].*
                    F £175 ($280) / **VF** £450 ($720) / **EF** £1,750 ($2,800)

1850   La. Rev. EX S C / P P / OB CIVES / SERVATOS in four lines within oak-wreath. RIC 112.
        BMCRE 185. CBN 207. C 38. *[Rome, AD 42].*
                    F £175 ($280) / **VF** £450 ($720) / **EF** £1,750 ($2,800)
        *Claudius received the title of Pater Patriae ('P P') in the first half of January, AD 42, and
        the production of aes coinage appears to have ceased before the end of the year.*

1851   Ka. Rev. NERO CLAVDIVS DRVSVS GERMAN IMP S C, triumphal arch of elaborate form,
        with four Ionic columns and pediment, surmounted by equestrian statue of Nero Claudius
        Drusus galloping r., thrusting downwards with spear, between two trophies. RIC 98.
        BMCRE 121. CBN 162. C 48. *[Rome, AD 41–2].*
                    F £250 ($400) / **VF** £650 ($1,040) / **EF** £2,500 ($4,000)
        *This ornate structure probably represents the Arcus Drusi, erected over the Via Appia, just
        north of its junction with the Via Latina, to commemorate the military exploits in Germany
        of Claudius' father, Nero Claudius Drusus (died 9 BC). For another depiction of this monu-
        ment, and possibly that of a different arch celebrating victories in Germany, see the issues
        in the sole name of Nero Claudius Drusus (nos. 1892 and 1894–5).*

1852

1852   La. Rev. As previous. RIC 114. BMCRE 187. CBN 212. C 48. *[Rome, AD 42].*
                    F £250 ($400) / **VF** £650 ($1,040) / **EF** £2,500 ($4,000)

1853   Ka. Rev. SPES AVGVSTA S C, Spes advancing l., holding flower. RIC 99. BMCRE 124.
        CBN 165. Cf. C 85. *[Rome, AD 41–2].*
                    F £150 ($240) / **VF** £400 ($640) / **EF** £1,500 ($2,400)

CLAUDIUS

367

1853

1854 **Brass sestertius.** La. Rev. As previous. RIC 115. BMCRE 192. CBN 216. Cf. C 85.
[Rome, AD 42]. **F** £150 ($240) / **VF** £400 ($640) / **EF** £1,500 ($2,400)
For a restoration of this type, see under Titus (no. 2601). For a similar restoration by Domitian (though with emperor's head to left), see no. 2898.

1855 **Brass dupondius.** Kc. Rev. CERES AVGVSTA S C, Ceres enthroned l., holding corn-ears and torch. RIC 94. BMCRE 136. CBN 174. C 1. *[Rome, AD 41–2].*
F £75 ($120) / **VF** £175 ($280) / **EF** £525 ($840)

1856

1856 Lc. Rev. As previous. RIC 110. BMCRE 197. CBN 222. C 1. *[Rome, AD 42].*
F £75 ($120) / **VF** £175 ($280) / **EF** £525 ($840)
For a restoration of this type, see under Titus (no. 2603).

1857 **Copper as.** Kc. Rev. CONSTANTIAE AVGVSTI S C, Constantia, helmeted, stg. l., r. hand raised, holding sceptre in l. RIC 95. BMCRE 140. CBN 176. C 14. *[Rome, AD 41–2].*
F £60 ($96) / **VF** £150 ($240) / **EF** £450 ($720)

1858

1858 Lc. Rev. As previous. RIC 111. BMCRE 199. CBN 226. C 14. *[Rome, AD 42].*
F £60 ($96) / **VF** £150 ($240) / **EF** £450 ($720)
For a restoration of this type, see under Titus (no. 2604).

1859 **Copper as.** Kc. Rev. LIBERTAS AVGVSTA S C, Libertas stg. facing, hd. r., holding pileus, l. hand extended. RIC 97. BMCRE 145. CBN 177. C 47. *[Rome, AD 41–2].*

F £55 ($88) / **VF** £135 ($216) / **EF** £400 ($640)

1860

1860 Lc. Rev. As previous. RIC 113. BMCRE 202. CBN 230. C 47. *[Rome, AD 42].*

F £55 ($88) / **VF** £135 ($216) / **EF** £400 ($640)

1861 Kc. Rev. S C, Minerva advancing r., brandishing spear and holding shield. RIC 100. BMCRE 149. CBN 179. C 84 var. *[Rome, AD 41–2].*

F £50 ($80) / **VF** £125 ($200) / **EF** £375 ($600)

1862

1862 Lc. Rev. As previous. RIC 116. BMCRE 206. CBN 233. C 84. *[Rome, AD 42].*

F £50 ($80) / **VF** £125 ($200) / **EF** £375 ($600)

For restorations of this type, see under Titus (no. 2606) and Domitian (no. 2899).

1863 **Copper quadrans.** J, modius. Rev. PON M TR P IMP COS DES IT around large S C. RIC 84. BMCRE 179. CBN 185. C 70. *[Rome, AD 41].*

F £20 ($32) / **VF** £45 ($72) / **EF** £110 ($176)

1864   1867

1864 J, r. hand holding scales, P N R between the pans. Rev. As previous. RIC 85. BMCRE 174. CBN 181. C 71. *[Rome, AD 41].*   F £20 ($32) / **VF** £45 ($72) / **EF** £110 ($176)

The expansion of the abbreviation P N R has not been satisfactorily resolved: pondus mummorum restitutum ('the weight of the coinage restored') and ponderum norma restituta ('the standard of weights restored') have both been suggested.

1865 **Copper quadrans.** Similar to 1863, but with rev. legend PON M TR P IMP P P COS II. RIC 90. BMCRE 182. CBN 195. C 72. *[Rome, AD 42].*

F £20 ($32) / **VF** £45 ($72) / **EF** £110 ($176)

1866 Similar to 1864, but with rev. legend as previous. RIC 91. BMCRE 181. CBN 192. C 73. *[Rome, AD 42].* **F** £20 ($32) / **VF** £45 ($72) / **EF** £110 ($176)

1867 Ka. Rev. ROM ET AVG, altar of the cult of Roma and Augustus at Lugdunum, flanked by two columns, each surmounted by statue of Victory. RIC 1. BMCRE 227. CBN 98. C 81. *[Lugdunum, AD 41].* **F** £110 ($176) / **VF** £275 ($440) / **EF** £650 ($1,040) *This remarkable issue, the first of its type since early in the reign of Tiberius, may be associated with the 50th anniversary of the dedication of the famous shrine by Augustus and with the birth of Claudius, both of which events took place in Lugdunum on the same day.*

For coins of Divus Claudius and later restorations, see under Nero (nos. 2051–7), Titus (nos. 2601–6), Domitian (nos. 2898–9), and Trajan.

Alexandrian Coinage

Under Claudius the Egyptian mint resumed the production of its tetradrachm coinage, initiated by Tiberius, as well as large scale minting of various bronze denominations.

1868

1868 **Billon tetradrachm.** ΤΙ ΚΛΑΥΔΙ ΚΑΙΣ ΣΕΒΑ ΓΕΡΜΑΝΙ ΑΥΤΟΚΡ, laur. hd. of Claudius r., L B (= regnal year 2) before. Rev. ΑΝΤΩΝΙΑ ΣΕΒΑΣΤΗ, dr. bust of Antonia r. RPC 5117. BMCG 65. Cologne 62. Milne 61. *[AD 41–2].* **F** £70 ($112) / **VF** £175 ($280)

1869

1869 Obv. Similar, but with L ς (= regnal year 6) before. Rev. ΜΕΣΣΑΛΙΝΑ ΚΑΙΣ ΣΕΒΑΣ, Messalina stg. l., resting on column and holding two small figures on extended r. hand and ears of corn in l. RPC 5164. BMCG 75. Cologne 88. Milne 106. *[AD 45–6].*

F £50 ($80) / **VF** £125 ($200)

The two small figures on reverse are sometimes identified as the children of Claudius and Messalina, Britannicus and Octavia.
NB *The illustration shows a variant dated regnal year 2 (= AD 41–2) with lituus in rev. field.*

1870   **Billon didrachm.** TIB KΛΑΥ ΚΑΙ CEBAC ΓΕΡΜ, laur. hd. r., L Γ (= regnal year 3) before. Rev.
AYTOKPA, crossed cornuacopiae, each surmounted by bust of child, a third bust between
them. RPC 5135. BMCG 68. Cologne —. Milne —. *[AD 42–3]*.
F £1,000 ($1,600) / **VF** £2,000 ($3,200)
*This extremely rare experimental issue depicts the three children of Claudius – Britannicus
and Octavia by Messalina, Antonia by a previous marriage to Aelia Paetina.*

1871   **Billon drachm.** TI KΛ ΚΑ CE ΓΕ ΑΥ, laur. hd. r., L Γ (= regnal year 3) before. Rev. Dr. bust
of Sarapis r., wearing modius. RPC 5136. BMCG 78. Cologne —. Milne (Supplement)
87a. *[AD 42–3]*.
F £225 ($360) / **VF** £550 ($880)
*Another extremely rare experimental denomination, the billon drachm was not issued by
any of Claudius' successors, with the possible exception of Nero (see no. 2017).*

1872   **Bronze obol** (25 mm. diam). TIB KΛΑΥ ΚΑΙ CEBAC ΓΕΡΜΑ, laur. hd. r., star before. Rev.
AYTOKPA, Nike advancing l., L B (= regnal year 2) in field. RPC 5121. BMCG 79. Cologne
68. Milne 68. *[AD 41–2]*.
F £30 ($48) / **VF** £75 ($120)

1873   Similar, but with rev. type bull butting r., and date L Γ (= regnal year 3) in ex. RPC 5138.
BMCG 85. Cologne 80. Milne 89. *[AD 42–3]*.
F £30 ($48) / **VF** £75 ($120)

1874   Similar, but with rev. type hippopotamus stg. r., and date L Δ (= regnal year 4) in ex. RPC
5151. BMCG 96–8 var. Cologne 84. Milne 100. *[AD 43–4]*.
F £30 ($48) / **VF** £75 ($120)

1875   Similar, but the date L I (= regnal year 10) is before hd. on obv., in place of star, and with
rev. type bust of Nilus r., cornucopiae at shoulder behind, child before. RPC 5174. BMCG
81. Cologne 98. Milne 113. *[AD 49–50]*.
F £35 ($56) / **VF** £85 ($136)

1876   Similar, but with date L IA (= regnal year 11) on obv., and with rev. type four ears of corn
with caduceus at centre. RPC 5182. BMCG 100. Cologne 100. Milne 119. *[AD 50–51]*.
F £30 ($48) / **VF** £75 ($120)

1877

1877   Obv. Similar to 1872, but without star. Rev. AYTOKPA, eagle stg. r. on thunderbolt, looking
back, L IΓ (= regnal year 13) in field. RPC 5193. BMCG 92. Cologne 105. Milne 128. *[AD
52–3]*.
F £30 ($48) / **VF** £75 ($120)
NB The illustration shows a variant dated regnal year 14 (= AD 53–4).

1878   **Bronze hemiobol** (20 mm). TIB KΛΑΥ ΚΑΙ CEBAC ΓΕΡΜ, laur. hd. r. Rev. AYTOKPA, hip-
popotamus stg. r., L B (= regnal year 2) in ex. RPC 5128. BMCG 97. Cologne 72. Milne 75.
[AD 41–2].
F £25 ($40) / **VF** £65 ($104)

1879   — Rev. AYTOKPA, clasped r. hands, L I (= regnal year 10) below. RPC 5176. BMCG 106.
Cologne 93. Milne 115. *[AD 49–50]*.
F £25 ($40) / **VF** £65 ($104)

1880   — Rev. — r. hand holding two ears of corn and two poppies, L IA (= regnal year 11) below.
RPC 5184. BMCG 105. Cologne —. Milne 121. *[AD 50–51]*. **F** £25 ($40) / **VF** £65 ($104)

1881   **Bronze hemiobol** (20 mm). — Rev. — r. hand holding caduceus, L IB (= regnal year 12) below. RPC 5189. BMCG –. Cologne 104. Milne —. *[AD 51–2].*
                                            F £25 ($40) / **VF** £65 ($104)

1882   **Bronze dichalkon** (15 mm). TIB KΛAY, laur. hd. r. Rev. Crocodile r., L I (= regnal year 10) above. RPC 5178. BMCG 87. Cologne 97. Milne 117. *[AD 49–50].*
                                            F £18 ($29) / **VF** £45 ($72)

1883   — Rev. Frog seated r., L I (= regnal year 10) above. RPC 5179. BMCG 94. Cologne 96. Milne —. *[AD 49–50].*   **F** £18 ($29) / **VF** £45 ($72)

1884   **Bronze chalkos** (10 mm). No legend, laur. hd. r. Rev. Capricorn r., L Δ (= regnal year 4). RPC 5159. BMCG —. Cologne 83. Milne —. *[AD 43–4].*   **F** £20 ($32) / **VF** £50 ($80)

For other local coinages of this reign, see *Roman Provincial Coinage,* vol. I, and *Greek Imperial Coins & Their Values,* pp. 39–48.

CLAUDIUS AND AGRIPPINA JUNIOR

1887

Claudius married his niece Agrippina as his fourth wife in AD 49. Later, she was elevated to the rank of Augusta and coins were struck in the joint names of the emperor and empress.

1885   **Gold aureus.** TI CLAVD CAESAR AVG GERM P M TRIB POT P P, laur hd. of Claudius r. Rev. AGRIPPINAE AVGVSTAE, dr. bust of Agrippina Junior r., wreathed with corn-ears. RIC 80. BMCRE 72. CBN 76. C *Agrippina and Claudius 3. [Lugdunum, AD 51].*
                                    VF £2,500 ($4,000) / **EF** £6,500 ($10,400)

1885   1886

1886   **Silver denarius.** Similar. RIC 81. BMCRE 75. CBN 82. RSC *Agrippina and Claudius 4. [Lugdunum, AD 51].*   **VF** £900 ($1,440) / **EF** £2,250 ($3,600)

1887   **Silver cistophorus.** TI CLAVD CAESAR AVG P M TR P X IMP XIIX, laur. hd. of Claudius r. Rev. AGRIPPINA AVGVSTA CAESARIS AVG, dr. bust of Agrippina Junior r. RPC 2223. RIC 117. BMCRE 234. CBN 294. RSC *Agrippina and Claudius 2. [Ephesus, AD 51].*
                                    VF £1,250 ($2,000) / **EF** £3,000 ($4,800)

1888

1888 **Silver cistophorus.** TI CLAVD CAES AVG AGRIPP AVGVSTA, conjoined laur. hd. of Claudius and dr. bust of Agrippina Junior l. Rev. DIANA EPHESIA, cultus-statue of the Ephesian Diana stg. facing. RPC 2224. RIC 119. BMCRE 231. CBN 302. RSC *Agrippina and Claudius* 1. *[Ephesus, AD 51].*   VF £1,250 ($2,000) / EF £3,000 ($4,800)

CLAUDIUS AND NERO

1890

Agrippina's son Nero was adopted by his imperial step-father as heir to the throne at about the same time as his mother's elevation to the rank of Augusta.

1889 **Gold aureus.** Obv. As 1885. Rev. NERO CLAVD CAES DRVSVS GERM PRINC IVVENT, bare-headed and dr. bust of young Nero l. RIC 82. BMCRE 79. CBN 85. Cf. C *Claudius and Nero/Nero and Claudius* 4. *[Lugdunum, AD 50].*
          VF £2,750 ($4,400) / EF £7,250 ($11,600)

1890 **Silver denarius.** Similar. RIC 83. BMCRE 80. CBN 89. RSC *Claudius and Nero/Nero and Claudius* 5. *[Lugdunum, AD 50].*   VF £1,100 ($1,760) / EF £2,750 ($4,400)

For coins of Nero and Divus Claudius, see nos. 2053–7.

Issues of Claudius in honour of Divus Augustus

1891 **Brass dupondius.** DIVVS AVGVSTVS, rad. hd. of Augustus l., dividing S – C. Rev. DIVA AVGVSTA, Livia enthroned l., holding corn-ears and torch. RIC 101. BMCRE 224. CBN 256. C *Augustus* 93. *[Rome, AD 41–2].*
          F £125 ($200) / VF £300 ($480) / EF £900 ($1,440)

Issues of Claudius in honour of his deceased father Nero Claudius Drusus († 9 BC)

Nero Claudius Drusus, the younger brother of Tiberius, was born in 38 BC and was brought up in the household of Augustus. He married Antonia, the daughter of Mark Antony and Octavia, about 16 BC and the union produced two sons, Germanicus and the future emperor Claudius. Augustus evidently considered him the ablest of his generals, and after campaigning for several seasons with his brother Tiberius he was entrusted with the projected conquest of Germany. He achieved considerable success during the course of four campaigns (12–9 BC), but following an accidental fall from his horse in summer camp he fell ill and died at the age of only twenty-nine. His Roman coinage in gold, silver, and orichalcum was issued half a century after his death, during the reign of his younger son Claudius.

1892   1893

1892   **Gold aureus.** NERO CLAVDIVS DRVSVS GERMANICVS IMP, laur. hd. of Nero Claudius Drusus l. Rev. DE GERM above and on architrave of triumphal arch with two Ionic columns, surmounted by equestrian statue of Nero Claudius Drusus galloping r., holding couched spear, between two trophies, each with captive at base. RIC 69. BMCRE 95. CBN 1. C *Nero Claudius Drusus 1. [Lugdunum, AD 41–2].*
VF £2,000 ($3,200) / EF £4,500 ($7,200)
This probably represents the Arcus Drusi erected over the Via Appia, just north of its junction with the Via Latina, to commemorate the military exploits in Germany of Claudius' father, Nero Claudius Drusus (died 9 BC). For another, more elaborate, depiction of this monument, see no. 1851.

1893   — Rev. DE GERMANIS, two oblong shields crossed, upright vexillum and crossed spears and trumpets in background. RIC 73. BMCRE 104. CBN 7. C *Nero Claudius Drusus 5. [Lugdunum, AD 41–2].*   VF £2,000 ($3,200) / EF £4,500 ($7,200)

1894   **Silver denarius.** Obv. As 1892. Rev. DE GERMANIS on architrave of wide single-span triumphal arch, surmounted by equestrian statue l. between two trophies. RIC 72. BMCRE 101. CBN 6. RSC *Nero Claudius Drusus 4. [Lugdunum, AD 41–2].*
VF £850 ($1,360) / EF £2,250 ($3,600)
This is clearly a different arch from the one depicted on no. 1892. Hill ('The Monuments of Ancient Rome as Coin Types', p. 50) calls it the Arcus Claudii, a monument erected to commemorate the success of Roman arms in Germany. Like the slightly later arch celebrating the Claudian conquest of Britain it was converted from one of the spans of the Aqua Virgo. Its scant remains are still extant in the courtyard of no. 14 Via Nazarene, near the Trevi Fountain.

1895

1895   **Silver didrachm.** Obv. Similar to 1892, but CLAVD for CLAVDIVS and the hd. of Drusus is to r. Rev. Similar to previous, but the equestrian statue is to r. RPC 3628. RIC 126. BMCRE p. 199, note *. CBN 289. Cf. RSC *Nero Claudius Drusus 4a. [Caesarea in Cappadocia, AD 46–8].*   VF £1,500 ($2,400) / EF £3,000 ($4,800)

1896

1896   **Brass sestertius.** Obv. Similar to 1892, but the hd. of Drusus is bare. Rev. TI CLAVDIVS
        CAESAR AVG P M TR P IMP S C, Claudius (or Drusus?) seated l. on curule chair, amidst an
        assortment of arms, holding branch. RIC 93. BMCRE 157. CBN 125. C *Nero Claudius
        Drusus* 8. *[Rome, AD 41–2].*   **F** £200 ($320) / **VF** £500 ($800) / **EF** £2,000 ($3,200)
        For a restoration of this type (obv. only), see under Titus (No. 2596).

1897   Similar, but with IMP P P instead of IMP on rev. RIC 109. BMCRE 208. CBN 198. C *Nero
        Claudius Drusus* 8. *[Rome, AD 42].*
                                      F £200 ($320) / **VF** £500 ($800) / **EF** £2,000 ($3,200)

See also no. 1851.

Issues of Claudius in honour of his deceased mother Antonia († AD 37)

*Antonia, younger daughter of Mark Antony and Octavia, sister of Augustus, was born 31 January
36 BC. At the age of twenty she was married to Nero Claudius Drusus, younger brother of Tiberius,
by whom she had two sons, Germanicus and the future emperor Claudius, and a daughter, Livilla.
Tragically widowed in 9 BC Antonia refused to marry again and devoted the remainder of her long
life to the interests of her family. Her wealth and important connections made her influential during
the reign of her brother-in-law, Tiberius, and it was she who brought about the downfall of Sejanus
by revealing to the emperor the true nature of the praetorian prefect's treacherous activities. On the
accession of her grandson Caligula in AD 37 Antonia initially received many honours, but the
unstable young emperor soon tired of her criticisms. She died later the same year at the age of
seventy-three, reputedly by her own hand, though there is no firm evidence to support the tradition
that Caligula was responsible for her death. However, she did not receive posthumous honours
until after the accession of her son Claudius in AD 41. As in the case of her husband, who had died
forty-six years before, all of the coinage in Antonia's name was issued early in the reign of
Claudius.*

1898   **Gold aureus.** ANTONIA AVGVSTA, dr. bust of Antonia r., wreathed with corn-ears. Rev.
        CONSTANTIAE AVGVSTI, Ceres stg. facing, holding long torch and cornucopiae. RIC 65.
        BMCRE 109. CBN 9. C *Antonia* 1. *[Lugdunum, AD 41–2].*
                                                VF £3,000 ($4,800) / **EF** £7,000 ($11,200)

1899   — Rev. SACERDOS DIVI AVGVSTI, two lighted torches linked by ribbon. RIC 67. BMCRE
        112. CBN 15. C *Antonia* 4. *[Lugdunum, AD 41–2].*
                                                VF £3,000 ($4,800) / **EF** £7,000 ($11,200)

1899   1900

1900   **Silver denarius.** As 1898. RIC 66. BMCRE 111. CBN 13. RSC *Antonia* 2. *[Lugdunum, AD 41–2].*   **VF** £1,200 ($1,920) / **EF** £2,500 ($4,000)

1901   As 1899. RIC 68. BMCRE 114. CBN —. RSC *Antonia* 5. *[Lugdunum, AD 41–2].*   **VF** £1,200 ($1,920) / **EF** £2,500 ($4,000)

1902   **Brass dupondius.** Obv. Similar, but Antonia is bare-headed. Rev. TI CLAVDIVS CAESAR AVG P M TR P IMP S C, Claudius, veiled and togate, stg. l., holding simpulum. RIC 92. BMCRE 166. CBN 143. C *Antonia* 6. *[Rome, AD 41–2].*   **F** £125 ($200) / **VF** £300 ($480) / **EF** £900 ($1,440)

1903

1903   Similar, but with IMP P P instead of IMP on rev. RIC 104. BMCRE 213. CBN 204. C *Antonia* 6. *[Rome, AD 42].*   **F** £125 ($200) / **VF** £300 ($480) / **EF** £900 ($1,440)

Issues of Claudius in honour of his deceased brother Germanicus († AD 19)

1904   **Brass sestertius.** GERMANICVS CAESAR TI AVG F DIVI AVG N, bare hd. of Germanicus r. Rev. TI CLAVDIVS CAESAR AVG GERM P M TR P IMP P P around large S C. RIC 105. BMCRE 214. CBN —. C *Germanicus* 8. *[Rome, AD 42].*   *(Extremely rare)*

1905

1905   **Copper as.** Similar. RIC 106. BMCRE 215. CBN 241. C *Germanicus* 9. *[Rome, AD 42].*   **F** £70 ($112) / **VF** £175 ($280) / **EF** £425 ($680)
       For a restoration of this type, see under Titus (no. 2597).

For earlier issues honouring Germanicus, see under Caligula (nos. 1813–22).

Issues of Claudius in honour of his deceased sister-in-law Agrippina Senior
(† AD 33)

1906

1906   **Brass sestertius.** AGRIPPINA M F GERMANICI CAESARIS, dr. bust of Agrippina Senior r.
Rev. TI CLAVDIVS CAESAR AVG GERM P M TR P IMP P P around large S C. RIC 102.
BMCRE 219. CBN 236. C *Agrippina Senior* 3. *[Rome, AD 42].*

F £350 ($560) / **VF** £850 ($1,360) / **EF** £2,500 ($4,000)
For a restoration of this type, see under Titus (no. 2600).

For earlier issues honouring Agrippina Senior, see under Caligula (nos. 1823–7).

MESSALINA

1907

*Valeria Messalina, a grand-daughter of Augustus' sister Octavia, was born about AD 25. At the age
of only fourteen she married her second cousin Claudius, already twice married before and thirty-
five years her senior. She bore him two children, Octavia and Britannicus, and became empress on
his elevation to the throne in AD 41. Unfortunately, her sexual profligacy was common knowledge
to all but her husband, and when the truth was eventually revealed to him by the freedman
Narcissus Messalina was immediately put to death (AD 48).*

1907   **Silver didrachm.** MESSALLINA AVGVSTI, dr. bust of Messalina r. Rev. OCTAVIA
BRITANNICVS ANTONIA, the three children of Claudius stg. side by side, the shorter figure
of Britannicus between his two sisters. RPC 3627. RIC *Claudius* 124. BMCRE *Claudius*
242. CBN *Claudius* 292. RSC 2. *[Caesarea in Cappadocia, AD 46–8].*

F £6,500 ($10,400) / **VF** £12,500 ($20,000)

See also no. 1869.

BRITANNICUS

1908

Tiberius Claudius Britannicus, son of Claudius by his third wife Messalina, was born in AD *41, soon after his father's accession to the throne. Originally called Germanicus, after his late uncle, the child's name was soon changed to Britannicus in celebration of Claudius' invasion and conquest of Britain. Following his mother's disgrace and execution in* AD *48 the young prince fell from favour and was eventually replaced as heir by Nero, son of Claudius' fourth wife Agrippina Junior. In* AD *55, the year following Nero's accession to the throne, the fourteen-year-old Britannicus died, almost certainly poisoned on the new emperor's orders.*

RIC and BMC favour an attribution of these enigmatic sestertii to the reign of Titus, as part of that emperor's 'restoration' coinage. However, they appear rather to be an integral part of the curious 'Balkan' group of aes which includes issues in the names of Agrippina Junior and her son Nero.

1908   **Brass sestertius.** TI CLAVDIVS CAESAR AVG F BRITANNICVS, bare-headed and dr. bust of Britannicus l. Rev. S C, Mars advancing l., holding spear and shield. Cf. RIC p. 130, note (re-attributing this type and the next to the reign of Titus). BMCRE *Claudius* 226 (later catalogued as *Titus* 306). CBN —. C 2. *[Uncertain Thracian mint,* AD *51].*
                          F £20,000 ($32,000) / **VF** £35,000 ($56,000)

1909   Similar, but the bust of Britannicus is to r. Cf. RIC p. 130, note. BMCRE *Claudius* 226, note (later catalogued as *Titus* 306, note). CBN *Claudius* 287. C 1. *[Uncertain Thracian mint,* AD *51].*
                          F £20,000 ($32,000) / **VF** £35,000 ($56,000)

See also nos. 1869–70 and 1907.

AGRIPPINA JUNIOR

1911

Agrippina Junior was born in AD *15, the eldest daughter of Germanicus and Agrippina Senior. At the age of thirteen she was betrothed to Cn. Domitius Ahenobarbus by whom, in* AD *37, she bore a son, the future emperor Nero. In* AD *39 she was banished by her brother, the emperor Caligula, who believed her to be implicated in a conspiracy against him. Fortunate to escape with her life she was later recalled by her uncle Claudius who, following the execution of Messalina, took her as his fourth wife in* AD *49. The following year Agrippina was elevated to the rank of Augusta and it was probably soon after this that extremely rare sestertii were issued in her name, apparently from an unidentified Balkan mint. On these she is identified as the daughter of Germanicus –* GERMANICI F[ilia], *and the wife of the emperor –* CAESARIS AVG[usti Uxor]. *The new empress used her influence over her husband to secure the advancement of Nero, her son by Domitius Ahenobarbus. Claudius' own son Britannicus, already in disgrace because of the behaviour of his mother Messalina, was ousted from his position as heir and replaced by Nero who was three years his senior. The death of Claudius in* AD *54 may have been due to poison administered by his wife with the object of gaining the throne for the seventeen-year-old Nero while he was still young enough to be influenced by his mother.*

1910   **Brass sestertius.** AGRIPPINA AVG GERMANICI F CAESARIS AVG, dr. bust of Agrippina Junior r. Rev. No legend, carpentum drawn l. by two mules. RIC *Claudius* 103. BMCRE *Claudius* p 195, note *, and pl. 37, 3. CBN —. C —. *[Uncertain Thracian mint,* AD *51].*
        F £2,000 ($3,200) / **VF** £5,000 ($8,000) / **EF** £15,000 ($24,000)

Alexandrian Coinage

1911   **Bronze obol** (25 mm. diam). ΑΓΡΙΠΠΙΝΑ ϹΕΒΑϹΤΗ, dr. bust of Agrippina Junior r., wreathed with corn. Rev. ΕΥΘΗΝΙΑ, dr. bust of Euthenia r., wreathed with corn and holding corn-ears, L IB (= regnal year 12 of Claudius) in field. RPC 5188. BMCG 108. Cologne 109. Milne 124. *[AD 51–2].*   **F** £60 ($96) / **VF** £150 ($240)

1912   **Bronze hemiobol** (20 mm). Obv. Similar. Rev. Modius between two torches, L IΓ (=regnal year 13 of Claudius) in ex. RPC 5196. BMCG —. Cologne —. Milne (Supplement) 130a. *[AD 52–3].*   **F** £50 ($80) / **VF** £125 ($200)

1913   **Bronze chalkos** (10 mm). Obv. Similar, but legend ΑΓΡΙΠ ϹΕΒΑϹ. Rev. Two ears of corn between two poppies, L IB (= regnal year 12 of Claudius) in field. RPC 5192. BMCG —. Cologne —. Milne —. *[AD 51–2].*   **F** £35 ($56) / **VF** £85 ($136)

See also the following, and nos. 1800, 1885–8, 1989, and 2041–50.

AGRIPPINA JUNIOR AND NERO

In the final years of Claudius' reign the imperial propaganda made it abundantly clear that Nero had now replaced Britannicus as the heir to the imperial throne. This denarius combines the head of the recently elevated prince with that of his mother, the empress Agrippina.

1914   **Silver denarius.** AGRIPPINAE AVGVSTAE, dr. bust of Agrippina Junior r., wreathed with corn-ears. Rev. NERO CLAVD CAES DRVSVS GERM PRINC IVVENT, bare-headed and dr. bust of young Nero l. RIC *Claudius* 75. BMCRE *Claudius* 82. Cf. CBN p. 172, 5. RSC 5. *[Lugdunum,* AD *51].*   (*May not exist*)
        Coins of this type are condemned as modern forgeries in CBN.

For coins of Nero and Agrippina struck during the reign of Nero, see nos. 2041–50.

NERO
13 Oct. AD 54–9 Jun. 68

1952

Born in AD 37 Nero originally bore the name L. Domitius Ahenobarbus and was the son of Cn. Domitius Ahenobarbus (consul AD 32) and Agrippina Junior, sister of Caligula. Later, when Agrippina married her uncle, the emperor Claudius, her son was adopted for the imperial succession and his name changed to Nero Claudius Caesar Drusus Germanicus. Three years later (AD 54) Claudius died, possibly poisoned by Agrippina, and Nero became the fifth emperor of Rome. In the early years of the new reign political power was in the hands of wise counselors, such as Seneca and Burrus, Agrippina quickly having been deprived of the position of influence which she had hoped to occupy under the new regime. But from AD 62 the young emperor fully asserted his independence, and with the encouragement of dissolute companions his behavior became increasingly erratic and unpredictable. In the summer of AD 64 a great fire laid waste much of central Rome and Nero, who was rumoured to have been the author of the conflagration, eagerly took advantage of the opportunity to build a magnificent extension of the imperial palace, known as the 'Domus Aurea' or Golden House. He also fancied himself as a great artist, poet, and theatrical performer and spent much time in Greece in the latter part of his reign. The Roman world eventually tired of his follies and revolts broke out in several provinces. Trouble arose initially in the East, where the outbreak in AD 66 of the First Jewish Revolt, known also as the Jewish War, led to the appointment of the future emperor Vespasian as supreme commander in the area. Unrest soon spread to the western provinces and serious uprisings in Spain and Gaul led ultimately to the proclamation of Galba as emperor and the suicide of Nero in the early summer of AD 68.

The precious-metal coinage of this reign falls into two distinct periods, AD 54–64 and 64–68. In the first phase the aureus and denarius types were very conservative and showed a remarkable deference to senatorial authority. The weight standards of the preceding reigns were also strictly maintained. But in AD 64 major changes were initiated by the young emperor. These resulted in significant weight reductions for the gold aureus and silver denarius denominations and a reintroduction of regular aes production for the first time since the early years of Claudius. The Elder Pliny actually records the enactment of Nero's currency reform in his 'Naturalis Historia'. RIC attributes all the regular precious metal issues to the mint of Rome, while CBN prefers to assign the pre-reform aurei and denarii to Lugdunum and the post-reform types to Rome. As the reform in 64 would have provided the obvious occasion for a transfer of the mint establishment Giard's arrangement has been preferred in this catalogue. The reintroduction of regular aes coinage took place at Rome and was quickly followed by the reform of the precious metal coinage. Lugdunum, now deprived of its role as the supplier of gold and silver, shared in the production of the new aes denominations which were produced in unprecedented quantities during the final four years of the reign.

For the titles and powers of this reign, including Alexandrian regnal dates, see table on pp. 307–8.

The following obv. legends and types are represented by upper and lower case letters. All other varieties are described in full:

A. IMP NERO CAESAR AVG GERM
B. IMP NERO CAESAR AVG P MAX TR P P P
C. IMP NERO CAESAR AVG P P
D. IMP NERO CAESAR AVG PONT MAX TR POT P P

E. IMP NERO CAESAR AVGVSTVS
F. NERO CAESAR AVG IMP
G. NERO CAESAR AVGVSTVS
H. NERO CLAVD CAESAR AVG GER (or GERM) P M TR P IMP P P
I. NERO CLAVDIVS CAESAR AVG GER (or GERM) P M TR P IMP P P

a. Bare hd. of Nero r.
b. Bare hd. of Nero l.
c. Laur. hd. of Nero r.
d. Laur. hd. of Nero l.
e. Laur. hd. of Nero r., with aegis on neck
f. Rad. hd. of Nero r.
g. Rad. hd. of Nero l.

NB The aes coinage attributed to the Lugdunum mint has a small globe at the point of the truncation.

Pre-accession issues under Claudius

1915 **Gold aureus.** NERO CLAVD CAES DRVSVS GERM PRINC IVVENT, young bare-headed and dr. bust l. Rev. SACERD COOPT IN OMN CONL SVPRA NVM EX S C, simpulum and lituus above tripod and patera (emblems of the four principal priestly colleges). RIC *Claudius* 76. BMCRE *Claudius* 84. CBN *Claudius* 91. C 311. *[Lugdunum, AD 51].*
VF £1,750 ($2,800) / **EF** £3,750 ($6,000)

1916 NERONI CLAVDIO DRVSO GERM COS DESIGN, young bare-headed and dr. bust r. Rev. EQVESTER / ORDO / PRINCIPI / IVVENT in four lines on circular shield, vertical spear in background. RIC *Claudius* 78. BMCRE *Claudius* 90. CBN *Claudius* 94. C 96. *[Lugdunum, AD 51].*   VF £1,750 ($2,800) / **EF** £3,750 ($6,000)

1916   1917

1917 **Silver denarius.** As 1915. RIC *Claudius* 77. BMCRE *Claudius* 87. CBN *Claudius* 93. RSC 312. *[Lugdunum, AD 51].*   **VF** £375 ($600) / **EF** £950 ($1,520)

1918 As 1916. RIC *Claudius* 79. BMCRE *Claudius* 93. CBN *Claudius* 96. RSC 97. *[Lugdunum, AD 51].*   **VF** £375 ($600) / **EF** £950 ($1,520)

1918   1919

1919 **Silver cistophorus.** NERONI CLAVD CAES DRVSO GERM, young bare-headed and dr. bust l. Rev. COS DES / PRINCI / IVVENT in three lines on shield encircled by laurel-wreath. RPC 2225. RIC *Claudius* 121. BMCRE *Claudius* 236. CBN *Claudius* 307. RSC 82a. *[Ephesus, AD 51].*   **VF** £1,000 ($1,600) / **EF** £2,500 ($4,000)

1920 **Brass sestertius.** NERONI CLAVDIO DRVSO GERMANICO COS DESIGN, young bare-headed and dr. bust r. Rev. EQVESTER / ORDO / PRINCIPI / IVVENT in four lines on circular shield, vertical spear in background. RIC *Claudius* 108. BMCRE *Claudius* p. 195, † note and pl. 37, 4. CBN *Claudius* 288. C 99. *[Uncertain Thracian mint, AD 51].*
F £7,500 ($12,000) / **VF** £15,000 ($24,000)

1921 **Brass dupondius.** NERO CLAVD CAES DRVS GERM PRINC IVVENT, young bare-headed and dr. bust l. Rev. SACERD COOPT IN OMN CONL SVPRA NVM EX S C, simpulum and lituus above tripod and patera (emblems of the four principal priestly colleges). RIC *Claudius* 107. BMCRE (Appendix) p. 397, 242 *bis.* CBN —. C —. *[Uncertain Thracian mint, AD 51].*   **F** £2,500 ($4,000) / **VF** £6,500 ($18,000)

For other coins depicting Nero struck during the reign of Claudius, see nos. 1889–90 and 1914.

Post-accession issues

1922 **Gold aureus (pre-reform).** Fa. Rev. Rev. PONTIF MAX TR P II P P around oak-wreath encircling EX S C. RIC 8. BMCRE 9. CBN 15. C 204. *[Lugdunum, AD 55–6].*
VF £1,500 ($2,400) / **EF** £3,250 ($5,200)

1923

1923 Fa. Rev. PONTIF MAX TR P VII COS IIII P P EX S C, Ceres stg. l., holding corn-ears and long torch. RIC 23. BMCRE 25. CBN 31. C 217. *[Lugdunum, AD 60–61].*
VF £1,500 ($2,400) / **EF** £3,250 ($5,200)

1924 Fa. Rev. — Roma stg. r., l. foot on arms, inscribing shield set on l. knee. RIC 27. BMCRE 29. CBN 38. C 221. *[Lugdunum, AD 60–61].*   **VF** £1,500 ($2,400) / **EF** £3,250 ($5,200)

1924   1925

1925 Fa. Rev. PONTIF MAX TR P X COS IIII P P EX S C, Virtus stg. l., r. foot on arms, holding parazonium and spear. RIC 40. BMCRE 45. CBN 46. C 232. *[Lugdunum, AD 63–4].*
VF £1,600 ($2,560) / **EF** £3,500 ($5,600)

1926　**Gold aureus (post-reform).** Gc. Rev. AVGVSTVS AVGVSTA, Augustus, rad., holding patera and sceptre and Livia, veiled, holding patera and cornucopiae, stg. l. side by side. RIC 44, 56. BMCRE 52. CBN 199. C 42. *[Rome, AD 64–5].*
　　　　　　　　　　　　　　　VF £1,400 ($2,240) / **EF** £3,000 ($4,800)
　　　The two figures on rev. are often identified as Nero and the Empress Poppaea.

1927　　　　　　　　　　　　　　　　　　1928

1927　NERO CAESAR, c. Rev. AVGVSTVS GERMANICVS, Nero, rad. and togate, stg. facing, holding branch and Victory on globe. RIC 46. BMCRE 56. CBN 202. C 44. *[Rome, AD 64–5].*
　　　　　　　　　　　　　　　VF £1,400 ($2,240) / **EF** £3,000 ($4,800)

1928　Gc. Rev. CONCORDIA AVGVSTA, Concordia seated l., holding patera and cornucopiae. RIC 48. BMCRE 61. CBN 207. C 66. *[Rome, AD 64–5].*
　　　　　　　　　　　　　　　VF £1,300 ($2,080) / **EF** £2,750 ($4,400)

1929　　　　　　　　　　　　　　　　　　1930

1929　Gc. Rev. IANVM CLVSIT PACE P R TERRA MARIQ PARTA, one end of the 'Twin Janus' (*Ianus Geminus*) showing closed double doors. RIC 50, 58. BMCRE 64. CBN 211. C 114. *[Rome, AD 65].*　　　　　　　**VF** £1,600 ($2,560) / **EF** £3,500 ($5,600)
　　　This curious rectangular structure, the precise location of which remains uncertain, consisted of two arched gateways joined by walls though lacking a roof. On the rare occasions when Rome was not at war with a foreign enemy the doors of the 'Twin Janus' were ceremonially closed, an event which Nero commemorated extensively on the coinage of AD 65–7 (see also nos. 1958–60, 1964–5, and 1973–4).

1930　Gc. Rev. IVPPITER CVSTOS, Jupiter seated l., holding thunderbolt and sceptre. RIC 52. BMCRE 67. CBN 213. C 118. *[Rome, AD 65–6].*
　　　　　　　　　　　　　　　VF £1,200 ($1,920) / **EF** £2,500 ($4,000)
　　　Referring, in all probability, to Nero's deliverance from the conspiracy of C. Calpurnius Piso in AD 65.

1931　Gc. Rev. ROMA, Roma seated l. on cuirass, holding Victory and parazonium. RIC 54. BMCRE 81. CBN 222. C 257. *[Rome, AD 65–6].*
　　　　　　　　　　　　　　　VF £1,300 ($2,080) / **EF** £2,750 ($4,400)
　　　This and the frequent depictions of Roma on the aes denominations are commemorative of the restoration of the city centre following the great fire of AD 64.

1931   1932

1932   **Gold aureus (post-reform).** Gc. Rev. SALVS, Salus enthroned l., holding patera. RIC 59.
       BMCRE 87. CBN 225. C 313. *[Rome, AD 65–6].*
       VF £1,200 ($1,920) / EF £2,500 ($4,000)

1933   Gc. Rev. VESTA, domed temple of Vesta, showing six columns and containing seated
       statue of the goddess. RIC 61. BMCRE 101. CBN 229. C 334. *[Rome, AD 65].*
       VF £1,500 ($2,400) / EF £3,250 ($5,200)
       *The celebrated temple of Vesta in the Roman Forum was destroyed in the great fire of
       AD 64. Nero rebuilt it and his structure, the sixth to be constructed on the site, survived
       until another catastrophic fire late in the reign of Commodus. See also no. 1946.*

1934   **Gold quinarius.** NERO CL DIVI F CAES AVG P M TR P II, a. Rev. VICT AVG, Victory alight-
       ing l., wings spread, r. hand resting on large circular shield. RIC 10. BMCRE 11. CBN —.
       C 336. *[Lugdunum, AD 55–6].*   *(Extremely rare)*

1935   **Silver didrachm.** NERO CLAVD DIVI CLAVD F CAESAR AVG GERMANI, c. Rev.
       ARMENIAC, Victory advancing r., holding wreath and palm. RPC 3634. RIC 615. BMCRE
       405. CBN 437. RSC 32a. *[Caesarea in Cappadocia, AD 58–60].*
       VF £350 ($560) / EF £850 ($1,360)
       *In commemoration of the military successes of the celebrated general Cn. Domitius
       Corbulo which resulted in the settlement of Armenia and the installation of Tigranes V as
       client king of the country (see also no. 1948).*

1936

1936   **Silver denarius (pre-reform).** Fa. Rev. Rev. PONTIF MAX TR P VII COS IIII P P around
       oak-wreath encircling EX S C. RIC 22. BMCRE 24. CBN 30. RSC 216. *[Lugdunum, AD
       60–61].*   VF £325 ($520) / EF £800 ($1,280)

1937   Fa. Rev. PONTIF MAX TR P VIII COS IIII P P EX S C, Ceres stg. l., holding corn-ears and long
       torch. RIC 30. BMCRE 32. CBN 41. RSC 224. *[Lugdunum, AD 61–2].*
       VF £350 ($560) / EF £850 ($1,360)

1938   Fa. Rev. — Virtus stg. l., r. foot on arms, holding parazonium and spear. RIC 32. BMCRE
       35. CBN 43. RSC 226. *[Lugdunum, AD 61–2].*   VF £350 ($560) / EF £850 ($1,360)

1939   Fa. Rev. PONTIF MAX TR P VIIII COS IIII P P EX S C, Roma stg. r., l. foot on arms, inscribing
       shield set on l. knee. RIC 39. BMCRE 44. CBN —. RSC 231. *[Lugdunum, AD 62–3].*
       VF £350 ($560) / EF £850 ($1,360)

1940   **Silver denarius (post-reform).** As 1926 (rev. AVGVSTVS AVGVSTA, Augustus and Livia stg.). RIC 45, 57. BMCRE 54. CBN 201. RSC 43. *[Rome, AD 64–5].*
          VF £300 ($480) / **EF** £750 ($1,200)

                    1941   1944

1941   As 1927 (rev. AVGVSTVS GERMANICVS, Nero stg. facing). RIC 47. BMCRE 60. CBN 206. RSC 45. *[Rome, AD 64–5].*   VF £300 ($480) / **EF** £750 ($1,200)

1942   As 1928 (rev. CONCORDIA AVGVSTA, Concordia seated). RIC 49. BMCRE 63. CBN 210. RSC 67. *[Rome, AD 64–5].*   VF £275 ($440) / **EF** £675 ($1,080)

1943   Cc. Rev. IVPPITER CVSTOS, Jupiter seated, as 1930. RIC 69. BMCRE 80. CBN 239. RSC 123. *[Rome, AD 67–8].*   VF £250 ($400) / **EF** £600 ($960)

1944   As 1931 (rev. ROMA, Roma seated). RIC 55. BMCRE 83. CBN 224. RSC 258. *[Rome, AD 65–6].*   VF £275 ($440) / **EF** £675 ($1,080)

1945   Ec. Rev. SALVS, Salus enthroned, as 1932. RIC 67. BMCRE 96. CBN 237. RSC 318. *[Rome, AD 66–7].*   VF £250 ($400) / **EF** £600 ($960)

                    1946

1946   As 1933 (rev. VESTA, temple of Vesta). RIC 62. BMCRE 104. CBN 230. RSC 335. *[Rome, AD 65].*   VF £325 ($520) / **EF** £800 ($1,280)

1947   Cc. Rev. No legend, legionary eagle between two standards. RIC 68. BMCRE 107. CBN 238. RSC 356. *[Rome, AD 68].*   VF £350 ($560) / **EF** £850 ($1,360)

                    1948   1949

1948   **Silver hemidrachm.** As 1935 (rev. ARMENIAC, Victory advancing). RPC 3644. RIC 616. BMCRE 406. CBN 438. RSC 32. *[Caesarea in Cappadocia, AD 58–60].*
          VF £100 ($160) / **EF** £250 ($400)
          See note following no. 1935.

1949 **Silver hemidrachm.** NERO CLAVD DIVI CLAVD F CAESAR AVG GERMANI, c. Rev. No legend, Victory seated r. on globe, holding wreath. RPC 3645. RIC 617. BMCRE 409. CBN 439. RSC 352. *[Caesarea in Cappadocia, AD 58–60].*   **VF** £75 ($120) / **EF** £175 ($280)

1950 — Rev. — Victory stg. r., foot on globe, inscribing shield set on r. knee. RPC 3646. RIC 618. BMCRE 411. CBN 440. RSC 351. *[Caesarea in Cappadocia, AD 58–60].*
VF £85 ($136) / **EF** £200 ($320)

1951

1951 **Brass sestertius.** I (GERM) d. Rev. ADLOCVT COH, Nero stg. l. on platform, accompanied by praetorian prefect, haranguing three soldiers, pillared building behind with curved walls of praetorian camp in background. RIC 97. BMCRE 126. CBN 254 var. (obv. type e). C 5. *[Rome, AD 64].*   **F** £375 ($600) / **VF** £950 ($1,520) / **EF** £3,750 ($6,000)
An early issue distinguished by the omission of the normal formula 'S C' on reverse. This type was subsequently revived by Nerva (see no. 3040).

1952 H (GER) c (globe). Rev. ANNONA AVGVSTI CERES S C, Annona stg. r., holding cornucopiae, facing Ceres seated l., holding corn-ears and torch, modius on garlanded altar between them, stern of ship in background. RIC 430. BMCRE 305. CBN 70. C 14. *[Lugdunum, AD 65].*   **F** £250 ($400) / **VF** £650 ($1,040) / **EF** £2,500 ($4,000)
This type was subsequently revived by Domitian (see no. 2760) and by Nerva (see no. 3041).

1953

1953 H (GER) e. Rev. AVGVSTI POR OST S C, aerial view of the harbour of Ostia, showing pier, breakwaters, lighthouse, and ships, figure of Tiber reclining l. in foreground, holding rudder and dolphin. RIC 178. BMCRE 131. CBN 300. C 37. *[Rome, AD 64].*
F £1,000 ($1,600) / **VF** £2,500 ($4,000) / **EF** £10,000 ($16,000)
The improvement of the harbour facilities at Ostia, Rome's port at the mouth of the Tiber, was initiated by Claudius but not completed until the reign of Nero.

1954   **Brass sestertius.** I (GER) e. Rev. CONG I DAT POP S C, Nero seated r. on platform, a second
        platform before him on which attendant is seated, distributing largess to citizen who
        mounts steps of platform, small boy behind him, statues of Minerva and Liberalitas stg. l.
        on pedestals in background. RIC 154. BMCRE 136. CBN 279. C 69. *[Rome, AD 64].*
                            F £350 ($560) / **VF** £900 ($1,440) / **EF** £3,500 ($5,600)
        This type was subsequently revived by Nerva (see no. 3043).

1955   Dd (globe). Rev. CONG II DAT POP S C, Nero seated l. on low platform, accompanied by
        stg. figure of the *praefectus annonae*, attendant stg. l. at foot of platform, handing tessera
        to citizen who stands before him, statue of Minerva stg. l. on pedestal behind attendant,
        flat-roofed tetrastyle building in background. RIC 505. BMCRE 310 var. CBN 134. C 80.
        [Lugdunum, AD 66].   **F** £375 ($600) / **VF** £950 ($1,520) / **EF** £3,750 ($6,000)

1956

1956   I (GERM) d. Rev. DECVRSIO, Nero on horseback prancing r., holding couched spear, soldier
        running r. before him, looking back, holding vexillum, a second soldier running beside the
        emperor in background. RIC 108. BMCRE 155. CBN 258. C 95. *[Rome, AD 64].*
                            F £300 ($480) / **VF** £750 ($1,200) / **EF** £3,000 ($4,800)
        An early issue distinguished by the omission of the normal formula 'S C' on reverse.

1957

1957   I (GER) e. Rev. DECVRSIO S C, Nero on horseback prancing r., holding couched spear,
        accompanied by second horseman in background, holding vexillum over shoulder. RIC
        170. BMCRE 143. CBN 283. C 83. *[Rome, AD 64].*
                            F £275 ($440) / **VF** £700 ($1,120) / **EF** £2,750 ($4,400)

1958

1958   **Brass sestertius.** H (GER) c (globe). Rev. PACE P R TERRA MARIQ PARTA IANVM CLVSIT
        S C, the 'Twin Janus' (*Ianus Geminus*) showing closed double doors and one side wall (on
        l.) with long latticed window. RIC 438. BMCRE 319. CBN 73. C 146. *[Lugdunum, AD 65].*
                                    F £250 ($400) / **VF** £600 ($960) / **EF** £2,250 ($3,600)
        See note following no. 1929.

1959   NERO CAESAR AVG IMP TR POT XI P P P, laur., dr.and cuir. bust r. Rev. As previous. RIC
        263. BMCRE 111. CBN 363. Cf. C 143. *[Rome, AD 65].*
                                    F £350 ($560) / **VF** £900 ($1,440) / **EF** £3,500 ($5,600)

1960   I (GER) e. Rev. Similar to previous, but the side wall of the 'Twin Janus' is shown on r. RIC
        270. BMCRE 164. CBN 366. C 134. *[Rome, AD 65].*
                                    F £250 ($400) / **VF** £600 ($960) / **EF** £2,250 ($3,600)

1961

1961   Dd (globe). Rev. ROMA S C, Roma seated l. on cuirass, r. foot on helmet, holding Victory
        and parazonium, shields on ground behind. RIC 517. BMCRE 328. CBN 138. C 268.
        [Lugdunum, AD 66].   **F** £200 ($320) / **VF** £500 ($800) / **EF** £1,750 ($2,800)

1962   I (GER) e. Rev. S C, view of triumphal arch, surmounted by group of statuary with Nero in
        facing quadriga between stg. figures of Victory and Pax, showing front festooned with
        wreath and side adorned with bas-relief of Mars stg. on pedestal. RIC 147. BMCRE 185.
        CBN 287. C 308. *[Rome, AD 64].*
                                    F £300 ($480) / **VF** £750 ($1,200) / **EF** £3,000 ($4,800)
        This arch has been identified as that decreed by the Senate in AD 58 (Tacitus Annals xiii,
        41) to commemorate the eastern victories of Cn. Domitius Corbulo. It was located on the
        Capitoline Hill but its exact site is uncertain, the structure probably having been demol-
        ished following Nero's downfall a decade later.

1962

1963   **Brass dupondius.** I (GER) f. Rev. MAC AVG S C, front view of Nero's two-storeyed provi-
       sion-market, showing domed central section approached by steps and containing statue on
       pedestal, flanked by wings, that on l. showing two columns on each storey, that on r. three,
       mark of value II in ex. RIC 187. BMCRE 195. CBN 312. C 130. *[Rome, AD 64].*
                   F £300 ($480) / **VF** £750 ($1,200) / **EF** £2,250 ($3,600)
       *The Great Provision-Market (Macellum Magnum) on Rome's Caelian Hill was completed
       in AD 59. Part of it was transformed into the church of S. Stefano Rotundo by Pope
       Simplicius at about the time of the fall of the Western Empire (cf. Hill, 'The Monuments of
       Ancient Rome as Coin Types', p. 40).*

1964   H (GER) g. Rev. PACE P R TERRA MARIQ PARTA IANVM CLVSIT S C, the 'Twin Janus'
       (*Ianus Geminus*) showing closed double doors and one side wall (on l.) with long latticed
       window. RIC 285. BMCRE 200. CBN 382. C 151. *[Rome, AD 65].*
                   F £100 ($160) / **VF** £250 ($400) / **EF** £750 ($1,200)
       See note following no. 1929.

1965   I (GER) f. Rev. PACE P R VBIQ PARTA IANVM CLVSIT S C, similar to previous, but the side
       wall of the 'Twin Janus' is shown on r. RIC 291. BMCRE 203. CBN —. C 165. *[Rome,
       AD 65].*   **F** £100 ($160) / **VF** £250 ($400) / **EF** £750 ($1,200)

1966   H (GER) f. Rev. ROMA S C, Roma seated l. on cuirass, r. foot on helmet, holding wreath and
       parazonium, arms on ground behind. RIC 296. BMCRE 206. CBN 388. C 282. *[Rome, AD
       65].*   **F** £90 ($144) / **VF** £225 ($360) / **EF** £675 ($1,080)

1966A

1966A IMP NERO CLAVD CAESAR AVG GERM P M TR P XIII P P, f. Rev. Similar to previous, but
       Roma's r. foot rests on stool, and she holds spear in r. hand and rests l. arm on shield. RIC
       363. BMCRE 120. CBN 431. C 286. *[Rome, AD 67].*
                   F £140 ($224) / **VF** £350 ($560) / **EF** £1,100 ($1,760)

1967   I (GERM) f. Rev. SECVRITAS AVGVSTI S C, Securitas, in relaxed pose, enthroned r., hd. rest-
       ing on r. hand, holding sceptre in l., lighted altar and torch at her feet, mark of value II in
       ex. RIC 195. BMCRE 213 var. CBN 307. C 326. *[Rome, AD 64].*
                   F £80 ($128) / **VF** £200 ($320) / **EF** £600 ($960)

1968

1968   **Brass dupondius.** Bd (globe). Rev. Similar to previous, but without mark of value. RIC
        597. BMCRE 347. CBN 195. C 325. *[Lugdunum, AD 67].*
        F £80 ($128) / **VF** £200 ($320) / **EF** £600 ($960)

1969

1969   H (GERM) g. Rev. VICTORIA AVGVSTI S C, Victory advancing l., holding wreath and palm,
        mark of value II in ex. RIC 199. BMCRE 219. CBN 310. C 348. *[Rome, AD 64].*
        F £80 ($128) / **VF** £200 ($320) / **EF** £600 ($960)
        NB The illustration shows a variant with head of Nero to right.

1970   Bd (globe). Rev. Similar to previous, but without mark of value. RIC 523. BMCRE 356.
        CBN 34. C 344. *[Lugdunum, AD 66].*   F £80 ($128) / **VF** £200 ($320) / **EF** £600 ($960)

1971   **Copper as (normal module).** H (GER) a (globe). Rev. ARA PACIS S C, façade of altar-
        enclosure of the *Ara Pacis* (Altar of Peace) with decorated panels and narrow central
        double doors, the horns of the altar visible above. RIC 458. BMCRE 360. CBN 120 var. C
        27. *[Lugdunum, AD 65].*   F £125 ($200) / **VF** £325 ($520) / **EF** £1,000 ($1,600)
        *The Ara Pacis was erected by Augustus between 13 and 9 BC beside the Via Flaminia in the
        northern Campus Martius. Its site was thoroughly explored in 1937–8 and the monument
        reconstructed, with most of its surviving sculptures, between the Mausoleum of Augustus
        and the Tiber. However, the Neronian asses of the 'Ara Pacis' type are confined to the
        Lugdunum mint, giving rise to speculation that the structure depicted may have been
        erected in the Gallic city in the late AD 50s in commemoration of Corbulo's Parthian
        victory.*

1972   Ba (globe). Rev. GENIO AVGVSTI S C, Genius of the emperor stg. l., sacrificing from patera
        over altar and holding cornucopiae. RIC 533. BMCRE 370. CBN 151. C 103. *[Lugdunum,
        AD 66].*   F £65 ($104) / **VF** £165 ($264) / **EF** £450 ($720)
        See also no. 1977.

1972

1973   **Copper as (normal module).** NERO CAESAR AVG GERM IMP, c. Rev. PACE P R TERRA
       MARIQ PARTA IANVM CLVSIT S C, the 'Twin Janus' (*Ianus Geminus*) showing closed
       double doors and one side wall (on r.) with long latticed window. RIC 304. BMCRE 226.
       CBN 398. C 132. *[Rome, AD 65].*   **F** £55 ($88) / **VF** £140 ($224) / **EF** £375 ($600)
       See note following no. 1929.

1974

1974   Similar, but with rev. legend PACE P R VBIQ PARTA IANVM CLVSIT S C, and the side wall
       of the 'Twin Janus' is shown on l. RIC 306. BMCRE 227. CBN 400. C 171. *[Rome, AD
       65].*   **F** £55 ($88) / **VF** £140 ($224) / **EF** £375 ($600)

1975

1975   NERO CLAVD CAESAR AVG GERMANICVS, a (globe). Rev. PONTIF MAX TR POT IMP P P S
       C, Nero as Apollo Citharoedus advancing r., playing lyre. RIC 416. BMCRE 376. CBN
       101. C 247. *[Lugdunum, AD 65].*   **F** £90 ($144) / **VF** £225 ($360) / **EF** £650 ($1,040)
       *A Graecophile and a passionate devotee of the arts, Nero regarded himself as an accom-
       plished musician and singer as well as a poet. The type of Apollo Citharoedus is doubtless
       intended to flatter this aspect of the emperor's character (see also no. 1978).*

1976

1976 **Copper as (normal module).** Obv. As 1973. Rev. S C, Victory alighting l., wings spread, holding shield inscribed S P Q R. RIC 312. BMCRE 241. CBN 399. C 288. *[Rome, AD 65]*.

F £50 ($80) / **VF** £125 ($200) / **EF** £325 ($520)

1977 **Brass as (small module).** H (GER) c. Rev. GENIO AVGVSTI S C, Genius of the emperor stg. l., sacrificing from patera over altar and holding cornucopiae, mark of value I in ex. RIC 214. BMCRE 252. CBN 322. C 107. *[Rome, AD 64]*.

F £80 ($128) / **VF** £200 ($320) / **EF** £550 ($880)

See also no. 1972.

1977   1978

1978 NERO CLAVDIVS CAESAR AVG GERMANIC, f. Rev. PONTIF MAX TR POT IMP P P S C, Nero as Apollo Citharoedus advancing r., playing lyre, mark of value I in ex. RIC 211. BMCRE 256. CBN 325. C 248. *[Rome, AD 64]*.

F £90 ($144) / **VF** £225 ($360) / **EF** £625 ($1,000)

See note following no. 1975.

1979   1981

1979 **Brass semis (normal module).** NERO CAES AVG IMP, c. Rev. CER QVINQ ROM CO S C, agonistic prize-table, ornamented on front with confronted gryphons and surmounted by prize-urn and wreath, discus (?) propped against leg of table below on r., mark of value S above. RIC 233. BMCRE 261. CBN 338. C 47. *[Rome, AD 64]*.

F £45 ($72) / **VF** £110 ($176) / **EF** £300 ($480)

The 'Certamen Quinquennale' was a festival instituted by Nero in AD 60. It included athletics, horse racing, and competitions in music and poetry, and was part of the emperor's policy of attempting to lead Rome away from gladiatorial shows to more noble entertainments.

1980 **Brass semis (normal module).** NERO CLAV CAESAR AVG, c (globe). Rev. CER QVIN ROM CON S C, agonistic prize-table, similar to previous, but with palm-branch attached to the wreath, and without mark of value. RIC —. BMCRE —. CBN 60. C 52 var. *[Lugdunum, AD 64].* **F** £50 ($80) / **VF** £120 ($192) / **EF** £325 ($520)

1981 Obv. As 1979. Rev. TR POT P P S C, Roma seated l. on cuirass, r. foot on helmet, holding wreath and parazonium, shield behind, mark of value S in upper field. RIC 226. BMCRE 281. CBN 349. C 332 var. *[Rome, AD 64].* **F** £55 ($88) / **VF** £130 ($208) / **EF** £350 ($560)

1982 **Copper semis (large module).** NERO CLAVD CAESAR AVG GERM, b (globe). Rev. CER QVINQ ROM CON S C, agonistic prize-table, similar to 1979, but without mark of value. RIC 487. BMCRE 392. CBN 127. C 53 var. *[Lugdunum, AD 65].* **F** £60 ($96) / **VF** £150 ($240) / **EF** £400 ($640)

1983 — a (globe). Rev. PONTIF MAX TR POT IMP P P S C, Roma seated l., as 1981, but without mark of value. RIC 482. BMCRE 399. CBN 125. C 236 var. *[Lugdunum, AD 65].* **F** £60 ($96) / **VF** £150 ($240) / **EF** £400 ($640)

1984 **Copper quadrans (normal module).** NERO CLAVD CAE AVG GER, column, surmounted by helmet and with shield propped against it on r., spear placed diagonally in background (sometimes omitted). Rev. P M TR P IMP P P S C, olive-branch. RIC 318. BMCRE 287. CBN 407. C —. *[Rome, AD 65].* **F** £20 ($32) / **VF** £50 ($80) / **EF** £125 ($200)

1985 NERO CLAV CAE AVG GER, owl, wings spread, stg. facing on garlanded altar. Rev. As previous. RIC 319. BMCRE 288. CBN 408. C 185. *[Rome, AD 65].* **F** £20 ($32) / **VF** £50 ($80) / **EF** £125 ($200)

1986 Obv. Similar. Rev. P M TR P IMP P P S C, column with helmet, etc., as obv. of 1984. RIC 322. BMCRE 290. CBN 410. C 183. *[Rome, AD 65].* **F** £25 ($40) / **VF** £60 ($96) / **EF** £150 ($240)

1987   1988

1987 **Brass quadrans (small module).** NERO CLAVD CAESAR AVG, column with helmet, etc., as 1984. Rev. GER P M TR P IMP P P S C, olive-branch, sometimes with mark of value three pellets below. RIC 250. BMCRE p. 257, * note. Cf. CBN 351–2. Cf. C 111. *[Rome, AD 64].* **F** £20 ($32) / **VF** £50 ($80) / **EF** £125 ($200)

1988 NERO CLAV CAE AVG GER, owl on altar, as 1985. Rev. P M TR P IMP P P S C, olive-branch. RIC 260. BMCRE p. 258, * note. CBN 360. C 185. *[Rome, AD 64].* **F** £20 ($32) / **VF** £50 ($80) / **EF** £125 ($200) *

Alexandrian Coinage

Under Nero the development of the complex system of coinage in Roman Egypt was finally completed with the introduction of the two largest bronze denominations (35 and 30 mm. diameter). These are often referred to as 'drachms' and 'hemidrachms', though 'hemidrachm' and 'diobol' respectively would seem to be preferable on the basis of the evidence provided by the coinage itself (see nos. 2035, 2038, and 2040). In reality, this merely represents a continuation of the system introduced by the last ruler of Ptolemaic Egypt, Queen Cleopatra VII. The Neronian tetradrachms were minted in unprecedented quantities in the emperor's later years, perhaps the result of the recoining of late Ptolemaic and Tiberian issues.

1989   **Billon tetradrachm.** ΝΕΡ ΚΛΑΥ ΚΑΙΣ ΣΕΒ ΓΕΡ ΑΥΤΟ, laur. hd. of Nero r. Rev. ΑΓΡΙΠΠΙΝΑ ΣΕΒΑΣΤΗ, dr. bust of Agrippina Junior r., L Γ (= regnal year 3) before. RPC 5201. BMCG 116. Cologne 114. Milne 131. *[AD 56–7].*   F £75 ($120) / VF £175 ($280)

1990 var. (year 4)

1990   Similar, but with rev. ΟΚΤΑΟΥΙΑ ΣΕΒΑΣΤΟΥ, dr. bust of Octavia r., L Γ (= regnal year 3) before. RPC 5202. BMCG 119. Cologne 122. Milne 133. *[AD 56–7].*
                                                      F £75 ($120) / VF £175 ($280)

1991   Similar, but with rev. ΠΡΟΝ ΝΕΟΥ ΣΕΒΑΣΤΟΥ, Nero., rad., enthroned l., holding scroll (?) and sceptre, L Γ (= regnal year 3) before. RPC 5203. BMCG 154. Cologne 121. Milne 145. *[AD 56–7].*   F £45 ($72) / VF £110 ($176)

1992   Similar, but with rev. ΟΜΟΝΟΙΑ, Homonoia (= Concordia) seated l., holding patera, L Γ (= regnal year 3) before. RPC 5208. BMCG (Supplement) 2693. Cologne 120. Milne 139. *[AD 56–7].*   F £30 ($48) / VF £75 ($120)

1993   ΝΕΡΩ ΚΛΑΥ ΚΑΙΣ ΣΕΒΑ ΓΕΡ ΑΥΤΟ, laur. hd. r. Rev. ΝΕΟ ΑΓΑΘ ΔΑΙΜ, serpent Agathodaemon r., with ears of corn and poppies, L Δ (= regnal year 4) before. RPC 5230. BMCG 172. Cologne 127. Milne 165. *[AD 57–8].*   F £40 ($64) / VF £100 ($160)

1994   Similar, but with rev. ΔΗΜΟΣ ΡΩΜΑΙΩΝ, the Roman Demos stg. r., holding sceptre and cornucopiae, L E (= regnal year 5) before. RPC 5234. BMCG 152. Cologne 140. Milne 179. *[AD 58–9].*   F £35 ($56) / VF £85 ($136)

1995   Similar, but with rev. ΡΩΜΗ, Roma seated l., holding Nike and sword in sheath, L E (= regnal year 5) behind. RPC 5239. BMCG 159. Cologne 141. Milne 177. *[AD 58–9].*
                                                      F £30 ($48) / VF £75 ($120)

1996   ΝΕΡΩΝ ΚΛΑΥ ΚΑΙΣ ΣΕΒΑ ΓΕΡ ΑΥΤΟ, laur. hd. r. Rev. ΔΗΜΗΤΕΡ, Demeter stg. l., holding corn-ears with poppies and long torch, L E (= regnal year 5) before. RPC 5244. BMCG (Supplement) 2675. Cologne 133 var. Milne 184. *[AD 58–9].*   F £30 ($48) / VF £75 ($120)

1997   Similar, but with rev. ΙΡΗΝΗ, Eirene (= Pax) stg. r., holding caduceus and helmet, L E (= regnal year 5) before. RPC 5246. BMCG 148. Cologne 135. Milne 186. *[AD 58–9].*
                                                      F £30 ($48) / VF £75 ($120)

1998   Similar, but with rev. ΔΙΚΑΙΟΣΥΝΗ, Dikaiosyne (= Aequitas) stg. l., holding scales, L ς (= regnal year 6) behind. RPC 5256. BMCG 147. Cologne 144. Milne 198. *[AD 59–60].*
                                                      F £30 ($48) / VF £75 ($120)

394   JULIO-CLAUDIAN DYNASTY

1999   **Billon tetradrachm.** ΝΕΡΩ ΚΛΑΥ ΚΑΙC CEB ΓEP ΑΥΤΟ, laur. hd. r. Rev. L ENAT (= regnal year 9), hippopotamus stg. r., star in ex. RPC 5269. BMCG 169. Cologne 154 var. Milne 213. *[AD 62–3].*   **F** £50 ($80) / **VF** £120 ($192)

2000   2002 var. (year 10)

2000   ΝΕΡΩ ΚΛΑΥ ΚΑΙΣ ΣΕΒ ΓEP, laur. hd. r. Rev. ΑΥΤΟΚΡΑ, bust of Nilus r., reeds over l. shoulder, cornucopiae and L I (= regnal year 10) before. RPC 5273. BMCG (Supplement) 2703. Cologne 156. Milne 216. *[AD 63–4].*   **F** £30 ($48) / **VF** £75 ($120)

2001   Similar, but emperor's hd. is rad., and with rev. type dr. bust of Sarapis r., wearing modius, L I (= regnal year 10) before. RPC 5274. BMCG 156. Cologne 160. Milne 222. *[AD 63–4].*   **F** £30 ($48) / **VF** £75 ($120)

2002   ΝΕΡΩ ΚΛΑΥ ΚΑΙΣ ΣΕΒ ΓEP ΑΥ, rad. hd. of Nero r. Rev. ΠΟΠΠΑΙΑ ΣΕΒΑΣΤΗ, dr. bust of Poppaea r., L IA (= regnal year 11) before. RPC 5282. BMCG 124. Cologne 168. Milne 223. *[AD 64–5].*   **F** £60 ($96) / **VF** £150 ($240)

2003   ΝΕΡΩ ΚΛΑΥ ΚΑΙΣ ΣΕΒ ΓEP, rad. bust r., wearing aegis. Rev. ΑΥΤΟΚΡΑ, eagle stg. l., palm-branch transversely in background, L IA (= regnal year 11) before, sometimes also with simpulum behind. RPC 5283–4. BMCG 165–6. Cologne 163, 167. Milne 228, 236. *[AD 64–5].*   **F** £25 ($40) / **VF** £65 ($104)

2004   Similar, but with rev. type dr. bust of Alexandria r., wearing elephant's skin head-dress, L IB (= regnal year 12) before. RPC 5289. BMCG 163. Cologne 172. Milne 238. *[AD 65–6].*   **F** £25 ($40) / **VF** £65 ($104)

2005   Similar, but with rev. type laur. bust of Apollo r., L IΓ (= regnal year 13) before. RPC 5292. BMCG 140. Cologne 175. Milne 248. *[AD 66–7].*   **F** £30 ($48) / **VF** £75 ($120)

2006   Similar, but with rev. type helmeted and cuir. bust of Roma r., L IΓ (= regnal year 13) before. RPC 5293. BMCG 162. Cologne 183. Milne 249. *[AD 66–7].*   **F** £30 ($48) / **VF** £75 ($120)

2007   2009

2007   ΝΕΡΩ ΚΛΑΥ ΚΑΙΣ ΣΕΒ ΓEP ΑΥ, rad. bust of Nero l., wearing aegis, L IΓ (= regnal year 13) before. Rev. ΘΕΟΣ ΣΕΒΑΣΤΟΣ, rad. hd. of Augustus r. RPC 5294. BMCG 112. Cologne 177. Milne 251. *[AD 66–7].*   **F** £50 ($80) / **VF** £120 ($192)

2008 **Billon tetradrachm.** Similar, but with rev. ΤΙΒΕΡΙΟΣ ΚΑΙΣΑΡ, laur. hd. of Tiberius r. RPC 5295. BMCG 114. Cologne 187. Milne 256. *[AD 66–7].* F £55 ($88) / VF £140 ($224)

2009 Similar, but with rev. ΣΕΒΑΣΤΟΦΟΡΟΣ, ship under sail r. RPC 5296. BMCG 176. Cologne 184. Milne 273. *[AD 66–7].* F £50 ($80) / VF £120 ($192)

2010 Similar, but with date L ΙΔ (= regnal year 14) on obv., and with rev. ΝΕΜΕΙΟΣ ΖΕΥΣ, bust of Nemean Zeus r., wreathed with oak and wearing aegis. RPC 5308. BMCG 131. Cologne 205 var. Milne 279. *[AD 67–8].* F £30 ($48) / VF £75 ($120)

2011 var. (star)

2011 Similar, but with rev. ΗΡΑ ΑΡΓΕΙΑ, veiled and diad. bust of Hera Argeia r. RPC 5309. BMCG 135. Cologne 199. Milne 281. *[AD 67–8].* F £30 ($48) / VF £75 ($120)

2012 Similar, but with rev. ΠΥΘΕΙΟΣ ΑΠΟΛΛΩΝ, laur. bust of Pythian Apollo r., quiver behind shoulder. RPC 5312. BMCG 141. Cologne 197 var. Milne 290. *[AD 67–8].* F £35 ($56) / VF £85 ($136)

2013 Similar, but with rev. ΔΙΟΣ ΟΛΥΜΠΙΟΥ, laur. bust of Olympian Zeus r., star before. RPC 5313. BMCG 127. Cologne 207. Milne 292. *[AD 67–8].* F £30 ($48) / VF £75 ($120)

2014 Similar, but with rev. ΠΟΣΕΙΔΩΝ ΙΣΘΜΙΟΣ, bust of Poseidon Isthmios r., wearing taenia, trident behind shoulder, star before. RPC 5316. BMCG 136. Cologne 204. Milne 298. *[AD 67–8].* F £35 ($56) / VF £85 ($136)

2015 Similar, but with rev. ΑΚΤΙΟΣ ΑΠΟΛΛΩΝ, laur. bust of Actian Apollo r., trident behind shoulder, star before. RPC 5317. BMCG 144. Cologne 195. Milne 300. *[AD 67–8].* F £30 ($48) / VF £75 ($120)
This remarkable series of tetradrachms (nos. 2010–2015) depicting and naming an array of important Greek deities is commemorative of Nero's sojourn in Greece in AD 67–68.

2016 **Billon didrachm.** ΝΕΡ ΚΛΑΥ ΚΑΙΣ ΣΕΒ ΓΕΡ ΑΥΤΟ, laur. hd. r. Rev. ΕΛΠΙΣ, Elpis (= Spes) advancing l., holding flower, L Δ (= regnal year 4) before. RPC 5220 (*Berlin*). BMCG —. Cologne —. Milne —. *[AD 57–8].* (*Unique*)

2017 **Billon drachm?** Obv. Similar. Rev. ΑΓΡΙΠ ΣΕΒ, dr. bust of Agrippina Junior r., L Γ (= regnal year 3) before. RPC 5211 (*Athens*). BMCG —. Cologne —. Milne —. *[AD 56–7].*(*Unique*)

2018 **Bronze hemidrachm** (35 mm. diam). ΝΕΡΩ ΚΛΑΥ ΚΑΙC ΣΕΒ ΓΕΡ ΑΥΤΟ, laur. hd. r. Rev. ΤΩΙ / CΩΤΗΡΙ / ΤΗC ΟΙΚΟΥ/ΜΕΝΗC / L ΕΝΑΤ (= regnal year 9) in five lines within wreath. RPC 5271 (*Paris and Athens*). BMCG —. Cologne —. Milne —. *[AD 62–3].* F £550 ($880) / VF £1,100 ($1,760)

2019 ΝΕΡΩ ΚΛΑΥ ΚΑΙΣ ΣΕΒ ΓΕΡ ΑΥ, laur. hd. r., L ΙΔ (= regnal year 14) before. Rev. Sarapis seated l., holding sceptre, Cerberus at feet. Cf. RPC 5286 (*Athens*; attributed to year 11, in error). BMCG —. Cologne —. Milne —. *[AD 67–8].* F £450 ($720) / VF £900 ($1,440)

R. Pincock (Numismatic Chronicle, 1995, pp. 266–71 and pl. 48) has demonstrated conclusively that specimens of this type and the next were all struck in year 14.

2020 **Bronze hemidrachm** (35 mm. diam). Similar, but with rev. ΖΕΥΣ ΚΑΠΕΤΩΛΙΟΣ, the Capitoline Zeus (Jupiter) enthroned l., holding sceptre and thunderbolt, eagle at feet. Cf. RPC 5285 (*ANS, New York*; attributed to year 11, in error). BMCG —. Cologne —. Milne —. *[AD 67–8].* **F** £450 ($720) / **VF** £900 ($1,440)

2021 **Bronze diobol** (30 mm). ΝΕΡΩ ΚΛΑΥ ΚΑΙΣ ΣΕΒ ΓΕΡ, laur. hd. r. Rev. ΑΥΤΟΚΡΑ, bust of Nilus r., cornucopiae and L I (= regnal year 10) before. RPC 5276 (*ANS, New York*). BMCG —. Cologne —. Milne —. *[AD 63–4].* **F** £200 ($320) / **VF** £400 ($640)

2022 ΝΕΡΩ ΚΛΑΥ ΚΑΙΣ ΣΕΒ ΓΕΡ ΑΥ, laur. hd. r. Rev. Tyche stg. l., holding rudder and cornucopiae, L ΙΔ (= regnal year 14) before. RPC 5319. BMCG —. Cologne 212, 216. Milne —. *[AD 67–8].* **F** £200 ($320) / **VF** £400 ($640)

2023 **Bronze obol** (25 mm). Obv. As 2018. Rev. L ΕΝΑΤΟΥ (= regnal year 9), hawk stg. r. RPC 5272. BMCG —. Cologne —. Milne (Supplement) 215a. *[AD 62–3].* **F** £90 ($144) / **VF** £200 ($320)

2024 Obv. As 2021. Rev. ΑΥΤΟΚΡΑ, winged caduceus, L ΙΒ (= regnal year 12) to r. RPC 5290 (*Paris*). BMCG —. Cologne —. Milne —. *[AD 65–6].* **F** £80 ($128) / **VF** £180 ($288)

2025 Similar, but with rev. type eagle stg. r., L ΙΓ (= regnal year 13) before. RPC 5304. BMCG 183. Cologne 192. Milne (Supplement) 276a. *[AD 66–7].* **F** £70 ($112) / **VF** £160 ($256)

2026 Obv. As 2022. Rev. Serpent Agathodaemon r., with ears of corn and poppies, L ΙΔ (= regnal year 14) in field. RPC 5320. BMCG — (cf. 185). Cologne 208. Milne 306. *[AD 67–8].* **F** £70 ($112) / **VF** £160 ($256)

2027 Similar, but with rev. type Uraeus snake r. RPC 5321. BMCG —. Cologne 213. Milne —. *[AD 67–8].* **F** £80 ($128) / **VF** £180 ($288)

2028 Similar, but with rev. type ritual vase r. RPC 5322. BMCG 188. Cologne 211. Milne —. *[AD 67–8].* **F** £80 ($128) / **VF** £180 ($288)

2029 Similar, but with rev. type Apis bull stg. r. (date above). RPC 5323. BMCG 182. Cologne 209. Milne (Supplement) 306a. *[AD 67–8].* **F** £80 ($128) / **VF** £180 ($288)

2030 **Bronze hemiobol** (20 mm). ΝΕΡ ΚΛΑΥ ΚΑΙC CΕΒ ΓΕΡ, laur. hd. r. Rev. ΑΥΤΟΚΡΑΤ, Roma stg. l., holding patera, shield and spear, L Η (= regnal year 8) before. RPC 5263. BMCG 179. Cologne 149. Milne 207. *[AD 61–2].* **F** £40 ($64) / **VF** £90 ($144)

2031 Similar, but with rev. type bust of Alexandria r., wearing elephant's skin head-dress. RPC 5264. BMCG 181. Cologne —. Milne (Supplement) 207a. *[AD 61–2].* **F** £45 ($72) / **VF** £100 ($160)

2032 Similar, but with rev. ΑΥΤΟΚΡΑ, hawk stg. r., L I (= regnal year 10) before. RPC 5277. BMCG —. Cologne 162. Milne (Supplement) 222a. *[AD 63–4].* **F** £45 ($72) / **VF** £100 ($160)

2033 Obv. As 2021. Rev. ΑΥΤΟΚΡΑ, five ears of corn tied together in bundle, L ΙΓ (= regnal year 13) to r. RPC 5305. BMCG —. Cologne 193. Milne —. *[AD 66–7].* **F** £45 ($72) / **VF** £100 ($160)

2034 **Bronze hemiobol** (20 mm). Obv. As 2022. Rev. Gryphon seated r., l. forepaw resting on wheel, L IΔ (= regnal year 14) above. RPC 5324. BMCG (Supplement) 2712. Cologne 210. Milne —. *[AD 67–8].* **F £50 ($80) / VF £110 ($176)**

2035 **Bronze dichalkon** (15 mm). NEP KΛAY KAI ΣEB ΓEP AYT around the letter-numeral K (= 20 bronze drachmas = 1 silver quarter-obol). Rev. Eagle stg. r., hd. l., standard before, L E (= regnal year 5) above. RPC 5250 (ANS, New York). BMCG —. Cologne —. Milne —. *[AD 58–9].* (*Unique*)
This remarkable type appear to be of considerable significance in the interpretation of the denominational values of the Alexandrian bronze coinage (see also nos. 2038 and 2040).

2036 No legend, laur. hd. r., L ς (= regnal year 6) before. Rev. Eagle stg. r., wings spread, hd. l. RPC 5261 (ANS, New York). BMCG —. Cologne 148. Milne —. *[AD 59–60].*
F £30 ($48) / VF £65 ($104)

2037 No legend, laur. hd. r. Rev. Trophy, with captive kneeling r. at base, L H (= regnal year 8) in field. RPC 5265. BMCG 186. Cologne 150. Milne (Supplement) 207b. *[AD 61–2].*
F £35 ($56) / VF £75 ($120)

2038 **Bronze chalkos** (10 mm). No legend, laur. hd. r., L ς (= regnal year 6) in field. Rev. Wreath containing letter-numeral I (= 10 bronze drachmas = 1 silver eighth-obol). RPC 5262. BMCG 189. Cologne 215. Milne —. *[AD 59–60].* **F £25 ($40) / VF £55 ($88)**
See note following no. 2035.

2039 No legend, laur. hd. r. Rev. Trophy, L H (= regnal year 8) in field. RPC 5266 (ANS, New York). BMCG —. Cologne —. Milne —. *[AD 61–2].* **F £30 ($48) / VF £65 ($104)**

2040 **Bronze hemichalkon** (8 mm). NEP KΛAY KAI . . . around letter-numeral ε (= 5 bronze drachmas = 1 silver sixteenth-obol). Rev. Uraeus snake r., L E (= regnal year 5) in field. RPC 5251 (Berlin). BMCG —. Cologne —. Milne —. *[AD 58–9].* (*Unique*)
See note following no. 2035.

For other local coinages of this reign, see *Roman Provincial Coinage,* vol. I, and *Greek Imperial Coins & Their Values,* pp. 51–63.

NERO AND AGRIPPINA JUNIOR

2045

Having succeeded in her designs to bring her young son to the imperial throne Agrippina initially enjoyed great influence in the government of the Empire. However, her ascendancy was short-lived and with the downfall of her powerful and influential ally, the freedman Pallas, Agrippina was ousted before the end of the year AD 55. At this point her name and image disappear from the regular Roman coinage, but she continued to be represented on various provincial issues down to the time of her murder in March, AD 59.

2041 **Gold aureus.** AGRIPP AVG DIVI CLAVD NERONIS CAES MATER, confronted busts of Nero r., bare-headed, and Agrippina Junior l., dr. Rev. NERONI CLAVD DIVI F CAES AVG GERM IMP TR P around oak-wreath encircling EX S C. RIC 1. BMCRE 1. CBN 4. C *Agrippina and Nero* 6. *[Lugdunum, AD 54].* **VF £3,250 ($5,200) / EF £7,500 ($12,000)**

2042   **Gold aureus.** NERO CLAVD DIVI F CAES AVG GERM IMP TR P COS, conjoined bare-headed
       and dr. busts of Nero and Agrippina Junior r., that of the emperor in foreground. Rev.
       AGRIPP AVG DIVI CLAVD NERONIS CAES MATER, seated statues of Augustus and Claudius
       on car drawn l. by four elephants, EX S C in field. RIC 6. BMCRE 7. CBN 10. C *Agrippina
       and Nero* 3. *[Lugdunum, AD 55].*   VF £3,250 ($5,200) / EF £7,500 ($12,000)

                    2042   2043

2043   **Silver denarius.** As 2041. RIC 2. BMCRE 3. CBN 8. RSC *Agrippina and Nero* 7.
       [Lugdunum, AD 54].   VF £1,000 ($1,600) / EF £2,500 ($4,000)

2044   As 2042. RIC 7. BMCRE 8. CBN 13. RSC *Agrippina and Nero* 4. *[Lugdunum, AD 55].*
                                      VF £1,000 ($1,600) / EF £2,500 ($4,000)

2045   **Silver didrachm.** NERO CLAVD DIVI CLAVD F CAESAR AVG GERMANI, laur. hd. of Nero r.
       Rev. AGRIPPINA AVGVSTA MATER AVGVSTI, dr. bust of Agrippina Junior r. RPC 3632.
       RIC 607. BMCRE 422. CBN 434. RSC *Agrippina and Nero* 1. *[Caesarea in Cappadocia,
       AD 58–9].*   VF £400 ($640) / EF £950 ($1,520)

2046   Similar, but Agrippina also wears veil. RPC 3633. RIC 608. BMCRE 423. CBN 433. RSC
       Agrippina and Nero 2. *[Caesarea in Cappadocia, AD 58–9].*
                                      VF £425 ($680) / EF £1,000 ($1,600)

2047   **Silver 24-as piece** (= 1½ denarii). Similar to 2045, but without rev. legend and with AC / IT
       behind hd. of Agrippina and KΔ before, all within laurel-wreath. RPC 3636. RIC 609.
       BMCRE 424. CBN —. RSC *Agrippina and Nero* 2e. *[Caesarea in Cappadocia, AD 58–9].*
                                      VF £1,100 ($1,760) / EF £2,500 ($4,000)
       *This remarkable issue, doubtless struck for the use of Roman troops operating in the East,
       clearly states its value (KΔ = 24) in terms of 'Italian asses' (see also no. 2056).*

2048   **Silver drachm.** Similar to 2045, but sometimes with K / K (Καισαρεια τησ Καππαδοκιασ)
       behind hd. of Agrippina. RPC 3637, 3641. RIC 611. BMCRE 426. CBN —. RSC
       Agrippina and Nero 2b. *[Caesarea in Cappadocia, AD 58–9].*
                                      VF £350 ($560) / EF £850 ($1,360)

2049   Similar, but Agrippina's bust is to l., sometimes veiled, and sometimes with K / K
       (Καισαρεια τησ Καππαδοκιασ) behind. RPC 3638, 3640, 3642. RIC 610. BMCRE 425.
       CBN —. RSC *Agrippina and Nero* 2a. *[Caesarea in Cappadocia, AD 58–9].*
                                      VF £350 ($560) / EF £850 ($1,360)

2050   **Silver 12-as piece** (= ¾ denarius). Similar to 2047, but with IB (= 12) instead of KΔ before
       hd. of Agrippina. RPC 3643. RIC 612. BMCRE 427. CBN —. RSC *Agrippina and Nero*
       2f. *[Caesarea in Cappadocia, AD 58–9].*   VF £750 ($1,200) / EF £1,750 ($2,800)
       See note following no. 2047.

See also nos. 1989 and 2017. For a denarius (of disputed authenticity) of Agrippina and Nero
struck during the reign of Claudius, see no. 1914.

Issues of Nero in honour of Divus Claudius

2051　**Gold aureus.** DIVVS CLAVDIVS AVGVSTVS, laur. hd. of Claudius l. Rev. EX S C, richly ornamented car drawn r. by four horses, surmounted by four miniature horses galloping r. between two Victories. RIC 4. BMCRE 4. CBN 1. C *Claudius* 31. *[Lugdunum, AD 54–5].*
VF £2,750 ($4,400) / **EF** £6,500 ($10,400)

2052

2052　**Silver denarius.** Similar. RIC 5. BMCRE 6. CBN 3. RSC *Claudius* 32. *[Lugdunum, AD 54–5].*
VF £750 ($1,200) / **EF** £1,750 ($2,800)

2053

2053　**Silver tetradrachm.** NERO CLAVD DIVI CLAVD F CAESAR AVG GER, laur. hd. of Nero r., usually with star behind. Rev. DIVOS CLAVD AVG GERMANIC PATER AVG, laur. hd. of Claudius r. RPC 4122–3. RIC —. BMCRE —. CBN 450. RSC *Claudius and Nero/Nero and Claudius* 2. *[Uncertain Syrian mint, AD 64].*
VF £225 ($360) / **EF** £550 ($880)

2054　**Silver didrachm.** NERO CLAVD DIVI CLAVD F CAESAR AVG GERMANI, laur. hd. of Nero r. Rev. DIVOS CLAVD AVGVST GERMANIC PATER AVG, laur. hd. of Claudius r. RPC 3631. RIC 613. BMCRE 413. CBN —. RSC *Claudius and Nero* 1b. *[Caesarea in Cappadocia, AD 59].*
VF £225 ($360) / **EF** £550 ($880)

2055　　　　　　　　　　　　　　2057

2055　Similar, but the obv. legend ends GERMA (rarely GERM) and with more mature portrait of Nero. RPC 3647. RIC 619–20. BMCRE 416. CBN 442, 444. RSC *Claudius and Nero* 1, 1a/*Nero and Claudius* 1. *[Caesarea in Cappadocia, AD 64].*
VF £200 ($320) / **EF** £500 ($800)

2056 **Silver 24-as piece** (= $1\frac{1}{2}$ denarii). Similar to 2054, but without rev. legend and with **AC / IT** behind hd. of Claudius and **KΔ** before, all within laurel-wreath. RPC 3635. RIC 614. BMCRE 417. CBN —. RSC *Nero and Claudius* 6. *[Caesarea in Cappadocia, AD 59].*
VF £1,100 ($1,760) / **EF** £2,500 ($4,000)
See also no. 2047 and note.

2057 **Silver drachm.** As 2055. RPC 3648. RIC 621–2. BMCRE 418, 420. CBN 448. RSC *Claudius and Nero* 3, 3a/*Nero and Claudius* 3. *[Caesarea in Cappadocia, AD 64].*
VF £125 ($200) / **EF** £325 ($520)

For a later issue in honour of Divus Claudius, see under Trajan.

OCTAVIA

The daughter of Claudius and Messalina, Octavia was born about AD 40. She was married to Nero in AD 53, the year before he ascended the imperial throne. Although their union lasted for nine years their relationship was very unhappy and eventually Nero divorced her to facilitate his marriage to Poppaea. Later in the same year Octavia was banished to the island of Pandateria, condemned on trumped-up charges of adultery and treason, and finally put to death. Her cruel fate inspired the praetexta 'Octavia', of unknown authorship, written soon after Nero's death.

For depictions of Octavia on the coinage of Claudius' reign, see nos. 1869–70 and 1907; and for a depiction on an Alexandrian tetradrachm of Nero, see no. 1990.

POPPAEA

Poppaea Sabina, named after her maternal grandfather C. Poppaeus Sabinus (consul AD 9) became Nero's second wife in AD 62. She had previously been married to Rufrius Crispinus, praetorian prefect under Claudius, and later to the future emperor M. Salvius Otho. Her association with Nero seems to have begun as early as AD 58 when Otho was sent to Lusitania as governor, his wife remaining in Rome as the emperor's mistress. Following her subsequent divorce from Otho Poppaea became empress in succession to Octavia and in AD 63 bore Nero a daughter, Claudia, who died within four months. Poppaea herself died two years later when, pregnant again, she was kicked by her husband in a fit of temper. Filled with remorse, Nero accorded her a public funeral and divine honours.

For a depiction of Poppaea on an Alexandrian tetradrachm of Nero, see no. 2002.

POPPAEA AND CLAUDIA

2058

The daughter of Nero and Poppaea, Claudia was born at Antium in AD 63 but survived for just four months. The only coins bearing her name were struck following her mother's death and deification two years later.

2058 **Æ 19** of Caesarea Paneas in Syria (Palestine). **DIVA POPPAEA AVG**, distyle temple containing statue of Poppaea seated l. Rev. **DIVA CLAVD NER F**, hexastyle temple with domed roof containing statue of Claudia stg. l. RPC 4846. C p. 315, 1. *[AD 65].*
F £150 ($240) / **VF** £350 ($560)

STATILIA MESSALINA

Statilia Messalina, probably the daughter of T. Statilius Taurus (consul AD 44), married Nero in AD 66, the year following the death of his second wife Poppaea. Beautiful and well educated, she was noted for her eloquence and successfully survived her husband's downfall in 68. She lived in great style under Nero's successors and it is said that Otho contemplated marriage with her during his brief reign.

2059   Æ **23** of Hypaepa in Asia (Lydia). ΝΕΡΩΝ ΜΕΣΣΑΛΕΙΝΑ, dr. bust of Statilia Messalina r. facing laur. hd. of Nero l. Rev. ΥΠΑΙ ΙΟΥ ΓΡ ΗΓΗΣΙΠΠΟΣ, cultus-statue of Artemis Anaitis facing. RPC 2543. *[AD 66].*   **F** £325 ($520) / **VF** £750 ($1,200)

THE TWELVE CAESARS:
2. CIVIL WARS AND FLAVIAN DYNASTY, AD 68–96

CIVIL WARS: REVOLT OF VINDEX
IN GAUL
Mar.–May AD 68

2061

Gaius Julius Vindex, descended from the kings of Aquitania and the son of a Roman senator, was governor of Gallia Lugdunensis at the time he raised the standards of revolt against Nero in March, AD 68. Having no Roman troops under his command Vindex appealed to other provincial governors to support his uprising, an invitation which was answered only by Servius Sulpicius Galba in Spain (Tarraconensis). Even his own provincial capital of Lugdunum refused to join his cause, though Vienna (modern Vienne) in Narbonensis did side with him and was the probable place of mintage of the coins struck during the period of his revolt (none of which bear his name or portrait). In May the rebellion of Vindex was crushed when his army was defeated at Vesontio (Besançon) by L. Verginius Rufus, governor of Upper Germany. Just a few weeks later Nero committed suicide and soon afterwards Galba was formally recognized as emperor by the Roman Senate.

2060   **Gold aureus.** MARS VLTOR, helmeted bust of bearded Mars r. Rev. SIGNA P R, legionary eagle between two standards, altar to r. of eagle. RIC 50. BMCRE 38. CBN 16. C *Galba* 405. *[Vienne].*   **VF** £6,500 ($10,400) / **EF** £14,000 ($22,400)

2061   **Silver denarius.** Similar. RIC 51. BMCRE 39. CBN 18. RSC *Civil War (Galba)* 406. *[Vienne].*   **VF** £600 ($960) / **EF** £1,400 ($2,240)

2062

2062   SALVS GENERIS HVMANI, Victory stg. l. on globe, holding wreath and palm. Rev. S P Q R in oak-wreath. RIC 72. BMCRE 34. CBN 37. RSC *Civil War (Galba)* 420. *[Vienne].*
                    VF £550 ($880) / **EF** £1,250 ($2,000)

402   CIVIL WARS

2063   **Silver denarius.** ROMA RESTITVTOR, helmeted bust of Roma r. Rev. IVPPITER LIBERATOR,
        Jupiter seated l., holding thunderbolt and sceptre. RIC 62. BMCRE 19. CBN 29. RSC
        Civil War (Galba) 374. *[Vienne].*   **VF** £750 ($1,200) / **EF** £1,750 ($2,800)
        The reverse is adapted from the coinage of Nero (see no. 1943).

2064   No legend, bare hd. of Augustus r. Rev. AVGVSTVS, capricorn r., holding globe and rudder,
        cornucopiae on its back. RIC 82. BMCRE 45. CBN 48. RSC *Civil War (Augustus)* 21a.
        [Vienne].   **VF** £500 ($800) / **EF** £1,100 ($1,760)
        *This is copied from the coinage of Augustus (see no. 1592) – cf. also the following two
        types.*

2065   CAESAR AVGVSTVS, laur. hd. of Augustus r. Rev. DIVVS IVLIVS, eight-rayed comet. RIC
        92. BMCRE 49. CBN —. RSC *Civil War (Augustus)* 98a. *[Vienne].*
                                                               VF £750 ($1,200) / **EF** £1,750 ($2,800)
        Copied from an Augustan prototype (see no. 1607).

2066   AVGVSTVS DIVI F, bare hd. of Augustus l. Rev. OB / CIVES / SERVAT in three lines within
        oak-wreath. RIC 102. BMCRE 52. CBN 56. RSC *Civil War (Augustus)* 209a. *[Vienne].*
                                                               VF £850 ($1,360) / **EF** £2,000 ($3,200)
        Copied from an Augustan prototype (see no. 1625).

**CIVIL WARS: REVOLT OF GALBA
IN SPAIN**
Apr.–June AD 68

2068 var. (rev. Pax)

*The elderly aristocrat Servius Sulpicius Galba was governor of Hispania Tarraconensis through-
out the latter part of Nero's reign. In April AD 68 he answered the appeal of Vindex, governor of
Gallia Lugdunensis, to join in a provincial revolt against the unpopular rule of Nero. Initially
accepting only his soldiers' acclamation as imperator and posing merely as the representative of
the Senate and People of Rome, he eventually took the titles of Caesar and Augustus following the
suicide of Nero early in June. His full recognition as emperor by the Senate came at a meeting with
a senatorial deputation at Narbo in July. Many of the coins struck under Galba's rebel regime bear
his name and portrait, but some of the Spanish issues were produced anonymously or with the head
of Divus Augustus as the obverse type. The mint was most likely situated at Tarraco, the capital city
of Galba's provincial command.*

2067   **Gold aureus.** LIBERTAS RESTITVTA, bust of Libertas r., wearing pearl necklace. Rev.
        S P Q R on round shield encircled by oak-wreath. RIC 26. BMCRE 12, note. CBN 9. C
        Galba 430. *[Tarraco].*   **VF** £7,000 ($11,200) / **EF** £15,000 ($24,000)

2068   DIVVS AVGVSTVS, rad. hd. of Augustus r. Rev. HISPANIA, Hispania stg. l., holding corn-
        ears and two short spears, shield slung on shoulders behind. RIC 112. BMCRE p. 304, §
        and pl. 51, 16. CBN 63. C *Augustus* 109. *[Tarraco].*
                                                               VF £6,000 ($9,600) / **EF** £12,500 ($20,000)

2069   **Silver denarius.** As 2067. RIC 27. BMCRE 12. CBN 10. RSC *Civil War (Galba)* 431.
        [Tarraco].   **VF** £550 ($880) / **EF** £1,250 ($2,000)

2070   **Silver denarius.** GENIO P R, young male hd. r., cornucopiae behind. Rev. MARTI VLTORI, Mars advancing r., brandishing spear and holding shield. RIC 17. BMCRE 1. CBN 4. RSC *Civil War (Galba)* 384a. *[Tarraco].*   VF £750 ($1,200) / EF £1,750 ($2,800)

2071   LIBERTAS, bust of Libertas r. Rev. P R RESTITVTA, pileus between two daggers. RIC 24. BMCRE 7. CBN 8. RSC *Civil War (Galba)* 394. *[Tarraco].*
                                    VF £2,000 ($3,200) / EF £4,500 ($7,200)
        This remarkable type revives the famous issue of M. Junius Brutus in 42 BC in celebration of the murder of Caesar on the Ides of March 44 (see no. 1439).

2072

2072   BON EVENT, hd. of Bonus Eventus r. Rev. ROM RENASC, Roma stg. r., holding Victory on globe and spear. RIC 9. BMCRE 9. CBN 2. RSC *Civil War (Galba)* 396. *[Tarraco].*
                                    VF £650 ($1,040) / EF £1,500 ($2,400)
        The obverse is copied from the Republican coinage of the moneyer L. Scribonius Libo (62 BC) – see no. 367.

2073   Obv. As 2068. Rev. SENATVS P Q ROMANVS, Victory alighting l., wings spread, holding shield inscribed VI / AV. RIC 116. BMCRE 59. CBN 69. RSC *Civil War (Augustus)* 254. *[Tarraco].*   VF £650 ($1,040) / EF £1,500 ($2,400)

For contemporary Spanish and Gallic issues bearing the name (and usually the portrait) of Galba as imperator, see below under the coinage of his reign (AD 68–69).

CIVIL WARS: CLODIUS MACER IN AFRICA
Apr.–Oct. AD 68

2074

Lucius Clodius Macer, legatus in Africa, rebelled against the rule of Nero about April of AD 68, thereby threatening Rome's vital corn supply. Following the suicide of Nero in June Macer appears not to have recognized the rule of the new emperor, Galba. Instead, he styled himself simply 'propraetor Africae' and set about raising a new legion (Legio I Macriana) to augment the military establishment already under his command (Legio III Augusta in Numidia). Both units were given the title 'Liberatrix'. His motives remain unclear, for his downfall occurred in October when Galba, concerned over the capital's corn supply, gave orders for his arrest and execution. The coinage of Macer – all of silver denarii – invariably bears his name, but only one type has his portrait. His mint seems to have been situated at Carthage, though Cirta in Numidia has also been suggested as a possible site.

2074   **Silver denarius.** L CLODIVS MACER S C, bare hd. of Clodius Macer r. Rev. PROPRAE AFRICAE, galley r. RIC 35. BMCRE 1. CBN 8. RSC 13. *[Carthage].*
                                    VF £12,500 ($20,000) / EF £35,000 ($56,000)

2075   **Silver denarius.** L CLODI MACRI S C, lion's hd. r. Rev. LIB AVG LEG III, legionary eagle between two standards. RIC 8. BMCRE 3. CBN 2. RSC 5. *[Carthage].*
VF £5,000 ($8,000) / **EF** £12,500 ($20,000)

2076

2076   Similar, but with obv. type winged bust of Victory r. RIC 13. BMCRE 4. CBN 4. RSC 4. *[Carthage].*
VF £5,500 ($8,800) / **EF** £13,500 ($21,600)

2077   Similar, but with obv. L CLODI MACRI LIBERA S C, bust of Africa r., wearing elephant's skin head-dress. RIC 2. BMCRE p. 286, † note. CBN 8. RSC 13. *[Carthage].*
VF £5,500 ($8,800) / **EF** £13,500 ($21,600)

2078   L CLODI MACRI S C, Libertas stg. l., holding pileus and patera. Rev. LIB LEG I MACRIANA, legionary eagle between two standards. RIC 21. BMCRE p. 286, * note. CBN 5. RSC 2. *[Carthage].*
VF £5,500 ($8,800) / **EF** £13,500 ($21,600)

2079   L CLODI MACRI CARTHAGO S C, turreted and dr. bust of Carthage r., cornucopiae behind. Rev. SICILIA, triskelis with Medusa hd. at centre, ear of corn between each pair of legs. RIC 26. BMCRE 5. CBN 7. RSC 10. *[Carthage].*
VF £6,000 ($9,600) / **EF** £15,000 ($24,000)

2080   ROMA S C, helmeted hd. of Roma r. Rev. L CLODI MACRI, trophy. RIC 30. BMCRE p. 287, * note. CBN —. RSC 9. *[Carthage].*
VF £6,500 ($10,400) / **EF** £16,000 ($25,600)

CIVIL WARS: PRO-VITELLIAN FORCES IN SOUTHERN GAUL
Mar. AD 69

2082

The most satisfactory interpretation of this controversial group of anonymous civil war issues was put forward by Kraay (Numismatic Chronicle 1949, pp. 78 ff.) who regarded them as a propaganda coinage produced on behalf of Vitellius for distribution amongst the praetorians and populace in Rome during the latter part of Otho's reign. In March of AD 69 the Vitellian commander Fabius Valens entered Italy from southern Gaul at the head of a small band of secret agents. Their mission was to infiltrate the capital, especially the ranks of the praetorians, with the object of disseminating pro-Vitellian propaganda and dissociating the guards from their allegiance to Otho. These coins, struck in advance in southern Gaul, would thus have played a vital role in the operation as bribe money. Despite these covert activities the praetorians remained loyal to their emperor, though all for nought as the following month the invading army of Vitellius was victorious at the battle of Bedriacum and Otho took his own life.

2081　**Gold aureus.** I O M CAPITOLINVS, diad. and dr. bust of the Capitoline Jupiter l., small palm-branch before. Rev. VESTA P R QVIRITIVM, Vesta enthroned l., holding patera and torch. RIC 124. BMCRE 72, note. CBN —. C —. *[Nemausus].* (*Unique*)

2082　**Silver denarius.** Similar. RIC 125a. BMCRE 72. CBN 78. RSC *Civil War (Galba)* 432. *[Nemausus].* **VF** £650 ($1,040) / **EF** £1,500 ($2,400)

2083　FIDES EXERCITVVM, clasped r. hands. Rev. CONCORDIA PRAETORIANORVM, Concordia stg. l., holding branch and cornucopiae. RIC 118. BMCRE 61. CBN 71. RSC *Civil War (Galba)* 359. *[Lugdunum].* **VF** £600 ($960) / **EF** £1,400 ($2,240)

2084

2084　Obv. Similar. Rev. FIDES PRAETORIANORVM, clasped r. hands. RIC 121. BMCRE 65. CBN 75. RSC *Civil War (Galba)* 363. *[Lugdunum].* **VF** £550 ($880) / **EF** £1,250 ($2,000)

2085　VESTA P R QVIRITIVM, veiled and dr. bust of Vesta r., lighted torch before. Rev. I O MAX CAPITOLINVS, distyle temple containing statue of Jupiter seated l., holding thunderbolt and sceptre. RIC 128. BMCRE 70. CBN 82. RSC *Civil War (Galba)* 368. *[Lugdunum].*
VF £700 ($1,120) / **EF** £1,600 ($2,560)
The celebrated temple of Jupiter Optimus Maximus on Rome's Capitoline Hill, the second such structure to occupy the site, was destined to be destroyed at the end of the year (AD 69) in the fighting between the forces supporting the two contenders for imperial power, Vitellius and Vespasian (see also no. 2194).

There is a Trajanic restoration of the aureus of this series (see Vol. II).

CIVIL WARS: GALLIC REVOLT
late AD 69–early AD 70

2086

Gaius Julius Civilis was a Batavian noble with Roman citizenship who had served in the auxiliary branch of the Roman army, where he had risen to the rank of cohort commander. For reasons unknown he harboured strong grievances against the Roman government, a circumstance which was to dictate his conduct during the civil war between Vitellius and Vespasian and its aftermath. When the Flavian army was advancing into Italy in the summer of AD 69 the legate of Legio VII, Antonius Primus, wrote to Civilis inciting him to create a diversion and so prevent Vitellian reinforcements from transferring to Italy. Grateful for the opportunity to strike against the Roman army Civilis fomented a war of liberation under the pretext of supporting Vespasian. With help from Germans beyond the Rhine he attacked the legionary camp of Castra Vetera (modern Xanten) but was beaten off. The revolt, however, spread widely, finding support in the winter of 69–70 among Gallic tribes, such as the Treveri and Lingones. Roman troops at Novaesium (Neuss) on the Rhine even took an oath of allegiance to the 'Imperium Galliarum' and Vetera finally fell, its garrison force of Legio XV Primigenia being turned out in shameful surrender. However, support for the rebels' cause was not as universal as Civilis had hoped and with the approach of the Flavian generals at the head of a mighty army the Gallic movement showed signs of disintegration. Vespasian's general Cerialis (later governor of Britain) won a battle near Trier, and after mixed fighting along the Rhine towards the Batavian territory Civilis finally capitulated. His fate is not recorded. A group of very rare denarii, together with a single aureus type, have been convincingly attributed to the revolt of Civilis and his allies. The rebel leader appears to have been extremely mobile, both on land and also up and down the Rhine, and he may well have possessed a mobile mint for the production of his very limited output of coinage.

2086 **Gold aureus. SALVTIS**, dr. bust of Salus r. Rev. **CONCORDIA**, Concordia stg. l., holding branch and cornucopiae. RIC 134. BMCRE p. 308(a) and pl. 51, 24. CBN —. C *Civil War (Galba)* 357. *[Lower Germany].*
VF £8,500 ($13,600) / **EF** £17,500 ($28,000)

2087 **Silver denarius. GALLIA**, diad. and dr. bust of Gallia r., trumpet behind. Rev. **FIDES**, clasped r. hands holding corn-ears and standard surmounted by boar r. RIC 131. BMCRE p. 308(c) and pl. 51, 26. CBN —. RSC *Civil War (Galba)* 361. *[Lower Germany].*
VF £2,500 ($4,000) / **EF** £5,500 ($8,800)

2088 **LIBERTAS RESTITVTA**, veiled, diad. and dr. bust of Libertas r., ear of corn before. Rev. **MARS ADSERTOR**, Mars stg. facing, hd. r., holding vexillum and shield. RIC 133. BMCRE p. 308, note. CBN 86. RSC *Civil War (Galba)* 376. *[Lower Germany].*
VF £2,000 ($3,200) / **EF** £4,500 ($7,200)

GALBA
3 Apr. AD 68–15 Jan. 69

2113 var.

Servius Sulpicius Galba, born of an aristocratic family in 3 BC and a favourite of the Empress Livia in his youth, had a most distinguished public career culminating in the governorhip of Hispania Tarraconensis in the latter part of Nero's reign. When Vindex, governor of Gallia Lugdunensis, rebelled against Nero in March, AD 68, he invited Galba to join him and promised to support him as Nero's replacement on the imperial throne. Vindex soon perished, but by then Galba had already committed himself to the revolt and Nero's suicide soon afterwards assured his success. Galba's reign was destined to be of short duration. He failed to gain popularity, principally because of his ruthlessness in implementing reforms and his notorious avarice. This caused a serious rift with the praetorian guards to whom he refused to pay a promised donative. His supporter in the revolt against Nero, M. Salvius Otho, had hoped to be adopted as his successor. But when, early in January 69, Galba selected a certain L. Calpurnius Piso as his heir the disgruntled Otho wasted no time in organizing a conspiracy of the praetorians. On January 15th Galba and Piso were both assassinated in the Forum, their severed heads being taken to Otho in the praetorian camp.

Galba's coinage commenced in Spain at the time of his revolt against Nero early in April AD 68 and coins were also struck for him in southern Gaul. Rome became Galba's principal mint after the Senate's recognition of his imperial authority in July, though his western provincial mints remained active.

For the titles and powers of this reign, including Alexandrian regnal dates, see table on p. 308.

2089   **Gold aureus (provincial series).** GALBA IMPERATOR, laur. hd. r., globe below. Rev. ROMA
RENASC, Roma walking r., holding Victory on globe and spear. RIC 40. BMCRE 178.
CBN 22. C 195. *[Tarraco, Apr.–Jun.* AD *68].*   **VF** £3,500 ($5,600) / **EF** £8,500 ($13,600)

2090   SER GALBA IMP CAESAR AVG P M TR P, laur. hd. r. Rev. CONCORDIA PROVINCIARVM,
Concordia stg. l., holding branch and cornucopiae. RIC 119. BMCRE 216. CBN —. C 37.
[Narbo, Nov. AD *68].*   **VF** £4,000 ($6,400) / **EF** £10,000 ($16,000)

2091   **Gold aureus (regular series).** IMP SER GALBA CAESAR AVG, laur. and dr. bust r. Rev.
DIVA AVGVSTA, Livia stg. l., holding patera and sceptre. RIC 188. BMCRE 3. CBN 82. C
54. *[Rome, Oct.–Nov.* AD *68].*   **VF** £3,000 ($4,800) / **EF** £7,500 ($12,000)
The Empress Livia, wife of Augustus, had died in AD *29, though her deification was
delayed until the reign of her grandson Claudius. Suetonius records that in his youth
Galba was a favourite of Livia through whose patronage he moved in the most elevated
social circles of the Julio-Claudian era.*

2092   SER GALBA CAESAR AVG, bare-headed and cuir. bust l. Rev. SALVS GEN HVMANI, female
figure stg. l. before lighted altar, r. foot on globe, holding patera and rudder. RIC 146.
BMCRE p. 314, note † and pl. 52, 19. CBN 66. C 232. *[Rome, Jul.–Aug.* AD *68].*
VF £5,000 ($8,000) / **EF** £12,500 ($20,000)

2093

2093   IMP SER GALBA AVG, bare hd. r. Rev. S P Q R / OB C S in two lines within oak-wreath. RIC
164. Cf. BMCRE 29 (obv. misdescribed). CBN 72. C 286. *[Rome, Aug.–Oct.* AD *68].*
VF £2,500 ($4,000) / **EF** £6,500 ($10,400)

2094   **Silver denarius (provincial series).** GALBA IMP, Galba on horseback galloping r., his r.
hand extended and trailing behind him. Rev. HISPANIA, dr. bust of Hispania r., two spears
and shield behind and below, two corn-ears before. RIC 1. BMCRE 161. CBN 1. RSC 76.
[Tarraco, Apr.–Jun. AD *68].*   **VF** £450 ($720) / **EF** £1,100 ($1,760)

2094 var. (emperor left)   2095

2095   Similar to 2089, but with legends GALBA IMP and ROMA RENASCENS. RIC 27. BMCRE
183. CBN 15. RSC 209. *[Tarraco, Apr.–Jun.* AD *68].*   **VF** £375 ($600) / **EF** £900 ($1,440)

2096   SER GALBA IMP CAESAR AVG P M TR P, laur. hd. r., globe below. Rev. ROMA VICTRIX,
Roma stg. l., r. foot on globe, holding branch and spear. RIC 60. BMCRE 189. CBN 30.
RSC 225. *[Tarraco, Nov.* AD *68].*   **VF** £400 ($640) / **EF** £950 ($1,520)

2097   **Silver denarius (provincial series).** SER GALBA IMP, Galba on horseback galloping r., brandishing spear. Rev. GALLIA, dr. bust of Gallia r., two spears and shield behind and below, two corn-ears before. RIC 85. BMCRE 206. CBN 42. RSC 72. *[Vienne, Apr.–Jun. AD 68].*   **VF** £500 ($800) / **EF** £1,250 ($2,000)

2098   SER GALBA IMP AVG, Galba on horseback r., as 2094. Rev. TRES GALLIAE, busts of the three Gauls (Aquitania, Lugdunensis, and Narbonensis) r., ear of corn before each. RIC 92. BMCRE 214. CBN 44. RSC 308. *[Vienne, July AD 68].*
        F £1,000 ($1,600) / **VF** £2,500 ($4,000) / **EF** £6,000 ($9,600)

2099   SER GALBA IMP, laur. hd. r., globe below. Rev. VICTORIA, Victory stg. r., inscribing P R on shield set on cippus. RIC 99. BMCRE 232. CBN 52. RSC 316. *[Narbo, May–Jun. AD 68].*
                                                      VF £450 ($720) / **EF** £1,100 ($1,760)

2100

2100   SER GALBA IMPERATOR, laur. hd. r. Rev. CONCORDIA PROVINCIARVM, Concordia stg. l., holding branch and cornucopiae. RIC 105. BMCRE 217. CBN 53. RSC 34. *[Narbo, May–Jun. AD 68].*   **VF** £375 ($600) / **EF** £900 ($1,440)

2101   IMP GALBA CAESAR AVG P P, laur. hd. r., globe below. Rev. FORTVNA AVG, Fortuna stg. l., holding rudder and cornucopiae. RIC 128. BMCRE 241a. CBN 60. RSC 70. *[Lugdunum, Nov. AD 68].*   **VF** £450 ($720) / **EF** £1,100 ($1,760)

2102 var,   2103

2102   **Silver denarius (regular series).** IMP SER GALBA CAESAR AVG P M, laur. hd. r. Rev. DIVA AVGVSTA, Livia stg. l., holding patera and sceptre. RIC 224. BMCRE 12. CBN 101. RSC 58. *[Rome, Nov. AD 68–Jan. 69].*   **VF** £375 ($600) / **EF** £900 ($1,440)

2103   IMP SER GALBA AVG, laur. hd. r. Rev. HISPANIA, Hispania advancing l., holding corn-ears and poppy in r. hand, shield and two spears in l. RIC 155. BMCRE 15. CBN 68. RSC 82. *[Rome, Aug.–Oct. AD 68].*   **VF** £400 ($640) / **EF** £950 ($1,520)

2104   SER GALBA AVG, laur. hd. r. Rev. IMP, Galba on horseback galloping r., his r. hand extended and trailing behind him. RIC 145. BMCRE 21. CBN —. RSC 93. *[Rome, Jul.–Aug. AD 68].*   **VF** £400 ($640) / **EF** £950 ($1,520)

2104 var.   2106

2105   **Silver denarius (regular series).** Obv. As 2103. Rev. LIBERTAS P R, Libertas stg. facing,
       hd. r., between two ears of corn, holding pileus in r. hand, l. hand extended. RIC 157.
       BMCRE 24. CBN 70. RSC 106. *[Rome, Aug.–Oct. AD 68]*.
       VF £400 ($640) / **EF** £950 ($1,520)

2106   IMP SER GALBA CAESAR AVG, laur. hd. r. Rev. ROMA RENASC, Roma stg. r., holding
       Victory and spear. RIC 199. BMCRE 25. CBN 91. RSC 200. *[Rome, Oct.–Nov. AD 68]*.
       VF £375 ($600) / **EF** £900 ($1,440)

2107   Obv. As 2102. Rev. ROMA RENASCES, Roma stg. l., holding Victory and eagle-tipped scep-
       tre. RIC 229. BMCRE p. 313, note †. CBN 103. RSC 208. *[Rome, Nov. AD 68–Jan. 69]*.
       VF £375 ($600) / **EF** £900 ($1,440)

2108   2109

2108   IMP SER GALBA CAESAR AVG, laur. and dr. bust r. Rev. SALVS GEN HVMANI, female stg. l.
       before altar, as 2092. RIC 214. BMCRE 43. CBN 95. RSC 236. *[Rome, Oct.–Nov. AD 68]*.
       VF £375 ($600) / **EF** £900 ($1,440)

2109   IMP SER GALBA AVG, bare hd. r. Rev. S P Q R / OB / C S in three lines within oak-wreath.
       RIC 167. Cf. BMCRE 34 (obv. misdescribed). CBN 76. RSC 287. *[Rome, Aug.–Oct.
       AD 68]*.   **VF** £350 ($560) / **EF** £850 ($1,360)

2110   Obv. As 2108. Rev. VICTORIA P R, Victory stg. l. on globe, holding wreath and palm. RIC
       217. BMCRE 49. CBN 97. RSC 328. *[Rome, Oct.–Nov. AD 68]*.
       VF £375 ($600) / **EF** £900 ($1,440)

2110   2112

2111 **Silver denarius (regular series).** Obv. As 2103. Rev. VIRTVS, Virtus stg. facing, holding parazonium and spear. RIC 179. BMCRE 50. CBN 80. RSC 341a. *[Rome, Aug.–Oct.* AD *68].* **VF** £400 ($640) / **EF** £950 ($1,520)

2112 **Silver quinarius.** SER GALBA IMP CAESAR AVG P M T P, laur. hd. r. Rev. VICTORIA GALBAE AVG, Victory stg. r. on globe, holding wreath and palm. RIC 132. BMCRE 244. CBN 63. RSC 317. *[Lugdunum, Nov.* AD *68–Jan. 69].* **VF** £300 ($480) / **EF** £750 ($1,200) *This remarkable revival of the half-denarius, the first issue of the denomination since early in the principate of Augustus (see nos. 1642–3), anticipates the resumption of limited production of the silver quinarius under the Flavian emperors.*

2113 **Brass sestertius.** SER SVLPI GALBA IMP CAESAR AVG TR P, laur. laur. hd. r. Rev. ADLOCVTIO S C, Galba, accompanied by praetorian praefect, stg. r. on low platform, addressing gathering of four soldiers. RIC 467. BMCRE 249 var. (hd. r.). CBN 236. C 2. *[Rome, Dec.* AD *68].* **F** £750 ($1,200) / **VF** £1,750 ($2,800) / **EF** £7,500 ($12,000)

2114 IMP SER GALBA CAE AVG TR P, hd. l., wreathed with oak. Rev. AVGVSTA S C, Livia seated l., holding patera and sceptre. RIC 334. BMCRE 54. CBN 161 var. (hd. r.). C 12 var. *[Rome, Sept.–Oct.* AD *68].* **F** £350 ($560) / **VF** £850 ($1,360) / **EF** £3,250 ($5,200)

2115 var.

2115 SER GALBA IMP CAESAR AVG TR P, laur. hd. l. Rev. CONCORD AVG S C, Concordia seated l., holding branch and sceptre. RIC 381. BMCRE 55. CBN 189. C 28. *[Rome, Oct.* AD *68].* **F** £325 ($520) / **VF** £800 ($1,280) / **EF** £3,000 ($4,800)

2116 SER SVLPI GALBA IMP CAESAR AVG P M TR P, laur. hd. r., with aegis. Rev. HISPANIA CLVNIA SVL S C, Galba seated l. on curule chair, holding parazonium and receiving Palladium from city-goddess Clunia stg. r. before him, holding cornucopiae. RIC 472. BMCRE 252. CBN 237. C 86. *[Rome, Dec.* AD *68].* **F** £800 ($1,280) / **VF** £2,000 ($3,200) / **EF** £8,000 ($12,800) *After the failure of the rebellion of Vindex in Gaul (May 68) his ally Galba sought refuge within the walls of Clunia in Tarraconensis. The following month, following Nero's suicide, Galba was proclaimed emperor in the city, as evidenced by this remarkable coin type.*

2117 Obv. Similar to 2113, but bust laur. and dr. r. Rev. HONOS ET VIRTVS S C, Honos stg. r., holding sceptre and cornucopiae, facing Virtus stg. l., holding parazonium and spear. RIC 475. BMCRE 256. CBN 239. C 89. *[Rome, Dec.* AD *68].* **F** £400 ($640) / **VF** £1,000 ($1,600) / **EF** £4,000 ($6,400)

2118 Obv. Similar to 2115, but laur. hd. r. Rev. LIBERTAS PVBLICA S C, Libertas stg. l., holding pileus and sceptre. RIC 387. BMCRE 68. CBN 195. C 108. *[Rome, Oct.* AD *68].* **F** £275 ($440) / **VF** £700 ($1,120) / **EF** £2,500 ($4,000)

2118 var.

2119

2119 **Brass sestertius.** SER GALBA IMP CAES AVG TR P, laur. and dr. bust r. Rev. ROMA S C, Roma seated l. on cuirass, holding spear and resting on shield set on heap of arms. RIC 241. BMCRE 89. CBN 112. C 169. *[Rome, Jul.–Aug. AD 68].*
F £300 ($480) / **VF** £750 ($1,200) / **EF** £2,750 ($4,400)

2120 Obv. Similar to 2115, but laur. and dr. bust r. Rev. — Roma stg. l., holding Victory and spear. RIC 393. BMCRE 80. CBN 198. C 186. *[Rome, Oct. AD 68].*
F £325 ($520) / **VF** £800 ($1,280) / **EF** £3,000 ($4,800)

2121

2121 Obv. Similar to 2119, but laur. hd. r. Rev. ROMA R XL S C, Roma stg. l. amidst arms, resting on trophy and holding statuette of Fortuna and eagle-tipped sceptre. RIC —. BMCRE 84. CBN 229. C 193. *[Rome, Nov. AD 68].*
F £500 ($800) / **VF** £1,250 ($2,000) / **EF** £5,000 ($8,000)

This rare type records the remission of the 2.5% customs duty on goods passing into south-ern Gaul. This popular measure was meant to reward the provinces of Gaul and Spain which had supported Galba in his bid for the throne. The tax was later restored by Vespasian (see also nos. 2126, 2133 and 2136).

2122   **Brass sestertius.** Obv. As 2118. Rev. SALVS AVGVSTA S C, Salus seated l., holding patera and sceptre. RIC 395. BMCRE 119. CBN 200. C 227. *[Rome, Oct. AD 68].*

F £325 ($520) / **VF** £800 ($1,280) / **EF** £3,000 ($4,800)

2123   Obv. As 2115. Rev. S C, Victory advancing r., holding wreath and palm. RIC 399. BMCRE 99. CBN 204. C 247. *[Rome, Oct. AD 68].*

F £350 ($560) / **VF** £850 ($1,360) / **EF** £3,250 ($5,200)

2124   Obv. Similar to 2116, but laur. hd. r., globe below. Rev. SENATVS PIETATI AVGVSTI S C, the Senate stg. l., holding branch and crowning Galba who stands facing on l., holding Victory and branch. RIC 489. BMCRE 260a. CBN 245. C 280. *[Rome, Dec. AD 68].*

F £650 ($1,040) / **VF** £1,600 ($2,560) / **EF** £6,500 ($10,400)

2125 var.

2125   IMP SER GALBA AVG TR P, dr. bust r., wreathed with oak. Rev. S P Q R / OB / CIV SER in three lines within oak-wreath. RIC 263. BMCRE 115. CBN 122. C 303. *[Rome, Jul.–Aug. AD 68].*   F £300 ($480) / **VF** £750 ($1,200) / **EF** £2,750 ($4,400)

2126   SER GALBA IMP CAESAR AVG P M TR P P P, laur. hd. r., globe below. Rev. XXXX REMISSA S C, triumphal arch, surmounted by group of statuary depicting Galba in quadriga, crowned by Victory. RIC 134. BMCRE p. 354, * and pl. 59, 4. CBN 261. C 348. *[Lugdunum, Dec. AD 68–Jan. 69].*   F £1,000 ($1,600) / **VF** £2,500 ($4,000) / **EF** £10,000 ($16,000) *See note following no. 2121.*

2127   **Brass dupondius.** SER GALBA IMP CAESAR AVG TR P, laur. hd. r. Rev. FELICITAS PVBLICA S C, Felicitas stg. l., holding caduceus and cornucopiae. RIC 411. BMCRE 120. CBN 213. C 67. *[Rome, Oct. AD 68].*   F £125 ($200) / **VF** £325 ($520) / **EF** £1,000 ($1,600)

2128   Obv. As 2126. Rev. LIBERTAS PVBLICA S C, Libertas stg. l., holding pileus and sceptre. RIC 136. BMCRE p. 354, † note. CBN 263. C 114. *[Lugdunum, Dec. AD 68–Jan. 69].*

F £150 ($240) / **VF** £375 ($600) / **EF** £1,200 ($1,920)

2129   Obv. As 2119. Rev. PAX AVGVST S C, Pax stg. l., holding olive-branch and caduceus. RIC 284. BMCRE 127. CBN 126. C 149. *[Rome, Jul.–Aug. AD 68].*

F £125 ($200) / **VF** £325 ($520) / **EF** £1,000 ($1,600)

2129 var.

2130

2130 **Brass dupondius.** Similar to 2125, but laur. and dr. bust r. RIC 287. BMCRE 135. CBN 127. C 298 var. (laur. hd. r.). *[Rome, Jul.–Aug. AD 68].*

F £125 ($200) / **VF** £325 ($520) / **EF** £1,000 ($1,600)

2131 **Copper as.** IMP SER SVLP GALBA CAES AVG TR P, laur. hd. r. Rev. CERES AVGVSTA S C, Ceres seated l., holding corn-ears and caduceus. RIC 324. BMCRE 141. CBN 155. C 18. *[Rome, Aug.–Sep. AD 68].*

F £110 ($176) / **VF** £275 ($440) / **EF** £850 ($1,360)

2132 SER GALBA IMP CAESAR AVG P M TR P, laur. hd. l., globe below. Rev. DIVA AVGVSTA S C, Livia stg. l., holding patera and sceptre. RIC 66. BMCRE 202. CBN 35. C 49. *[Tarraco, Nov. AD 68].*

F £125 ($200) / **VF** £300 ($480) / **EF** £950 ($1,520)

2133 Obv. As 2119. Rev. LIB AVG R XL S C, Libertas stg. l., holding pileus and sceptre. RIC 293. BMCRE 142, note. CBN 140. C 99. *[Rome, Jul.–Aug. AD 68].*

F £175 ($280) / **VF** £450 ($720) / **EF** £1,400 ($2,240)

See note following no. 2121.

2134 var.

2134 Obv. As 2131. Rev. LIBERTAS PVBLICA S C, Libertas, as previous. Cf. RIC 328 (bare hd. r.). BMCRE 144. CBN 159. C 129. *[Rome, Aug.–Sep. AD 68].*

F £100 ($160) / **VF** £250 ($400) / **EF** £750 ($1,200)

For a restoration of this reverse type, see under Titus (no. 2609).

2135   **Copper as.** SER GALBA IMP CAESAR AVG PON M TR P P P, laur. hd. r., globe below. Rev.
        PAX AVG S C, Pax stg. l., sacrificing from patera over lighted altar and holding olive-
        branch and caduceus. RIC 140. BMCRE p. 354, † note. CBN 266. C 142. *[Lugdunum,
        Dec. AD 68–Jan. 69].*   **F** £125 ($200) / **VF** £300 ($480) / **EF** £950 ($1,520)

2136   Obv. As 2132. Rev. QVADRAGENS REMISSAE S C, triumphal arch surmounted by two
        equestrian statues l., procession of three prisoners followed by officer approaching the
        monument on l., the leading figure passing beneath the arch. RIC 80. BMCRE 205. CBN
        40 var. C 165 var. *[Tarraco, Nov. AD 68].*
                                                 F £275 ($440) / **VF** £700 ($1,120) / **EF** £2,500 ($4,000)
        *See note following no. 2121. The three prisoners doubtless represent Nero's rapacious
        procurators in Spain who, having denounced Galba at the time of his revolt, later paid the
        price with their lives.*

2137 var. (without prows)

2137   Obv. Similar to 2119, but laur. hd. r. Rev. S C, legionary eagle between two standards, all
        three resting on prows. RIC 304. BMCRE 156. CBN 143. C 267. *[Rome, Jul.–Aug. AD 68].*
                                                 F £125 ($200) / **VF** £325 ($520) / **EF** £1,000 ($1,600)
        This distinctive reverse type was revived by Vespasian (see no. 2364).

2138   IMP SER GALBA CAESAR AVG TR P, bare hd. r. Rev. VESTA S C, Vesta seated l., holding
        Palladium and sceptre. RIC 376. BMCRE 160. CBN 186 var. (CAES for CAESAR). C 310.
        [Rome, Sep.–Oct. AD 68].   **F** £110 ($176) / **VF** £275 ($440) / **EF** £850 ($1,360)

For anonymous coins of the revolt of Galba against Nero, see nos 2067–73. For restorations of the
coinage of Galba, see under Titus (nos. 2607–9) and Trajan.

Alexandrian Coinage

2139   2140

2139   **Billon tetradrachm.** ΛΟΥΚ ΛΙΒ ΣΟΥΛΠ ΓΑΛΒΑ ΚΑΙΣ ΣΕΒ ΑΥΤ, laur. hd. r., L A (= regnal
        year 1) before. Rev. ΑΛΕΞΑΝΔΡΕΑ, dr. bust of Alexandria r., wearing elephant's skin head-
        dress. RPC 5326. BMCG 199. Cologne 217. Milne 320. *[Jun.–Aug. AD 68].*
                                                                         F £60 ($96) / **VF** £150 ($240)

2140   **Billon tetradrachm.** Similar, but with rev. ΕΛΕΥΘΕΡΙΑ, Eleutheria (= Libertas) stg. l., resting on column and holding wreath and sceptre. RPC 5327. BMCG 192. Cologne 220.
Milne 307. *[Jun.–Aug. AD 68].*   **F** £60 ($96) / **VF** £150 ($240)

2141   ΛΟΥΚ ΛΙΒ ΣΟΥΛΠ ΓΑΛΒΑ ΣΕΒ ΑΥ, laur. hd. r., L B (= regnal year 2) before. Rev. ΕΙΡΗΝΗ,
veiled and dr. bust of Eirene (= Pax) r., wreathed with olive, caduceus behind. RPC 5333.
BMCG —. Cologne 228. Milne —. *[Sep. AD 68–Jan. 69].*   **F** £60 ($96) / **VF** £150 ($240)

2142   ΣΕΡΟΥΙ ΓΑΛΒΑ ΑΥΤΟ ΚΑΙΣ ΣΕΒΑ, laur. hd. r., L B (= regnal year 2) before. Rev. ΚΡΑΤΗΣΙΣ,
Kratesis stg. facing, hd. l., holding Nike and trophy, star in field to l. RPC 5339. BMCG
196. Cologne 235. Milne 331. *[Sep. AD 68–Jan. 69].*   **F** £60 ($96) / **VF** £150 ($240)

2143   Similar, but with rev. ΡΩΜΗ, helmeted and cuir. bust of Roma r., holding spear and shield,
simpulum in field before. RPC 5345. BMCG (Supplement) 2719. Cologne 239. Milne 346.
[Sep. AD 68–Jan. 69].   **F** £60 ($96) / **VF** £150 ($240)

2144   **Bronze hemidrachm** (35 mm. diam). ΣΕΡΟΥΙ ΓΑΛΒΑ ΑΥΤΟ ΚΑΙΣ ΣΕΒΑ, laur. hd. r. Rev.
Winged bust of Nike r., L B (= regnal year 2) before. RPC 5346. BMCG —. Cologne 243.
Milne 352. *[Sep. AD 68–Jan. 69].*   **F** £350 ($560) / **VF** £750 ($1,200)

2145   **Bronze diobol** (30 mm). Similar, but with rev. bust of Nilus r., cornucopiae behind, L B
(= regnal year 2) before. RPC 5348. BMCG 205. Cologne —. Milne 353. *[Sep. AD 68–Jan.
69].*   **F** £150 ($240) / **VF** £350 ($560)

2146   **Bronze obol** (25 mm). Similar, but with rev. bust of Sarapis r., wearing modius, L B (= regnal year 2) before. RPC 5350. BMCG 201. Cologne 244. Milne 354. *[Sep. AD 68–Jan. 69].*
                                                              F £80 ($128) / **VF** £180 ($288)

2147   Similar, but with rev. bust of Isis r., wearing crown composed of horns and disk, L B (= regnal year 2) before. RPC 5351. BMCG 202. Cologne 241. Milne 356. *[Sep. AD 68–Jan. 69].*
                                                              F £80 ($128) / **VF** £180 ($288)

2148   **Bronze hemiobol** (20 mm). Similar, but with rev. Canopus of Osiris r., L B (= regnal year
2) before. RPC 5352. BMCG 204. Cologne —. Milne 357. *[Sep. AD 68–Jan. 69].*
                                                              F £50 ($80) / **VF** £110 ($176)

For other local coinages of this reign, see *Roman Provincial Coinage*, vol. I, and *Greek Imperial
Coins & Their Values*, pp. 64–6.

OTHO
15 Jan.–17 Apr. AD 69

2151

*Marcus Salvius Otho, born in AD 32 of a family only recently risen to nobility, was prominent in
Roman society in the 50s and became a close friend of the young emperor Nero. However, Otho's
wife, the beautiful Poppaea Sabina, attracted the emperor's attention and Otho found himself
posted to distant Lusitania as governor (AD 58), an office which he retained for the following
decade. Poppaea remained in Rome as Nero's mistress and in AD 62 became his second wife,
though three years later she died from the effects of a kick from her imperial husband. The*

governor of Lusitania thus had little reason to love his emperor and in fact gave his enthusiastic support to Galba's revolt in 68. Disappointed in his hopes of being adopted as Galba's heir, Otho fomented disaffection amongst the praetorian guard and seized the throne in a coup d'etat on 15 January AD 69. However, just two weeks earlier the Rhine legions had declared for Vitellius and the inevitable trial of strength between the two rival emperors took place within three months. Otho's army was routed in a battle fought near Bedriacum in northern Italy and he committed suicide on hearing of the magnitude of the defeat (17 April).

Otho's Roman coinage is of gold and silver only and comprises just two denominations, aureus and denarius. Because of the abundance of aes struck recently under his two immediate predecessors, and his urgent need for precious metal coinage with which to pay the praetorians and other troops loyal to him, no base metal coinage was issued at Rome between the downfall of Galba in January of 69 and the recognition of Vitellius' rule in the capital in the latter part of April

For the titles and powers of this reign, see table on p. 308.

2149 2152

2149 **Gold aureus.** IMP M OTHO CAESAR AVG TR P, bare hd. r. PAX ORBIS TERRARVM, Pax stg. l., holding olive-branch and caduceus. RIC 3. BMCRE 1. CBN 2. C 2. *[Rome, Jan.–Feb. AD 69].*   **VF** £6,500 ($10,400) / **EF** £17,500 ($28,000)

2150 IMP OTHO CAESAR AVG TR P, bare hd. r. Rev. PONT MAX, Aequitas stg. l., holding scales and sceptre. RIC 18. BMCRE 5. CBN —. C —. *[Rome, Mar.–Apr. AD 69].*
                                            VF £6,500 ($10,400) / **EF** £17,500 ($28,000)

2151 Obv. As 2149. Rev. SECVRITAS P R, Securitas stg. l., holding wreath and sceptre. RIC 7. BMCRE 13. CBN 7. C 16. *[Rome, Jan.–Feb. AD 69].*
                                            VF £6,500 ($10,400) / **EF** £17,500 ($28,000)

2152 Similar, but with obv. IMP OTHO CAESAR AVG TR P, bare hd. l. RIC 11. BMCRE 16. CBN —. C 18. *[Rome, Feb.–Mar. AD 69].*   **VF** £7,500 ($12,000) / **EF** £20,000 ($32,000)

2153 Obv. As 2149. Rev. VICTORIA OTHONIS, Victory alighting r., wings spread, holding wreath and palm. RIC 13. BMCRE 21. CBN 18. C 26. *[Rome, Jan.–Feb. AD 69].*
                                            VF £6,500 ($10,400) / **EF** £17,500 ($28,000)
This type and the next are probably best interpreted as being in anticipation of the defeat of Otho's rival for the imperial throne, Aulus Vitellius (see also nos. 2164–5)

2154 Similar, but Victory is advancing l. RIC 15. BMCRE 23. CBN 20. C 23. *[Rome, Jan.–Feb. AD 69].*   **VF** £6,500 ($10,400) / **EF** £17,500 ($28,000)

2155 **Silver denarius.** IMP OTHO CAESAR AVG TR P, bare hd. r. Rev. CERES AVG, Ceres stg. l., holding corn-ears and cornucopiae. RIC 2. BMCRE p. 364, † note. CBN 1. RSC 1. *[Rome, Feb.–Mar. AD 69].*   **VF** £700 ($1,120) / **EF** £1,700 ($2,720)

2156 As 2149 (rev. PAX ORBIS TERRARVM, Pax stg. l.). RIC 4. BMCRE 3. CBN 3. RSC 3. *[Rome, Jan.–Feb. AD 69].*   **VF** £650 ($1,040) / **EF** £1,600 ($2,560)

2156   2157

2157   **Silver denarius.** Similar, but with obv. IMP OTHO CAESAR AVG TR P, bare hd. l. RIC 6. BMCRE 4. CBN —. RSC 5. *[Rome, Feb.–Mar. AD 69].*

VF £750 ($1,200) / EF £1,800 ($2,880)

2158   2159

2158   Obv. As 2155. Rev. PONT MAX, Aequitas stg. l., holding scales and sceptre. RIC 19. BMCRE 6. CBN 22. RSC 9. *[Rome, Mar.–Apr. AD 69].*

VF £700 ($1,120) / EF £1,700 ($2,720)

2159   — Rev. — Jupiter enthroned r., holding thunderbolt and sceptre. RIC 21. BMCRE 10. CBN 26. RSC 8. *[Rome, Mar.–Apr. AD 69].*   VF £700 ($1,120) / EF £1,700 ($2,720)

2160   — Rev. — Otho on horseback galloping r., brandishing spear. RIC 22. BMCRE 12. CBN 27. RSC 12. *[Rome, Mar.–Apr. AD 69].*   VF £750 ($1,200) / EF £1,800 ($2,880)

2161   — Rev. — Vesta seated l., holding patera and sceptre. RIC 24. BMCRE 11. CBN 29. RSC 7. *[Rome, Mar.–Apr. AD 69].*   VF £700 ($1,120) / EF £1,700 ($2,720)

2162   As 2151 (rev. SECVRITAS P R, Securitas stg. l.). RIC 8. BMCRE 17. CBN 10. RSC 17. *[Rome, Jan.–Feb. AD 69].*   VF £600 ($960) / EF £1,500 ($2,400)

2163   2164

2163   Similar, but with obv. legend IMP OTHO CAESAR AVG TR P. RIC 10. BMCRE 19. CBN 11. RSC 15. *[Rome, Feb.–Mar. AD 69].*   VF £600 ($960) / EF £1,500 ($2,400)

2164   As 2153 (rev. VICTORIA OTHONIS, Victory alighting r.). RIC 14. BMCRE 22. CBN 19. RSC 27. *[Rome, Jan.–Feb. AD 69].*   VF £650 ($1,040) / EF £1,600 ($2,560)
This type and the next are probably best interpreted as being in anticipation of the defeat of Otho's rival for the imperial throne, Aulus Vitellius.

2165 **Silver denarius.** As 2154 (rev. VICTORIA OTHONIS, Victory advancing l.). RIC 16. BMCRE 24. CBN 21. RSC 24. *[Rome, Jan.–Feb. AD 69].*

VF £650 ($1,040) / **EF** £1,600 ($2,560)

Alexandrian Coinage

2166 var. (no simpulum)   2168

2166 **Billon tetradrachm.** AYTOK MAPK OΘΩNOΣ KAIΣ ΣEB, laur. hd. r., L A (= regnal year 1) before. Rev. EΛEYΘEPIA, Eleutheria (= Libertas) stg. l., resting on column and holding wreath and sceptre, simpulum in field to l. RPC 5354. BMCG 208. Cologne —. Milne 359. *[Jan.–Apr. AD 69].* F £100 ($160) / **VF** £250 ($400)

2167 Similar, but with rev. AΛEΞANΔPEA, dr. bust of Alexandria r., wearing elephant's skin head-dress. RPC 5358. BMCG 212. Cologne 245. Milne 368. *[Jan.–Apr. AD 69].*

F £100 ($160) / **VF** £250 ($400)

2168 Similar, but with rev. EIPHNH, veiled and dr. bust of Eirene (= Pax) r., wreathed with olive, caduceus behind. RPC 5360. BMCG 206. Cologne 246. Milne 363. *[Jan.–Apr. AD 69].*

F £100 ($160) / **VF** £250 ($400)

2169 Similar, but with rev. KPATHΣIΣ, Kratesis stg. facing, hd. l., holding Nike and trophy. RPC 5361. BMCG 210. Cologne 249. Milne 366. *[Jan.–Apr. AD 69].*

F £100 ($160) / **VF** £250 ($400)

2170 Similar, but with rev. PΩMH, helmeted and cuir. bust of Roma r., holding spear and shield. RPC 5362. BMCG 211. Cologne 250. Milne 367. *[Jan.–Apr. AD 69].*

F £100 ($160) / **VF** £250 ($400)

2171 **Bronze hemidrachm** (35 mm. diam). AYTOK MAPK OΘΩNOΣ KAIΣ ΣEB, laur. hd. r. Rev. Winged bust of Nike r., L A (= regnal year 1) before. RPC 5363. BMCG (Supplement) 2723. Cologne —. Milne —. *[Jan.–Apr. AD 69].* F £400 ($640) / **VF** £850 ($1,360)

2172 **Bronze diobol** (30 mm). Similar, but with rev. bust of Nilus r., cornucopiae behind, L A (= regnal year 1) before. RPC 5364. BMCG 217. Cologne 257. Milne (Supplement) 368a. *[Jan.–Apr. AD 69].* F £175 ($280) / **VF** £400-($640)

2173 **Bronze obol** (25 mm). Similar, but with rev. bust of Sarapis r., wearing modius, L A (= regnal year 1) before. RPC 5366. BMCG 213. Cologne 258. Milne 369. *[Jan.–Apr. AD 69].* F £90 ($144) / **VF** £200 ($320)

2174 MAPK OΘΩN KAIΣ ΣEB AYT, laur. hd. r. Rev. Bust of Isis r., wearing crown composed of horns and disk, L A (= regnal year 1) before. RPC 5369. BMCG 215. Cologne —. Milne 370. *[Jan.–Apr. AD 69].* F £100 ($160) / **VF** £225 ($360)

2175   **Bronze hemiobol** (20 mm). Similar, but with rev. Canopus of Osiris r., L A (= regnal year
        1) before. RPC 5371. BMCG 216. Cologne 252. Milne 371 var. *[Jan.–Apr. AD 69].*
        F £55 ($88) / **VF** £125 ($200)

For other local coinages of this reign, see *Roman Provincial Coinage,* vol. I, and *Greek Imperial
Coins & Their Values,* p. 66.

VITELLIUS
2 Jan.–20 Dec. AD 69

2204

*Aulus Vitellius, born in AD 15, was the son of the illustrious Lucius Vitellius who had been one of
Claudius' principal advisers. Aulus thus moved in elevated circles and was a close friend of all the
emperors from Caligula to Nero. He held the consulship in AD 48 and was proconsul of Africa.
Towards the close of the year AD 68 Galba appointed him to the important military command of
Lower Germany, believing that his reputed indolence made him less of a threat in this important
posting. At the beginning of the new year (69) the legions of the German frontier refused to take the
oath of loyalty to Galba and on 2 January Vitellius was proclaimed emperor by his troops. Two
weeks later Galba was overthrown in Rome and his place taken by M. Salvius Otho. The army of
Vitellius, under the command of two of his principal generals, advanced slowly on Rome and was
eventually victorious against the forces of Otho at the battle of Bedriacum (16 April). Vitellius was
now undisputed master of the Empire and proceeded in a leisurely manner to the capital, not arriving there until July. It was only then that he assumed the title of Augustus. In the meantime, however, T. Flavius Vespasianus had been proclaimed emperor by the legions in the East (July 1st)
where he had been sent by Nero to quell the First Jewish Revolt. Vitellius' unpopular regime was
finally overthrown towards the close of the year when forces loyal to Vespasian invaded Italy and
advanced slowly on Rome. The emperor was arrested in his palace, dragged through the streets of
the city and brutally murdered by the mob (20 December).*

*Prior to 19 April, when his rule was officially recognized in Rome, the coinage of Vitellius had
all been produced by a provincial mint, probably located at Tarraco in Spain. Rome then became
his main mint, but its products were augmented by continued production at Tarraco and at the
Gallic mint of Lugdunum. These provincial coinages appear to have ceased in July when Vitellius
took up residence in Rome and was first styled Augustus.*

For the titles and powers of this reign, see table on p. 308.

2176   **Gold aureus (provincial series).** A VITELLIVS IMP GERMANICVS, laur. hd. l., globe below.
        Rev. CLEMENTIA IMP GERMAN, Clementia seated l., holding branch and sceptre. RIC 1.
        BMCRE 78. CBN —. C 9. *[Tarraco, Jan.–May AD 69].*
        VF £3,500 ($5,600) / **EF** £9,000 ($14,400)

2177   Similar, but with rev. LIBERTAS RESTITVTA, Libertas stg. facing, hd. r., holding pileus and
        sceptre. RIC 9. BMCRE 88. CBN —. C 50. *[Tarraco, Jan.–May AD 69].*
        VF £3,500 ($5,600) / **EF** £9,000 ($14,400)

2178   Similar, but with rev. SECVRITAS IMP GERMAN, Securitas seated r., hd. resting on r. hand,
        holding sceptre in l., lighted altar and torch at her feet. RIC 12. BMCRE 89. CBN —.
        C 82. *[Tarraco, Jan.–May AD 69].*   **VF** £3,500 ($5,600) / **EF** £9,000 ($14,400)

2177   2179

2179 **Gold aureus (provincial series).** A VITELLIVS IMP GERMAN, laur. hd. l., globe below. Rev.
      VICTORIA AVGVSTI, Victory alighting l., wings spread, holding shield inscribed S P / Q R.
      RIC 34. BMCRE 91. CBN 12 var. C —. *[Tarraco, May–Jul. AD 69].*
                                    VF £3,250 ($5,200) / **EF** £8,000 ($12,800)

2180 Similar, but with rev. CONSENSVS EXERCITVVM, Mars advancing l., holding spear and
      legionary eagle with vexillum. RIC 22. BMCRE 82. CBN —. C 23. *[Tarraco, May–Jul.
      AD 69].*   **VF** £3,250 ($5,200) / **EF** £8,000 ($12,800)

2181 Similar, but emperor's hd. r., and the VM of EXERCITVVM is in monogram. RIC 49.
      BMCRE p. 390, note. CBN 26. C 27. *[Lugdunum, May–Jul. AD 69].*
                                    VF £3,750 ($6,000) / **EF** £10,000 ($16,000)

2182   2185 var.

2182 **Gold aureus (regular series).** A VITELLIVS GERMAN IMP TR P, laur. hd. r. Rev.
      CONCORDIA P R, Concordia seated l., holding patera and cornucopiae. RIC 72. BMCRE 6.
      CBN —. C 19. *[Rome, May–Jul. AD 69].*   **VF** £3,500 ($5,600) / **EF** £9,000 ($14,400)

2183 Similar, but with rev. IVPPITER VICTOR, Jupiter seated l., holding Victory and sceptre. RIC
      74. BMCRE 9, note. CBN 39. C 43. *[Rome, May–Jul. AD 69].*
                                    VF £3,750 ($6,000) / **EF** £10,000 ($16,000)

2184 Similar, but with rev. S P Q R / OB / C S in three lines within oak-wreath. RIC 82. BMCRE
      14. CBN 42. C 85. *[Rome, May–Jul. AD 69].*   **VF** £3,500 ($5,600) / **EF** £9,000 ($14,400)

2185 A VITELLIVS GERM IMP AVG TR P, laur. hd. r. Rev. LIBERTAS RESTITVTA, Libertas stg. fac-
      ing, hd. r., as 2177. RIC 104. BMCRE 30. CBN 63. C 46. *[Rome, Jul.–Dec. AD 69].*
                                    VF £3,750 ($6,000) / **EF** £10,000 ($16,000)

2186 Similar, but with rev. PONT MAXIM, Vesta enthroned r., holding patera and sceptre. RIC
      106. BMCRE 33. CBN 70. C 71. *[Rome, Jul.–Dec. AD 69].*
                                    VF £3,750 ($6,000) / **EF** £10,000 ($16,000)

2186   2187

2187   **Gold aureus (regular series).** Similar, but with rev. XV VIR SACR FAC, tripod-lebes sur-
       mounted by dolphin r., raven r. below. RIC 108. BMCRE 38. CBN 75. C 110. *[Rome,
       Jul.–Dec. AD 69].*   **VF** £3,750 ($6,000) / **EF** £10,000 ($16,000)
       *This refers to Vitellius' membership in the priestly college of the Quindecimviri Sacris
       Faciundis, 'fifteen men for the conduct of sacred matters'. This body had care of the
       Sibylline prophecies and were famous for the opulence of their banquets, a feature of the
       priesthood which particularly appealed to the gluttonous emperor.*

2188   **Silver denarius (provincial series).** A VITELLIVS IMP GERMANICVS, laur. hd. l., globe
       below. Rev. LIBERTAS RESTITVTA, Libertas stg. facing, hd. r., as 2177. RIC 10. BMCRE
       88, note. CBN 3 RSC 51. *[Tarraco, Jan.–May AD 69].*
                                                            VF £375 ($600) / **EF** £900 ($1,440)

2189 var.   2191

2189   A VITELLIVS IMP GERMAN, laur. hd. l., globe below. Rev. CLEMENTIA IMP GERMAN,
       Clementia seated l., as 2176. RIC 18. BMCRE 80. CBN —. RSC 7a. *[Tarraco, May–Jul.
       AD 69].*   **VF** £375 ($600) / **EF** £900 ($1,440)

2190   Similar, but with rev. CONSENSVS EXERCITVVM, Mars advancing l., as 2180. RIC 23.
       BMCRE 84. CBN 8. RSC 24. *[Tarraco, May–Jul. AD 69].*
                                                            VF £375 ($600) / **EF** £900 ($1,440)

2191   Obv. Similar, but also with palm before emperor's hd. Rev. VICTORIA AVGVSTI, Victory
       alighting l., as 2179. RIC 36. BMCRE 94. CBN 13. RSC 101. *[Tarraco, May–Jul. AD 69].*
                                                            VF £350 ($560) / **EF** £850 ($1,360)

2192   Obv. Similar, but laur. hd. r., globe below, palm before. Rev. FIDES EXERCITVVM, clasped r.
       hands. RIC 28. BMCRE 86. Cf. CBN 11 (with palm?). RSC 31a. *[Tarraco, May–Jul.
       AD 69].*   **VF** £375 ($600) / **EF** £900 ($1,440)

2193   Similar, but without palm before emperor's hd., and the VM of EXERCITVVM is in mono-
       gram. RIC 53. BMCRE 114. CBN —. RSC 33a. *[Lugdunum, May–Jul. AD 69].*
                                                            VF £400 ($640) / **EF** £950 ($1,520)

2194   Obv. Similar. Rev. I O MAX CAPITOLINVS, distyle temple containing statue of Jupiter
       seated l., holding thunderbolt and sceptre. RIC 56. BMCRE 118. CBN 27. RSC 39.
       [Lugdunum, May–Jul. AD 69].   **VF** £500 ($800) / **EF** £1,200 ($1,920)

The celebrated temple of Jupiter Optimus Maximus on Rome's Capitoline Hill, the second such structure to occupy the site, was destined to be destroyed at the end of the year in the fighting between the forces supporting Vitellius and those of his rival Vespasian (see also no. 2085).

2195   **Silver denarius (provincial series).** Obv. Similar, but with legend A VITELLIVS GER IMP AVG P MAX TR P. Rev. VESTA P R QVIRITIVM (VM in monogram), Vesta enthroned l., holding patera and torch. RIC 65. BMCRE 123. CBN —. RSC 91. *[Lugdunum, Jul. AD 69].*   **VF** £450 ($720) / **EF** £1,100 ($1,760)

2196 var.   2198 var.

2196   **Silver denarius (regular series).** A VITELLIVS GERMANICVS IMP, bare hd. r. Rev. CONCORDIA P R, Concordia seated l., as 2182. RIC 66. BMCRE 1. CBN 31. RSC 21. *[Rome, Apr.–May AD 69].*   **VF** £350 ($560) / **EF** £850 ($1,360)

2197   A VITELLIVS GERMAN IMP TR P, laur. hd. r. Rev. IVPPITER VICTOR, Jupiter seated l., as 2183. RIC 75. BMCRE 8. CBN 40. RSC 44. *[Rome, May–Jul. AD 69].*
                                        VF £400 ($640) / **EF** £950 ($1,520)

2198   Similar, but with rev. LIBERTAS RESTITVTA, Libertas stg. facing, hd. r., as 2177. RIC 81. BMCRE 13. CBN 41. RSC 48. *[Rome, May–Jul. AD 69].*
                                        VF £400 ($640) / **EF** £950 ($1,520)

2199   2201

2199   Similar, but with rev. S P Q R / OB / C S in wreath, as 2184. RIC 83. BMCRE 15. CBN 45. RSC 86. *[Rome, May–Jul. AD 69].*   **VF** £350 ($560) / **EF** £850 ($1,360)

2200   A VITELLIVS GERM IMP AVG TR P, laur. hd. r. Rev. PONT MAXIM, Vesta enthroned r., as 2186. RIC 107. BMCRE 34. CBN 71. RSC 72. *[Rome, Jul.–Dec. AD 69].*
                                        VF £375 ($600) / **EF** £900 ($1,440)

2201   Similar, but with rev. XV VIR SACR FAC, tripod-lebes, as 2187. RIC 109. BMCRE 39. CBN 77. RSC 111. *[Rome, Jul.–Dec. AD 69].*   **VF** £350 ($560) / **EF** £850 ($1,360)

2202   Similar, but with rev. type Victory seated l., holding patera and palm (no legend). RIC 110. BMCRE 41. CBN 78. RSC 117. *[Rome, Jul.–Dec. AD 69].*
                                        VF £375 ($600) / **EF** £900 ($1,440)

2203 **Brass sestertius.** A VITELLIVS GERMANICVS IMP AVG P M TR P, laur. and dr. bust r. Rev. HONOS ET VIRTVS S C, Honos stg. r., holding sceptre and cornucopiae, facing Virtus stg. l., holding parazonium and spear. RIC 113. BMCRE p. 375, †. CBN 88. C 38. *[Rome, Jul.–Sep. AD 69].* **F** £900 ($1,440) / **VF** £3,250 ($5,200) / **EF** £9,000 ($14,400)

2204 Similar, but with rev. MARS VICTOR S C, Mars advancing l., holding Victory and trophy (or standard with eagle). RIC 115–16. BMCRE 53. CBN 91. C 57, 61. *[Rome, Jul.–Sep. AD 69].* **F** £800 ($1,280) / **VF** £2,750 ($4,400) / **EF** £8,000 ($12,800)

2205

2205 Similar, but with rev. PAX AVGVSTI S C, Pax stg. l., holding olive-branch and cornucopiae. RIC 118. BMCRE p. 377, †. CBN 92. C 67. *[Rome, Jul.–Sep. AD 69].* **F** £750 ($1,200) / **VF** £2,500 ($4,000) / **EF** £7,500 ($12,000)

2206

2206 Similar, but with rev. VICTORIA AVGVSTI S C, Victory stg. r., l. foot on helmet, inscribing OB / CIVIS / SERV in three lines on shield attached to trunk of palm-tree. RIC 123. BMCRE 62. CBN 96. C 105. *[Rome, Jul.–Sep. AD 69].* **F** £850 ($1,360) / **VF** £3,000 ($4,800) / **EF** £8,500 ($13,600) *This would appear to represent an attempt on the part of Vitellius to claim credit for the victories achieved in Judaea by Vespasian, his rival for the imperial throne.*

2207 A VITELLIVS GERMAN IMP AVG P M TR P, laur. and dr. bust r. Rev. CONCORD AVG S C, Concordia seated l., holding olive-branch and sceptre. RIC 133. BMCRE 48. Cf. CBN 101 (rev. type misdescribed). Cf. C 12 (rev. type misdescribed). *[Rome, Sep.–Oct. AD 69].* **F** £800 ($1,280) / **VF** £2,750 ($4,400) / **EF** £8,000 ($12,800)

2208 Similar, but with rev. S C, Mars advancing r., carrying spear and trophy. RIC 141. BMCRE 58. CBN 108. C 79. *[Rome, Sep.–Oct. AD 69].* **F** £750 ($1,200) / **VF** £2,500 ($4,000) / **EF** £7,500 ($12,000)

2208 var.

2209 **Brass sestertius.** Similar, but with obv. A VITELLIVS GERMA IMP AVG P M TR P, laur. hd. l. RIC 158. BMCRE 59. CBN —. C 77. *[Rome, Oct.–Nov. AD 69].*
F £750 ($1,200) / **VF** £2,500 ($4,000) / **EF** £7,500 ($12,000)

2210 A VITELLIVS GERM IMP AVG P M TR P, laur. and dr. bust r. Rev. ANNONA AVG S C, Vitellius stg. r., holding spear and parazonium, facing Ceres seated l., holding patera and torch, lighted altar between them, stern of ship in background. RIC 166. BMCRE 47. CBN —. Cf. C 3. *[Rome, Nov.–Dec. AD 69].*
F £950 ($1,520) / **VF** £3,500 ($5,600) / **EF** £9,500 ($15,200)

2211 **Brass dupondius.** A VITELLIVS GERMAN IMP AVG P M TR P, laur. hd. r. Rev. PAX AVGVSTI S C, Pax stg. l., as 2205. RIC 146. BMCRE 66. CBN —. C 64. *[Rome, Sep.–Oct. AD 69].*
F £300 ($480) / **VF** £750 ($1,200) / **EF** £2,200 ($3,520)

2212 Obv. Similar. Rev. — Vitellius, togate, stg. l., clasping hands with Roma stg. r., holding spear and shield. RIC 147. BMCRE 67. CBN —. Cf. C 68. *[Rome, Sep.–Oct. AD 69].*
F £350 ($560) / **VF** £850 ($1,360) / **EF** £2,600 ($4,160)

, 2213

2213 A VITELLIVS GERMA IMP AVG P M TR P, laur. and dr. bust r. Rev. CONCORDIA AVGVSTI S C, Concordia seated l., holding patera and cornucopiae, lighted altar at feet. RIC 162. BMCRE 65. CBN 116. C 15. *[Rome, Oct.–Nov. AD 69].*
F £300 ($480) / **VF** £750 ($1,200) / **EF** £2,200 ($3,520)

2214 Similar, but with rev. PAXS AVG S C, Pax stg. l., setting fire with torch to heap of arms at her feet and holding cornucopiae. RIC 164. BMCRE p. 383. CBN 117. C 70. *[Rome, Oct.–Nov. AD 69].*
F £325 ($520) / **VF** £800 ($1,280) / **EF** £2,400 ($3,840)

2215 **Copper as (provincial series).** A VITELLIVS IMP GERMAN, laur. hd. l., globe below. Rev. CLEMENTIA IMP GERMAN S C, Clementia seated l., as 2176. RIC 39. BMCRE p. 388, † note. CBN 15. C 8. *[Tarraco, Jan.–Jul. AD 69].*
F £150 ($240) / **VF** £375 ($600) / **EF** £1,000 ($1,600)

2216   **Copper as (provincial series).** Similar, but with rev. CONSENSVS EXERCITVVM S C, Mars
       advancing l., as 2180. RIC 40. BMCRE 99. CBN 16. C 25. *[Tarraco, Jan.–Jul. AD 69].*
                                   F £150 ($240) / **VF** £375 ($600) / **EF** £1,000 ($1,600)

2217

2217   Similar, but with rev. FIDES EXERCITVVM S C, clasped r. hands. RIC 42. BMCRE 103. CBN
       17. C 34. *[Tarraco, Jan.–Jul. AD 69].*
                                   F £140 ($224) / **VF** £350 ($560) / **EF** £950 ($1,520)

2218   Similar, but with rev. LIBERTAS RESTITVTA S C, Libertas stg. facing, hd. r., as 2177. RIC
       43. BMCRE 105. CBN 19. C 49. *[Tarraco, Jan.–Jul. AD 69].*
                                   F £150 ($240) / **VF** £375 ($600) / **EF** £1,000 ($1,600)

2219   Similar, but with rev. VICTORIA AVGVSTI S C, Victory alighting l., as 2179. RIC 46.
       BMCRE 107. CBN 24. C 103. *[Tarraco, Jan.–Jul. AD 69].*
                                   F £150 ($240) / **VF** £375 ($600) / **EF** £1,000 ($1,600)

2220   **Copper as (regular series).** A VITELLIVS GERMANICVS IMP AVG P M TR P, laur. hd. r. Rev.
       AEQVITAS AVGVSTI S C, Aequitas stg. l., holding scales and sceptre. RIC 125. BMCRE
       69. CBN 98. C 1. *[Rome, Jul.–Sep. AD 69].*
                                   F £250 ($400) / **VF** £650 ($1,040) / **EF** £1,850 ($2,960)

2221   Obv. Similar, but GERMAN for GERMANICVS. Rev. CERES AVG S C, Ceres seated l., holding
       corn-ears and torch. RIC 145. BMCRE 71. CBN 112. C 5. *[Rome, Sep.–Oct. AD 69].*
                                   F £250 ($400) / **VF** £650 ($1,040) / **EF** £1,850 ($2,960)

2222 var.

2222   Obv. Similar, but GERMA for GERMAN. Rev. PROVIDENT S C, façade of altar-enclosure of
       the *Ara Providentiae Augusti*, with double panelled door and horns of the altar visible
       above. RIC 163. BMCRE 74. CBN 119. C 74. *[Rome, Oct.–Nov. AD 69].*
                                   F £250 ($400) / **VF** £650 ($1,040) / **EF** £1,850 ($2,960)
       *The reverse is a revival of a Divus Augustus type issued by Tiberius in the AD 20s (see no.
       1789). It depicts the altar dedicated to the 'providence' of Augustus which may have stood
       in the Campus Martius (see also nos. 2360, 2477, 2581–2, 2657, and 2892).*

2223   **Copper as (regular series).** Similar, but with rev. VICTOR AVGVSTI S C, Victory advancing l., setting shield on trophy at foot of which captive is seated l. on globe. RIC 165. BMCRE 76. CBN 120. C 93. *[Rome, Oct.–Nov. AD 69].*
F £275 ($432) / **VF** £700 ($1,120) / **EF** £2,000 ($3,200)

For anonymous issues of the pro-Vitellian forces in southern Gaul, March-April AD 69, see nos 2081–5.

Alexandrian Coinage

These issues were restricted to a period of little more than two months, from Vitellius' recognition as emperor on 19 April to Vespasian's proclamation at Alexandria on 1 July.

2224

2224   **Billon tetradrachm.** ΩΛΟΥ ΟΥΙΤ ΚΑΙΣ ΣΕΒ ΓΕΡΜ ΑΥΤ, laur. hd. r.. Rev. Nike advancing l., holding wreath and palm, L A (= regnal year 1) before. RPC 5372. BMCG 218. Cologne 260. Milne 372. *[Apr.–Jul. AD 69].*   **F** £140 ($224) / **VF** £350 ($560)

2225   Similar, but on rev. Nike advances to r. RPC 5373. BMCG (Supplement) 2725. Cologne 259. Milne 375. *[Apr.–Jul. AD 69].*   **F** £150 ($240) / **VF** £375 ($600)

2226   **Bronze hemidrachm** (35 mm. diam). Similar, but with rev. winged bust of Nike r., L A (= regnal year 1) before. RPC 5374. BMCG —. Cologne —. Milne —. *[Apr.–Jul. AD 69].*
F £500 ($800) / **VF** £1,000 ($1,600)

2227   **Bronze diobol** (30 mm). Similar, but with rev. bust of Nilus r., cornucopiae behind, L A (= regnal year 1) before. RPC 5375. BMCG —. Cologne 264. Milne 376. *[Apr.–Jul. AD 69].*   **F** £225 ($360) / **VF** £450 ($720)

2228   **Bronze obol** (25 mm). Similar, but with rev. bust of Sarapis r., wearing modius, L A (= regnal year 1) before. RPC 5376. BMCG 219. Cologne —. Milne 378. *[Apr.–Jul. AD 69].*   **F** £125 ($200) / **VF** £250 ($400)

2229   Similar, but with rev. bust of Isis r., wearing crown composed of horns and disk, L A (= regnal year 1) before. RPC 5377. BMCG —. Cologne 263. Milne 379. *[Apr.–Jul. AD 69].*
F £125 ($200) / **VF** £250 ($400)

2230   **Bronze hemiobol** (20 mm). Similar, but with rev. Canopus of Osiris r., L A (= regnal year 1) before. RPC 5378. BMCG 220. Cologne —. Milne —. *[Apr.–Jul. AD 69].*   **F** £75 ($120) / **VF** £150 ($240)

For other local coinages of this reign, which appear to be restricted to the Macedonian Koinon, see *Roman Provincial Coinage,* vol. I, p. 304 and *Greek Imperial Coins & Their Values,* pp. 66–7.

VITELLIUS AND HIS CHILDREN

2232

The young son and daughter of Vitellius and Galeria Fundana are depicted on several issues of aurei and denarii from the mint of Rome. During the reign of Otho the children remained in the capital and were treated with respect by Vitellius' rival for imperial power. The young Vitellius is reported to have suffered from a serious speech impediment. Following the Vitellian victory at Bedriacum he joined his father at Lugdunum, the whole army being ordered to march out to meet him. On this occasion Vitellius, holding the youngster in his arms wrapped in a general's cloak, bestowed on him the cognomen Germanicus. Soon after the downfall and death of Vitellius the unfortunate boy was executed on the orders of Vespasian's general C. Licinius Mucianus (early AD 70). His sister, Vitellia, was spared and was even given a dowry by Vespasian.

2231   **Gold aureus.** A VITELLIVS GERMAN IMP TR P, laur. hd. of Vitellius r. Rev. LIBERI IMP GERMAN, confronted bare-headed busts of Vitellius' son r. and daughter l. RIC 78. BMCRE 12. CBN —. C 6. *[Rome, May–Jul. AD 69].*   **VF** £7,500 ($12,000) / **EF** £18,000 ($28,800)

2232   Similar, but with legends A VITELLIVS GERM IMP AVG TR P and LIBERI IMP GERM AVG. RIC 100. BMCRE 27. CBN —. C 3. *[Rome, Jul.–Dec. AD 69].*
        VF £7,500 ($12,000) / **EF** £18,000 ($28,800)

2233   **Silver denarius.** Similar. RIC 101. BMCRE 28. CBN —. RSC 4. *[Rome, Jul.–Dec. AD 69].*   **VF** £1,000 ($1,600) / **EF** £2,500 ($4,000)

2234   Similar, but with rev. as 2231. RIC 103. BMCRE 29. CBN 62. RSC 2. *[Rome, Jul.–Dec. AD 69].*   **VF** £1,000 ($1,600) / **EF** £2,500 ($4,000)

Issues of Vitellius in honour of his deceased father Lucius Vitellius († AD 51)

Lucius Vitellius, the father of the emperor, had a far more distinguished career than his son. His first consulship was in AD 34 and was followed by a highly successful term as legate of Syria under Tiberius (AD 35–7) during which he was responsible for the dismissal of Pontius Pilate, prefect of Judaea. A favourite of Antonia, he became a close friend and adviser of her younger son, later the emperor Claudius. His second and third consulships were in partnership with Claudius in AD 43 and 47 and in the latter year he was also the emperor's colleague in the censorship. Claudius even left his trusted friend in charge of the government during the invasion of Britain in AD 43. One of Lucius Vitellius' last political acts was to advocate Agrippina's marriage to the emperor in AD 49. On his death, two years later, he received a public funeral and a statue in the Forum bearing an epitaph commemorating his 'unswerving devotion to the Princeps' (pietatis immobilis erga principem). It was small wonder that Aulus Vitellius commemorated his father's memory so extensively on the coinage, for without the lustre of this association it is doubtful if he would ever have been proclaimed emperor.

2235   **Gold aureus.** A VITELLIVS GERMAN IMP TR P, laur. hd. of Vitellius r. Rev. L VITELLIVS COS III CENSOR, laur. and dr. bust of Lucius Vitellius r, eagle-tipped sceptre before. RIC 76. BMCRE 10. CBN —. C *Lucius Vitellius 3. [Rome, May–Jul. AD 69].*
        VF £12,500 ($20,000) / **EF** £30,000 ($48,000)

2236   2237

2236   **Gold aureus.** A VITELLIVS GERM IMP AVG TR P, laur. hd. of Vitellius r. Rev. L VITELLIVS
        COS III CENSOR, Lucius Vitellius seated l. on curule chair, r. hand extended, holding eagle-
        tipped sceptre in l. RIC 94. BMCRE 23. CBN 54. Cf. C *Vitellius* 54. *[Rome, Jul.–Dec.* AD
        69].   VF £4,750 ($7,600) / **EF** £12,500 ($20,000)

2237   **Silver denarius.** Obv. Similar. Rev. As 2235. RIC 99. BMCRE 26. CBN 58. RSC *Lucius
        Vitellius* 2. *[Rome, Jul.–Dec.* AD *69].*   VF £1,500 ($2,400) / **EF** £3,750 ($6,000)

2238   As 2236. RIC 95. BMCRE 24. CBN 56. RSC *Vitellius* 55a. *[Rome, Jul.–Dec.* AD *69].*
                                                             VF £600 ($960) / **EF** £1,500 ($2,400)

2239   **Brass sestertius.** A VITELLIVS GERMAN IMP AVG P M TR P, laur. and dr. bust of Vitellius r.
        Rev. L VITELL CENSOR II S C, Lucius Vitellius seated l. on platform, clasping hands with the
        foremost of three togate figures stg. r. at foot of platform, another togate figure seated r. in
        background in elevated position behind the stg. figures. RIC 134. BMCRE 49. CBN 103.
        C *Vitellius* 53. *[Rome, Sep.–Oct.* AD *69].*
                              F £1,250 ($2,000) / **VF** £4,000 ($6,400) / **EF** £12,500 ($20,000)
        *Mattingly's interpretation of this remarkable type (BMCRE i, p. ccxxv) is that it represents
        the 'lectio senatus', i.e. the ceremony in which the senators passed before the censor to be
        approved for a continuation of their office and function, a process recorded by the scribe
        placed unobtrusively in the background.*

VESPASIAN
1 Jul. AD 69–24 Jun. 79

2327

*T. Flavius Vespasianus, son of a middle-class tax gatherer, was born at Reate in Sabine country in
AD 9. He rose from his relatively obscure origins to enjoy a most successful military career, playing
an important role in the Claudian invasion of Britain in AD 43 as commander of Legio II Augusta.
At the time of the outbreak of the Jewish Revolt in AD 66 Vespasian was already in his late fifties
and living in semi-retirement. Nevertheless, the following year Nero appointed him to supreme military command in the East with orders to put down the serious uprising. With the help of his elder
son, Titus, he achieved great success in this task, but in the meantime the Julio-Claudian dynasty
had been overthrown and the Empire plunged into civil war. After three emperors had been proclaimed in rapid succession (Galba, Otho and Vitellius) Vespasian decided to use his power base in
the East to make his own bid for the throne. Leaving Titus to prosecute the Jewish War he returned*

to Rome where his authority had already been established following the collapse of Vitellius' regime before the advance of armies loyal to the Flavian cause. The accession of Vespasian saw the rise of Rome's second great imperial dynasty and his decade of power (AD 69–79) marked a return to strong government after the disruption occasioned by Nero's misrule and the ensuing civil conflict. Discipline was restored to the armies and the praetorian guard was reduced to its old size. The year following his capture of Jerusalem in AD 70 Titus returned to Rome and celebrated a magnificent joint triumph with his father. He become a full partner in the government of the Empire, receiving the tribunician power and sharing the office of censor with Vespasian. This led to the recruitment to the Senate of many new Italian and provincial members. The emperor's younger son, Domitian, remained very much in the background, though he was accorded a not inconsiderable share in the coinage. Vespasian's industry and simple life style made him popular with the people and on his death in AD 79 there was genuine public sorrow. His deification the following year was the first such honour bestowed on an emperor since Claudius in AD 54 and only the third in the history of the Empire. The succession of Titus was smooth and Domitian became heir to his brother's throne. Vespasian's wife, Flavia Domitilla, and a daughter (also Domitilla) both died prior to his accession. He then lived with Caenis, a freedwoman of Antonia, who had once been his mistress.

Following a proliferation of provincial mints in the opening years of Vespasian's reign, especially in the East (a legacy of the civil wars), production came to be concentrated at the Capitoline establishment in Rome. Lugdunum in Gaul had a considerable output of aes towards the close of the reign, and an eastern mint, which seems to have been situated in Commagene, also struck a range of denominations in orichalcum. Vespasian adopted a number of coin types from previous issues (mostly Julio-Claudian but some earlier) in order to strengthen the popular perception of the constitutional validity of his new dynasty. Attention has been drawn to the more obvious instances in the following listings. This practice may well have given rise to the idea behind the remarkable series of 'restorations' of various aes types produced under Titus and Domitian. Vespasian's extensive coinage was augmented by large numbers of types in all metals struck in the names of his two sons, both of whom bore the rank of Caesar.

For the titles and powers of this reign, including Alexandrian regnal dates, see table on p. 308.

The following obv. legends and types are represented by upper and lower case letters. All other varieties are described in full:

A. CAESAR VESPASIANVS AVG
B. IMP CAES VESP AVG CENS
C. IMP CAES VESP AVG P M
D. IMP CAES VESP AVG P M COS IIII
E. IMP CAES VESP AVG P M T P COS IIII CENS
F. IMP CAES VESPASIAN AVG COS III
G. IMP CAES VESPASIAN AVG P M TR P P P COS III
H. IMP CAESAR VESPASIANVS AVG

a. Laur. hd. of Vespasian r.
b. Laur. hd. of Vespasian l.
c. Rad. hd. of Vespasian r.
d. Rad. hd. of Vespasian l.

2240   **Gold aureus (provincial series).** IMP CAESAR AVG VESPASIANVS, a. Rev. MARS VLTOR, Mars advancing r., carrying spear and trophy. RIC 257. BMCRE 350. CBN 312. C 270. *[Tarraco, AD 69–70].*   **VF** £1,100 ($1,760) / **EF** £2,750 ($4,400)

2241   IMP CAES VESPAS AVG P M TR P IIII P P COS IIII, a. Rev. DE IVDAEIS, trophy. RIC 301. BMCRE 402. CBN 305. C 139. *[Lugdunum, AD 72].*
                                    VF £7,500 ($12,000) / **EF** £18,000 ($28,800)
        The reverse type celebrates the success of Vespasian and Titus in quelling the First Jewish Revolt (see also nos. 2252, 2262, 2278, 2296–7, 2321, 2325–7, 2343–4, 2357–8, 2370–73, 2561, and 2565; see also under Titus).

2241 2245

2242   **Gold aureus (provincial series).** Ga. Rev. PACI AVGVSTI, winged Pax-Nemesis advancing r., drawing out fold of drapery from neck and holding caduceus, snake at feet. Cf. RIC 297. BMCRE 399. Cf. CBN 303. C 283. *[Lugdunum, AD 71].*
VF £1,100 ($1,760) / **EF** £2,750 ($4,400)
This reverse is copied from the coinage of Claudius (see nos. 1833 and 1846).

2243   Ga. Rev. S P Q R / P P / OB C S in three lines within oak-wreath. RIC 298. BMCRE 401. CBN 304. Cf. C 524. *[Lugdunum, AD 71].*   **VF** £1,200 ($1,920) / **EF** £3,000 ($4,800)

2244   IMP CAESAR VESPASIANVS AVG TR P, a. Rev. TRIVMP AVG, Vespasian in triumphal quadriga r., crowned by Victory stg. behind him, captive escorted by soldier before horses, trumpeter in background. RIC 294. BMCRE 397. CBN 301. C 567. *[Lugdunum, AD 71].*
VF £5,000 ($8,000) / **EF** £12,500 ($20,000)
The reverse type commemorates the triumph of Vespasian and Titus in June 71 for their victory in the Jewish War (see also nos. 2257, 2279, 2337, 2562, and 2566; see also under Titus as Caesar and Domitian as Caesar).

2245   IMP VESPAS AVG P M TRI P P P COS IIII, laur. and dr. bust l. Rev. PAX AVGVSTI, Vespasian (?) stg. l., raising turreted female figure kneeling r. and holding spear. RIC 356. BMCRE 504. CBN 317. Cf. C 322. *[Antioch, AD 72].*   **VF** £2,500 ($4,000) / **EF** £6,000 ($9,600)

2246   **Gold aureus (regular series).** Hb. Rev. AETERNITAS, Aeternitas stg. l., holding hds. of Sol and Luna, altar at feet. RIC 121(b). BMCRE 272. CBN 245. C 23. *[Rome, AD 75–9].*
VF £1,200 ($1,920) / **EF** £3,000 ($4,800)

2247 2248

2247   Aa. Rev. ANNONA AVG, Annona enthroned l., holding sack of corn-ears on lap. RIC 131(a). BMCRE 290. CBN 256. Cf. C 27. *[Rome, AD 78–9].*
VF £1,000 ($1,600) / **EF** £2,500 ($4,000)

2248   Ha. Rev. COS ITER TR POT, Aequitas stg. l., holding scales and sceptre. RIC 5. BMCRE 16. CBN 8. C — (omitted in error, cf. 30 in 1st edition). *[Rome, AD 70].*
VF £1,000 ($1,600) / **EF** £2,500 ($4,000)

2249   Ha. Rev. COS VI, bull butting r. RIC 87. BMCRE 159. CBN 137. Cf. C 112. *[Rome, AD 75].*   **VF** £1,200 ($1,920) / **EF** £3,000 ($4,800)
The reverse type is copied from the coinage of Augustus (see no. 1610). See also no. 2415.

2249 2252

2250   **Gold aureus (regular series).** Ha. Rev. COS VIII, Vespasian stg. l., holding spear and parazonium, crowned by Victory stg. behind him, holding palm. RIC 105. BMCRE 204. CBN 181. C 130. *[Rome, AD 77–8].*   **VF** £1,300 ($2,080) / **EF** £3,250 ($5,200)

2251   IMP CAESAR VESP AVG, a. Rev. FORTVNA AVGVST, Fortuna stg. l. on garlanded base, holding rudder and cornucopiae. RIC 81. BMCRE 145. CBN 117. C 174. *[Rome, AD 74].*
VF £1,100 ($1,760) / **EF** £2,750 ($4,400)

2252   Ha. Rev. IVDAEA, Judaea, as mourning captive, seated r. on ground at foot of trophy. RIC 15. BMCRE 31. CBN 20. C 225. *[Rome, AD 69–70].*
VF £4,000 ($6,400) / **EF** £10,000 ($16,000)
The reverse type celebrates the success of Vespasian and Titus in quelling the First Jewish Revolt (see also nos. 2241, 2262, 2278, 2296–7, 2321, 2325–7, 2243–4, 2357–8, 2370–73, 2561, and 2565; see also under Titus).

2253   Ba. Rev. PAX AVG, Pax stg. l., resting on column and holding caduceus and branch, purse on tripod at her feet. RIC 63(c). BMCRE 96. CBN 81. Cf. C 297. *[Rome, AD 73].*
VF £1,100 ($1,760) / **EF** £2,750 ($4,400)

2254 2255 var.

2254   Ha. Rev. PON MAX TR P COS VI, Victory stg. l. on cista mystica flanked by snakes, holding wreath and palm. RIC 92. BMCRE 168. CBN 143. C 370. *[Rome, AD 75].*
VF £1,200 ($1,920) / **EF** £3,000 ($4,800)
The reverse type is inspired by the triumviral cistophoric coinage of Provincia Asia (see nos. 1512–13). See also no. 2421.

2255   B (but CEN for CENS) a. Rev. VESTA, circular shrine of Vesta on the Palatine, showing four columns, flanked by two statues on pedestals, statue of Vesta within. RIC 69(a). BMCRE 107. CBN 92. C 578. *[Rome, AD 73].*   **VF** £2,250 ($3,600) / **EF** £5,500 ($8,800)
The Aedicula Vestae was built by Augustus in 12 BC and was located close to his house on the Palatine. It had already appeared on a dupondius of Divus Augustus issued under Tiberius in AD 22–3 (see no. 1785) half a century before its appearance on a series of aurei issued under Vespasian (see also nos. 2423 and 2626).

2256   Da. Rev. VIC AVG, Victory stg. r. on globe, holding wreath and palm. RIC 51. BMCRE 72. CBN 57. C 586. *[Rome, AD 72–3].*   **VF** £1,100 ($1,760) / **EF** £2,750 ($4,400)
The reverse type appears to be copied from the coinage of Octavian (see no. 1554). See also no. 2424.

2257

2257 **Gold aureus (regular series).** Da. Rev. No legend, Vespasian in triumphal quadriga r., holding branch and sceptre. RIC 54. BMCRE 79. CBN 61. C 642. *[Rome, AD 72–3]*.
   VF £2,500 ($4,000) / **EF** £6,000 ($9,600)
   This reverse commemorates the triumph of Vespasian and Titus in June 71 for their victory in the Jewish War (see also nos. 2244, 2279, 2337, 2562, and 2566; see also under Titus as Caesar and Domitian as Caesar).

2258 **Gold quinarius.** Ha. Rev. VICTORIA AVGVST, Victory seated l., holding wreath and palm. RIC 125. BMCRE 283. CBN —. C 593. *[Rome, AD 75–9]*.
   VF £1,500 ($2,400) / **EF** £3,750 ($6,000)

2259 **Silver cistophorus.** IMP VESP CAES AVG PONT MAX TRIB POT COS II P P, a. Rev. COM – ASI either side of distyle temple containing stg. figures of Vespasian crowned by female deity, ROM ET AVG on entablature. RIC —. BMCRE 449. CBN —. RSC 61a. *[Pergamum, AD 70]*.
   VF £2,000 ($3,200) / **EF** £4,500 ($7,200)
   The reverse type is copied from the coinage of Claudius (see no. 1838).

2260 **Silver denarius (provincial series).** Hb. Rev. VICTORIA IMP VESPASIANI, Victory stg. l. on globe, holding wreath and palm. RIC 268. BMCRE 362. CBN 30 (attributed to Rome). RSC 630. *[Tarraco, AD 70]*.
   VF £225 ($360) / **EF** £550 ($880)
   This reverse appears to be copied from the coinage of Octavian (see no. 1552).

2261 IMP CAESAR VESPASIANVS AVG TR P, a. Rev. COS ITER TR POT, Neptune stg. l., r. foot on prow, holding dolphin and trident. RIC 279. BMCRE 375. CBN —. RSC 93. *[Lugdunum, AD 70]*.
   VF £125 ($200) / **EF** £325 ($520)

2262 — Rev. IVDAEA DEVICTA, Judaea, as bound captive, stg. l. before palm-tree. RIC 289. BMCRE 388. CBN 297. RSC 243. *[Lugdunum, AD 70–71]*.
   VF £550 ($880) / **EF** £1,250 ($2,000)
   The reverse type celebrates the success of Vespasian and Titus in quelling the First Jewish Revolt (see also nos. 2241, 2252, 2278, 2296–7, 2321, 2325–7, 2343–4, 2357–8, 2370–73, 2561, and 2565; see also under Titus).

2263 Ha. Rev. PACIS EVENTVM, Bonus Eventus stg. l., holding patera and corn-ears with poppy. RIC 308. BMCRE 421. CBN 379 (Uncertain Eastern Mint). RSC 295. *[Aquileia, AD 69–70]*.
   VF £200 ($320) / **EF** £500 ($800)

2264 Ha. Rev. ROMA PERPETVA, Roma seated l. on cuirass and shield, holding Victory and parazonium. RIC 309. BMCRE 423. CBN 380 (Uncertain Eastern Mint). RSC 423. *[Aquileia, AD 69–70]*.
   VF £225 ($360) / **EF** £550 ($880)

2265 IMP CAESAR VESPAS AVG COS III TR P P P, a. Rev. AVG, EPHE (PHE in monogram) below, all within oak-wreath. RIC 328. BMCRE 452. CBN 341. RSC 40. *[Ephesus, AD 71]*.
   VF £140 ($224) / **EF** £350 ($560)

433

2265

NB The attribution to Ephesus of virtually all the types within the 'Balkan and Asia Minor' group, regardless of mint mark, follows the arguments of R.A.G. Carson in *Coins of The Roman Empire* (1990), p. 25.

2266   **Silver denarius (provincial series).** Similar, but with obv. legend IMP CAES VESPAS AVG, and with mint mark Ө below legend on rev. RIC 311. BMCRE 434. CBN 32. RSC 37. *[Ephesus, AD 69–70].*   VF £125 ($200) / **EF** £325 ($520)

2267   Similar, but with obv. legend IMP CAESAR VESPAS AVG COS V TR P P P, and with mint mark star below legend on rev. RIC 335. Cf. BMCRE p. 99, *. CBN 367. RSC 39. *[Ephesus, AD 74].*   VF £125 ($200) / **EF** £325 ($520)

2268   As 2266, but without mint mark on rev. RIC 311. BMCRE 427. CBN –. RSC 36b. *[Ephesus, AD 69–70].*   VF £110 ($176) / **EF** £300 ($480)

2269   Obv. As 2265. Rev. CONCORDIA AVG, Ceres enthroned l., holding corn-ears and cornucopiae, EPHE (PHE in monogram) in ex. RIC 329. BMCRE 453. CBN 343. RSC 67. *[Ephesus, AD 71].*   VF £125 ($200) / **EF** £325 ($520)

2270   — Rev. PACI AVGVSTAE, Victory advancing r., holding wreath and palm, EPHE (PHE in monogram) in lower field to r. RIC 333. BMCRE 457. CBN 351. RSC 276. *[Ephesus, AD 71].*   VF £140 ($224) / **EF** £350 ($560)

2271   Similar, but with obv. as 2267, and with mint mark star in lower field to r. on rev. RIC 337. BMCRE 475. CBN 368. RSC 277. *[Ephesus, AD 74].*   VF £125 ($200) / **EF** £325 ($520)

2272   IMP CAESAR VESPAS AVG COS II TR P P P, a. Rev. PACI AVGVSTAE, Victory advancing l., holding wreath and palm, BY monogram in lower field to l. RIC 323. BMCRE 446. Cf. CBN 330. RSC 278. *[Ephesus, AD 70].*   VF £150 ($240) / **EF** £375 ($600)

2273   IMP CAES VESPAS AVG, a. Rev. PACI ORB TERR AVG, turreted and dr. female bust r., Ө below. RIC 317. BMCRE 437. CBN 335. RSC 291. *[Ephesus, AD 69–70].*   VF £225 ($360) / **EF** £550 ($880)

2274

2274   Similar, but with obv. as 2265, and with mint mark EPHE (PHE in monogram) below bust on rev. RIC 334. BMCRE 459. CBN 356. RSC 293. *[Ephesus, AD 71].*   VF £225 ($360) / **EF** £550 ($880)

2275   **Silver denarius (provincial series).** Ha (with mint mark small 'O' below bust). Rev. PON
       MAX TR P COS VII, winged caduceus. Cf. RIC 377. BMCRE 483. CBN 371. RSC 375a.
       [Ephesus, AD 76].   **VF** £110 ($176) / **EF** £300 ($480)

2276   Da. Rev. NEP RED, Neptune stg. l., r. foot on globe, holding aplustre and sceptre. RIC 361.
       BMCRE 506. CBN —. RSC 274. *[Antioch, AD 72].*   **VF** £125 ($200) / **EF** £325 ($520)
       *The reverse type is copied from the coinage of Octavian (see no. 1553). See also nos. 2418
       and 2433.*

2277   Ha. Rev. VIRTVS AVGVST, Virtus stg. r., l. foot on prow, holding spear and parazonium,
       shield behind. RIC 354. BMCRE 499. CBN 315. RSC 640. *[Antioch, AD 69–70].*
                                                               VF £165 ($264) / **EF** £400 ($640)

2278   2279

2278   Da. Rev. No legend, Vespasian stg. r., l. foot on helmet, holding spear and parazonium,
       palm-tree before him at foot of which Judaea, as mourning captive, is seated r. on ground.
       RIC 363. BMCRE 510. CBN 318. RSC 645. *[Antioch, AD 72].*
                                                            VF £450 ($720) / **EF** £1,100 ($1,760)
       *The reverse type celebrates the success of Vespasian and Titus in quelling the First Jewish
       Revolt (see also nos. 2241, 2252, 2262, 2296–7, 2321, 2325–7, 2343–4, 2357–8, 2370–73,
       2561, and 2565; see also under Titus).*

2279   Da. Rev. — Vespasian in triumphal quadriga r., holding branch and sceptre. RIC 364.
       BMCRE 512. CBN 320. RSC 643. *[Antioch, AD 72].*   **VF** £150 ($240) / **EF** £375 ($600)
       *This reverse commemorates the triumph of Vespasian and Titus in June 71 for their victory
       in the Jewish War (see also nos. 2244, 2257, 2337, 2562, and 2566; see also under Titus as
       Caesar and Domitian as Caesar).*

2280   **Silver denarius (regular series).** Ab. Rev. ANNONA AVG, Annona enthroned l., as 2247.
       RIC 131(b). BMCRE 298. CBN 260. RSC 30. *[Rome, AD 78–9].*
                                                               VF £65 ($104) / **EF** £185 ($296)

2281   Ca. Rev. AVGVR PON MAX, simpulum, sprinkler, jug and lituus (emblems of the augurate
       and pontificate). RIC 29. BMCRE 48. CBN 35. RSC 42. *[Rome, AD 70–1].*
                                                               VF £65 ($104) / **EF** £185 ($296)
       The reverse type is copied from the coinage of Octavian (see no. 1544).

2282   2285

2282   **Silver denarius (regular series).** Similar, but with obv. Da, and with rev. legend AVGVR
        TRI POT. RIC 42. BMCRE 64. CBN 49. RSC 45. *[Rome, AD 72–3].*
                                                VF £65 ($104) / EF £185 ($296)

2283   Aa. Rev. CERES AVGVST, Ceres stg. l., holding corn-ears and long torch. RIC 132. BMCRE
        300. CBN 263. RSC 54. *[Rome, AD 78–9].*   VF £65 ($104) / EF £185 ($296)

2284   Ha. Rev. COS ITER TR POT, Aequitas stg. l., holding scales and sceptre. RIC 5. BMCRE 17.
        CBN 10. RSC 94a. *[Rome, AD 70].*   VF £65 ($104) / EF £185 ($296)

2285   Similar, but with rev. type Pax seated l., holding olive-branch and caduceus. RIC 10.
        BMCRE 26. CBN 18. RSC 94h. *[Rome, AD 70].*   VF £65 ($104) / EF £185 ($296)

2286   IMP CAESAR VESP AVG, a. Rev. COS V, two laurel-branches. RIC 72. BMCRE 133. CBN
        108. RSC 110. *[Rome, AD 74].*   VF £85 ($136) / EF £240 ($384)

           2287   2288

2287   Ha. Rev. COS VII, eagle stg. facing on garlanded base, hd. l. RIC 99(a). BMCRE 180. CBN
        156. RSC 121. *[Rome, AD 76].*   VF £75 ($120) / EF £210 ($336)

2288   Hb. Rev. COS VIII, Mars stg. l., holding spear and trophy. RIC 103. BMCRE 202. CBN
        178. RSC 126. *[Rome, AD 77–8].*   VF £65 ($104) / EF £185 ($296)

2289   Ha. Rev. — pair of oxen under yoke l. RIC 107. BMCRE 206. CBN 184. RSC 133a.
        [Rome, AD 77–8].   VF £125 ($200) / EF £325 ($520)

           2290 var.   2292

2290   Hb. Rev. — prow of galley r., large star above. RIC 108. BMCRE 211. CBN 187. RSC
        137. *[Rome, AD 77–8].*   VF £100 ($160) / EF £275 ($440)
        *The reverse type is copied from the triumviral coinage of Mark Antony (see nos. 1461 and
        1472). See also no. 2441.*

2291   IMP CAES VESP AVG P M COS IIII CEN, a. Rev. FIDES PVBL, clasped r. hands holding winged
        caduceus between corn-ears and poppies. RIC 55. BMCRE 86. CBN 75. RSC 164. *[Rome,
        AD 73].*   VF £80 ($128) / EF £225 ($360)

2292   Aa. Rev. IMP XIX, sow walking l., with three young. RIC 109. BMCRE 212. CBN 188.
        RSC 213. *[Rome, AD 78].*   VF £150 ($240) / EF £375 ($600)

2293 **Silver denarius (regular series).** Ab. Rev. IMP XIX, modius containing corn-ears. RIC 110. BMCRE 218. CBN 192. RSC 215. *[Rome, AD 78].* VF £90 ($144) / **EF** £250 ($400)

2294

2294 Aa. Rev. — goatherd seated l. on stone, milking she-goat over bowl. RIC 111. BMCRE 220. CBN 193. RSC 220. *[Rome, AD 78].* **VF** £250 ($400) / **EF** £600 ($960)

2295 Ha. Rev. IOVIS CVSTOS, Jupiter stg. facing, sacrificing from patera over altar and holding sceptre. RIC 124(a). BMCRE 276. CBN 249. RSC 222. *[Rome, AD 75–9].* VF £75 ($120) / **EF** £210 ($336)

2296   2297

2296 Ha. Rev. IVDAEA, Judaea seated beside trophy, as 2252. RIC 15. BMCRE 35. CBN 23. RSC 226. *[Rome, AD 69–70].* VF £200 ($320) / **EF** £500 ($800)
The reverse types of this and the following celebrate the success of Vespasian and Titus in quelling the First Jewish Revolt (see also nos. 2241, 2252, 2262, 2278, 2321, 2325–7, 2343–4, 2357–8, 2370–73, 2561, and 2565; see also under Titus).

2297 Ha. Rev. — Judaea, as bound captive, seated r. on ground at foot of palm-tree. Cf. RIC 16. BMCRE 43. CBN —. RSC 229. *[Rome, AD 69–70].* VF £325 ($520) / **EF** £800 ($1,280)

2298 Ca. Rev. PON MAX, Vesta seated l., holding simpulum. RIC 36. BMCRE 55. CBN 38. RSC 358. *[Rome, AD 70–71].* VF £75 ($120) / **EF** £210 ($336)

2299 Ha. Rev. PON MAX TR P COS V, winged caduceus. RIC 75. BMCRE 138. CBN 113. RSC 362. *[Rome, AD 74].* VF £75 ($120) / **EF** £210 ($336)

2300 IMP CAESAR VESP AVG, a. Rev. — Vespasian seated r. on curule chair, holding sceptre and branch. RIC 76. BMCRE 135. CBN 109. RSC 363. *[Rome, AD 74].* VF £65 ($104) / **EF** £185 ($296)

2301 Ha. Rev. PON MAX TR P COS VI, Pax seated l., holding olive-branch, l. hand at side. RIC 90. BMCRE 161. CBN 139. RSC 366. *[Rome, AD 75].* VF £65 ($104) / **EF** £185 ($296)

2302 Ha. Rev. — Securitas, in relaxed pose, enthroned l., r. hand on hd., l. resting at her side. RIC 91. BMCRE 165. CBN 141. RSC 367. *[Rome, AD 75].* VF £75 ($120) / **EF** £210 ($336)

2301   2303

2303   **Silver denarius (regular series).** Ha. Rev. — Victory stg. l. on prow of galley, holding
        wreath and palm. RIC 93. BMCRE 166. CBN 142. RSC 368. *[Rome, AD 75].*
        VF £80 ($128) / **EF** £225 ($360)

2304   Ba. Rev. **PONTIF MAXIM,** winged Pax-Nemesis advancing r., drawing out fold of drapery
        from neck and holding caduceus, snake at feet. RIC 64. BMCRE 97. CBN 85. RSC 385.
        [Rome, AD 73].   **VF** £85 ($136) / **EF** £240 ($384)
        The reverse type is copied from the coinage of Claudius (see nos. 1833 and 1846).

2305   2308

2305   Ba. Rev. — Vespasian seated r., holding sceptre and branch. RIC 65. BMCRE 98. CBN 86.
        RSC 387. *[Rome, AD 73].*   **VF** £65 ($104) / **EF** £185 ($296)
        *Although the seated figure is male, this reverse is strongly reminiscent of the 'Tribute
        Penny' type of Tiberius (see nos. 1760 and 1763).*

2306   **IMP CAESAR VESP AVG,** a. Rev. — winged caduceus. RIC 84. BMCRE 146. CBN 120.
        RSC 390. *[Rome, AD 74].*   **VF** £75 ($120) / **EF** £210 ($336)

2307   **IMP CAES VESP AVG P M COS IIII CEN,** a. Rev. **SALVS AVG,** Salus seated l., holding patera,
        l. hand at side. RIC 58. BMCRE 87. CBN 76. RSC 432. *[Rome, AD 73].*
        VF £65 ($104) / **EF** £185 ($296)

2308   Ha. Rev. **TR POT X COS VIIII,** Ceres seated l., holding corn-ear with poppy and torch. RIC
        113. BMCRE 244. CBN 213. RSC 550. *[Rome, AD 79].* **VF** £65 ($104) / **EF** £185 ($296)

2309   Hb. Rev. — Victory stepping l., attaching shield to trophy at base of which mourning cap-
        tive is seated to l. RIC 115. BMCRE 248. CBN 216. RSC 553. *[Rome, AD 79].*
        VF £85 ($136) / **EF** £240 ($384)
        *This reverse refers either to the victory in Judaea or, alternatively, may be associated with
        the activities in northern Britain of the celebrated governor Gnaeus Julius Agricola,
        father-in-law of the historian Tacitus (see also nos. 2449, 2493, 2505, and 2511).*

2310   Ha. Rev. — capricorn l., globe below. RIC 118. BMCRE 251. CBN 219. RSC 554. *[Rome,
        AD 79].*   **VF** £90 ($144) / **EF** £250 ($400)
        *The reverse type is based on the coinage of Augustus (see nos. 1585 and 1592). See also
        nos. 2492 and 2510.*

2310   2311

2311   **Silver denarius (regular series).** Ha. Rev. TR POT X COS VIIII, naked rad. figure stg. facing, holding spear and parazonium, atop rostral column ornamented with anchor and beaks of galleys. RIC 119. BMCRE 254. CBN 222. RSC 559. *[Rome, AD 79].*
        VF £80 ($128) / **EF** £225 ($360)
        This reverse is copied from the coinage of Octavian (see no. 1559). See also nos. 2488 and 2509.

2312   2313

2312   Ca. Rev. TRI POT, Vesta seated l., holding simpulum. RIC 37. BMCRE 57. CBN 39. RSC 561. *[Rome, AD 70–71].*
        VF £65 ($104) / **EF** £185 ($296)

2313   Ca. Rev. TRI POT II COS III P P, Pax seated l., holding olive-branch and caduceus. RIC 39. BMCRE 61. CBN 45. RSC 566. *[Rome, AD 71].*
        VF £75 ($120) / **EF** £210 ($336)

2314   IMP CAESAR, Vespasian in triumphal quadriga r., holding branch and sceptre. Rev. VESP AVG, Victory stg. r. on prow of galley, holding wreath and palm. RIC 85. BMCRE 147. CBN 121. RSC 569. *[Rome, AD 70].*
        VF £500 ($800) / **EF** £1,100 ($1,760)
        This is an almost exact copy of the denarius issued by Octavian at the time of his conquest of Egypt in 30 BC (see no. 1555). It is tempting to associate the revival of the type with the centenary of this pivotal event which saw the suicides of Antony and Cleopatra and the commencement of Octavian's supremacy in the Roman world.

2315   No legend, rad. and dr. bust of Sol facing. Rev. VESPASIANVS, Vespasian, in military attire, stg. l., his r. hand extended and holding spear in l. RIC 28. BMCRE 47. CBN —. RSC 571. *[Rome, AD 70].*
        VF £1,500 ($2,400) / **EF** £3,000 ($4,800)
        The obverse of this remarkable type is clearly inspired by an issue of the moneyer L. Mussidius Longus (see no. 496) who held office under the triumviral government in Rome at the time of the victory over Brutus and Cassius at Philippi (42 BC). The symbolism on that occasion was the imminence of a new age, a sentiment most appropriate to Vespasian as he established Rome's second imperial dynasty. The reverse bears a close resemblance to an issue of Octavian made just prior to the battle of Actium in 31 BC (see no. 1549), though the figure faces in the opposite direction.

2316   Da. Rev. VESTA, Vesta stg. l., holding simpulum and sceptre. RIC 50. BMCRE 71. CBN 55. RSC 574. *[Rome, AD 72].*
        VF £75 ($120) / **EF** £210 ($336)

2316   2317

2317 **Silver denarius (regular series).** Da. Rev. VICTORIA AVGVSTI, Victory advancing r.,
      placing wreath on standard and holding palm. Cf. RIC 52. BMCRE 74. CBN 60. RSC 618.
      [Rome, AD 72].   **VF** £80 ($128) / **EF** £225 ($360)

2318 **Silver quinarius.** IMP CAES VESP AVG P M COS V CENS, a. Rev. VICTORIA AVGVSTI,
      Victory advancing r., holding wreath and palm. RIC 78. BMCRE 142. CBN 116. RSC 613.
      [Rome, AD 74].   **VF** £225 ($360) / **EF** £550 ($880)
      *The silver half-denarius here makes its first appearance at the Rome mint in Imperial
      times. However, the quinarius had never been an integral part of the Roman currency
      system and was produced only in very limited quantities by the emperors down to its final
      disappearance late in the 3rd century.*

2319

2319 Ha. Rev. VICTORIA AVGVST, Victory seated l., holding wreath and palm. RIC 125.
      BMCRE 285. CBN 252. RSC 594. *[Rome, AD 75–9].*   **VF** £225 ($360) / **EF** £550 ($880)

2320 **Brass sestertius.** G (but COS VIII), b. Rev. ANNONA AVGVST S C, Annona enthroned l., as
      2247. RIC 587(b). BMCRE 731. CBN 767. C 34. *[Rome, AD 77–8].*
                         F £120 ($192) / **VF** £300 ($480) / **EF** £900 ($1,440)

2321 IMP CAESAR VESPASIANVS AVG P M T P P P COS III, a. Rev. DEVICTA IVDAEA S C, Victory
      stg. r., l. foot on helmet, inscribing S P Q R on shield attached to palm-tree at foot of which
      Judaea, as mourning captive, is seated r. RIC 419. BMCRE p. 184, * (attributed to
      Tarraco). Cf. CBN 480. C 142. *[Rome, AD 71].*
                         F £600 ($960) / **VF** £1,500 ($2,400) / **EF** £4,500 ($7,200)
      *The reverse type celebrates the success of Vespasian and Titus in quelling the First Jewish
      Revolt (see also nos. 2241, 2252, 2262, 2278, 2296–7, 2325–7, 2343–4, 2357–8, 2370–73,
      2561, and 2565; see also under Titus).*

2322 Gb. Rev. FIDES EXERCITVVM S C, clasped r. hands holding legionary eagle set on prow. RIC
      420. BMCRE 756 (attributed to Tarraco). CBN 482. C 160. *[Rome, AD 71].*
                         F £180 ($288) / **VF** £450 ($720) / **EF** £1,350 ($2,160)

2323 G (but VESPAS), a. Rev. FORTVNAE REDVCI S C, Fortuna stg. l., holding olive-branch and
      rudder in r. hand, cornucopiae in l. RIC 422. BMCRE 529. CBN 484. Cf. C 188. *[Rome,
      AD 71].*   **F** £120 ($192) / **VF** £300 ($480) / **EF** £900 ($1,440)

2324   **Brass sestertius.** G (but **VESPAS**), a. Rev. HONOS ET VIRTVS S C, Honos stg. r., holding sceptre and cornucopiae, facing Virtus stg. l., holding parazonium and spear. RIC 423. BMCRE 530. CBN 488. C 202. *[Rome, AD 71].*
F £200 ($320) / **VF** £500 ($800) / **EF** £1,500 ($2,400)

2325

2325   Ga. Rev. IVDAEA CAPTA S C, palm-tree, to l. of which bound male Jewish captive stands r., and to r. of which Judaea, as mourning female captive, is seated r., arms on ground around. RIC 424. BMCRE 533. CBN 489. C 232. *[Rome, AD 71].*
F £375 ($600) / **VF** £950 ($1,520) / **EF** £2,750 ($4,400)
The reverses of this and the following two types celebrate the success of Vespasian and Titus in quelling the First Jewish Revolt (see also nos. 2241, 2252, 2262, 2278, 2296–7, 2321, 2343–4, 2357–8, 2370–73, 2561, and 2565; see also under Titus).

2326   Similar, but on rev. the male captive stands l. to r. of palm-tree, and mourning Judaea is seated l. on other side of tree. RIC 426. BMCRE 540. CBN 494. C 238. *[Rome, AD 71].*
F £450 ($720) / **VF** £1,100 ($1,760) / **EF** £3,250 ($5,200)

2327   Similar, but with rev. type Vespasian stg. r., l. foot on helmet, holding spear and parazonium, palm-tree before him at foot of which Judaea, as mourning captive, is seated r. on ground. RIC 427. BMCRE 543. CBN 498. C 239. *[Rome, AD 71].*
F £350 ($560) / **VF** £850 ($1,360) / **EF** £2,500 ($4,000)

2328 var.

2328   Ga. Rev. LIBERTAS PVBLICA S C, Libertas stg. l., holding pileus and sceptre. RIC 429. BMCRE 548. CBN 504. C 252. *[Rome, AD 71].*
F £120 ($192) / **VF** £300 ($480) / **EF** £900 ($1,440)

2329   Ga. Rev. MARS VICTOR S C, Mars running l., holding Victory and trophy, parazonium at waist. RIC 433. BMCRE 551. CBN 508. C 267. *[Rome, AD 71].*
F £120 ($192) / **VF** £300 ($480) / **EF** £900 ($1,440)

2330

2330   **Brass sestertius.** G (but VESPAS), a. Rev. PAX AVGVSTI S C, Pax stg. l., holding olive-
branch and cornucopiae. RIC 437. BMCRE 555. CBN 516. Cf. C 326. *[Rome, AD 71].*
                  F £110 ($176) / **VF** £275 ($440) / **EF** £850 ($1,360)

2331

2331   Ga. Rev. ROMA S C, Roma stg. l., holding Victory and spear. RIC 443. Cf. BMCRE 560.
       CBN 525. C 419. *[Rome, AD 71].*   **F** £120 ($192) / **VF** £300 ($480) / **EF** £900 ($1,440)

2332   Ga (globe below). Rev. — Roma seated l. on cuirass, r. foot on helmet, holding Victory
       and parazonium, on ground behind. RIC 441. BMCRE 802. CBN 799. C 407. *[Lugdunum,
       AD 71].*   **F** £180 ($288) / **VF** £450 ($720) / **EF** £1,350 ($2,160)

2333   Ga (drapery on chest). Rev. ROMA RESVRGES S C, Vespasian, togate, stg. l., raising female
       figure who kneels r. before him, Roma stg. r. in background, holding spear and shield. RIC
       445. BMCRE 565. CBN 531. C 425. *[Rome, AD 71].*
                  F £250 ($400) / **VF** £650 ($1,040) / **EF** £2,000 ($3,200)

2334   G (but COS VIII), a (globe below). Rev. SALVS AVGVSTA S C, Salus seated l., holding pat-
       era and sceptre. RIC 752. BMCRE 827. CBN 822. C 436. *[Lugdunum, AD 77–8].*
                  F £150 ($240) / **VF** £350 ($560) / **EF** £1,000 ($1,600)

2335   G (but VESPAS and COS IIII), a. Rev. S C, Mars advancing r., carrying spear and trophy. RIC
       522. BMCRE 621. CBN 609. C 446. *[Rome, AD 72].*
                  F £110 ($176) / **VF** £275 ($440) / **EF** £850 ($1,360)

2335 var.

2336   **Brass sestertius.** G (but COS VII), b. Rev. S C, Spes advancing l., holding flower. RIC
       576(b). BMCRE 720. CBN 750. C 456. *[Rome, AD 76].*
                                    F £110 ($176) / **VF** £275 ($440) / **EF** £850 ($1,360)

2337   E (but T P P P), a. Rev. — Vespasian in triumphal quadriga r., holding branch and sceptre.
       RIC 536. BMCRE 659. CBN —. Cf. C 477. *[Rome, AD 73].*
                                    F £225 ($360) / **VF** £550 ($880) / **EF** £1,600 ($2,560)
       *The reverse type commemorates the triumph of Vespasian and Titus in June 71 for their
       victory in the Jewish War (see also nos. 2244, 2257, 2279, 2562, and 2566; see also under
       Titus as Caesar and Domitian as Caesar).*

2338   G (but COS VII), a. Rev. — hexastyle temple of Jupiter Optimus Maximus Capitolinus,
       richly ornamented with statuary and bas-reliefs and containing cult-statue of the god at
       centre. RIC 577. BMCRE 721. CBN 751. C 492. *[Rome, AD 76].*
                                    F £600 ($960) / **VF** £1,500 ($2,400) / **EF** £4,500 ($7,200)
       *Following the destruction of the second temple of Jupiter Capitolinus, in the fighting for
       the capital at the end of AD 69, Vespasian rebuilt the celebrated structure and dedicated it
       in AD 75. Just five years later, however, it was again destroyed in the great fire which
       engulfed central Rome, one of the two major disasters which afflicted the Empire during
       the brief reign of Titus (see also nos. 2363, 2481, and 2662).*

2339   Ga. Rev. SPES AVGVSTA S C, Spes advancing l., offering flower to Vespasian, in military
       dress, stg. r. before her, holding spear, flanked by Titus and Domitian, one holding para-
       zonium and vexillum, the other legionary eagle. RIC 462. BMCRE 782 (attributed to
       Tarraco). CBN 545. C 514. *[Rome, AD 71].*
                                    F £300 ($480) / **VF** £750 ($1,200) / **EF** £2,250 ($3,600)

2340   G (but VESPAS), a. Rev. S P Q R / ADSERTORI / LIBERTATIS / PVBLICAE in four lines within
       oak-wreath. RIC 456. BMCRE p. 123, note. CBN 549. C 521. *[Rome, AD 71].*
                                    F £225 ($360) / **VF** £550 ($880) / **EF** £1,600 ($2,560)

2341   — Rev. S P Q R / OB / CIVES / SERVATOS in four lines within oak-wreath. RIC 458.
       BMCRE 573. CBN 551. C 528. *[Rome, AD 71].*
                                    F £130 ($208) / **VF** £325 ($520) / **EF** £950 ($1,520)

2342   Obv. As 2321. Rev. VICTORIA AVGVSTI S C, Victory stepping r., holding palm and pre-
       senting Palladium to Vespasian stg. l., in military dress, resting on spear. RIC 465.
       BMCRE 586. CBN 553 var. C 620. *[Rome, AD 71].*
                                    F £225 ($360) / **VF** £550 ($880) / **EF** £1,600 ($2,560)

2343   G (but VESPAS), a. Rev. — Victory stg. r., l. foot on helmet, inscribing OB / CIV / SER on
       shield attached to palm-tree. RIC 466. BMCRE 577, note. CBN 555. C 621. *[Rome, AD
       71].*
                                    F £180 ($288) / **VF** £450 ($720) / **EF** £1,350 ($2,160)

The reverse types of this and the following celebrate the success of Vespasian and Titus in quelling the First Jewish Revolt (see also nos. 2241, 2252, 2262, 2278, 2296–7, 2321, 2325–7, 2357–8, 2370–73, 2561, and 2565; see also under Titus).

2344

2344   **Brass sestertius.** Ga. Rev. — Victory inscribing shield, as previous, but at foot of palm-tree Judaea seated r., as mourning captive. RIC 467. BMCRE 582. CBN 559. C 624. *[Rome, AD 71].*   **F** £225 ($360) / **VF** £550 ($880) / **EF** £1,600 ($2,560)

2345   **Brass dupondius.** Fc. Rev. CONCORDIA AVGVSTI S C, Concordia seated l., holding patera and cornucopiae, lighted altar at feet. RIC 471. BMCRE 588. CBN 566. C 71. *[Rome, AD 71].*   **F** £50 ($80) / **VF** £125 ($200) / **EF** £375 ($600)

2346 var.

2346   E (but COS V CENS), d. Rev. FELICITAS PVBLICA S C, Felicitas stg. l., holding caduceus and cornucopiae. RIC 555. BMCRE 698. CBN 714. C 152. *[Rome, AD 74].*   **F** £50 ($80) / **VF** £125 ($200) / **EF** £375 ($600)

2347   IMP CAES VESPASIAN AVG COS VIII P P, a (globe below). Rev. FIDES PVBLICA S C, Fides stg. l., holding patera and cornucopiae. RIC 753(b). BMCRE 828. CBN 825. C 166/7. *[Lugdunum, AD 77–8].*   **F** £50 ($80) / **VF** £125 ($200) / **EF** £375 ($600)

2348   — — Rev. FORTVNAE REDVCI S C, Fortuna stg. l., holding rudder set on globe and cornucopiae. RIC 754(b). BMCRE 833. CBN 828. C 181. *[Lugdunum, AD 77–8].*   **F** £50 ($80) / **VF** £125 ($200) / **EF** £375 ($600)

2349   IMP CAESAR VESPASIAN AVG COS IIII, c (globe below). Rev. PAX AVG S C, Pax stg. l., sacrificing from patera over garlanded altar and holding caduceus and olive-branch. RIC 740. BMCRE 816. CBN 817. C 301. *[Lugdunum, AD 72–3].*   **F** £55 ($88) / **VF** £135 ($216) / **EF** £400 ($640)

2350

2350   **Brass dupondius.** H (but VESPASIAN), b. Rev. PON MAX TR POT P P COS V CENS, winged
        caduceus between two crossed cornuacopiae. RIC 798(b). BMCRE 888. CBN 904. C 377.
        [Samosata in Commagene, AD 74].   F £55 ($88) / **VF** £135 ($216) / **EF** £400 ($640)

2351

2351   Fc. Rev. ROMA S C, Roma seated l. on cuirass, holding wreath and parazonium, shields
        behind. RIC 476. BMCRE 592. CBN 568. C 411. *[Rome, AD 71].*
                                                  F £55 ($88) / **VF** £135 ($216) / **EF** £400 ($640)

2352   Fc. Rev. ROMA VICTRIX S C, Roma seated, similar to previous, but holding Victory and
        spear. RIC 477. BMCRE p. 128, *. CBN 571. C 429. *[Rome, AD 71].*
                                                  F £60 ($96) / **VF** £150 ($240) / **EF** £450 ($720)

2353   IMP CAES VESPASIAN AVG COS VIII P P, c (globe below). Rev. S C, Victory alighting l.,
        wings spread, holding shield inscribed S P Q R. RIC 757(a). BMCRE 841. CBN 835. C
        468. *[Lugdunum, AD 77–8].*   F £55 ($88) / **VF** £135 ($216) / **EF** £400 ($640)

2354   Fc. Rev. TVTELA AVGVSTI S C, Tutela seated l., her hands extended to two children stg.
        either side. RIC 480. BMCRE 596. CBN 572. C 568. *[Rome, AD 71].*
                                                  F £120 ($192) / **VF** £300 ($480) / **EF** £900 ($1,440)

2355 var. (Lugdunum)

2355   Fc. Rev. VICTORIA NAVALIS S C, Victory stg. r. on forepart of galley, holding wreath and
        palm. RIC 481. BMCRE 597. CBN 574. C 633. *[Rome, AD 71].*
                                                  F £60 ($96) / **VF** £150 ($240) / **EF** £450 ($720)

2356

2356 **Copper as.** Fa. Rev. AEQVITAS AVGVSTI S C, Aequitas stg. l., holding scales and sceptre. RIC 482. BMCRE 600. CBN 575. C 13. *[Rome, AD 71].*
F £45 ($72) / **VF** £110 ($176) / **EF** £325 ($520)

2357 Fa. Rev. IVDEA CAPTA S C, Judaea, as mourning captive, seated r. amidst arms at foot of palm-tree. RIC 490. BMCRE 605. CBN 580. C 244. *[Rome, AD 71].*
F £175 ($280) / **VF** £450 ($720) / **EF** £1,350 ($2,160)
The reverse types of this and the following celebrate the success of Vespasian and Titus in quelling the First Jewish Revolt (see also nos. 2241, 2252, 2262, 2278, 2296–7, 2321, 2325–7, 2343–4, 2370–73, 2561, and 2565; see also under Titus).

2358 Similar, but mourning Judaea is seated l. RIC 491. BMCRE 609. CBN 584. C 245. *[Rome, AD 71].*
F £175 ($280) / **VF** £450 ($720) / **EF** £1,350 ($2,160)

2359 Eb. Rev. PAX AVGVST S C, Pax stg. l., holding caduceus and olive-branch and resting on column. RIC 543(b). BMCRE 663. CBN 656. C 305. *[Rome, AD 73].*
F £45 ($72) / **VF** £110 ($176) / **EF** £325 ($520)

2360 var. (Lugdunum)

2360 Fa. Rev. PROVIDENT S C (the NT sometimes in monogram), façade of altar-enclosure of the *Ara Providentiae Augusti*, with double panelled door and horns of the altar visible above. RIC 494. BMCRE 611. CBN 586. C 396. *[Rome, AD 71].*
F £50 ($80) / **VF** £125 ($200) / **EF** £375 ($600)
The reverse is a revival of a Divus Augustus type issued by Tiberius in the AD 20s (see no. 1789). It had been revived previously by Vitellius (see no. 2222) and depicts the altar dedicated to the 'providence' of Augustus which may have stood in the Campus Martius (see also nos. 2477, 2581–2, 2657, and 2892).

2361 IMP CAESAR VESP AVG COS V CENS, a. Rev. S C, Spes advancing l., holding flower. RIC 560(a). BMCRE 703. CBN 721. C 452. *[Rome, AD 74].*
F £45 ($72) / **VF** £110 ($176) / **EF** £325 ($520)

2361

2362 var. (COS III)

2362   **Copper as.** IMP CAES VESPASIAN AVG COS VIII P P, a (globe below). Rev. S C, eagle stg.
        facing on globe, hd. r., wings spread. RIC 764(a). BMCRE 848. CBN 849. C 482.
        [Lugdunum, AD 77–8].   **F** £50 ($80) / **VF** £125 ($200) / **EF** £375 ($600)

2363   Fa. Rev. — hexastyle temple of Jupiter Optimus Maximus Capitolinus, richly ornamented
        with statuary and bas-reliefs and containing statues of Jupiter between Juno and Minerva.
        RIC 496. BMCRE 614. CBN 588. C 486. *[Rome, AD 71].*
                                        F £250 ($400) / **VF** £650 ($1,040) / **EF** £2,000 ($3,200)
        See note following no. 2338. See also nos. 2481 and 2662.

2364   Fa. Rev. — legionary eagle between two standards, all three resting on prows. RIC 499.
        BMCRE 613. CBN 591. C 500. *[Rome, AD 71].*
                                        F £60 ($96) / **VF** £150 ($240) / **EF** £450 ($720)
        This revives a Galban reverse type (see no. 2137).

2365   Ea. Rev. VESTA S C, domed temple of Vesta in the Forum, showing four columns and con-
        taining statue of the goddess on pedestal. RIC 548. BMCRE 664. CBN 663. C 577. *[Rome,
        AD 73].*   **F** £175 ($280) / **VF** £450 ($720) / **EF** £1,350 ($2,160)
        *This celebrated temple had been rebuilt by Nero following the great fire of AD 64 (see nos.
        1933 and 1946). The Neronian structure survived until another conflagration late in the
        reign of Commodus and was again restored early in the 3rd century by Julia Domna (see
        also nos. 2482 and 2663).*

2366   IMP CAESAR VESP AVG COS V CENS, b. Rev. VICTORIA AVGVST S C, Victory stg. r. on
        forepart of galley, holding wreath and palm. RIC 561(b). BMCRE 705. CBN 724. C 602.
        [Rome, AD 74].   **F** £50 ($80) / **VF** £125 ($200) / **EF** £375 ($600)

2367   **Brass as (small module).** IMP CAESAR VESP AVG, b. Rev. S C in laurel-wreath. RIC 796.
        BMCRE 894. CBN 913. C 501. *[Samosata in Commagene].*
                                        F £50 ($80) / **VF** £125 ($200) / **EF** £375 ($600)

2368   **Brass semis.** IMP VESP AVG, b. Rev. P M TR POT P P, winged caduceus. RIC 794. BMCRE
        880. CBN 894. Cf. C 349. *[Samosata in Commagene, AD 70].*
                                        F £45 ($72) / **VF** £110 ($176) / **EF** £325 ($520)

2369   **Brass semis.** IMP VESP AVG COS VIII, winged caduceus between two crossed cornua-
        copiae. Rev. S C in laurel-wreath. RIC 802. BMCRE 741. CBN 911. C 505. *[Samosata in
        Commagene, AD 77–8].*   **F** £35 ($56) / **VF** £90 ($144) / **EF** £225 ($360)

2370 var.

2370   **Copper quadrans.** IMP VESPASIAN AVG, palm-tree. Rev. P M TR P P P COS III S C, vexil-
        lum. RIC 504. BMCRE 618. CBN 600 var. C 343. *[Rome, AD 71].*
                                                 F £30 ($48) / **VF** £75 ($120) / **EF** £185 ($296)

2371   **Copper quadrans.** IMP CAES VESPASIAN AVG, trophy. Rev. – two crossed spears between
        two shields. RIC 508. BMCRE p. 135, †. CBN 599. C 345. *[Rome, AD 71].*
                                                 F £30 ($48) / **VF** £75 ($120) / **EF** £185 ($296)

2372   Obv. As 2370. Rev. PON M TR P P P COS III S C, sprinkler, patera and lituus (emblems of the
        priestly colleges). RIC 512. BMCRE p. 135, *. CBN 605. C 355. *[Rome, AD 71].*
                                                 F £30 ($48) / **VF** £75 ($120) / **EF** £185 ($296)

2373 var.

2373   Obv. As 2371. Rev. – vexillum. RIC 511. BMCRE p. 134, * note. CBN 603. C 353.
        [Rome, AD 71].   **F** £30 ($48) / **VF** £75 ($120) / **EF** £185 ($296)

*The quadrantes of AD 71 appear all to be connected with the celebration of the victory in
Judaea. It seems reasonable to surmise that they were struck for distribution at the great
triumph of Vespasian and Titus which took place in June of that year.*

For coins of Divus Vespasian and later restorations, see under Titus (nos. 2561–76), Domitian (no.
2887), Trajan, and Trajan Decius.

Alexandrian Coinage

Vespasian was proclaimed emperor at Alexandria on 1 July AD 69, thus cutting short the coinage of
Vitellius at the Egyptian capital which had begun little more than two months before.

2374

2374 **Billon tetradrachm.** ΑΥΤ ΤΙΤ ΦΛΑΥΙ ΟΥΕΣΠΑΣΙΑΝ ΚΑΙΣ, laur. hd. r., L A (= regnal year 1) before. Rev. ΕΙΡΗΝΗ, Eirene (= Pax) stg. l., holding flowers (?) and caduceus. Dattari 356. BMCG 229. Cologne 266. Milne 380. *[Jul.–Aug.* AD *69].*   **F** £50 ($80) / **VF** £125 ($200)

2375 Similar, but with rev. ΦΛΑΥΙ ΟΥΕΣΠΑΣΙΑΝΟΣ ΚΑΙΣ, laur. and cuir. bust of Titus r. Dattari 343. BMCG 221. Cologne 269. Milne 387. *[Jul.–Aug.* AD *69].*
F £80 ($128) / **VF** £200 ($320)

2376 ΑΥΤΟΚ ΚΑΙΣ ΣΕΒΑ ΟΥΕΣΠΑΣΙΑΝΟΥ, laur. hd. r., L B (= regnal year 2) before. Rev. No legend, Nike advancing l., holding wreath nd palm (no legend). Dattari 360. BMCG 236. Cologne 276. Milne 393. *[AD 69–70].*   **F** £40 ($64) / **VF** £100 ($160)

2377 Similar, but with rev. ΡΩΜΗ, Roma stg. l., holding spear and shield. Dattari 241. BMCG 365. Cologne 278. Milne 396. *[AD 69–70].*   **F** £40 ($64) / **VF** £100 ($160)

2378 Obv. Similar, but with L Γ (= regnal year 3) before. Rev. ΑΛΕΞΑΝΔΡΕΙΑ, Alexandria stg. l., with elephant's skin head-dress, holding wreath and sceptre. Dattari 355. BMCG 244. Cologne 284. Milne 410. *[AD 70–71].*   **F** £40 ($64) / **VF** £100 ($160)

2379

2379 Obv. Similar, but with L H (= regnal year 8) before. Rev. ΑΥΤΟΚΡΑΤΩΡ ΤΙΤΟΣ ΚΑΙΣΑΡ, laur. hd. of Titus r. Dattari 348. BMCG 225. Cologne 303. Milne 441. *[AD 75–6].*
F £70 ($112) / **VF** £175 ($280)

2380 **Bronze hemidrachm** (35 mm. diam). ΑΥΤΟΚ ΚΑΙΣ ΣΕΒΑ ΟΥΕΣΠΑΣΙΑΝΟΥ, laur. hd. r. Rev. Winged bust of Nike r., L B (= regnal year 2) before. Dattari 388. BMCG 248. Cologne 282. Milne 403. *[AD 69–70].*   **F** £125 ($200) / **VF** £275 ($440)

2381 ΑΥΤΟΚ ΚΑΙΣ ΣΕΒΑ ΟΥΕΣΠΑΣΙΑΝΟΥ L ENAT (= regnal year 9), laur. hd. of Vespasian r. Rev. ΑΥΤΟΚΡΑΤΟΡΟΣ ΤΙΤΟΥ ΚΑΙΣΑΡΟΣ, laur. hd. of Titus r. Dattari 352. BMCG 226. Cologne 313. Milne 449. *[AD 76–7].*   **F** £225 ($360) / **VF** £475 ($760)

2382 **Bronze diobol** (30 mm). ΑΥΤ ΤΙΤ ΦΛΑΥΙ ΟΥΕΣΠΑΣΙΑΝ ΚΑΙΣ, laur. hd. r. Rev. Bust of Nilus r., crowned with reeds, cornucopiae behind, L A (= regnal year 1) before. Dattari 394. BMCG 269. Cologne 271. Milne —. *[Jul.–Aug.* AD *69].*   **F** £65 ($104) / **VF** £150 ($240)

2383 **Bronze obol** (25 mm). ΑΥΤΟΚ ΚΑΙΣ ΣΕΒΑ ΟΥΕΣΠΑΣΙΑΝΟΥ, laur. hd. r. Rev. Bust of Sarapis r., wearing modius, L B (= regnal year 2) before. Dattari 397. BMCG 252. Cologne 283. Milne 404. *[AD 69–70].*   **F** £30 ($48) / **VF** £65 ($104)

2384 Similar, but with rev. bust of Isis r., wearing crown composed of horns and disk, L Δ (= regnal year 4) before. Dattari 397. BMCG 252. Cologne 283. Milne 404. *[AD 71–2].*
F £30 ($48) / **VF** £65 ($104)

2385 ΑΥΤΟΚΡ ΚΑΙΣΑΡΟΣ ΟΥΕΣΠΑΣΙΑΝΟΥ, laur. hd. r. Rev. ΣΕΒΑΣΤΟΥ L ENAT (= regnal year 9), bust of Alexandria r., wearing elephant's skin head-dress. Dattari 370. BMCG 272. Cologne 309. Milne 451. *[AD 76–7].*   **F** £30 ($48) / **VF** £65 ($104)

2386   **Bronze hemiobol** (20 mm). Obv. As 2383. Rev. Canopus of Osiris r., L Δ (= regnal year 4) before. Dattari 371. BMCG 268. Cologne 291. Milne 422. *[AD 71–2]*.
F £25 ($40) / **VF** £55 ($88)

2387   — Rev. Hawk stg. r., L ϛ (= regnal year 6) behind. Dattari 417. BMCG 276. Cologne 298. Milne 436. *[AD 73–4]*.
F £20 ($32) / **VF** £45 ($72)

2388   — Rev. ΔΙΚΑΙΟΣΥΝΗ L ΕΝΑΤ (= regnal year 9), Dikaiosyne (= Aequitas) stg. l., holding scales and sceptre. Dattari 377. BMCG 245. Cologne 311. Milne 453. *[AD 76–7]*.
F £20 ($32) / **VF** £45 ($72)

2389   **Bronze dichalkon** (15 mm). No legend, laur. hd. r. Rev. L ΕΝΑΤ (= regnal year 9), Nike advancing l., holding wreath and palm. Dattari 391 var. (Nike r.). BMCG 251. Cologne 312 var. (L Θ). Milne —. *[AD 76–7]*.
F £22 ($35) / **VF** £50 ($80)

For other local coinages of this reign, see *Greek Imperial Coins & Their Values*, pp. 67–73.

VESPASIAN AND TITUS

2392

Titus played a leading role in the East at the time of the establishment of the Flavian dynasty. His father gave him supreme command of the Roman army in the Jewish War, a task which he successfully accomplished, with the result that he was commemorated extensively on coin issues in the region. The following aurei were struck in Syria and Egypt in the names of both father and son.

2390   **Gold aureus.** IMP CAESAR VESPASIA AVG, laur. hd. of Vespasian l. Rev. T ELAVI (*sic*) VESPASIANVS CAESAR, laur. hd. of Titus r. Cf. RIC 352. BMCRE 525. CBN —. C —. *[Alexandria, AD 69]*.
VF £7,500 ($12,000) / **EF** £18,000 ($28,800)

2391   IMP CAESAR VESPASIANVS AVG, laur. hd. of Vespasian r. Rev. IMP T FLAVIVS CAESAR AVG F, laur. hd. of Titus r. RIC 351. BMCRE 496. CBN 314 var. Cf. C 6 (= the BM coin imperfectly described). *[Antioch, AD 69–70]*.
VF £6,500 ($10,400) / **EF** £16,000 ($25,600)

2392   IMP CAES VESP AVG P M, laur. hd. of Vespasian r. Rev. IMP CAES VESP AVG P TRI P COS II, bare hd. of Titus r. RIC 359. BMCRE p. 105, *. CBN 316. C 1. *[Antioch, AD 72]*.
VF £6,500 ($10,400) / **EF** £16,000 ($25,600)

2393   IMP VESPA CAESAR AVGVS, laur. hd. of Vespasian r. Rev. IMP / T / CAESAR in three lines on circular shield, two crossed spears in background. RIC 369. BMCRE p. 109, *. CBN —. C —. *[Tyre, AD 69]*.
VF £5,000 ($8,000) / **EF** £12,500 ($20,000)

See also nos. 2375, 2379, and 2381.

VESPASIAN, TITUS AND DOMITIAN

2399

One of the strengths of the new regime was that its elderly founder had two adult sons who carried with them the prospect of the establishment of a successful dynasty. The propaganda value of this theme was fully exploited on the coinage, and issues in all metals were made in the early years of the reign combining the head of Vespasian with the portraits and figures of both Titus and Domitian.

2394   **Gold aureus.** IMP CAESAR VESPASIANVS AVG, laur. hd. of Vespasian r. Rev. CAESAR AVG F COS CAESAR AVG F PR, confronted bare hds. of Titus and Domitian. RIC 2. BMCRE 1. CBN —. C 4. *[Rome, AD 69–70].*   **VF** £3,000 ($4,800) / **EF** £7,500 ($12,000)

2395   IMP VESPAS AVG P M TRI P P P COS IIII, laur. and dr. bust of Vespasian l. Rev. CAE DVM (*sic*) ET T CAES IMP VESPAS, as previous. RIC 358. BMCRE p. 106, *. CBN —. Cf. C 8. *[Antioch, AD 72].*   **VF** £5,000 ($8,000) / **EF** £12,500 ($20,000)

2396   Obv. As 2394. Rev. CAESERES (*sic*) VESP AVG FILI (the last word retrograde), togate figures of Titus and Domitian stg. facing one another, each holding patera and scroll. RIC 3. BMCRE 6. CBN 4. Cf. C *Vespasian* 52, 570. *[Rome, AD 69–70].*
VF £2,500 ($4,000) / **EF** £6,000 ($9,600)

2397   2400 var. (COS II, mint mark Ϙ)

2397   IMP CAESAR VESPASIANVS AVG TR P, laur. hd. of Vespasian r. Rev. TITVS ET DOMITIAN CAESARES PRIN IVEN, Titus and Domitian galloping r., each holding spear. RIC 292. BMCRE 395. CBN 299. C *Vespasian* 538. *[Lugdunum, AD 70–71].*
VF £1,750 ($2,800) / **EF** £3,500 ($5,600)

2398   Similar, but with rev. type Titus and Domitian seated l. on curule chairs side by side, each holding branch. RIC 293. BMCRE 392. CBN 300. C *Vespasian* 543. *[Lugdunum, AD 70–71].*
VF £1,750 ($2,800) / **EE** £3,500 ($5,600)

2399   **Silver denarius.** As 2394. RIC 2. BMCRE 2. CBN 1. RSC 5. *[Rome, AD 69–70].*
VF £350 ($560) / **EF** £850 ($1,360)

2400   IMP CAESAR VESPAS AVG COS III TR P P P, laur. hd. of Vespasian r. Rev. LIBERI IMP AVG VESPAS, confronted bare hds. of Titus and Domitian, EPHE (PHE in monogram) between them. RIC 330. BMCRE 455. CBN 347. RSC 2a. *[Ephesus, AD 71].*
VF £700 ($1,120) / **EF** £1,500 ($2,400)

2401 **Silver denarius.** Similar, but with rev. type veiled and togate figures of Titus and Domitian stg. l. side by side, each holding patera, EPHE (PHE in monogram) in ex. RIC 331. BMCRE 456. CBN 349. RSC *Vespasian* 250. *[Ephesus, AD 71].* **VF** £175 ($280) / **EF** £425 ($680)

2402 Obv. As 2394. Rev. TITVS ET DOMITIAN CAES PRIN IV, Titus and Domitian galloping r., their r. hands raised. Cf. RIC 23 (princes seated, in error). Cf. BMCRE p. 7, // (holding spears, in error). CBN 28. Cf. RSC *Vespasian* 539. *[Rome, AD 69–70].*
VF £300 ($480) / **EF** £750 ($1,200)

2403 — Rev. TITVS ET DOMITIAN CAESARES PRIN IVEN, Titus and Domitian seated, as 2398. RIC 25. BMCRE 45. CBN —. RSC *Vespasian* 541b. *[Rome, AD 69–70].*
VF £150 ($240) / **EF** £375 ($600)

2404 var. (Lugdunum)

2404 **Brass sestertius.** IMP CAES VESPASIAN AVG P M TR P P P COS III, laur. hd. of Vespasian r. Rev. CAES AVG F DES IMP AVG F COS DES IT S C, Titus and Domitian stg. facing each other, holding spears, the figure on l. also holding scroll, the one on r. holding parazonium. RIC 413. BMCRE 528. CBN 473. C *Vespasian* 46. *[Rome, AD 71].*
F £225 ($360) / **VF** £550 ($880) / **EF** £1,600 ($2,560)

2405 IMP CAESAR VESPASIANVS AVG P M TR P, laur. hd. of Vespasian r. Rev. T ET DOMIT CAESARES PRINC IVVENT S C, Titus and Domitian galloping r., each holding couched spear, preceded by infantryman holding vexillum. RIC 390. BMCRE 878. CBN p. 5, D3/R4. Cf. C *Vespasian* 534. *[Rome, AD 70].* **F** £350 ($560) / **VF** £850 ($1,360) / **EF** £2,500 ($4,000)

2406 IMP CAESAR VESPASIANVS AVG, laur. hd. of Vespasian r., small globe below. Rev. TITVS CAESAR AVG F COS DOMITIAN CAESAR AVG F PR S C, military figure of Titus stg. r., holding Victory, facing togate figure of Domitian stg. l., holding sceptre. RIC —. BMCRE —. CBN p. 182, * (Oxford). C —. *[Tarraco, AD 70].*
F £300 ($480) / **VF** £750 ($1,200) / **EF** £2,250 ($3,600)

2407 **Copper as.** Obv. Similar. Rev. CAESAR AVG F COS CAESAR AVG F PR S C, confronted bare hds. of Titus and Domitian. RIC 386. BMCRE 748B. CBN 797. Cf. C 12. *[Tarraco, AD 70].*
F £350 ($560) / **VF** £850 ($1,360) / **EF** £2,500 ($4,000)

2408 IMP CAES VESPASIAN AVG P M T P P P COS II D III, laur. and dr. bust of Vespasian r. Rev. IMP T VES COS DESIGN D CAESAR AVG F COS DESIG, as previous. RIC 412. BMCRE p. 182, §. CBN 472. C 13. *[Rome, late AD 70].*
F £350 ($560) / **VF** £850 ($1,360) / **EF** £2,500 ($4,000)

2409　**Copper as.** IMP CAESAR VESPASIANVS AVG P M TR P, laur. hd. of Vespasian r., with aegis. Rev. T ET DOMITIAN CAESARES PRIN IVVENT S C, Titus and Domitian galloping r., their r. hands raised. RIC 391. BMCRE 750. CBN 469. Cf. C *Vespasian* 535 (holding spears, in error). *[Rome, AD 69–70].*　　　　　　　　　**F** £100 ($160) / **VF** £250 ($400) / **EF** £750 ($1,200)

TITUS
24 Jun. AD 79–13 Sep. 81

2459 var.

Titus Flavius Vespasianus, the elder son of Vespasian and Flavia Domitilla, was born in AD 39. He was a close boyhood friend of Britannicus, son of the Emperor Claudius, with whom he was educated. During the reign of Nero he served as a military tribune in Germany and Britain and in AD 67 accompanied his father to Judaea, where he commanded Legio XV Apollinaris. When his father made his bid for the imperial throne in AD 69 Titus was given supreme command over the Jewish War. In September AD 70 he captured Jerusalem, thus effectively ending the Jewish Revolt which had begun four years earlier during the reign of Nero. Although he bore only the junior rank of Caesar throughout Vespasian's reign Titus was, in all other respects, his father's colleague in the government of the Empire. They celebrated a magnificent joint triumph in Rome for the Jewish victory (June AD 71) and Titus was accorded a considerable share in the imperial coinage, with large scale issues in all metals. The share of his younger brother, Domitian, was considerably smaller and there can be little doubt that the latter felt bitterly resentful of his inferior status (a resentment which was to find expression in the tyranny of Domitian's own reign a decade later). Titus succeeded to the imperial throne on the death of Vespasian on June 24, AD 79. He reigned for little more than two years, but this brief period witnessed a series of natural disasters. Most famous is the eruption of Vesuvius, which destroyed the towns of Pompeii and Herculaneum in AD 79, but in the following year the capital suffered from both plague and a devastating fire. It was in connection with these disasters that Titus issued a series of coins commemorating the services of prayer and propitiation through which he attempted to allay public alarm. One of the rare highlights of the reign was the dedication in June AD 80 of the great 'Amphitheatrum Flavium', better known today as the Colosseum. This magnificent arena, still one of the principal landmarks of modern Rome, had been commenced by Vespasian in AD 71 on the site of the stagnum (pool) formerly in the gardens of Nero's Golden House. The dedication by Titus was accompanied by lavish celebrations for the Roman populace. Probably exhausted and depressed by his ordeals, Titus died on 13 September AD 81 at the early age of forty-two. He was succeeded by his younger brother Domitian who, as heir to the throne, had been accorded a considerable coinage in all metals during the reign of Titus.

　　The precious metal coinage of this reign was terminated by the great fire which destroyed large areas of central Rome, including the imperial mint on the Capitoline Hill, before the emperor attained his tenth tribunician year on 1 July AD 80. The facility was subsequently moved to a new location on the Caelian Hill, a little to the east of the Colosseum. The same fate may have befallen the aes coinage as the senatorial mint also stood on the Capitoline, a region which is known to have suffered greatly in the conflagration. The traditional attribution to Lugdunum of certain aes issues of this reign (and that of Domitian), characterized by massive portraits, seriffed lettering, and flat reverse fields, has been challenged by Michael Grant (Essays in Roman Coinage presented to Harold Mattingly, 1956) and more recently by H.A. Cahn ('An imperial mint in Bithynia', Israel

Numismatic Journal, 1984–5). Ian Carradice ('Coinage and Finances in the Reign of Domitian', pp. 118–21) rejects the Bithynian attribution and prefers to integrate these coins into the main sequence of issues from the senatorial mint, seeing in them the output of a single officina exhibiting distinctive characteristics. The question can hardly be regarded as settled, but for the purposes of this catalogue all the aes coinage of Titus' reign (with the exception of the semis of Commagene, no. 2553) has been given to Rome.

For the titles and powers of this reign, including Alexandrian regnal dates, see table on p. 309.

The following obv. legends and types are represented by upper and lower case letters. All other varieties are described in full:

As Caesar

    A. T CAES IMP PON TR P COS II CENS
    B. T CAES IMP VESP CENS
    C. T CAES IMP VESP PON TR POT
    D. T CAES VESPASIAN IMP P TR P COS II
    E. T CAES VESPASIAN IMP PON TR POT COS II
    F. T CAESAR IMP COS III CENS
    G. T CAESAR IMP VESP
    H. T CAESAR IMP VESPASIAN
    I. T CAESAR IMP VESPASIANVS
    J. T CAESAR VESPASIANVS

As Augustus

    K. IMP T CAES VESP AVG P M TR P COS VIII
    L. IMP T CAES VESP AVG P M TR P P P COS VIII
    M. IMP TITVS CAES VESPASIAN AVG P M

    a. Laur. hd. of Titus r.
    b. Laur. hd. of Titus l.
    c. Rad. hd. of Titus r.
    d. Rad. hd. of Titus l.

Issues as Caesar under Vespasian, AD 69–79

(All RIC, BMCRE and CBN references are to the coinage of Vespasian)

2410   **Gold aureus (provincial series).** IMPERATOR T CAESAR AVGVSTI F, a. Rev. CONCORDIA AVG, Ceres enthroned l., holding corn-ears and cornucopiae, EPHE (PHE in monogram) in ex. RIC 340. BMCRE 465. CBN —. Cf. C 38. *[Ephesus, AD 71].*
                                 VF £3,500 ($5,600) / **EF** £8,500 ($13,600)

2411   IMP T CAESAR VESPASIANVS, a (with aegis). Rev. — Concordia seated l., holding patera and cornucopiae. RIC 372. BMCRE 524. CBN —. C 37. *[Tyre, AD 69].*
                                   VF £3,000 ($4,800) / **EF** £7,500 ($12,000)

2412   — — Rev. IVDAEA DEVICTA, Victory stg. r., l. foot on helmet, inscribing IMP / T / CAES in three lines on shield attached to palm-tree. RIC 373. BMCRE p. 110, *. CBN 384. C 119. *[Tyre, AD 69].*   **VF** £10,000 ($16,000) / **EF** £25,000 ($40,000)
    The reverse type celebrates the success of Vespasian and Titus in quelling the First Jewish Revolt (see also nos. 2426, 2434, 2455, 2463, 2475, and 2524–5; see also under Vespasian and Divus Vespasian).

2413   **Gold aureus (regular series).** Ha. Rev. **AETERNITAS**, Aeternitas stg. l., holding hds. of Sol and Luna, altar at feet. RIC 209. BMCRE 302. CBN 265. C 13. *[Rome, AD 75–9].*
                                       VF £1,300 ($2,080) / **EF** £3,250 ($5,200)

             2414   2416 var.

2414   Ja. Rev. **ANNONA AVG**, Annona enthroned l., holding sack of corn-ears on lap. RIC 218. BMCRE 316. CBN 278. C 16. *[Rome, AD 78–9].*
                                         VF £1,100 ($1,760) / **EF** £2,750 ($4,400)

2415   Ha. Rev. **COS IIII**, bull butting r. RIC 181. BMCRE 171. CBN 145. C 48. *[Rome, AD 75].*
                                         VF £1,300 ($2,080) / **EF** £3,250 ($5,200)
    The reverse type is copied from the coinage of Augustus (see no. 1610). See also no. 2249.

2416   Ia. Rev. **COS V**, heifer walking r. RIC 188. BMCRE 187. CBN 164. C 53. *[Rome, AD 76].*
                                         VF £1,300 ($2,080) / **EF** £3,250 ($5,200)
    Another reverse type of Augustan origin (see no. 1577).

             2417   2418

2417   Ia. Rev. **COS VI**, Roma seated r. on pile of shields, holding spear, two birds flying in field to l. and to r., she-wolf suckling twins at Roma's feet. RIC 194. BMCRE 223. CBN 199. C 64. *[Rome, AD 77–8].*   **VF** £1,400 ($2,240) / **EF** £3,500 ($5,600)
    Remarkably, the seated Roma is an exact copy of an anonymous Republican denarius issued almost 200 years before (see no. 164).

2418   Ca. Rev. **NEP RED**, Neptune stg. l., r. foot on globe, holding aplustre and sceptre. RIC 155. BMCRE 80, note. CBN 65. C 120. *[Rome, AD 72–3].*
                                         VF £1,400 ($2,240) / **EF** £3,500 ($5,600)
    This reverse is copied from the coinage of Octavian (see no. 1553). See also nos. 2276 and 2433.

                              2419 var.

2419   Ba. Rev. **PAX AVG**, Pax stg. l., resting on column and holding caduceus and branch, purse on tripod at her feet. RIC 168(b). BMCRE 111. CBN 94. C 131. *[Rome, AD 73].*
                                         VF £1,300 ($2,080) / **EF** £3,250 ($5,200)

2420   **Gold aureus (regular series).** Ha. Rec. PAX AVGVST, Pax enthroned l., holding olive-branch and sceptre. RIC 212. BMCRE 310. CBN 271. C 134. *[Rome, AD 75–9].*
VF £1,200 ($1,920) / EF £3,000 ($4,800)

2421   2423

2421   Ha. Rev. PONTIF TR P COS IIII, Victory stg. l. on cista mystica flanked by snakes, holding wreath and palm. RIC 184. BMCRE 173. CBN 151. C 163. *[Rome, AD 75].*
VF £1,300 ($2,080) / EF £3,250 ($5,200)
The reverse type is inspired by the triumviral cistophoric coinage of Provincia Asia (see nos. 1512–13). See also no. 2254

2422   Ga. Rev. PONTIF TR POT, Fortuna stg. l. on garlanded base, holding rudder and cornu-copiae. RIC 177(a). BMCRE 153. CBN 127. Cf. C 165. *[Rome, AD 74].* ·
VF £1,200 ($1,920) / EF £3,000 ($4,800)

2423   Ba. Rev. VESTA, circular shrine of Vesta on the Palatine, showing four columns, flanked by two statues on pedestals, statue of Vesta within. RIC 171(b). BMCRE 120. CBN 98 var. (CEN for CENS). C 348. *[Rome, AD 73].*   VF £2,250 ($3,600) / EF £5,500 ($8,800)
The Aedicula Vestae was built by Augustus in 12 BC and was located close to his house on the Palatine. It had already appeared on a dupondius of Divus Augustus issued under Tiberius in AD 22–3 (see no. 1785) half a century before its appearance on a series of aurei issued under Vespasian (see also nos. 2255 and 2626).

2424   Ca. Rev. VIC AVG, Victory stg. r. on globe, holding wreath and palm. RIC 158. BMCRE 81. CBN 71. C 352. *[Rome, AD 72–3].*   VF £1,200 ($1,920) / EF £3,000 ($4,800)
The reverse type appears to be copied from the coinage of Octavian (see no. 1554). See also no. 2256.

2425   2426

2425   Ca. Rev. No legend, Titus in triumphal quadriga r., holding branch and sceptre. RIC 159. BMCRE p. 15, † (cf. 520 catalogued under Antioch). CBN 73. C 393. *[Rome, AD 72–3].*
VF £2,500 ($4,000) / EF £6,000 ($9,600)
This reverse commemorates the triumph of Vespasian and Titus in June 71 for their victory in the Jewish War (see also nos. 2435, 2461, and 2479; see also under Vespasian, Divus Vespasian, and Domitian as Caesar).

2426   Ca. Rev. — Titus stg. r., l. foot on helmet, holding spear and parazonium, palm-tree before him at foot of which Judaea, as mourning captive, is seated r. on ground. RIC 160. BMCRE 83. CBN 74. C 391. *[Rome, AD 72–3].*
VF £6,000 ($9,600) / EF £15,000 ($24,000)

This reverse celebrates the success of Vespasian and Titus in quelling the First Jewish Revolt (see also nos. 2412, 2434, 2455, 2463, 2475, and 2524–5; see also under Vespasian and Divus Vespasian).

2427   **Silver denarius (provincial series).** IMPERATOR T CAESAR AVGVSTI F, a. Rev. AVG, EPHE (PHE in monogram) below, all within oak-wreath. RIC 339. BMCRE 464. CBN 357. RSC 23. *[Ephesus, AD 71].*   **VF** £200 ($320) / **EF** £500 ($800)

2428   2433

2428   — — Rev. CONCORDIA AVG, Ceres enthroned, as 2410. RIC 340. BMCRE 467. CBN 358. RSC 39. *[Ephesus, AD 71].*   **VF** £250 ($400) / **EF** £600 ($960)

2429   — — Rev. PACI AVGVSTAE, Victory advancing r., holding wreath and palm, EPHE (PHE in monogram) in lower field to r. RIC 341. BMCRE 468. CBN 361. RSC 125. *[Ephesus, AD 71].*   **VF** £225 ($360) / **EF** £550 ($880)

2430   Ba (with mint mark small 'O' below bust). Rev. COS V, eagle stg. facing on garlanded base, hd. r. RIC 379. BMCRE 485. CBN 373. Cf. RSC 61. *[Ephesus, AD 76].*
                                         VF £150 ($240) / **EF** £375 ($600)

2431   — — Rev. FIDES PVBL, clasped r. hands holding winged caduceus between corn-ears and poppies. Cf. RIC 167 (misattributed to Rome). BMCRE p. 102, *. CBN 375. RSC 87a. *[Ephesus, AD 76].*   **VF** £150 ($240) / **EF** £375 ($600)

2432   C, laur. and dr. bust r. Rev. CONCORDIA AVGVSTI, Concordia seated l., holding patera and cornucopiae. RIC 365. BMCRE 514. CBN —. RSC 44. *[Antioch, AD 72].*
                                         VF £225 ($360) / **EF** £550 ($880)

2433   — — Rev. NEP RED, Neptune stg., as 2418. RIC 366. BMCRE 516. CBN 321. RSC 122. *[Antioch, AD 72].*   **VF** £175 ($280) / **EF** £425 ($680)

2434   2435

2434   — — Rev. No legend, Titus and captive Judaea, as 2426. RIC 367. BMCRE 518. CBN 322. Cf. RSC 392 (rev. misdescribed). *[Antioch, AD 72].*
                                         VF £300 ($480) / **EF** £750 ($1,200)
        The reverse type celebrates the success of Vespasian and Titus in quelling the First Jewish Revolt (see also no. 2412, 2426, 2455, 2463, 2475, and 2524–5; see also under Vespasian and Divus Vespasian).

2435 **Silver denarius (provincial series).** IMPERATOR T CAESAR AVGVSTI F, a. Rev. — Titus in quadriga, as 2425. RIC 368. BMCRE 521. CBN 324. RSC 395. *[Antioch, AD 72].*
VF £185 ($296) / **EF** £450 ($720)
This reverse commemorates the triumph of Vespasian and Titus in June 71 for their victory in the Jewish War (see also nos. 2425, 2461, and 2479; see also under Vespasian, Divus Vespasian, and Domitian as Caesar).

2436   2446

2436 **Silver denarius (regular series).** As 2414 (rev. ANNONA AVG, Annona enthroned). RIC 218. BMCRE 319. CBN 280. RSC 17. *[Rome, AD 78–9].*
VF £100 ($160) / **EF** £275 ($440)

2437 Ja. Rev. CERES AVGVST, Ceres stg. l., holding corn-ears and long torch. RIC 219. BMCRE 321. CBN 282. RSC 31. *[Rome, AD 78–9].* VF £100 ($160) / **EF** £275 ($440)

2438 Ha. Rev. COS V, eagle stg. facing on garlanded base, hd. l. RIC 191(a). BMCRE 191. CBN 166. RSC 59a. *[Rome, AD 76].* VF £110 ($176) / **EF** £300 ($480)

2439 Ia. Rev. COS VI, Mars stg. l., holding spear and trophy, corn-ear in ground on r. RIC 196. BMCRE 222. CBN 196. RSC 66. *[Rome, AD 77–8].* VF £100 ($160) / **EF** £275 ($440)

2440 Ia. Rev. — pair of oxen under yoke l. RIC 197. BMCRE 225. CBN 201. RSC 67. *[Rome, AD 77–8].* VF £150 ($240) / **EF** £375 ($600)

2441 Ia. Rev. — prow of galley r., large star above. RIC 198. BMCRE 226. CBN 202. RSC 68. *[Rome, AD 77–8].* VF £125 ($200) / **EF** £325 ($520)
The reverse type is copied from the triumviral coinage of Mark Antony (see nos. 1461 and 1472). See also no. 2290.

2442 Ja. Rev. IMP XIII, goatherd seated l. on stone, milking she-goat over bowl. Cf. RIC 221. BMCRE 230. CBN 204. RSC 103. *[Rome, AD 78].* VF £275 ($440) / **EF** £650 ($1,040)

2443 Ja. Rev. — sow walking l., with three young. Cf. RIC 220. BMCRE 227. CBN 203. RSC 104. *[Rome, AD 78].* VF £175 ($280) / **EF** £425 ($680)

2444 Ia. Rev. IOVIS CVSTOS, Jupiter stg. facing, sacrificing from patera over altar and holding sceptre. RIC 176 (= 211). BMCRE 305. CBN 268. RSC 106. *[Rome, AD 75–9].*
VF £110 ($176) / **EF** £300 ($480)

2445 Ga. Rev. PONTIF TR P COS III, winged caduceus. RIC 173. BMCRE 152. CBN 125. RSC 159. *[Rome, AD 74].* VF £110 ($176) / **EF** £300 ($480)

2446 Ha. Rev. PONTIF TR P COS IIII, Pax seated l., holding olive-branch, l. hand at side. RIC 185. BMCRE 172. CBN 148. RSC 162. *[Rome, AD 75].* VF £100 ($160) / **EF** £275 ($440)

2447 Ba. Rev. PONTIF TRI POT, Titus seated r., holding sceptre and branch. RIC 169. BMCRE 116. CBN —. RSC 169. *[Rome, AD 73].* VF £110 ($176) / **EF** £300 ($480)

2448   **Silver denarius (regular series).** Ia. Rev. TR POT VIII COS VII, Venus stg. r., her back
        turned towards spectator, holding helmet and transverse spear and resting on column. RIC
        205. BMCRE 255. CBN 223. RSC 332. *[Rome, AD 79].*
                                                    VF £125 ($200) / **EF** £325 ($520)
        *The reverse type is copied from the coinage of Octavian (see no. 1547). See also no. 2489
        and 2507.*

2449   Ia. Rev. — bound captive kneeling r. at foot of trophy. RIC 208. BMCRE 258. CBN 229.
        RSC 334. *[Rome, AD 79].*   **VF** £175 ($280) / **EF** £425 ($680)
        *This reverse refers either to the victory in Judaea or, alternatively, may be associated with
        the activities in northern Britain of the celebrated governor Gnaeus Julius Agricola,
        father-in-law of the historian Tacitus (see also nos. 2309, 2493, 2505, and 2511).*

                    2450   2452 var.

2450   Ia. Rev. — triumphal quadriga l., containing ears of corn (?). Cf. RIC 206. BMCRE 256.
        CBN 226. RSC 336. *[Rome, AD 79].*   **VF** £165 ($264) / **EF** £400 ($640)

2451   **Silver quinarius.** T CAES IMP VESP P TR P CENS, a. Rev. VICTORIA AVGVSTI, Victory
        advancing r., holding wreath and palm. RIC 165. BMCRE 92. CBN 79. RSC 374. *[Rome,
        AD 73].*   **VF** £250 ($400) / **EF** £600 ($960)

2452   Ha. Rev. — Victory seated l., holding wreath and palm. RIC 217. BMCRE 314. CBN 277.
        RSC 375. *[Rome, AD 75–9].*   **VF** £250 ($400) / **EF** £600 ($960)

2453   **Brass sestertius.** T CAES VESPASIAN IMP PON TR POT COS VI, a (with aegis). Rev.
        ANNONA AVGVST S C, Annona enthroned l., holding sack of corn-ears on lap. RIC 680a.
        BMCRE p. 175, †. CBN 781. C 18. *[Rome, AD 77–8].*
                                    F £150 ($240) / **VF** £375 ($600) / **EF** £1,100 ($1,760)

2454   Ea. Rev. FORTVNAE REDVCI S C, Fortuna stg. l., holding branch and rudder on globe in r.
        hand, cornucopiae in l. RIC 607. BMCRE 630. CBN 617. Cf. C 93. *[Rome, AD 72].*
                                    F £170 ($272) / **VF** £425 ($680) / **EF** £1,250 ($2,000)

2455   Ea. Rev. IVDAEA CAPTA S C, Titus stg. r., l. foot on helmet, holding spear and parazonium,
        palm-tree before him at foot of which Judaea, as mourning captive, is seated r. on ground.
        RIC 608. BMCRE 631. CBN 618. C 113. *[Rome, AD 72].*
                                    F £400 ($640) / **VF** £1,000 ($1,600) / **EF** £3,000 ($4,800)
        *The reverse type celebrates the success of Vespasian and Titus in quelling the First Jewish
        Revolt (see also nos. 2412, 2426, 2434, 2463, 2475, and 2524–5; see also under Vespasian
        and Divus Vespasian).*

2456   Ea. Rev. PAX AVGVSTI S C, Pax stg. l., holding olive-branch and cornucopiae. RIC 609.
        BMCRE 633. CBN 619. Cf. C 150. *[Rome, AD 72].*
                                    F £150 ($240) / **VF** £375 ($600) / **EF** £1,100 ($1,760)

2457   Ea. Rev. ROMA S C, Roma stg. l., holding Victory and spear. RIC 610. BMCRE p. 140 *.
        CBN 620. C 181. *[Rome, AD 72].*   **F** £150 ($240) / **VF** £375 ($600) / **EF** £1,100 ($1,760)

2458   **Brass sestertius.** T CAES IMP AVG F PON TR P COS VI CENSOR, a (globe below). Rev.
       SALVS AVGVSTA S C, Salus seated l., holding patera and sceptre. RIC 774. BMCRE p.
       212, *. CBN 857. C 196. *[Lugdunum, AD 77–8].*
                    F £170 ($272) / **VF** £425 ($680) / **EF** £1,250 ($2,000)

2459   T CAESAR VESPASIAN IMP IIII PON TR POT II COS II, a. Rev. S C, Mars advancing r., carry-
       ing spear and trophy. RIC 636. BMCRE p. 146, ¶. CBN 645. C 201. *[Rome, AD 73].*
                    F £150 ($240) / **VF** £375 ($600) / **EF** £1,100 ($1,760)

2460   T CAES VESPASIAN IMP PON TR POT COS V, a. Rev. — Spes advancing l., holding flower.
       Cf. RIC 674. BMCRE p. 170, §. CBN 760. C 214. *[Rome, AD 76].*
                    F £150 ($240) / **VF** £375 ($600) / **EF** £1,100 ($1,760)

2461   T CAES VESP IMP PON TR POT COS II CENS, a. Rev. — Titus in triumphal quadriga r., hold-
       ing branch and sceptre. RIC 645. BMCRE 668. CBN 671. C 226. *[Rome, AD 73].*
                    F £250 ($400) / **VF** £650 ($1,040) / **EF** £2,000 ($3,200)
       *The reverse type commemorates the triumph of Vespasian and Titus in June 71 for their
       victory in the Jewish War (see also nos. 2425, 2435, and 2479; see also under Vespasian,
       Divus Vespasian, and Domitian as Caesar).*

2462 var.

2462   T CAESAR VESPASIAN IMP IIII PON TR POT III COS II, a. Rev. — Titus on horseback gallop-
       ing r., spearing prostrate enemy on ground beneath him. RIC 642. BMCRE 653. Cf. CBN
       647. Cf. C 238. *[Rome, AD 73].*   **F** £250 ($400) / **VF** £650 ($1,040) / **EF** £2,000 ($3,200)
       This reverse records the personal bravery of Titus during the conduct of the war in Judaea

2463

2463   Ea. Rev. VICTORIA AVGVSTI S C, Victory stg. r., l. foot on helmet, inscribing VIC / AVG
       on shield attached to palm-tree. RIC 614. BMCRE 637. CBN 624. C 385. *[Rome, AD 72].*
                    F £225 ($360) / **VF** £550 ($880) / **EF** £1,600 ($2,560)
       *This reverse celebrates the success of Vespasian and Titus in quelling the First Jewish
       Revolt (see also nos. 2412, 2426, 2434, 2455, 2475, and 2524–5; see also under Vespasian
       and Divus Vespasian).*

       See also no. 2560.

2464   **Brass dupondius.** T CAESAR VESPASIANVS TR P COS VI, c. Rev. CERES AVGVST S C,
        Ceres stg. l., holding corn-ears and torch. Cf. RIC 682. BMCRE p. 175, §. CBN 783. Cf. C
        32. *[Rome, AD 77–8].*   **F** £60 ($96) / **VF** £150 ($240) / **VF** £450 ($720)

2465   Ac. Rev. CONCORDIA AVGVSTI S C, Concordia seated l., holding patera and cornucopiae.
        RIC 647. BMCRE 669. CBN 673. C 45. *[Rome, AD 73].*
                                             F £60 ($96) / **VF** £150 ($240) / **VF** £450 ($720)

2466 var.

2466   Ac. Rev. FELICITAS PVBLICA S C, Felicitas stg. l., holding caduceus and cornucopiae. RIC
        648(a). BMCRE 670. CBN 675. C 80. *[Rome, AD 73].*
                                             F £60 ($96) / **VF** £150 ($240) / **VF** £450 ($720)

2467   T CAES IMP AVG F TR P COS VI CENSOR, a (globe below). Rev. PAX AVG S C, Pax stg. l.,
        sacrificing from patera over lighted altar and holding caduceus and olive-branch. RIC
        777(b). BMCRE 860, note. CBN 864. C 129. *[Lugdunum, AD 77–8].*
                                             F £65 ($104) / **VF** £160 ($256) / **VF** £475 ($760)

2468   Ac. Rev. ROMA S C, Roma seated l. on cuirass, holding Victory and spear, shields behind.
        RIC 649. BMCRE 671. CBN 676. C 185. *[Rome, AD 73].*
                                             F £65 ($104) / **VF** £160 ($256) / **VF** £475 ($760)

2469   Dc. Rev. Similar to previous, but with legend ROMA VICTRIX S C. RIC 617. BMCRE 641.
        CBN 630. C 192. *[Rome, AD 72].*   **F** £70 ($112) / **VF** £175 ($280) / **VF** £525 ($840)

2470   Obv. As 2467, but hd. rad. Rev. SECVRITAS AVGVSTI S C, Securitas, in relaxed pose,
        enthroned r., hd. resting on r. hand, holding sceptre in l., altar at feet. RIC 782(a). BMCRE
        861. CBN 867. C 261. *[Lugdunum, AD 77–8].*
                                             F £65 ($104) / **VF** £160 ($256) / **VF** £475 ($760)

2471   Ac. Rev. S P Q R / OB / CIV SER in three lines within oak-wreath. RIC 651. BMCRE p. 154,
        †. CBN 679. C 265. *[Rome, AD 73].*   **F** £75 ($120) / **VF** £185 ($296) / **VF** £550 ($880)

2472

2472   T CAESAR IMP PONT, a. Rev. TR POT COS III CENSOR, winged caduceus between two
        crossed cornuacopiae. RIC 813(a). BMCRE 891. CBN 907. Cf. C 326. *[Samosata in
        Commagene, AD 74].*   **F** £65 ($104) / **VF** £160 ($256) / **VF** £475 ($760)

2473   **Copper as.** Da. Rev. AEQVITAS AVGVSTI S C, Aequitas stg. l., holding scales and sceptre.
RIC 618. BMCRE —. CBN 631. C 6. *[Rome, AD 72].*
F £55 ($88) / **VF** £140 ($224) / **VF** £425 ($680)

2474   Da. Rev. FIDES PVBLICA S C, clasped r. hands holding caduceus between two corn-ears. RIC
619. BMCRE 642. CBN 632. C 89. *[Rome, AD 72].*
F £60 ($96) / **VF** £150 ($240) / **VF** £450 ($720)

2475 var. (Rome)

2475   Obv. As 2467. Rev. IVDAEA CAPTA S C, Judaea, as mourning captive, seated r. amidst
arms at foot of palm-tree. RIC 784. BMCRE 862. CBN 869. C 117–18. *[Lugdunum,
AD 77–8].*   F £175 ($280) / **VF** £450 ($720) / **VF** £1,350 ($2,160)
*The reverse type celebrates the success of Vespasian and Titus in quelling the First Jewish
Revolt (see also nos. 2412, 2426, 2434, 2455, 2463, and 2524–5; see also under Vespasian
and Divus Vespasian).*

2476   Aa. Rev. PAX AVGVST S C, Pax stg l., holding caduceus and olive-branch and resting on
column. RIC 654. BMCRE p. 155, *. CBN 682. C 143. *[Rome, AD 73].*
F £55 ($88) / **VF** £140 ($224) / **VF** £425 ($680)

2477   Obv. As 2467. Rev. PROVIDENT (NT in monogram) S C, façade of altar-enclosure of the
Ara Providentiae Augusti, with double panelled door and horns of the altar visible above.
RIC 785. BMCRE 867. CBN 878. C 176. *[Lugdunum, AD 77–8].*
F £60 ($96) / **VF** £150 ($240) / **VF** £450 ($720)
*The reverse is a revival of a Divus Augustus type issued by Tiberius in the AD 20s (see no.
1789). It had been revived previously by Vitellius (see no. 2222) and depicts the altar dedi-
cated to the 'providence' of Augustus which may have stood in the Campus Martius (see
also nos. 2360, 2581–2, 2657, and 2892).*

2478   T CAESAR IMP COS V, a. Rev. S C, Spes advancing l., holding flower. RIC 678. BMCRE
728. CBN —. C 212. *[Rome, AD 76].*   F £55 ($88) / **VF** £140 ($224) / **VF** £425 ($680)

2479   Aa. Rev. — Titus in triumphal quadriga r., holding branch and sceptre. RIC 658. BMCRE
p.155, §. CBN 688. C 227. *[Rome, AD 73].*
F £100 ($160) / **VF** £250 ($400) / **VF** £750 ($1,200)
*The reverse type commemorates the triumph of Vespasian and Titus in June 71 for their
victory in the Jewish War (see also nos. 2425, 2435, and 2461; see also under Vespasian,
Divus Vespasian, and Domitian as Caesar).*

2480   Aa. Rev. — eagle stg. facing on globe, hd. r. RIC 656. BMCRE 673. CBN 684. C 239.
[Rome, AD 73].   F £60 ($96) / **VF** £150 ($240) / **VF** £450 ($720)

2481   Aa. Rev. — hexastyle temple of Jupiter Optimus Maximus Capitolinus, richly ornamented
with statuary and bas-reliefs and containing statues of Jupiter between Juno and Minerva.
RIC 656(a). BMCRE p. 155,⫽. CBN 685. C 242. *[Rome, AD 73].*
F £250 ($400) / **VF** £650 ($1,040) / **VF** £2,000 ($3,200)

*Following the destruction of the second temple of Jupiter Capitolinus, in the fighting for
the capital at the end of AD 69, Vespasian rebuilt the celebrated structure and dedicated it
in AD 75. Just five years later, however, it was again destroyed in the great fire which
engulfed central Rome, one of the two major disasters which afflicted the Empire during
the brief reign of Titus (see also nos. 2338, 2363, and 2662).*

2482   **Copper as.** Aa. Rev. VESTA S C, domed temple of Vesta in the Forum, showing four
columns and containing statue of the goddess on pedestal. RIC 659. BMCRE 674. CBN
689. C 351. *[Rome, AD 73].*   **F** £175 ($280) / **VF** £450 ($720) / **VF** £1,350 ($2,160)
*This celebrated temple had been rebuilt by Nero following the great fire of AD 64 (see nos.
1933 and 1946). The Neronian structure survived until another conflagration late in the
reign of Commodus and was again restored early in the 3rd century by Julia Domna (see
also no. 2365 and 2663).*

2483

2483   T CAESAR VESPASIANVS TR P COS VI, a. Rev. VICTORIA AVGVST S C, Victory stg. r. on
forepart of galley, holding wreath and palm. RIC 686. BMCRE 742. CBN 787. C 364.
[Rome, AD 77–8].   **F** £60 ($96) / **VF** £150 ($240) / **VF** £450 ($720)

2484   Da. Rev. VICTORIA AVGVSTI S C, Victory stepping r., crowning standard and holding
palm-branch. RIC 626. BMCRE 645. CBN 636. C 381. *[Rome, AD 72].*
F £70 ($112) / **VF** £175 ($280) / **VF** £525 ($840)

2485   Aa. Rev. Similar to 2483, but with legend VICTORIA NAVALIS S C. RIC 662. BMCRE
677. CBN 691. C 386. *[Rome, AD 73].*   **F** £65 ($104) / **VF** £160 ($256) / **VF** £475 ($760)

2486   **Brass as (small module).** T CAES IMP TR POT, a. Rev. S C in laurel-wreath. RIC 804.
BMCRE p. 218, *. CBN 897. C 250. *[Samosata in Commagene, AD 71–2].*
F £60 ($96) / **VF** £150 ($240) / **VF** £450 ($720)

2487   **Brass semis.** T CAES IMP, a. Rev. PON TR POT, winged caduceus. RIC 807. BMCRE 882.
CBN 898. C 156. *[Samosata in Commagene, AD 71–2].*
F £55 ($88) / **VF** £140 ($224) / **VF** £425 ($680)

Issues as Augustus, AD 79–81

2488   **Gold aureus.** Ma. Rev. TR P VIIII IMP XIIII COS VII, naked rad. figure stg. facing, holding
spear and parazonium, atop rostral column ornamented with anchor and beaks of galleys.
RIC 4. BMCRE p. 224, * note. CBN 2. C 271. *[Rome, AD 79].*
VF £1,500 ($2,400) / **EF** £3,750 ($6,000)
*The reverse type is copied from the coinage of Octavian (see no. 1559). See also nos. 2311
and 2509.*

2489 var. 2493 var.

2489   **Gold aureus.** Ma. Rev. TR P VIIII IMP XIIII COS VII P P, Venus stg. r., her back turned
towards spectator, holding helmet and transverse spear and resting on column. RIC 9.
BMCRE 8. CBN 8. C 267. *[Rome, AD 79].*   **VF** £1,400 ($2,240) / **EF** £3,500 ($5,600)
*This reverse is also copied from the coinage of Octavian (see no. 1547). See also nos. 2448
and 2507.*

2490   Ma. Rev. — Ceres seated l., holding corn-ear with poppy and torch. RIC 8. BMCRE 6.
CBN 6. C 269. *[Rome, AD 79].*   **VF** £1,400 ($2,240) / **EF** £3,500 ($5,600)

2491   Ma. Rev. — triumphal quadriga l., containing ears of corn (?). RIC 12. BMCRE 16. CBN
13. C 277. *[Rome, AD 79].*   **VF** £2,000 ($3,200) / **EF** £5,000 ($8,000)

2492   Ma. Rev. TR P VIIII IMP XV COS VII P P, capricorn l., globe below. RIC 19. BMCRE 34.
CBN 31. C 293. *[Rome, AD 79].*   **VF** £1,500 ($2,400) / **EF** £3,750 ($6,000)
*The reverse type is based on the coinage of Augustus (see nos. 1585 and 1592). See also
nos. 2310 and 2510.*

2493   Ma. Rev. — bound captive kneeling r. at foot of trophy. RIC 17. BMCRE 30. CBN —. C
296. *[Rome, AD 79].*   **VF** £2,500 ($4,000) / **EF** £6,000 ($9,600)
*This reverse and the following refer either to the victory in Judaea or, alternatively, may be
associated with the activities in northern Britain of the celebrated governor Gnaeus Julius
Agricola, father-in-law of the historian Tacitus (see also nos. 2309, 2449, 2505, and 2511).*

2494   Ma. Rev. TR P IX IMP XV COS VIII P P, trophy between two seated captives, a female in
mourning on l., a bound male on r. RIC 21a. BMCRE 36. CBN 33. C 305. *[Rome, AD 80].*
VF £2,500 ($4,000) / **EF** £6,000 ($9,600)

2495 2497

2495   Ma. Rev. — elephant walking l. RIC 22a. BMCRE 42. CBN 35. C 300. *[Rome, AD 80].*
VF £2,000 ($3,200) / **EF** £5,000 ($8,000)

2496   Mb. Rev. — winged thunderbolt on draped seat or table. RIC 23(b). BMCRE 55. CBN —.
C —. *[Rome, AD 80].*   **VF** £1,500 ($2,400) / **EF** £3,750 ($6,000)

2497   Ma. Rev. — ornamented semicircular diadem (?) on draped seat or table. RIC 24a.
BMCRE 57. CBN 46. C 312. *[Rome, AD 80].*   **VF** £1,400 ($2,240) / **EF** £3,500 ($5,600)

2498   2499 var.

2498   **Gold aureus.** Ma. Rev. TR P IX IMP XV COS VIII P P, wreath on curule chair. RIC 25a.
       BMCRE 64. CBN 52. C 317. *[Rome, AD 80].*   **VF** £1,400 ($2,240) / **EF** £3,500 ($5,600)

2499   Mb. Rev. — dolphin entwined around anchor. RIC 26(b). BMCRE 76. CBN —. C —.
       [Rome, AD 80].   **VF** £1,750 ($2,800) / **EF** £4,250 ($6,800)

2500

2500   Ma. Rev. — tripod surmounted by dolphin r. RIC 27(a). BMCRE 77. CBN 65. Cf. C 320.
       [Rome, AD 80].   **VF** £1,500 ($2,400) / **EF** £3,750 ($6,000)

2501   **Silver cistophorus.** Ma. Rev. CAPIT RESTIT, tetrastyle temple of Jupiter Optimus Maximus
       Capitolinus, containing statues of the Capitoline Triad (Jupiter enthroned between stg. fig-
       ures of Juno and Minerva). RIC —. BMCRE —. CBN 111. RSC —. *[Ephesus, AD 80–81].*
                                         VF £1,500 ($2,400) / **EF** £3,500 ($5,600)
       *The third temple of Jupiter Capitolinus, which had been dedicated by Vespasian only five
       years before, was destroyed in the great fire of AD 80. Plans to restore this important sym-
       bol of Roman power were drawn up with the minimum of delay, as evidenced by this
       remarkable type. Titus did not live to see the grandiose fourth temple completed and it was
       dedicated by Domitian in 82, the year following his accession (see no. 2715). It was to sur-
       vive the downfall of paganism and the victory of Christianity, gradually falling into dis-
       repair through deliberate neglect.*

2502

2502   Ma. Rev. No legend, legionary eagle between two standards. RIC 74. BMCRE 149.
       CBN —. RSC 398. *[Ephesus, AD 80–81].*   **VF** £750 ($1,200) / **EF** £1,750 ($2,800)

2503 **Silver denarius.** Ma. Rev. BONVS EVENTVS AVGVSTI, Bonus Eventus stg. l., holding patera and corn-ears with poppy. RIC 31. BMCRE 106. CBN 83. RSC 25. *[Rome, AD 79–80].*
VF £140 ($224) / **EF** £360 ($576)

2504 IMP T CAESAR VESPASIANVS AVG, a. Rev. CERES AVGVST, Ceres stg. l., holding corn-ears and sceptre. RIC 28. BMCRE 105. CBN —. RSC 31a. *[Rome, AD 79].*
VF £150 ($240) / **EF** £375 ($600)

2505 — — Rev. TR POT VIII COS VII, bound captive kneeling r. at foot of trophy. RIC 1. BMCRE 1. CBN 116. RSC 334a. *[Rome, AD 79].* VF £175 ($280) / **EF** £425 ($680)
See note following no. 2493.

2506 var.

2506 Ma. Rev. TR P VIIII IMP XIIII COS VII, triumphal quadriga l., containing corn-ears (?). RIC 6. BMCRE p. 224, * note. CBN 5. RSC 276. *[Rome, AD 79].*
VF £165 ($264) / **EF** £400 ($640)

2507 Ma. Rev. TR P VIIII IMP XIIII COS VII P P, Venus stg. r., as 2489. RIC 9. BMCRE 9. CBN 9. RSC 268. *[Rome, AD 79].* VF £130 ($208) / **EF** £340 ($544)
The reverse type is copied from the coinage of Octavian (see no. 1547). See also nos. 2448 and 2489.

2508 Ma. Rev. — Ceres seated l., as 2490. RIC 8. BMCRE 7. CBN 7. RSC 270. *[Rome, AD 79].*
VF £120 ($192) / **EF** £320 ($512)

2509 var.   2510

2509 Mb. Rev. TR P VIIII IMP XV COS VII P P, rad. figure on rostral column, as 2488. RIC 16(b). BMCRE 28. CBN 27. RSC 291. *[Rome, AD 79].* VF £140 ($224) / **EF** £360 ($576)
The reverse type is copied from the coinage of Octavian (see no. 1559). See also nos. 2311 and 2488.

2510 Ma. Rev. — capricorn l., globe below. RIC 19. BMCRE 35. CBN 32. RSC 294. *[Rome, AD 79].* VF £140 ($224) / **EF** £360 ($576)
The reverse type is based on the coinage of Augustus (see nos. 1585 and 1592). See also nos. 2310 and 2492.

2511 Ma. Rev. TR P IX IMP XV COS VIII P P, trophy between two captives, as 2494. RIC 21a. BMCRE 37. CBN 34. RSC 306. *[Rome, AD 80].* VF £165 ($264) / **EF** £400 ($640)
The reverse type refers either to the victory in Judaea or, alternatively, may be associated with the activities in northern Britain of the celebrated governor Gnaeus Julius Agricola, father-in-law of the historian Tacitus (see also nos. 2309, 2449, 2493–4, and 2505).

466 FLAVIAN DYNASTY

2512 **Silver denarius.** Ma. Rev. TR P IX IMP XV COS VIII P P, elephant walking l. RIC 22a.
BMCRE 43. CBN 37. RSC 303. *[Rome, AD 80].* **VF** £130 ($208) / **EF** £340 ($544)

2513 Ma. Rev. — winged thunderbolt on draped seat or table. RIC 23(a). BMCRE 51. CBN 43.
RSC 316. *[Rome, AD 80].* **VF** £120 ($192) / **EF** £320 ($512)

2514 Ma. Rev. — ornamented semicircular diadem (?) on draped seat or table. RIC 24a.
BMCRE 58. CBN 47. RSC 313. *[Rome, AD 80].* **VF** £120 ($192) / **EF** £320 ($512)

2515 Ma. Rev. — similar, but the diadem (?) is of triangular form. RIC —. BMCRE 61. CBN
49. RSC 313a. *[Rome, AD 80].* **VF** £120 ($192) / **EF** £320 ($512)

2516 var. 2517

2516 Mb. Rev. — wreath on curule chair. RIC 25b. BMCRE 70. CBN 55. RSC 319. *[Rome, AD
80].* **VF** £120 ($192) / **EF** £320 ($512)

2517 Ma. Rev. — dolphin entwined around anchor. RIC 26(a). BMCRE 72. CBN 60. RSC 309.
[Rome, AD 80]. **VF** £130 ($208) / **EF** £340 ($544)

2518 Mb. Rev. — tripod surmounted by dolphin r. RIC 27(b). BMCRE 80. CBN 69. RSC 323.
[Rome, AD 80]. **VF** £120 ($192) / **EF** £320 ($512)

2519

2519 **Silver quinarius.** Ma. Rev. VICTORIA AVGVST, Victory advancing r., holding wreath and
palm. RIC 34. BMCRE 108. CBN 87. RSC 356. *[Rome, AD 79–80].*
VF £275 ($440) / **EF** £650 ($1,040)

2520 Ma. Rev. — Victory seated l., holding wreath and palm. RIC 35(a). BMCRE 110. CBN 88.
RSC 370a. *[Rome, AD 79–80].* **VF** £275 ($440) / **EF** £650 ($1,040)

2521 **Brass sestertius.** IMP TITVS CAES VESP AVG P M TR P P P COS VII, a. Rev. VESTA S C Vesta
seated l., holding Palladium and sceptre. RIC 78. BMCRE p. 253, §. CBN 146. C 341.
[Rome, AD 79]. **F** £170 ($272) / **VF** £425 ($680) / **EF** £1,250 ($2,000)
For a similar issue of the following year, see no. 2534.

2522 La. Rev. ANNONA AVG (no S C), Annona stg. l., between modius and stern of ship, holding statuette of Aequitas and cornucopiae. Cf. RIC 86. BMCRE 152. CBN 151. Cf. C 14.
[Rome, AD 80]. **F** £170 ($272) / **VF** £425 ($680) / **EF** £1,250 ($2,000)

2523 **Brass sestertius.** Lb. Rev. FELICIT PVBLIC S C, Felicitas stg. l., holding sceptre and cornucopiae. RIC 89. BMCRE 158. CBN 154. C 74. *[Rome, AD 80].*
F £150 ($240) / VF £375 ($600) / EF £1,100 ($1,760)

2524 La. Rev. IVD CAP S C, palm-tree, to l. of which bound male Jewish captive stands l., and to r. of which Judaea, as mourning female captive, is seated r., arms on ground around. RIC 92. BMCRE 161. CBN 160. C 111. *[Rome, AD 80].*
F £450 ($720) / VF £1,100 ($1,760) / EF £3,250 ($5,200)
The reverses of this and the following commemorate Titus' role, a decade before, in the quelling of the First Jewish Revolt (see also nos. 2412, 2426, 2434, 2455, 2463, and 2475; see also under Vespasian and Divus Vespasian).

2525 Lb. Rev. — similar, but the male captive stands r. to r. of palm-tree, and mourning Judaea is seated l. on other side of tree. RIC 91. BMCRE 169. CBN 159. C 109. *[Rome, AD 80].*
F £450 ($720) / VF £1,100 ($1,760) / EF £3,250 ($5,200)

2526 var.

2526 Lb. Rev. PAX AVGVST S C, Pax stg. l., holding olive-branch and cornucopiae. RIC 94. BMCRE 171. CBN 162. C 140. *[Rome, AD 80].*
F £150 ($240) / VF £375 ($600) / EF £1,100 ($1,760)

2527 Similar, but with obv. IMP T CAES DIVI VESP F AVG P M TR P P P COS VIII, a. RIC 181 (attributed to Lugdunum). BMCRE 309 (Lugdunum). CBN 323 (Bithynia). Cf. C 141. *[Rome, AD 80].*
F £160 ($256) / VF £400 ($640) / EF £1,200 ($1,920)

2528 Lb. Rev. PIETAS AVGVST S C, Titus and Domitian, togate, stg. facing each other, clasping r. hands and holding sceptres in l., Concordia (or Pietas) stg. facing, looking r., in background between them. RIC 96. BMCRE 177. CBN 167. Cf. C 152. *[Rome, AD 80].*
F £250 ($400) / VF £650 ($1,040) / EF £2,000 ($3,200)

2529

2529 Lb. Rev. PROVIDENT AVGVST S C, Vespasian and Titus, togate, stg. facing each other, holding between them globe with rudder below. RIC 98. BMCRE 180. CBN 170. C 179. *[Rome, AD 80].*
F £225 ($360) / VF £550 ($880) / EF £1,600 ($2,560)

2530

2530   **Brass sestertius.** La. Rev. S C, Spes advancing l., holding flower. RIC 100. BMCRE 186.
       CBN 73. C 221. *[Rome, AD 80].*   **F** £150 ($240) / **VF** £375 ($600) / **EF** £1,100 ($1,760)

2531

2531   Obv. As 2527. Rev. — Mars advancing r., carrying spear and trophy. RIC 182 (attributed to
       Lugdunum). BMCRE 310 (Lugdunum). CBN 324 (Bithynia). Cf. C 203. *[Rome, AD 80].*
                                          F £160 ($256) / **VF** £400 ($640) / **EF** £1,200 ($1,920)

2532   Lb. Rev. — Victory advancing l., holding wreath and palm. RIC 103. BMCRE 187. CBN
       178. Cf. C 205. *[Rome, AD 80].*   **F** £160 ($256) / **VF** £400 ($640) / **EF** £1,200 ($1,920)

2533   La. Rev. — Titus on horseback pacing l., holding sceptre, receiving Palladium from Roma
       stg. r. before him, r. foot on globe and holding sceptre. RIC 104. BMCRE 188. CBN 180.
       C 223. *[Rome, AD 80].*   **F** £300 ($480) / **VF** £750 ($1,200) / **EF** £2,250 ($3,600)

2534   La. Rev. **VESTA S C,** Vesta seated l., holding Palladium and sceptre. RIC 106. BMCRE p.
       261, ‡. CBN 183. C 343. *[Rome, AD 80].*
                                          F £160 ($256) / **VF** £400 ($640) / **EF** £1,200 ($1,920)
       For a similar issue of the preceding year, see no. 2521.

2535   Lb. Rev. **VICTORIA AVG S C,** Victory stg. l., resting on column and holding cornucopiae
       and palm. RIC 107. BMCRE p. 261, §. CBN 186. C 353. *[Rome, AD 80].*
                                          F £225 ($360) / **VF** £550 ($880) / **EF** £1,600 ($2,560)

2536   L, Titus seated l. on curule chair amidst arms, holding branch and scroll, S – C in field.
       Rev. No legend, view of the Colosseum (Amphitheatrum Flavium), showing part of the
       interior, with gangways, arch, and rows of spectators, obelisk (Meta Sudans) to l. of the
       building, two-storied porticoed structure to r. Cf. RIC 110. BMCRE 190. CBN 189. C 400.
       [Rome, AD 80].   **F** £2,500 ($4,000) / **VF** £6,250 ($10,000) / **EF** £20,000 ($32,000)

2536

The great Flavian Amphitheatre, better known by its popular name of the Colosseum,
remains to this day one of the principal landmarks of Rome. Begun by Vespasian in AD 71,
the completed building was dedicated with much celebration by Titus in June of 80. It
appears again on coins of Severus Alexander, who was commemorating its reopening fol-
lowing extensive damage caused by lightning in 217; and on a medallion of Gordian III,
who completed the restoration which had begun under Elagabalus. The last recorded wild
beast hunts in the Colosseum took place in Ostrogothic times, following a restoration of
the building by Eutharich, son-in-law of Theodoric the Great, in 523 (cf. Hill, 'The
Monuments of Ancient Rome as Coin Types', p. 40).

2537 **Brass dupondius.** Kc. Rev. CERES AVGVST S C, Ceres stg., as 2464. RIC 111(a). BMCRE
191A. CBN 191. Cf. C 34. *[Rome, AD 80].*
F £60 ($96) / **VF** £150 ($240) / **EF** £450 ($720)

2538 Kd. Rev. CONCORDIA AVGVST S C, Concordia seated, as 2465. RIC 112(b). BMCRE 194,
note. CBN 193. Cf. C 43. *[Rome, AD 80].*
F £60 ($96) / **VF** £150 ($240) / **EF** £450 ($720)

2539 Kc. Rev. PAX AVGVST S C, Pax stg. l., holding caduceus and olive-branch and resting on
column. RIC 114. BMCRE 195, note. CBN 195. C 149. *[Rome, AD 80].*
F £60 ($96) / **VF** £150 ($240) / **EF** £450 ($720)

2540 IMP T CAES DIVI VESP F AVG P M TR P P P COS VIII, c. Rev. ROMA S C, Roma seated l. on
cuirass, holding wreath and parazonium, shields behind. RIC 183 (attributed to
Lugdunum). BMCRE 314 (Lugdunum). CBN 325 (Bithynia). C 189. *[Rome, AD 80].*
F £70 ($112) / **VF** £175 ($280) / **EF** £525 ($840)

2541 Kd. Rev. SALVS AVG S C, Salus enthroned l., holding patera. RIC 116(b). BMCRE 197.
CBN 198. C 195. *[Rome, AD 80].*   F £60 ($96) / **VF** £150 ($240) / **EF** £450 ($720)

2542 Kd. Rev. SECVRITAS AVGVST S C, Securitas, in relaxed pose, enthroned l., holding sceptre
in r. hand, hd. propped on l., lighted altar at feet. Cf. RIC 118. Cf. BMCRE 199, note. CBN
200. C 257. *[Rome, AD 80].*   F £65 ($104) / **VF** £160 ($256) / **EF** £475 ($760)

2543 Kd. Rev. SECVRITAS P R S C, Securitas enthroned l., holding sceptre and resting l. arm on
throne, lighted altar at feet. Cf. RIC 119(b). BMCRE 199. CBN 202. C 263. *[Rome,*
AD 80].   F £60 ($96) / **VF** £150 ($240) / **EF** £450 ($720)

2544 Kc. Rev. VESTA S C, Vesta seated l., holding Palladium and sceptre. RIC 120(a). BMCRE
200. CBN 203. Cf. C 345. *[Rome, AD 80].*
F £60 ($96) / **VF** £150 ($240) / **EF** £450 ($720)

2545

2545   **Copper as.** Ka. Rev. AEQVITAS AVGVST S C, Aequitas stg. l., holding scales and sceptre. RIC 121(a). BMCRE 203. CBN 206. C 4. *[Rome, AD 80]*.

                                       F £55 ($88) / **VF** £140 ($224) / **EF** £425 ($680)

2546   Kb. Rev. AETERNIT AVG S C, Aeternitas stg. r., l. foot on globe, holding sceptre and cornucopiae. RIC 122(b). BMCRE 206. CBN 209. C 11. *[Rome, AD 80]*.

                                       F £65 ($104) / **VF** £160 ($256) / **EF** £475 ($760)

2547   Ka. Rev. FIDES PVBLICA S C, clasped hands holding caduceus, as 2474. RIC 125. BMCRE 266, †. CBN 214. C 90. *[Rome, AD 80]*.   **F** £60 ($96) / **VF** £150 ($240) / **EF** £450 ($720)

2548   Ka. Rev. GENI P R S C, Genius of the Roman People stg. l., sacrificing from patera over lighted altar and holding cornucopiae. RIC 126. BMCRE 209. CBN 215. C 96. *[Rome, AD 80]*.   **F** £60 ($96) / **VF** £150 ($240) / **EF** £450 ($720)

2549   Kb. Rev. PAX AVGVST S C, Pax stg. l., holding olive-branch and caduceus. RIC 129(b). BMCRE 212. CBN 219. C — (omitted in error, cf. 201 in 1st edition). *[Rome, AD 80]*.

                                       F £55 ($88) / **VF** £140 ($224) / **EF** £425 ($680)

2550   Ka. Rev. S C, Spes advancing l., holding flower. RIC 130. BMCRE 216. CBN 220. C 219. *[Rome, AD 80]*.   **F** £55 ($88) / **VF** £140 ($224) / **EF** £425 ($680)

2551 var.

2551   IMP T CAES VESP AVG P M TR P COS VII, b. Rev. VICTORIA AVGVST S C, Victory stg. r. on forepart of galley, as 2483. RIC 85. BMCRE p. 254, ‡ note. CBN 150. C 365. *[Rome, AD 79]*.   **F** £65 ($104) / **VF** £160 ($256) / **EF** £475 ($760)

2552   Similar, but with obv. Ka. RIC 133. BMCRE 217. CBN 222. C 368. *[Rome, AD 80]*.   **F** £60 ($96) / **VF** £150 ($240) / **EF** £450 ($720)

2553   **Brass semis.** IMP T VESP AVG COS VIII, winged caduceus between two crossed cornucopiae. Rev. S C in laurel-wreath. RIC —. BMCRE —. CBN —. C —. *[Samosata in Commagene, AD 80]*.   **F** £50 ($80) / **VF** £125 ($200) / **EF** £350 ($560)

2554   **Copper quadrans.** IMP T VESP AVG COS VIII, helmeted hd. of Minerva r. Rev. S C in lau-
        rel-wreath. RIC 135. BMCRE 219. CBN 225. C 251. *[Rome, AD 80].*
        F £40 ($64) / **VF** £100 ($160) / **EF** £250 ($400)

2555   Similar, but with obv. type modius. RIC 136. BMCRE 220. CBN 228. C 252. *[Rome, AD
        80].*   F £35 ($56) / **VF** £90 ($144) / **EF** £225 ($360)

For coins of Divus Titus and later restorations, see under Domitian (nos. 2885–6), Trajan, and
Trajan Decius.

Alexandrian Coinage

2556 var. (year 3)

2556   **Billon tetradrachm.** ΑΥΤΟΚ ΤΙΤΟΥ ΚΑΙΣ ΟΥΕΣΠΑΣΙΑΝΟΥ ΣΕΒ, laur. hd. r. Rev. ΟΜΟΝΟΙΑ,
        Homonoia (= Concordia) seated l., holding olive-branch, L B (= regnal year 2) before.
        Dattari 422. BMCG 278. Cologne 317. Milne 454. *[AD 79–80].*
        F £50 ($80) / **VF** £125 ($200)

2557   —— Rev. ΣΑΡΑΠΙΣ, bust of Sarapis r., wearing modius, L B (= regnal year 2) before.
        Dattari 426. BMCG —. Cologne 319. Milne 456. *[AD 79–80].*
        F £50 ($80) / **VF** £125 ($200)

2558   —— Rev. ΕΥΘΗΝΙΑ, bust of Euthenia (= Abundantia) r., wreathed with corn, corn-ears
        and poppies on breast, L Γ (= regnal year 3) before, star behind. Dattari 421. BMCG —.
        Cologne 321. Milne 464. *[AD 80–81].*   F £50 ($80) / **VF** £125 ($200)

2559   —— Rev. ΝΙΛΟΣ, bust of Nilus r., lotus-flower over r. shoulder, L Γ (= regnal year 3)
        before). Dattari 425 var. BMCG —. Cologne 324. Milne 462. *[AD 80–81].*
        F £50 ($80) / **VF** £125 ($200)

See also nos. 2375, 2379, and 2381. For other local coinages of this reign, see *Greek Imperial
Coins & Their Values*, pp. 73–6.

TITUS AND DOMITIAN CAESARS

*This type issued early in the reign of Vespasian features the names and images of his two sons,
Titus occupying the senior position on the obverse.*

2560   **Brass sestertius.** T CAES VESPASIAN IMP PON TR POT COS II, laur. hd. of Titus r. Rev.
        CAESAR DOMITIAN COS DES II S C, Domitian on horseback prancing l., holding sceptre
        surmounted by human hd. RIC *Vespasian* 605. BMCRE *Vespasian* 628. CBN *Vespasian*
        615. C *Titus* 27. *[Rome, AD 72].*   F £180 ($288) / **VF** £450 ($720) / **EF** £1,350 ($2,160)

Issues of Titus in honour of Divus Vespasian

2561　**Gold aureus.** DIVVS AVGVSTVS VESPASIANVS, laur. hd. of Vespasian r. Rev. EX S C, Victory advancing l., attaching shield to trophy, at foot of which mourning captive is seated l. RIC 59(a). BMCRE 112, note. CBN 89. C *Vespasian* 143. *[Rome, AD 80].*

　　　　　　　　　　　　　　　　　VF £5,000 ($8,000) / **EF** £12,500 ($20,000)

　　　This represents a final tribute to Vespasian's victory in the Jewish War (see also no. 2565).

2562　Obv. Similar. Rev. — empty triumphal quadriga l., surmounted by model of temple pediment with quadriga at centre flanked by two wreath-bearing Victories. RIC 60. BMCRE 118. CBN 92. C *Vespasian* 145. *[Rome, AD 80].*

　　　　　　　　　　　　　　　　　　VF £2,500 ($4,000) / **EF** £6,250 ($10,000)

　　　A last reference to the great triumph of Vespasian and Titus nine years before (see also no. 2566).

2563　Obv. Similar. Rev. — circular shield attached to lower part of column which is surmounted by urn and flanked by two laurel-branches (the S C inscribed on the shield). RIC 62. BMCRE 123. CBN 96. C *Vespasian* 148. *[Rome, AD 80].*

　　　　　　　　　　　　　　　　　　VF £2,500 ($4,000) / **EF** £6,250 ($10,000)

2564　Obv. Similar. Rev. S C on circular shield supported by two capricorns, back to back, globe below. RIC 63. BMCRE 128. CBN 100. C *Vespasian* 496. *[Rome, AD 80].*

　　　　　　　　　　　　　　　　　　VF £2,000 ($3,200) / **EF** £5,000 ($8,000)

　　　　　　　2565　　　　　　　　　　　　　2567

2565　**Silver denarius.** As 2561. RIC 59(a). BMCRE 112. CBN 90. RSC *Vespasian* 144. *[Rome, AD 80].*　　　　　　　　　　　　　　　　　**VF** £175 ($280) / **EF** £425 ($680)

2566　As 2562. RIC 60. BMCRE 119. CBN 94. RSC *Vespasian* 146. *[Rome, AD 80].*

　　　　　　　　　　　　　　　　　　　　　　VF £110 ($176) / **EF** £300 ($480)

2567　Similar, but with obv. legend DIVVS VESPASIANVS AVGVSTVS, and the quadriga on rev. is to r. Cf. RIC 61. BMCRE 117. CBN 91 RSC *Vespasian* 147a. *[Rome, AD 80].*

　　　　　　　　　　　　　　　　　　　　　　VF £140 ($224) / **EF** £350 ($560)

　　　　　　　2568　　　　　　　　　　　　　2569

2568　As 2563. RIC 62. BMCRE 125. CBN 98. RSC *Vespasian* 149. *[Rome, AD 80].*

　　　　　　　　　　　　　　　　　　　　　　VF £100 ($160) / **EF** £275 ($440)

2569   **Silver denarius.** As 2564. RIC 63. BMCRE 129. CBN 101. RSC *Vespasian* 497. *[Rome,*
       AD 80].   **VF** £90 ($144) / **EF** £250 ($400)

2570   **Silver quinarius.** DIVVS AVGVSTVS VESPASIANVS, laur. hd. of Vespasian r. Rev. VICTORIA
       AVGVST, Victory advancing r., holding wreath and palm. RIC 64. BMCRE 135. CBN —.
       RSC *Vespasian* 596b (= 616). *[Rome, AD 80].*   **VF** £250 ($400) / **EF** £600 ($960)

2571   **Brass sestertius.** Obv. Similar. Rev. S C, Spes advancing l., holding flower. RIC 147.
       BMCRE 249. CBN 261. C *Vespasian* 461. *[Rome, AD 80].*
                              F £180 ($288) / **VF** £450 ($720) / **EF** £1,350 ($2,160)

2572   DIVO AVG VESP S P Q R, team of four elephants drawing ornamented car r., surmounted by
       seated statue of Vespasian, holding sceptre and Victory. Rev. IMP T CAES DIVI VESP F AVG
       P M TR P P P COS VIII around large S C. RIC 143. BMCRE 221. CBN 229. C *Vespasian*
       205. *[Rome, AD 80].*   **F** £160 ($256) / **VF** £400 ($640) / **EF** £1,200 ($1,920)
       The obv. type is inspired by the coinage of Divus Augustus issued by Tiberius (see no.
       1784).

2573   Similar, but with obv. DIVVS AVGVSTVS VESP, Vespasian, rad., seated l., holding branch
       and sceptre. RIC 145. BMCRE 224. CBN 232. C *Vespasian* 207. *[Rome, AD 80].*
                              F £160 ($256) / **VF** £400 ($640) / **EF** £1,200 ($1,920)
       Another type based on a Divus Augustus issue of Tiberius (see no. 1782). Domitian also
       adopted this design for his coinage in honour of Divus Titus (see no. 2886).

2574   **Brass dupondius.** DIVVS AVGVSTVS VESPASIANVS, rad. hd. of Vespasian r. Rev. CONCORD
       AVGVST S C, Concordia seated l., holding patera and cornucopiae. RIC 149. BMCRE 251.
       CBN —. C *Vespasian* 63. *[Rome, AD 80].*
                              F £90 ($144) / **VF** £225 ($360) / **EF** £675 ($1,080)

2575   Obv. Similar, but hd. l. Rev. VESTA S C, Vesta enthroned l., holding Palladium and sceptre.
       RIC 150. BMCRE p. 277, †. CBN 262. C *Vespasian* 576. *[Rome, AD 80].*
                              F £90 ($144) / **VF** £225 ($360) / **EF** £675 ($1,080)

2576   **Copper as.** Obv. As 2574. Rev. AEQVITAS AVGVST S C, Aequitas stg. l., holding scales
       and sceptre. RIC 151. BMCRE p. 277, ‡. CBN 263. C *Vespasian* 7. *[Rome, AD 80].*
                              F £80 ($128) / **VF** £200 ($320) / **EF** £600 ($960)

For later issues in honour of Divus Vespasian, see under Domitian (no. 2887), Trajan, and Trajan
Decius.

Issues of Titus in honour of his deceased mother Domitilla († before AD 69)

Flavia Domitilla, the wife of Vespasian, was honoured by both her sons on the coinages of their
reigns. It was scandalously rumoured that she possessed only Latin status, until her father
Liberalis produced evidence of her Roman citizenship. She was the mother not only of Titus and
Domitian but also of a daughter (another Flavia Domitilla) who, like her mother, died prior to
Vespasian's accession to the throne. The sestertii issued under Titus accord her neither the rank
of Augusta nor the title Diva, whereas Domitian's gold and silver, struck several years later, give
her both. It would seem she was granted these honours early in Domitian's reign to bring her
coinage into line with the contemporary issues celebrating the other Flavian 'Divi', Vespasian
and Titus.

2577

2577   **Brass sestertius.** MEMORIAE DOMITILLAE S P Q R, carpentum drawn r. by two mules. Rev.
         IMP T CAES DIVI VESP F AVG P M TR P P P COS VIII around large S C. RIC 153. BMCRE
         226. CBN 234. C *Domitilla Junior* 1. *[Rome, AD 80].*
                                    F £300 ($480) / **VF** £750 ($1,200) / **EF** £2,250 ($3,600)

2578

2578   Similar, but with obv. legend DOMITILLAE IMP CAES VES (or VESP) AVG S P Q R. RIC 154.
         BMCRE 229. CBN 235. C *Domitilla Junior* 3. *[Rome, AD 80].*
                                    F £500 ($800) / **VF** £1,250 ($2,000) / **EF** £3,750 ($6,000)

For coins issued in the name of Diva Domitilla, see under Domitian (nos. 2887–8).

The Restoration Coinage of Titus

*This remarkable series was intended to recall memories of Rome's imperial (i.e. Julio-Claudian)
past. The recently established Flavian dynasty was anxious to strengthen its position by emphasiz-
ing continuity with the old regime and to that end Vespasian had adopted a number of coin types
from earlier issues. This was carried a step further by Titus who, in AD 80, restored a whole range
of Julio-Claudian aes types from Divus Augustus to Claudius, with the surprising addition of
Galba. The reason for Galba's inclusion is uncertain, though the intent may have been to stress
that membership of the Julio-Claudian family was not a prerequisite for imperial office, Galba having been the first 'outsider' to occupy the throne following the downfall of Nero. The idea was
revived at the beginning of each of the following two reigns, though the Domitianic series is of
more limited scope (see nos. 2892–9) and that of Nerva is restricted to Divus Augustus and
includes a silver denarius (see nos. 3075–83).*

Divus Augustus

2579 var.

2579 **Brass sestertius.** DIVVS AVGVSTVS PATER, Augustus, rad., seated l., holding branch and sceptre, altar at feet. Rev. IMP T CAES DIVI VESP F AVG P M TR P P P COS VIII around large S C above which, REST. RIC 184. BMCRE 261. CBN 276. C *Augustus* 548. *[Rome, AD 80].*
                                                                F £160 ($256) / **VF** £400 ($640) / **EF** £1,200 ($1,920)
For the prototype of this restoration, see no. 1782.

2580

2580 **Brass dupondius.** DIVVS AVGVSTS PATER, rad. hd. of Augustus l. Rev. IMP T VESP AVG REST S C, Victory alighting l., wings spread, holding shield inscribed S P Q R. RIC 189. BMCRE 265. CBN 278. C *Augustus* 557. *[Rome, AD 80].*
                                                                F £120 ($192) / **VF** £300 ($480) / **EF** £900 ($1,440)
For the prototype of this restoration, see no. 1786.

2581

2581 **Copper as.** Obv. Similar. Rev. IMP T VESP AVG REST S C, façade of altar-enclosure of the *Ara Providentiae Augusti*, with double panelled door and horns of the altar visible above, PROVIDENT (NT in monogram) below. RIC 191. BMCRE 268. CBN 281. C *Augustus* 559. *[Rome, AD 80].*   F £80 ($128) / **VF** £200 ($320) / **EF** £600 ($960)
For the prototype of this restoration, see no. 1789. For a similar restoration by Domitian, see no. 2892, and for another by Nerva, see no. 3080.

Divus Augustus

2582 **Copper as.** Similar, but with star above hd. of Augustus, and with rev. legend IMP T CAES AVG REST S C. RIC —. BMCRE 271. CBN 280. Cf. C *Augustus* 558. *[Rome, AD 80]*
F £90 ($144) / **VF** £225 ($360) / **EF** £675 ($1,080)

2583 DIVVS AVGVSTVS PATER, rad. hd. of Augustus l. Rev. IMP T VESP AVG REST S C, eagle stg. facing on globe, hd. r., wings open. RIC 197. BMCRE 272. CBN 284. C *Augustus* 551. *[Rome, AD 80]*. F £80 ($128) / **VF** £200 ($320) / **EF** £600 ($960)
For the prototype of this restoration, see no.1790. For a similar restoration by Domitian, see no. 2893, and for another by Nerva, see no. 3082.

2584 Similar, but with star above hd. of Augustus, and with rev. legend IMP T CAES AVG RESTITVIT S C. Cf. RIC 198. BMCRE 275. CBN —. C *Augustus* —. *[Rome, AD 80]*.
F £90 ($144) / **VF** £225 ($360) / **EF** £675 ($1,080)

2585 Similar to 2583, but the eagle stands on thunderbolt, its hd. turned to l. RIC 206. BMCRE 278. CBN 287. C *Augustus* 554. *[Rome, AD 80]*.
F £80 ($128) / **VF** £200 ($320) / **EF** £600 ($960)
Although lacking a true prototype, this variety was issued also under Nerva (see no. 3083).

Livia

2586 **Brass dupondius.** IVSTITIA, diad. and dr. bust of Livia, as Justitia, r. Rev. IMP T CAES DIVI VESP F AVG REST around large S C. RIC 218. BMCRE 289. CBN 301. C *Livia* 9. *[Rome, AD 80]*. F £175 ($280) / **VF** £450 ($720) / **EF** £1,500 ($2,400)
For the prototype of this restoration, see no. 1739.

2587 Similar, but with rev. IMP T CAES DIVI VESP F AVG P M / TR P P P COS VIII RESTITV in two concentric circles around large S C. RIC 220. BMCRE 290, note. CBN 303. C *Livia* 10. *[Rome, AD 80]*. F £200 ($320) / **VF** £500 ($800) / **EF** £1,650 ($2,640)

2588 PIETAS, veiled, diad. and dr. bust of Livia, as Pietas, r. Rev. IMP T CAES DIVI VESP F AVG RESTIT around large S C. RIC 222. BMCRE 291, note. CBN 304. C *Livia* 11. *[Rome, AD 80]*. F £175 ($280) / **VF** £450 ($720) / **EF** £1,500 ($2,400)
For the prototype of this restoration, see no. 1741.

Agrippa

2589

2589 **Copper as.** M AGRIPPA L F COS III, hd. of Agrippa l., wearing rostral crown. Rev. IMP T VESP AVG REST S C, Neptune stg. l., holding dolphin and trident. RIC 209. BMCRE 281. CBN 289. C *Agrippa* 6. *[Rome, AD 80]*. F £80 ($128) / **VF** £200 ($320) / **EF** £600 ($960)
For the prototype of this restoration, see no. 1812. For a similar restoration by Domitian, see no. 2894.

Tiberius

2590   **Brass sestertius.** CIVITATIBVS ASIAE RESTITVT, Tiberius seated l. on curule chair, holding
        patera and sceptre. Rev. IMP T CAES DIVI VESP F AVG P M TR P P P COS VIII around large
        S C above which, REST. RIC 210. BMCRE 282. CBN 291. Cf. C *Tiberius* 71. *[Rome,*
        AD 80].   **F** £200 ($320) / **VF** £500 ($800) / **EF** £1,750 ($2,800)
        For the prototype of this restoration, see no. 1764.

2591   **Copper as.** TI CAESAR DIVI AVG F AVGVST IMP VIII, bare hd. of Tiberius l. Rev. IMP T
        CAES DIVI VESP F AVG REST around large S C. RIC 211. BMCRE 284. CBN 293. C
        Tiberius 73. *[Rome, AD 80].*   **F** £80 ($128) / **VF** £200 ($320) / **EF** £600 ($960)
        For the prototype of this restoration, see no. 1770.

2592   Similar, but with rev. IMP T CAES DIVI VESP F AVG P M / TR P P P COS VIII RESTITVIT in
        two concentric circles around large S C. RIC 212. BMCRE 285. CBN 295. C *Tiberius* 75.
        [Rome, AD 80].   **F** £90 ($144) / **VF** £225 ($360) / **EF** £675 ($1,080)

2593   Similar, but with rev. IMP T CAES DIVI VESP F AVG REST S C, winged caduceus. RIC 215.
        BMCRE p. 286, †. CBN 297. C *Tiberius* 72. *[Rome, AD 80].*
                                            F £80 ($128) / **VF** £200 ($320) / **EF** £600 ($960)
        For the prototype of this restoration, see no. 1771.

Drusus

2594   **Copper as.** DRVSVS CAESAR TI AVG F DIVI AVG N, bare hd. of Drusus l. Rev. IMP T CAES
        DIVI VESP F AVG REST around large S C. RIC 216. BMCRE 286. CBN 298. Cf. C *Drusus* 6.
        [Rome, AD 80].   **F** £90 ($144) / **VF** £225 ($360) / **EF** £675 ($1,080)
        For the prototype of this restoration, see no. 1794. For a similar restoration by Domitian,
        see no. 2896.

2595   Similar, but with rev. IMP T CAES DIVI VESP F AVG P M / TR P P P COS VIII RESTITV in two
        concentric circles around large S C. RIC 217. Cf. BMCRE 288. CBN 300. C *Drusus* 7.
        [Rome, AD 80].   **F** £100 ($160) / **VF** £250 ($400) / **EF** £750 ($1,200)

Nero Claudius Drusus

2596   **Brass sestertius.** NERO CLAVDIVS DRVSVS GERMANICVS IMP, bare hd. of Nero Claudius
        Drusus l. Rev. IMP T CAES DIVI VESP F AVG P M TR P P P COS VIII around large SC above
        which, REST. RIC 225. BMCRE 292. CBN —. Cf. C *Nero Claudius Drusus* 10. *[Rome,*
        AD 80].   **F** £400 ($640) / **VF** £1,000 ($1,600) / **EF** £3,000 ($4,800)
        For the prototypes, see nos. 1896–7. The obverse type only is depicted on the restored
        issue.

Germanicus

2597   **Copper as.** GERMANICVS CAESAR TI AVG F DIVI AVG N, bare hd. of Germanicus r. Rev.
        IMP T CAES DIVI VESP F AVG REST around large S C. RIC 226. BMCRE 283, note. CBN
        306. C *Germanicus* 12. *[Rome, AD 80].*   **F** £80 ($128) / **VF** £200 ($320) / **EF** £600 ($960)
        For the prototype of this restoration, see no. 1905.

Germanicus

2597

2598   **Copper as.** Similar, but with bare hd. of Germanicus l. RIC 228. BMCRE 293. CBN —. C
—. *[Rome, AD 80].*   **F** £90 ($144) / **VF** £225 ($360) / **EF** £675 ($1,080)
*For the prototype of this restoration, see no. 1822. For a similar restoration by Domitian,
see no. 2897.*

2599   Similar, but with rev. IMP T CAES DIVI VESP F AVG P M / TR P P P COS VIII RESTITVIT in
two concentric circles around large S C. RIC 230. BMCRE 295. CBN —. C *Germanicus*
14. *[Rome, AD 80].*   **F** £100 ($160) / **VF** £250 ($400) / **EF** £750 ($1,200)

Agrippina Senior

2600   **Brass sestertius.** AGRIPPINA M F GERMANICI CAESARIS, dr. bust of Agrippina Senior r.
Rev. IMP T CAES DIVI VESP F AVG P M TR P P P COS VIII around large S C above which,
REST. RIC 231. BMCRE 296. CBN 307. C *Agrippina Senior* 4. *[Rome, AD 80].*
F £500 ($800) / **VF** £1,250 ($2,000) / **EF** £3,750 ($6,000)
For the prototype of this restoration, see no. 1906.

Claudius

2601

2601   **Brass sestertius.** TI CLAVDIVS CAESAR AVG P M TR P IMP P P, laur. hd. of Claudius r. Rev.
IMP T VESP AVG REST S C, Spes advancing l., holding flower. RIC 234. BMCRE 297. CBN
308. C *Claudius* 103. *[Rome, AD 80].*
F £175 ($280) / **VF** £450 ($720) / **EF** £1,500 ($2,400)
For the prototype of this restoration, see no. 1854.

2602   Similar, but laur. hd. of Claudius l. RIC 232. BMCRE 298. CBN 309. C *Claudius* 104.
[Rome, AD 80].   **F** £200 ($320) / **VF** £500 ($800) / **EF** £1,650 ($2,640)
For a similar restoration by Domitian, see no. 2898.

Claudius

2603 var.

2603 **Brass dupondius.** TI CLAVDIVS CAES AVG P M TR P IMP P P, bare hd. of Claudius r. Rev. IMP T VESP AVG REST S C, Ceres enthroned l., holding corn-ears and torch. RIC 236. BMCRE p. 290, *. Cf. CBN 312. C *Claudius* 102. *[Rome, AD 80].*
F £100 ($160) / **VF** £250 ($400) / **EF** £750 ($1,200)
For the prototype, see no. 1856. The original issue has CAESAR *for* CAES *and the emperor's head is to left.*

2604 **Copper as.** TI CL CAESAR AVG P M TR P IMP P P, bare hd. of Claudius r. Rev. IMP TITVS VESP REST S C, Constantia, helmeted, stg. l., r. hand raised, holding sceptre in l. RIC 239. BMCRE p. 290, † note. CBN 314. C *Claudius* 107. *[Rome, AD 80].*
F £90 ($144) / **VF** £225 ($360) / **EF** £675 ($1,080)
For the prototype, see no. 1858. The original issue has CLAVDIVS *for* CL *and the emperor's head is to left.*

2605 TI CLAVDIVS CAESAR AVG P M TR P IMP P P, bare hd. of Claudius r. Rev. IMP T VESP AVG REST S C, Minerva advancing r., brandishing spear and holding shield. RIC 241. BMCRE 300. CBN 315. Cf. C *Claudius* 105. *[Rome, AD 80].*
F £80 ($128) / **VF** £200 ($320) / **EF** £600 ($960)

2606 Similar, but bare hd. of Claudius l. RIC 243. BMCRE 300, note. CBN 317. Cf. C *Claudius* 106. *[Rome, AD 80].*
F £90 ($144) / **VF** £225 ($360) / **EF** £675 ($1,080)
For the prototype of this restoration, see no. 1862. For a similar restoration by Domitian, see no. 2899.

Galba

2607 **Brass sestertius.** IMP SER SVLP GALBA CAES AVG TR P, laur. hd. of Galba r. Rev. IMP T CAES DIVI VESP F AVG P M TR P P P COS VIII around large S C above which, REST. RIC 245. BMCRE 305. CBN 319. C *Galba* 350. *[Rome, AD 80].*
F £500 ($800) / **VF** £1,250 ($2,000) / **EF** £3,750 ($6,000)
This is merely a restoration of a typical obverse type of a Galba sestertius.

2608 **Brass dupondius.** SER GALBA IMP CAES AVG TR P , laur. hd. of Galba r. Rev. IMP T VESP AVG REST S C, Pax stg. l., firing heap of arms with torch and holding cornucopiae. RIC 249. BMCRE p. 292, ‡. CBN 320. C *Galba* 353. *[Rome, AD 80].*
F £250 ($400) / **VF** £600 ($960) / **EF** £1,750 ($2,800)
This is a restoration of a Galba as with legend PAXS AVGVSTI *(cf. RIC 496–8, for the reverse type).*

2609 **Copper as.** Obv. Similar. Rev. — Libertas stg. l., holding pileus and sceptre. RIC 248. BMCRE p. 292, †. CBN 322. C *Galba* 352. *[Rome, AD 80].*
F £200 ($320) / **VF** £500 ($800) / **EF** £1,500 ($2,400)
For the prototype of the reverse, see no. 2134.

JULIA

2611

Flavia Julia was the daughter of Titus by his second wife, Marcia Furnilla, and was born about AD 65, shortly before her parents' divorce. She married her cousin Flavius Sabinus and was granted the title of Augusta during her father's reign (AD 79–81). Her husband was Domitian's colleague in the consulship in AD 82 but two years later he was executed on the emperor's orders. Thereafter, Julia lived with her uncle Domitian as his mistress and on her death, circa AD 89, she was deified. Coins in the name of Julia were struck in gold, silver and aes. The earlier issues belong to the reign of Titus and were probably produced on the occasion of Julia's elevation to the rank of Augusta. Her later coinage was struck under Domitian, the final issues being posthumous aurei and sestertii. It is of some interest that Julia was the first Roman empress to be honoured with the issue of regular Roman coin denominations – in precious metal as well as aes – produced solely in her own name.

2610   **Silver denarius.** IVLIA AVGVSTA T AVG F, diad. and dr. bust of Julia r. Rev. SALVS AVG, Salus seated l., holding patera. RIC *Titus* 54. BMCRE *Titus* 139. CBN —. RSC 11. *[Rome, AD 79–80].*   **VF** £850 ($1,360) / **EF** £2,200 ($3,520)

2611   Obv. Similar. Rev. VENVS AVG, Venus stg. r., viewed partially from behind, holding helmet and spear and resting on column. RIC *Titus* 55a. BMCRE *Titus* 140. CBN *Titus* 103. RSC 12. *[Rome, AD 79–80].*   **VF** £650 ($1,040) / **EF** £1,650 ($2,640)

2612

2612   Similar, but with obv. legend IVLIA AVGVSTA TITI AVGVSTI F and rev. legend VENVS AVGVST. RIC *Titus* 56. BMCRE *Titus* 141. CBN *Titus* 106. RSC 14. *[Rome, AD 79–80].*
                                       VF £600 ($960) / **EF** £1,500 ($2,400)

2613   IVLIA IMP T AVG F AVGVSTA, dr. bust of Julia r., hair in short queue. Rev. VESTA, Vesta seated l., holding Palladium and sceptre. RIC *Titus* 57. BMCRE *Titus* p. 424, 143 *bis.* CBN *Titus* 103. RSC 16. *[Rome, AD 79–80].*   **VF** £750 ($1,200) / **EF** £1,850 ($2,960)

2614   Similar, but Julia's hair is piled in bun behind, and with rev. legend VESTA S C. RIC *Titus* 58. BMCRE *Titus* 144. CBN *Titus* 110. RSC 17. *[Rome, AD 79–80].*
                                       VF £800 ($1,280) / **EF** £2,000 ($3,200)

2615   **Brass dupondius.** Obv. As 2613 or 2614. Rev. CERES AVGVST S C, Ceres stg. l., holding corn-ears and long torch. RIC *Titus* 177. BMCRE *Titus* 253, 255. CBN *Titus* 264, 265. C 2. *[Rome, AD 79–80].*   **F** £250 ($400) / **VF** £600 ($960) / **EF** £1,800 ($2,880)

2615

2616   **Brass dupondius.** Obv. As 2614. Rev. CONCORDIA AVG S C, Concordia seated l., holding
patera and cornucopiae. RIC *Titus* 178. BMCRE *Titus* p. 279, *. CBN *Titus* 268. C 3.
[Rome, AD 79–80].   **F** £275 ($440) / **VF** £650 ($1,040) / **EF** £2,000 ($3,200)

2617

2617   Obv. As 2613 or 2614. Rev. VESTA S C, Vesta seated l., holding Palladium and sceptre. RIC
Titus 180. BMCRE *Titus* 256, 257. CBN *Titus* 270, 271. C 18. *[Rome, AD 79–80].*
F £225 ($360) / **VF** £550 ($880) / **EF** £1,600 ($2,560)

For later issues in the name of Julia, see under Domitian (nos. 2885, 2889–91, and 2912–14).

DOMITIAN
13 Sep. AD 81–18 Sep. 96

2780 var.

*Titus Flavius Domitianus, the younger son of Vespasian and Flavia Domitilla, was born on
24 October AD 51. He was in Rome at the time of his father's rebellion against Vitellius in the summer of AD 69 and was lucky to escape with his life when he and his uncle, Flavius Sabinus, were
besieged on the Capitol in the final days of Vitellius' regime. Although given the rank of Caesar,
like his elder brother Titus, he was kept very much in the background during the 10-year reign of
Vespasian. The bitter resentment which he felt over his treatment at this time and the inferiority of
his status in the imperial family eventually found expression in the highly autocratic behaviour
which he exhibited when he succeeded to the imperial throne on the early death of Titus in AD 81.*

Domitian has gone down in history as one of the worst of the Roman tyrants and it is true that his memory was condemned by the Senate immediately following his death. But this harsh judgement is not fully borne out by the facts and owes much to the bitter feelings of a resentful aristocracy. He certainly exhibited cruelty in dealing with those he considered to be his enemies and this increased with the discovery of plots against his regime, especially after the rebellion in AD 89 of Saturninus, governor of Upper Germany. However, he exhibited some aptitude as a military commander during his campaigns on the Rhine and Danube and the frontier arrangements between the two rivers were improved. He was, in fact, the first emperor since Claudius in AD 43 to campaign in person. He maintained high moral standards in public performances and showed respect for religious ritual. As a builder he was tireless, restoring the temple of Jupiter on the Capitol in monumental style and adding significantly to the imperial palace on the Palatine. In financial affairs, he improved the weight and quality of the precious metal coinage and raised military pay by one-third, thereby ensuring his continued popularity with the army and the praetorian guard. The people were entertained with frequent public spectacles and banquets, and in October of AD 88 the Secular Games were celebrated in Rome with great pomp and ceremony. Domitian's relations with the Senate, however, remained strained at best and were sometimes openly hostile. The executions of at least twelve ex-consuls are recorded during this reign, a state of affairs which led inevitably to further conspiracies and ultimately to the emperor's violent downfall. In the late summer of AD 96 a palace cabal, involving the court chamberlain and possibly even the Empress Domitia Longina, hatched a plot against the emperor's life and on 18 September Domitian fell victim to the assassin's knife in his private apartments. Thus ended Rome's second imperial dynasty which had lasted a mere twenty-seven years.

The traditional attribution to Lugdunum of certain aes issues of the early part of this reign, characterized by massive portraits, seriffed lettering, and flat reverse fields, has been challenged by Michael Grant (Essays in Roman Coinage presented to Harold Mattingly, 1956) and more recently by H.A. Cahn ('An imperial mint in Bithynia', Israel Numismatic Journal, 1984–5). These issues were in continuation of a series which had commenced under Titus. Ian Carradice ('Coinage and Finances in the Reign of Domitian', pp. 118–21) rejects the Bithynian attribution and prefers to integrate these coins into the main sequence of issues from the senatorial mint, seeing in them the output of a single officina exhibiting distinctive characteristics. The question can hardly be regarded as settled, but for the purposes of this catalogue all the aes coinage of Domitian's reign has been given to Rome.

For the titles and powers of this reign, including Alexandrian regnal dates, see table on p. 309.

The following obv. legends and types are represented by upper and lower case letters. All other varieties are described in full:

As Caesar

A. CAES DIVI AVG VESP F DOMITIAN (or DOMITIANVS) COS VII
B. CAES DIVI VESP F DOMITIAN (or DOMITIANVS) COS VII
C. CAES (or CAESAR) AVG F DOMIT (or DOMITIAN or DOMITIANVS) COS II (- VII)
D. CAESAR AVG F DOMITIANVS
E. CAESAR DIVI F DOMITIANVS COS VII

As Augustus

F. DOMITIANVS AVGVSTVS
G. IMP CAES DIVI VESP F DOMITIAN AVG P M
H. IMP CAES DOMIT AVG GERM COS XI CENS POT P P
I. IMP CAES DOMIT AVG GERM COS XI (- XVII) CENS PER P P
J. IMP CAES DOMIT AVG GERM P M TR P IIII (- XVI)
K. IMP CAES DOMIT AVG GERM P M TR P VIII CENS PER P P
L. IMP CAES DOMIT (or DOMITIAN) AVG GERM COS X (or XI)
M. IMP CAES DOMITIANVS AVG GERMANIC (or GERMANICVS)
N. IMP CAES DOMITIANVS AVG P M

a. Laur. hd. of Domitian r.
b. Laur. hd. of Domitian r., with aegis on neck
c. Rad. hd. of Domitian r.
d. Rad. hd. of Domitian r., with aegis on neck

Issues as Caesar under Vespasian, AD 69–79

(All RIC, BMCRE and CBN references are to the coinage of Vespasian)

         2618   2619

2618   **Gold aureus.** Da. Rev. CERES AVGVST, Ceres stg. l., holding corn-ears and long torch. RIC
        248. BMCRE 322. CBN 283. C 29. *[Rome, AD 76–8].*
                              VF £1,100 ($1,760) / **EF** £2,750 ($4,400)

2619   Da. Rev. COS IIII, cornucopiae. RIC 237. BMCRE 196. CBN 171. C 46. *[Rome, AD 76].*
                              VF £1,100 ($1,760) / **EF** £2,750 ($4,400)

         2620   2621

2620   Da. Rev. COS V, barbarian kneeling r., presenting standard with vexillum. RIC 240.
        BMCRE 231. CBN 205. C 48. *[Rome, AD 77–8].*
                              VF £1,200 ($1,920) / **EF** £3,000 ($4,800)
        The reverse type is copied from the coinage of Augustus (see no. 1603).

2621   Da. Rev. — she-wolf stg. l., suckling the twins Romulus and Remus, boat in ex. RIC 241.
        BMCRE 237. CBN 210. C 50. *[Rome, AD 77–8].*
                              VF £1,200 ($1,920) / **EF** £3,000 ($4,800)

2622   C (CAES, DOMIT COS III) a. Rev. PRINCEPS IVVENTVT, Spes advancing l., holding flower.
        RIC 233. BMCRE 155. CBN 131. C 374. *[Rome, AD 74–5].*
                              VF £1,100 ($1,760) / **EF** £2,750 ($4,400)

2623   C (CAESAR, DOMITIANVS COS VI) a. Rev. PRINCEPS IVVENTVTIS, Vesta enthroned l., hold-
        ing Palladium and sceptre. RIC 244. BMCRE 260. CBN 231. C 377. *[Rome, AD 79].*
                              VF £1,100 ($1,760) / **EF** £2,750 ($4,400)

2624   C (CAESAR, DOMITIANVS COS VI) a. Rev. — Salus stg. r., feeding snake and resting on
        column. RIC 243. BMCRE 264. CBN 235. C 383. *[Rome, AD 79].*
                              VF £1,100 ($1,760) / **EF** £2,750 ($4,400)

2625   **Gold aureus.** C (CAESAR, DOMITIANVS COS VI) a. Rev. PRINCEPS IVVENTVTIS, clasped r.
        hands holding legionary eagle set on prow. RIC 246. BMCRE 267. CBN 239. C 392.
        [Rome, AD 79].   **VF** £1,200 ($1,920) / **EF** £3,000 ($4,800)

2626   C (CAES, DOMIT COS II) a. Rev. VESTA, circular shrine of Vesta on the Palatine, showing
        four columns, flanked by two statues on pedestals, statue of Vesta within. RIC 230.
        BMCRE 412 (attributed to Lugdunum). CBN —. C 614 var. *[Rome, AD 73].*
                                                            VF £2,500 ($4,000) / **EF** £6,000 ($9,600)
        *The Aedicula Vestae was built by Augustus in 12 BC and was located close to his house on
        the Palatine. It had already appeared on a dupondius of Divus Augustus issued under
        Tiberius in AD 22–3 (see no. 1785) half a century before its appearance on a series of aurei
        issued under Vespasian (see also nos. 2255 and 2423).*

                        2622   2627

2627   C (CAES, DOMIT COS II) a. Rev. No legend, Domitian on horseback prancing l., r. hand
        raised, holding human-headed sceptre in l. RIC 232. BMCRE 123. CBN 100. C 663.
        [Rome, AD 73].   **VF** £1,200 ($1,920) / **EF** £3,000 ($4,800)

2628   **Silver denarius (provincial series).** DOMITIANVS CAESAR AVG F, bare-headed, dr. and
        cuir. bust r. Rev. AVG, EPHE (PHE in monogram) below, all within oak-wreath. RIC 247.
        BMCRE 469. CBN 362. RSC 22. *[Ephesus, AD 71].*   **VF** £200 ($320) / **EF** £500 ($800)

2629   Similar, but with rev. CONCORDIA AVG, Ceres enthroned l., holding corn-ears and cornu-
        copiae, EPHE (PHE in monogram) in ex. RIC 348. BMCRE 470. CBN 363. RSC 38.
        [Ephesus, AD 71].   **VF** £175 ($280) / **EF** £450 ($720)

                        2630   2631

2630   Similar, but with rev. PACI AVGVSTAE, Victory advancing r., holding wreath and palm,
        EPHE (PHE in monogram) in lower field to r. RIC 349. BMCRE 473. CBN 365. RSC 336.
        [Ephesus, AD 71].   **VF** £200 ($320) / **EF** £500 ($800)

2631   Similar, but with rev. PACI ORB TERR AVG, turreted and dr. female bust r., EPHE (PHE in
        monogram) below. RIC 350. BMCRE 474. CBN —. RSC 337. *[Ephesus, AD 71].*
                                                            VF £225 ($360) / **EF** £550 ($880)

2632   C (CAES, DOMIT COS III) a (with mint mark small 'O' below bust). Rev. FIDES PVBL, clasped
        r. hands holding winged caduceus between corn-ears and poppies. RIC —. BMCRE 480.
        CBN —. RSC 117a. *[Ephesus, AD 76].*   **VF** £110 ($176) / **EF** £300 ($480)

2633 **Silver denarius (provincial series).** C (CAES, DOMIT COS III) a (with mint mark small 'O' below bust). Rev. PRINCEPS IVVENTVT, Spes advancing l., holding flower. RIC 380. BMCRE 481. CBN —. RSC 375a. *[Ephesus, AD 76].*   **VF** £110 ($176) / **EF** £300 ($480)

2634 Da (with mint mark small 'O' below bust). Rev. COS IIII, eagle stg. facing on garlanded base, hd. r. RIC 381. BMCRE 487. CBN —. RSC 45c. *[Ephesus, AD 76].*
VF £110 ($176) / **EF** £300 ($480)

2635 —— Rev. PON MAX TR P COS IIII, winged caduceus. RIC 383. BMCRE 489. CBN 377. RSC 369. *[Ephesus, AD 76].*   **VF** £110 ($176) / **EF** £300 ($480)

2636 **Silver denarius (regular series).** As 2618 (rev. CERES AVGVST, Ceres stg.). RIC 248. BMCRE 323. CBN 285. RSC 30. *[Rome, AD 76–8].*   **VF** £75 ($120) / **EF** £210 ($336)

2637   2638

2637 Da. Rev. COS IIII, Pegasus stepping r. RIC 238. BMCRE 193. CBN 169. RSC 47. *[Rome, AD 76].*   **VF** £85 ($136) / **EF** £240 ($384)
The reverse type is copied from the coinage of Augustus (see no. 1629).

2638 Da. Rev. COS V, helmeted horseman galloping r., his r. hand extended and trailing behind him. RIC 242. BMCRE 234. CBN 207. RSC 49. *[Rome, AD 77–8].*
VF £85 ($136) / **EF** £240 ($384)
The reverse type would appear to be inspired by the coinage of Galba (see nos. 2094 and 2104).

2639   2643

2639 As 2621 (rev. COS V, wolf and twins). RIC 241. BMCRE 240. CBN 208. RSC 51. *[Rome, AD 77–8].*   **VF** £85 ($136) / **EF** £240 ($384)

2640 Similar to 2633 (rev. PRINCEPS IVVENTVT, Spes) but without mint mark below hd. on obv. RIC 233. BMCRE 156. CBN 135. RSC 375. *[Rome, AD 74].*
VF £75 ($120) / **EF** £210 ($336)

2641 As 2623 (rev. PRINCEPS IVVENTVTIS, Vesta enthroned). RIC 244. BMCRE 262. CBN 233. RSC 378. *[Rome, AD 79].*   **VF** £75 ($120) / **EF** £210 ($336)

2642 As 2624 (rev. PRINCEPS IVVENTVTIS, Salus resting on column). RIC 243. BMCRE 265. CBN 237. RSC 384. *[Rome, AD 79].*   **VF** £75 ($120) / **EF** £210 ($336)

2643 **Silver denarius (regular series).** As 2625 (rev. PRINCEPS IVVENTVTIS, clasped hands
      holding legionary eagle). RIC 246. BMCRE 269. CBN 240. RSC 393. *[Rome, AD 79]*.
                                                     VF £85 ($136) / **EF** £240 ($384)

2644

2644 As 2627 (rev. no legend, Domitian on horseback). RIC 232. BMCRE 129. CBN 105. RSC
      664. *[Rome, AD 73]*.   **VF** £100 ($160) / **EF** £275 ($440)

2645 **Silver quinarius.** C (CAES, DOMIT COS II) a. Rev. VICTORIA AVGVSTI, Victory advancing
      r., holding wreath and palm. Cf. RIC 231. Cf. BMCRE p. 23, †. CBN 107. RSC 632.
      [Rome, AD 73].   **VF** £200 ($320) / **EF** £500 ($800)

2646 var.

2646 C (CAESAR, DOMITIANVS COS VI) a. Rev. VICTORIA AVGVST, Victory seated l., holding
      wreath and palm. Cf. RIC 247. BMCRE p. 48, *. CBN 243. RSC 623. *[Rome, AD 79]*.
                                                     VF £200 ($320) / **EF** £500 ($800)

2647 **Brass sestertius.** C (CAESAR, DOMITIANVS COS V) a. Rev. ANNONA AVGVST S C,
      Annona enthroned l., holding sack of corn-ears on lap. RIC 717. BMCRE 743. CBN 788.
      C 21. *[Rome, AD 77–8]*.   **F** £130 ($208) / **VF** £325 ($520) / **EF** £950 ($1,520)

2648 C (CAESAR, DOMITIANVS COS II) a. Rev. PAX AVGVST S C, Pax stg. l., holding olive-
      branch and cornucopiae. RIC 693. BMCRE 678. CBN —. C —. *[Rome, AD 73]*.
                                     F £130 ($208) / **VF** £325 ($520) / **EF** £950 ($1,520)

2649 — laur., dr. and cuir. bust r. Rev. S C, Spes advancing l., holding flower. RIC 694(b).
      BMCRE 679, note. CBN 692. C 445. *[Rome, AD 73]*.
                                     F £130 ($208) / **VF** £325 ($520) / **EF** £950 ($1,520)

2650 **Brass dupondius.** C (CAESAR, DOMITIAN COS V), laur. and dr. bust r. Rev. CERES AVGVST
      S C, Ceres stg. l., holding corn-ears and long torch. RIC 720. BMCRE p. 176, ‡. CBN 790.
      C 31. *[Rome, AD 77–8]*.   **F** £55 ($88) / **VF** £130 ($208) / **EF** £350 ($560)

2651 C (CAESAR, DOMITIAN COS II), laur. and dr. bust r. Rev. FELICITAS PVBLICA S C, Felicitas
      stg. l., holding caduceus and cornucopiae. Cf. RIC 695(a). BMCRE p. 157, * note. CBN
      693. Cf. C 98. *[Rome, AD 73]*. **F** £55 ($88) / **VF** £130 ($208) / **EF** £350 ($560)

2652 Similar, but with obv. bust to l. Cf. RIC 695(b). BMCRE p. 157, * note. CBN 695. Cf. C
      99. *[Rome, AD 73]*.   **F** £60 ($96) / **VF** £140 ($224) / **EF** £375 ($600)

2653   **Brass dupondius.** CAESAR AVGVSTI F, laur. hd. l. Rev. DOMITIANVS COS II, winged caduceus between two crossed cornuacopiae. RIC 816. BMCRE 883. CBN 901. C 97. *[Samosata in Commagene, AD 73].*   **F** £65 ($104) / **VF** £150 ($240) / **EF** £400 ($640)

2654   **Copper as.** C (CAESAR, DOMITIAN COS II) a. Rev. AEQVITAS AVGVST S C, Aequitas stg. l., holding scales and sceptre. RIC 694A(a). BMCRE 680. CBN 697. Cf. C 1. *[Rome, AD 73].*   **F** £50 ($80) / **VF** £120 ($192) / **EF** £325 ($520)

2655   C (CAESAR, DOMITIAN COS II), laur. hd. l. Rev. PAX AVGVST S C, Pax stg. l., holding caduceus and olive-branch and resting on column. RIC 696(b). BMCRE 682. CBN 700. Cf. C 348 (sestertius–in error). *[Rome, AD 73].*
                    F £55 ($88) / **VF** £130 ($208) / **EF** £350 ($560)

2656   C (CAESAR, DOMITIAN COS III) a. Rev. PRINCIP IVVENT S C, Domitian on horseback prancing l., r. hand raised, holding sceptre in l. RIC 711. BMCRE p. 164, †. CBN 736. C 401. *[Rome, AD 74].*   **F** £75 ($120) / **VF** £175 ($280) / **EF** £475 ($760)

2657   C (CAESAR, DOMITIAN COS II) a. Rev. PROVIDENT S C, façade of altar-enclosure of the *Ara Providentiae Augusti*, with double panelled door and horns of the altar visible above. RIC 698. BMCRE 687. CBN 701. Cf. C 405. *[Rome, AD 73].*
                    F £55 ($88) / **VF** £130 ($208) / **EF** £350 ($560)
        The reverse is a revival of a Divus Augustus type issued by Tiberius in the AD 20s (see no. 1789). It had been revived previously by Vitellius (see no. 2222) and depicts the altar dedi-cated to the 'providence' of Augustus which may have stood in the Campus Martius (see also nos. 2360, 2477, 2581–2, and 2892).

2658   C (CAESAR, DOMITIAN COS II), laur. hd. l. Rev. S C, Spes advancing l., holding flower. RIC 699. BMCRE 688. CBN 703. C 447. *[Rome, AD 73].*
                    F £55 ($88) / **VF** £130 ($208) / **EF** £350 ($560)

2659   C (CAESAR, DOMITIANVS COS V) a (globe below). Rev. — as previous. RIC 791(a). BMCRE 873. CBN 885. Cf. C 454. *[Lugdunum, AD 77–8].*
                    F £50 ($80) / **VF** £120 ($192) / **EF** £325 ($520)

2660   C (CAESAR, DOMITIAN COS II) a. Rev. — Domitian on horseback prancing l., r. hand raised, holding human-headed sceptre in l. RIC 701(a). BMCRE 690. CBN 704. C 478. *[Rome, AD 73].*   **F** £75 ($120) / **VF** £175 ($280) / **EF** £475 ($760)

2661   CAESAR AVG F DOMITIANVS COS DES II, a. Rev. — Vespasian in triumphal quadriga r., holding branch and sceptre. RIC 688. Cf. BMCRE 646 (dupondius?). CBN 639. C 476. *[Rome, AD 72].*   **F** £100 ($160) / **VF** £250 ($400) / **EF** £700 ($1,120)
        The reverse type commemorates the triumph of Vespasian and Titus in June 71 for their victory in the Jewish War (see also under Vespasian, Titus as Caesar, and Divus Vespasian).

2662   —— Rev. — hexastyle temple of Jupiter Optimus Maximus Capitolinus, richly orna-mented with statuary and bas-reliefs and containing statues of Jupiter between Juno and Minerva. RIC 689. BMCRE 647. CBN 638. Cf. C 533. *[Rome, AD 72].*
                    F £250 ($400) / **VF** £650 ($1,040) / **EF** £1,800 ($2,880)
        Following the destruction of the second temple of Jupiter Capitolinus, in the fighting for the capital at the end of AD 69, Vespasian rebuilt the celebrated structure and dedicated it in AD 75. Just five years later, however, it was again destroyed in the great fire which engulfed central Rome, one of the two major disasters which afflicted the Empire during the brief reign of Titus (see also nos. 2338, 2363, and 2481).

2663   **Copper as.** C (CAESAR, DOMITIAN COS II) a. Rev. VESTA S C, domed temple of Vesta in the Forum, showing four columns and containing statue of the goddess on pedestal. RIC 705. BMCRE 691. CBN 705. C 615. *[Rome, AD 73].*
F £175 ($280) / **VF** £450 ($720) / **EF** £1,250 ($2,000)
This celebrated temple had been rebuilt by Nero following the great fire of AD 64 (see nos. 1933 and 1946). The Neronian structure survived until another conflagration late in the reign of Commodus and was again restored early in the 3rd century by Julia Domna (see also nos. 2365 and 2482).

2664 var.

2664   C (CAESAR, DOMITIAN COS V) a. Rev. VICTORIA AVGVST S C, Victory stg. r. on forepart of galley, holding wreath and palm. RIC 725. BMCRE p. 177, §. CBN 793. C 630. *[Rome, AD 77–8].*   **F** £55 ($88) / **VF** £130 ($208) / **EF** £350 ($560)

2665   C (CAESAR, DOMITIAN COS II) a. Rev. VICTORIA NAVALIS S C, as previous. Cf. RIC 707. Cf. BMCRE p. 159, *. CBN 708. Cf. C 637 (misdescribed). *[Rome, AD 73].*
F £60 ($96) / **VF** £140 ($224) / **EF** £375 ($600)

2666   **Brass as (small module).** CAESAR DOMIT COS II, laur. hd. l. Rev. S C within laurel-wreath. RIC 817. BMCRE 884. CBN —. C —. *[Samosata in Commagene, AD 73].*
F £55 ($88) / **VF** £130 ($208) / **EF** £350 ($560)

2667   **Brass semis.** CAES AVG F, laur. hd. l. Rev. DOMIT COS II, winged caduceus. RIC 818. BMCRE 885. CBN 902. C 96. *[Samosata in Commagene, AD 73].*
F £50 ($80) / **VF** £120 ($192) / **EF** £325 ($520)

Issues as Caesar under Titus, AD 79–81

(All RIC, BMCRE and CBN references are to the coinage of Titus)

2668   **Gold aureus.** Ea. Rev. PRINCEPS IVVENTVTIS, garlanded and lighted altar. RIC 50. BMCRE 91. CBN 74. Cf. C 396 (misdescribed). *[Rome, AD 80].*
VF £1,300 ($2,080) / **EF** £3,250 ($5,200)

2669   Ea. Rev. — crested Corinthian helmet r. on draped seat or table. RIC 51. BMCRE 97. CBN 78. Cf. C 398 (misdescribed). *[Rome, AD 80].*   **VF** £1,300 ($2,080) / **EF** £3,250 ($5,200)

2670   **Silver cistophorus.** E (but CAES) a. Rev. DIVO VESP either side of façade of altar-enclosure, with double panelled door and horns of altar visible above. RIC 75. BMCRE 150. CBN 112. RSC 95. *[Ephesus, AD 80–81].*   **VF** £450 ($720) / **EF** £1,100 ($1,760)

2671   **Silver denarius.** C (CAESAR, DOMITIANVS COS VII) a. Rev. PRINCEPS IVVENTVTIS, Vesta enthroned l., holding Palladium and sceptre. RIC 42. BMCRE 83. CBN 70. RSC 380a. *[Rome, AD 80].*   **VF** £75 ($120) / **EF** £210 ($336)

2672   **Silver denarius.** C (CAESAR, DOMITIANVS COS VII) a. Rev. PRINCEPS IVVENTVTIS, Salus stg. r., feeding snake and resting on column. RIC 40. BMCRE 84. CBN —. RSC 386. *[Rome, AD 80].*   **VF** £75 ($120) / **EF** £210 ($336)

2673   — — Rev. — clasped r. hands holding legionary eagle set on prow. RIC 45. BMCRE 85. CBN 71. RSC 395. *[Rome, AD 80].*   **VF** £85 ($136) / **EF** £240 ($384)

2674   Ea. Rev. — Minerva advancing r., brandishing javelin and holding shield. RIC —. BMCRE 86. CBN 72. RSC 381a. *[Rome, AD 80].*   **VF** £75 ($120) / **EF** £210 ($336)

2675   2676

2675   Ea. Rev. — goat stg. l., within laurel-wreath. RIC 49. BMCRE 88. CBN 73. RSC 390. *[Rome, AD 80].*   **VF** £100 ($160) / **EF** £275 ($440)

2676   Ea. Rev. — garlanded and lighted altar. RIC 50. BMCRE 92. CBN 76. RSC 397a. *[Rome, AD 80].*   **VF** £85 ($136) / **EF** £240 ($384)

2677

2677   Ea. Rev. — crested Corinthian helmet r. on draped seat or table. RIC 51. BMCRE 98. CBN 79. RSC 399a. *[Rome, AD 80].*   **VF** £85 ($136) / **EF** £240 ($384)

2678   **Silver quinarius.** Ea. Rev. VICTORIA AVGVST, Victory advancing r., holding wreath and palm. RIC 52. BMCRE 104. CBN 81. RSC 620. *[Rome, AD 80].*   **VF** £175 ($280) / **EF** £425 ($680)

2679   Ea. Rev. — Victory seated l., holding wreath and palm. RIC 53. BMCRE 104A. CBN —. RSC 624. *[Rome, AD 80].*   **VF** £175 ($280) / **EF** £425 ($680)

2680

2680   **Brass sestertius.** A (DOMITIANVS) a. Rev. PAX AVGVST S C, Pax stg. l., holding olive-branch and cornucopiae. RIC 155(b). BMCRE 230, note. CBN 236. C 343. *[Rome, AD 80].*   **F** £120 ($192) / **VF** £300 ($480) / **EF** £900 ($1,440)

2681 **Brass sestertius.** A (DOMITIANVS) a. Rev. ROMA S C, Roma seated l. on cuirass amidst arms, holding Victory and parazonium. RIC 156. BMCRE 316 (attributed to Lugdunum). CBN —. Cf. C 408 (incomplete description). *[Rome, AD 80].*
F £225 ($360) / **VF** £550 ($880) / **EF** £1,600 ($2,560)

2682 A (DOMITIANVS) a. Rev. S C, Mars advancing r., carrying spear and trophy. RIC 159. BMCRE p. 296, * (attributed to Lugdunum). CBN 326 (Bithynia). C 422. *[Rome, AD 80].*
F £130 ($208) / **VF** £325 ($520) / **EF** £950 ($1,520)

2683 B (DOMITIANVS), laur. hd. l. Rev. — Minerva advancing r., brandishing javelin and holding shield. RIC 157, note. BMCRE 233, note. CBN 241. C 435. *[Rome, AD 80].*
F £150 ($240) / **VF** £350 ($560) / **EF** £1,000 ($1,600)

2684 A (DOMITIANVS) a. Rev. — Spes advancing l., holding flower. RIC 158(b). BMCRE 234. CBN 243. C 460. *[Rome, AD 80].* **F** £120 ($192) / **VF** £300 ($480) / **EF** £900 ($1,440)

2685 A (DOMITIANVS) a. Rev. VICTORIA AVG S C, Victory stg. l., holding cornucopiae and palm and resting on column. RIC 161. BMCRE 235. CBN 245. C 617. *[Rome, AD 80].*
F £150 ($240) / **VF** £350 ($560) / **EF** £1,000 ($1,600)

2686 A (DOMITIANVS) a. Rev. VICTORIA AVGVST S C, Victory advancing l., holding wreath and palm. RIC 162A. BMCRE 236. CBN —. C —. *[Rome, AD 80].*
F £150 ($240) / **VF** £350 ($560) / **EF** £1,000 ($1,600)

2687 **Brass dupondius.** A (DOMITIAN) a. Rev. CERES AVGVST S C, Ceres stg. l., holding corn-ears and long torch. RIC 165(a). BMCRE 237. CBN 246. C 32. *[Rome, AD 80].*
F £55 ($88) / **VF** £130 ($208) / **EF** £350 ($560)

2688 B (DOMITIAN), laur. hd. l. Rev. CONCORDIA AVG S C, Concordia seated l., holding patera and cornucopiae. RIC 166(c). BMCRE 240. CBN 248 var. C 40. *[Rome, AD 80].*
F £60 ($96) / **VF** £140 ($224) / **EF** £375 ($600)

2689 A (DOMITIAN) a. Rev. VESTA S C, Vesta seated l., holding Palladium and sceptre. RIC 173. BMCRE p. 276, *. CBN 259. C 612. *[Rome, AD 80].*
F £60 ($96) / **VF** £140 ($224) / **EF** £375 ($600)

2690 **Copper as.** A (DOMITIANVS) a. Rev. AEQVITAS AVGVST S C, Aequitas stg. l., holding scales and sceptre. RIC 163(c). BMCRE p. 274, † note. CBN 251. Cf. C 5. *[Rome, AD 80].*
F £50 ($80) / **VF** £120 ($192) / **EF** £325 ($520)

2691 A (DOMITIAN) a. Rev. S C, Minerva advancing r., brandishing javelin and holding shield. RIC 170(c). BMCRE 247. CBN 252 var. Cf. C 438. *[Rome, AD 80].*
F £50 ($80) / **VF** £120 ($192) / **EF** £325 ($520)

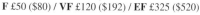

2692

2692 B (DOMITIAN), laur. hd. l. Rev. — Minerva stg. l., holding thunderbolt and spear, shield at side. RIC 169(b). BMCRE 246, note. CBN 256. C 443. *[Rome, AD 80].*
F £55 ($88) / **VF** £130 ($208) / **EF** £350 ($560)

2693   **Copper as.** A (DOMITIAN) a. Rev. S C, Spes advancing l., holding flower. RIC 168(b).
        BMCRE 248. CBN 257. C 459. *[Rome, AD 80].*
        F £50 ($80) / **VF** £120 ($192) / **EF** £325 ($520)

2694   CAESAR DIVI AVG F DOMITIANVS COS VII, a. Rev. VICTORIA AVGVST S C, Victory stg. r.,
        holding wreath and palm. RIC —. Cf. BMCRE p. 276, † note. CBN 260. Cf. C 631 (mis-
        described). *[Rome, AD 80].*   **F** £60 ($96) / **VF** £140 ($224) / **EF** £375 ($600)

2695   Similar, but with obv. legend A (DOMITIANVS), and on rev. Victory stands on forepart of
        galley. RIC 174. BMCRE 320 (attributed to Lugdunum). CBN —. C —. *[Rome, AD 80].*
        F £60 ($96) / **VF** £140 ($224) / **EF** £375 ($600)

Issues as Augustus, AD 81–96

2696   **Gold aureus.** IMP CAES DOMITIAN AVG PONT, a. Rev. COS VII DES VIII P P, wreath on
        curule chair. Cf. RIC 7. BMCRE p. 299, * note. CBN 6. C 57. *[Rome, AD 81].*
        VF £1,400 ($2,240) / **EF** £3,500 ($5,600)

2697   DOMITIANVS AVGVSTVS GERMANICVS, a. Rev. COS XIIII LVD SAEC FEC, herald advancing
        l., wearing feathered cap and holding wand and shield. RIC 119. BMCRE 130. CBN —. C
        75. *[Rome, AD 88].*   **VF** £4,000 ($6,400) / **EF** £10,000 ($16,000)
        *This commemorates the Secular Games celebrated in Rome by Domitian in October of AD
        88 (see also nos. 2723–5, 2755, 2761–4, 2783–4, and 2802–3).*

2698   Fa. Rev. GERMANICVS COS XIIII, Minerva stg. l., holding thunderbolt and spear, shield at
        side. RIC 125. BMCRE 142. CBN 131. C 142. *[Rome, AD 88–9].*
        VF £1,200 ($1,920) / **EF** £3,000 ($4,800)

2699   Fa. Rev. GERMANICVS COS XV, Minerva stg. l., holding spear, l. hand on side. RIC 163.
        BMCRE 173. CBN 162. C 150. *[Rome, AD 90–91].*
        VF £1,200 ($1,920) / **EF** £3,000 ($4,800)

2700   Fa. Rev. GERMANICVS COS XVI, Minerva stg. r. on galley, brandishing javelin and holding
        shield, owl at feet. RIC 182. BMCRE 208. CBN —. C 159. *[Rome, AD 92–4].*
        VF £1,300 ($2,080) / **EF** £3,250 ($5,200)

2701 var.   2702 var.

2701   F, bare hd. r. Rev. — Domitian in triumphal quadriga l., holding branch and sceptre. RIC
        185a. BMCRE 213. CBN 190. C —. *[Rome, AD 92–4].*
        VF £2,000 ($3,200) / **EF** £5,000 ($8,000)

2702   Fa. Rev. GERMANICVS COS XVII, Germania, as mourning captive, naked to waist, seated r.
        on oblong shield, broken spear below. RIC 202. BMCRE 228. CBN 205. C 169. *[Rome, AD
        95–6].*   **VF** £1,400 ($2,240) / **EF** £3,500 ($5,600)

2703   **Gold aureus.** J (TR P V) a. Rev. IMP VIIII COS XI CENS POT P P, as previous. RIC 72.
        BMCRE 85, note. CBN 88. C 188. *[Rome, AD 85].*
                                        VF £1,500 ($2,400) / **EF** £3,750 ($6,000)

2704   — — Rev. IMP XI COS XII CENS P P P, Minerva stg. r. on galley, as 2700. RIC 74. BMCRE
        89. CBN —. C 195. *[Rome, AD 86].*   **VF** £1,300 ($2,080) / **EF** £3,250 ($5,200)

2705 var.   2706

2705   J (TR P VI) a. Rev. IMP XIIII COS XIII CENS P P P, Minerva stg. l., holding spear, as 2699.
        RIC 94. BMCRE 107, note. CBN 106. Cf. C 212. *[Rome, AD 87].*
                                        VF £1,200 ($1,920) / **EF** £3,000 ($4,800)

2706   Na. Rev. IVPPITER CONSERVATOR, eagle stg. facing on thunderbolt, wings spread, hd. l.
        RIC 40. BMCRE 51. CBN 49. C 319. *[Rome, AD 82–3].*
                                        VF £1,400 ($2,240) / **EF** £3,500 ($5,600)

2707   M (GERMANIC), laur. and dr. bust l. Rev. P M TR POT III IMP V COS X P P, helmeted and dr.
        bust of Minerva r. RIC 48. BMCRE 45. CBN 45 var. C —. *[Rome, AD 84].*
                                        VF £1,750 ($2,800) / **EF** £4,250 ($6,800)

2708   M (GERMANIC) a. Rev. P M TR POT IIII IMP VIII COS XI P P, Minerva advancing r., bran-
        dishing javelin and holding shield. RIC 52. BMCRE 70. CBN —. C 363. *[Rome, AD 85].*
                                        VF £1,300 ($2,080) / **EF** £3,250 ($5,200)

2709   Na. Rev. TR P COS VII DES VIII P P, winged thunderbolt on draped seat or table. RIC 16.
        BMCRE 15, note. CBN 12. C 574. *[Rome, AD 81].*
                                        VF £1,300 ($2,080) / **EF** £3,250 ($5,200)

2710   Na. Rev. TR POT COS VIII P P, garlanded and lighted altar. Cf. RIC 29. BMCRE 31.
        CBN —. C —. *[Rome, AD 82].*   **VF** £1,300 ($2,080) / **EF** £3,250 ($5,200)

2711 var.

2711   Na. Rev. TR POT IMP II COS VIII DES IX P P, helmeted bust of Minerva l., wearing aegis,
        sceptre over r. shoulder. RIC 33a. BMCRE 33. CBN 36 var. C 609. *[Rome, AD 82].*
                                        VF £1,500 ($2,400) / **EF** £3,750 ($6,000)

2712   Na. Rev. TR POT II COS VIIII DES X P P, Minerva stg. l., holding spear, as 2699. RIC 38.
        BMCRE 44. CBN 41. C 600. *[Rome, AD 83].*   **VF** £1,300 ($2,080) / **EF** £3,250 ($5,200)

NB A large gold multiple, possibly of 5 aurei, has also been recorded (rev. Minerva stg. on galley). The only known specimen (C 237) was formerly in the Paris Cabinet, but was lost in the great robbery of 1831. A cast in the British Museum is illustrated in BMC (pl. 63, 8).

2713   **Gold quinarius.** J (TR P VII) a. Rev. IMP XIIII COS XIIII CENS P P P, Victory advancing r., holding wreath and palm. RIC 112. BMCRE 126. CBN —. Cf. C 238. *[Rome, AD 88].*
VF £2,000 ($3,200) / **EF** £5,000 ($8,000)

2714   **Silver cistophorus.** IMP CAES DOMITIANVS, a. Rev. AVG GERM, six ears of corn tied together in bundle. RIC 221. BMCRE 254. CBN —. RSC 22a. *[Ephesus, ca. AD 95].*
VF £350 ($560) / **EF** £850 ($1,360)

2715   IMP CAES DOMITIAN AVG P M COS VIII, a. Rev. CAPIT RESTIT, tetrastyle temple of Jupiter Optimus Maximus Capitolinus, containing statues of the Capitoline Triad (Jupiter seated between stg. figures of Juno and Minerva). RIC 222. BMCRE 251. CBN 221. RSC 23. *[Ephesus, AD 82].*   VF £450 ($720) / **EF** £1,100 ($1,760)
The third temple to occupy this site was destroyed during the great fire of AD 80, just five years after its dedication by Vespasian. The celebrated structure was soon rebuilt and dedicated with great ceremony by Domitian in 82. This fourth temple was destined to survive for more than 400 years, being left to decay gradually following the triumph of Christianity in the 4th century (cf. Hill, 'The Monuments of Ancient Rome as Coin Types', pp. 24–6). See also no. 2726.

2716

2716   IMP CAES DOMIT AVG GERM P M TR P XIIII IMP XXII, a. Rev. COS XVII CENS P P P, legionary eagle between two standards, G below. RIC 223. BMCRE 253. CBN —. RSC 94. *[Ephesus, AD 95].*   VF £350 ($560) / **EF** £850 ($1,360)

2717   IMP CAES DOMITIANVS, a. Rev. ROM ET AVG on entablature of distyle temple containing stg. figures of emperor crowned by female deity, G below. RIC 224. BMCRE p. 352, *. CBN 223. RSC 407. *[Ephesus, ca. AD 95].*   VF £450 ($720) / **EF** £1,100 ($1,760)

2718   Obv. As 2715. Rev. No legend, legionary eagle between two standards. RIC 226. BMCRE 252. CBN 222. RSC 667. *[Ephesus, AD 82].*   VF £325 ($520) / **EF** £800 ($1,280)

2719   **Silver denarius.** IMP CAES DOMIT AVG GERMANIC COS XIIII, a. Rev. CENS — P P P (across field), Minerva stg. l., holding thunderbolt and spear, shield at side. RIC 120. BMCRE 139. CBN 129. RSC 27. *[Rome, AD 88–9].*   VF £75 ($120) / **EF** £210 ($336)

2720   IMP CAES DOMITIANVS AVG PONT, a. Rev. COS VII DES VIII P P, ornamented semicircular diadem (?) on draped seat or table. RIC 8. BMCRE 7. CBN 7. RSC 59. *[Rome, AD 81].*
VF £85 ($136) / **EF** £240 ($384)

2721   Na. Rev. — winged thunderbolt on draped seat or table. RIC 13. BMCRE 9. CBN 10. RSC 62. *[Rome, AD 81].*   VF £75 ($120) / **EF** £210 ($336)

2722   **Silver denarius.** J (TR P VII) a. Rev. COS — XIIII (across field), Minerva stg. l., holding spear, l. hand on side. RIC 106. BMCRE p. 324, ‡. CBN 113. RSC 66. *[Rome, AD 88]*.
                                   VF £75 ($120) / **EF** £210 ($336)

               2723   2724

2723   J (TR P VIII) a. Rev. COS XIIII LVD SAEC FEC, herald advancing l., wearing feathered cap and holding wand and shield. RIC 117. BMCRE 131. CBN 120. RSC 76/77. *[Rome, AD 88]*.   **VF** £150 ($240) / **EF** £375 ($600)
This, and the following two types, commemorate the Secular Games celebrated in Rome by Domitian in October of AD 88 (see also nos. 2697, 2755, 2761–4, 2783–4, and 2802–3).

2724   — — Rev. COS / XIIII / LVD / SAEC / FEC in five lines on cippus, to r. of which herald stands l. before candelabrum, holding wand and shield. RIC 116. BMCRE 135. CBN 124. RSC 73. *[Rome, AD 88]*.   **VF** £175 ($280) / **EF** £425 ($680)

                                   2725

2725   — — Rev. COS — XIIII divided by cippus inscribed LVD / SAEC / FEC in three lines, all within laurel-wreath. RIC 115. BMCRE 137. CBN 126. RSC 70. *[Rome, AD 88]*.
                                   VF £125 ($200) / **EF** £325 ($520)

2726   DOMITIANVS AVG GERM, bare hd. r. Rev. IMP CAES on entablature of hexastyle temple of Jupiter Optimus Maximus Capitolinus, containing statues of Jupiter between Juno and Minerva. RIC 207. BMCRE 242. CBN 216. RSC 174, 174a. *[Rome, ca. AD 95–6]*.
                                 VF £500 ($800) / **EF** £1,500 ($2,400)
See note following no. 2715. Other temple types appear on denarii of this series: tetrastyle sanctuaries of Serapis, Cybele (Magna Mater), and Minerva Chalcidica; and an octastyle edifice of uncertain identity, possibly that of Jupiter Victor at the north-eastern corner of the Palatine (cf. Hill, 'The Monuments of Ancient Rome as Coin Types', pp. 28, 29, 33–6, and 36–7).

2727   J (TR P IIII) b. Rev. IMP VIIII COS XI CENS POT P P, Minerva stg. l., holding thunderbolt, as 2719. RIC 64. BMCRE 79. CBN 81. RSC 178a. *[Rome, AD 85]*.
                                 VF £60 ($96) / **EF** £175 ($280)

2728   — — Rev. IMP VIIII COS XI CENS POTES P P, Germania, as mourning captive, naked to waist, seated r. on oblong shield, broken spear below. RIC 66a. BMCRE 82. CBN 84. RSC 181. *[Rome, AD 85]*.   **VF** £250 ($400) / **EF** £650 ($1,040)

2729 **Silver denarius.** J (TR P V) b. Rev. IMP XII COS XII CENS P P P, Minerva advancing r., brandishing javelin and holding shield. RIC 79. BMCRE 93. CBN 97. RSC 201b. *[Rome, AD 86].* **VF** £55 ($88) / **EF** £160 ($256)

2730 var. 2731

2730 J (TR P VI) a. Rev. IMP XIIII COS XIII CENS P P P, Minerva stg. r. on galley, brandishing javelin and holding shield, owl at feet. RIC 92. BMCRE 103. CBN 104. RSC 218. *[Rome, AD 87].* **VF** £55 ($88) / **EF** £160 ($256)

2731 J (TR P VII) a. Rev. IMP XIIII COS XIIII CENS P P P, Minerva stg. l., holding spear, as 2722. RIC 110. BMCRE 122. CBN 117. RSC 233. *[Rome, AD 88].*
VF £55 ($88) / **EF** £160 ($256)

2732 2734

2732 J (TR P VIII) a. Rev. IMP XIX COS XIIII CENS P P P, Minerva stg. l., holding thunderbolt, as 2719. RIC 139. BMCRE 153. CBN 147. RSC 251. *[Rome, AD 89].*
VF £55 ($88) / **EF** £160 ($256)

2733 — — Rev. — Victory advancing r., holding branch. RIC 141. BMCRE 156. CBN 150. RSC 254a. *[Rome, AD 89].* **VF** £150 ($240) / **EF** £375 ($600)

2734 J (TR P VIIII) a. Rev. IMP XXI COS XV CENS P P P, Minerva advancing r., as 2729. RIC 147. BMCRE 164. CBN 157. RSC 261. *[Rome, AD 90].* **VF** £55 ($88) / **EF** £160 ($256)

2735 J (TR P X) a. Rev. — Minerva stg. r. on galley, as 2730. RIC 153. BMCRE 179. CBN 168. RSC 266. *[Rome, AD 90–91].* **VF** £55 ($88) / **EF** £160 ($256)

2736 J (TR P XII) a. Rev. IMP XXII COS XVI CENS P P P, Minerva stg. l., holding spear, as 2722. RIC 174. BMCRE 207. CBN 186. RSC 278. *[Rome, AD 92–3].*
VF £55 ($88) / **EF** £160 ($256)

2737 J (TR P XIIII) a. Rev. IMP XXII COS XVII CENS P P P, Minerva stg. l., holding thunderbolt, as 2719. RIC 188. BMCRE 224. CBN 202. RSC 287. *[Rome, AD 95].*
VF £55 ($88) / **EF** £160 ($256)

2738 J (TR P XV) a. Rev. — winged Minerva advancing l., holding javelin and shield. RIC 194. BMCRE 237. CBN 210. RSC 294. *[Rome, AD 95–6].* **VF** £125 ($200) / **EF** £325 ($520)

2738   2740

2739   **Silver denarius.** J (TR P XV) a. Rev. IMP XXII COS XVII CENS P P P, large rectangular altar,
       flanked by two legionary eagles. RIC 195. BMCRE p. 344, †. CBN 212. RSC 296. *[Rome,*
       AD 95–6].   **VF** £375 ($600) / **EF** £1,000 ($1,600)

2740   As 2706 (rev. IVPPITER CONSERVATOR, eagle on thunderbolt). RIC 40. BMCRE 52. CBN
       53. RSC 320. *[Rome, AD 82–3].*   **VF** £100 ($160) / **EF** £275 ($440)

2741   M (GERMANIC), laur. and dr. bust l. Rev. P M TR POT III IMP V COS X P P, eagle on thunder-
       bolt, as 2706. RIC 49. BMCRE 50, note. CBN 48. RSC 359. *[Rome, AD 84].*
                                                                   VF £150 ($240) / **EF** £375 ($600)

2742   M (GERMANIC) b. Rev. P M TR POT IIII IMP VIII COS XI P P, Minerva stg. l., holding spear,
       as 2722. RIC 55. BMCRE 74, note. CBN 77. RSC 360. *[Rome, AD 85].*
                                                                   VF £75 ($120) / **EF** £210 ($336)

2743   Na. Rev. SALVS AVGVST, Salus enthroned l., holding corn-ears and poppy. RIC 41.
       BMCRE 54. CBN 54. RSC 412. *[Rome, AD 82–3].*   **VF** £65 ($104) / **EF** £185 ($296)

2744   IMP CAESAR DOMITIANVS AVG, a. Rev. TR P COS VII, winged thunderbolt on draped seat
       or table. RIC 1. BMCRE 1. CBN 1. RSC 554. *[Rome, AD 81].*
                                                                   VF £75 ($120) / **EF** £210 ($336)

2745   Similar, but with rev. type dolphin entwined around anchor. RIC 4. BMCRE 3. CBN 3.
       RSC 551. *[Rome, AD 81].*   **VF** £85 ($136) / **EF** £240 ($384)

2746   2750 var.

2746   Na. Rev. TR P COS VII DES VIII P P, Minerva stg. l., holding Victory and spear, shield at
       side. RIC 23. BMCRE 13. CBN 29. RSC 564. *[Rome, AD 81].*
                                                                   VF £65 ($104) / **EF** £185 ($296)

2747   Similar, but with rev. type wreath on curule chair. RIC 18. BMCRE 18. CBN 17. RSC 570.
       [Rome, AD 81].   **VF** £75 ($120) / **EF** £210 ($336)

2748   Similar, but with rev. type garlanded and lighted altar. RIC 19. BMCRE 23. CBN 22. RSC
       577. *[Rome, AD 81].*   **VF** £75 ($120) / **EF** £210 ($336)

2749   Na. Rev. TR POT COS VIII P P, Minerva advancing r., as 2729. RIC 30. BMCRE 24. CBN
       34. RSC 592. *[Rome, AD 82].*   **VF** £65 ($104) / **EF** £185 ($296)

2750 **Silver denarius.** Similar, but with rev. type tripod surmounted by dolphin r. RIC 27.
BMCRE 30. CBN 33. RSC 594. *[Rome, AD 82].*   **VF** £75 ($120) / **EF** £210 ($336)

2751 Similar, but with rev. type ornamented semicircular diadem (?) on draped seat or table.
RIC 25. BMCRE 27. CBN 31. RSC 596. *[Rome, AD 82].*
VF £75 ($120) / **EF** £210 ($336)

2752 Na. Rev. TR POT IMP II COS VIII DES VIIII P P, Fortuna stg. l., holding rudder and cornucopiae. RIC 32. BMCRE 34. CBN 35. RSC 610. *[Rome, AD 82].*
VF £100 ($160) / **EF** £275 ($440)

2753 Na. Rev. TR POT II COS VIIII DES X P P, Minerva stg. l., holding spear, as 2722. RIC 38.
BMCRE 44, note. CBN 42. RSC 601. *[Rome, AD 83].*   **VF** £60 ($96) / **EF** £175 ($280)

2754 Similar, but Minerva holds thunderbolt, as 2719. RIC 37. BMCRE 43. CBN 40. RSC 604.
[Rome, AD 83].   **VF** £60 ($96) / **EF** £175 ($280)

NB Large silver multiples, possibly of 8, 5, and 4 denarii, have also been recorded: the 8-denarius
piece has rev. Minerva enthroned (BMC 83, pl. 62, 3); the 5-denarius pieces have revs. captive
Germania seated (BMC 85, pl. 62, 6) and Minerva stg. on galley (BMC 191, pl. 65, 13); and the 4-
denarius piece also has Minerva stg. on galley (BMC 191, note).

2755

2755 **Silver quinarius.** J (TR P VIII) a. Rev. COS XIIII LVD SAEC FEC, herald advancing l., wear-
ing feathered cap and holding wand and shield. RIC 118. BMCRE 134. CBN 122. RSC 78.
[Rome, AD 88].   **VF** £225 ($360) / **EF** £550 ($880)
*This commemorates the Secular Games celebrated in Rome by Domitian in October of
AD 88 (see also nos. 2697, 2723–5, 2761–4, 2783–4, and 2802–3).*

2756 var.   2757 var.

2756 J (TR P V) a. Rev. IMP XI COS XII CENS P P P, Victory advancing r., holding wreath and
palm. RIC 78. BMCRE 92. CBN 94. RSC 197. *[Rome, AD 86].*
VF £150 ($240) / **EF** £375 ($600)

2757 J (TR P VII) a. Rev. IMP XIIII COS XIIII CENS P P P, Victory seated l., holding wreath and
palm. RIC 113. BMCRE 128. CBN 118. RSC 240. *[Rome, AD 88].*
VF £150 ($240) / **EF** £375 ($600)

2758   **Silver quinarius.** IMP CAES DOMITIAN AVG GERMANICVS, a. Rev. P M TR POT III IMP V
        COS X P P, Victory advancing r., as 2756. RIC 51. BMCRE 50A. CBN —. RSC 357.
        [Rome, AD 84].   **VF** £175 ($280) / **EF** £425 ($680)

2759   Na. Rev. TR POT COS VIIII P P, winged caduceus. RIC 35. BMCRE 38. CBN 38. RSC 599.
        [Rome, AD 83].   **VF** £250 ($400) / **EF** £600 ($960)

2760   **Brass sestertius.** Hb. Rev. ANNONA AVGVST S C, Annona stg. r., holding cornucopiae,
        facing Ceres seated l., holding corn-ears and torch, modius on garlanded altar between
        them, stern of ship in background. RIC 277(a). BMCRE 323. CBN 349. C 17. *[Rome,
        AD 85].*   **F** £150 ($240) / **VF** £375 ($600) / **EF** £1,100 ($1,760)
        *This is a revival of a Neronian type (see no. 1952). About a decade later it was again repli-
        cated by Nerva (see no. 3041).*

2761   Ka. Rev. COS XIIII LVD SAEC A POP S C, Domitian, holding patera, seated r. on low plat-
        form inscribed FRVG AC, three baskets at his feet, two togate citizens stg. l. before him,
        holding paterae, tetrastyle temple in background viewed partially from side. RIC 375(a).
        BMCRE 422. CBN 458. C 83. *[Rome, AD 88].*
                     F £400 ($640) / **VF** £1,000 ($1,600) / **EF** £3,500 ($5,600)
        *This, and the following three types, commemorate the Secular Games celebrated in Rome
        by Domitian in October of AD 88 (see also nos. 2697, 2723–5, 2755, 2783–4, and 2802–3).*

2762   Ka. Rev. COS XIIII LVD SAEC FEC S C, Domitian stg. r., his r. hand extended, addressing
        three matrons who kneel l. before him, their hands held out in prayer, tetrastyle temple in
        background viewed partially from side. RIC 377. BMCRE 424. CBN 460. C 80. *[Rome,
        AD 88].*   **F** £350 ($560) / **VF** £900 ($1,440) / **EF** £3,000 ($4,800)

2763 var.

2763   Kb. Rev. — Domitian stg. r., sacrificing from patera over garlanded altar, to r. of which
        victimarius holds sacrificial pig, Tellus reclining r. in foreground, holding cornucopiae,
        lyre-player and flute-player in background. RIC 378. BMCRE 425. CBN — (cf. p. 344,
        42). Cf. C 84. *[Rome, AD 88].*   **F** £400 ($640) / **VF** £1,000 ($1,600) / **EF** £3,500 ($5,600)

2764   Ka. Rev. COS XIIII LVD SAEC S C, Domitian seated l. on low platform inscribed SVF P D, two
        vessels at his feet, his r. hand extended to give incense or fumigants (*suffimenta*) to togate
        citizen stg. r. before him, accompanied by child, tetrastyle temple in background viewed
        partially from side. RIC 376. BMCRE 428. CBN 462. C 81. *[Rome, AD 88].*
                     F £400 ($640) / **VF** £1,000 ($1,600) / **EF** £3,500 ($5,600)

2765   Hb. Rev. GERMANIA CAPTA S C, trophy, to l. of which Germania, as mourning female cap-
        tive, is seated l., and to r. of which bound male German captive stands r., arms on ground
        around. RIC 278 (a). BMCRE 325. CBN 350. C 136. *[Rome, AD 85].*
                     F £300 ($480) / **VF** £750 ($1,200) / **EF** £2,500 ($4,000)

2765 var.

2766 var.

2766 **Brass sestertius.** I (COS XIIII) a. Rev. IOVI VICTORI S C, Jupiter seated l., holding Victory and sceptre. RIC 358. BMCRE 406. CBN 436. C 313. *[Rome, AD 88–9].*
F £110 ($176) / **VF** £275 ($440) / **EF** £850 ($1,360)

2767 IMP DOMITIAN CAES DIVI VESP F AVG P M TR P P P COS VIII, a. Rev. PAX AVGVST S C, Pax stg. l., holding olive-branch and cornucopiae. RIC 448 (attributed to Lugdunum). BMCRE 516 (Lugdunum). CBN 551 (Bithynia). C 345. *[Rome, AD 82].*
F £130 ($208) / **VF** £325 ($520) / **EF** £950 ($1,520)

2768 — — Rev. S C, Mars advancing r., carrying spear and trophy. RIC 449 (attributed to Lugdunum). BMCRE 517 (Lugdunum). CBN 552 (Bithynia). C 423. *[Rome, AD 82].*
F £130 ($208) / **VF** £325 ($520) / **EF** £950 ($1,520)

2769 L (DOMITIAN, COS XI) b. Rev. S C, Pax stg. l., setting fire with torch to heap of arms and holding cornucopiae. RIC 254. BMCRE 295. CBN 314. C — (omitted in error, cf. 445 in 1st edition). *[Rome, AD 85].* F £180 ($288) / **VF** £450 ($720) / **EF** £1,350 ($2,160)

2770 Hb. Rev. S C, Victory stg. r., inscribing DE / GER in two lines on shield set on trophy, at foot of which is Germania, as mourning captive, seated r. RIC 282(a). BMCRE 330. CBN 355. C 472. *[Rome, AD 85].* F £250 ($400) / **VF** £650 ($1,040) / **EF** £2,000 ($3,200)

2771 Hb. Rev. S C, Domitian on horseback galloping r., about to spear fallen German warrior. RIC 284. BMCRE 339. CBN 359. C 484. *[Rome, AD 85].*
F £225 ($360) / **VF** £550 ($880) / **EF** £1,600 ($2,560)

2772 L (DOMITIAN, COS XI) b. Rev. S C, Domitian stg. l., holding spear, receiving supplication of German warrior kneeling r., resting on shield. RIC 258. BMCRE 299. CBN 320. C 488. *[Rome, AD 85].* F £250 ($400) / **VF** £650 ($1,040) / **EF** £2,000 ($3,200)

2771

2773   **Brass sestertius.** I (COS XII) b. Rev. S C, Domitian stg. l., holding parazonium and spear,
       river-god Rhenus reclining r. at his feet, holding reed. RIC 319. BMCRE 377. CBN 399. C
       505. *[Rome, AD 86].*   **F** £180 ($288) / **VF** £450 ($720) / **EF** £1,350 ($2,160)

2774 var.

2774   — — Rev. S C, Domitian stg. l., holding thunderbolt and spear, crowned by Victory who
       stands l. behind him, holding palm. Cf. RIC 322. BMCRE 381. CBN 406. C 510. *[Rome,
       AD 86].*   **F** £180 ($288) / **VF** £450 ($720) / **EF** £1,350 ($2,160)

2775 var.

2775   Hb. Rev. S C, Domitian, togate, stg. r., clasping hands over altar with officer stg. l., accom-
       panied by three soldiers, two of whom bear standards. RIC 288B. BMCRE 344. CBN 361.
       C 501. *[Rome, AD 85].*   **F** £250 ($400) / **VF** £650 ($1,040) / **EF** £2,000 ($3,200)
       *This type has sometimes been interpreted as commemorating the return to Rome of the cel-
       ebrated general Gnaeus Julius Agricola, whose remarkable achievements as governor of
       Britain spanned the reigns of all three Flavian emperors.*

2776

2776   **Brass sestertius.** L (DOMITIAN, COS XI) b. Rev. S C, Domitian, togate, stg. l., sacrificing
from patera over lighted altar, shrine in background showing three columns and containing
statuette of Minerva stg. r. RIC 256. BMCRE 296. CBN 316. C 491. *[Rome, AD 85].*
F £180 ($288) / **VF** £450 ($720) / **EF** £1,350 ($2,160)
*Hill ('The Monuments of Ancient Rome as Coin Types', pp. 30–31) identifies this shrine
with the lararium, or private chapel, in Domitian's palace on the Palatine.*

2777   L (DOMITIAN, COS XI) b. Rev. S C, four-portalled triumphal arch, surmounted by two
quadrigae of elephants back to back, each with driver. RIC 261. BMCRE p. 364, †. CBN
324. C 530. *[Rome, AD 85].*
F £1,000 ($1,600) / **VF** £2,500 ($4,000) / **EF** £10,000 ($16,000)
*Hill (op. cit., p. 51) believes that this elaborate structure was the arch erected by Domitian
at the intersection of the Via Flaminia and the Vicus Pallacinae, near the present Piazza
Venezia.*

2778   Ga. Rev. TR P COS VII DES VIII P P S C, Minerva advancing r., brandishing javelin and holding shield. RIC 232(a). BMCRE 260. CBN 274. C 561. *[Rome, AD 81].*
F £120 ($192) / **VF** £300 ($480) / **EF** £900 ($1,440)

2779   Ga. Rev. — Domitian, togate, stg. l., holding Palladium. RIC 234. BMCRE 265. CBN 278.
C 566. *[Rome, AD 81].*   **F** £150 ($240) / **VF** £350 ($560) / **EF** £1,000 ($1,600)

2780   G, laur. hd. l. Rev. TR P COS VIII DES VIIII P P S C, Minerva stg. l., holding spear, l. hand on
side. RIC 240(b). BMCRE 276. Cf. CBN 286. C 582. *[Rome, AD 82].*
F £150 ($240) / **VF** £350 ($560) / **EF** £1,000 ($1,600)

2781   **Brass dupondius.** Hd. Rev. AETERNITATI AVGVST S C, Aeternitas stg. l., holding hds. of
Sol and Luna. RIC 289. BMCRE 346. CBN 363. C 8. *[Rome, AD 85].*
F £65 ($104) / **VF** £150 ($240) / **EF** £400 ($640)

2782   L (DOMITIAN, COS X) c. Rev. ANNONA AVG S C, Annona seated r., holding open bag of
corn-ears on lap, which is also held by child stg. l. before her, large stern of ship l. in background. RIC 243. BMCRE p. 360, *. CBN 298. Cf. C 10. *[Rome, AD 84].*
F £75 ($120) / **VF** £175 ($280) / **EF** £475 ($760)

2783   Kc. Rev. COS — XIIII (across field), S C (in ex.), herald stg. l. before candelabrum, holding
wand and shield, cippus on l. inscribed LVD / SAEC / FEC in three lines. RIC 380. BMCRE
429. CBN 463. Cf. C 72. *[Rome, AD 88].*
F £225 ($360) / **VF** £550 ($880) / **EF** £1,500 ($2,400)
*This type and the next commemorate the Secular Games celebrated in Rome by Domitian
in October of AD 88 (see also nos. 2697, 2723–5, 2755, 2761–4, and 2802–3).*

2784 **Brass dupondius.** Kc. Rev. COS XIIII LVD SAEC FEC S C, Domitian, togate, stg. l., sacrificing from patera over garlanded altar on other side of which victimarius kneels beside sacrificial goat and sheep, two flute-players facing the emperor, hexastyle temple of Jupiter Capitolinus in background. RIC 381. BMCRE 430. CBN 464. C 87. *[Rome, AD 88].*
F £95 ($152) / VF £225 ($360) / EF £625 ($1,000)

2785 L (DOMITIAN, COS XI) d. Rev. FIDEI PVBLICAE S C, Fides stg. l., holding dish of fruits and corn-ears with poppy. RIC 263. BMCRE 306. CBN 327. C 107. *[Rome, AD 85].*
F £45 ($72) / VF £110 ($176) / EF £300 ($480)

2786 I (COS XV) c. Rev. FORTVNAE AVGVSTI S C, Fortuna stg. l., holding rudder and cornucopiae. RIC 392. BMCRE 444. CBN 479. C 132. *[Rome, AD 90–91].*
F £45 ($72) / VF £110 ($176) / EF £300 ($480)

2787 J (TR P VI) d. Rev. IMP XIIII COS XIII CENSOR PERPETVVS P P around large S C. Cf. RIC 357. Cf. BMCRE 398. CBN 425. Cf. C 231. *[Rome, AD 87].*
F £100 ($160) / VF £240 ($384) / EF £650 ($1,040)

2788 IMP D CAES DIVI VESP F AVG P M TR P P P COS VII, c. Rev. ROMA S C, Roma seated l. on cuirass, holding wreath and parazonium, shields behind. RIC 446 (attributed to Lugdunum). BMCRE 514 (Lugdunum). CBN 549 (Bithynia). C 409. *[Rome, AD 81].*
F £75 ($120) / VF £175 ($280) / EF £475 ($760)

2789 L (DOMITIAN, COS X) d. Rev. S C, Mars advancing l., holding Victory and trophy. RIC 245(a). BMCRE 287. CBN 300. C 424. *[Rome, AD 84].*
F £65 ($104) / VF £150 ($240) / EF £400 ($640)

2790 I (COS XVII) c. Rev. S C, Victory stg. l. on globe, holding wreath and trophy. RIC 420. BMCRE p. 407, §. CBN 511. C 466. *[Rome, AD 95–6].*
F £65 ($104) / VF £150 ($240) / EF £400 ($640)

2791 L (DOMITIAN, COS XI) d. Rev. S C, trophy, at base of which male and female German captives seated l. and r. RIC 266. BMCRE 310. CBN 332. C 539. *[Rome, AD 85].*
F £85 ($136) / VF £200 ($320) / EF £550 ($880)

2792

2792 — — Rev. S C, two oval shields crossed, with vexillum, spears, trumpets, etc. in background. RIC 267. BMCRE 311. CBN 333. C 537. *[Rome, AD 85].*
F £85 ($136) / VF £200 ($320) / EF £550 ($880)

2793 I (COS XVII) c. Rev. S C, helmet, on l., and shield, on r., in front of olive-tree. RIC 419. BMCRE 478. CBN —. Cf. C 535. *[Rome, AD 95–6].*
F £185 ($296) / VF £450 ($720) / EF £1,250 ($2,000)

2794 Gc. Rev. TR P COS VII DES VIII P P S C, Felicitas stg. l., holding branch and caduceus and resting on column. RIC 235. BMCRE 267. CBN —. C —. *[Rome, AD 81].*
F £55 ($88) / VF £130 ($208) / EF £350 ($560)

2795   **Brass dupondius.** Ga. Rev. TR P COS VIII DES VIIII P P S C, Minerva stg. l., holding thunderbolt and spear, shield at side. RIC 241(a). BMCRE 277. CBN 287. C 583. *[Rome, AD 82].*   **F** £55 ($88) / **VF** £130 ($208) / **EF** £350 ($560)

2796   Similar, but with obv. type rad. hd. l. RIC 241(b). BMCRE 280. CBN 289. C 585. *[Rome, AD 82].*   **F** £60 ($96) / **VF** £140 ($224) / **EF** £375 ($600)

2797   Hd. Rev. VICTORIAE AVGVSTI S C, Victory stg. l., inscribing shield on trophy attached to palm-trunk and holding palm-branch. RIC 296. BMCRE p. 374, *. CBN 368. C 640. *[Rome, AD 85].*   **F** £65 ($104) / **VF** £150 ($240) / **EF** £400 ($640)

2798   I (COS XVI) c. Rev. VIRTVTI AVGVSTI S C, Virtus stg. r., l. foot on helmet, holding spear and parazonium. RIC 406. BMCRE 468. CBN 496. C 659. *[Rome, AD 92–4].*   **F** £45 ($72) / **VF** £110 ($176) / **EF** £300 ($480)

2799   **Copper as.** Hb. Rev. AETERNITATI AVGVST S C, Aeternitas stg., as 2781. RIC 297. BMCRE 353. CBN 369. C 7. *[Rome, AD 85].*   **F** £60 ($96) / **VF** £140 ($224) / **EF** £375 ($600)

2800   I (COS XIIII) a. Rev. ANNONA AVG S C, Annona seated, as 2782. RIC 369 var. BMCRE 415. CBN 450. C 16 var. *[Rome, AD 88–9].*   **F** £70 ($112) / **VF** £165 ($264) / **EF** £450 ($720)

2801 var.

2801   IMP D CAES DIVI VESP F AVG P M TR P P P COS VII, a. Rev. CERES AVGVST S C, Ceres stg. l., holding corn-ears and long torch. RIC 447 (attributed to Lugdunum). BMCRE 515 (Lugdunum). CBN 550 (Bithynia). C 33. *[Rome, AD 81].*   **F** £50 ($80) / **VF** £120 ($192) / **EF** £325 ($520)

2802   Ka. Rev. COS XIIII LVD SAEC FEC S C, Domitian sacrificing before temple, similar to 2784, but the victimarius is slaying a sacrificial bull, the head of which is held by a kneeling attendant, and one of the musicians plays a lyre instead of flute. RIC 386. BMCRE 438. CBN 469. C 90. *[Rome, AD 88].*   **F** £95 ($152) / **VF** £225 ($360) / **EF** £625 ($1,000)
This type and the next commemorate the Secular Games celebrated in Rome by Domitian in October of AD 88 (see also nos. 2697, 2723–5, 2755, 2761–4, and 2783–4).

2803

2803   Similar, but without the victimarius, bull, and attendant. RIC 385(a). BMCRE 434. CBN 471. C 85. *[Rome, AD 88].*   **F** £85 ($136) / **VF** £200 ($320) / **EF** £550 ($880)

2804   **Copper as.** I (COS XII) b. Rev. FIDEI PVBLICAE S C, Fides stg. r., holding corn-ears with poppy and dish of fruits. RIC 332. BMCRE 385. CBN 415. C 111. *[Rome, AD 86].*
F £40 ($64) / **VF** £100 ($160) / **EF** £275 ($440)

2805 var.

2805   I (COS XIIII) a. Rev. FORTVNAE AVGVSTI S C, Fortuna stg., as 2786. RIC 371. BMCRE 416. CBN 452. C 128. *[Rome, AD 88–9].*   F £40 ($64) / **VF** £100 ($160) / **EF** £275 ($440)

2806   Hb. Rev. IOVI CONSERVAT S C, Jupiter stg. l., holding thunderbolt and sceptre. RIC 300. BMCRE 354. CBN 372. C 303. *[Rome, AD 85].*
F £60 ($96) / **VF** £140 ($224) / **EF** £375 ($600)

2807 var.

2807   I (COS XV) a. Rev. MONETA AVGVSTI S C, Moneta stg. l., holding scales and cornucopiae. RIC 395. BMCRE 449. CBN 481. Cf. C 332. *[Rome, AD 90–91].*
F £40 ($64) / **VF** £100 ($160) / **EF** £275 ($440)

2808 var.

2808   Hb. Rev. SALVTI AVGVSTI S C, façade of altar-enclosure of the *Ara Salutis Augusti*, with double panelled door and horns of the altar visible above. RIC 304(a). BMCRE 358. CBN 379. C 418. *[Rome, AD 85].*   F £50 ($80) / **VF** £120 ($192) / **EF** £325 ($520)
The identification of this altar is wholly uncertain. Hill ('The Monuments of Ancient Rome as Coin Types', p. 64) suggests that it may have been erected under Titus because of that emperor's failing health, but its precise location and subsequent history are unknown.

2809   **Copper as.** I (COS XIII) a. Rev. S C, Mars advancing, as 2789. RIC 355. BMCRE —. CBN
433. C 433. *[Rome, AD 87].*   **F** £60 ($96) / **VF** £140 ($224) / **EF** £375 ($600)

2810   L (DOMITIAN, COS X) b. Rev. S C, Victory advancing r., holding with both hands a
legionary eagle over l. shoulder. Cf. RIC 249(a). BMCRE 290. CBN 305. C 463. *[Rome,
AD 84].*   **F** £65 ($104) / **VF** £150 ($240) / **EF** £400 ($640)

2811 var.

2811   Hb. Rev. S C, Victory alighting l., wings spread, holding shield inscribed S P Q R. RIC
302(a). BMCRE 355. CBN 376. C 468. *[Rome, AD 85].*
F £55 ($88) / **VF** £130 ($208) / **EF** £350 ($560)

2812   I (COS XVII) a. Rev. S C, eagle stg. facing on palm-branch, hd. r., wings spread, holding
wreath in beak. Cf RIC 418 (midescribed as a dupondius). BMCRE p. 408, ‡. CBN 515.
Cf. C 519 (misdescribed). *[Rome, AD 95–6].*
F £110 ($176) / **VF** £275 ($440) / **EF** £750 ($1,200)

2813   Similar, but with rev. type owl stg. l. on branch, hd. facing. RIC 424. BMCRE p. 408, §.
CBN —. C —. *[Rome, AD 95–6].*   **F** £225 ($360) / **VF** £550 ($880) / **EF** £1,500 ($2,400)

2814 var.

2814   G, laur. hd. l. Rev. TR P COS VII DES VIII P P S C, Minerva stg. l., holding thunderbolt and
spear, shield at side. RIC 238(b). BMCRE 270, note. CBN 282. C 558. *[Rome, AD 81].*
F £55 ($88) / **VF** £130 ($208) / **EF** £350 ($560)

2815   Ga. Rev. TR P COS VIII DES VIIII P P S C, Minerva advancing r., brandishing javelin and
holding shield. RIC 242(a). BMCRE 281. CBN 290. C 587. *[Rome, AD 82].*
F £50 ($80) / **VF** £120 ($192) / **EF** £325 ($520)

2816   I (COS XII) b. Rev. VICTORIAE AVGVSTI S C, Victory inscribing shield, as 2797. RIC 339.
BMCRE p. 385, ‡. CBN 419. C 643. *[Rome, AD 86].*
F £60 ($96) / **VF** £140 ($224) / **EF** £375 ($600)

2817 var.

2817 **Copper as.** I (COS XV) a. Rev. VIRTVTI AVGVSTI S C, Virtus stg., as 2798. RIC 397. BMCRE 452. CBN 482. C 656. *[Rome, AD 90–91].*
F £40 ($64) / **VF** £100 ($160) / **EF** £275 ($440)

2818

2818 **Brass semis.** IMP DOMITIANVS AVG, a. Rev. S C, cornucopiae. RIC 425. BMCRE 481. CBN 517. C 543. *[Rome, AD 81–2].* F £45 ($72) / **VF** £110 ($176) / **EF** £325 ($520)

2819 IMP DOMIT AVG GERM COS XI, laur. and dr. bust of Apollo r. Rev. S C, tripod, with snake entwined around the central leg. RIC 274. BMCRE 319 var. CBN 340. C 546. *[Rome, AD 85].* F £40 ($64) / **VF** £95 ($152) / **EF** £250 ($400)

2820 Similar, but with laurel-branch before bust of Apollo, and rev. type lyre. RIC —. BMCRE 318. CBN 341 var. C 541 var. *[Rome, AD 85].*
F £40 ($64) / **VF** £95 ($152) / **EF** £250 ($400)

2821 2822

2821 IMP DOMIT AVG GERM COS XII, bust of Minerva r., wearing crested Corinthian helmet and aegis. Rev. S C, owl stg. l., hd. facing. RIC 308. BMCRE 369. CBN 390. C 523. *[Rome, AD 86].* F £35 ($56) / **VF** £85 ($136) / **EF** £225 ($360)

2822 IMP DOMIT AVG GERM COS XV, laur. and dr. bust of Apollo r., laurel-branch before. Rev. S C, raven stg. r. on laurel-branch. RIC 398(a). BMCRE 453. CBN 484. C 527. *[Rome, AD 90–91].* F £35 ($56) / **VF** £85 ($136) / **EF** £225 ($360)

2823 **Copper quadrans.** IMP DOM AVG, helmeted hd. of Minerva r. Rev. S C within laurel-wreath. RIC 436. BMCRE 485. CBN 521. C —. *[Rome, AD 81–2].*
F £25 ($40) / **VF** £65 ($104) / **EF** £175 ($280)

2823   2827

2824   **Copper quadrans.** Similar, but with obv. IMP DOMIT AVG GERM, helmeted and dr. bust of
        Minerva r. RIC 427. BMCRE 484. CBN 519. C —. *[Rome, AD 83 or later].*
                                            F £25 ($40) / **VF** £65 ($104) / **EF** £175 ($280)

2825   Obv. Similar. Rev. IMP DOMIT AVG GERM around large S C. RIC 426. BMCRE 482. CBN
        —. C —. *[Rome, AD 83 or later].*   **F** £30 ($48) / **VF** £75 ($120) / **EF** £200 ($320)

2826   Obv. Similar. Rev. S C, owl stg. r., hd. facing. RIC 429. BMCRE 487. CBN 527. C 521 var.
        [Rome, AD 83 or later].   **F** £20 ($32) / **VF** £55 ($88) / **EF** £150 ($240)

2827   Obv. Similar. Rev. S C, olive-branch. RIC 428. BMCRE 488. CBN 524. C 544. *[Rome,*
        AD 83 or later].   **F** £20 ($32) / **VF** £55 ($88) / **EF** £150 ($240)

2828   2832

2828   IMP DOMIT AVG GERM COS XI, dr. bust of Ceres l., wreathed with corn. Rev. S C, basket
        containing corn-ears. RIC 276(b). BMCRE 321, note. CBN 347. C *Domitia* 14. *[Rome,*
        AD 85].   **F** £35 ($56) / **VF** £85 ($136) / **EF** £225 ($360)

2829   Similar, but with obv. legend IMP DOMIT AVG GERM. RIC 432. BMCRE 493. CBN 532. C
        Domitia 15. *[Rome, AD 83 or later].*   **F** £35 ($56) / **VF** £85 ($136) / **EF** £225 ($360)

2830   IMP DOMITIAN AVG GERM COS XII, dr. bust of Ceres r., wreathed with corn. Rev. S C, four
        corn-ears and three poppies tied together in bundle. RIC 392. BMCRE 370. CBN 392. C
        Domitia 18 var. *[Rome, AD 86].*   **F** £35 ($56) / **VF** £85 ($136) / **EF** £225 ($360)

2831   Similar, but with obv. legend IMP DOMIT AVG GERM and the bust of Ceres is to l. RIC 431.
        BMCRE 492. CBN 531. C *Domitia* 17. *[Rome, AD 83 or later].*
                                            F £35 ($56) / **VF** £85 ($136) / **EF** £225 ($360)

2832   Obv. Similar. Rev. S C, ship under sail r. RIC 431A. BMCRE p. 410, †. CBN 530. C
        Domitia 16. *[Rome, AD 83 or later].*   **F** £60 ($96) / **VF** £150 ($240) / **EF** £400 ($640)

2833   IMP DOMIT AVG GERM, trophy. Rev. S C, olive-branch. RIC 433. BMCRE 494. Cf. CBN
        534. C 545. *[Rome, AD 83 or later].*   **F** £25 ($40) / **VF** £65 ($104) / **EF** £175 ($280)

2834   No legend, rhinoceros walking r. Rev. IMP DOMIT AVG GERM around large S C. RIC 434.
        BMCRE 496. CBN 535. C 673. *[Rome, AD 83 or later].*
                                            F £30 ($48) / **VF** £75 ($120) / **EF** £200 ($320)

2834   2835

2835   **Copper quadrans.** Similar, but rhinoceros l. RIC 435. BMCRE 498. CBN 539. C 674.
       [Rome, AD 83 or later].   **F** £30 ($48) / **VF** £75 ($120) / **EF** £200 ($320)

Alexandrian Coinage

2836   **Billon tetradrachm.** AYTOK KAIΣAPOΣ ΔOMITIANOY ΣEB, laur. hd. r. Rev. ETOYΣ
       ΔEYTEPOY (= regnal year 2), Athena stg. r., brandishing javelin and holding shield. Dattari
       445. BMCG —. Cologne —. Milne —. *[AD 82–3].*   **F** £70 ($112) / **VF** £175 ($280)

2837   — — Rev. ETOYΣ ΔEYTEPOY (= regnal year 2), bust of Nilus r., crowned with papyrus,
       lotus-flower over r. shoulder. Dattari 440 var. BMCG 285. Cologne 327 var. Milne —.
       [AD 82–3].   **F** £70 ($112) / **VF** £175 ($280)

2838   — — Rev. ETOYΣ ΔEYTEPOY (= regnal year 2), Homonoia (= Concordia) seated l., holding
       olive-branch. Cf. Dattari 438. BMCG —. Cologne —. Milne 465. *[AD 82–3].*
                                                   F £60 ($96) / **VF** £150 ($240)

2839   — — Rev. ETOYΣ ΔEYTEPOY (= regnal year 2), Dikaiosyne (= Aequitas) stg. l., holding
       scales and sceptre. Dattari —. BMCG —. Cologne 326. Milne —. *[AD 82–3].*
                                                   F £60 ($96) / **VF** £150 ($240)

2840   AYT KAIΣAP ΔOMITIANOΣ ΣEB ΓEPM, laur. hd. r. Rev. Dr. bust of Alexandria r., wearing
       elephant's skin head-dress, L – ς (= regnal year 6) in field. Dattari 434. BMCG —. Cologne
       —. Milne —. *[AD 86–7].*   **F** £70 ($112) / **VF** £175 ($280)

2841   — — Rev. HΛIOΣ ΣAPAΠIΣ, Helios-Sarapis stg. l., rad. and wearing modius, r. hand
       extended, holding sceptre in l., Kerberos at feet, L ς (= regnal year 6) before. Dattari 446.
       BMCG 284. Cologne —. Milne 482. *[AD 86–7].*   **F** £70 ($112) / **VF** £175 ($280)

2842   — — Rev. NEIΛOΣ, Nilus reclining l., holding corn-ears and cornucopiae, hippopotamus r.
       behind, water-plants below, L ς (= regnal year 6) before. Dattari 442. BMCG —. Cologne
       348. Milne 483 var. *[AD 86–7].*   **F** £70 ($112) / **VF** £175 ($280)

2843   — — Rev. NIKH KAIΣAP ΓEPMΩN, Nike stg. r., inscribing shield set on Germania, as
       mourning female captive, seated r. on ground, L ς (= regnal year 6) before. Dattari 439.
       BMCG —. Cologne —. Milne —. *[AD 86–7].*   **F** £90 ($144) / **VF** £225 ($360)

2844   — — Rev. Triumphal arch with three portals, surmounted by elaborate group of statuary
       comprising emperor in quadriga flanked by trophies with captives, L – ς (= regnal year 6)
       in field. Dattari 449. BMCG 286. Cologne 349. Milne 484. *[AD 86–7].*
                                                   F £80 ($128) / **VF** £200 ($320)

2845   — — Rev. Athena stg. l., holding Nike and resting on shield, L H (= regnal year 8) before.
       Dattari 435 *bis.* BMCG —. Cologne —. Milne —. *[AD 88–9].* **F** £60 ($96) / **VF** £150 ($240)

2845

2846 **Billon tetradrachm.** ΑΥΤ ΚΑΙΣΑΡ ΔΟΜΙΤΙΑΝΟΣ ΣΕΒ ΓΕΡΜ, laur. hd. r. Rev. Zeus-Sarapis enthroned l., holding sceptre, Kerberos at feet, L H (= regnal year 8) before. Dattari 447. BMCG —. Cologne 358. Milne 492. *[AD 88–9].* **F** £70 ($112) / **VF** £175 ($280)

2847 — — Rev. Canopus of Osiris r., L – H (= regnal year 8) in field. Dattari 436. BMCG —. Cologne 357. Milne 493. *[AD 88–9].* **F** £70 ($112) / **VF** £175 ($280)

2848 var. (year 13)

2848 **Bronze hemidrachm** (35 mm. diam). ΑΥΤ ΚΑΙC ΘΕΟ ΥΙΟC ΄ΔΟΜΙΤ ΣΕΒ ΓΕΡΜ, laur. hd. r. Rev. Domitian in biga of Centaurs r., holding branch and sceptre, L ΙΔ (= regnal year 14) in ex. Dattari 453. BMCG 338 var. Cologne 406. Milne 523 var. *[AD 94–5].* **F** £110 ($176) / **VF** £250 ($400)

2849 ΑΥΤ ΚΑΙC ΘΕΟΥ ΥΙΟC ΔΟΜΙΤ ΣΕΒ ΓΕΡΜ, laur. hd. r. Rev. Domitian in quadriga of elephants r., holding branch and eagle-tipped sceptre, Nike r. above elephants, L ΙΕ (= regnal year 15) in ex. Dattari 462 var. BMCG 339. Cologne 411. Milne 528. *[AD 95–6].* **F** £110 ($176) / **VF** £250 ($400)

2850

2850 — — Rev. Triumphal arch, similar to 2844, L – ΙΕ (= regnal year 15) in field. Dattari 544 var. Cf. BMCG 342. Cologne 415. Milne 532. *[AD 95–6].* **F** £130 ($208) / **VF** £300 ($480)

2851	**Bronze diobol** (28–30 mm). ΑΥΤ ΚΑΙCΑΡ ΔΟΜΙΤ CΕΒ ΓΕΡΜ, hd. r., wreathed with corn, wearing aegis. Rev. ΑΘΗΝΑ CΕΒΑCΤ, Athena stg. l., holding corn-ears and resting on shield, L I (= regnal year 10) before. Dattari 468 var. BMCG 288. Cologne 369. Milne 496. *[AD 90–91].*					**F** £65 ($104) / **VF** £150 ($240)

2852	— — Rev. ΔΟΜΙΤΙΑ CΕΒΑCΤΗ, Domitia, as Euthenia (Abundantia), seated l., holding corn-ears and sceptre, L ΙΑ (= regnal year 11) before. Dattari 432 var. BMCG 292 var. Cologne 384. Milne —. *[AD 91–2].*					**F** £100 ($160) / **VF** £225 ($360)

2853	ΑΥΤ ΚΑΙC ΘΕΟ ΥΙΟC ΔΟΜΙΤ CΕΒ ΓΕΡΜ, hd. r., wreathed with corn. Rev. Isis Pharia advancing r., holding inflated sail, L ΙΑ (= regnal year 11) behind. Dattari 509 var. BMCG 305 var. Cologne 390. Milne —. *[AD 91–2].*					**F** £80 ($128) / **VF** £175 ($280)

2854	— laur. hd. r., wearing aegis. Rev. Domitian in triumphal quadriga r., holding branch and sceptre, L ΙΒ (= regnal year 12) above horses. Dattari 455 var. Cf. BMCG 340. Cologne 403. Milne (Supplement) 517a. *[AD 92–3].*					**F** £80 ($128) / **VF** £175 ($280)

2855	— laur. hd. r. Rev. Pharos (lighthouse) of Alexandria, surmounted by lantern, Tritons, and statue of stg. figure, L – ΙΒ (= regnal year 12) in field. Dattari 550. Cf. BMCG 343. Cologne —. Milne —. *[AD 92–3].*					**F** £90 ($144) / **VF** £200 ($320)

2856	— — Rev. Nike advancing l., holding wreath and palm, L ΙΕ (= regnal year 15) before. Dattari 514 var. BMCG 295. Cologne 413. Milne — *[AD 95–6].*					**F** £65 ($104) / **VF** £150 ($240)

2857

2857	**Bronze obol** (23–5 mm). ΑΥΤΟΚ ΚΑΙCΑΡ ΔΟΜΙΤΙΑΝΟC CΕΒ, laur. hd. r. Rev. ΕΤΟΥC ΔΕΥΤΕΡΟΥ (= regnal year 2), bust of Isis r., wearing crown composed of horns and disk. Dattari 502 var. BMCG 302. Cologne 329. Milne 467. *[AD 82–3].*					**F** £30 ($48) / **VF** £65 ($104)

2858	— — Rev. ΕΤΟΥC ΤΡΙΤΟΥ (= regnal year 3), eagle stg. r., wings closed. Dattari 584. BMCG 320. Cologne 331. Milne 474. *[AD 83–4].*					**F** £30 ($48) / **VF** £65 ($104)

2859	— — Rev. ΕΤΟΥC ΤΡΙΤΟΥ (= regnal year 3), bust of Alexandria r., wearing elephant's skin head-dress. Dattari 465 var. BMCG 310. Cologne 334. Milne 473. *[AD 83–4].*					**F** £30 ($48) / **VF** £65 ($104)

2860	ΑΥΤ ΚΑΙCΑΡ ΔΟΜΙΤΙΑΝΟC CΕΒ ΓΕΡΜ, laur. hd. r. Rev. Bull Apis stg. r., altar before, L Δ (= regnal year 4) above. Dattari 574. BMCG —. Cologne 338. Milne 478. *[AD 84–5].*					**F** £35 ($56) / **VF** £75 ($120))

2861	— — Rev. ΕΤΟΥC ΠΕΜΠΤΟΥ (= regnal year 5), bust of Sarapis r., wearing modius. Dattari —. BMCG —. Cologne 347. Milne —. *[AD 85–6].*					**F** £30 ($48) / **VF** £65 ($104)

2862 **Bronze obol** (23–5 mm). ΑΥΤ ΚΑΙΣΑΡ ΔΟΜΙΤΙΑΝΟΣ ΣΕΒ ΓΕΡΜ, laur. hd. r. Rev. ΕΥΘΗΝΙΑ, Euthenia (= Abundantia) stg. l., holding corn-ears and cornucopiae, L ϛ (= regnal year 6) before. Dattari 492. BMCG —. Cologne 352. Milne —. *[AD 86–7].*
F £30 ($48) / **VF** £65 ($104)

2863 —— Rev. ΕΤΟΥΣ ΟΓΔΟΟΥ (= regnal year 8), horned bust of Zeus Ammon r. Dattari 535. BMCG —. Cologne 363. Milne —. *[AD 88–9].*
F £30 ($48) / **VF** £65 ($104)

2864 ΑΥΤ ΚΑΙΣΑΡ ΔΟΜΙΤ ΣΕΒ ΓΕΡΜ, laur. hd. r. Rev. Canopus of Osiris r., L – I (= regnal year 10) in field. Dattari 471. BMCG —. Cologne 371. Milne —. *[AD 90–91].*
F £35 ($56) / **VF** £75 ($120)

2865 —— Rev. Harpokrates stg. l., his r. hand raised to mouth, holding cornucopiae in l., L ΙΑ (= regnal year 11) before. Dattari 494. BMCG 306. Cologne 386 var. Milne 504 var. *[AD 91–2].*
F £35 ($56) / **VF** £75 ($120)

2866 — hd. r., wreathed with corn. Rev. ΕΛΠΙΣ ΣΕΒΑΣΤΗ, Elpis (= Spes) advancing l., holding flower, L – ΙΑ (= regnal year 11) in field. Dattari 490 var. BMCG 291. Cologne —. Milne 501. *[AD 91–2].*
F £30 ($48) / **VF** £65 ($104)

2867 — hd. r., wreathed with corn, wearing aegis. Rev. ΤΥΧΗ ΣΕΒΑΣΤΗ, Tyche stg. l., holding rudder and cornucopiae, L – ΙΑ (= regnal year 11) in field. Dattari 531 var. BMCG 297 var. Cologne 398 var. Milne 503. *[AD 91–2].*
F £30 ($48) / **VF** £65 ($104)

2868 var. (year 10, horse left)

2868 —— Rev. Serpent Agathodaemon on back of horse galloping r., L ΙΑ (= regnal year 11) below. Dattari 565 var. BMCG 334 var. Cologne 378. Milne 507. *[AD 91–2].*
F £40 ($64) / **VF** £85 ($136)

2869 — laur. hd. r. Rev. Serpent Agathodaemon r., with caduceus and ear of corn, L ΙΒ (= regnal year 12) in ex. Dattari 560. BMCG —. Cologne 401. Milne 519. *[AD 92–3].*
F £35 ($56) / **VF** £75 ($120)

2870 **Bronze hemiobol** (18–20 mm). ΑΥΤΟΚ ΚΑΙΣΑΡ ΔΟΜΙΤΙΑΝΟΣ ΣΕΒ, laur. hd. r. Rev. Hawk stg. r., L Β (= regnal year 2) before. Dattari 618 var. BMCG 328. Cologne —. Milne 469. *[AD 82–3].*
F £20 ($32) / **VF** £45 ($72)

2871 ΑΥΤ ΚΑΙΣΑΡ ΔΟΜΙΤΙΑΝΟΣ ΣΕΒ ΓΕΡΜ, laur. hd. r., L Δ (= regnal year 4) before. Rev. ΡΩΜΗ, Roma stg. r., holding Nike and spear. Dattari 525. BMCG —. Cologne 340. Milne —. *[AD 84–5].*
F £20 ($32) / **VF** £45 ($72)

2872 Obv. Similar, but with L Ε (= regnal year 5) before hd. Rev. ΔΟΜΙΤΙΑ ΣΕΒΑΣΤΗ, bust of Domitia r. Cf. Dattari 429–30. BMCG 283. Cologne 343. Milne (Supplement) 481a. *[AD 85–6].*
F £50 ($80) / **VF** £110 ($176)

512   FLAVIAN DYNASTY

2873   **Bronze hemiobol** (18–20 mm). Obv. Similar, but with L ς (= regnal year 6) before hd. Rev.
       ΔΙΚΑΙΟΣΥΝΗ, Dikaiosyne (= Aequitas) stg. l., holding scales and sceptre. Dattari 484.
       BMCG 290. Cologne 351. Milne —. *[AD 86–7].*   **F** £20 ($32) / **VF** £45 ($72)

2874   ΑΥΤ ΚΑΙΣΑΡ ΔΟΜΙΤΙΑΝΟΣ ΣΕΒ ΓΕΡΜ, laur. hd. r. Rev. Gryphon seated r., l. forepaw resting
       on wheel, L ΕΝΑΤ (= regnal year 9) in ex. Dattari 609. BMCG 326. Cologne 365.
       Milne —. *[AD 89–90].*   **F** £20 ($32) / **VF** £45 ($72)

2875   ΑΥΤ ΚΑΙΣΑΡ ΔΟΜΙΤ ΣΕΒ ΓΕΡΜ, laur. hd. r., wearing aegis. Rev. Uraeus l., with head-dress
       of Isis, L – I (= regnal year 10) in field. Dattari 625 var. BMCG —. Cologne 377.
       Milne —. *[AD 90–91].*   **F** £25 ($40) / **VF** £55 ($88)

2876   — laur. hd. r. Rev. Canopus of Osiris r., L – I (= regnal year 10) in field. Dattari 476.
       BMCG —. Cologne 372. Milne —. *[AD 90–91].*   **F** £25 ($40) / **VF** £55 ($88)

2877   — — Rev. Dolphin entwined around anchor, L – ΙΑ (= regnal year 11) in field. Dattari 600.
       BMCG 318. Cologne 381. Milne 512 var. *[AD 91–2].*   **F** £20 ($32) / **VF** £45 ($72)

2878   — — Rev. Modius, containing corn-ears and poppies, between two torches, L – ΙΑ (= reg-
       nal year 11) in ex. Dattari 547. BMCG 345 var. Cologne 392. Milne 514 var. *[AD 91–2].*
                                                             F £20 ($32) / **VF** £45 ($72)

2879   — laur. hd. l. Rev. Sphinx recumbent r., L ΙΑ (= regnal year 11) above. Dattari 571. BMCG
       336. Cologne 396. Milne 510 var. *[AD 91–2].*   **F** £25 ($40) / **VF** £55 ($88)

2880   — laur. hd. r. Rev. Eagle stg. l. on thunderbolt, wings wings open, L ΙΒ (= regnal year 12) in
       ex. Dattari 594 var. BMCG —. Cologne 400. Milne 520 var. *[AD 92–3].*
                                                             F £20 ($32) / **VF** £45 ($72)

2881   **Bronze dichalkon** (13–15 mm). No legend, laur. hd. r. Rev. Crocodile r., disk on head, L ς
       (= regnal year 6) above. Dattari 598. BMCG 317. Cologne 353. Milne —. *[AD 86–7].*
                                                             F £22 ($35) / **VF** £50 ($80)

2882   — — Rev. Ibis walking r., L Ι (= regnal year 10) above. Dattari 613. BMCG —. Cologne
       374. Milne (Supplement) 500a. *[AD 90–91].*   **F** £22 ($35) / **VF** £50 ($80)

For other local coinages of this reign, see *Greek Imperial Coins & Their Values*, pp. 77–85.

DOMITIAN AND DOMITIA

2883

*Domitian's wife, Domitia Longina, received the title of Augusta in AD 82, the year following her
husband's accession to the imperial throne. These issues combining the portraits of emperor and
empress appear to have been struck to commemorate her elevation.*

2883   **Gold aureus.** IMP CAES DOMITIANVS AVG P M, laur. hd. of Domitian r. Rev. DOMITIA
       AVGVSTA IMP DOMIT, dr. bust of Domitia . RIC 210. BMCRE 58. CBN 58. C *Domitia
       and Domitian 3. [Rome, AD 82–3].*   **VF** £5,000 ($8,000) / **EF** £12,500 ($20,000)

2884   **Silver cistophorus.** IMP CAES DOMITIAN AVG P M COS VIII, laur. hd. of Domitian r. Rev.
       DOMITIA AVGVSTA, dr. bust of Domitia r. RIC 228. BMCRE 255. CBN —. RSC *Domitia
       and Domitian 2. [Ephesus, AD 82].*   **VF** £550 ($880) / **EF** £1,350 ($2,160)

See also nos. 2852 and 2872. For issues in the sole name of Domitia, see nos. 2900–2911.

Issues of Domitian in honour of Divus Titus

2885   **Gold aureus.** DIVVS TITVS AVGVSTVS, rad. hd. of Titus r. Rev. IVLIA AVGVSTA DIVI TITI
F, dr. bust of Julia, daughter of Titus, r. RIC 216. BMCRE 69. CBN 74. C *Julia and Titus* 1.
[Rome, AD 82–3].   **VF** £20,000 ($32,000) / **EF** £45,000 ($72,000)
*In addition to the deified Titus this aureus honours the late emperor's daughter, the young
empress Julia.*

2886   **Brass sestertius.** DIVO AVG T (or T DIVO AVG) DIVI VESP F VESPASIANO, Titus, rad.,
enthroned l., holding branch and sceptre, altar at feet. Rev. IMP CAES DIVI VESP F DOMIT
AVG P M TR P P P around large S C. RIC 437–8. BMCRE 284–5. CBN 293–4. C *Titus*
98–9. *[Rome, AD 81–2].*   **F** £180 ($288) / **VF** £450 ($720) / **EF** £1,350 ($2,160)
*The obv. type revives one of Titus' issues in honour of Divus Vespasian (see no. 2573)
which was itself inspired by the coinage of Divus Augustus struck under Tiberius (see no.
1782).*

Issues of Domitian in honour of his deified parents Vespasian († AD 79) and Domitilla († before AD 69)

2887   **Gold aureus.** DIVVS AVGVSTVS VESPASIANVS, rad. hd. of Vespasian r. Rev. DIVA DOMITILLA
AVGVSTA, dr. bust of Domitilla r. RIC *Titus* 69. BMCRE 68. CBN 73. C *Domitilla and
Vespasian* 1. *[Rome, AD 82–3].*   **VF** £12,500 ($20,000) / **EF** £30,000 ($48,000)

2888

2888   **Silver denarius.** DIVA DOMITILLA AVGVSTA, dr. bust of Domitilla r. Rev. FORTVNA
AVGVST, Fortuna stg. l., holding rudder and cornucopiae. RIC *Titus* 71. BMCRE *Titus*
137. CBN *Titus* 102. RSC *Domitilla* 3. *[Rome, AD 82–3].*
VF £5,000 ($8,000) / **EF** £12,500 ($20,000)

For other coins issued in the name of Domitilla, see under Titus (nos. 2577–8).

Issues of Domitian in honour of his deified niece Julia, daughter of Titus († ca. AD 89)

2889   **Gold aureus.** DIVA IVLIA AVGVSTA, dr. bust of Julia r. Rev. No legend, ornamented
funeral car, surmounted by seated statue of Julia r., holding sceptre and branch, drawn r. by
two elephants ridden by drivers. RIC 220. Cf. BMCRE p. 351, *. CBN —. C *Julia* 19.
[Rome, AD 90].   **VF** £30,000 ($48,000) / **EF** £65,000 ($104,000)

2890   **Brass sestertius.** DIVAE IVLIAE AVG DIVI TITI F S P Q R, carpentum drawn r. by two
mules. Rev. IMP CAES DOMIT AVG GERM COS XV CENS PER P P around large S C. RIC 400.
BMCRE 458. CBN 490. C *Julia* 9. *[Rome, AD 90–91].*
F £225 ($360) / **VF** £550 ($880) / **EF** £1,500 ($2,400)

2890

2891 **Brass sestertius.** Similar, but with COS XVI on rev. RIC 411. BMCRE 471. CBN 502. C *Julia* 10. *[Rome, AD 92–4].* **F** £225 ($360) / **VF** £550 ($880) / **EF** £1,500 ($2,400)

For lifetime issues of Julia struck under Domitian, see nos. 2885 and 2912–14; and for issues under Titus, see nos. 2610–17.

The Restoration Coinage of Domitian

Domitian's restoration coinage was but a pale reflection of that of his brother issued a year or two before. It is far more limited in scope and honours only six of the ten individuals included in Titus' series. It is also restricted to asses, with the sole exception of a sestertius type of Claudius. The emperor's motivation in reviving the series in this way is unclear, though he must have felt some necessity to continue stressing the concept of continuity with Rome's first imperial dynasty.

Divus Augustus

2892 **Copper as.** DIVVS AVGVSTVS PATER, rad. hd. of Augustus l., star above. Rev. IMP D AVG REST S C, façade of altar-enclosure of the *Ara Providentiae Augusti*, with double panelled door and horns of the altar visible above, PROVIDENT (NT in monogram) below. RIC 455. BMCRE 505. CBN —. C *Augustus* 563. *[Rome, AD 81–2].*
F £100 ($160) / **VF** £250 ($400) / **EF** £750 ($1,200)
For the prototype of this restoration, see no. 1789. For a similar restoration by Titus, see nos. 2581–2, and for another by Nerva, see no. 3080.

2893 — — Rev. IMP D CAES AVG RESTITVIT S C, eagle stg. facing on globe, hd. r., wings open. RIC 456. BMCRE 506. CBN 555 (attributed to Bithynian mint). C *Augustus* 562. *[Rome, AD 81–2].* **F** £100 ($160) / **VF** £250 ($400) / **EF** £750 ($1,200)
For the prototype of this restoration, see no. 1790. For similar restorations by Titus, see nos. 2583–4, and for another by Nerva, see no. 3082.

Agrippa

2894 **Copper as.** M AGRIPPA L F COS III, hd. of Agrippa l., wearing rostral crown. Rev. IMP D AVG REST S C, Neptune stg. l., holding dolphin and trident. RIC 457. BMCRE 510. CBN 556 (attributed to Bithynian mint). C *Agrippa* 7. *[Rome, AD 81–2].*
F £100 ($160) / **VF** £250 ($400) / **EF** £750 ($1,200)
For the prototype of this restoration, see no. 1812. For a similar restoration by Titus, see no. 2589.

Tiberius

2895

2895 **Copper as.** TI CAESAR DIVI AVG F AVGVST IMP VIII, bare hd. of Tiberius l. Rev. IMP D
CAES DIVI VESP F AVG REST around large S C. Cf. RIC 458. BMCRE 509. CBN 558 (attrib-
uted to Bithynian mint). Cf. C *Tiberius* 76. *[Rome, AD 81–2].*
F £100 ($160) / **VF** £250 ($400) / **EF** £750 ($1,200)
*For the prototype of this restoration, see no. 1770. For a similar restoration by Titus, see
no. 2591.*

Drusus

2896 **Copper as.** DRVSVS CAESAR TI AVG F DIVI AVG N, bare hd. of Drusus l. Rev. IMP D CAES
DIVI VESP F AVG REST around large S C. RIC 459. BMCRE p. 416, *. CBN 559 (attributed
to Bithynian mint). C *Drusus* 8. *[Rome, AD 81–2].*
F £110 ($176) / **VF** £275 ($440) / **EF** £800 ($1,280)
*For the prototype of this restoration, see no. 1794. For a similar restoration by Titus, see
no. 2594.*

Germanicus

2897 **Copper as.** GERMANICVS CAESAR TI AVG F DIVI AVG N, bare hd. of Germanicus l. Rev.
IMP D CAES DIVI VESP F AVG REST around large S C. RIC 460. BMCRE 511. Cf. CBN 560
(attributed to Bithynian mint). C *Germanicus* 15. *[Rome, AD 81–2].*
F £110 ($176) / **VF** £275 ($440) / **EF** £800 ($1,280)
*For the prototype of this restoration, see no. 1822. For a similar restoration by Titus, see
no. 2598.*

Claudius

2898 **Brass sestertius.** TI CLAVDIVS CAESAR AVG P M TR P IMP P P, laur. hd. of Claudius l. Rev.
IMP D CAES AVG REST S C, Spes advancing l., holding flower. RIC 461. BMCRE p. 417, *.
CBN 564 (attributed to Bithynian mint). C *Claudius* 108. *[Rome, AD 81–2].*
F £225 ($360) / **VF** £550 ($880) / **EF** £1,750 ($2,800)
*For the prototype of this restoration, see no. 1854 (with emperor's head to right). For a
similar restoration by Titus, see no. 2602.*

2899 **Copper as.** Obv. Similar, but hd. bare. Rev. IMP D AVG REST S C, Minerva advancing r.,
brandishing spear and holding shield. RIC 462. BMCRE 512. CBN —. C —. *[Rome, AD
81–2].* **F** £110 ($176) / **VF** £275 ($440) / **EF** £800 ($1,280)
*For the prototype of this restoration, see no. 1862. For a similar restoration by Titus, see
no. 2606.*

DOMITIA

2906

Domitia Longina was the daughter of Gnaeus Domitius Corbulo, the great general who com-manded the Roman forces in the war against Parthia during the reign of Nero. Corbulo was later forced to commit suicide (October AD 66) in the aftermath of the Pisonian conspiracy in which his son-in-law Vinicianus had been implicated. Soon after Vespasian's establishment of the new Flavian dynasty at the end of AD 69 Domitia became the wife of the emperor's younger son, Domitian (AD 70). Vespasian himself had been a leading general in Nero's later years, having received the supreme command in the East in AD 67, so it was natural that he would wish to honour the memory of the great Corbulo by adopting the late general's daughter into his own family. Domitian became emperor in AD 81 on the death of his brother Titus and Domitia received the title of Augusta the following year. Quite early in her husband's reign the empress fell from favour, doubtless as a result of her alleged adultery with the actor Paris, but the couple were reconciled some years later. Domitia's coinage thus falls into two distinct phases (AD 82–3 and 88–9). She was suspected of having been involved in the court conspiracy which led to Domitian's assassination in AD 96, though this has not been proven and she continued to style herself the 'wife of Domitian' on inscriptions dating as late as the reign of Hadrian. The actual year of her death is uncertain, though she seems to have survived to a very advanced age, perhaps even into the reign of Antoninus Pius (after AD 138).

All RIC, BMCRE and CBN references are to the coinage of Domitian.

2900 **Gold aureus.** DOMITIA AVGVSTA IMP DOMIT, dr. bust of Domitia r. Rev. CONCORDIA AVGVST, peacock stg. r. RIC 212. BMCRE 60. CBN 62. Cf. C 1. *[Rome, AD 82–3].*
VF £5,000 ($8,000) / **EF** £12,500 ($20,000)

2901 Similar, but with obv. legend DOMITIA AVG IMP DOMITIAN AVG GERM. RIC 215A. Cf. BMCRE 249. CBN 217. Cf. C 4. *[Rome, AD 88–9].*
VF £6,000 ($9,600) / **EF** £15,000 ($24,000)

2902 Obv. As 2900. Rev. DIVVS CAESAR IMP DOMITIANI F, naked infant boy seated l. on celes-tial globe, his hands outstretched towards seven encircling stars. RIC 213. BMCRE 62. CBN 70. C 10. *[Rome, AD 82–3].* **VF** £6,000 ($9,600) / **EF** £15,000 ($24,000)
The reverse type commemorates the son of Domitian and Domitia who died in infancy and was deified by his father.

2903

2903 **Silver cistophorus.** DOMITIA AVGVSTA, dr. bust of Domitia r. Rev. VENVS AVG, Venus stg. r., her back turned towards spectator, holding helmet and transverse sceptre and resting on column. RIC 230. BMCRE 256. CBN 226. RSC 19. *[Ephesus, AD 82].*
VF £750 ($1,200) / **EF** £1,850 ($2,960)

2904 **Silver denarius.** As 2900. RIC 212. BMCRE 61. CBN 65. RSC 2. *[Rome, AD 82–3]*.
VF £1,200 ($1,920) / **EF** £3,000 ($4,800)

2905 Similar to 2901, but rev. legend ends AVGVSTI. RIC 215, note. BMCRE 249, note. Cf. CBN 219. RSC 4b. *[Rome, AD 88–9]*. VF £1,400 ($2,240) / **EF** £3,500 ($5,600)

2906 As 2902. RIC 213. BMCRE 63. CBN 71. RSC 11. *[Rome, AD 82–3]*.
VF £1,600 ($2,560) / **EF** £4,000 ($6,400)

2904   2907

2907 Obv. As 2900. Rev. PIETAS AVGVST, Domitia, as Pietas, enthroned l., holding sceptre and extending r. hand towards child stg. l. at her feet, its r. hand raised. RIC 214. BMCRE 65. CBN 72. RSC 12. *[Rome, AD 82–3]*. VF £1,400 ($2,240) / **EF** £3,500 ($5,600)
The reverses of this and the following two types depict the empress with her deceased son.

2908 **Brass sestertius.** DOMITIAE AVG IMP CAES DIVI F DOMITIAN AVG, dr. bust of Domitia r. Rev. DIVI CAESAR MATRI S C, Domitia as Pietas, similar to previous. RIC 440. BMCRE 501. CBN 544. C 7. *[Rome, AD 82]*.
F £6,000 ($9,600) / **VF** £15,000 ($24,000) / **EF** £45,000 ($72,000)

2909 Similar, but DOMITIA for DOMITIAE on obv., and with rev. legend DIVI CAESARIS MATER S C. RIC 441. BMCRE 502, note. CBN 547. C 8. *[Rome, AD 82]*.
F £6,000 ($9,600) / **VF** £15,000 ($24,000) / **EF** £45,000 ($72,000)

2910 **Brass dupondius.** Similar to previous, but with rev. type Domitia, veiled, stg. l., sacrificing from patera over garlanded altar and holding sceptre. RIC 442. BMCRE 503. CBN —. C 9. *[Rome, AD 82]*. F £1,400 ($2,240) / **VF** £3,500 ($5,600) / **EF** £10,000 ($16,000)

See also nos. 2883–4.

Alexandrian Coinage

2911 **Bronze diobol** (28–30 mm). ΔOMITIA CEB ΔOMITIANOY KAICAPOC CEB ΓEPM, dr. bust of Domitia l. Rev. EIPHNE, Eirene (Pax) stg. l., holding corn-ears and caduceus, L IA (= regnal year 11) before. Dattari 629. BMCG —. Cologne —. Milne —. *[AD 91–2]*.
F £150 ($240) / **VF** £375 ($600)

For other Alexandrian issues depicting Domitia, see nos. 2852 and 2872. For other local coinages depicting this empress, see *Greek Imperial Coins & Their Values*, pp. 84–7.

JULIA

2912

Julia, daughter of Titus, lived with her uncle Domitian as his mistress between AD 84, when her husband Flavius Sabinus was executed, and her own death which seems to have occurred late in AD 89. It is said that she died as a result of an abortion which was forced on her by the emperor (Suetonius, Domitian 22). She was subsequently deified, an event commemorated on the coinage (see nos. 2889–91).

2912   **Gold aureus.** IVLIA AVGVSTA, dr. bust of Julia r. Rev. DIVI TITI FILIA, peacock stg. facing, its tail in splendour. RIC *Domitian* 218. BMCRE *Domitian* 250. CBN *Domitian* 220. C 6. *[Rome, AD 88–9].*   **VF** £17,500 ($28,000) / **EF** £40,000 ($64,000)

2913   Similar, but bust to l. on obv. RIC *Domitian* 218a. BMCRE *Domitian* 250, note. CBN —. Cf. C 8. *[Rome, AD 88–9].*   **VF** £22,000 ($35,200) / **EF** £50,000 ($80,000)

2914

2914   **Silver cistophorus.** IVLIA AVGVSTA DIVI TITI F, dr. bust of Julia r. Rev. VESTA, Vesta seated l., holding Palladium and sceptre. RIC *Domitian* 231. BMCRE *Domitian* 258. CBN *Domitian* 227. RSC 15. *[Ephesus, AD 82].*   **VF** £750 ($1,200) / **EF** £1,850 ($2,960)

See also no. 2885. For earlier issues in the name of Julia, see under Titus (nos. 2610–17).

VESPASIAN JUNIOR

2915 var.

Vespasian Junior and Domitian Junior were the sons of Flavius Clemens and Flavia Domitilla, respectively cousin and niece of Domitian. The two boys were adopted by the childless emperor and made heirs to the imperial throne. However, in AD 95, towards the end of his consulship, their father was executed on a trumped-up charge of 'maiestas' and their mother exiled. There was talk that the couple had been converted to Christianity, though it seems more likely that they were pros-

elytes to Judaism. The fate of the two boys is unknown as they are not mentioned again after this tragic episode. Provincial coinage was produced bearing the name and portrait of the young Vespasian, though none has yet been identified attributable to his brother.

2915   Æ **17** of Smyrna in Asia (Ionia). OYECΠACIANOC NEΩTEPOC, bare-headed and dr. bust of Vespasian Junior r. Rev. ZMYPNAIΩN, Nike stg. l., holding wreath and palm. BMCG (Ionia) 316. C 1 var. *[before AD 95].*   **F** £200 ($320) / **VF** £500 ($800)

ANONYMOUS QUADRANTES

2922

The series of so-called 'anonymous quadrantes' is generally ascribed to the late 1st century through the mid-2nd century AD (period of Domitian to Antoninus Pius). They usually depict the head of a deity on the obverse with a complementary design on the reverse (e.g. Jupiter/eagle, Minerva/owl, etc.). Their origin and purpose is as uncertain as their date, and some may even be semisses rather than quadrantes. The authors of RIC suggest that by a dispensation of the emperor the Senate may have been allowed to issue these anonymous coins in connection with special occasions, such as public festivals. Alternatively, they propose that their purpose may have been for use as small change at mining centers owned by the Senate, though the two theories need not be mutually exclusive. Likenesses to certain members of the imperial families have occasionally been noted in the features of the obverse deities. While such characteristics can provide an approximate indication of date, it has to be acknowledged that some of the suggestions amount to nothing more than optimistic speculation.

RIC references are to Vol. II, pp. 216–19; Cohen references are to Vol. VIII, pp. 267–71.

2916   **Copper quadrans.** No legend, laur. hd. of Jupiter r. Rev. **S C**, eagle stg. facing on thunderbolt, hd. r. RIC 1. C 14.   **F** £30 ($48) / **VF** £75 ($120) / **EF** £200 ($320)

2917   Similar, but with rev. type winged thunderbolt. RIC 6. C 13.
                F £30 ($48) / **VF** £75 ($120) / **EF** £200 ($320)

2918   No legend, helmeted and dr. bust of Minerva r. Rev. **S C**, owl stg. r., hd. facing. RIC 7. C 7.
                F £20 ($32) / **VF** £55 ($88) / **EF** £150 ($240)

2919   Similar, but with rev. type olive-tree. RIC 9. C 4.
                F £20 ($32) / **VF** £55 ($88) / **EF** £150 ($240)

2920   No legend, diad. and dr. bust of Neptune l., trident behind. Rev. **S C**, dolphin entwined around anchor. RIC 14. C 21 var.   **F** £35 ($56) / **VF** £85 ($136) / **EF** £225 ($360)

2921

2921   — bearded hd. of river-god Tiber r., crowned with reeds. Rev. **S C**, she-wolf stg. r., suckling the twins Romulus and Remus. RIC 17. C 22.
                F £40 ($64) / **VF** £100 ($160) / **EF** £275 ($440)

2922   **Copper quadrans.** No legend, helmeted and cuir. bust of Mars r. Rev. S C, cuirass. RIC
       19. Cf. C 26, 27.   **F** £20 ($32) / **VF** £55 ($88) / **EF** £150 ($240)

2923   — helmeted hd. of Mars r. Rev. S C, legionary eagle between two standards. RIC 22. C 19.
                                                            F £25 ($40) / **VF** £65 ($104) / **EF** £175 ($280)

2924   — diad. and dr. bust of Venus r. Rev. S C, dove stg. r. RIC 24. C 10.
                                                            F £25 ($40) / **VF** £65 ($104) / **EF** £175 ($280)

2925   — laur. and dr. bust of Apollo r. Rev. S C, tripod. RIC 26. Cf. C 40, 41.
                                                            F £30 ($48) / **VF** £75 ($120) / **EF** £200 ($320)

2926 var.

2926   Similar, but with obv. type gryphon seated r., l. forepaw on wheel. RIC 27. C 39.
                                                            F £35 ($56) / **VF** £85 ($136) / **EF** £225 ($360)

2927   No legend, dr. bust of Mercury r., wearing winged petasus. Rev. S C, winged caduceus.
       RIC 31. C 34.   **F** £25 ($40) / **VF** £65 ($104) / **EF** £175 ($280)

2928   Similar, but with obv. type winged petasus. RIC 32. C 36.
                                                            F £30 ($48) / **VF** £75 ($120) / **EF** £200 ($320)

2929   No legend, hd. of infant (Bacchus?) r., crowned with vine-leaves and with grape-clusters
       around neck. Rev. S C within wreath of vine-leaves and grapes. RIC 34. C 31.
                                                            F £35 ($56) / **VF** £85 ($136) / **EF** £225 ($360)

2930   — veiled infant hd. r., crowned with reeds. Rev. S C within wreath of olive or laurel. RIC
       35. C 30.   **F** £35 ($56) / **VF** £85 ($136) / **EF** £225 ($360)

2931   — rhinoceros walking l. Rev. S C, olive-branch. RIC 36. C 2.
                                                            F £30 ($48) / **VF** £75 ($120) / **EF** £200 ($320)

(Continued in Volume II)

BOOKS AND MONOGRAPHS ON ROMAN COINS

Where a letter appears in brackets preceding the author's name this indicates the abbreviation used in the catalogue listings in this book when referring to the work in question.

REPUBLICAN

(**B**) BABELON, E. *Description Historique et Chronologique des Monnaies de la République Romaine*. 2 vols. 1885–6.
BANTI, A. *Corpus Nummorum Romanorum, Monetazione Repubblicana*. 9 vols. 1980–1.
BELLONI, G.G. *Le Monete Romane dell'età Repubblicana*. 1960.
(**BMCRR**) GRUEBER, H.A. *Coins of the Roman Republic in the British Musem*. 3 vols. 1910 (revised edition 1970).
BUTTREY, T.V. *The Triumviral Portrait Gold of the Quattuorviri Monetales of 42 BC*. 1956.
CARSON, R.A.G. *Principal Coins of the Romans*. Vol. I. The Republic, *c*. 290–31 BC. 1978.
COHEN, H. *Description Générale des Monnaies de la République Romaine*. 1857.
CRAWFORD, M.H. *Roman Republican Coin Hoards*. 1969.
CRAWFORD, M.H. *Coinage and Money under the Roman Republic*. 1985.
(**CRI**) SEAR, D.R. *The History and Coinage of the Roman Imperators, 49–27 BC*. 1998.
(**CRR**) SYDENHAM, E.A. *The Coinage of the Roman Republic*. 1952.
HAEBERLIN, E.J. *Aes Grave. Das Schwergeld Roms und Mittel Italiens*. 2 vols. 1910.
(**ICC**) THURLOW, B.K. and VECCHI, *Italian Cast Coinage*. 1979.
PINK, K. *The Triumviri Monetales and the Structure of the Coinage of the Roman Republic*. 1952.
ROLLAND, H. *Numismatique de la République Romaine*. 1924.
(**RRC**) CRAWFORD, M.H. *Roman Republican Coinage*. 2 vols. 1974.
(**RRM**) HARLAN, M. *Roman Republican Moneyers and Their Coins, 63 BC–49 BC*. 1995.
(**RSC**) SEABY, H.A. *Roman Silver Coins*. Vol. I. Republic–Augustus. 3rd edition. 1978.
SYDENHAM, E.A. *Aes Grave*. 1926.
THOMSEN, R. *Early Roman Coinage. A Study of the Chronology*. 3 vols. 1957–61.

IMPERIAL

AKERMAN, J.Y. *Coins of the Romans relating to Britain*. 1844.
ALFÖLDI, A. & E. and CLAY, C.L. *Die Kontorniat-Medaillons*. 2 vols. 1976.
ASKEW, G. *The Coinage of Roman Britain*. 2nd edition. 1980.
BALDUS, H.R. *Uranius Antoninus – Münzprägung und Geschichte*. 1971.
BANTI, A. *I Grande Bronzi Imperiali*. 9 vols. 1983–6.

BANTI, A. and SIMONETTI, L. *Corpus Nummorum Romanorum*. 18 vols. 1972–8.

BASTIEN, P. *Le Monnayage de Magnence (350–353)*. 1964.

BASTIEN, P. *Le Monnayage de Bronze de Postume*. 1967.

BASTIEN, P. *Le Monnayage de l'Atelier de Lyon. De la réouverture de l'Atelier par Aurélien à la mort de Carin (fin 274–285)*. 1976.

BASTIEN, P. *Le Monnayage de l'Atelier de Lyon. Dioclétien et ses corégents avant la Réforme Monétaire (285–294)*. 1972.

BASTIEN, P. *Le Monnayage de l'Atelier de Lyon. De la Réforme de Dioclétien à la fermeture temporaire de l'Atelier en 316 (294–316)*. 1980.

BASTIEN, P. *Le Monnayage de l'Atelier de Lyon. De la réouverture de l'Atelier en 318 à la mort de Constantin (318–337)*. 1982.

BASTIEN, P. *Le Monnayage de l'Atelier de Lyon. De la mort de Constantin à la mort to Julien (337–363)*. 1985.

BASTIEN, P. *Le Monnayage de l'Atelier de Lyon du règne de Jovien à la mort de Jovin (363–413)*. 1987.

BASTIEN, P. and HUVELIN, H. *Trouvaille de Folles de la Periode Constantinienne (307–317)*. 1969.

BASTIEN, P. and METZGER, C. *Le Trésor de Beaurains (dit d'Arras)*. 1977.

BASTIEN, P. and VASSELLE, F. *Le Trésor Monetaire de Domqueur (Somme)*. 1965.

BESLEY, E. and BLAND, R. *The Cunetio Treasure, Roman Coinage of the Third Century* AD. 1983.

BLAND, R. (editor). *The Chalfont Hoard and other Roman Coin Hoards*. 1992.

BLAND, R. and BURNETT, A. (editors). *The Normanby Hoard and other Roman Coin Hoards*. 1988.

(**BMCRE**) *Coins of the Roman Empire in the British Museum*.
    Vol. I. Augustus–Vitellius, by H. Mattingly. 1923 (revised edition 1976).
    Vol. II. Vespasian–Domitian, by H. Mattingly. 1930 (revised edition 1976).
    Vol. III. Nerva–Hadrian, by H. Mattingly. 1936 (revised edition 1966).
    Vol. IV. Antoninus Pius–Commodus, by H. Mattingly. 1940 (revised edition, in 2 vols., 1968).
    Vol. V. Pertinax–Elagabalus, by H. Mattingly. 2 vols. 1950 (revised edition in 2 vols., 1976).
    Vol. VI. Severus Alexander–Balbinus and Pupienus, by R.A.G. Carson. 1962.

BREGLIA, L. *Roman Imperial Coins, Their Art and Technique*. 1968.

BRUCK, G. *Die Spätrömische Kupferprägung*. 1961.

(**C**) COHEN, H. *Description Historique des Monnaies frappées sous l'Empire Romain*. 2nd edition. 8 vols. 1880–92.

CARRADICE, I. *Coinage and Finances in the Reign of Domitian*, AD 81–96. 1983.

CARSON, R.A.G. *Principal Coins of the Romans*. Vol. 2. The Principate, 31 BC–AD 296. 1979.

CARSON, R.A.G. *Principal Coins of the Romans*. Vol. 3. The Dominate, AD 294–498. 1981.

CARSON, R.A.G., HILL, P.V. and KENT, J.P.C. *Late Roman Bronze Coinage, AD 324–498*. 1960.

CASEY, P.J. *Roman Coinage in Britain*. 1980.

CAYÓN, J.R. *Los Sestercios del Imperio Romano*. 1984.
    Vol. I. De Pompeyo Magno a Matidia (del 81 a.C. al 117 d.C.).
    Vol. II. De Adriano a Faustina Madre (del 117 d.C. al 161 d.C.).
    Vol. III. De Marco Aurelio a Caracalla (del 161 d.C. al 217 d.C.).

(**CBN**) GIARD, J.-P. *Catalogue des Monnaies de l'Empire Romain*.
    Vol. I. Auguste. 1976 (revised edition 1988).
    Vol. II. De Tibère à Néron. 1988
    Vol. III. Du Soulèvement de 68 après J.-C. à Nerva. 1998.

(**CSS**) HILL, P.V. *The Coinage of Septimius Severus and his Family of the Mint of Rome, AD 193–217*. 1977.

EDDY, S.K. *The Minting of Antoniniani AD 238–249 and the Smyrna Hoard*. 1967.

FRANKE, P.R. and HIRMER, M. *Römische Kaiserporträts im Münzbild*. 3rd edition. 1972.

FROEHNER, W. *Medaillons de l'Empire Romain*. 1878.

GILLJAM, H.H. *Antoniniani und Aurei des Ulpius Cornelius Laelianus, Gegenkaiser des Postumus*. 1982.

GNECCHI, F. *The Coin Types of Imperial Rome.* 1908.
GNECCHI, F. *I Medaglioni Romani.* 3 vols. 1912.
GÖBL, R. *Regalianus und Dryantilla.* 1970.
GRANT, M. *Roman Anniversary Issues: an exploratory study of the numismatic and medallic commemoration of anniversary years, 49 B.C.–A.D. 375.* 1950.
GRANT, M. *Roman Imperial Money.* 1954.
GRANT, M. *Roman History from Coins: some uses of the Imperial coinage to the historian.* 1958.
GRANT, M. *The Six Main Aes Coinages of Augustus.* 1953.
GRIERSON, P. and MAYS, M. *Catalogue of Late Roman Coins in the Dumbarton Oaks Collection and in the Whittemore Collection, from Arcadius and Honorius to the Accession of Anastasius.* 1992.
GRUEBER, H.A. *Roman Medallions in the British Museum.* 1874.
HAHN, W. *Moneta Imperii Romani-Byzantini: Die Ostprägung des Römischen Reiches im 5. Jahrhundert (408–491).* 1989.
HILL, P.V. *'Barbarous Radiates' – Imitations of Third-Century Roman Coins.* 1949.
KING, C.E. (see SEABY, H.A., *Roman Silver Coins*, Vol. V).
KRAAY, C.M. *The Aes Coinage of Galba.* 1956.
MAC DOWALL, D.W. *The Western Coinages of Nero.* 1979.
MARTIN, P.-H. *Die Anonymen Münzen des Jahres 68 nach Christus.* 1974.
MAURICE, J. *Numismatique Constantinienne.* 3 vols. 1908–12.
MAZZINI, G. *Monete Imperiali Romane.* 5 vols. 1957–8.
METCALF, W.E. *The Cistophori of Hadrian.* 1980.
MILLER, D. *Coins of Roman Britain.* 1976.
Moneta Imperii Romani.
    Vols. 2 and 3. Die Münzprägung der Kaiser Tiberius und Caius (Caligula) 14/41, by W. Szaivert. 1984.
    Vol. 18. Die Münzprägung der Kaiser Marcus Aurelius, Lucius Verus und Commodus (161/192), by W. Szaivert. 1986.
    Vol. 27. Die Münzprägung des Kaisers Maximinus I Thrax (235/238), by M. Alram. 1989.
    Vol. 47. Die Münzprägung des Kaisers Aurelianus (270/275), by R. Göbl. 2 vols.1995.
MONTENEGRO, E. *Monete Imperiali Romane.* 1988.
REECE, R. *Coinage in Roman Britain.* 1987.
(**RIC**) *Roman Imperial Coinage.*
    Vol. I. Augustus–Vitellius, by H. Mattingly and E.A. Sydenham. 1923 (revised edition 1984 by C.H.V. Sutherland).
    Vol. II. Vespasian–Hadrian, by H. Mattingly and E.A. Sydenham. 1926.
    Vol. III. Antoninus Pius–Commodus, by H. Mattingly and E.A. Sydenham. 1930.
    Vol. IV, part I. Pertinax–Geta, by H. Mattingly and E.A. Sydenham. 1936.
    Vol. IV, part II. Macrinus–Pupienus, by H. Mattingly, E.A. Sydenham and C.H.V. Sutherland. 1938.
    Vol. IV, part III. Gordian III–Uranius Antoninus, by H. Mattingly, E.A. Sydenham and C.H.V. Sutherland. 1949.
    Vol. V, part I. Valerian–Florian, by P.H. Webb. 1927.
    Vol. V, part II. Probus–Amandus, by P.H. Webb. 1933.
    Vol. VI. Diocletian–Maximinus, by C.H.V. Sutherland. 1967.
    Vol. VII. Constantine and Licinius, by P.M. Bruun. 1966.
    Vol. VIII. The Family of Constantine, by J.P.C. Kent. 1981.
    Vol. IX. Valentinian I–Theodosius I, by J.W.E. Pearce. 1951.
    Vol. X. The Divided Empire and the Fall of the Western Parts, AD 395–491, by J.P.C. Kent. 1994.
ROBERTSON, A.S. *Roman Imperial Coins in the Hunter Coin Cabinet, University of Glasgow.*
    Vol. I. Augustus–Nerva. 1962.
    Vol. II. Trajan–Commodus. 1971.
    Vol. III. Pertinax–Aemilian. 1977.

Vol. IV. Valerian I–Allectus. 1978.
Vol. V. Diocletian (Reform)–Zeno. 1982.
RODEWALD, C. *Money in the Age of Tiberius.* 1976.
(**RSC**) SEABY, H.A. *Roman Silver Coins.*
Vol. I. The Republic–Augustus. 3rd edition. 1978.
Vol. II. Tiberius–Commodus. 3rd edition. 1979.
Vol. III. Pertinax–Balbinus and Pupienus. 2nd edition. 1982.
Vol. IV. Gordian III–Postumus. 2nd edition. 1982.
Vol. V. Carausius–Romulus Augustus (by C.E. King). 1987.
SABATIER, J. *Medaillons Contorniates.* 1860.
SCHULTE, B. *Die Goldprägung der Gallischen Kaiser von Postumus bis Tetricus.* 1983.
SHIEL, N. *The Episode of Carausius and Allectus.* 1977.
STRACK, P.L. *Untersuchungen zur Römischen Reichsprägung des Zweiten Jahrhunderts.* 3 vols. 1931–7.
SUTHERLAND, C.H.V. *Romano-British Imitations of Bronze Coins of Claudius I.* 1935.
SUTHERLAND, C.H.V. *Coinage and Currency in Roman Britain.* 1937.
SUTHERLAND, C.H.V. *Coinage in Roman Imperial Policy, 31 BC–AD 68.* 1951.
SUTHERLAND, C.H.V. *The Emperor and the Coinage: Julio-Claudian Studies.* 1976.
SUTHERLAND, C.H.V. and KRAAY, C.M. *Catalogue of Coins of the Roman Empire in the Ashmolean Museum.* Part I. Augustus. 1975.
SUTHERLAND, C.H.V., OLCAY, N. and MERRINGTON, K.E. *The Cistophori of Augustus.* 1970.
SYDENHAM, E.A. *The Coinage of Nero.* 1920.
SYDENHAM, E.A. *Historical References on Coins of the Roman Empire from Augustus to Gallienus.* 1917.
THIRION, M. *Les Monnaies d'Elagabale.* 1968.
TOYNBEE, J.M.C. *Roman Historical Portraits.* 1978.
TOYNBEE, J.M.C. *Roman Medallions.* 1944.
TRILLMICH, W. *Familienpropaganda der Kaiser Caligula und Claudius.* 1978.
TURNER, P.J. *Roman Coins from India.* 1989.
(**UCR**) HILL, P.V. *The Dating and Arrangement of the Undated Coins of Rome, AD 98–148.* 1970.
ULRICH-BANSA, O. *Moneta Mediolanensis.* 1947.
VAGI, D.L. *Coinage and History of the Roman Empire.* 2 vols. 1999.
VAN METER, D. *The Handbook of Roman Imperial Coins.* 1991.
VOETTER, O. *Die Münzen der Römischen Kaiser, Kaiserinnen und Caesaren von Diocletianus bis Romulus (284–476).* 1921.
WEBB, P.H. *The Reign and Coinage of Carausius.* 1908.

PROVINCIAL

BELLINGER, A.R. *The Syrian Tetradrachms of Caracalla and Macrinus.* 1940.
(**BMCG**) *Catalogue of the Greek Coins in the British Museum.* 29 vols. 1873–1927.
(**BMCG Supplement**) CHRISTIANSEN, E. *Coins of Alexandria and the Nomes, a Supplement to the British Museum Catalogue.* 1991.
BUTCHER, K. *Roman Provincial Coins: an Introduction to the Greek Imperials.* 1988.
(**Cologne**) GEISSEN, A. and WEISER, W. *Katalog Alexandrinischer Kaisermünzen der Sammlung des Instituts für Altertumskunde der Universität zu Köln.* 5 vols. 1974–83.
CURTIS, J.W. *The Tetradrachms of Roman Egypt.* 1957 (reprinted with supplements 1990).
(**Dattari**) DATTARI, G. *Monete Imperiali Greche. Numi Augg. Alexandrini.* 2 vols. 1901.
Die Antiken Münzen Nord-Griechenlands.
Vol. I. Dacien und Moesien, by B. Pick and K. Regling. 2 parts, 1898 and 1910.
Vol. II. Thrakien, by M.L. Strack. 1912.
Vol. III. Makedonia und Paionia, by H. Gaebler. 2 parts, 1906 and 1935.
FORRER, L., *The Weber Collection of Greek Coins.* 3 vols. 1922–9.

BOOKS AND MONOGRAPHS ON ROMAN COINS 525

GRANT, M. *From Imperium to Auctoritas: a historical study of the aes coinage in the Roman Empire, 49 BC–AD 14.* 1946.

GRANT, M. *Aspects of the Principate of Tiberius: historical comments on the colonial coinage issued outside Spain.* 1950.

GROSE, S.W. *Catalogue of the McClean Collection of Greek Coins (Fitzwilliam Museum).* 3 vols. 1923–9.

HEAD, B.V. *Historia Numorum.* 2nd edition. 1911.

HEISS, A. *Description Général des Monnaies Antiques de l'Espagne.* 1870.

HOWGEGO, C.J. *Greek Imperial Countermarks, Studies in the Provincial Coinage of the Roman Empire.* 1985.

KADMAN, L. *Corpus Nummorum Palaestinensium.*
  Vol. I. The Coins of Aelia Capitolina. 1956.
  Vol. II. The Coins of Caesarea Maritima. 1957.
  Vol. IV. The Coins of Akko Ptolemais. 1961.

KRAFT, K. *Das System der Kaiserzeitlichen Münzprägung in Kleinasien, Materialien und Entwürfe.* 1972.

LINDGREN, H.C. *Ancient Greek Bronze Coins: European Mints.* 1989.

LINDGREN, H.C. and KOVACS, F.L. *Ancient Bronze Coins of Asia Minor and the Levant.* 1985.

MACDONALD, G. *Catalogue of Greek Coins in the Hunterian Collection, University of Glasgow.* 1899–1905.

(**Milne**) MILNE, J.G. *Catalogue of Alexandrian Coins, University of Oxford, Ashmolean Museum.* 1933 (revised edition 1971 with supplement by C.M. Kraay).

MIONNET, T.-E. *Description des Médailles antiques, grecques et Romaines.* 1806–8 (supplement 1819–37).

MULLER, L. *Numismatique de l'Ancienne Afrique.* 1860–3.

ROSENBERGER, M. *City-Coins of Palestine.* 3 vols. 1972–7.

ROSENBERGER, M. *The Coinage of Eastern Palestine.* 1978.

(**RPC**) *Roman Provincial Coinage.*
  Vol. I. From the Death of Caesar to the Death of Vitellius, 44 BC–AD 69. 2 vols. 1992 (Supplement 1998).
  Vol. II. From Vespasian to Domitian, AD 69–96. 2 vols. 1999.

SEAR, D.R. *Greek Imperial Coins and Their Values.* 1982.

SPIJKERMAN, A. *The Coins of the Decapolis and Provincia Arabia.* 1978.

SUTHERLAND, C.H.V. and KRAAY, C.M. *Catalogue of Coins of the Roman Empire in the Ashmolean Museum.* Part I. Augustus. 1975.

SVORONOS, J.N. *Numismatique de la Crète Ancienne.* 1890.

SYDENHAM, E.A. *The Coinage of Caesarea in Cappadocia.* 1933.

Sylloge Nummorum Graecorum.
  Danish Series. The Royal Collection of Coins and Medals, Danish National Museum, Copenhagen. In 43 parts, 1942–77.
  German Series. Sammlung von Aulock. In 18 parts. 1957–68.
  Switzerland. Levante–Cilicia. 1986 (Supplement 1993).

VON FRITZE, H. *Die Antiken Münzen Mysiens: Adramytion–Kisthene.* 1913.

WADDINGTON, W.H., BABELON, E. and REINACH, T. *Recueil Général des Monnaies Grecques d'Asie Mineure.* 4 vols. 1904–12.

WRUCK, W. *Die Syrische Provinzialprägung von Augustus bis Traian.* 1931.

GENERAL

AKERMAN, J.Y. *A Descriptive Catalogue of Rare and Unedited Roman Coins.* 2 vols. 1834.

BOYNE, W. *A Manual of Roman Coins; from the Earliest Period to the Extinction of the Empire; with Rarity Guide.* 1865 (revised reprint 1968).

BRITISH MUSEUM. *A Guide to the Exhibition of Roman Coins in the British Museum.* 1963.

BURNETT, A. *Coinage in the Roman World.* 1987.

FOSS, C. *Roman Historical Coins*. 1988.

GNECCHI, F. *Roman Coins: Elementary Manual*. 1903.

HILL, G.F. *Historical Roman Coins*. 1909.

HILL, G.F. *Handbook of Greek and Roman Coins*. 1899.

JONES, J. MELVILLE. *A Dictionary of Ancient Roman Coins*. 1990.

KENT, J.P.C. and HIRMER, M. and A. *Roman Coins*. 1978.

LEVY, BOB (with Introduction by David R. Sear). *From the Coin's Point of View*. 1993.

MATTINGLY, H. *Roman Coins from the Earliest Times to the Fall of the Western Empire*. 2nd edition. 1960.

MILNE, J.G. *Greek and Roman Coins and the Study of History*. 1939.

MOMMSEN, T. *Die Geschichte des RömischenMünzwesens*. 1860 (reprinted edition 1956).

PENN, R.G. *Medicine on Ancient Greek and Roman Coins*. 1994.

SEAR, D.R. *The Emperors of Rome and Byzantium*. 2nd edition. 1981.

STEVENSON, S.W. *A Dictionary of Roman Coins*. 1889 (reprinted edition 1964).

SUTHERLAND, C.H.V. *Roman Coins*. 1974.

INDEX

References in this index are either to page numbers, in the case of text, or to catalogue entry numbers, in the case of coin listings.